Final Cut Pro Cookbook

Develop pro editing skills with over 70 recipes for advanced creative effects and efficient workflows

Mike Eddy

Final Cut Pro Cookbook

Portfolio Director: Pavan Ramchandani

Relationship Lead: Alok Dhuri

Content Engineer: Mohd Hammad

Technical Editor: Vidhisha Patidar

Copy Editor: Safis Editing

Indexer: Manju Arasan

Proofreader: Mohd Hammad

Production Designer: Nilesh Mohite

Growth Lead: Priya Bhanushali

First published: July 2025

Production reference: 2010725

Published by Packt Publishing Ltd.
Grosvenor House
11 St Paul's Square
Birmingham
B3 1RB, UK.

ISBN 978-1-83588-846-9

www.packtpub.com

This book is dedicated to my wife and family, who have supported me throughout my career, and most recently, during the writing of this book. Also, to the many students I have enjoyed teaching the coolness of Final Cut Pro.

In addition, I testify to the deep love of Jesus that has saturated my life.

Taste and see that the Lord is good – Psalm 34:8

Foreword

I first met Mike Eddy nearly 20 years ago when I was serving as a Master Trainer for Apple's inaugural Final Cut Pro certification program. During one of our early four-day Train-the-Trainer workshops in Cupertino, I had the opportunity to see Mike in action. Even then, it was clear – Mike wasn't just another editor. He was a born educator.

With a rare blend of technical precision, creative insight, and a gift for simplifying the complex, Mike had the ability to make even the most advanced workflows feel accessible. Watching him train others reminded me why we teach in the first place: to equip and empower people to tell meaningful stories.

Fast-forward to today, and the demands on editors have only increased. In a fast-paced content landscape, speed and efficiency are everything. Turnaround times are tighter. Expectations are higher. Editors don't just need knowledge – they need clarity, confidence, and shortcuts that work.

That's exactly what *Final Cut Pro Cookbook* delivers. Whether you're brand new to Final Cut Pro or a seasoned pro looking to refine your workflow, this book offers practical, well-structured solutions to everyday editing challenges. From importing and organizing to editing, sweetening audio, and color correction, each "recipe" is built for the way modern editors actually work: fast, focused, and under pressure.

What I admire most is how approachable this guide is. Mike doesn't just walk you through the buttons – he explains the purpose behind each step and shows how it fits into a larger editorial strategy. The tone is friendly, the instructions are crystal clear, and the layout is designed for quick reference and immediate application.

After more than two decades in the world of editing and training, I can tell you this: truly great resources are rare. This book is one of them. Whether you're cutting a short film, a YouTube series, or a corporate piece, Final Cut Pro Cookbook deserves a permanent spot on your desk – or better yet, within arm's reach of your edit bay.

Steve Martin

Founder and CEO, RippleTraining.com

Contributors

About the author

Mike Eddy is an Apple Certified Final Cut Pro Trainer with over 30 years of experience in video production, photography, print, web, and stage productions. Mike was a 2023 National Teacher of the Year finalist for the Association of Career and Technical Educators. He is a retired instructor from Century College in Minnesota, where he taught filmmaking and video production since 2007. Mike got his start scripting interactive projects in HyperCard on a Mac II. He has had the privilege to work with General Mills, Federated Insurance, 3M, Andersen Windows, Apple, Compassion International, 5 Eyewitness News, and many other leading companies.

I would like to extend my thanks to my family for the time to work on this book, which seemed to grow larger the more time I spent on it. I would like to thank Mohd Hammad for his patience. Special thanks to Alok Dhuri and the entire Packt team for their support during the course of writing this book, developing a cover image, and creating a marketing plan.

About the reviewers

Maarten J. Boer is a video editor, director, and Final Cut Pro specialist with over 20 years of experience in filmmaking. As an editor, he loves shaping stories, isn't afraid to make tough decisions, and is obsessed with clean timelines. He currently works for the largest museums in the Netherlands and produces numerous documentary portraits of international artists. A Final Cut Pro user since 2003, he was among the first FCP X specialists in the country.

Jonathan Mercieca is a Maltese freelance video content creator with 20 years of experience, specializing in Final Cut Pro. An Apple Certified Pro User in FCPX since 2019, he has worked on documentaries, TV productions, commercials, and international events, collaborating with major names such as Euronews and IMG Media. Jonathan is passionate about crafting high-quality visual stories that engage and inspire audiences.

Table of Contents

Preface   **xvii**

Chapter 1: Utilizing the Final Cut Pro Interface for Workflow Success   **1**

Technical requirements 2

Working with the Final Cut Pro interface and workspaces 2

Getting ready • 2

How to do it... • 2

Changing the Event Browser's appearance 10

Getting ready • 11

How to do it... • 11

Customizing the Event Browser's filtering order 15

Getting ready • 16

How to do it... • 16

There's more... • 18

Taking advantage of the Magnetic Timeline and the Position tool 21

Getting ready • 21

How to do it... • 22

There's more • 24

Working with the Precision Editor view 26

How to do it... • 26

Chapter 2: Organizing Media and Using the Event Browser Effectively   31

Technical requirements 32

Creating a camera archive 32

Getting ready • 32

How to do it... • 32

There's more... • 35

Importing media into Final Cut Pro 36

How to do it... • 36

There's more... • 43

Importing media with drag and drop 46

Getting ready • 47

How to do it... • 47

Understanding optimized versus proxy media 50

How to do it... • 51

There's more... • 52

Using keywords 53

Getting ready • 54

How to do it... • 54

Using the Event Browser List view 58

Getting ready • 59

How to do it... • 59

Making an assembly edit 66

Getting ready • 67

How to do it... • 67

Creating Smart Collections 68

Getting ready • 68

How to do it... • 68

Relinking media 72

Getting ready • 72

How to do it... • 72

There's more... • 75

Chapter 3: Sculpting Clips in the Final Cut Pro Timeline 77

Technical requirements 78

Appending, inserting, connecting, and overwriting clips 78

How to do it... • 78

There's more... • 84

Quickly selecting clips with keyboard shortcuts 85

Getting ready • 86

How to do it... • 86

There's more... • 89

Adjusting the timeline's appearance 89

Getting ready • 89

How to do it... • 89

There's more... • 93

Replacing clips 94

Getting ready • 94

How to do it... • 94

Adding transitions 97

How to do it... • 98

There's more... • 105

Creating secondary storyline transitions 106

Getting ready • 107

How to do it... • 108

There's more... • 112

Using the Blade tool 114

Getting ready • 114

How to do it... • 114

Changing a clip's duration 116

How to do it... • 117

There's more... • 119

Chapter 4: Improving Your Editing Efficiency   121

Getting to grips with ripple, roll, slip, and slide edits 122

Getting ready • 123

How to do it... • 123

Using gap clips and placeholder clips 127

How to do it... • 127

There's more... • 134

Creating J- and L-cuts 135

Getting ready • 135

How to do it... • 136

There's more... • 138

Using markers and the Timeline Index 139

How to do it... • 139

Creating an audition 143

Getting ready • 144

How to do it... • 144

Creating compound clips 150

How to do it... • 150

Color coding your clips 153

How to do it... • 154

Using multicam editing 157

Getting ready • 157

How to do it... • 157

Chapter 5: Exploring Color Correction and Stylizing   167

Utilizing white balance 168

Getting ready • 168

How to do it... • 169

How it works... • 172

There's more... • 172

Using the Match Color feature 173

Getting ready • 173

How to do it... • 173

Using Color Board, Wheels, and Curves 176

Getting ready • 176

How to do it... • 177

There's more... • 187

Using Shape Masks and Color Masks 190

How to do it... • 191

Fixing exposure with the luma waveform monitor 196

Getting ready • 196

How to do it... • 196

Adding secondary color corrections 199

How to do it... • 200

There's more... • 204

Applying LUTs to raw files 204

Getting ready • 205

How to do it... • 205

Chapter 6: Applying Visual Effects 211

Stacking visual effects 212

How to do it... • 212

There's more... • 217

Stacking adjustment clips 220

How to do it... • 221

Creating a custom Color Board preset effect 226

How to do it... • 226

There's more... • 230

Using the Color Adjustments effect **231**

Getting ready • 231

How to do it... • 232

There's more... • 237

Using the Custom LUT effect **237**

Getting ready • 237

How to do it... • 237

Using blend modes **240**

Getting ready • 240

How to do it... • 241

   Creating a freeze-frame effect • 244

How it works... • 248

Chapter 7: Transforming Visual Elements   251

Unmasking the mystery of masks **252**

How to do it... • 252

Using the Green Screen Keyer effect **256**

Getting ready • 256

How to do it... • 256

There's more... • 263

Using the Magnetic Mask effect **264**

Getting ready • 264

How to do it... • 264

Keyframing clip position and effects **271**

How to do it... • 271

There's more... • 276

Retiming clips **276**

How to do it... • 277

Stabilizing clips **283**

Getting ready • 283

How to do it... • 283

There's more... • 286

Reframing clip resolution 286

Getting ready • 286

How to do it... • 287

Cropping, distorting, and who is Ken Burns anyway? 290

Getting ready • 291

How to do it... • 291

Chapter 8: Correcting and Enhancing Audio   299

Technical requirements 300

Setting audio roles 303

Getting ready • 304

How to do it... • 304

There's more... • 308

Using the Range Selection tool to duck audio 309

How to do it... • 309

Adjusting levels with keyboard shortcuts 313

Getting ready • 313

How to do it... • 314

Keyframing audio spikes 322

Getting ready • 322

How to do it... • 322

Using the Audio Enhancement functions 324

How to do it... • 325

There's more... • 332

Syncing audio from an external recorder 335

Getting ready • 335

How to do it... • 335

There's more... • 338

Recording scratch audio 339

Getting ready • 340

How to do it... • 340

See also • 344

Using audio effects 344

How to do it... • 344

Fixing a mono recording 351

Getting ready • 351

How to do it... • 351

Chapter 9: Building Titles   355

Customizing titles 356

How to do it... • 356

Replacing titles 362

How to do it... • 363

Using safe zones 364

How to do it... • 364

Using themes in titles and generators 367

How to do it... • 367

There's more... • 370

Creating a title object tracker 371

Getting ready • 371

How to do it... • 371

There's more... • 378

Revealing text animation 381

Getting ready • 381

How to do it... • 382

There's more... • 388

Chapter 10: Accelerating Real-World Projects 389

Creating assets for a workgroup 390

Getting ready • 390

How to do it... • 390

Controlling project versions 394

Getting ready • 395

How to do it... • 395

Planning for project versatility 397

Getting ready • 397

How to do it... • 398

Creating a repeatable project intro and outro 403

Getting ready • 403

How to do it... • 403

There's more... • 410

Creating closed captions 410

Getting ready • 411

How to do it... • 411

Gathering accurate client feedback 413

Getting ready • 414

How to do it... • 414

Chapter 11: Sharing Your Projects 417

Technical requirements 417

Sharing for Apple devices 418

How to do it... • 419

Sharing for other devices 426

How to do it... • 427

There's more... • 436

Customizing share settings 437

How to do it... • 437

There's more... • 447

Sharing roles 449

Getting ready • 449

How to do it... • 453

Sharing closed and burned-in captions 456

Getting ready • 457

How to do it... • 458

There's more... • 461

Exporting an XML project 461

Getting ready • 462

How to do it... • 466

Saving a project archive 469

How to do it... • 469

How it works... • 478

Other Books You May Enjoy   **483**

Index   **485**

Preface

Final Cut Pro is an incredible piece of software. It's built for fast, focused, digital video production. From the single main viewer window to its database-driven clip tagging, every tool is designed with one central goal: smooth, efficient, digital delivery. Is it perfect for every project? No – but I believe Final Cut Pro does 98% of what 98% of people need.

The inspiration to write this book came from my students at Century College in St. Paul, MN. Teaching Final Cut Pro has always been a joy – it's intuitive enough to dive into right away, yet deep enough to keep revealing new possibilities the more you use it. I wanted this book to reflect that balance in a format that supports learning at your own pace.

This book is structured into chapters of recipes. The content generally builds on itself: we begin with the interface and importing media, then move into editing clips, adding effects, and beyond. But each recipe also stands on its own – you can jump in anywhere to learn a specific technique and apply it immediately.

I hope you enjoy the cooking metaphors peppered throughout. I've kept the tone conversational and included plenty of supporting screenshots to guide the way.

Unlike the how-to videos scattered online, this cookbook brings everything together in one place. It's organized, practical, and designed with real-world editing scenarios in mind. You won't waste time digging through tutorials – you can head straight to a clear, step-by-step recipe and work at your own tempo.

My aim was to explain techniques and tools through specific examples, hoping you will be inspired to explore similar features and apply them to your own projects. This book isn't meant to be an exhaustive reference of every possible function or effect – it's a starting point. A sharpened chef's knife.

After 17 years of teaching Final Cut Pro at the college level, I feel confident sharing what I've learned. I hope this book helps you get creative, get editing, and get cooking.

Who this book is for

Among others, this book will be especially helpful for the independent producer – the kind of person who wears all the hats on a video project. Whether they are a freelancer juggling multiple clients or the one-person video department inside a company, this guide will get them cooking.

What this book covers

Chapter 1, Utilizing the Final Cut Pro Interface for Workflow Success: Just as a chef arranges their kitchen setup for each recipe, this chapter shows how customizing Final Cut Pro's interface and using features such as tagging, the Magnetic Timeline, and the Precision Editor view can help you cook up a smoother, more flavorful editing workflow.

Chapter 2, Organizing Media and Using the Event Browser Effectively: Just as a great chef preps their ingredients before the heat is on, this chapter shows how organizing and importing media sets the stage for an efficient and stress-free edit.

Chapter 3, Sculpting Clips in the Final Cut Pro Timeline: Like a seasoned chef perfecting a signature dish, this chapter focuses on refining your edit with advanced trimming, transitions, and timeline tools to shape your project into a polished creation.

Chapter 4, Improving Your Editing Efficiency: Just as a skilled chef prepares ingredients with precision and speed, we'll uncover time-saving shortcuts as this chapter serves up advanced editing techniques and workflow strategies to help you slice through projects with precision and speed.

Chapter 5, Exploring Color Correction and Stylizing: Just as a skilled chef uses spices to transform a dish, this chapter explores how to use Final Cut Pro's powerful color tools to elevate your footage with emotion and visual flair.

Chapter 6, Applying Visual Effects: Just as a chef layers flavors to craft a signature dish, this chapter shows how to apply visual effects to enhance storytelling with precision, style, and purpose.

Chapter 7, Transforming Visual Elements: Just as a chef perfects a dish with careful plating and garnish, this chapter teaches how to refine and position visual elements to enhance clarity, motion, and storytelling impact.

Chapter 8, Correcting and Enhancing Audio: Just as a master chef balances flavors for a perfect dish, this chapter shows how to shape, enhance, and refine audio in Final Cut Pro to create a rich and immersive storytelling experience.

Chapter 9, Building Titles: Just as an event chef ensures every place setting is picture-perfect, this chapter teaches you how to craft and finesse titles to add clarity, personality, and polish to your video productions.

Chapter 10, Accelerating Real-World Projects: Just as a master chef shares secret recipes to perfect their dishes, this chapter offers essential practical tips and workflow strategies to help you efficiently manage and elevate your projects.

Chapter 11, Sharing Your Projects: Just as a great chef presents a carefully prepared feast to guests, this chapter guides you through sharing your Final Cut Pro projects with the world using tailored export and collaboration techniques.

To get the most out of this book

We are going to assume you are at least a little familiar with Final Cut Pro. The first chapters explore the interface and organizing clips, so you should know how to import clips and add them to a project in the Timeline panel.

You will also need some footage to work with. You will need a variety of clips, including some action, someone talking, and clips that need color correction. Most can be obtained from stock media websites, but you can also use clips from your smartphone camera.

Software/hardware covered in the book	Operating system requirements
Final Cut Pro version 11.1 or later	macOS 14.6 or later
A Mac with 8 GB of memory (16 GB recommended) – some features require a Mac with Apple Silicon	

Disclaimer about AI usage

The author acknowledges the use of ChatGPT during the development of this book. It was used to generate some text, which was later edited, as well as to rewrite certain passages that the author may have further refined, thereby ensuring a smooth reading experience for readers. ChatGPT was also used in designing the book cover; however, no images within the chapters were created using AI. It's essential to note that all content and ideas were crafted by the author and refined by a professional publishing team.

Download the color images

We also provide a PDF file that has color images of the screenshots/diagrams used in this book. You can download it here: https://packt.link/gbp/9781835888469.

Conventions used

There are a number of text conventions used throughout this book.

`CodeInText`: Indicates code words in text, database table names, folder names, filenames, file extensions, pathnames, dummy URLs, user input, and Twitter handles. For example: "Note that `.cube` files are the files that will work as LUTs."

Bold: Indicates a new term, an important word, or words that you see on the screen. For instance, words in menus or dialog boxes appear in the text like this. For example: "Go to the **Window** menu and select **Show in Workspace**."

Warnings or important notes appear like this.

Tips and tricks appear like this.

Get in touch

Feedback from our readers is always welcome.

General feedback: If you have questions about any aspect of this book or have any general feedback, please email us at `customercare@packt.com` and mention the book's title in the subject of your message.

Errata: Although we have taken every care to ensure the accuracy of our content, mistakes do happen. If you have found a mistake in this book, we would be grateful if you reported this to us. Please visit `http://www.packtpub.com/submit-errata`, click **Submit Errata**, and fill in the form.

Piracy: If you come across any illegal copies of our works in any form on the internet, we would be grateful if you would provide us with the location address or website name. Please contact us at `copyright@packtpub.com` with a link to the material.

If you are interested in becoming an author: If there is a topic that you have expertise in and you are interested in either writing or contributing to a book, please visit `http://authors.packtpub.com/`.

Share your thoughts

Once you've read *Final Cut Pro Cookbook*, we'd love to hear your thoughts! Scan the QR code below to go straight to the Amazon review page for this book and share your feedback.

https://packt.link/r/183588847X

Your review is important to us and the tech community and will help us make sure we're delivering excellent quality content.

Download a Free PDF Copy of This Book

Thanks for purchasing this book!

Do you like to read on the go but are unable to carry your print books everywhere?

Is your eBook purchase not compatible with the device of your choice?

Don't worry, now with every Packt book you get a DRM-free PDF version of that book at no cost.

Read anywhere, any place, on any device. Search, copy, and paste code from your favorite technical books directly into your application.

The perks don't stop there, you can get exclusive access to discounts, newsletters, and great free content in your inbox daily.

Follow these simple steps to get the benefits:

1. Scan the QR code or visit the link below:

https://packt.link/free-ebook/9781835888469

2. Submit your proof of purchase.

3. That's it! We'll send your free PDF and other benefits to your email directly.

1

Utilizing the Final Cut Pro Interface for Workflow Success

Just like a chef meticulously plans each ingredient for a delectable dish, a skilled editor carefully crafts every element of a video to tell a compelling story. The **Final Cut Pro** interface is straightforward yet seasoned with special features that will help you with all kinds of different tasks.

In this chapter, we will explore how the Final Cut Pro interface can be changed to your advantage during different editing tasks. We will start with pre-set and custom workspaces and how to change the appearance of the Event Browser panel. But we will also tap into the power of tagging footage, as well as the benefit of the **Magnetic Timeline** and the unique Precision Editor view.

Throughout, you'll discover the essential ingredients for a successful workflow, so get ready to whip up cinematic masterpieces as we uncover the recipe for editing success in Final Cut Pro.

In this chapter, you will complete the following recipes:

- Working with the Final Cut Pro interface and workspaces
- Changing the Event Browser's appearance
- Customizing the Event Browser filtering order
- Taking advantage of the Magnetic Timeline and the Position tool
- Using the Precision Editor view

Technical requirements

For this chapter, you will need a Mac running Final Cut Pro version 11.1 or higher.

Working with the Final Cut Pro interface and workspaces

Just as a chef might customize their work surface for a specific task, Final Cut Pro allows you to arrange tools, timelines, and media in a way that best fits your editing style and workflow needs. By configuring your workspace, you can keep essential tools accessible and minimize distractions, making it easier to focus on creative tasks without getting bogged down by interface clutter. The advantage of setting up personalized workspaces is improved efficiency and a smoother editing process, as you can switch between layouts that suit different phases of your project, from organizing assets to initial edits and color correction.

In this recipe, we'll explore the Final Cut Pro interface, unlocking its intuitive design and powerful features. We will see how workspaces help you concentrate on specific tasks and how they can be customized and saved.

Getting ready

Create a new library and import some sample footage or open an existing video project. If you need more information about importing footage, see *Chapter 2* and the recipe called *Importing media into Final Cut Pro*.

How to do it...

Let's get cooking with the Final Cut Pro interface:

1. Open Final Cut Pro, and you will be greeted with its interface – it is essentially one window with different panes.

Figure 1.1: Note the panels of the Final Cut Pro interface

You can explore the interface as a single window by dragging the top window frame to see that the whole interface is made up of smaller panels that all stay together. Personally, I am not a big fan of the Mac's single window "fullscreen mode" as I like to have the menus visible and adjust the size of the window to my preference. Depending on the size of your monitor, you can adjust the Final Cut Pro interface window by dragging the lower-right corner.

Let's break down some of the panels:

- **Sidebar**: This panel holds libraries and events:

  - **Libraries** are the largest containers of media. They are essentially Final Cut Pro documents that are used in the Finder. Libraries can contain multiple events, which is why their icon looks like four event icons in a group.

  - **Events** are organized inside libraries. Their icon looks like a square with a star in the middle. They contain footage and projects (projects essentially being edited timelines).

When an event is created, the default name is the current date, which is often how footage is organized.

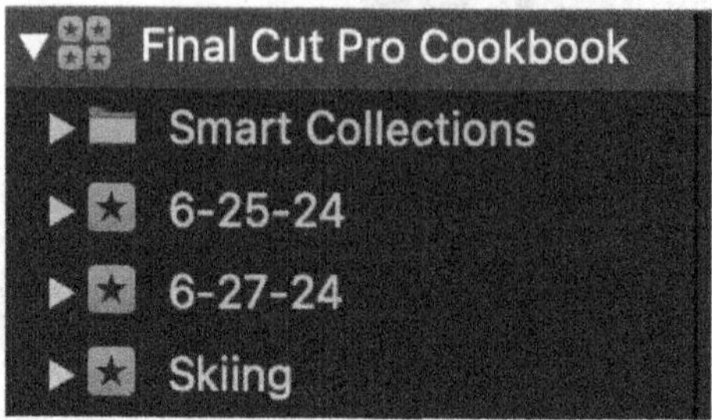

Figure 1.2: A library selected in the sidebar displaying its contained events

 You may see the terms projects and timelines used interchangeably.

- **Event Browser**: This panel organizes your footage and project timelines. As you hover the mouse over a clip, the cursor changes to a red line (known as a skimmer). As you move the skimmer over the clips, their image is displayed in the Viewer.

- **Inspector**: This panel provides full control over the properties and settings of your selected libraries and clips. It is a centralized place for precise adjustments to parameters such as color, transitions, effects, and titles.

- **Timeline** (or the **Project panel**): This panel is a visual representation of your project's sequence. It is where you assemble, arrange, layer, and fine-tune your video and audio clips. Final Cut Pro uses a primary storyline and secondary storylines connected to the primary storyline. Audio clips are also connected to the primary storyline.

- **Viewer**: This panel changes based on what we're mousing over. If we're viewing clips in the Event Browser, that's what we see in the Viewer. If we're looking at clips in the Timeline or Project panel, that's what the Viewer will show.

The panels have tool icons right above them that are associated with things that you can do within that panel. We will get into more detail about the tools and settings in later chapters and recipes.

Figure 1.3: Note the tool icons for each panel

2.   Different panes can be changed in size by moving your mouse between the panels and dragging them to make them bigger/smaller.

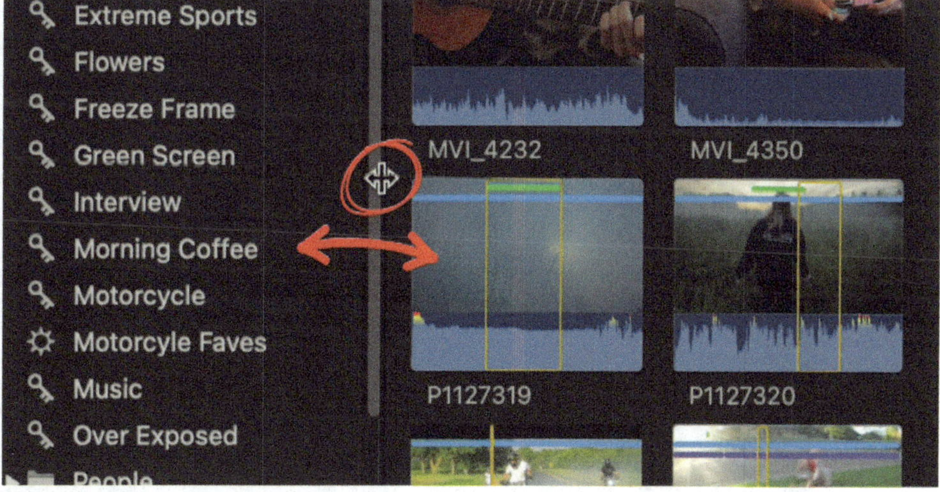

Figure 1.4: Drag the edges of panels to resize them

Don't hesitate to quickly change the size of panels to suit your editing task.

3. By clicking on the icons in the upper-right corner of the interface, you can hide or show three of the main panels of the interface – the Library Sidebar, the Timeline, or the Inspector (note that the Viewer always remains active).

Figure 1.5: Use the icons to hide or show the main panels

4. Final Cut Pro also has different looks, called **workspaces**. Click on the **Window** menu, scroll down, and select **Workspaces**. Currently, we're looking at the **Default** workspace; however, let's select the **Organize** workspace.

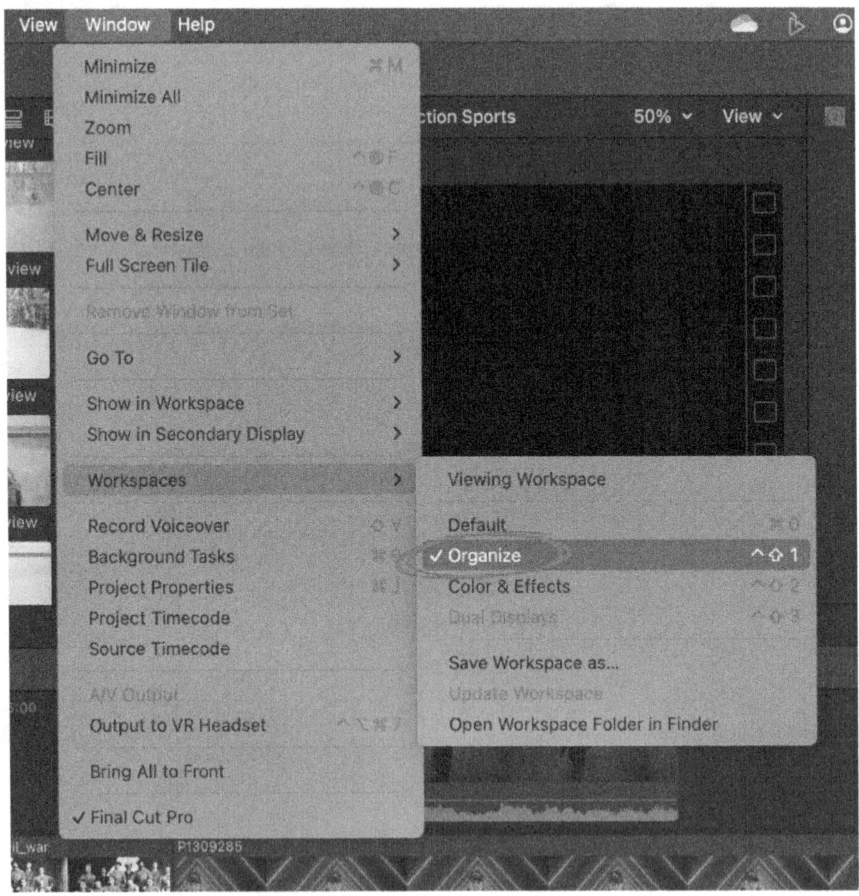

Figure 1.6: Select Organize from the Workspaces menu

You'll see that the interface hides the Timeline panel and lets you focus on the Event Browser, Viewer, and Inspector.

Figure 1.7: Note the Organize workspace interface

5. Now, from **Windows** | **Workspaces**, select **Color & Effects**. This hides the Event Browser and lets you work with the color scopes associated with the clips that you skim over with your mouse in the project timeline.

It also opens up the Effects Browser panel and keeps the Inspector open.

Figure 1.8: Note the Color & Effects workspace interface

It is also possible to make your own custom workspace.

6.   Go to the **Window** menu and select **Show in Workspace**. From there, you can check the interface panels that you want to make visible/invisible.

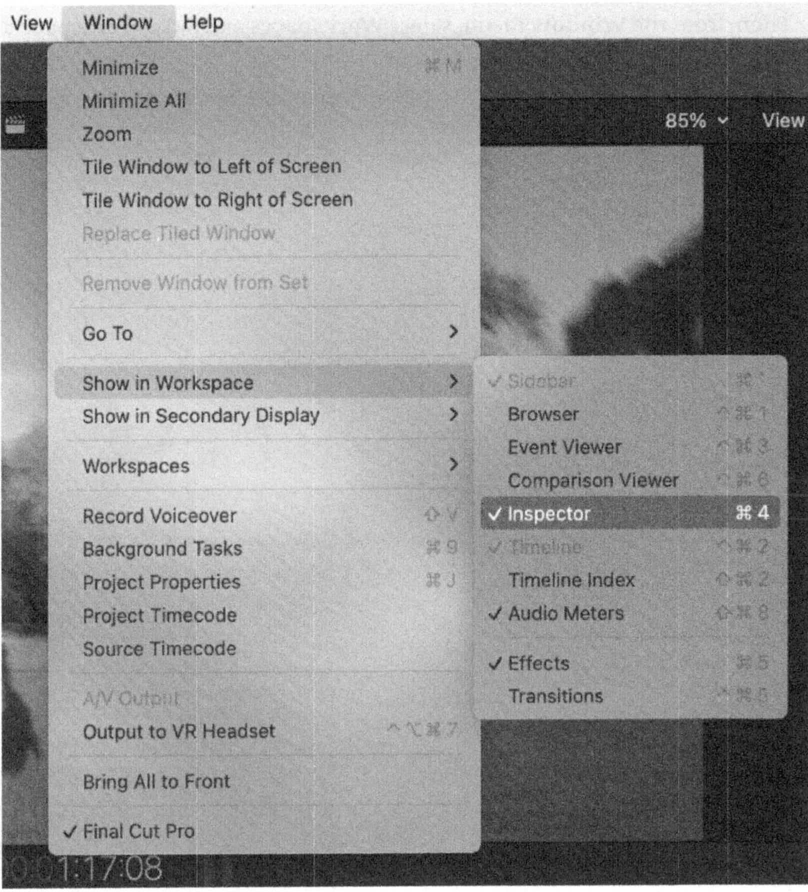

Figure 1.9: Explore the panel layout with the Show in Workspace menu

7. With the panels selected, resize them to your preference.

8. Then, from the **Window** menu, select **Workspaces** and **Save Workspace as....**

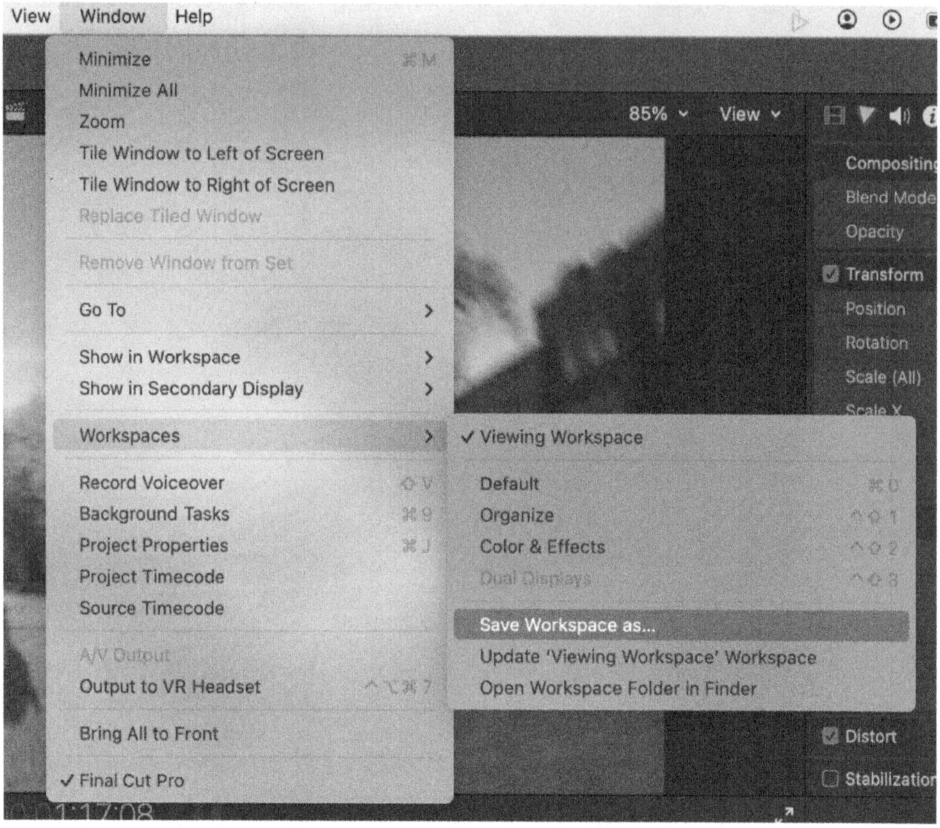

Figure 1.10: Save your custom workspace

9. Once you have created a workspace, you can update it by clicking **Update '…' Workspace** (where **…** would be your workspace name).

10. In addition, you can use this menu to open the Workspace folder in the Finder, copy your custom workspace, and transfer it to a different computer so you always have your screen preference readily available.

Changing the Event Browser's appearance

Changing the Event Browser's appearance in Final Cut Pro lets you customize how your clips are displayed, making it easier to locate and organize your clips. By using the **Clip Appearance** menu, you can tailor the clips and layout to fit your workflow. You can adjust the height and length of clips, as well as how they are grouped and sorted, making it easier to manage your media efficiently and speeding up the process of selecting and preparing footage for the timeline.

In this recipe, we'll see how to adjust the height and length of clips and how to sort and group media in the Event Browser.

Getting ready

We are going to practice sorting a variety of types of media. If you don't have project footage already, import a variety of footage, including clips that have audio. Clips with dialogue and music will be needed. You could get sample footage for free from any of the main stock media websites. If you need more information about importing footage, see *Chapter 2* and the recipe called *Importing media into Final Cut Pro*.

How to do it...

Creating your signature dish is easier when your ingredients are laid out and displayed in order. Let's explore how to customize the way your clips are displayed:

1. Along the top edge of the Event Browser, click on the **Clip Appearance** menu icon (the one that looks like a filmstrip). The **Clip Appearance** window will drop down, which contains controls that help you visualize your clips better and organize them in ways that will help you edit faster.

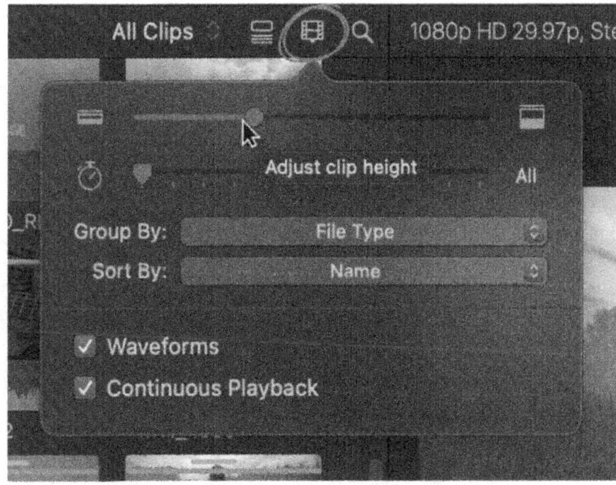

Figure 1.11: Click on the Clip Appearance button to see the drop-down window

2. Click and drag on the first slider – the **Clip Height** slider – to increase or decrease the size of the thumbnail that we're viewing in the Event Browser.

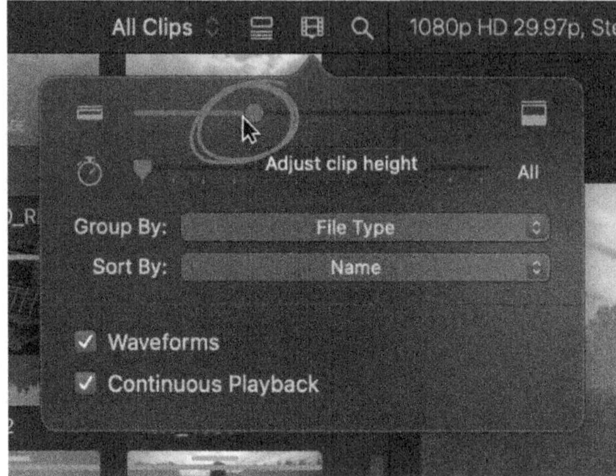

Figure 1.12: Drag the Clip Height slider

3. You can also change the amount of footage seen – that is, the number of thumbnail images per clip. To do so, click the second slider – the **Duration** slider – and move it to the right. This essentially zooms into the clip.

Figure 1.13: Drag the Duration slider

As we zoom into clips, note the jagged edge on the right end of the clip that matches with the jagged edge on the left of the next line – this shows that it is one continuous clip. In my case, as the **Duration** slider is set to **5s**, and because my clip has six images, I know the total length of the clip is about 30 seconds.

Figure 1.14: Note the jagged edges indicating a long clip in the Event Browser

4. Now click and drag the **Duration** slider to the right, so that the setting changes from **5s** to **10s**. In my case, I will see that the clip is represented by just three thumbnail images.

So, using this slider can help quickly visualize the approximate length of your clips to help organize your footage.

5.   What is also useful is the ability to group and sort your footage. Currently, the **Group By** drop-down menu shows the default option, **File Type** – which will separate video clips from photos and audio files, but there are other options, such as **Content Created** and **Date Imported**, that you could group footage by instead.

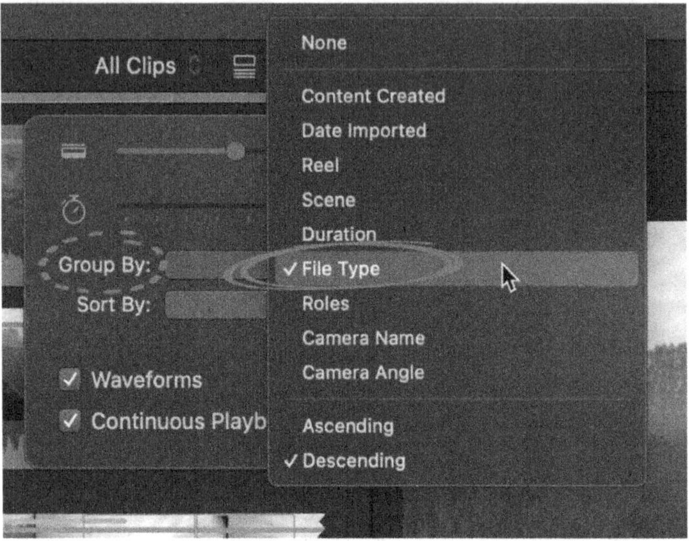

Figure 1.15: Select from the Group By drop-down menu

6.   Within these groups, clips can be sorted using the **Sort By** drop-down menu. If you are familiar with your footage and know the order in which it was shot, it might make sense to sort by the date it was created (**Content Created**). But you can also sort by **Name**, **Take**, or **Duration**.

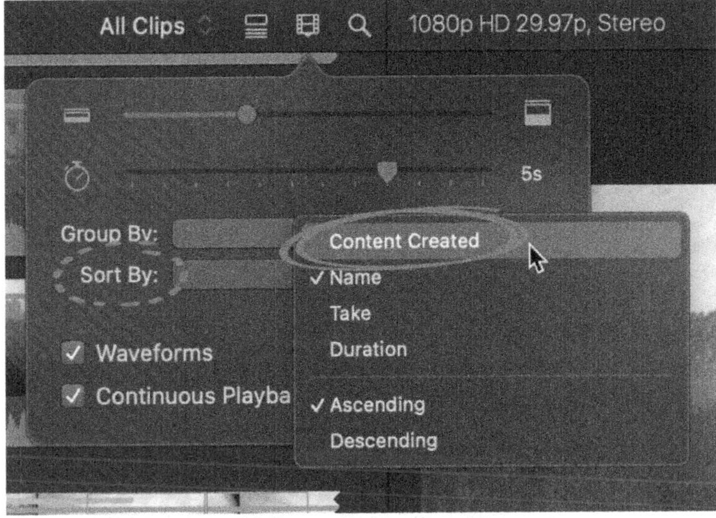

Figure 1.16: Select from the Sort By drop-down menu

7. There are two more options in the **Clip Appearance** menu you can use:

    - The **Waveforms** checkbox shows the audio visualization waveforms within our clips, to give us an idea of the dialogue or the audio levels.

    - The **Continuous Playback** checkbox allows you to play clips one after another in the Event Browser. This becomes something of an "assembly edit" (more on that in *Chapter 2*).

Customizing the Event Browser's filtering order

When working in the Event Browser, you can rate your clips as **Favourites** or **Rejected**. Then, you can customize the Browser's filtering order to quickly find and categorize your media to suit the unique needs of each project, reducing the time spent searching for clips. This personalized approach enhances efficiency and ensures that the most relevant footage is always at your fingertips, making the editing process smoother and more intuitive.

In this recipe, we will learn how to rate clips and then explore several ways to display clips based on our rating system.

Getting ready

Import some sample footage or open an existing video project. If you need more information about importing footage, see *Chapter 2* and the recipe called *Importing media into Final Cut Pro*.

How to do it...

Like a stack of your favorite recipe cards, let's rate and filter your clips:

1. Click on the **Clip Filtering** menu at the top of the Event Browser. From the list, you can choose which items you want to view and hide.

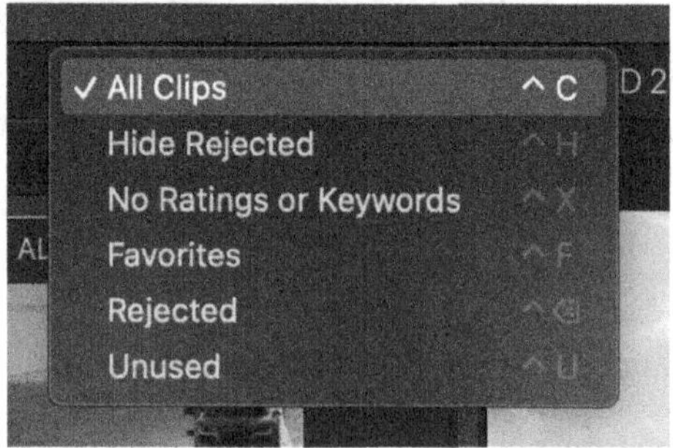

Figure 1.17: Select from the Clip Filtering menu

At the moment, **All Clips** is selected, but let's change that.

2. Click on a clip or a portion of a clip in the Event Browser. Then give it a **Favorite** rating by simply clicking on the *F* key as a keyboard shortcut. You could also use a menu command by going to the **Mark** menu and selecting **Favorite**.

3. Select another clip, and press the *Delete* key shortcut. Don't freak out – it doesn't delete the clip; it just rates the clip as rejected! Again, you could use a menu command by going to the **Mark** menu and selecting **Reject**.

Now, looking at the clips, the **Favorite** rating is indicated by a green bar above the clip, while the **Rejected** rating is indicated by a red bar:

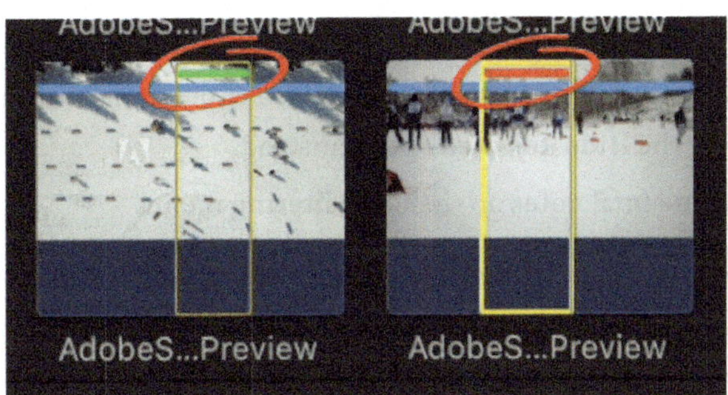

Figure 1.18: Note the green Favorite and red Rejected rating bars on clips

How you choose to create favorites is up to you. You can favorite all of the clips that you like, even if you don't end up using them, or you can reserve the favorite function for just those things that you're absolutely sure you're going to use. The same goes for rejecting clips. Remember that they are not gone, but rather easier to hide.

4. Once you have favorited and rejected some clips, return to the **Clip Filtering** menu and select **Favorites**. Now you will only see clips and portions of clips that have the **Favorite** rating.

5. It should be pointed out that the **Favorite** or **Rejected** rating is not lost if the rated portion of a clip becomes unselected, that is, not highlighted in yellow. To re-select just the rated portion of a clip, simply click on the green or red bar along the top edge of the clip.

Figure 1.19: Re-select the rated portion of a clip by clicking on the rating bar

6. Now, from the **Clip Filtering** menu, click **Rejected** to view just the clips, or portions of clips, rated as **Rejected**. We can also keep rejected clips from cluttering up the Event Browser by selecting the **Hide Rejected** option instead.

7. Here are some final notes on the **Clip Filtering** menu:

    - Sometimes, with large projects, there are so many clips that it is good to review which clips have not been used in the timeline. You can specifically filter clips that are marked as **Unused**.

    - Also, if you have used all of your favorite clips, try viewing clips using the **No Ratings or Keywords** option.

    - Finally, if you want to remove a **Favorite** or **Rejected** rating, select the clip and simply use the keyboard shortcut *U*. Or, from the **Mark** menu, select **Unrate**.

There's more...

There are two other sets of media that share the sidebar and browser panels: **Photos, Videos, and Audio,** and **Titles and Generators**.

In the upper-right corner of the Final Cut Pro interface, click on the **Photos, Videos, and Audio** icon that looks like a musical note in a circle on top of a camera. This tab gives you a quick link to the Apple ecosystem and access to the photos you have taken, as well as media you have purchased from Apple Music and Apple TV. There is also a variety of sound effects.

Figure 1.20: Select Sound Effects in the Photos, Videos, and Audio Browser

Take some time to explore the media available in this tab. We will be using some sound effects in *Chapter 7*.

Also located in the upper-right corner of the Final Cut Pro interface, click on the **Titles and Generators** icon that looks like a capital T in a square on top of a film countdown frame. Titles and generators are pre-built assets such as animated text, backgrounds, textures, and elements, allowing for seamless integration of additional visual content.

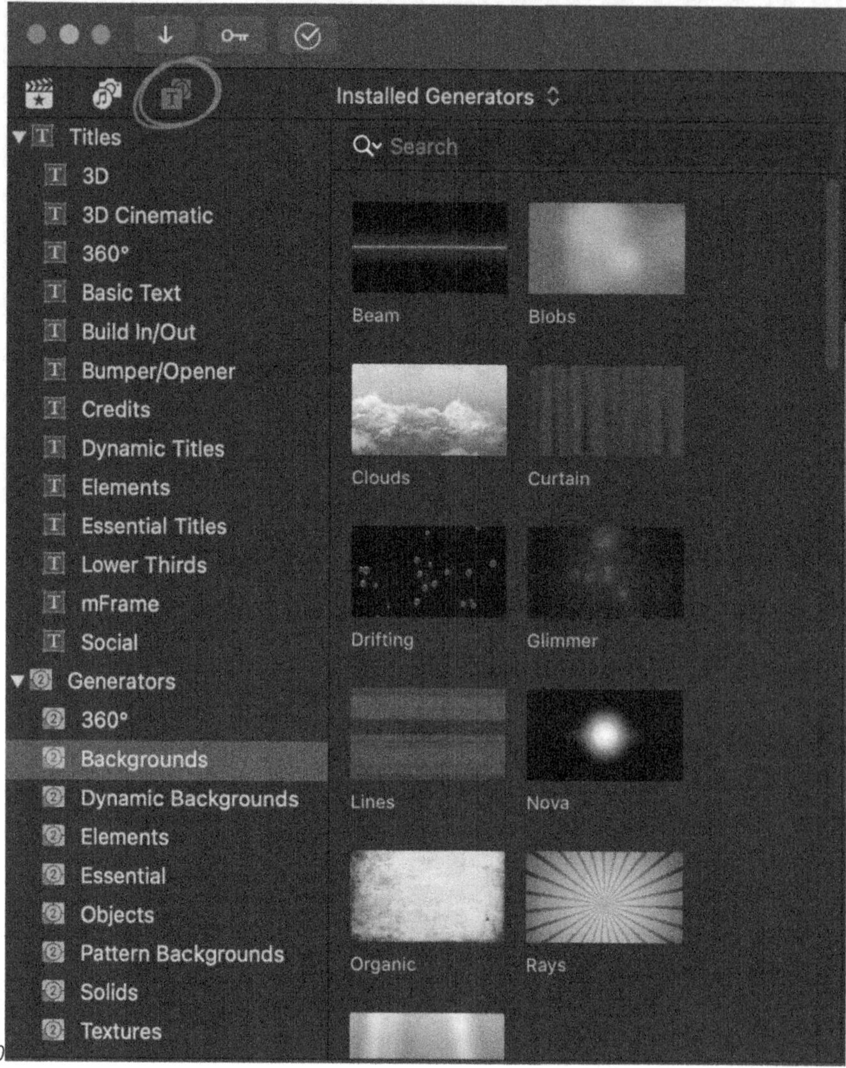

Figure 1.21: Select Backgrounds in the Titles and Generators Browser

Again, take some time to explore the possibilities available to you in this tab. We will be using some generators in *Chapter 6*, and we will have an entire chapter on titles in *Chapter 9*.

Overall, these tabs provide a quick and efficient way to enrich your project with diverse visual components, saving time while expanding your creative possibilities.

Taking advantage of the Magnetic Timeline and the Position tool

Instead of tracks, Final Cut Pro uses the metaphor of primary and secondary storylines:

- The primary storyline is the main stream of video. It is what drives the timing of the story.
- Secondary storylines are sequences of connected clips. These secondary storylines are stacked on top of the primary storyline.

Now, the primary storyline is a Magnetic Timeline. This means that, starting at the beginning of the timeline, clips simply *snap* together, so you don't have to worry about black gaps or missing frames between clips. This ensures your edits stay perfectly synchronized and your workflow remains smooth.

Meanwhile, the **Position** tool allows an editor to seamlessly position clips anywhere on the Magnetic Timeline. You can build portions of your story at any point in time that you choose.

We'll look at both of these features in this recipe.

Getting ready

Import some sample footage or open an existing video project. If you need more information about importing footage, see *Chapter 2* and the recipe called *Importing media into Final Cut Pro*.

How to do it...

The Magnetic Timeline is the non-stick skillet of video editing–ingredients stay in order, even when you shake things up. Let's explore it:

1. Take a clip from the Event Browser and drag it into the primary storyline. When you release the mouse, the clip will snap toward the left and connect to the right of an existing clip.

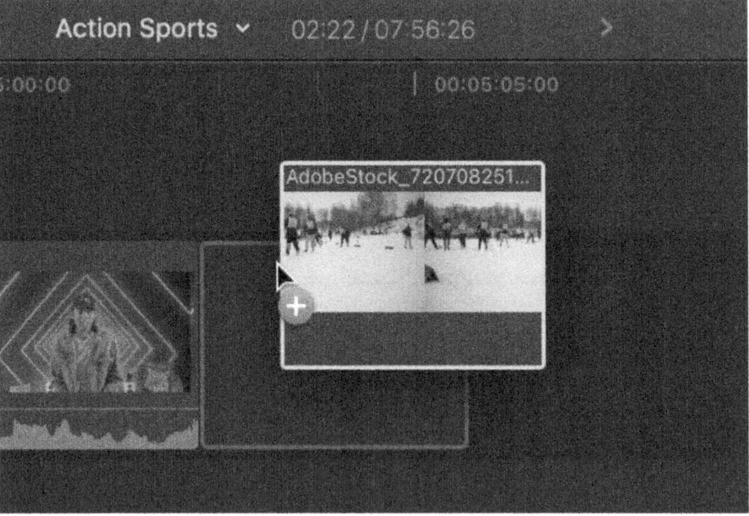

Figure 1.22: Note how a new clip snaps into place on the Magnetic Timeline

2. In addition, when you move clips to a different place on the timeline, other clips will shift position to allow the clip to snap into a new location without any gaps.

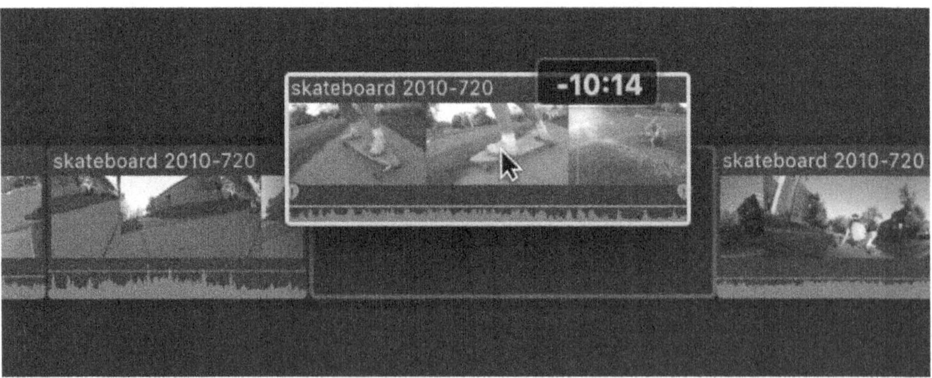

Figure 1.23: Note how the moved clips snap into place within the Magnetic Timeline

3. Besides the behavior of the Magnetic Timeline, you can also turn on **Snapping**. This option can be found above the timeline and looks like two clips clicking together. Alternatively, you can use the keyboard shortcut *N* for *"snnnnaping"*.

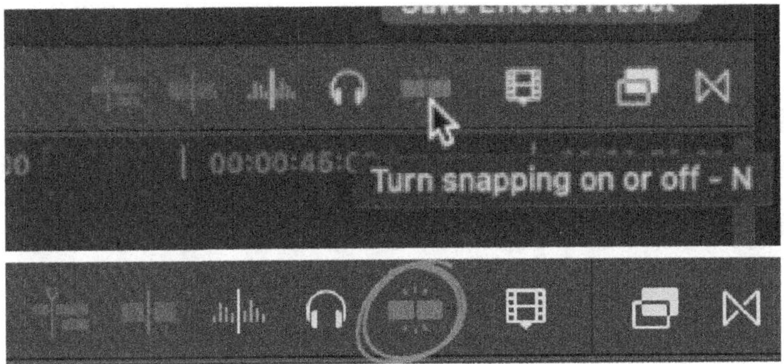

Figure 1.24: Click on the Snapping function icon

With **Snapping** turned on, clips and edit points will snap to the edges of your playhead, markers, or other connected clips in the timeline. Besides the magnetic behavior of the primary storyline, **Snapping** keeps other clips and edit points neat and tidy.

Moving on, sometimes you want to work on a portion of your project that's nearer the end of the project than the start. Perhaps you have an idea for a dramatic ending to your story and want to edit that together. That's possible in Final Cut Pro while keeping the Magnetic Timeline functioning perfectly. Enter the **Position** tool:

4. Above the Timeline panel, toward the right-hand side, is the **Tools** dropdown menu. The **Select** tool (with the keyboard shortcut *A*) is the most common tool people use while editing, but the **Position** tool (shortcut *P*) is what we're going to use right now.

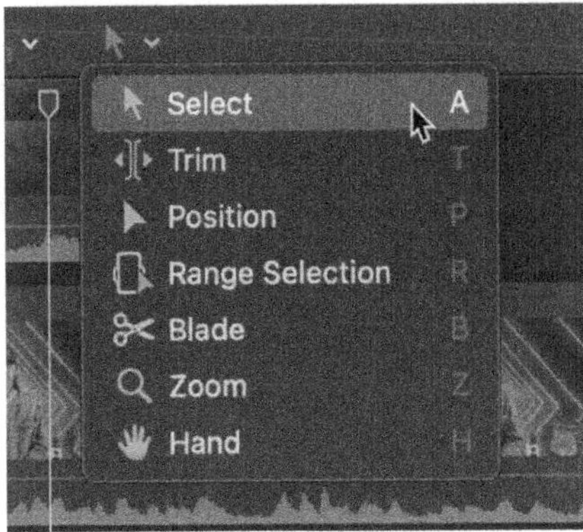

Figure 1.25: Select from the Tools menu or use the quick keyboard shortcuts

5. Using the **Position** tool, select a new clip or a portion of a clip from the Event Browser panel, and drag it to the primary storyline, making sure to place the clip toward the end of your project. Once done, Final Cut Pro will automatically make a **gap clip** (a blank clip, sometimes called a slug) between your new clip and where you left off in the Magnetic Timeline. Now you can build a new portion of your project, further down the timeline.

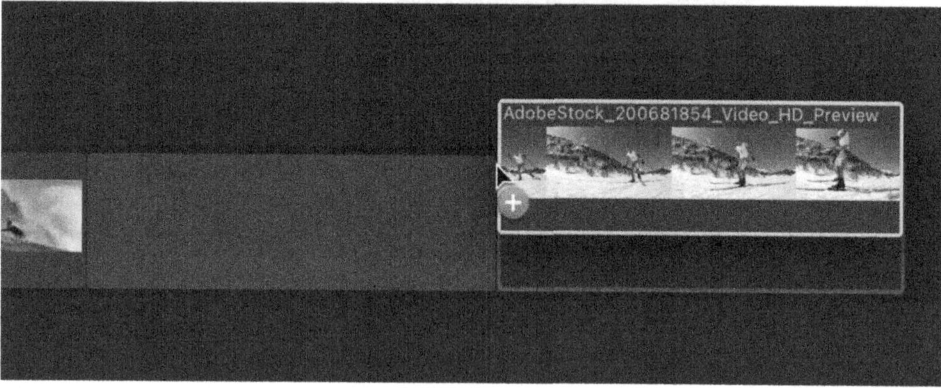

Figure 1.26: Note the Timeline with a gap clip created by the Position tool

6. As you build the project with the **Position** tool, you can put clips anywhere inside that gap clip. Be careful though, because the **Position** tool will also automatically override clips that you already have in your timeline. You can switch back to the **Select** tool, and your clips will work magnetically and not be overridden.

There's more

Let's explore continuous timeline scrolling, which means the timeline will keep scrolling as the video is played. You can find this option in the timeline control icons. It looks like a playhead over two clips. Or, you can use the keyboard shortcut *Option + Shift + S* to toggle the option on or off.

Figure 1.27: Select Continuous Scrolling from the Timeline panel control icons

So, with continuous scrolling turned off, the clips in the timeline stay where they are, and the playhead moves to the right.

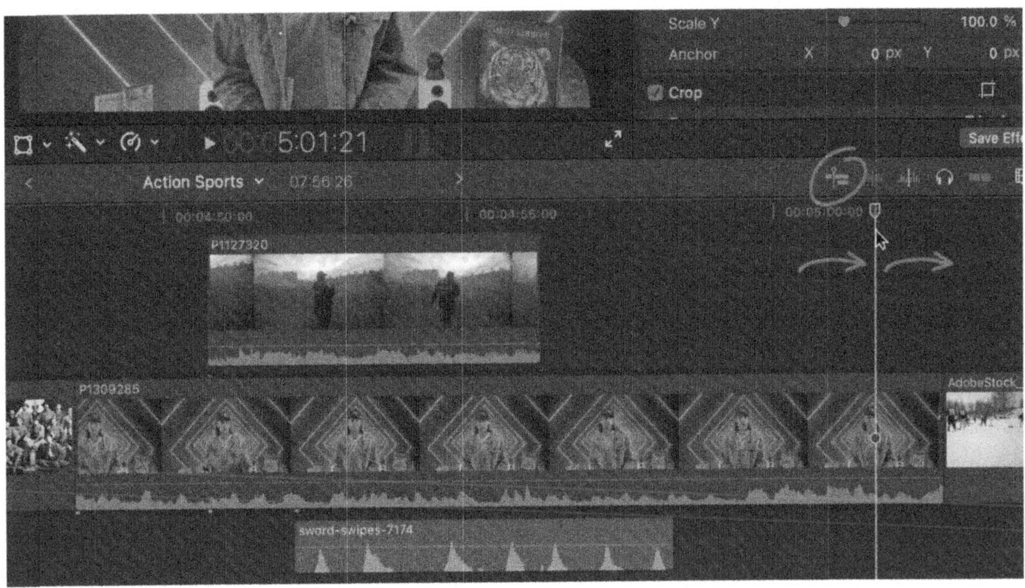

Figure 1.28: Note how the playhead scrolls to the right with continuous scrolling off

With it turned on, while located in the first half of the timeline, the playhead moves to the right as it normally would, but when it reaches the center of the timeline, the playhead remains where it is, and the clips scroll continuously to the left.

Figure 1.29: Note how clips scroll to the left with continuous scrolling on

Interestingly, if continuous scrolling is turned on and the clips start playing while the playhead is in the left half of the timeline, both the playhead and the clips will scroll to the left until the playhead is in the center of the panel, where it will remain while the clips continue to scroll to the left.

Working with the Precision Editor view

Just as a master chef might use an extremely sharp knife to make precision slices, the Precision Editor is a tool designed for careful clip trimming. Although an advanced tool, we are exploring its use to visualize how clips are interlinked in the Magnetic Timeline. This view lets you see extra footage on either side of a cut, so you can precisely trim, extend, or shorten clips to perfect the pace and enhance your storytelling.

In this recipe, we'll explore the Precision Editor view and the relationship between clips in the primary storyline.

How to do it...

Sharpen your editing knives and let's start cutting with the Precision Editor:

1. In the timeline, we can normally look at the edit point of two clips next to each other. Each clip can be adjusted in relation to the other, having its in and out points changed by dragging the edge of the clip.

Figure 1.30: Note the normal view of an edit point

But if you double-click on the edit point, you open up the view of the Precision Editor. This view expands the timeline and shows you the two clips – the first at the top and the second at the bottom. It also shows the point at which the clips have their edit point and what footage is tucked underneath (this is footage that exists, but it is not visible).

Figure 1.31: Note the Precision Editor view of an edit point

2.   In the Precision Editor view, the cursor changes to a small hand with arrows on it. If we click and hold the mouse, the cursor changes to an icon of a hand gripping the clip. Now we can move the clip in relation to the edit point.

Figure 1.32: Note how the hand cursor animates to "grip" footage when moving left or right

3. Move the mouse to the right side of the edit point for the top footage that is tucked underneath. Click, hold, and slide to see that the hand can grip and move the footage on either side of the edit point. This is in contrast to the regular view of editing where you can only change the edit point from the footage you can see.

Figure 1.33: Grip and adjust the edit point with the hidden footage

4. This is also the case with the clip on the bottom layer. Click, hold, and grab the footage with the hand cursor, then move it in relation to the edit point, which will remain in the center of the timeline.

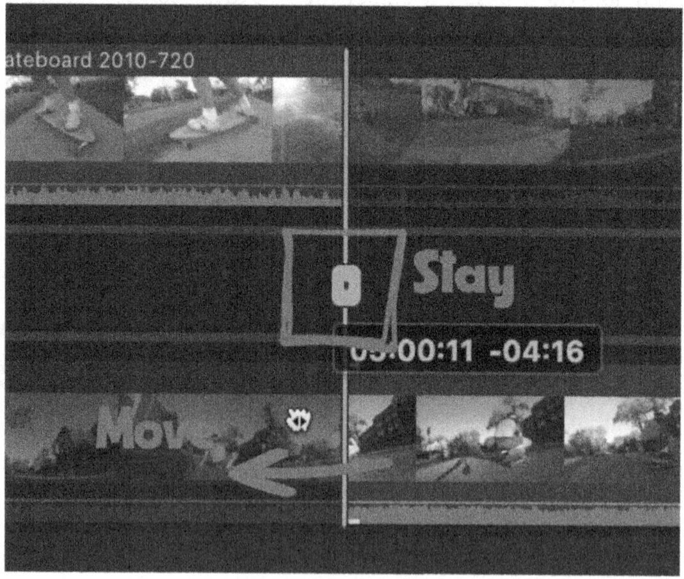

Figure 1.34: Note how the center edit point remains still as clips move

Note that when you are moving a clip, the Viewer changes to a two-up display, showing the out point of the top layer and the in point of the bottom layer.

Figure 1.35: Note how the Viewer panel window changes to a two-up display when editing the center point

5. You can also click, hold, and drag the edit point from the center of the panel. This is known as a rolling edit and changes the out point of the first clip and the in point of the second clip simultaneously. This allows you to adjust both clips at once, instead of individually, saving you time while editing.

Figure 1.36: Roll the edit point by dragging the center edit point

6. Once done, to close the Precision Editor panel, double-click on the edit point in the center of the timeline.

7. You may or may not incorporate the Precision Editor into your everyday workflow, but again, we are exploring it here to visualize how clips are interlinked in the Magnetic Timeline. This view lets you see the footage on either side of an edit point. This visualization will be helpful in advanced recipes such as *Getting to grips with ripple, roll, slip, and slide edits* in *Chapter 4*.

2

Organizing Media and Using the Event Browser Effectively

In the bustling kitchen of video editing, organization is the key ingredient for a smooth and efficient workflow. Just as a chef carefully arranges ingredients before cooking, mastering Final Cut Pro's Event Browser ensures your media is neatly sorted and easily accessible before you lay any clips onto the timeline.

In this chapter, we will start with organizing and importing media efficiently, and exploring the differences between optimized and proxy media. With media imported, we will discuss ways of using the Event Browser panel to its full potential. We will see the power behind tagging your clips with keywords and then how to locate your clips quickly with different views and by saving Smart Collections.

In this chapter, we will cover the following recipes:

- Creating a camera archive
- Importing media into Final Cut Pro
- Importing media with drag and drop
- Understanding optimized versus proxy media
- Using keywords

- Using the Event Browser List view
- Making an assembly edit
- Creating Smart Collections
- Relinking media

Technical requirements

To work with media in these recipes, you will need some sample clips. You can download free sample files with watermarks from any of the major stock media websites, or you can use the footage from your camera's SD card.

Creating a camera archive

You should treat your SD cards as precious jewels. If you are videoing a wedding and lose or damage the SD card, imagine trying to get the entire wedding party back together and ask them to look surprised as you recreate the wedding ceremony. That would probably not work, so keep those SD cards safe until you can make a backup on an external hard drive.

In this recipe, we will see how to save precious footage with a camera archive – a disk copy of an SD card on your hard drive.

Getting ready

To follow along, you need to have an SD card with footage recorded from a video camera.

How to do it...

That container of pasta at the back of your refrigerator won't keep for long, but a camera archive will. Let's make one:

1. With Final Cut Pro open, insert an SD card from your camera.
2. Once inserted, the **Media Import** window should come up automatically. On the left, you should see your SD card show up in the list of cameras.

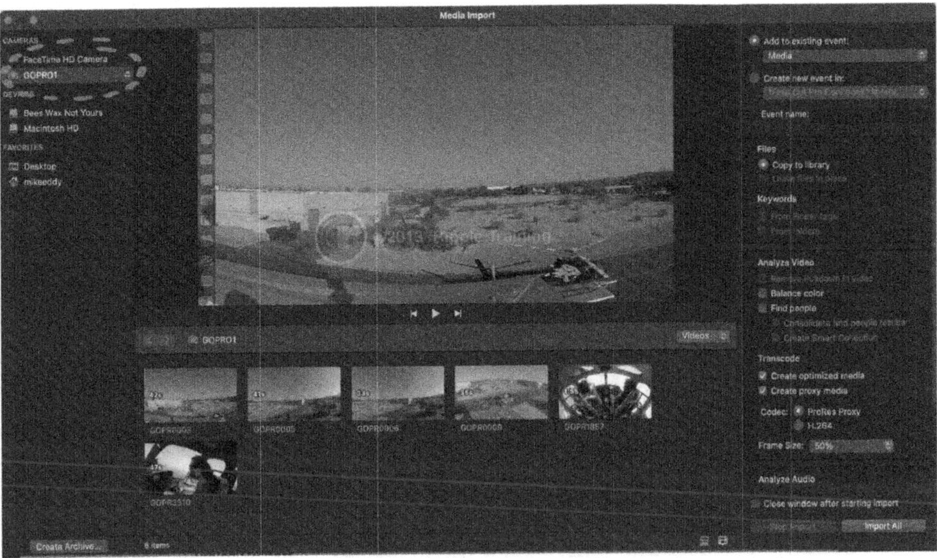

Figure 2.1: Select your SD card in the Media Import window

We will look at the **Media Import** window more closely in the next recipe, *Importing media into Final Cut Pro*. If the window doesn't appear automatically when you insert your SD card, you will find alternative ways to access the window there, too.

3. With the SD card selected, click on the **Create Archive...** button located in the lower-left corner of the interface. This will simply make a disk image of that SD card.

Figure 2.2: Click on the Create Archive... button first

4. When you create the archive, you can give the disk image a specific name, which will help you quickly know what media it contains, and choose a save location to help organize the footage further.

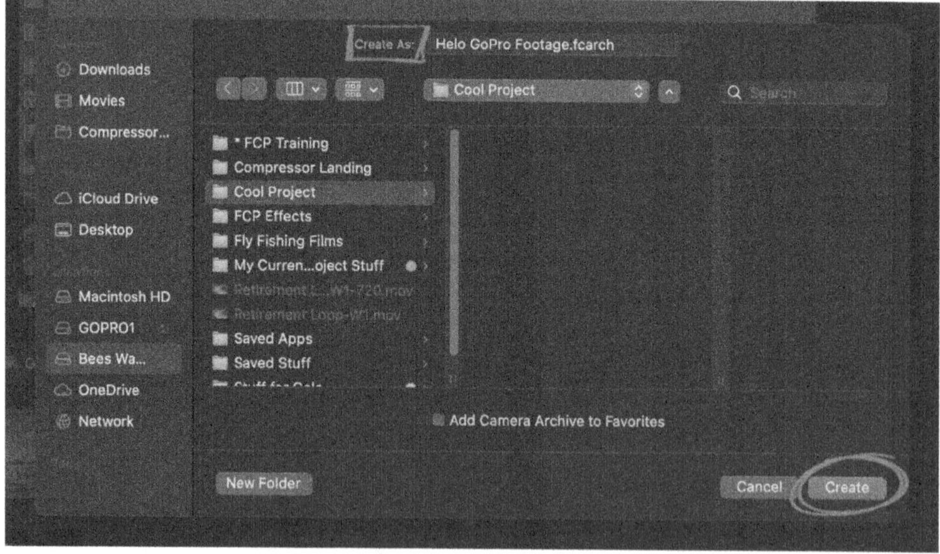

Figure 2.3: Give your card archive a new name

Here is the created camera archive (the **camera archive** icon looks like a round movie film canister with a keyhole):

Figure 2.4: The camera archive file icon in the Finder

 You can also import from a camera archive file later as if it were an SD card. This will be mentioned in the next recipe, *Importing media into Final Cut Pro*.

There's more...

Ideally, you will be working with three hard drives:

- One is the internal hard drive of your computer. This will contain the operating system and software such as Final Cut Pro.

- The second external drive will contain your current project libraries and footage. That way, the computer can run faster when Final Cut Pro does not have to switch between reading software data and footage data within the same hard drive.

- The third external drive, or cloud storage, will be backups of projects, libraries, and camera archives. It's a good idea to have the camera archive on a hard drive different from the project itself in case the project's hard drive fails.

This strategy of having multiple hard drives reduces your risk of content loss if a drive fails. Trying to recreate an event, film, or interview would be nearly impossible. In that regard, your footage is practically priceless.

Remember the *3-2-1 rule*: *three* copies, in *two* locations, and *one* on a different type of media, such as a server.

Importing media into Final Cut Pro

Just like gathering the freshest ingredients before a great meal, importing media is the first (and most important) step in crafting your edit. Final Cut Pro makes this process seamless with features such as automatic file organization, keyword tagging, and footage transcoding. These tools ensure your footage is prepped and ready to go, letting you focus on creative storytelling instead of digging through the pantry.

In this recipe, we'll explore the essential steps for importing media into Final Cut Pro, ensuring your footage is organized and ready for editing.

How to do it...

To import media into Final Cut Pro, follow these steps:

1. First, open the **Media Import** window. There are multiple ways to do this:

    - Click on the **Media Import** icon, which looks like an arrow pointing down and is located in the upper-left corner of the interface. From the drop-down menu, select **Media....**

Figure 2.5: Use the Media Import icon or keyboard shortcut of Command + I

    - From the **File** menu, select **Import**, then **Media**.
    - Use the keyboard shortcut of *Command + I*.

    We will discuss importing from **Image Playground...** in *Chapter 4*, in a recipe called *Using gap clips and placeholder clips*.

2. With the **Media Import** window open, we can see several areas:

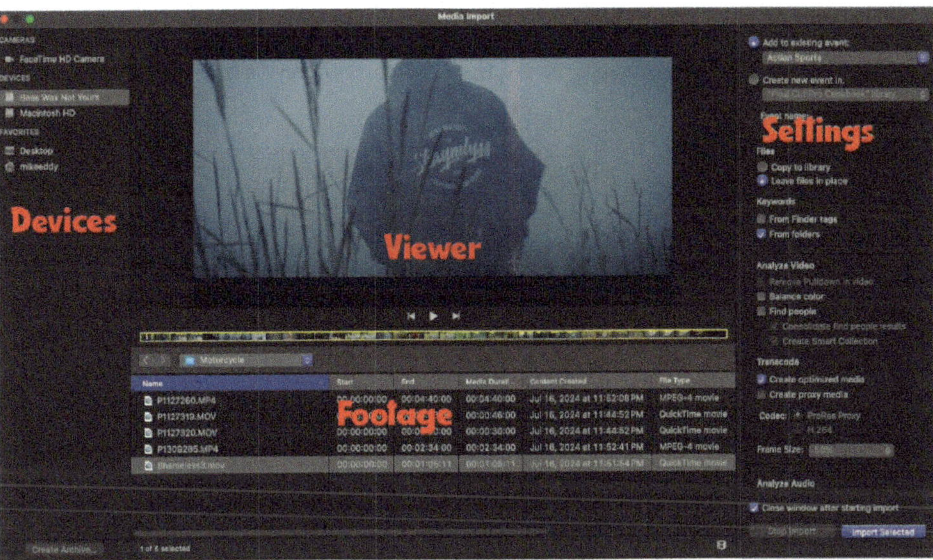

Figure 2.6: Note the panels in the Media Import window

On the left-hand side is the list of devices – this includes cameras, hard drives, and SD cards. For ease of access, you can set a list of your favorite devices here as well.

Based on the device selected, in the lower center of the interface, you will find a list of footage that the device contains. You can use the disclosure triangle to drill down and look inside the folders, although that can sometimes get a little bit confusing with so many files and folders. I prefer to double-click on the folder, and then the contents of the window reveal just the media in that folder.

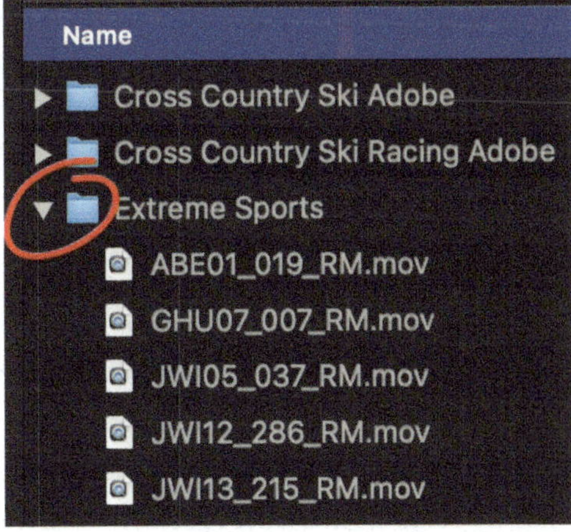

Figure 2.7: Clicking on a folder disclosure triangle

To aid in navigation, there are **forward** and **back** arrow icons along the top edge of the footage area. Like a web browser, these buttons will cycle back and forward between the folders you have been viewing.

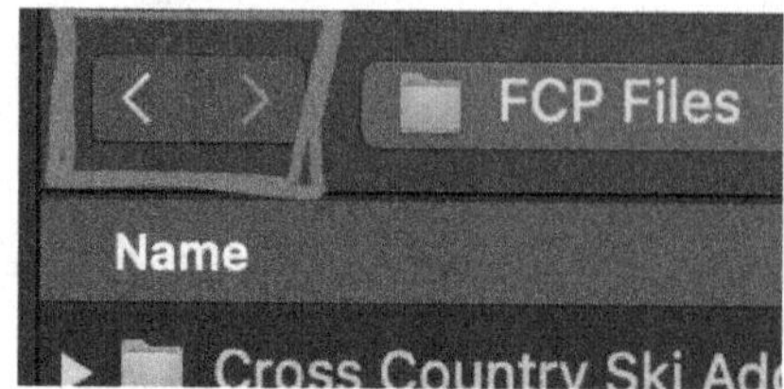

Figure 2.8: Note the forward and back navigation arrow icons

Alternatively, you can use a drop-down menu to show the backward path of where you've been navigating:

Figure 2.9: Navigate to a folder's backward path with the pop-up menu

When you click on a footage file, it shows up in the Viewer panel. Using the viewer icons, you can play/stop the media or go to the beginning/end of the footage.

On the right-hand side panel, there are the various settings that can be applied to your import session:

- The first two options deal with which library and event they will connect to:

    - **Add to existing event**: This option opens a list of libraries and events to which your footage will be added. In the drop-down menu shown in *Figure 2.9*, I have one library currently open, and it has two events to select from. If there were more libraries and their events, they'd also show up in this list. By default, Final Cut Pro selects the library and event you had selected in the Sidebar panel before starting the import process.

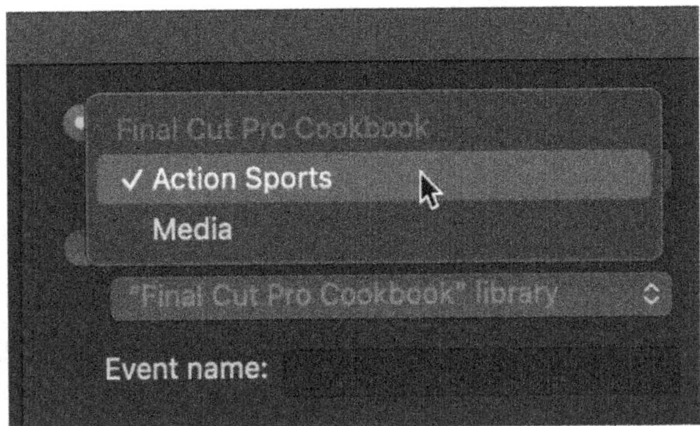

Figure 2.10: Select an event in which to import your footage

- **Create new event in**: Using this, we could choose a library and give the new event a name.

- Under **Files**, we have two options that are related to where our files will be physically imported, not just the event that they're listed in. We have a **Copy to library** option – where files will be copied and internal to the file size of the library – or a **Leave files in place** option, such as leaving them on a hard drive and just referencing those files. Final Cut Pro will create a link to remember the path to those files and not duplicate them into the library file.

Figure 2.11: Select either to copy footage to your library or leave it in place on your hard drive

- The next section of settings contains the **Keywords** settings. Keywords are tags related to our footage. At the time of importing, we can automatically assign keywords in two ways:

  - One is **From Finder tags**, which you can use if you've tagged folders with names and colors in the finder.

- The other is to assign keywords from folder names where these clips are located. I normally have the **From folders** checked because I want to organize my footage based on how I've already organized it by folder name on the hard drive.

Figure 2.12: Use the checkboxes to automatically add Finder keywords when importing

 We will work with keywords in the *Using keywords* recipe later in this chapter.

- Moving on, we have **Analyze Video** settings. At this point in importing, we can do several things to analyze our video:

  - We can check **Remove Pulldown in video** to eliminate pulldown patterns. This is currently grayed out because that has to do with footage from a tape-based camera or device.

  - We can also check **Balance color** so that, if our footage has a tint, it will be automatically fixed. Sometimes, outdoor shots tend to have a blue cast, and indoor shots are orange.

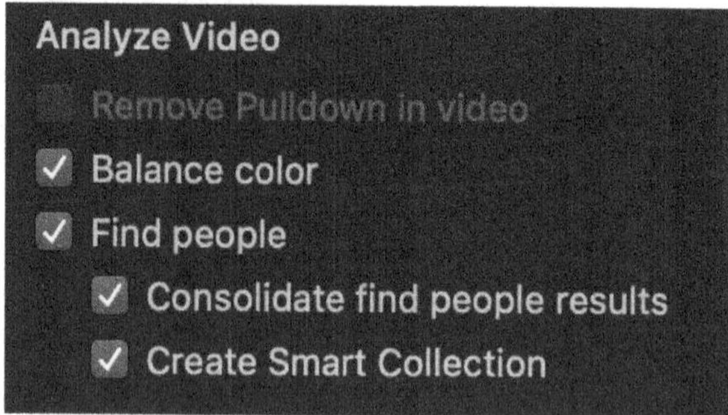

Figure 2.13: The options available to analyze video on import

- Plus, we can do a **Find people** analysis in the footage. Final Cut Pro will complete facial recognition on footage and still images to find people and shot angles, and give that footage keywords.

- I recommend checking **Consolidate find people results** and **Create Smart Collection**, too. This way, you can easily find the results of the analysis in the event listed in the Sidebar. The results of the Smart Collection will be in a folder called `People`, containing `Close Up Shot`, `Medium Shot`, `One Person`, `Two Persons`, and `Wide Shot` sub-folders, like so:

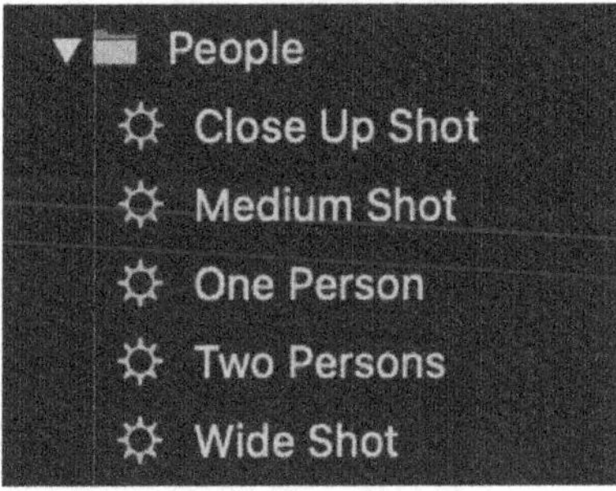

Figure 2.14: The Smart Collection results in the Event Browser from the Find people analysis

- Next up, we have the **Transcode** settings. Final Cut Pro imports the original media, but there are options to create alternate versions of the media or to transcode (change) it. One option is **Create optimized media**; as the word indicates, this version is optimal for editing in Final Cut Pro. You can also check **Create proxy media**, which is a smaller file size.

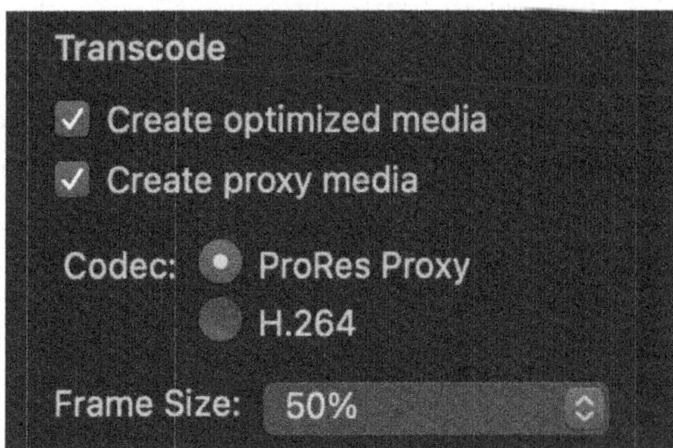

Figure 2.15: The options available to transcode your video when importing

We will dig deeper into this topic in the *Understanding optimized versus proxy media* recipe later in this chapter.

- Further down are the **Analyze Audio** settings.

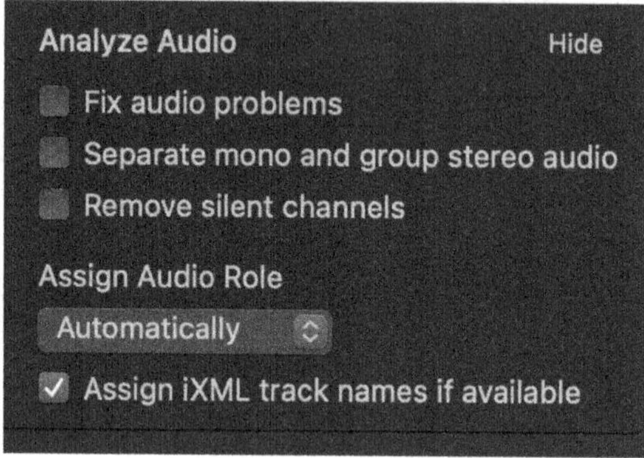

Figure 2.16: The options available in the Analyze Audio section

- Here, we can do the following:

    - Automatically fix most audio problems.

    - Separate mono and group stereo audio if we've recorded on separate channels. In that regard, we can remove silent channels if we have one microphone recording to a channel and another channel is not recording.

    - There's also the ability to assign an audio role when the footage is being imported. Most of the time, we know that the footage being imported is dialogue, visual effects, or music, so we can select one of those options. Alternatively, we can select automatically and use the iXML track information if it's available. We will dig deeper into audio in *Chapter 8*.

- Lastly, there is the **Close window after starting import** checkbox. I will often leave this unchecked so that when footage from an SD card is done importing, I can confirm that it is done and then eject the card by clicking on the **eject** icon next to the card listed in the **CAMERAS** area.

Figure 2.17: Click on the device eject icon

3. After reviewing those settings, with a clip or a folder selected, we can click on the **Import Selected** or **Import All** button to start the process.

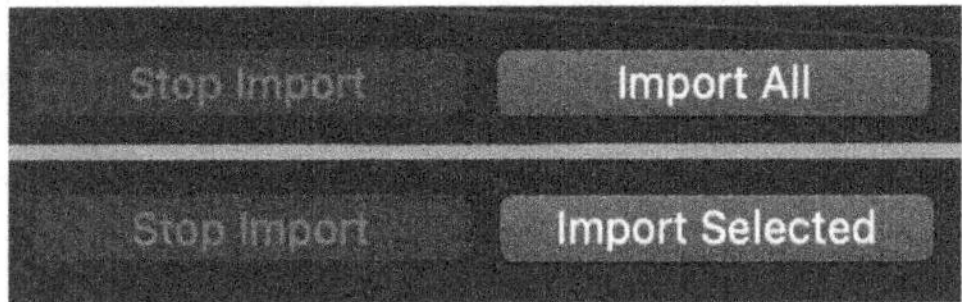

Figure 2.18: Click on the Import All or Import Selected button

There's more...

When importing from an SD card, the process is slightly different. Currently, I have an SD card inserted, and the SD card should show up in the upper-left corner in the **CAMERAS** category. Depending on the format and the camera, your SD card may be listed under **DEVICES**. Click on the SD card device.

The clips stored on your card will be lined up in the lower center of the window. The Viewer area looks slightly different compared to importing from a hard drive.

For example, from an SD card, you can select portions of clips to import.

Figure 2.19: Select a portion of a clip when importing from an SD card

When using an SD card, you will notice several things are grayed out in the Settings panel. One is the ability to leave files in place. This makes sense, as an SD card is often only inserted into your computer temporarily. So, the only option is to copy the footage to the library.

Figure 2.20: An SD card creates different settings options

The other change is that of the **Keywords** settings. As we discussed earlier in this recipe, the **From Finder tags** option refers to tagged folders with names and colors in the Finder, and **From folders** refers to the names of the folders. However, because an SD card is not a hard drive, there are no folder names or tags, so the options are grayed out.

It should also be noted that SD cards are not computer hard drives. Although it may be possible to use the Macintosh Finder to look at files and footage on an SD card, it is not recommended to drag those files from the SD card to the Finder folders. There's database information embedded in the SD card. It is formatted for a camera, not for a computer.

The safest way to keep SD cards intact is to extract the video with software such as Final Cut Pro, iMovie, and so on. Again, footage on an SD card, formatted for a camera, needs to be carefully processed and extracted onto the computer's hard drive.

Keep in mind that you need to let the import process complete before ejecting your SD card. This can be confusing because you may see the low-resolution thumbnails of the clips in the Event Browser panel, but the media will be offline. If you did not make a card archive and then reformat the SD card, there will be no way to recover the footage. To be safe, I watch the import progress to be sure the transfer is complete. Uncheck the checkbox next to **Close window after starting import**. This is located in the lower-right corner of the **Media Import** window.

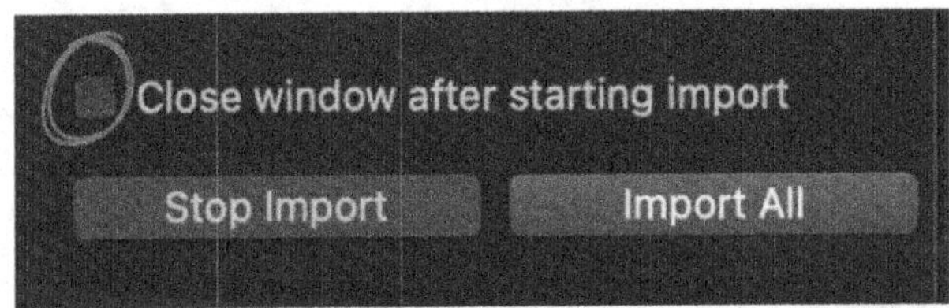

Figure 2.21: Turn off the checkbox next to Close window after starting import

By doing this, you keep the window open while the footage is imported from the SD card. Click on the **Import All** or **Import Selected** button. Notice the progress circles in the lower-left corner of the clips selected for importing. Watch to see that they have all been completed and are clear. Now, you can eject the SD card and close the **Media Import** window.

Figure 2.22: Note the import progress circles on each clip

In addition, once you have made a camera archive on your hard drive, you can import footage from it without the SD card inserted. Navigate to it in the **Media Import** window like you would a folder on a hard drive, but once you open the archive, the interface of the **Media Import** window functions like an SD card.

Figure 2.23: The ability to import from a camera archive

Importing media with drag and drop

Importing media quickly into an event can be done by dragging media from a Finder window into the Final Cut Pro interface. Like an omelet, it seems simple, but there is some prep work that needs to happen first using the Final Cut Pro preferences.

In this recipe, we'll explore the preparation and importing process so you can quickly drag files into Final Cut Pro.

Getting ready

Make sure you have some files on your hard drive ready to import.

How to do it...

Sometimes, you just want to hurry up and get the files into Final Cut Pro with the settings that you normally use. Here is a no-fuss, no-mess way to do it:

1. The preparation work we need to do is to set up our import preferences. From the **Final Cut Pro** menu, select **Settings...**. Alternatively, use the *Command +,* (comma) keyboard shortcut.

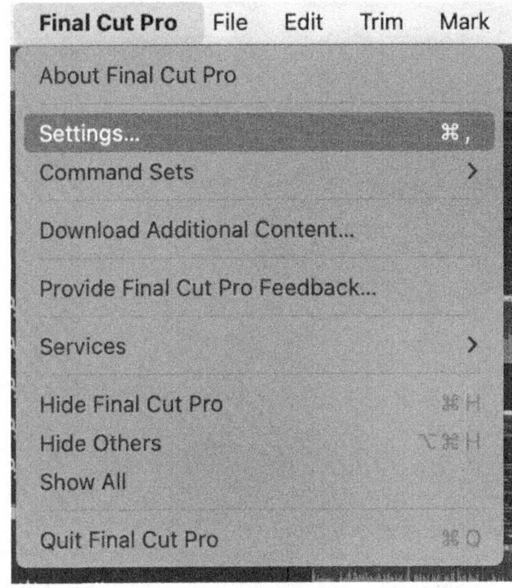

Figure 2.24: Select Settings... from the Final Cut Pro menu

2. From the **Settings** menu, click on the **Import** tab on the top row. This option opens the **Import** screen:

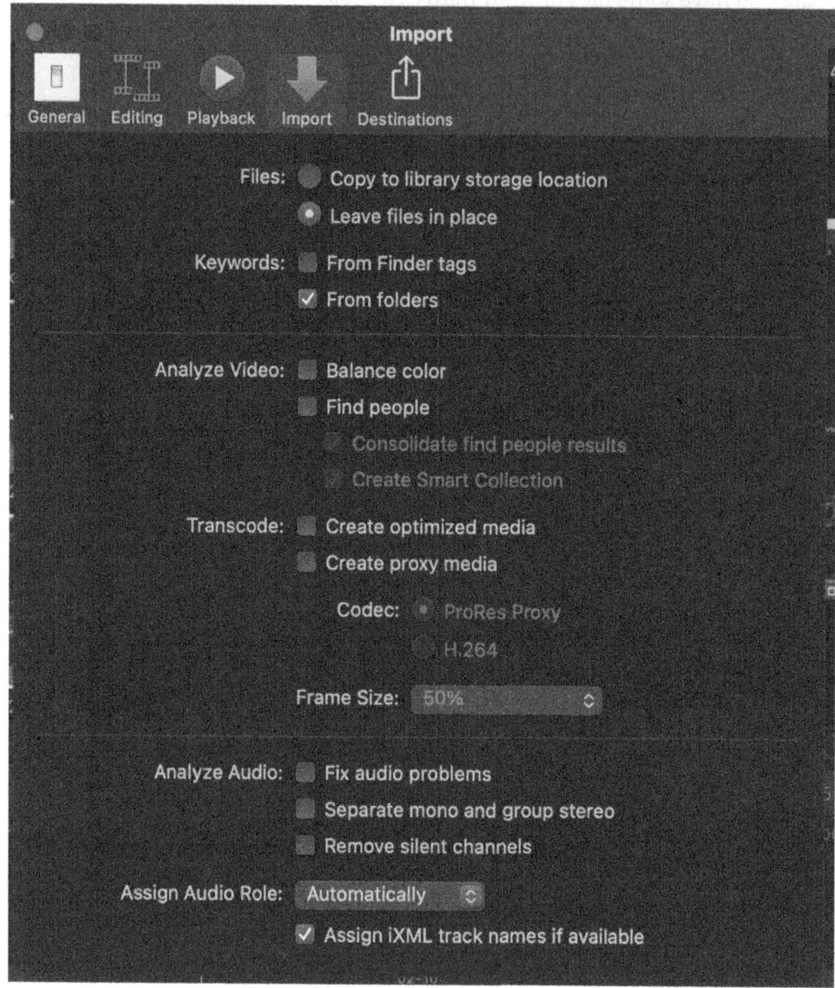

Figure 2.25: The Import tab of the Settings window

3. Select the settings according to your preference and the way you want media to be analyzed or transcoded. This preparatory work will establish the settings that the media will have when you drag and drop it into the Final Cut Pro interface.

Check the *Importing media into Final Cut Pro* recipe for a breakdown of the **Import** options.

4. Next, from the Finder, select the files or folder that you want to import. Then, drag them onto the event in the Final Cut Pro Sidebar panel into which you want to import. If you have set the **Files** preference to **Copy to library storage location**, you will see the cursor icon change to a green plus sign, indicating that the files you are dragging are being copied.

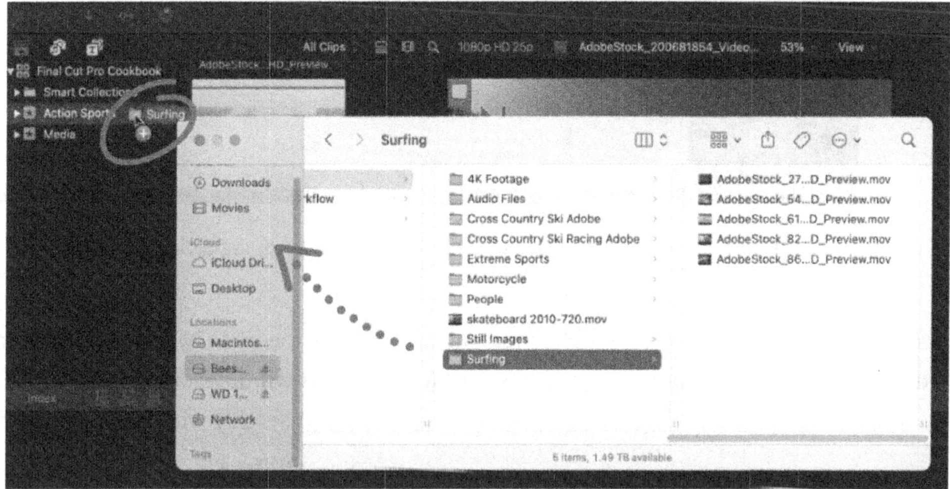

Figure 2.26: Note the cursor when dragging a folder to import with Copy to library storage location selected

5. Alternatively, if you set the **Files** preference to **Leave files in place** and then drag a file or a folder onto the event in the Final Cut Pro Sidebar panel into which you want to import, you will see the cursor icon change to a curved arrow alias sign, indicating that the files you are dragging are not being copied but instead referenced and left in place. There is a link established instead of actually making a copy of the file in the library.

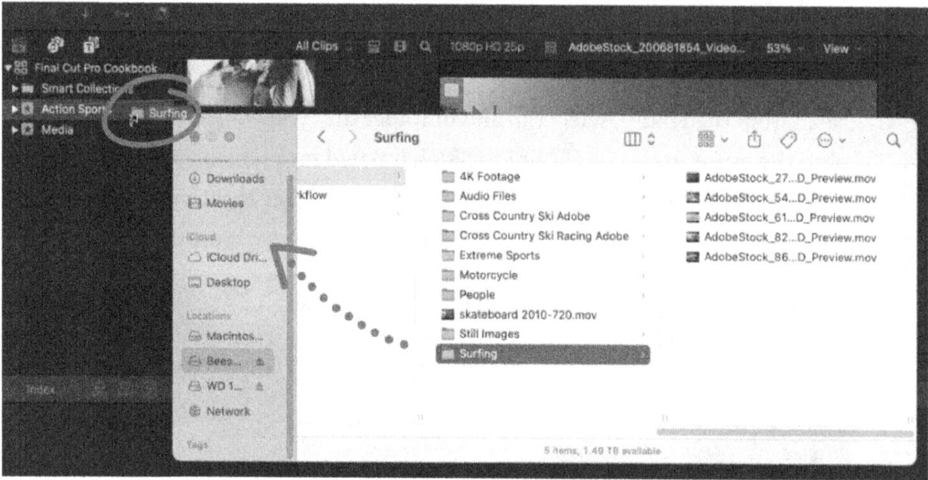

Figure 2.27: Note the cursor when dragging a folder to import with Leave files in place selected

As you can see, by setting a few preferences on how you like media to be analyzed and transcoded when imported, you not only pre-set your **Media Import** window, but you set up the ability to drag and drop your footage from the Finder smoothly and quickly with those same settings.

Understanding optimized versus proxy media

When transcoding (i.e., changing the code or format of media) in Final Cut Pro, there are two main options:

- The codec of optimized media will be the Apple ProRes 422 format, which is native to Final Cut Pro.

- The other option, proxy media, will have a smaller file size. You can choose a codec, or format, of ProRes Proxy or H.264.

In this recipe, we will explore the procedure of how to set these processes and what their purposes are.

How to do it...

Let's dig deeper into the process of transcoding media:

1. Start by importing some media into Final Cut Pro. The original format of the media will be saved into the library or folder of your choosing, but you have two options when transcoding (or creating alternate versions of media) when importing: optimized or proxy.

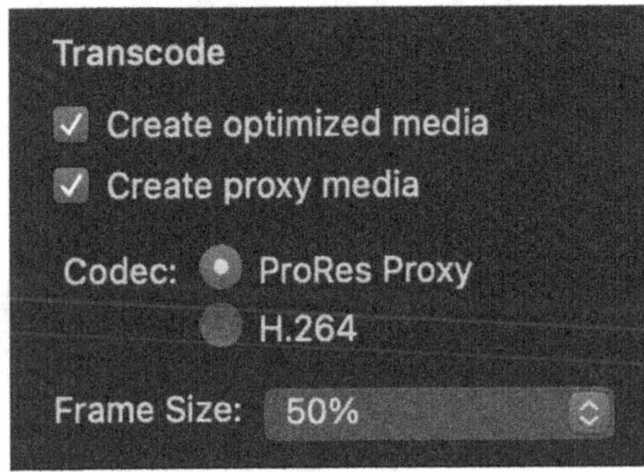

Figure 2.28: The Transcode options when importing media

Let's look at the two options:

*   The first option is **Create optimized media**. Optimized media, as the name implies, is optimal for editing. The format (that is, the codec) of optimized media is Apple's ProRes 422. This format is the Final Cut Pro native format.

*   The second option is **Create proxy media**. Sometimes, your situation is such that you want to work with smaller file sizes to speed up your editing. Perhaps you have a big project and you are working on a laptop, and you don't want to use large file sizes. This option is best for that.

2. When creating proxy media, you have settings for **Codec** and **Frame Size**. There are two format choices next to **Codec**. *Codec* stands for *compression-decompression*, and our codec for proxy media is a choice between **ProRes Proxy** or **H.264** compressed files:

*   **ProRes Proxy** has a better image quality with low data rates.

*   **H.264** files may be a bit smaller. This is a popular video compression standard with widespread use for internet streaming video. Images look good with small file sizes.

3. We can also choose to change the size of the files by selecting the **Frame Size** option's **SCALE** settings. The choices are to use the same as the source, reduce it by a specific percentage, or set an actual pixel size.

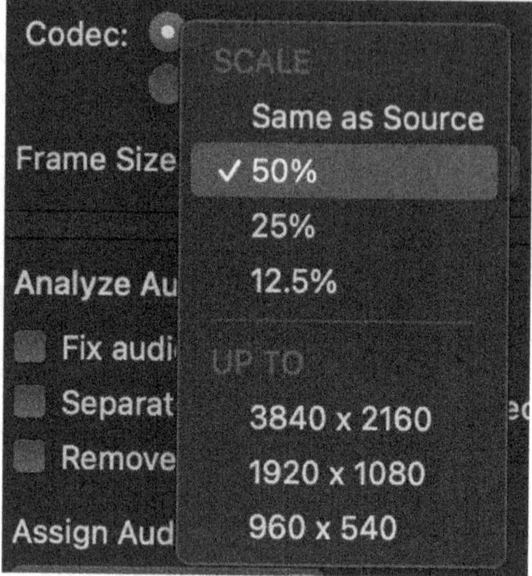

Figure 2.29: The proxy Frame Size options

Having fewer pixels means the graphics card needs less speed to display the images. However, you may find yourself in a situation where you don't need a crystal-clear image and would rather work fast with a smaller frame size.

There's more...

When footage is compressed, the media is made up of a **group of pictures (GOP)** that reference a true image, or iFrame, every several frames. Depending on the compression format, the GOP that references an image will be longer or shorter. Fewer iFrames and a longer GOP that references it will create a smaller file size.

In essence, not all of the video data actually exists. There are just references to images spaced out every several frames. You don't see the missing data when the video is played because the software displays images referenced from the iFrames.

Note that footage inside a camera is compressed. This format might be AVCHD or some other format, depending on the camera manufacturer. Proxy media is compressed with a group of pictures referencing an iFrame.

Conversely, Apple ProRes 422 optimizes media so that every frame is an iFrame, meaning there is a true picture in every frame. If you were to put an edit point on media that's referenced, it would look okay, but it's not optimal. By having a true image on every frame, the footage is optimized and looks best when applying effects and transitions. As you would imagine, this takes more disk space, which has to be accounted for, but the footage is optimized for editing and effects.

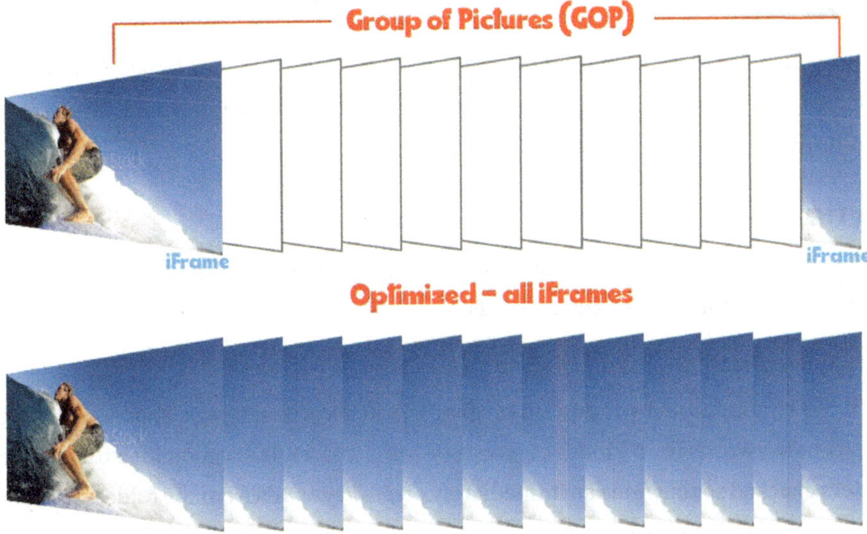

Figure 2.30: Comparing GOP media to optimized media

Using keywords

Tagging clips with keywords is like custom labeling your spice jars – it helps you find exactly what you need when the heat is on. With Final Cut Pro's powerful keyword tools, you can quickly organize, search, and group related clips. Organizing your footage is not limited to dealing with the file type or alphabetical names of your clips. Final Cut Pro uses a database and a modern method of tagging footage with different characteristics. This is known as **metadata**.

Meta means referencing itself, so metadata is data about data. In Final Cut Pro, metadata usually comes from three sources:

- From the camera, such as the date, the type of format, and the timecode on the clip
- Automatically from Final Cut Pro when media is imported, such as keywords entered from folder names
- Entered by the user, such as favorite or rejected ratings, as well as keywords

In this recipe, we will focus on ways to add custom keywords to your clips.

Getting ready

To follow this recipe, it would be helpful to read the *Customizing the Event Browser filtering order* recipe in *Chapter 1*. With that context, before starting, click on the **Clip Filtering** menu at the top of the Event Browser panel and select **All Clips**.

How to do it...

Let's first review how Final Cut Pro can automatically add keywords as part of the import process, and then we will look at user-entered keywords:

1. Press the keyboard shortcut of *Command + I*.

2. With the **Media Import** window open, go to the **Keywords** settings. You have the option to gather keywords from Finder tags and/or from folders. It's a good idea to leave **From folders** checked so that you can immediately create keywords from the folders that you've got your footage organized into.

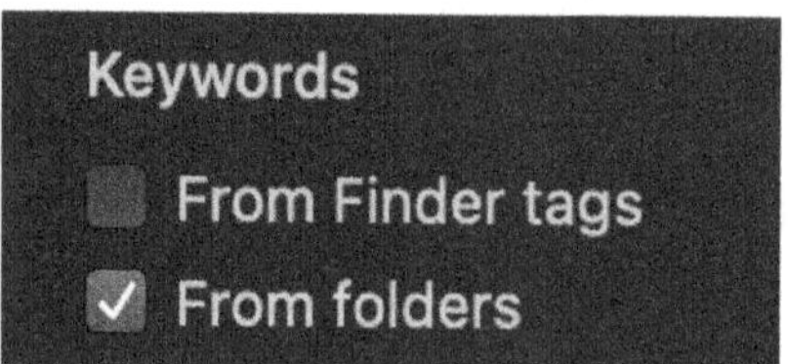

Figure 2.31: The automatic Keywords entry options in the Media Import window

3. Once done, close the **Media Import** window.

4. For my example, in the Sidebar, if I click on the disclosure triangle next to the **Action Sports** event, I can see there's a little key icon next to the word **Motorcycle**. That indicates a keyword group. The keyword group was created because, when we imported our footage, the clips were contained in a folder called Motorcycle.

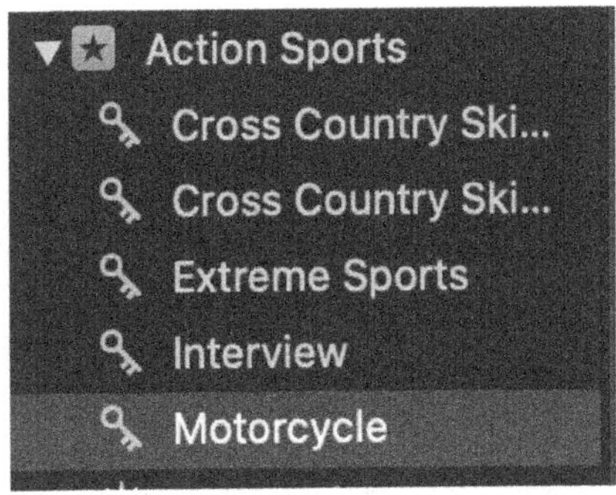

Figure 2.32: The keyword groups inside an event

5.   Click on the **Keyword Editor** icon (it looks like a key) in the top-left corner of the interface:

Figure 2.33: Click on the Keyword Editor icon

Alternatively, under the **Mark** menu, select **Show Keyword Editor**.

6.   A **Keywords for [File Name]** floating window will appear. This can be moved wherever on the screen it makes sense for you. When you select different clips, this window will show you which keywords are associated with that clip.

Click on the disclosure triangle to reveal the keyword shortcuts:

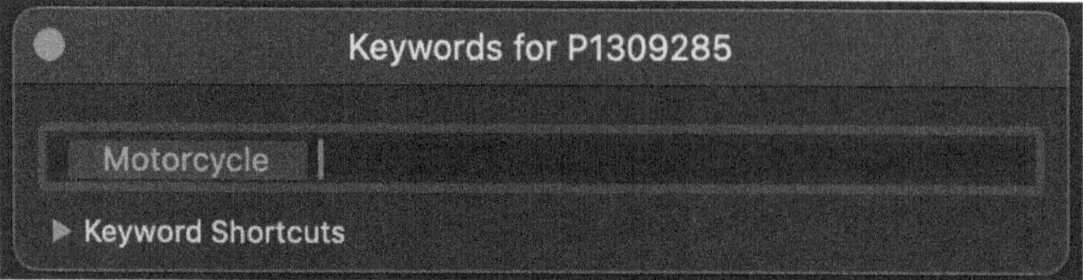

Figure 2.34: Add keywords in the Keyword Editor window

7. You can create keywords and organize your footage with keywords however you like. For instance, I know I have interview footage, so one of my keywords will be Interview. I also have some footage that is in super slow motion as well as some interior studio space, so I will give them keyword names accordingly.

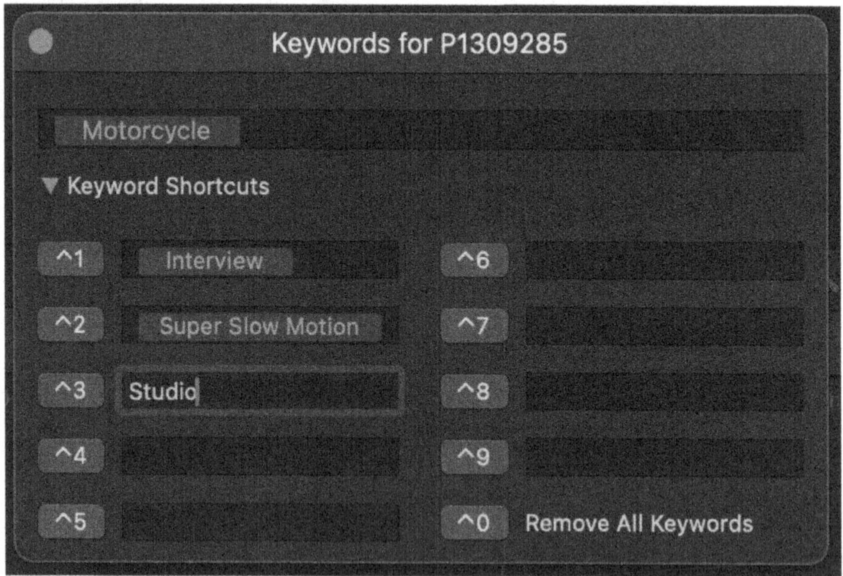

Figure 2.35: Add keyword shortcuts in the expanded Keyword Editor window

8. Now, those keywords are created, but they're not visible in my event until I apply them to some footage. Select several of your clips in the **Event Browser** window. Then, to apply the first keyword – in my case, **Interview** – click on the ^1 button next to the keyword. We can see that our selected clip has the keywords **Motorcycle** and **Interview** listed along the top of the **Keywords** window.

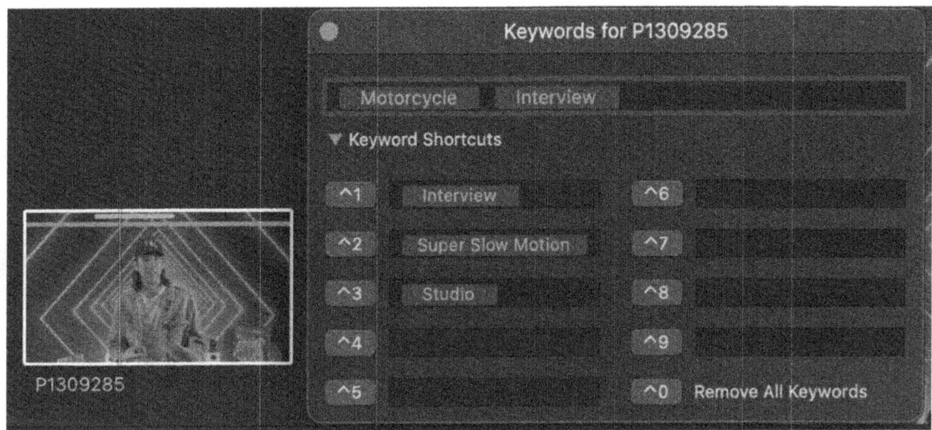

Figure 2.36: The Keyword Editor window lists all keywords tagged to a clip

9. Now that the new keyword of **Interview** has been added to a clip for the first time, the Sidebar panel will list the keyword group of **Interview** in my active event.

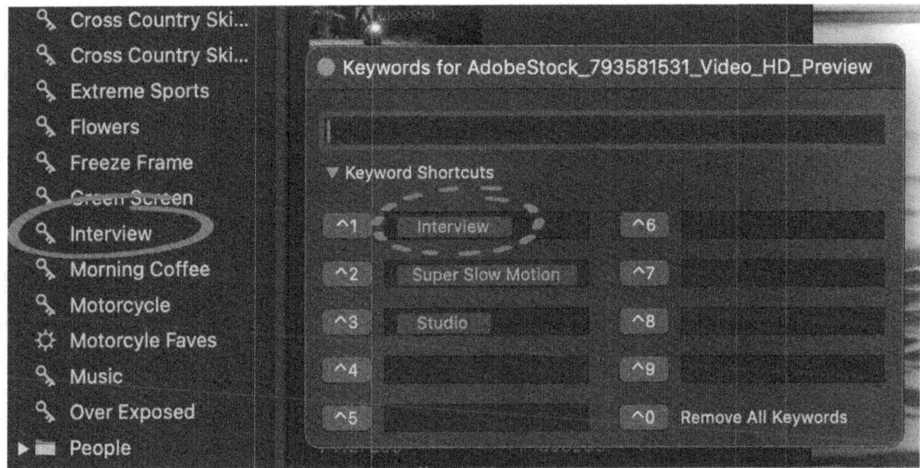

Figure 2.37: The keyword group of Interview is created in the active event

10. For the clips that are in super slow motion, I'm going to select just two of the three and tag them with the **Super Slow Motion** keyword button labeled ^2 (alternatively, you can use the keyboard shortcut *Control + 2*). Now, close the **Keyword Editor** window to review what you have done.

11. I can see that I have one more clip that is in super slow motion. Let's use another method of adding a keyword. You can simply drag the desired clip from the Event Browser panel onto the **Super Slow Motion** keyword group inside the event in the Sidebar panel. When you let go, that keyword will be added to that clip. This is a quick way to add a keyword to a group of clips.

Figure 2.38: Drag a clip onto a keyword group to tag the clip with that keyword

12. Practice applying keywords with either the buttons in the **Keyword Editor** window, the keyboard shortcuts, or by dragging the clips onto the keyword groups in the Sidebar panel.

Using the Event Browser List view

Think of the Event Browser List view as your well-organized recipe binder, laying out every ingredient (or clip) with clear, sortable details. Switching to List view lets you see essential metadata such as duration, scene, and custom keywords at a glance. This bird's-eye view makes it easier to sift, sort, and serve up the right clips quickly, keeping your workflow efficient and your edit on track.

In this recipe, we will explore the hidden advantages behind the List (or Column) view of the Event Browser panel. The power of organizing and sorting your media with detailed metadata will streamline your search process, making it easier to find and select the right footage for your project.

Getting ready

You might consider changing your workspace so that the Event Browser panel is larger. Go to the **Window** menu and select **Workspaces**, followed by **Organize** (or use the *Control + Shift + 1* keyboard shortcut).

Also, if you followed along with the previous recipe, click on the **Clip Filtering** menu at the top of the Event Browser panel and select **All Clips**.

How to do it...

It's like serving up your favorite food in a whole new way. Let's get a new perspective on the Event Browser:

1. To change our Event Browser view to a list, click on the **Toggle the clip display** icon, located in the upper-right corner of the Event Browser panel.

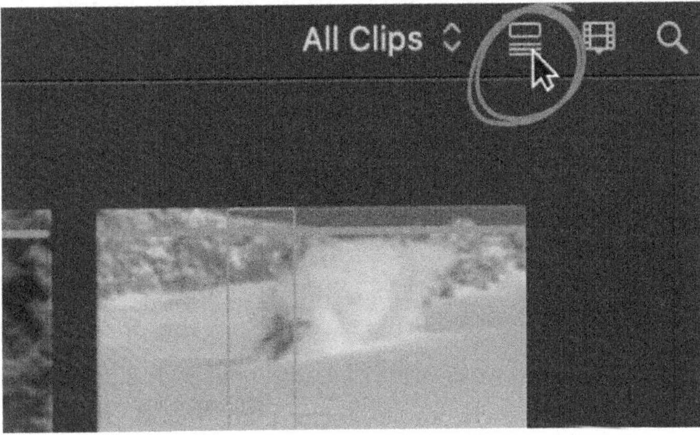

Figure 2.39: Click on the clip display toggle icon

Compared to the Filmstrip view, in which we can change how many thumbnail images represent the length of a clip, the List view has one length, and that's the size of the Event Browser panel. The entire clip, highlighted in yellow, is shown along the top of the Event Browser panel.

Figure 2.40: The Event Browser panel in the List view

2. Just like the Filmstrip view, we can make selections, change the selection's size, mark favorites, and so on, on the clip represented along the top of the Event Browser panel.

3. In the columns below, we have information about each clip. Interestingly, this is a mix of metadata from the camera, from user input, and from Final Cut Pro.

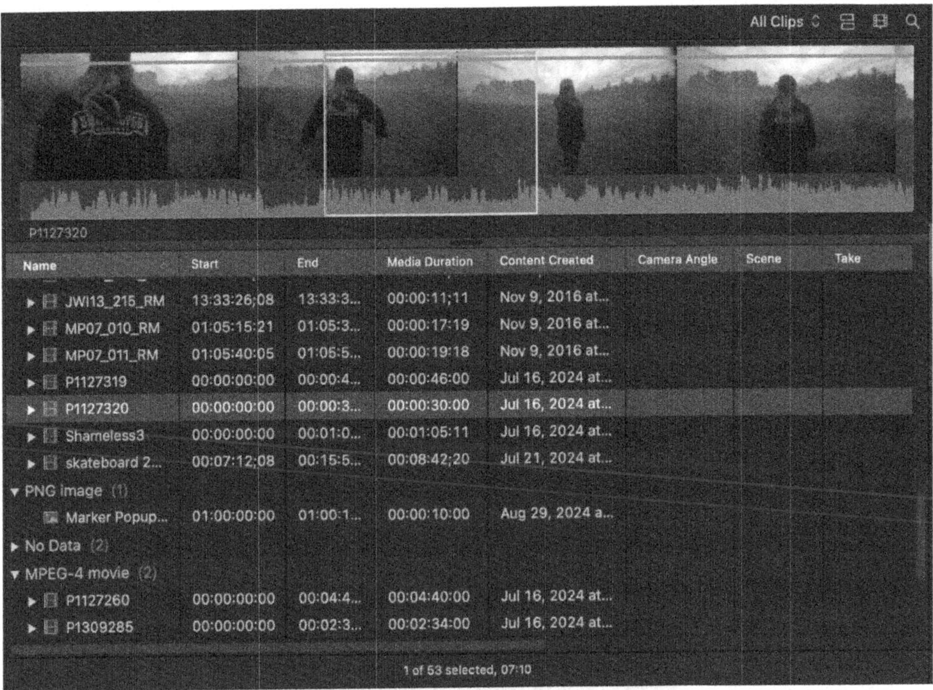

Figure 2.41: The metadata displayed for each clip in the List view

4.   Next to the name of each clip in the list is a **disclosure triangle** and a **filmstrip** icon. By flipping the disclosure triangle down, we can see the keywords applied to that clip.

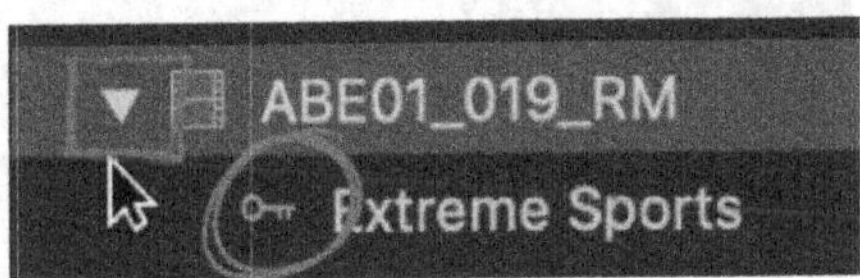

Figure 2.42: Clicking on a clip's disclosure triangle to show keywords

5.   Besides the detail of each line or clip, the List view format can be very useful because we can sort clips in different ways:

   •   By clicking on the header of a different column, it becomes highlighted in blue, indicating that this is the column with which the media is sorted. For example, instead of sorting by the names of the clips, click on the **Media Duration** column header, and now the clips are sorted by length of time.

- By clicking on the small triangle in the column header, you can sort data in ascending or descending order.

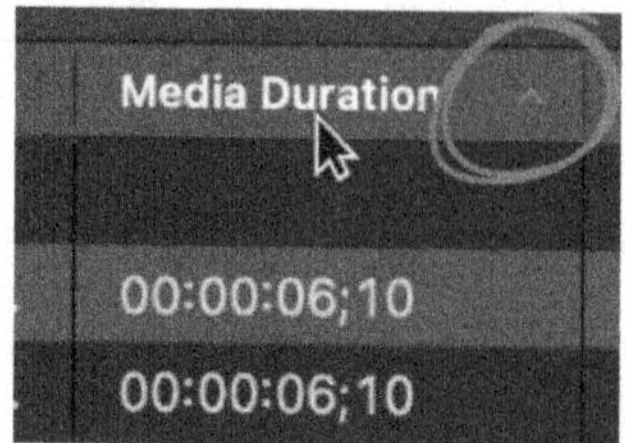

Figure 2.43: Click on a column header to sort by that data

6. You can also adjust the width of the columns. Notice a column in which the content ends with an ellipsis (...), indicating that the information does not fit in the column space. Move the cursor to the edge of the column header, and it will change to a vertical line with arrows pointing to the right and left. Click and drag the column width to make it larger to accommodate the information.

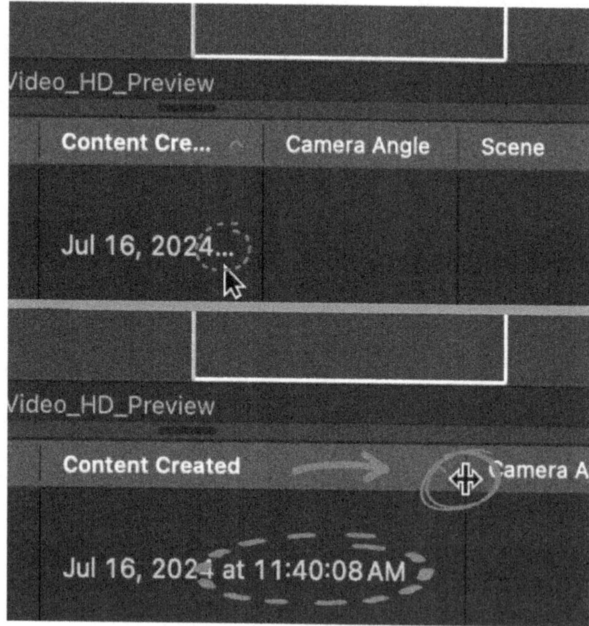

Figure 2.44: Adjust the column width by dragging the edge of the headers

7. But wait, there's more. Right-click in the column header, and you will be presented with a pop-up menu with two parts. The first part has commands for sizing, hiding, and showing columns. You can save custom column settings.

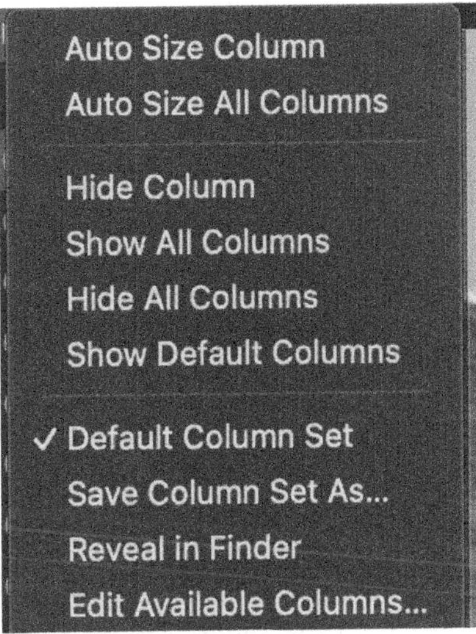

Figure 2.45: The first section of the column customization menu

Practice arranging columns and then select **Save Column Set As…** in the pop-up menu. A dialog box appears, and you can give your custom set a name. It will now be in the pop-up menu for you to use again.

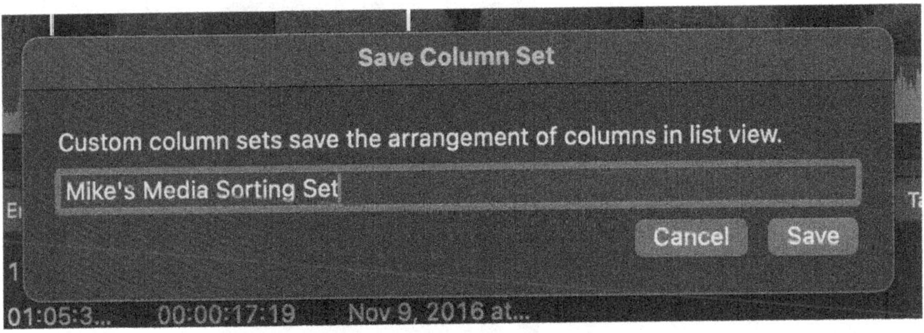

Figure 2.46: Save your custom column set

Note that the **Reveal in Finder** command will take you to your settings file in the Application Support folder. Then, you can copy your custom column set to another computer and have your clips organized in a streamlined way that works best for you.

In the second section of the column menu, we can see checkmarks indicating which columns are currently visible in the List view of the Event Browser panel. To hide or show different columns of metadata for our clips, simply select them to toggle their visibility.

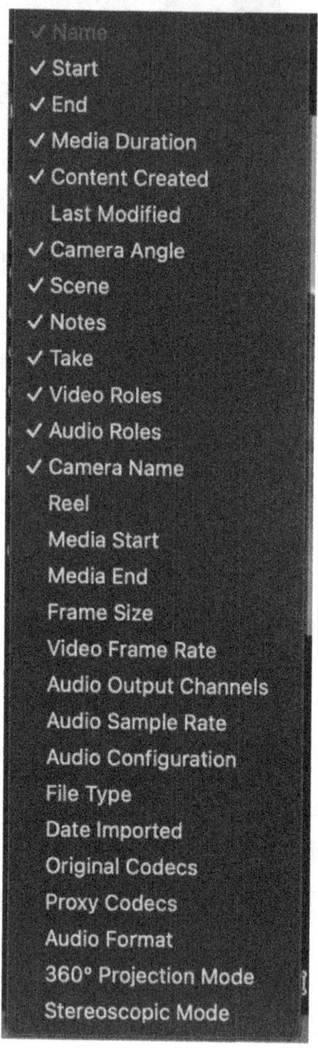

Figure 2.47: The second section of data options of the column customization menu

8. When making a short film, often there's information about the reel, the scene, and the take (the latter being a scene filmed or televised at one time without stopping the camera; directors may have the actors perform several *takes* with subtle differences). By adding **Scene** and **Take** as columns to our List view, we open up some possibilities for organizing our footage.

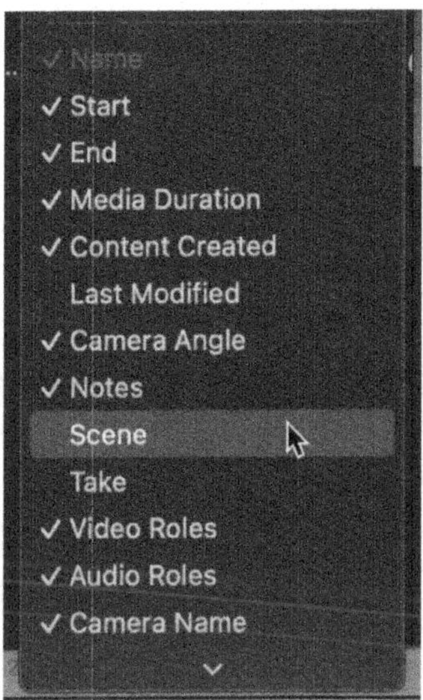

Figure 2.48: Select data items in the pop-up menu to add them as a column in the List view

9. With **Scene** and **Take** added to your columns in the List view, click once in the blank field for a clip, that is, the line under the **Scene** column. It becomes highlighted, and we can add information. For example, we can label this clip, naming **Scene** as 3 and **Take** as 1.

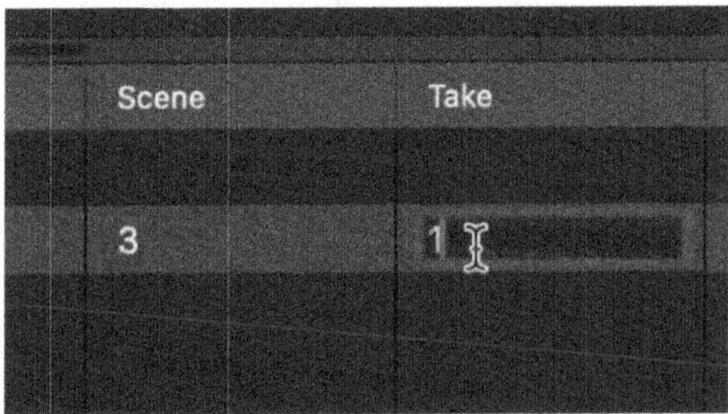

Figure 2.49: Click on a text field to enter data

10. In addition, if we want to make the columns easier to see, we can click and drag the column header to the place we desire.

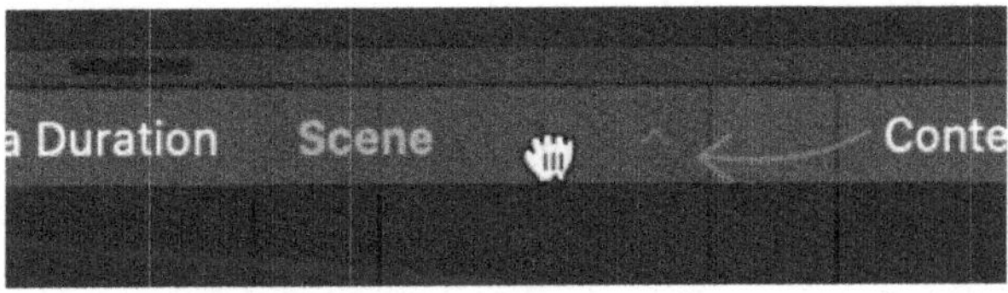

Figure 2.50: Click and drag column headers to a desired order

11. Once you have entered data into the **Scene** and **Take** fields, even if for practice and experimentation, click on the **Take** column header to sort by that data. Then, click on the **Scene** column header to sort by that data, too.

By clicking on **Take** first and then **Scene**, the **Take** data becomes the secondary sort order, and **Scene** becomes the primary sort order. You can see that all the **Take** numbers are in order within the **Scene** groupings.

Scene	Take
1	1
1	2
2	4
3	3
4	1

Figure 2.51: Clips sorted by Scene and Take

Wow, you have nearly organized your entire film without regard to the date on which the media was shot. This makes for some amazing organization!

Making an assembly edit

Sometimes, when making a project, especially a short film, directors want to review all the footage from a particular day or a series of days. Looking at the footage on a daily basis is called **dailies**.

When a director sits down with the editor and wants to see all the footage shot in order, that's sometimes called an **assembly edit**. The assembly edit is like prepping every ingredient (even the ones you might not use) because you never know which flavor might surprise you. You might think that you need to put all the clips into a timeline for the director to see the footage assembled. But Final Cut Pro has a quick technique to play all the footage right from the Event Browser panel.

In this recipe, we will find the quick setting that will save the day.

Getting ready

If you have previously altered the Event Browser's filtering options, click on the **Clip Filtering** menu at the top of the Event Browser panel and select **All Clips**.

How to do it...

Let's see the shortcut that Final Cut Pro uses to provide a director with an assembly edit:

1. In the upper-right corner of the Event Browser, click on the **Clip Appearance** icon.

2. In the drop-down window, for **Group By**, choose **File Type** so that photos and audio files are kept separate from video files. Then, for **Sort By**, choose **Content Created**. This is most likely the order in which it was shot for the different scenes.

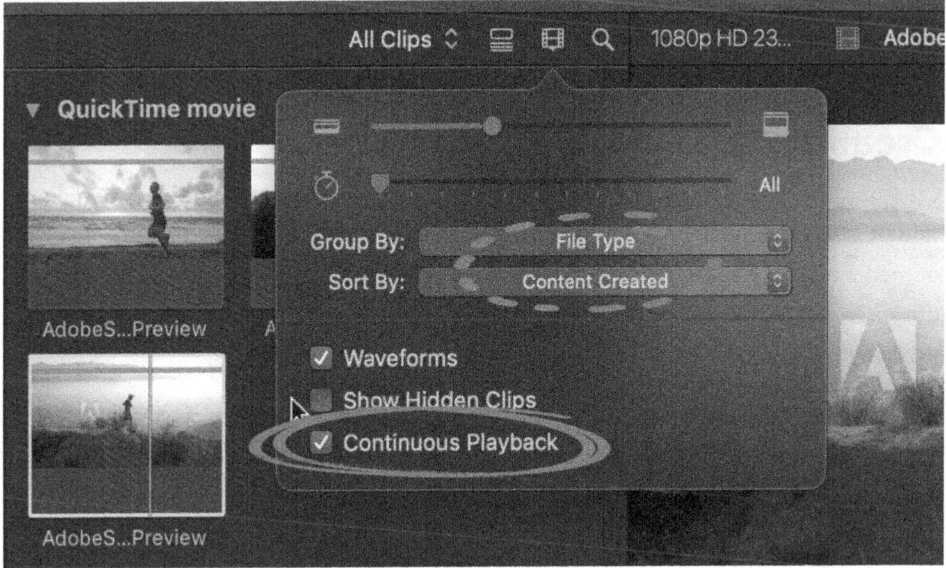

Figure 2.52: The Clip Appearance setting and Continuous Playback checkbox

3. Now, at the bottom of the window, check **Continuous Playback**. You have it! This is the trick that's going to play one clip after another in the Event Browser panel!

4. Click outside of the **Clip Appearance** message box to dismiss it, and now select the first clip in the event that you wish to play in the Event Browser panel. Then, press the *spacebar* as the keyboard shortcut to start playing the media. Clips will continually play from one to another until the end of the Event Browser.

Figure 2.53: Clips play one after another in the Event Browser

Creating Smart Collections

Creating Smart Collections is like sorting your ingredients based on a variety of flavor combinations. Collections automatically gather clips based on criteria you define, such as keywords, roles, or media type. It's a fast, efficient way to keep your media organized and accessible throughout the entire editing process. Perhaps you would like to organize interview clips by date or categorize B-roll by keyword. This is the right place.

In this recipe, we'll explore how to set up collections that group clips based on specific criteria, such as keywords, ratings, and more, streamlining your workflow and keeping you organized.

Getting ready

If you have previously altered the Event Browser's filtering options, click on the **Clip Filtering** menu at the top of the Event Browser panel and select **All Clips**.

How to do it...

To create a Smart Collection, follow these steps:

1. In the Event Browser, click on the **Search Field** icon (the magnifying glass in the upper-right corner).

2. Once clicked, this brings up a small dialog box. Try typing in some words that might match some of your clip names. This search field only deals with the names of clips and text from the **List View Note** column. This is helpful, but not very much. Let's do more.

Figure 2.54: Click on the Search Field icon to start a search and the X button to clear text

3. Click on the **X** button on the right side of the search field to cancel the text search.

4. Instead, click on the **Smart Search** icon (which looks like a small dialog box) located on the right next to the search field.

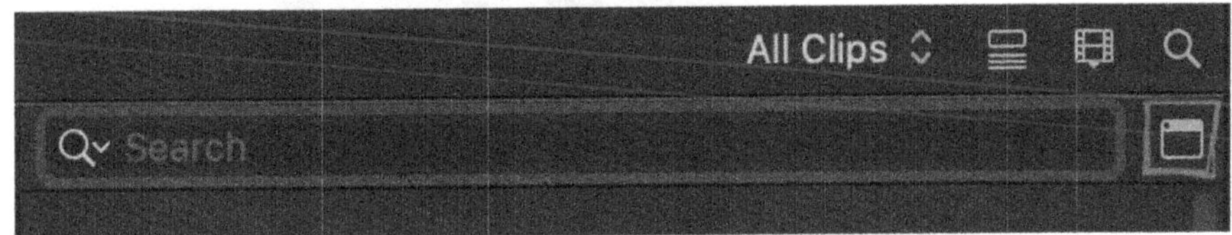

Figure 2.55: Click on the Smart Search icon to open the Smart Search filter window

5. This brings up the **Filter** window. A default search item of **Text** is created, but there is so much more.

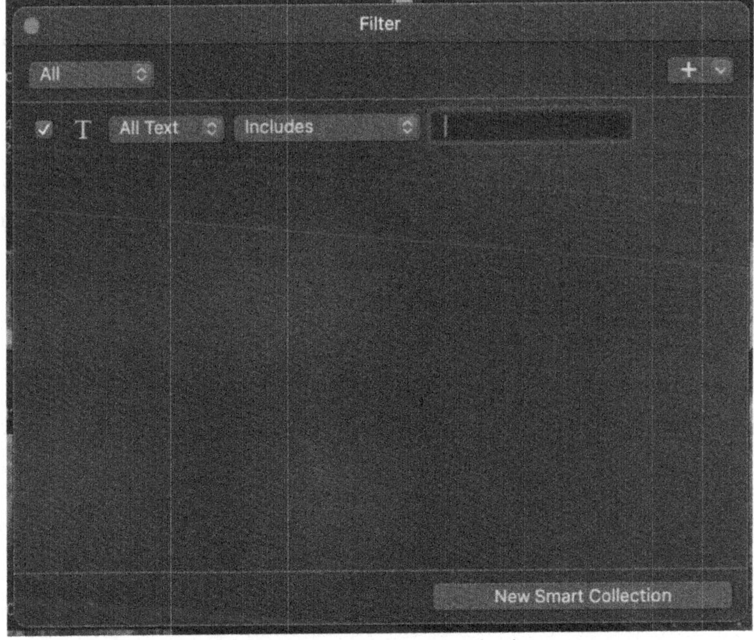

Figure 2.56: The initial Filter window

6. Click on the **Add Search Criteria** icon, which is the + button in the upper-right corner, and you will be presented with a menu of items that you can use as search criteria.

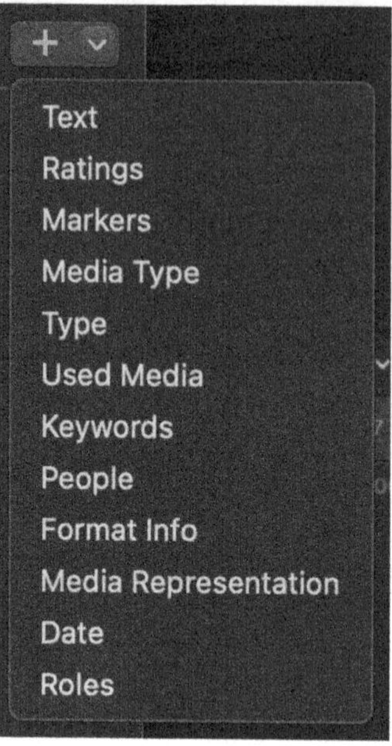

Figure 2.57: The criteria available to add from the Smart Search menu

For our example, let's say we want to find some clips in which we have used favorite ratings. Click on the **Add Search Criteria** button again, select **Ratings** from the menu, and select **Favorites** from the drop-down list.

7. Now, let's say that we also only want to find clips with the keyword **Motorcycle**. Click on the **Add Search Criteria** icon again and select **Keywords** from the menu, then put a checkmark next to **Motorcycle** in the list of keyword group choices.

8. And of course, we want clips that have audio with the video. Click on the **Add Search Criteria** icon again and select **Media Type** in the menu, then select **Is** and **Video with Audio** from the list of choices. In my example, I found several clips that have video with audio that are also part of my **Motorcycle** footage, and they've been marked as Favorites.

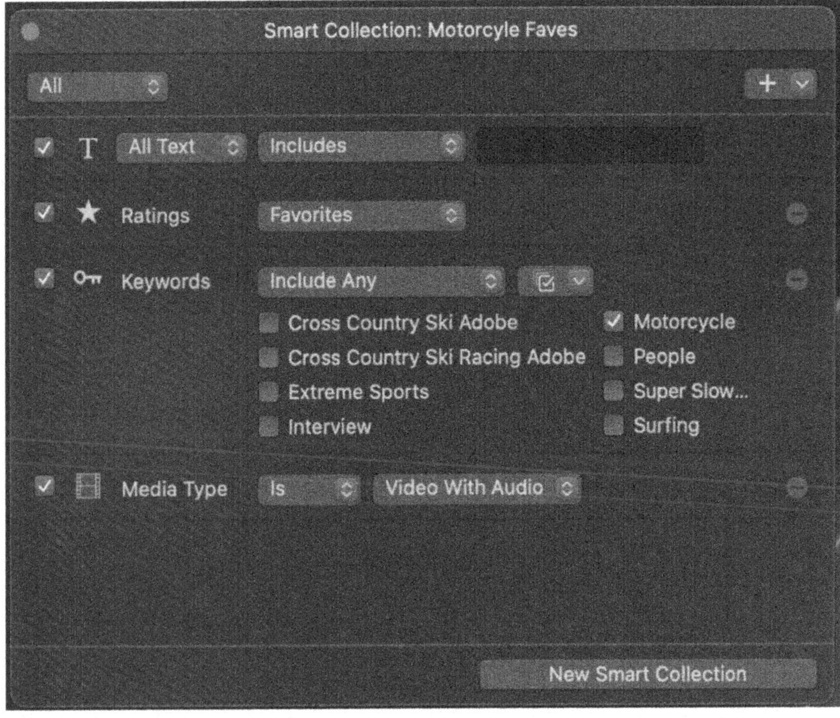

Figure 2.58: Explore the smorgasbord of Smart Search filters

9. Let's save this custom search setting by clicking **New Smart Collection**.

10. The **Filter** window will automatically close, and a new Smart Collection (represented by a gear icon) will be created in the event we have been using. The title of the Smart Collection is **Untitled**, and it is highlighted, so it is ready for you to just type a name that makes sense for organizing your footage. Let's call this Motorcycle Faves instead.

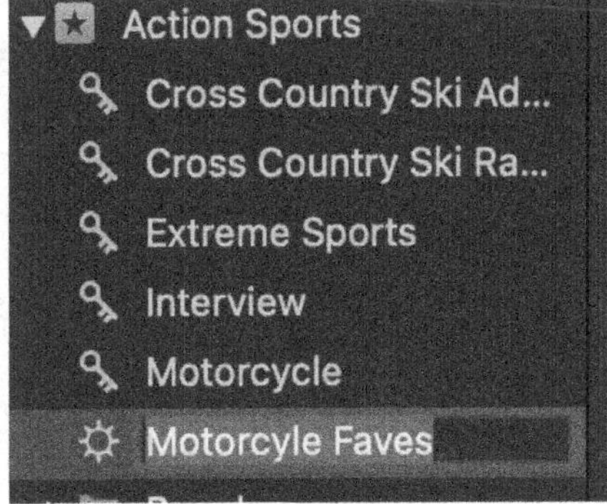

Figure 2.59: Give your Smart Collection a name

11. As you click on various saved Smart Collections and keyword groups, clips matching those tags are revealed in the Event Browser panel.

Relinking media

Let's say you have been marinating and prepping ingredients for days, but when you open the refrigerator, it's empty! Or, you open an editing project that you have not worked on in a while, and all your clips are red, saying **Missing File**!

Well, don't panic. It could be that the files are not lost but just moved. In this recipe, we will help direct Final Cut Pro to find them and put everything right.

Getting ready

For this, you will need to create a new library and import some media from a hard drive into it, using the **Leave files in place** import setting. Then, quit Final Cut Pro, move the file to another hard drive, delete the original files, and relaunch Final Cut Pro.

How to do it...

As mentioned, if your files appear to be disconnected, they'll appear in red, with a warning message that says **Missing File**, but have no fear. Your project may look like this:

Figure 2.60: The Final Cut Pro interface displaying missing files

If you encounter this, follow these steps:

1. Select the clips that are disconnected.

2. Go to the **File** menu, and select **Relink Media / Original Media**.

3. The **Relink Original Files** dialog box will display the original media filenames. Click on the **Locate All…** button present in the lower-right corner.

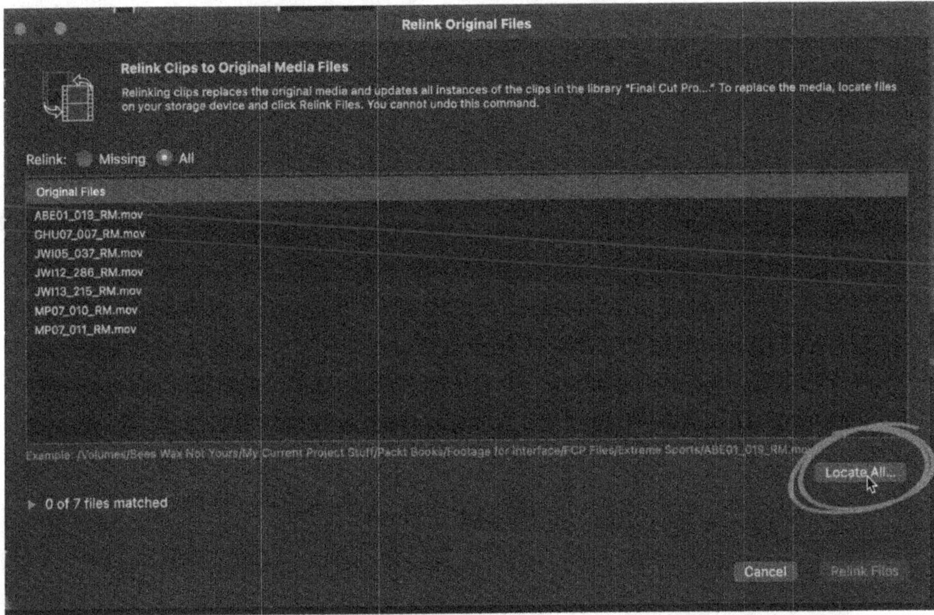

Figure 2.61: Click on the Locate All… button in the Relink Original Files dialog box

4. The next **Relink Original Files** page allows you to find the files. We are presented with a familiar column view of folder paths. A good tip is to look at the previous path to find where the file may have been moved to or how the filename might have been changed.

   In my example, I am looking for a folder called Extreme Sports and a particular filename. Take a look at *Figure 2.62* to see the original path underlined in the middle of the window. Use this as a clue to find the folder and file. In my case, searching for that folder, I navigated to my personal hard drive, and there I found the Extreme Sports folder.

Once you have found your file, click on the **Choose** button in the lower-right corner.

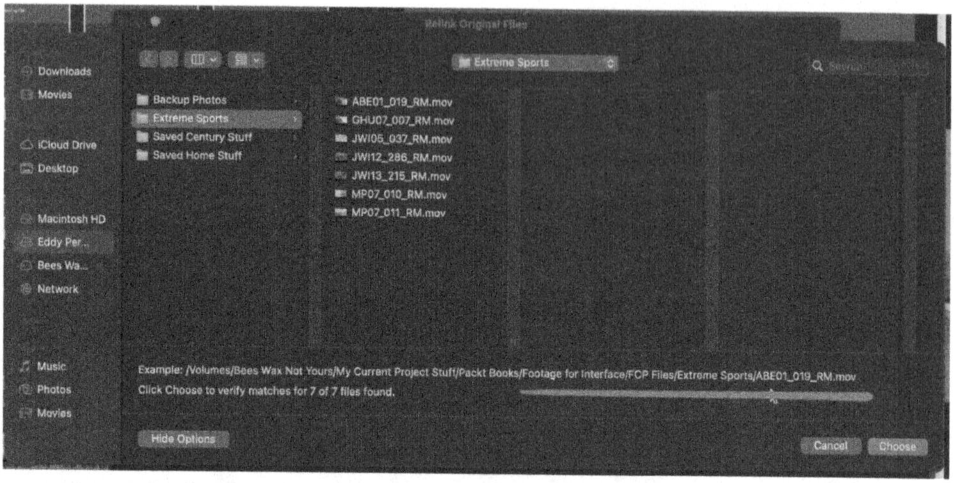

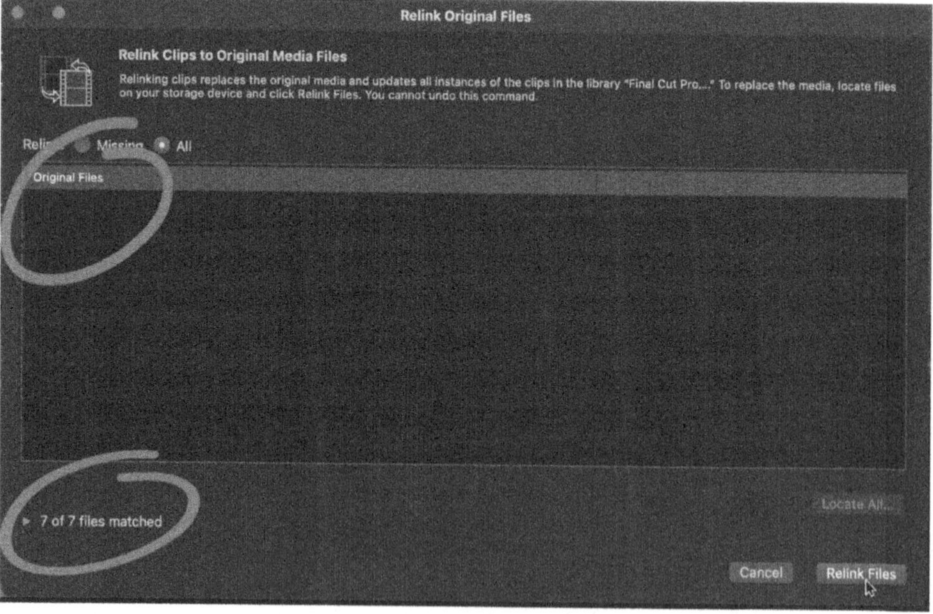

Figure 2.62: Use the clip's previous path as a clue to its new location

5. You will be taken back to the previous **Relink Original Files** dialog box, where you can verify that your files now have matching paths. In my case, seven files have been fixed. Now, click on the **Relink Files** button in the lower-right corner of the window.

Figure 2.63: Note that the files match and are ready to relink

When you return to the Event Browser, you will see that your files are relinked, no longer red, and the **Missing Files** message is no longer present:

Figure 2.64: The Final Cut Pro interface displaying relinked files

As you can see, the red files and warning messages can seem scary at first, but the linking problem can be easily fixed!

There's more...

In some cases, the clips match and are in the right place, but still do not relink. Final Cut Pro will relink files that have been processed or converted outside of Final Cut Pro, even if the frame size or the codec is different. However, Final Cut Pro has trouble if the timecode of the clip or the number of audio channels has changed.

The other situation is if, indeed, you have lost the files, but we will cover how to back up a project in *Chapter 11*, in a recipe called *Saving a project archive*.

3

Sculpting Clips in the Final Cut Pro Timeline

Step into the editing studio, where the timeline serves as your materials, and your creativity serves as the sculptor's chisel.

In this chapter, we delve deeper into the art of refining your project from its raw form to a polished masterpiece. Like a seasoned chef honing their signature dish, we'll explore advanced techniques for trimming, layering, and perfecting your edit. We will examine transitions, secondary storylines, and tools. We will look into how to speed up your editing with keyboard shortcuts, by adjusting clip durations, and by adjusting the timeline's appearance.

From mastering connected clips to fine-tuning pacing, join us as we elevate your editing skills to the next level in Final Cut Pro.

In this chapter, you will complete the following recipes:

- Appending, inserting, connecting, and overwriting clips
- Quickly selecting clips with keyboard shortcuts
- Adjusting the timeline's appearance
- Replacing clips
- Adding transitions
- Creating secondary storyline transitions
- Using the Blade tool
- Changing a clip's duration

Technical requirements

To test the process of adding clips to the timeline, you will need some sample clips. You can download free sample files with watermarks from any of the major stock media websites or use your own clips. Also, try to import some media with audio.

Appending, inserting, connecting, and overwriting clips

Well, that is a mouthful! Think of your timeline like a layered cake – every clip added brings a new flavor, whether you're spreading it on top, tucking it in, or swapping out an undercooked slice. Mastering these techniques will give you greater control, allowing you to build your sequence and make precise adjustments as you shape your narrative. Whether you're adding new clips, integrating footage into an existing sequence, or refining your edits, these skills are essential for creating a polished and professional final product.

In this recipe, we'll dive into the core editing actions in Final Cut Pro. So, let's get started.

How to do it...

As with most tools in Final Cut Pro, there are several ways to work with footage in the timeline. Let's get it connected:

1. We'll start by simply adding a clip to the primary storyline. One of the easiest ways, and the most intuitive, is to click, hold, and drag the clip from the Event Browser panel to the Timeline panel and into the primary storyline.

Figure 3.1: Drag a clip to the Timeline panel

2. With the clip in the primary storyline, let's look at the editing actions. Select a clip in the Event Browser panel, then look at the tools in the upper-left corner of the Timeline panel. If you slowly hover the mouse over the icons, you'll see pop-up messages telling you about each tool. There are **Append, Insert, Connect**, and **Overwrite** icons.

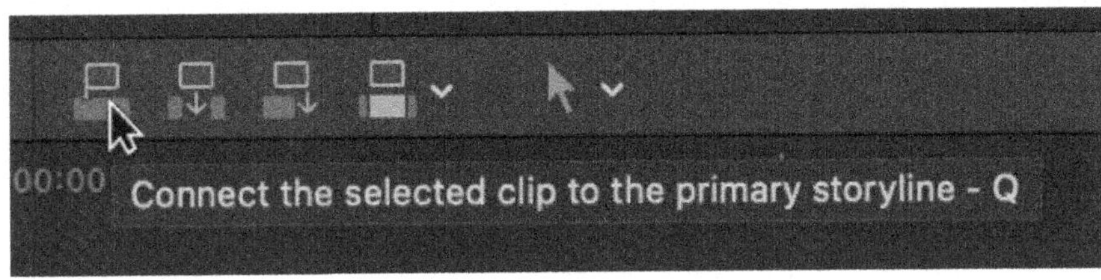

Figure 3.2: Note the icons to add clips

3. Compared to icons, though, keyboard shortcuts are faster. Hover the mouse slowly over the icons again, and you'll see the pop-up tool tips. Notice that at the end of the text of the tools' descriptions are the keyboard shortcuts. The shortcuts for **Connect, Insert**, and **Append** correspond to the top row of your keyboard – Q, W, and E, respectively. The keys are right next to each other and are easy to use with your left hand. The shortcut for **Overwrite** is D – this is not on the top row of the keyboard, but just below the E key – still accessible.

4. Let's start with appending clips. Select one clip in the Event Browser and press E to append the clip. I like using the E shortcut because it doesn't matter where the playhead is in the timeline, and even if you are not viewing the end of the project, E will put the selected clip right at the end of the primary storyline.

Being able to quickly append clips really works well when you have your clips organized in the Event Browser. See *Chapter 2* for more tips on using the Event Browser effectively. In fact, you can select multiple clips in the Event Browser panel and add them all, in the order of your selection, to the timeline with the E shortcut.

 I try to remember the "e" in append for a shortcut to add a clip to the end of the timeline.

5. Let's pause here and review the magnetic behavior of the primary storyline. There is more information in the *Taking advantage of the Magnetic Timeline and the Position tool* recipe in *Chapter 1*. The magnetic function of the timeline is always on and works well when we click, drag, and place footage in the primary storyline, as it snaps the clips into place.

    In the upper-right corner of the Timeline panel are a series of tool icons. The icon that looks like two blocks colliding is the **Snapping** toggle icon. Before clicking it, drag clips from the Event Browser panel to your Timeline project. Notice that, when dragging clips to connect above the primary storyline, they do not snap to the playhead, edit points in the primary storyline, or other connected clips.

Figure 3.3: Note the Snapping tool toggle icon

The keyboard shortcut for **Snapping** is *n*. Perhaps the folks at Apple have a sense of humor to remember the shortcut with *snnnapping*.

Now turn **Snapping** on. With snapping turned on, the red skimmer line snaps to the edge of edit points and the edges of clips. Also, when you drag a clip from the Event Browser panel and connect it on top of the primary storyline, the front or the back edge of the clip snaps to the playhead. With **Snapping** turned on, clips will also snap to the edges of other connected clips or edit points in the primary storyline.

6. With the behavior of **Snapping** covered, let's turn our attention to the playhead and the skimmer in the Timeline panel. The relationship between the playhead and skimmer seems to be a very basic concept in Final Cut Pro. But, like the use of certain spices, the distinctions between the two become pronounced in this recipe and how they impact inserting, connecting, and overwriting clips. Let me explain.

I like working with the skimmer turned on. I am able to quickly slide the mouse through clips to skim the visuals in the Viewer.

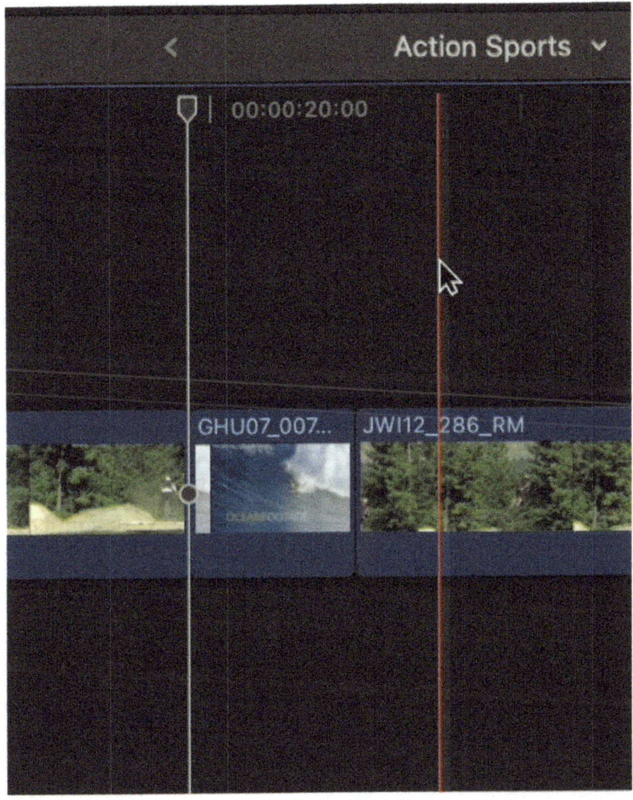

Figure 3.4: Note the red skimmer line turned on next to the white playhead

Then, when I click the mouse in the timeline, I position the playhead and the skimmer together, almost like an anchor point.

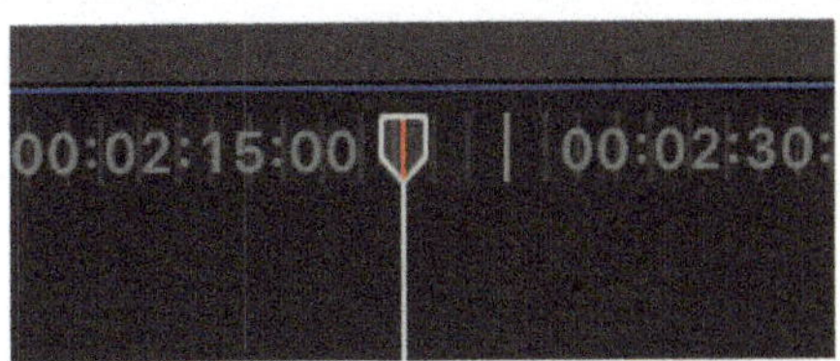

Figure 3.5: Click in the timeline to position the playhead and skimmer together

It is possible to turn the skimmer off. Click on the **Skimmer** toggle icon in the upper-right corner of the Timeline panel. Note that the playhead turns red. Then, you would click to position the playhead on the timeline. But if you wanted to scroll, or skim, through the clips, you would need to drag the top edge of the playhead along the timeline.

Figure 3.6: Note the red playhead when the Skimmer toggle icon is off

Let's move on to connecting, inserting, and overwriting clips.

7. If you first select a clip, or a portion of a clip, in the Event Browser, move your mouse onto the Timeline panel, and use the keyboard shortcut *Q* to connect the clip to the primary storyline, it will be connected at the location of the skimmer. This is also true for using the keyboard shortcuts of *W* to insert a clip and *D* to overwrite a clip into the primary storyline.

    But if you move your mouse to the Event Browser so that there is no longer a skimmer line in the Timeline panel, and then use the keyboard shortcut *Q* to connect a clip, it will connect the selected clip at the point of the playhead. This is also true for the keyboard shortcuts of *Q* to insert a clip and *D* to overwrite a clip into the primary storyline.

It is logical that if you are clicking on the **Connect, Insert,** and **Overwrite** icons, you have moved your mouse out of the Timeline panel, and there is no longer a skimmer line, so the actions will take place at the point of the playhead. So, pay attention to your skimmer line and make sure it is visible in the timeline or you have clicked the playhead at an edit point or in a position where you want clips to be connected, inserted, or overwritten.

8. The **Insert** and **Overwrite** commands seem similar in that they place video in the primary storyline, but there is a specific difference. Try this – zoom out in the Timeline panel so you can see all of your clips with some blank space to the right. Then select a clip in the Event Browser and use the **Insert** command somewhere in the middle of your timeline. Notice that it adds the video clip and pushes the rest of the clips downstream, that is, to the right.

Now, prepare the Timeline panel and use the **Overwrite** command. Notice how it replaces a section of video without pushing the footage downstream. It is overwritten in place.

That is the difference – **Insert** will add the clips and increase the length of the project, but **Overwrite** will replace the video and preserve the length of the project. Both are useful in their particular situation.

9. There is one more enhancement to the **Connect, Insert, Append,** and **Overwrite** commands that should be pointed out here. Just to the right of the four icons that we have been using is a small disclosure triangle. Click on it and you will see a drop-down menu that allows you to select whether you will add clips as **Video Only, Audio Only,** or **All** – both video and audio. Note the difference in the appearance of the add icons depending on the video or audio tracks selected.

    Try changing these selections and notice that the keyboard shortcuts will also add video only, audio only, or both tracks, depending on what is checked in the menu.

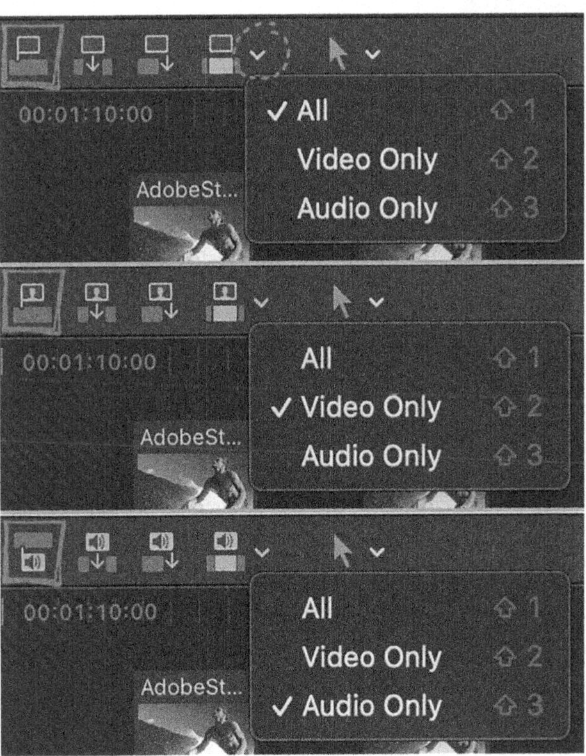

Figure 3.7: Note the changes in the add clip icons in relation to the track selection drop-down menu

There's more...

Another quick tip regarding connected clips involves the position of the mouse when skimming through the timeline. If you skim with the mouse above your connected clips, the Viewer will reflect the expected result of the timeline. That is, we see the connected clip because it covers the primary storyline.

Figure 3.8: Notice the Viewer when skimming over connected clips

But if you skim with your mouse in the primary storyline and below the connected clips, the Viewer will reflect the clip in the timeline, letting you review the clips under the connected clips.

Figure 3.9: Note the Viewer when skimming below connected clips

Quickly selecting clips with keyboard shortcuts

Keyboard shortcuts are the sharp knives of the editing kitchen – master them, and you'll slice through your workload with precision. We will practice how to quickly fast forward through clips and define sections of your footage, how to tag clips with ratings and keywords, and how to seamlessly place them in the timeline, all with an efficiency of motion. Mastering keyboard shortcuts with unique hand placement can make your editing process smoother and more intuitive, significantly speeding up your editing workflow in Final Cut Pro.

In this recipe, we'll cover essential shortcuts that allow you to navigate your timeline quickly.

Getting ready

It would be helpful to import some footage that is several minutes long.

How to do it...

As I have learned in the business, you have to be good, but you also have to be fast. Be sharp because here we go:

1. To speed up the editing process, I am going to try reducing the amount of time that I move my right hand from the mouse to the keyboard and back again. To do this, I will try to keep my right hand on the mouse and do all the keyboard shortcuts in this process with my left hand. To make my left hand efficient, I like to tilt the keyboard slightly clockwise so that my left wrist is mostly straight.

Figure 3.10: Pro tip – slant the keyboard for your left hand

2. Now we are going to use the keyboard shortcuts *J*, *K*, and *L*. There is no modifier key needed, just the simple key. With a clip selected in the Event Browser panel or with your mouse over the timeline, press *L* to play your clip forward. Use *K* to stop playing and *J* to play in reverse. Practice this with your left hand.

3. As you practice, notice that if you press *L* or *J* multiple times, the clip plays forward or backward two, four, or eight times faster. In this way, you can *skim* through the footage without needing to use the mouse, while the white playhead indicates where you are in the clip. This editing method is beneficial when you are unfamiliar with the footage and need to listen to find edit points.

Figure 3.11: Note the white playhead visible on a clip in the Event Browser

4. What about slow motion, you might ask? Hold down *K* and press *L*. The clips now play at one-half speed. This works in reverse with *K* and *J*. In addition, hold *K* and press *L* or *J* repeatedly to play forward or reverse one frame at a time.

5. When using keyboard shortcuts to play through footage in the Event Browser panel, we can find the rough locations for the beginning and end of our clip selections. With the white playhead line located at the start of the portion of a clip, press the *I* key. This keyboard shortcut creates an in point. Keeping your left hand on the keyboard, press *L* to play the clip forward. Then, use *K* to stop the playhead near the end of the clip, and press *O* to create an out point. The selection is surrounded in yellow.

Figure 3.12: Note the yellow selection that is a result of using keyboard shortcuts

The *I* and *O* keys – for in and out – are conveniently located just above *J*, *K*, and *L*. Try making selections quickly. Press *L* to play forward, *K* to stop, *I* to mark an in point, *L* to play again, *K* to stop, and *O* to create an out point.

6. Now, with the ability to make selections of clips with that group of keys, it takes a quick movement of the left hand to apply all sorts of commands to the selection you just made:

    - Try using the keyboard shortcuts to rate your selections. Use *F* to mark a favorite or the *Delete* key to reject a section of footage.

    - With a portion of a clip selected in the Event Browser, add a keyword with the keyboard shortcut of *^ + 1*.

Rating clips was covered in the *Customizing the Event Browser filtering order* recipe in *Chapter 1*, while keywords were covered in the recipe called *Using keywords* in Chapter 2.

    - And, of course, as discussed in the previous recipe, we can use keyboard shortcuts to work with our clips. Press *Q* to **Connect** your selection to the primary storyline at the place of the timeline playhead. Press *W* to **Insert** your selection. Press *D* to have your clip **Overwrite** the footage in the timeline. Press *E* to quickly **Append** your selection to the primary storyline. It is a quick movement of your left hand to the group of keys *Q*, *W*, *D*, and *E*.

Just a reminder that editing is like sculpting – you start with a rough shape and work at refining and smoothing it until you reach the final product. This recipe is just about creating selections, tagging them, and adding them to the timeline *quickly*, so the selection does not have to be perfect. You will work on refining the edits as we go further in later chapters.

There's more...

Knowing lots of keyboard shortcuts could shave minutes off your editing time, but you could lose it all if you spend half an hour looking for a particular file. Don't forget to keep your footage organized and backed up. Check out the recipes in *Chapters 2* and *9* for more details on this.

Adjusting the timeline's appearance

Just like arranging ingredients on a cutting board, a well-organized timeline sets the stage for a smooth edit. Customizing the appearance of your Timeline is key to creating an editing environment that suits your workflow.

In this recipe, we'll explore how to adjust the timeline's layout and visual settings, helping you to optimize your workspace for better clarity and efficiency as you craft your story.

Getting ready

It will be helpful to have a variety of clips in your Timeline panel, including clips with audio.

How to do it...

Similar to the ability to adjust the appearance of the Event Browser, as seen in *Chapter 1*, we can adjust the appearance of the timeline:

1. With clips in the Timeline panel, click on the **Clip Appearance** icon – the one that looks like a film strip – located in the upper-right corner of the Timeline panel.

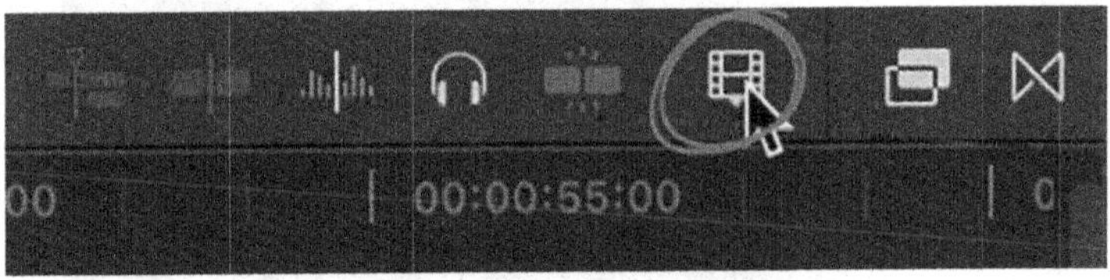

Figure 3.13: Click on the Clip Appearance icon

2. The **Clip Appearance** menu will appear. The top slider adjusts the timeline's zoom level. You can zoom in to see more detail and fewer frames in the length of the Timeline panel, or you can zoom out to see less detail and more seconds or minutes in the Timeline panel. Notice that zoom in and zoom out are centered at the point of the playhead.

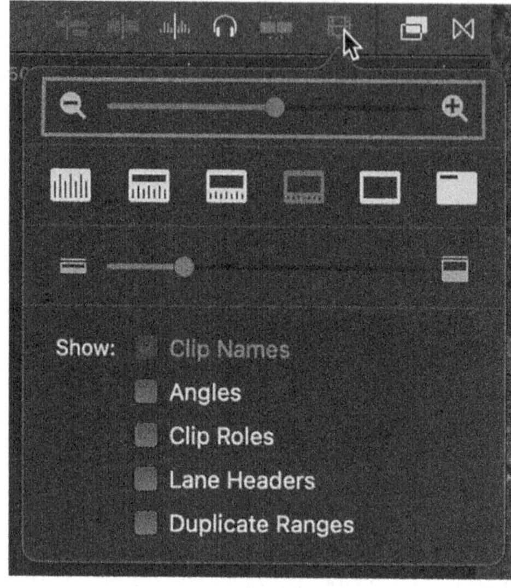

Figure 3.14: Use the slider to change the zoom setting in the Clip Appearance menu

3. The next row of icons represents the **Clip Appearance** options:

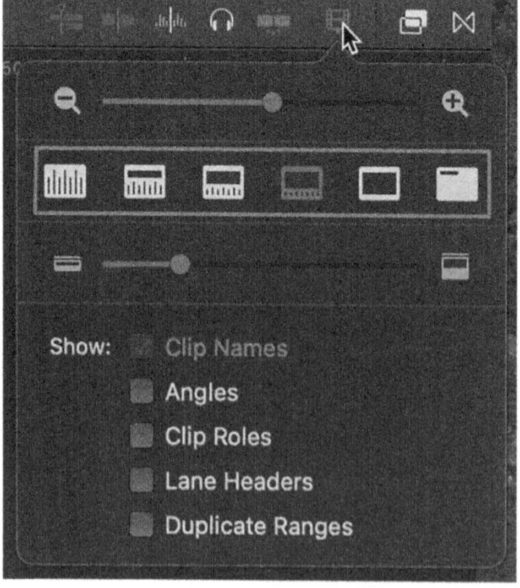

Figure 3.15: Note the filmstrip and waveform viewing options in the Clip Appearance menu

Clicking on the far-left icon will display only the clip's audio waveform:

Figure 3.16: Click on the waveform-only icon in the Clip Appearance menu

As you may notice from the way the icons look, using the icons from left to right will display less audio and more video, until the icon that is second from the right, which will display all video and no audio waveform.

Figure 3.17: Click on the video-only icon in the Clip Appearance menu

The icon on the far right will show the clips as small rectangles with just their clip labels and no video or audio. This might be helpful when organizing a very large project to get the big picture.

Figure 3.18: Click on the clip-labels-only icon in the Clip Appearance menu

4. You'll also want to get in the habit of changing the clip appearance depending on what phase you are in your editing. Having *all audio* turned on, the far-left icon works well in combination with the next slider, which is the Clip Height adjustment.

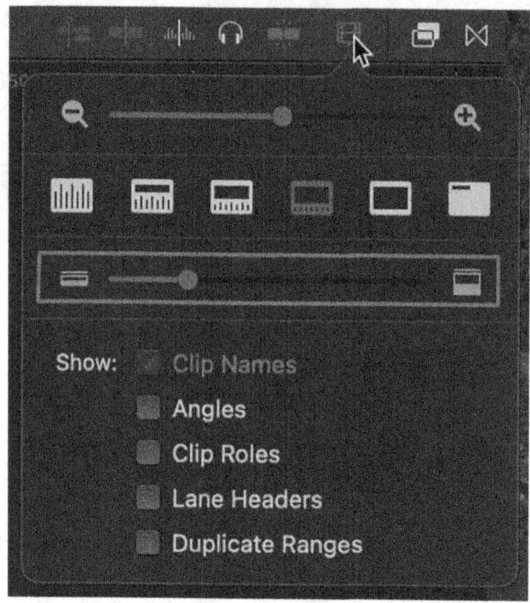

Figure 3.19: Use the slider to change the Clip Height adjustment in the Clip Appearance menu

Being able to increase the height of the timeline, combined with seeing all audio, or mostly audio, waveforms, makes it much easier to see the exact ups and downs of the audio in the waveforms, particularly when finding natural places to cut between dialogue.

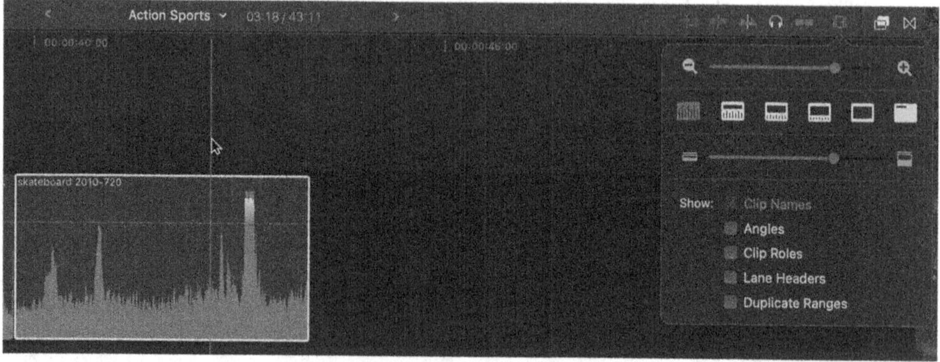

Figure 3.20: Pro tip – increase the clip height along with the waveform only for audio editing

5. In the bottom section of the **Clip Appearance** menu are the **Show** checkboxes. The **Clip Names** option is always on, but you can choose to have other labels visible, such as **Angles, Clip Roles, Lane Headers**, and **Duplicate Ranges**. Normally, just having **Clip Names** is enough.

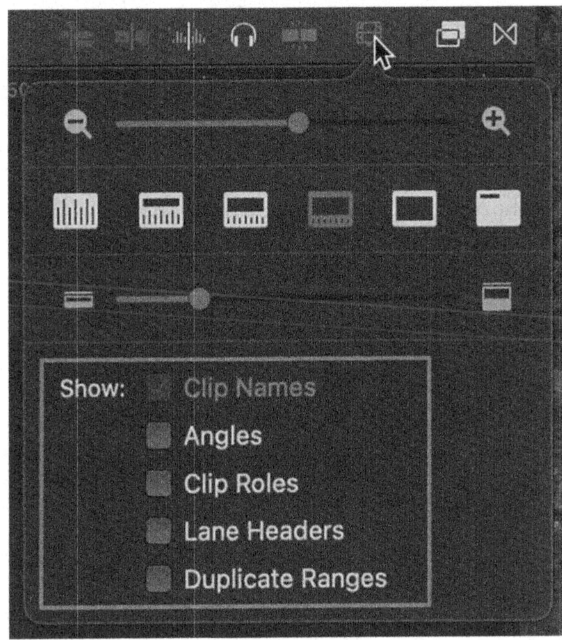

Figure 3.21: Use the checkboxes to select labels on clips other than Clip Names

There's more...

When navigating the Timeline panel, it can be helpful to know a few other keyboard shortcuts.

The + and - icons are the logical choice for zooming in and out of the detail on our clips in the timeline. But there is a subtlety to address. Because many of our Final Cut Pro shortcuts use only one modifier key, such as the *Command* key, the "plus" action actually uses the = symbol and not the "+" symbol, which is technically "Uppercase =". To use the actual "+" symbol, we would need to use the *Shift* key along with the *Command* key, but it would be awkward to add the *Shift* key to one command just to be technically right.

So, don't be thrown by the keyboard shortcut listed in the **View** menu for **Zoom In**. You can still think of it as "plus" and "minus" by using *Command + =* to zoom in and *Command + -* to zoom out.

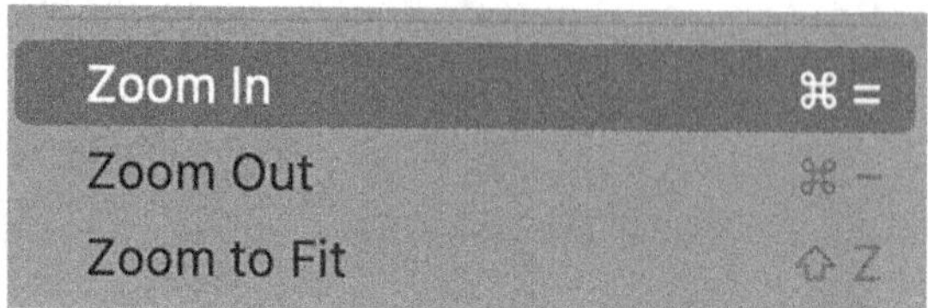

Figure 3.22: Note the zoom action keyboard shortcuts

Here is another good shortcut: *Shift + Z* will zoom the contents of the timeline to fit the size of the Timeline panel. If you zoom too far in or out, using this shortcut can feel like returning to home base, allowing you to see your whole project.

Replacing clips

When the dish doesn't quite sizzle, swap in a spicier ingredient. Mastering the various replace commands in Final Cut Pro will give you the flexibility to swap out clips seamlessly while preserving the integrity of your timeline.

In this recipe, we'll explore how to use these powerful tools to efficiently update your edits, ensuring that your revisions are both precise and effortless.

Getting ready

It will be helpful to have a variety of clips in the Event Browser panel and in the Timeline panel.

How to do it...

Perhaps you have heard old-timers talk about the three-point edit. That is, placing a new clip into a slot by only needing to know three edit points. Well, here is the modernized method that all the cool kids are using:

1. Identify a clip in the timeline that you want to replace. Then, in the Event Browser, select the clip that you want to replace the timeline clip with.

2. Click and drag the clip from the Event Browser and place it on top of the clip in the timeline. Hold the clip there until the cursor changes to an image of a filmstrip with a + sign.

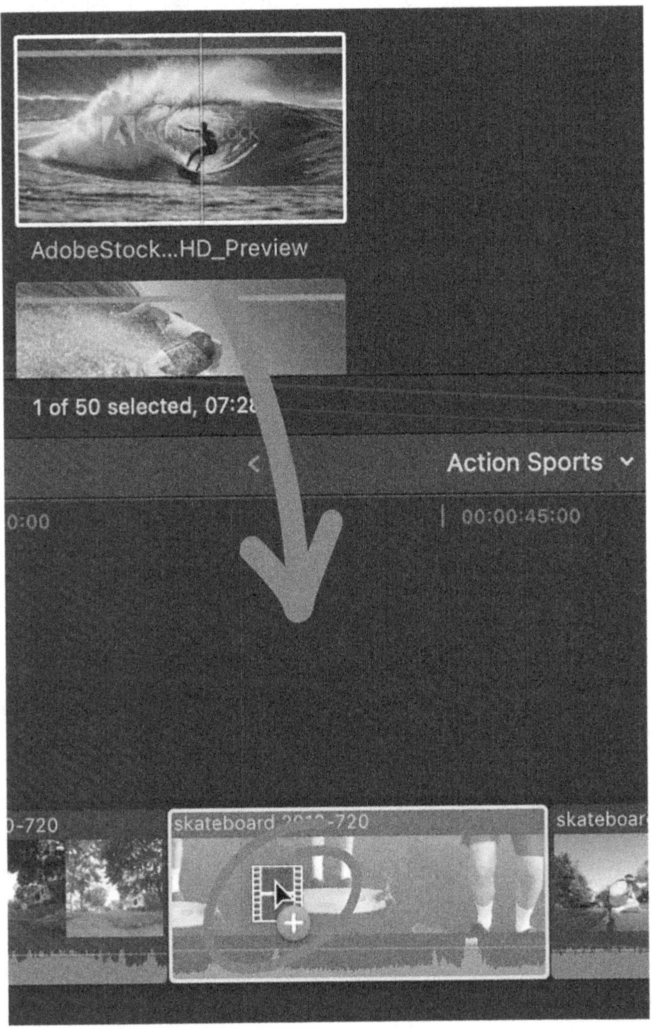

Figure 3.23: Drag a clip from the Event Browser on top of a clip in the timeline

When you let go, you will see a pop-up menu with several items in it.

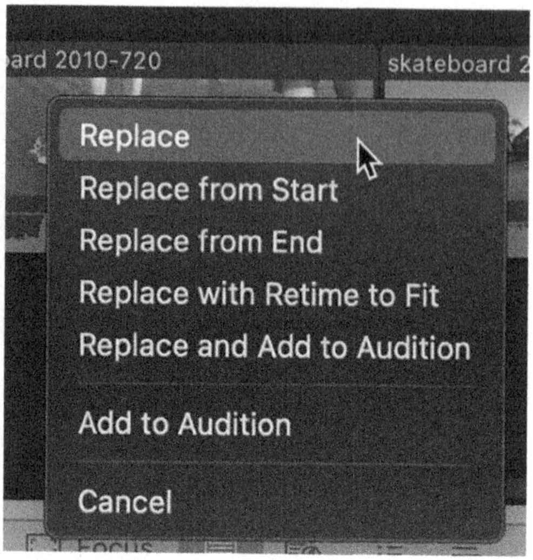

Figure 3.24: Note the options in the Replace command menu

Let's go through the options. First is the **Replace** command – this will do just that, it will replace that clip with the other, regardless of the length.

However, there is a problem. In my example, the clip I am using from the Event Browser is longer than the original. If I were to simply replace the clip, the longer clip would *ripple* time forward to the right, down the timeline, and change the size of my overall project. Oftentimes, though, you've already worked out the timing of a project based on music, or the fact that it is a 60-second commercial, and you want the clip that you're bringing down to have the exact same length of time. This is where the other commands and the three-point edit come in.

3. One option is **Replace from Start**. This means you're going to take the start point and end point from the clip in the timeline and use just the start point from the clip in the Event Browser. This command replaces the original clip and keeps the integrity of our timeline by using whatever it needs from the *first part* of the new clip.

4. Sometimes it is the other way around. Let's say it's the ending of the clip in the Event Browser that applies to your story, and it is still the case that you want to keep the same timing of the project. Then you would use **Replace from End**. This command replaces the original clip and keeps the integrity of our timeline by using whatever it needs from the *last part* of the new clip. Those are the three points: in and out of the original clip and either in or out of the new clip.

5. But, you know, sometimes you want both ends of the original clip in the Event Browser. Perhaps, if the clips are close enough in length, you can use **Replace with Retime to Fit**. This command replaces the original clip and keeps the integrity of our timeline by *stretching* or *shrinking* the timing of the new clip to fit the space. You have to decide whether the retiming looks right for the story you are trying to tell.

6. Fortunately, there is a **Cancel** command at the bottom in case you change your mind.

Auditions are a way to test several clips by bundling them in a way that does not disrupt your Timeline project. They are a special kind of topic and area of investigation. So, the **Replace and Add to Audition** command and the **Add to Audition** command will be covered in more depth in *Chapter 4*, in a recipe called *Creating an audition*.

Adding transitions

A seamless transition is the wine pairing of the edit – elevating the whole meal. Transitions bind your clips together, guiding your audience smoothly from one scene to the next.

In this recipe, we'll explore how to effectively apply transitions in the Final Cut Pro Timeline. We will investigate how transitions use extra media beyond a clip's edge and what to do when a message says there is not enough media.

How to do it...

Transitions are the dynamic blending of one clip into another, enhancing the flow of your edits and adding a polished, professional touch to your videos. Let's get to it:

1. To view the Transition Browser panel, click on the **Hide or Show Transition Browser** icon in the upper-right corner of the Timeline panel. It looks like a crisscross transition bow tie type of icon.

Figure 3.25: Click on the Hide or Show Transition Browser icon

2. Transitions are listed alphabetically, although **Cross Dissolve** is first because it is used the most. You can view all transitions or choose a specific category. Explore the variety of transitions by skimming your mouse slowly through the thumbnails in the Transition Browser panel to get an idea of what they look like. Final Cut Pro uses an image of orange mountains transitioning to blue mountains to illustrate the effects.

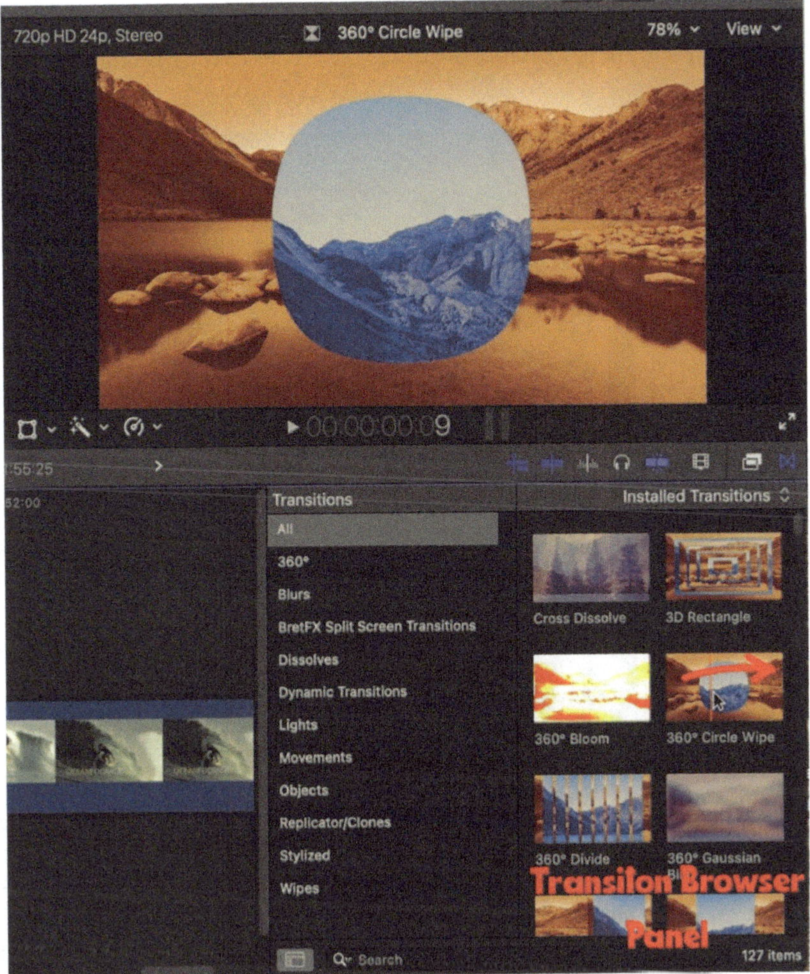

Chapter 399

Figure 3.26: Skim over samples in the Transition Browser panel

3. To apply a transition, simply select it in the Transition Browser panel and drag it on top of an edit point in the timeline. When you release the mouse, it is applied to the edit point between the two clips.

4. Another way to apply a transition is to click the edit point and use the keyboard shortcut *Command + T*. This will apply the default transition – **Cross Dissolve** – but you can change that in the **Settings** window.

5. The default transition length is one second, as we can see in the time code area at the top of the Timeline panel. The yellow timecode relates to the selection that is highlighted in yellow.

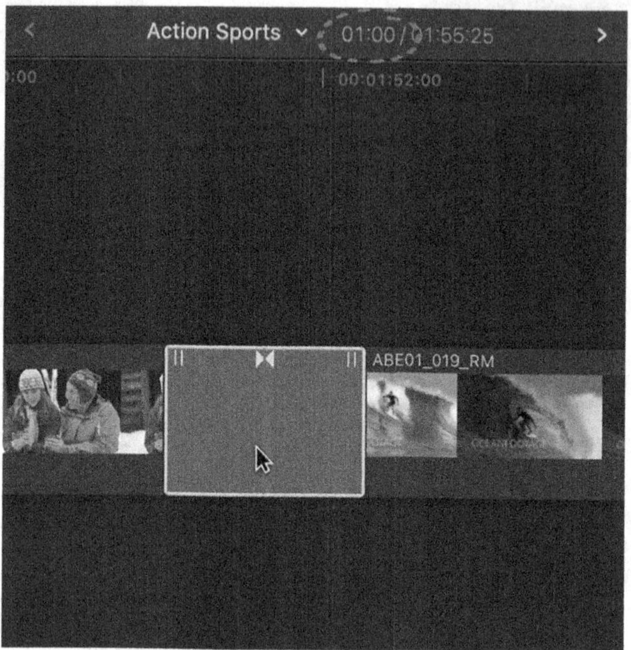

Figure 3.27: Note that the default duration of a transition is one second

Of course, you can change the timing of a transition. Simply click and drag on the lower edge on either side of the transition to make it longer or shorter according to the story you are telling. Notice that both sides of the transition are highlighted in yellow and turn in toward the center.

Figure 3.28: Drag the bottom corner to change the timing of a transition

6. But, take notice that if you click and drag on the two small white lines at either top corner of the transition, you will drag the edit point of either clip and not the transition. Notice in *Figure 3.29* how the top of the yellow highlighted lines turns in toward the transition, indicating that the drag action will only affect the in point of the clip to the right. The in point of the clip starts at the beginning of the transition. Anytime you change the in or out point of one clip, it is a ripple edit that changes the overall time of the project.

Figure 3.29: Drag the top corner to change the edit point of a clip

Conversely, if you were to click and drag the center *bow tie* of the transition, you would roll the edit point of both clips and change the position of the transition. This is called a rolling edit and does not change the overall time of the project. Note, we will explore this in *Chapter 4*, in a recipe called *Getting to grips with ripple, roll, slip, and slide edits*.

Figure 3.30: Drag the center of a transition to roll the edit point of both clips

7. Now let's look inside a transition. Choose a transition in your timeline and double-click inside the transition area. This opens the Precision Editor view (we looked at this in the *Using the Precision Editor view* recipe in *Chapter 1*), which helps us visualize the transition from one clip to the next.

    In the top clip, note the gradual angle of lightness to darkness of the image during the length of the transition. This indicates the gradual change from 100% to 0% opacity. Conversely, the change in the bottom clip goes from dark to light, 0% to 100% opacity. Notice that, halfway through, both clips are at 50% opacity. That is what goes on inside a transition. The image of the first clip decreases while the image of the second clip increases, with them both at 50% exactly in the center.

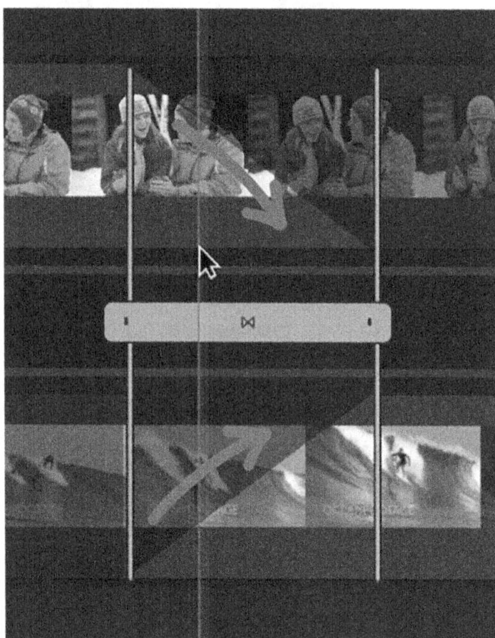

Figure 3.31: Note the Precision Editor view of a transition

8. Let's explore how transitions can use extra media beyond a clip's edge. In the Event Browser panel, select an entire clip, that is, edge to edge, and append it to the end of your Timeline project.

9.   Then, try dragging and holding the transition over the edit point – notice that it doesn't snap onto the timeline like it did on previous edit points.

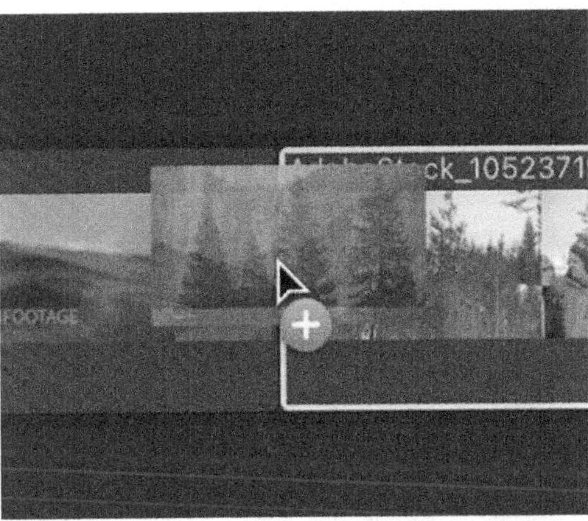

Figure 3.32: Note the situation when a transition does not snap into place

10. Release the mouse button – note that we get a message saying that there's not enough extra media. Don't worry, there is an easy solution.

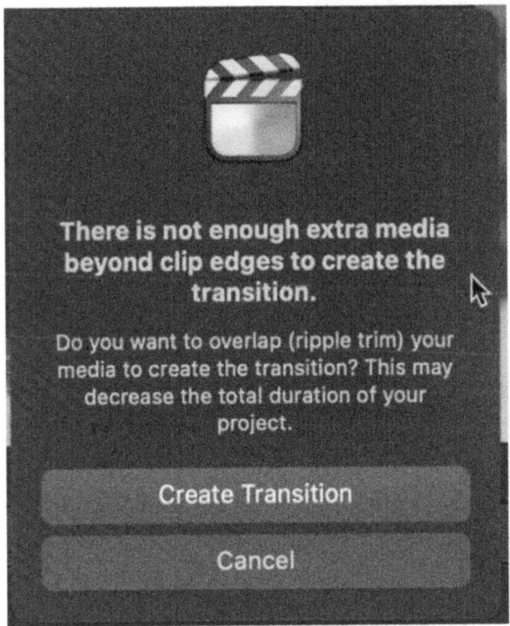

Figure 3.33: Carefully read the alert message regarding media beyond the clip edge

Click on the **Cancel** button for now, and let's look into this.

11. In the Timeline panel, double-click on the edit point to bring up the Precision Editor view. Note that our new clip – the one at the bottom – does not have any buffer media ahead of the edit point.

Figure 3.34: Note that the Precision Editor shows no extra media

12. Double-click on the center button to close the Precision Editor view.

13. Now apply the transition again. This time, when the message box comes up, click on the **Create Transition** button to see what happens.

14. The transition is applied. Now, double-click on the edit point to bring up the Precision Editor view again. Notice that Final Cut Pro shifted the new clip to the left to use one second of transition media so that the image could go from 0% to 100%.

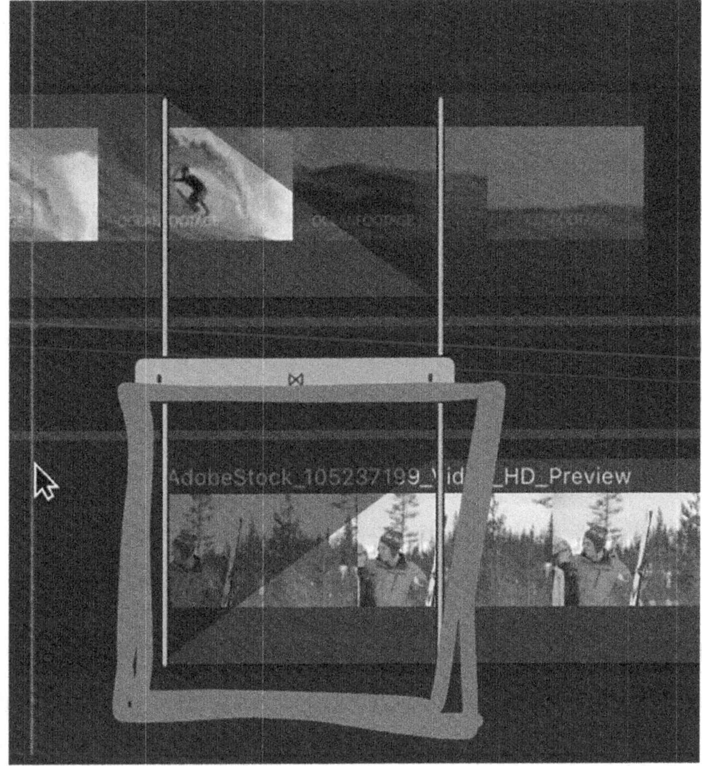

Figure 3.35: Note that the Precision Editor shows extra media added

That message isn't all bad. It just means that Final Cut Pro needs to use part of the clip for the graduated transition.

There's more...

An edit point between two clips with no transition is considered a *cut*. In the grammar of editing, a cut edit is used as a blink of the eye. Without distracting transitions, a cut allows the viewer to track your story more readily because a cut more closely mimics real life. That is why most films and TV shows with stories are assembled with cut edits. The viewer gets wrapped up in the story.

Although the cut may seem invisible because there is no transition symbol, it is actually quite powerful. When two clips are next to each other, there is a connection. If an actor looks offscreen, the audience assumes that whatever image is displayed next is the thing that the actor is looking at. Or, if we see the outside of a building, a la Seinfeld, and the next clip is a group of actors in a room, we assume the room is in that building. This is the power that an editor has.

However, keep in mind that certain transitions have meaning to audiences:

- A dissolve transition represents a change in time. Dissolving between clips represents a montage of actions that take place over time and not necessarily one right after another.
- A fade to black represents a great amount of time change. This might be used to represent an entire day or even several years that have changed from one scene to the next.
- A ripple dissolve, in a viewer's mind, will represent a dream or a flashback.

Big, dramatically changing transitions, such as checkerboards, circles, and chevrons, represent exclamation points in the grammar of editing. They're special and should be used sparingly to remain special.

With that in mind, enjoy using transitions – but remember, *the story should always drive production*. You should not add transitions just because they are available and look cool!

Creating secondary storyline transitions

When adding a new layer to the dish, stir gently; secondary storylines should mix, not overwhelm. Creating transitions within secondary storylines allows you to add depth and complexity to your edits, seamlessly blending clips that sit outside the main narrative.

In this recipe, we'll delve into how to create secondary storylines and the techniques for crafting smooth transitions within them, helping you to enhance the visual flow and cohesion of your project.

Getting ready

We will be using the right mouse button to easily bring up contextual pop-up menus. Out of the box, Mac does not have *right-click* turned on. So, if you have not already done so, in the **System Settings | Mouse** panel, set **Secondary click** to **Click Right Side**.

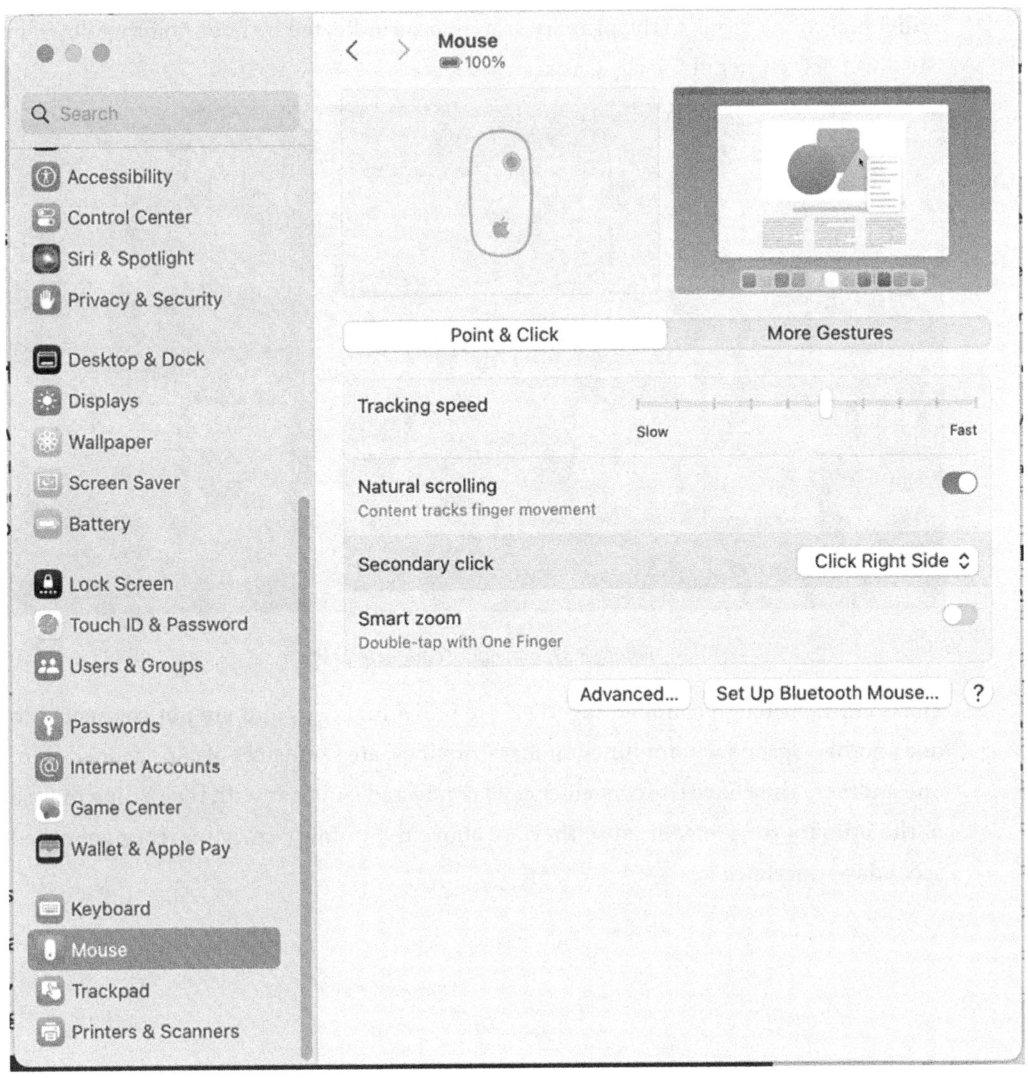

Figure 3.36: Use System Settings | Mouse to turn on right-click

How to do it...

Before we work with the secondary storyline, let's look at the primary storyline first:

1. When you have connected clips above, or on top of, the primary storyline, that is just what they are: individual clips. They are not in a relationship with each other and have individual connections to the primary storyline, as indicated by lines pointing down in the lower-left corner of the clips, as seen in *Figure 3.37*.

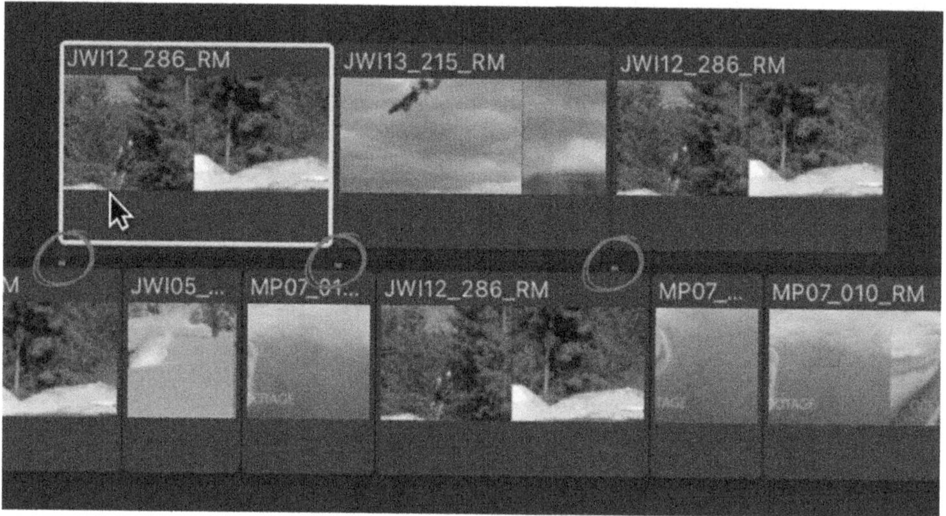

Figure 3.37: Individual connected clips

These clips, although snapped together, are individual clips and are not connected to one another. Secondary storylines, or just storylines, are sequences of clips connected to one another. They have the convenience of connected clips but with the editing finesse of the primary storyline. Because they are above the primary storyline, they are called secondary storylines.

2. Let's demonstrate how individual clips will function differently from clips formed into a storyline. Let's try to apply a transition between two clips. Drag a transition from the Transition Browser panel onto the *edit point* between two connected clips. Notice that the transition tries to apply itself to both sides of that clip.

Figure 3.38: Note a transition applied wrongly to multiple clips

3. That is not what we want. Let's undo this action with the keyboard shortcut *Command + Z*. Instead, to have these clips function together, we want to connect them into a secondary storyline.

4. Select the clips to bundle together. Then, right-click anywhere on the selected clips, and in the clip pop-up menu, select **Create Storyline** (or use the keyboard shortcut *Command + G*).

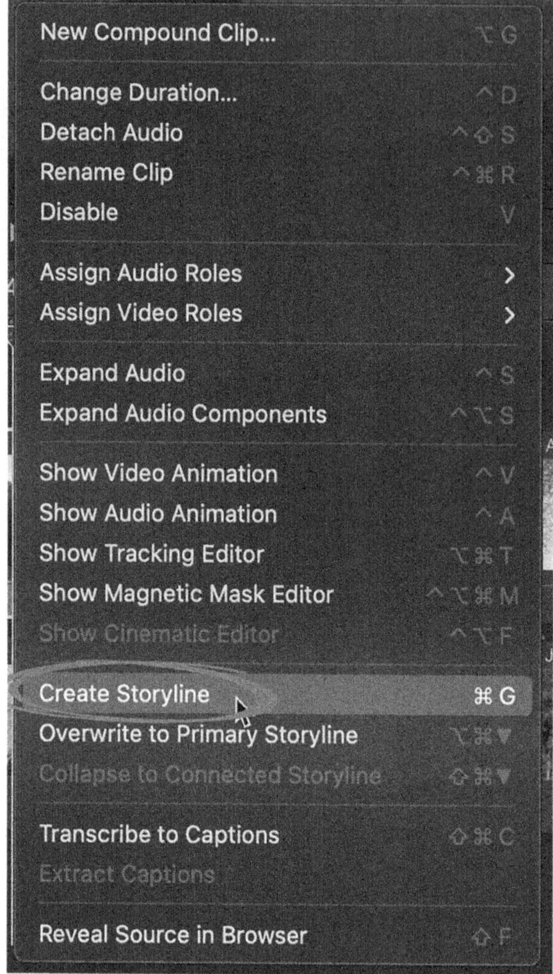

Figure 3.39: Select Create Storyline from the clip pop-up menu

Now these clips are connected as a storyline. We can see this from the shelf that runs across the top of the bundle. We can also see there is one connection line in the bottom-left corner of the storyline. These clips will stay connected and move together.

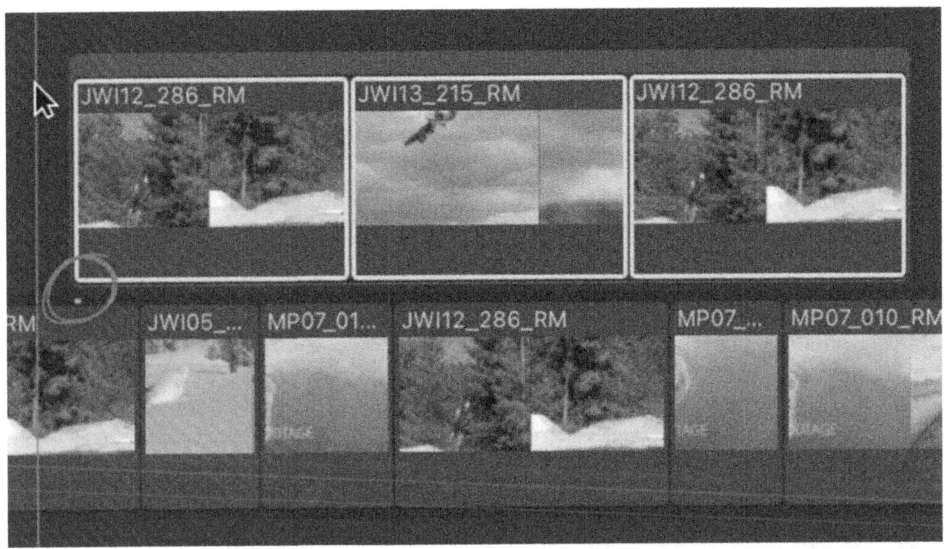

Figure 3.40: Note that the clips are connected in one storyline

5. Now add a transition between clips. This time, notice that the edit point between the clips functions similarly to the primary storyline, where the transitions are applied to just that one edit point.

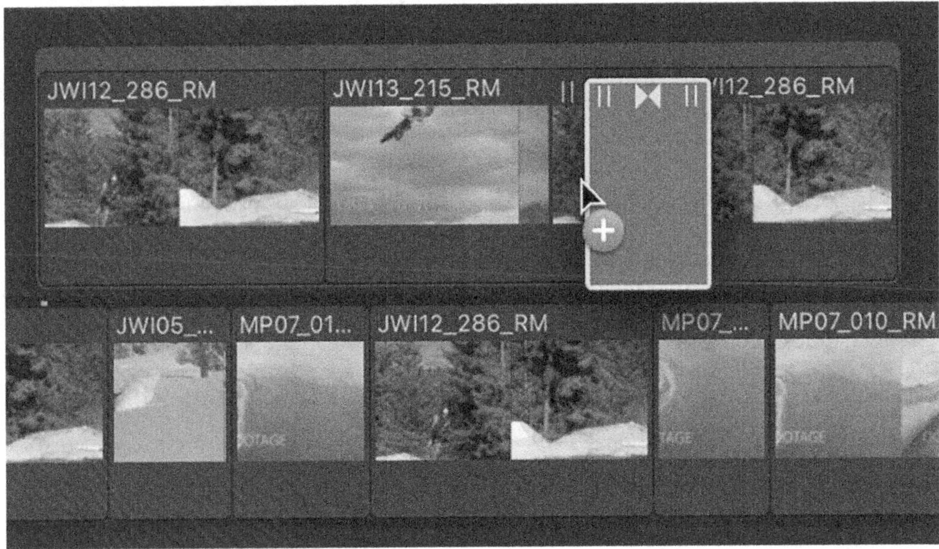

Figure 3.41: Note that transitions are applied to one edit point in a secondary storyline

Secondary storylines can be as complex as your primary storyline, adding depth to your overall narrative. Besides transitions, secondary storylines can contain titles, effects, and generators, and you can expand the audio to create J-cuts and L-cuts (we will look at some of these in the next chapter). Take some time to explore all the capabilities of secondary storylines.

There's more...

Another cool tip involves connected clips or secondary storylines – you can change the location of the connection point between a clip and the primary storyline.

When a clip is connected to the primary storyline, it moves along with the clip that it's connected to. In my example, you can see the primary storyline connection point in the lower-left corner of the connected clip. The connected clip moves with the clip before it in the primary storyline.

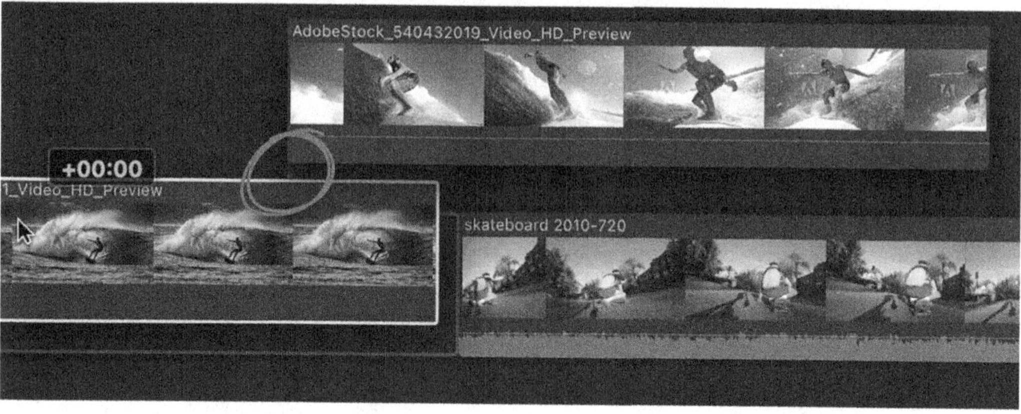

Figure 3.42: Note the connection point at the beginning of a connected clip

Sometimes we want a clip to be connected in a different place and not at the far left edge. In my example, I want the connected clip to be connected with the clip behind it, not the one in front. There's a quick keyboard shortcut for changing the connected position.

Select the clip in the primary storyline that you want your connected clip to be attached to. Then, while holding down the *Option + Command* keys, click inside the connected clip at the point at which you want the connection point.

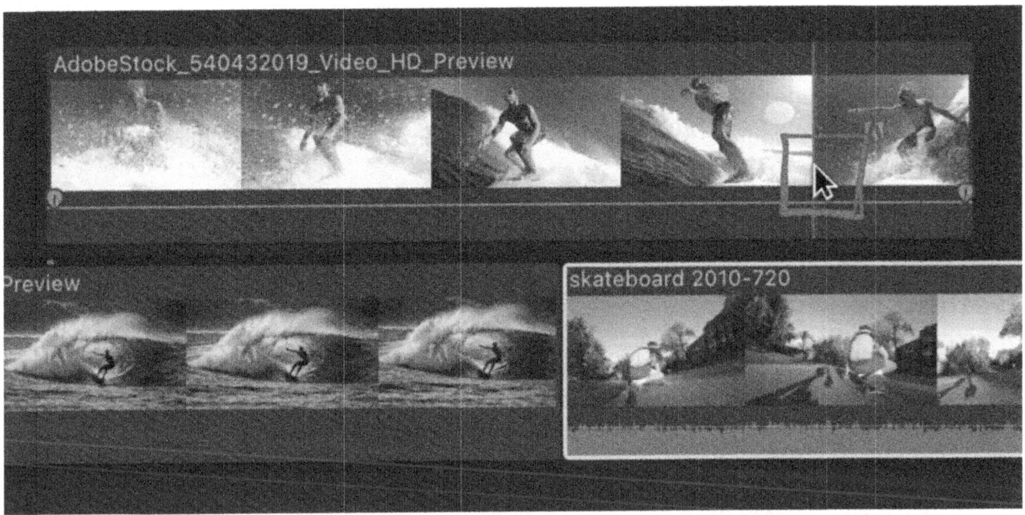

Figure 3.43: Click in the connected clip to change the connection to a selected clip

That will change the connection position to the place that you clicked. Now, that clip, or a secondary storyline, will be connected to the new point on the primary storyline, and they will move together.

Figure 3.44: Note that the connection point is in a new location

Using the Blade tool

Editing with the **Blade** tool is like slicing sushi – sharp, clean, and artfully arranged. The **Blade** tool in Final Cut Pro is your go-to for making cuts and splitting clips exactly where you need them.

In this recipe, we'll cover how to effectively use the **Blade** tool to refine your edits on long sections of footage, allowing you to carve out the perfect moments and edit your timeline with accuracy.

Getting ready

It would be helpful to import some footage that is several minutes long.

How to do it...

As we said, editing is like sculpting. You make a rough draft of what you need and gradually refine the edges – time to slice and dice:

1. It is easier to work with the **Blade** tool on a long clip, so select a long clip in the Event Browser and quickly append it to the end of the timeline with the keyboard shortcut *E*.

2. Click in the Timeline panel and use the keyboard shortcut of *Shift + Z* to show the entire project in the Timeline panel.

Figure 3.45: A long clip in the Timeline project

We could set in and out points in the browser window, as we did in the *Quickly selecting clips with keyboard shortcuts* recipe. But as we have our clip in the timeline, we'll use the **Blade** tool.

3. Select the **Blade** tool from the toolbar to the left of the Timeline panel, or use the keyboard shortcut *B*.

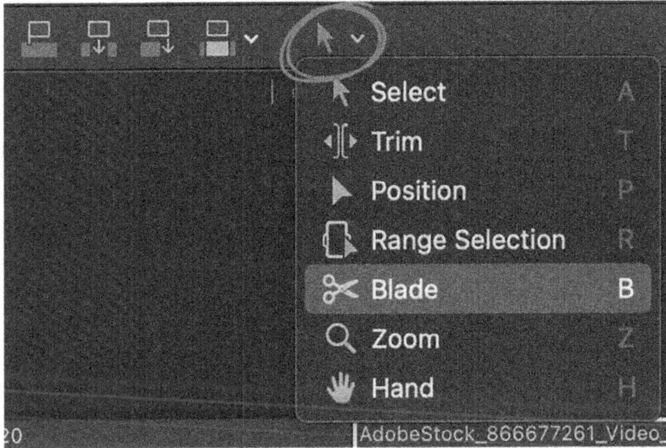

Figure 3.46: Select the Blade tool from the tool drop-down menu

4. Play through your long clip and find a place in the clip to create an edit point. Then click once with the **Blade** tool cursor.

   An edit point has been created, but, interestingly, you may notice it has dotted lines – this represents the fact that, even though it is an edit point, one frame blends into the next frame naturally without any breaks.

5. Next, from the toolbar, return to the **Select** tool (or use the keyboard shortcut *A*). Now, when you click and drag the edit point, you no longer have a dotted line because there are frames tucked underneath the two clips.

Figure 3.47: Note an edit point with no breaks and an edit point with breaks

6. Finally, let's quickly do some editing. Returning to the **Blade** tool (*B*), skim through your long clip, and click to create rough edit points. Next, quickly switch back to the **Select** tool (*A*) and click on a section of the clip that you don't want. Then, keeping your right hand on the mouse, reach over and press the *Delete* key with your left hand to delete the section from the timeline (this is quicker than using your right hand).

Figure 3.48: Use the Blade tool to cut the clip into sections

This editing method with the **Blade** tool is beneficial when you are familiar with the footage and don't need to listen carefully to find edit points. Perhaps it is an interview, and you want to cut out the sections where they look off camera, or there is some other audio or visual cue that you can quickly find by skimming through the footage.

Changing a clip's duration

Too long and it's burnt, too short and it's raw; dial in duration like a master chef. Achieving precise timing in your edits is crucial for creating a polished final product. The story drives production, so there may be a reason your project or clip needs to be an exact length of time.

In this recipe, we'll explore how to change a clip's or transition's duration by typing in exact values, giving you full control over the length of each clip and ensuring that every moment fits perfectly within your timeline.

How to do it...

Here's how to alter clip durations:

1. *Right-click* on a clip that you would like to change the duration of and, from the pop-up menu, select **Change Duration...**.

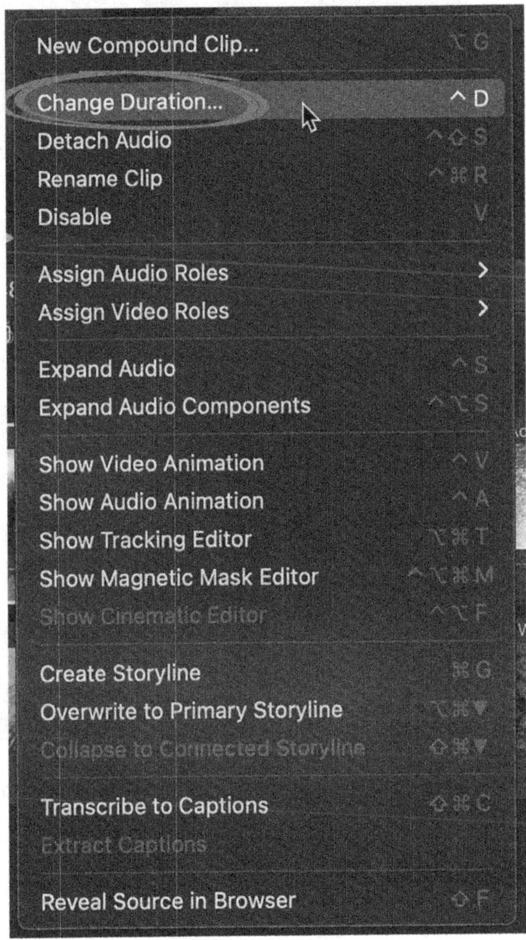

Figure 3.49: Select Change Duration… from the clip pop-up menu

2. Along the bottom edge of the Viewer, there is a purple icon representing a clip with its
    edges tucked underneath itself, along with a purple time code. The time code numbers
    represent hours, minutes, seconds, and frames.

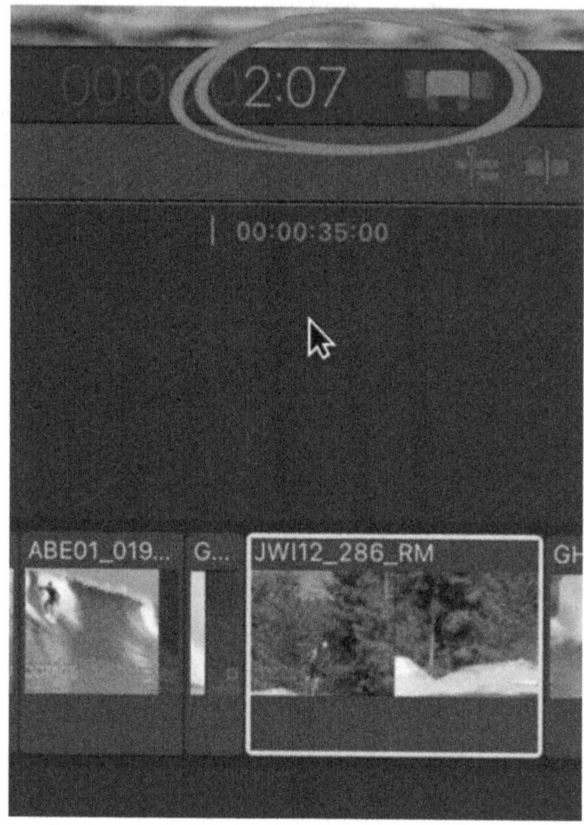

*Figure 3.50: Note the timecode and icon in the Viewer, indicating that a clip is ready
to be changed*

The purple timecode is ready to be changed simply by typing a new number. Note that
you need to include frames, not just minutes or seconds. In my example, if I want this
clip to be exactly 2 seconds, I will need to type 200, not 2, and then lock it in by pressing
the *Return* or *Enter* key.

3. Let's do it again, but with a transition. Find a transition in your timeline or add one be-
    tween two clips. Click on the transition to select it and use the easy keyboard shortcut
    Control + D to enter the **Change Duration** mode.

4. I want my transition to be one and a half seconds. I know that my project, or timeline, is set to 29.97 frames per second. So, one and a half seconds would be 1 second and 15 frames. The purple duration number is ready to be changed, so I will type 115 and hit *Return*.

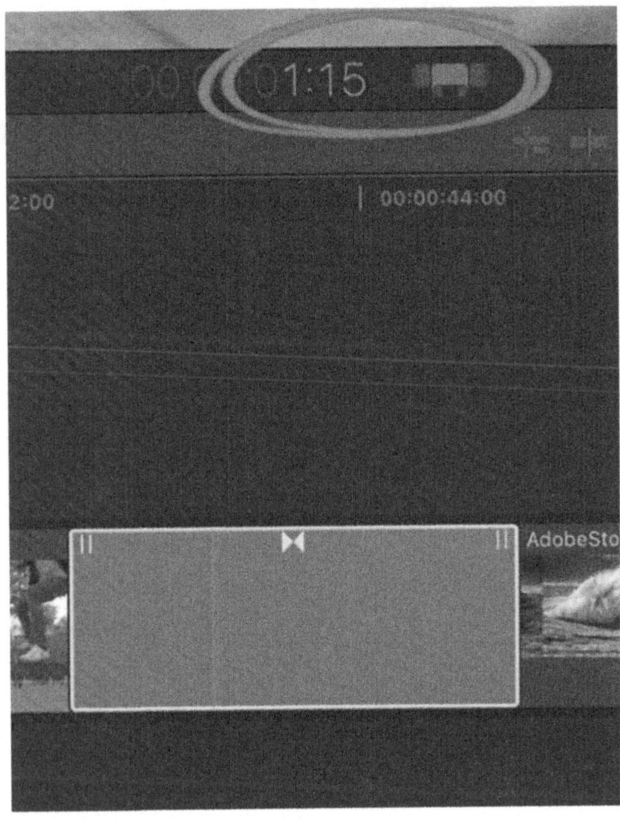

Figure 3.51: Note the timecode and icon in the Viewer, indicating that a transition is ready to be changed

There's more...

In this recipe, we used the example of changing the duration of a clip to one and a half seconds. If you are not sure how many frames are in a half-second in your project, you will need to check the project's **Frame Rate** settings:

1. In the Sidebar, select the library that contains the project.

2. Click on the project thumbnail in the Event Browser panel.

3. Look in the Inspector for the settings of the project.

Figure 3.52: Note a project's frame rate information in the Inspector

4. Notice that, near the top-right corner of the Inspector panel, there is information about the aspect ratio and the frame rate of your project.

4

Improving Your Editing Efficiency

Welcome to the bustling kitchen of video editing, where efficiency is the key to success. In this chapter, we'll sharpen our knives and hone our skills as we explore a bounty of techniques designed to streamline your workflow in Final Cut Pro. We'll uncover time-saving shortcuts, organizational strategies, and advanced editing tools to help you work smarter, not harder.

In this chapter, you will delve into advanced editing topics such as ripple and roll, and slip and slide, gaining mastery over precise clip adjustments to refine your edits with finesse in Final Cut Pro. You'll also learn how to enhance storytelling through creative editing methods such as using gap and placeholder clips, creating J- and L-cuts, utilizing markers and the Timeline Index, creating compound clips and auditions, changing clip colors, and seamlessly integrating multicam footage for dynamic and engaging video productions.

In this chapter, you will complete the following recipes:

- Getting to grips with ripple, roll, slip, and slide edits
- Using gap clips and placeholder clips
- Creating J- and L-cuts
- Using markers and the Timeline Index
- Creating an audition

- Creating compound clips
- Color coding your clips
- Using multicam editing

So far in this book, we have talked about quite a few keyboard shortcuts and the modifier keys that go with them. Some keyboards now list the word and symbol on the keys, but many don't. *Shift* (⇧) is used for capital letters, of course, and we take it for granted, but it is often used in combination with other modifiers. *Command* (⌘) is fairly common, and most users are familiar with using it for copy and paste.

Less common modifier keys are *Control* (∧) and *Option* (⌥), which can get mixed up. This is how I remember them. The *Control* symbol looks like handlebars, which you would use to *control* a bike. The *Option* symbol looks like an escalator – and an escalator is one "option" to reach the next floor of a building, instead of the stairs. Note that menu commands that have keyboard shortcuts will have them listed on the right side of the menu. The *Control* and *Option* keys, like the *Command* key, will have many functions to change or create a new option for a function or process. For example, we will use the *Option* key to modify the function of the **Trim** tool. In addition, we will use the *Control* key as part of a keyboard shortcut to expand the audio of a clip.

Getting to grips with ripple, roll, slip, and slide edits

Trimming is the knife work of editing – precise, essential, and transformative. Mastering these edits lets you fine-tune the flavor of your story, one clean cut at a time, without affecting the overall sequence length of your project. By learning these techniques, you'll enhance your ability to create smooth, professional edits that align perfectly with your creative vision.

In this recipe, we'll explore how to use the **Trim** tool. We will use the techniques of slipping and sliding clips and discuss the concepts of ripple and rolling edits.

Getting ready

In preparation for my example, I have three portions of clips lined up in a row in the primary storyline of my Timeline panel. Do not use the entire clip – it works best to have short portions from the middle of clips to demonstrate the **Trim** tool.

How to do it...

Trim is a versatile and specialized tool, and is worth getting to know well. Let's take a look:

1. From the **Tool** menu in the upper-left corner of the Timeline panel, select the **Trim** tool. Alternatively, you can simply use the keyboard shortcut *T*.

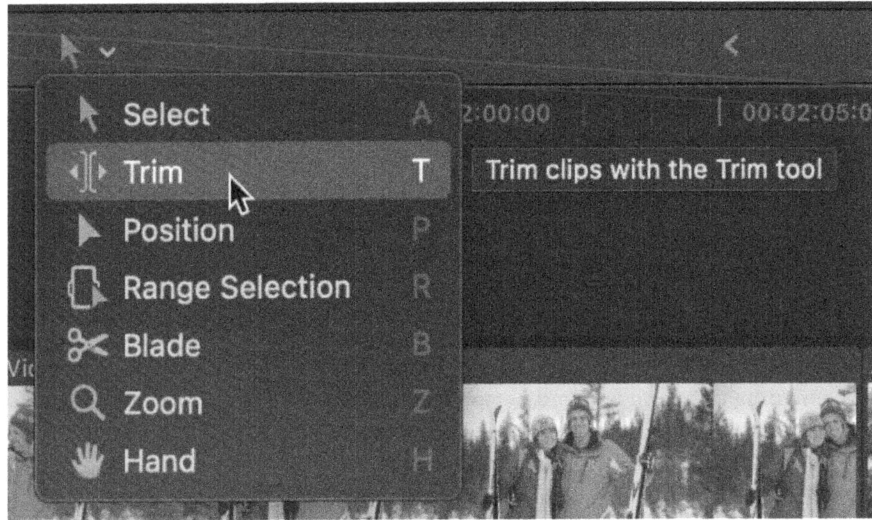

Figure 4.1: Select the Trim tool from the Tool menu

2. Understanding how the cursor looks is key to understanding what action the **Trim** tool will perform. Place your mouse to the left of an edit point and note that the cursor has two arrows with a line between the arrows and their top corners pointing to the left. There is also an icon of a film strip rolling in on itself. Click and drag that edit point either right or left – notice that the right edge of the left clip is highlighted in yellow matching the edge line in the cursor.

Figure 4.2: Hold and drag to trim one edge of a clip

3.   Test this on the right side of an edit point. Notice that the edge line in the center of the cursor now faces to the right, and the film strip canister rolls the other way. As you click and drag these single edit points, you will see that the length of your project changes. This is defined as a **ripple edit**. This type of edit ripples time downstream as you change an edit point.

4.   Still using the **Trim** tool, place the mouse directly over an edit point and note that the cursor changes to have two edges and two film strips rolling in on themselves. Then, click and drag right and left, and notice that the edit point moves the edges, *in* and *out* points, of both clips at the same time.

Figure 4.3: Hold and drag the Trim tool to roll the edit point between two clips

While changing the length of either of these two clips, the footage appears to roll into their respective canisters, as indicated by the image of the cursor; the result is that the overall length of our project has not changed. This is called a **rolling edit**. This edit rolls the time of the clips into themselves and does not affect the downstream time.

5. Let's slide into the next steps. Position the **Trim** tool in the center of a clip, and you will notice that the cursor changes with two edges facing each other and one film strip rolling in on both ends. Based on the image of the cursor, take a moment and try to guess what will happen when you clip and drag. What does the filmstrip indicate?

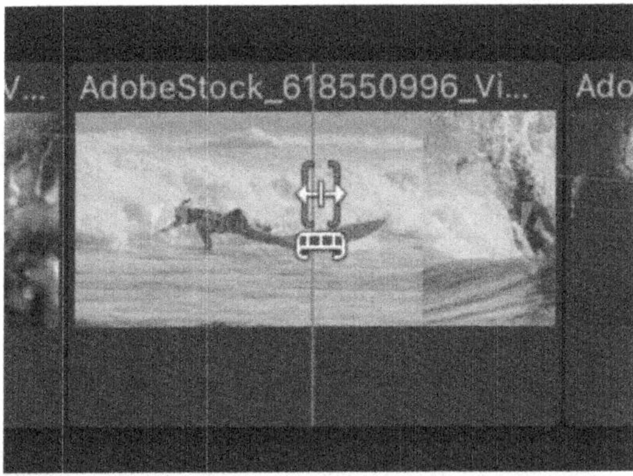

Figure 4.4: Notice the Trim tool cursor inside a clip

6. Now, click and drag within this clip. As you will see, images of the video change within the length of the clip. Almost like a window frame, the filmstrip is moved along under the clip's frame size. Is this what you expected? Note that this, too, is a rolling edit, as the length of the overall project does not change.

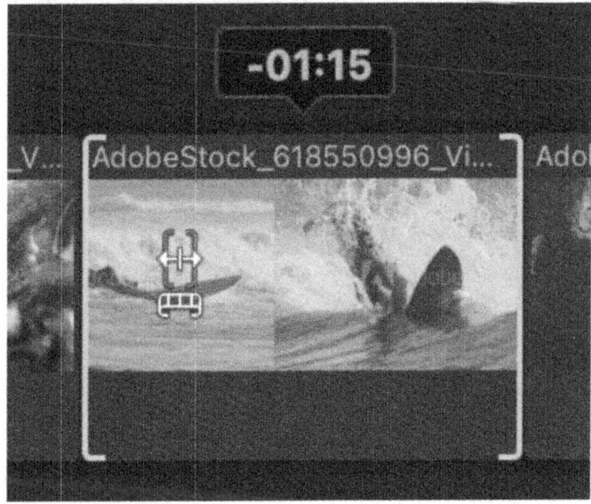

Figure 4.5: Hold and drag the Trim tool inside to slip the footage of a clip

This is a **slip edit**. Slip means that you change the in and out points of the clip simultaneously, effectively shifting the content of the clip while keeping its duration and position in the timeline unchanged. This is useful for selecting a different portion of the clip without altering the overall timing of your edit.

7. But wait, there's more. With the **Trim** tool cursor still in the center of a clip, hold down the *Option* key – you will see that the cursor changes to two edges facing inward, but the film strip canisters are rolling opposite one another. Now, click, hold, and drag the clip. The size of the clip doesn't change, but the position of the clip changes in relation to the two clips next to it. As indicated by the cursor icon, the edges of those outside clips roll in on themselves while this clip in the center stays static.

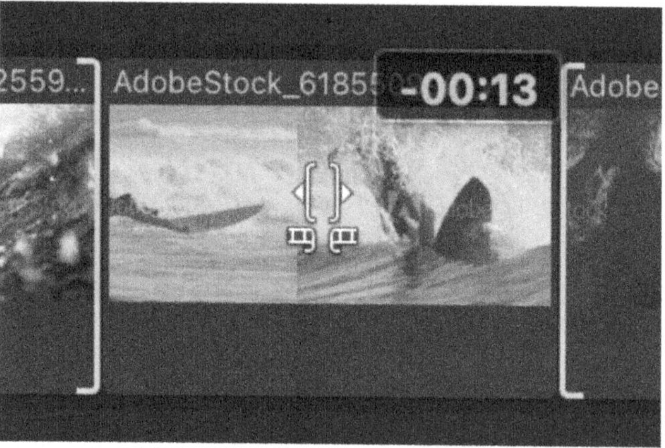

Figure 4.6: Hold and drag the Trim tool with the Option key to slide a clip

This is a **slide edit**. Slide means that you adjust a clip's position in the timeline while maintaining its in and out points. When you slide a clip, the clips on either side automatically adjust to fill the gap created by the move, allowing you to change the placement of a clip within your sequence without affecting its content. This technique is useful for altering the timing of your edits to achieve a more cohesive flow in your project.

Both slipping and sliding effects create rolling edits; you noticed that the overall length of your project didn't change.

Sometimes it's hard to remember the right terminology, but it is important, especially when speaking with other editors. This is how I remember them: consider slipping inside the clip like slipping *in* the shower. Meanwhile, sliding affects the other clips outside, and you would slide *out* a car door.

Using gap clips and placeholder clips

Mise en place is a French culinary term that means *everything in its place*. It refers to the practice of preparing and organizing all your ingredients and tools before cooking begins. But in our case, if an ingredient is missing, we don't have to hold up the entire production. Gap clips and placeholder clips are powerful tools that help you maintain the structure of your timeline and plan out your edit. By incorporating these tools into your workflow, you can keep your projects organized and make the editing process more flexible and efficient.

In this recipe, we'll cover how to use **gap clips** to create space between clips without shifting the rest of your timeline, and **placeholder clips** to temporarily stand in for footage you haven't yet added.

How to do it...

Let's learn how to add gap clips and placeholder clips:

1. With the playhead positioned on an edit point between two clips, go to the **Edit** menu and select **Insert Generator / Gap**. Alternatively, you can use the keyboard shortcut *Option + W*. This will insert a three-second gap clip (or a black slug, as we called it back in the tape editing days) into the primary storyline.

2. A gap clip behaves like any other clip, including having its length edited. This works great if, for example, you want to slow down an interview and add some breathing room, while covering the gap clip with some B-roll.

Figure 4.7: Place gap clips into the primary storyline

However, gap clips are just blank. When you need a temporary clip in the timeline while you continue to tell your story, there's a way to insert something that is a bit more professional.

3. In the upper-left corner of the Sidebar panel are three icon buttons. The icon to the right is the **Show or Hide Title and Generator Sidebar** icon. Click this once and you'll see the **Titles** and **Generators** collections.

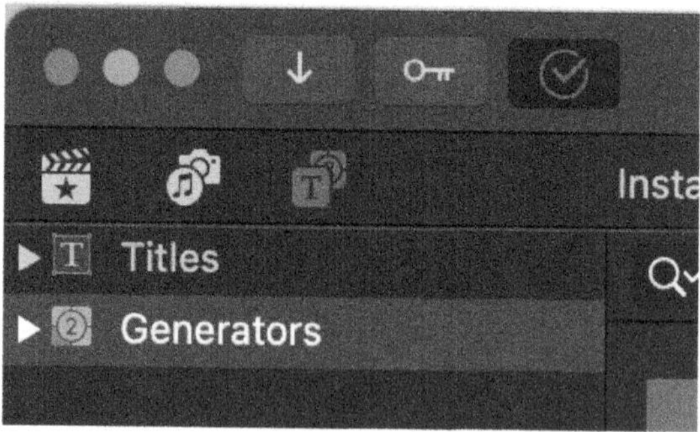

Figure 4.8: Click on the icon for the Title and Generator Browser panel

4. Click on the disclosure triangle for **Generators**. Under **Elements**, you'll see a generator called **Placeholder**. Click, hold, and drag this placeholder into the timeline.

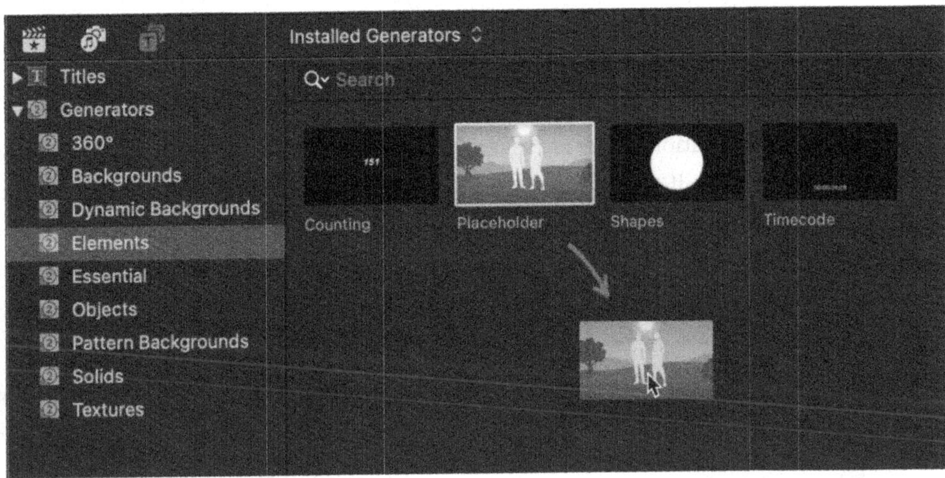

Figure 4.9: Drag a Placeholder generator to the timeline

You can also add a **Placeholder** generator by first positioning your playhead in the desired location, then selecting **Insert Generator / Placeholder** from the **Edit** menu. Plus, you can use the keyboard shortcut *Option + Command + W*.

5. With a **Placeholder** generator in the timeline, let's take a look at its details in the Inspector panel. If it's not already open, in the upper-right corner of the Final Cut Pro interface, click on the **Show or Hide Inspector panel** icon (the icon furthest to the right that looks like parameter sliders). An easier option is to use the keyboard shortcut *Command + 4*.

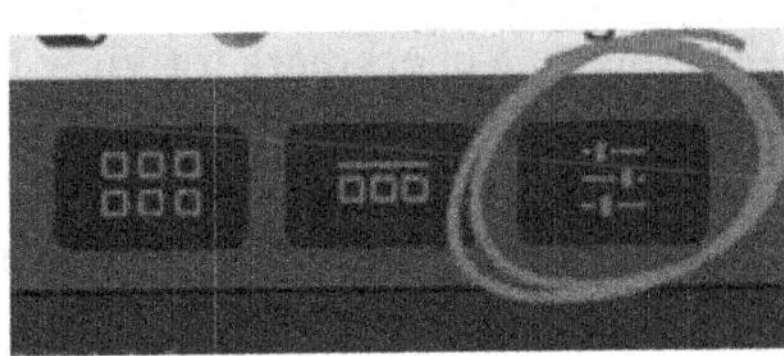

Figure 4.10: Click on the Show or Hide Inspector panel icon

6. Select the **Placeholder** generator in the timeline and click in the Timeline panel above the clip to park the playhead on the clip. By selecting the clip, we view its parameters in the Inspector panel. By parking the playhead on the clip, we see the parameter changes in the Viewer panel.

7. Click on the first icon in the upper-left corner of the Inspector panel to view the main inspector information. There are several settings that can be changed, from **Framing** to **Sky**. Click on the small arrows next to the parameter to see a drop-down menu of settings for each parameter. Experiment with these settings and note the changes in the Viewer panel.

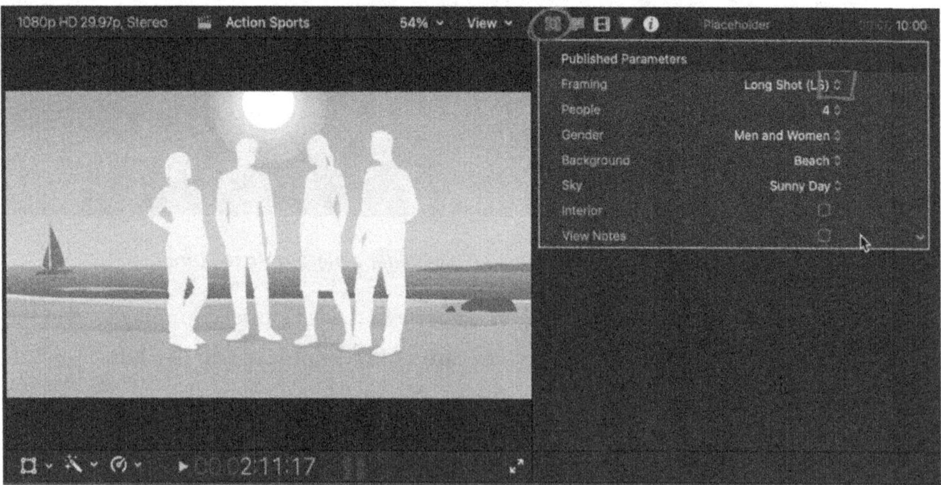

Figure 4.11: Experiment with the Placeholder parameters in the Inspector panel

The default is an exterior shot, but you will see a checkmark near the bottom for creating an **Interior** shot. Also, there's a checkmark for **View Notes**. With this checked, we can add text directly on the screen.

8. Another placeholder that might come in handy is to use the AI image generator called **Image Playground**, which is built into the Mac ecosystem. Click on the **Import** icon, which is the downward arrow in the upper-left corner of the Final Cut Pro interface, and select **Image Playground...** from the drop-down menu, or press *Option + Shift + P* as a keyboard shortcut.

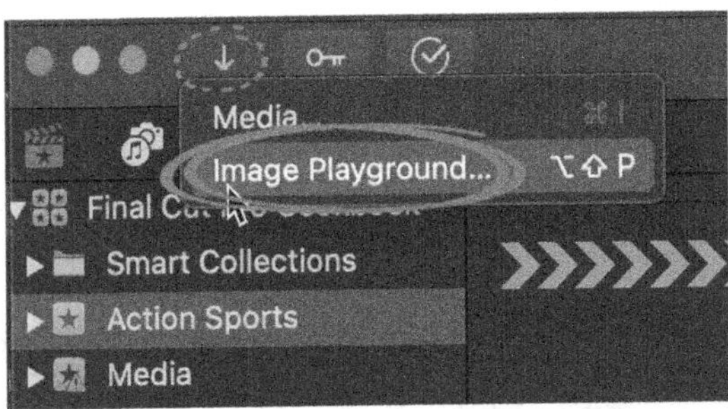

Figure 4.12: Click on the Import icon and selecting Image Playground... from the drop-down menu

9. Use any of the suggestions already provided in the interface or type in your own descriptions. I'm going to type in `city on a hill` and press the *Return* key. Add more prompts as needed. Click on the floating image in the center of the screen, then use the *arrow* icons to scroll through the generated images to find one that you like. Click on the **Done** button.

Figure 4.13: Type in prompts and use the arrow icons to view results

10. The image is added to your project as a **High-Efficiency Image File (HEIF)**. Click on it once to select a four-second portion. Press the *Q* key to add it to the timeline as a connected clip at the position of the skimmer. It is a square image. I would like to cover the screen. So, with the image clip still selected, let's examine it in the Inspector panel. Scroll down to **Spatial Conform** and, for the **Type** parameter, select **Fill** from the drop-down menu.

Figure 4.14: Select Fill for the Type parameter in Spatial Conform

11. Although the image now fills the screen, it needs to be framed differently. Click on the **Transform** icon, which looks like a square with dots in the corners and is located in the lower-left corner of the Viewer panel. Click and drag the image down to reposition it into the horizontal video frame. Click on the **Done** button.

Figure 4.15: Click on the Transform icon, reposition your image, and click on the Done button

12. Wow, you are one of the cool kids!

There's more...

Knowing the industry terminology for shot framing is important. Final Cut Pro gives a short list of framing options along with their abbreviations in the **Framing** drop-down menu in the Inspector panel for the **Placeholder** generator.

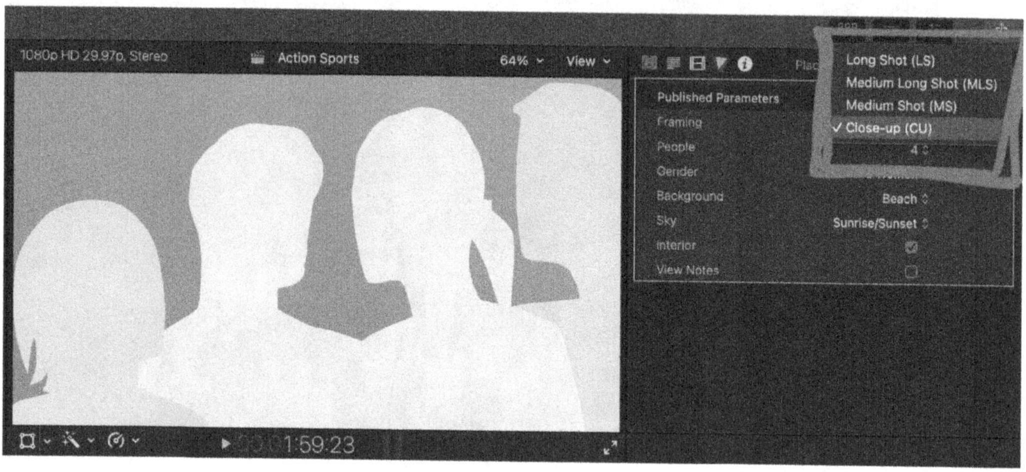

Figure 4.16: Note the four options for the Framing parameter in the Placeholder generator

Here's a quick look at the options:

- **Long Shot (LS)**: Also called a wide shot, a long shot captures the full subject in its surroundings, often used to establish context, location, and the relationship between the subject and the environment. This type of shot is great for showcasing scale, allowing viewers to absorb both the character and the world they inhabit.

- **Medium Long Shot (MLS)**: The medium long shot typically frames the subject from the knees up, balancing both the subject and their environment. It's ideal for scenes where you want to show body language while still maintaining a connection to the background. The slang for this shot is the *cowboy shot*, framed from the guns up.

- **Medium Shot (MS)**: A medium shot frames the subject from the waist up, focusing more on their expressions and gestures while still providing some environmental context. This shot is often used for dialogue scenes or interactions, as it strikes a balance between the subject and background.

- **Close-Up (CU)**: A close-up shot frames the subject's shoulders and face or a specific object, drawing attention to details or emotions. It's perfect for highlighting facial expressions or important narrative elements, making the viewer feel intimately connected to the subject. Note that a close-up shot includes the subject's chest and shoulders. Not to be confused with a shot tightly framed on the face, which may even cut off the top of the head. This is referred to as a **big close-up (BCU)**. Said the film production nerd.

To learn more about industry standard terminology for shot framing, there are plenty of resources on the web. You can also do a quick internet search for `camera shot framing` and look at the resulting images.

Creating J- and L-cuts

Just like a well-timed seasoning can elevate a dish, J and L cuts add flavor to your edits by letting audio and video overlap in creative ways. These edits allow the sound from one clip to lead into – or linger beyond – the visual of another, creating smoother, more natural transitions. Whether you're enhancing emotional impact or improving the rhythm of a scene, J and L edits are essential tools for cooking up seamless, professional storytelling.

Final Cut Pro does not split audio and video into separate tracks. Audio is kept with video in a synchronized clip in a storyline. So, in this recipe, we'll explore how to expand the audio portion of a clip to create J and L cuts.

Getting ready

In preparation for my example, I have two portions of clips lined up in a row in the primary storyline of my Timeline panel. Do not use the entire clip – it works best to have short portions from the middle of clips to demonstrate how to overlap audio.

How to do it...

J and L cuts build anticipation. I can't wait to get started:

1. Select the first of your two adjacent clips in the primary storyline. Then, right-click on that clip and select **Expand Audio** from the **Clip** pop-up menu.

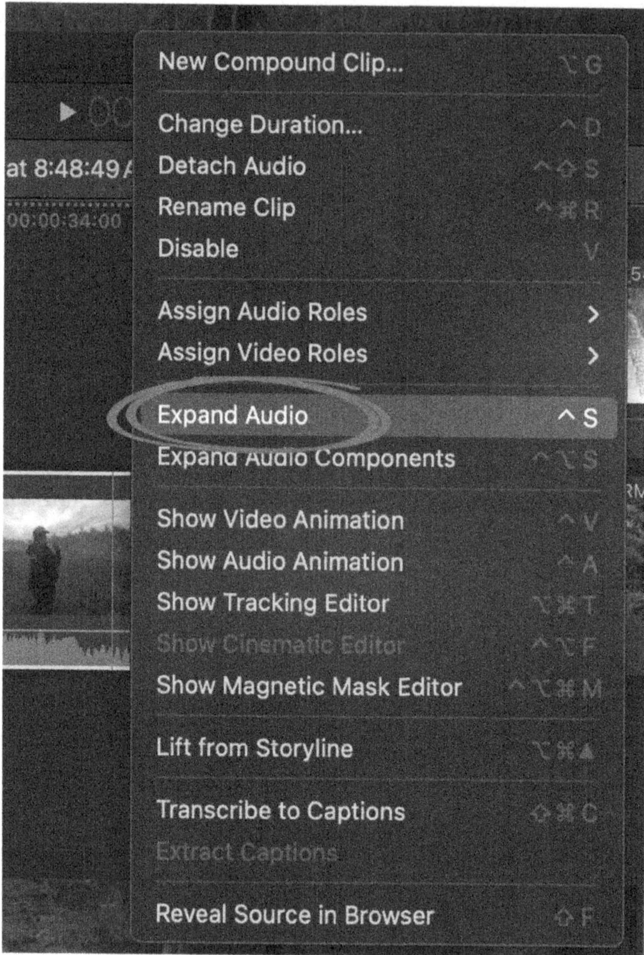

Figure 4.17: Select Expand Audio from the Clip pop-up menu

Once you have selected **Expand Audio**, notice that the clip stays within the primary storyline. The audio and the video appear to be separated, but they're connected and synchronized.

Figure 4.18: A clip with expanded audio

It is possible to choose the **Detach Audio** option from the menu in *Figure 4.17*, but in this situation, we want to keep the audio and video synchronized.

2. Let's do the same command to our second clip, but this time, let's use the keyboard shortcut *Control + S*. We want the sound of the second clip to start during the clip before it. This is a good opportunity to use the **Trim** tool (see the first recipe in this chapter, *Getting to grips with ripple, roll, slip, and slide edits*). The **Trim** tool will roll both clips on either side of an edit point at the same time. Press the keyboard shortcut of *T* to enable the **Trim** tool. Click and drag the edit point of the audio portion of the expanded clips to the left.

Figure 4.19: Click and drag the edit point of the expanded audio left to create a J-cut

This is called a **J-cut** as it mimics a capital *J*. The lower audio portion of the clip slides to the left under the clip next to it in the shape of an uppercase *J*.

3.   An **L-cut** goes the other way where the clip's audio segment slides to the right, under the clip next to it, mimicking a capital *L*. Using the **Trim** tool again, click and drag the edit point of the audio portion of the expanded clips to the right, like the shape of an uppercase *L*.

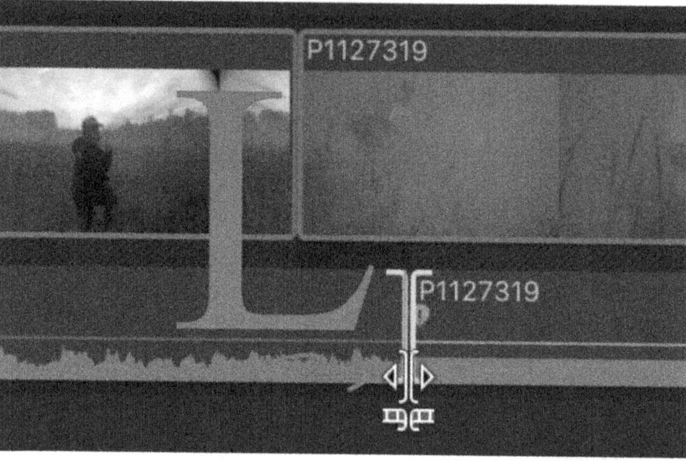

Figure 4.20: Click and drag the edit point of the expanded audio right to create an L-cut

4.   Notice that you can create J-cuts and L-cuts by dragging the edge of the video portion of clips as well, not just the audio segments. These methods will impact your storytelling and emphasize certain audio portions or images as they're linked in your audience's mind with the clips before or after the edit point.

There's more...

In previous recipes in this book, we have mentioned snapping, as well as in this recipe. I like to keep snapping turned on, but sometimes I just want to nudge an edit point without having it snap to another clip or marker. Here is a clever trick. You can keep snapping turned on, but temporarily turn it off by first holding down the *n* key, and then dragging your clip or edit point. While the *n* key is held down, the edit point will not jump to a snapping point. Release the *n* key, and snapping is still turned on. Especially when zoomed into the timeline, this can add some nice precision.

Of course, when you are editing and getting your story just right, you will also want to play your video to review the changes you have made. There is a handy shortcut to play around with the skimmer. Use *Shift + ?* to play two seconds before and two seconds after the position of the skimmer.

Using markers and the Timeline Index

Think of markers and the Timeline Index as the recipe cards and ingredient list of your editing kitchen – they help keep everything organized and easy to find. Markers let you flag key moments, leave notes, or set up to-do reminders directly in your timeline. Paired with the Timeline Index, you can quickly jump to those spots, sort by clip type or role, and streamline your workflow like a master chef prepping for service.

In this recipe, we'll dive into how to effectively use **markers** to create specific notes or instructions, reminders for future adjustments, or tasks to complete later. We'll also explore the **Timeline Index**, which allows you to quickly locate markers, clips, and effects, ensuring a more streamlined and efficient editing workflow.

How to do it...

I've marked this as a good recipe. Let's get to it:

1. Markers are perfect for marking a music or visual cue that you want to snap onto with a clip or edit point. So, place the skimmer above a clip, at the place where you want to mark a cue. Then, press the simple keyboard shortcut *M*. It is that simple. You have now created a standard marker (indicated in blue), and the playhead moves to that position.

2. By double-clicking on an existing marker, we get a dialog box. The title of the marker, by default, is a numbering sequence, but you can change the title to anything you like. Practice adding a title to this marker that references a task to be completed later.

Figure 4.21: The Marker dialog box

3. When you have typed a message, click **Done** or press the keyboard shortcut *Return*.

> The *Return* or *Enter* key is always the keyboard shortcut for whatever is the default button highlighted in a dialog box.

4. Rather than clicking *M* to create a marker and then double-clicking it to open the **Marker** dialog box, there's actually an easier way – just hit *M* twice. This quick shortcut adds a marker and automatically opens the dialog box together.

5. Practice this on a new clip and give your marker a new name. For my example, I am going to type `Add sound f/x here`. Also, let's make this a to-do item. Across the top of the dialog box, you see there are three icons – the first is for a standard marker (which we just created), the second is for a to-do marker, and the third is for a chapter marker, which can be used for DVDs and other media. We want to click the middle icon.

Figure 4.22: Click on the middle icon to create a to-do marker

Notice that now there is an added checkbox labeled **Completed** in the lower-left corner of the dialog box. When a to-do item is created, the marker turns red. If we check the **Completed** checkbox, the marker turns green.

6. Although you can drag a marker to move it, you only move the marker within its current clip. You can't drag a marker to another clip. You can, however, remove a marker. Click, hold, and drag a marker up and off a clip to remove it.

Figure 4.23: Click, hold, and drag a marker up and off a clip

7. You can also change markers in other ways:

    •   You can double-click on a marker to bring up the dialog box, and from there, change the type of marker, rename the marker, or delete it with the **Delete** button.

    •   You can also right-click on a marker to open a pop-up menu. From here, you can cut or copy the marker, change its type, or delete it. Choosing **Modify** simply brings up the marker's dialog box.

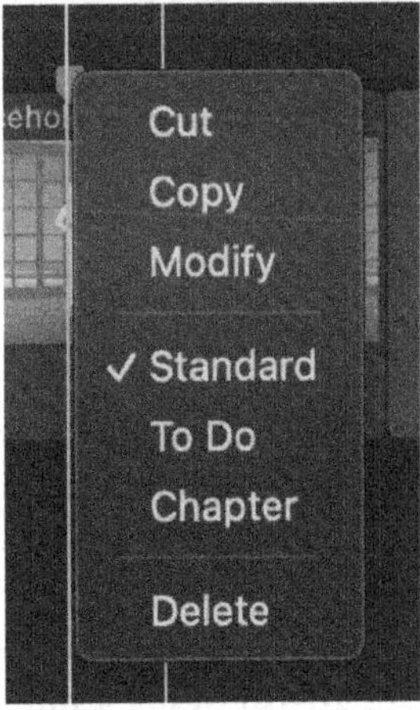

Figure 4.24: Select Modify from the Marker pop-up menu

8. Practice making several markers – a mixture of standard and to-do markers.

9. Once you have multiple markers, a great way to keep track of them is to take advantage of the Timeline **Index** panel. In the upper-left corner of the **Timeline** pane, click on the **Index** button to reveal the Timeline **Index** panel. This is a chronological list of all the items in your project.

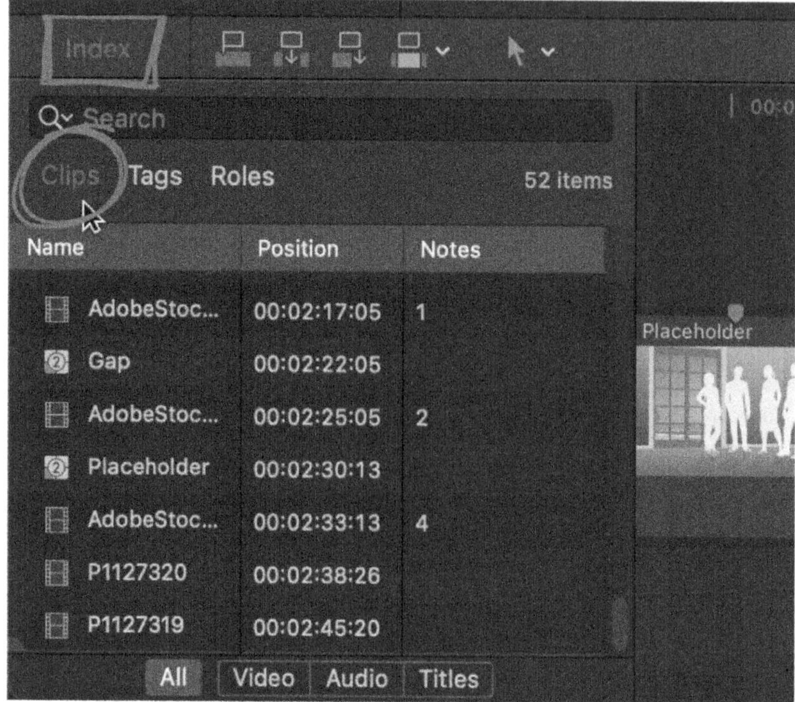

Figure 4.25: Click on the Clips tab in the Timeline Index panel

At the moment, we're looking at the **Clips** tab – this is a list of all the clips in the timeline. Using the buttons at the bottom of the tab, we can list all the clips, or filter the list by just videos, just audio, or just titles.

10. There are also tabs for **Tags** and **Roles**. Practice clicking on clips in the list and notice that the playhead jumps to that clip in the Timeline panel.

11. Now, click on the **Tags** tab. The icons at the bottom of the tab have now changed. We can choose to list all the tags or filter them by **Standard Markers, Keywords, Analysis Keywords, Incomplete To-Do Items, Completed To-Do Items,** and **Chapter Markers**. Click on the **Incomplete To-Do Items** icon (circled in *Figure 4.26*). This gives us the list of markers that are to-do items that have not been completed.

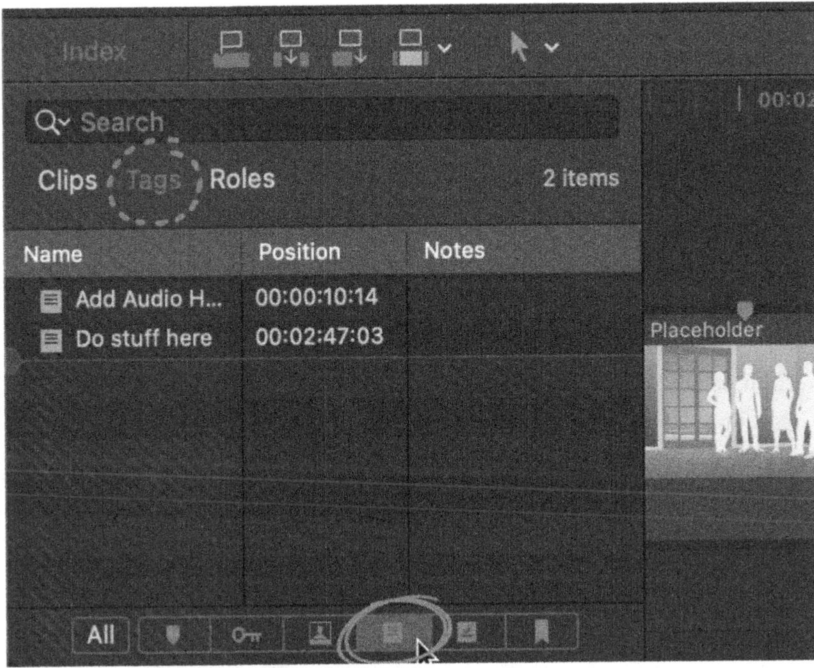

Figure 4.26: Click on the Incomplete To-Do markers icon in the Tags tab of the Timeline Index panel

12. Click on your to-do markers one by one in the Timeline **Index** panel and notice that the playhead jumps to that position in your project in the Timeline panel. This will be very helpful for you and your team when tracking to-do items that are yet to be completed in any size project.

13. Feel free to explore all the ways to view your content in the Timeline **Index** panel!

Creating an audition

Auditions in Final Cut Pro let you taste-test different creative options without committing to just one. Like trying out several sauces before plating the perfect dish, you can swap clips, performances, or effects to see which flavor fits your story best. This non-destructive flexibility makes it easy to compare, collaborate, and fine-tune your edit with confidence.

In this recipe, we'll explore how to create and use auditions to test different shots or effects, giving you and your team the flexibility to compare options and make informed creative decisions.

Getting ready

In a sense, we are picking up where we left off in the recipe from *Chapter 3* titled *Replacing clips*. But instead of replacing clips using a pop-up menu, we will scroll down and use the **Audition** command instead.

How to do it...

Let's start working with auditions (you will be a star of stage and screen in no time!):

1. Identify a clip in the timeline that you want to test with other clips.

2. Then, select a clip in the Event Browser that you want to use to bundle and *audition* with the clip in the timeline.

3. Click and drag the clip from the Event Browser and place it on top of the clip in the timeline; hold it there until the cursor changes to an image of a filmstrip with a + sign.

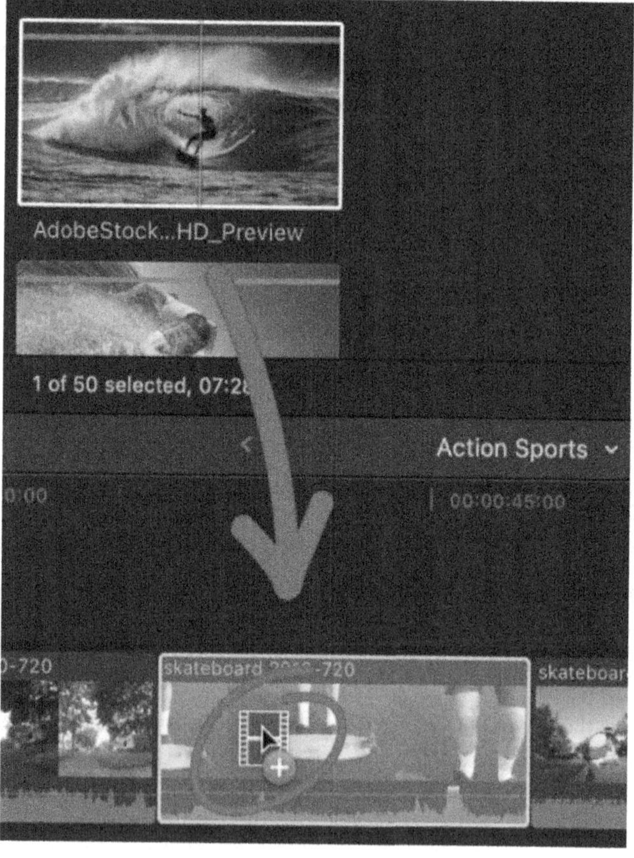

Figure 4.27: Drag a clip from the Event Browser on top of a clip in the timeline

4. When you let go, you will see the pop-up menu we saw if you followed the *Chapter 3* recipe, *Replacing clips*. Back then, we focused on the **Replace** commands, but here we will focus on the ones relating to auditions.

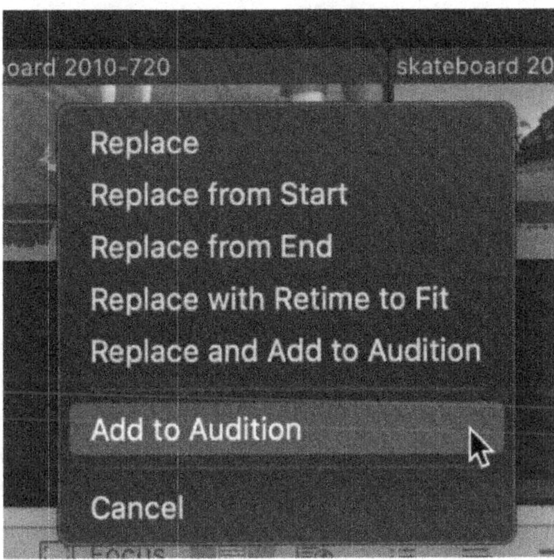

Figure 4.28: Select Add to Audition from the Replace and Audition pop-up menu

You can create an audition and have two things happen:

- The first choice is **Replace and Add to Audition** – this will put the new clip into the storyline, replacing the original clip and, at the same time, bundling the original clip with it into an audition.

- The second option is **Add to Audition** – the new clip you are dragging from the Event Browser panel is bundled with the original clip, which remains visible, and the storyline is unchanged.

An audition or bundle of clips is created in a storyline. Notice that an audition bundle is indicated by the icon in the upper right corner next to the name of the clip, and it looks like a little spotlight shining on a stage for an audition.

5. Now, right-click on the audition clip to see the **Clip** pop-up menu. From there, select
    Audition | Open Audition.

Figure 4.29: Select Audition | Open Audition from the Clip pop-up menu

6. This brings up a small **Audition** pop-up window above the storyline – this is where you
    can click and make selections between the clips that are in that audition bundle. The
    clips keep their original length and so the length is also part of something you're trying
    to decide between your clips. There is no limit to the number of clips that can be in an
    audition, so it comes down to your organizational style.

Figure 4.30: The Audition pop-up window

7. Click on the thumbnail images of the clips in your audition to test the variations they make to your timeline project. Notice that there are dots under the images. These represent the number of clips in your audition and give you an indication of where you are in the list of clips. The star indicates the clip that was originally in the storyline before you opened the **Audition** window.

8. When you select a clip, it becomes highlighted in yellow. Click on the **Done** button or close the window with the red dot button in the upper-left corner of the window, and the selected clip becomes visible in the storyline. You can also double-click on the clip of your choice to close the **Audition** window and make it visible in the storyline.

9. Now, right-click on the audition bundle in the storyline again and select **Audition** from the **Clip** pop-up menu. But this time, instead of clicking **Open Audition**, let's look at the other commands:

   - **Preview**: This will open the **Audition** window and play around the clip that is selected

   - **Duplicate as Audition**: This makes a duplicate of that clip in the audition bundle without opening the **Audition** window

   - **Next Pick**: The next clip in the audition bundle is selected and displayed without opening the **Audition** window

   - **Previous Pick**: The previous clip in the audition bundle is selected and displayed without opening the **Audition** window

   - **Finalize Audition**: This keeps the selection that you have and closes the audition bundle

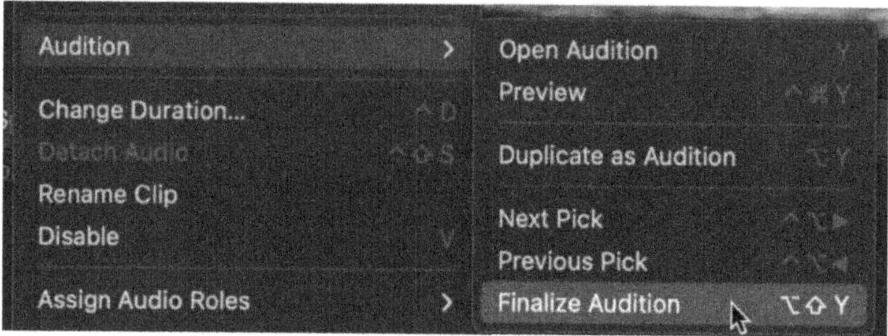

Figure 4.31: Select Audition | Finalize Audition from the Clip pop-up menu

Notice that the **Audition** keyboard shortcuts are a combination of *Y*, *Control*, *Option*, and *arrow* keys, making it easier to switch between the **Audition** commands. You don't have to open the **Audition** window. Instead, select the audition bundle and perform the command with the keyboard shortcut. **Next Pick** and **Previous Pick** shortcuts, in particular, make it quick to try out different clip options.

But wait, there is more. Often, you know the clip you want, but you have not decided on the effect or color change on that clip. Auditions are perfect for this. Without disrupting the timeline or creating duplicate projects, you can test out different effects or other changes in a clip. Let's see how to do this.

10. In the timeline, identify and clip to test an effect audition. Click on it once to select it, and then click in the Timeline panel above the clip to park the playhead on the clip as well.

11. Then, right-click on the clip, and from the **Clip** pop-up menu, select **Reveal in Browser**. This will select the same clip in the Event Browser.

12. Now, click, hold, and drag the selection from the Event Browser on top of the same clip on the timeline. Release the mouse button.

13. When the **Replace and Audition** pop-up menu appears, select **Add to Audition**.

14. Then, with the audition bundle still selected in the timeline, press the keyboard shortcut *Y* to open the **Audition** window. Click on the **Duplicate** button a few times to create a few clips for testing.

15. Click through the duplicate clips you have created and, from the Effects Browser panel, drag an effect across and place it directly on a clip in the **Audition** window.

Figure 4.32: Drag an effect directly into the Audition window to apply it to a clip

This works for color correcting or stylizing the clip that is selected in the **Audition** window as well. Now, you can more easily make decisions between clips when they are side by side.

Creating compound clips

Compound clips are like prepping your ingredients into a single bowl before cooking – they let you group multiple elements together and treat them as one. This makes complex timelines more manageable, allowing you to apply effects, transitions, or edits to an entire section with a single move. It's a great way to streamline your workflow, stay organized, and keep your project tidy and efficient.

In this recipe, we'll explore how to create and use compound clips to manage your timeline more efficiently.

How to do it...

To work with compound clips, follow these steps:

1. Start by creating several clips, connected video clips, connected audio clips, and titles in your Timeline panel. Then, click, hold, and drag your mouse over them to select them all at once. They should all be highlighted in yellow.

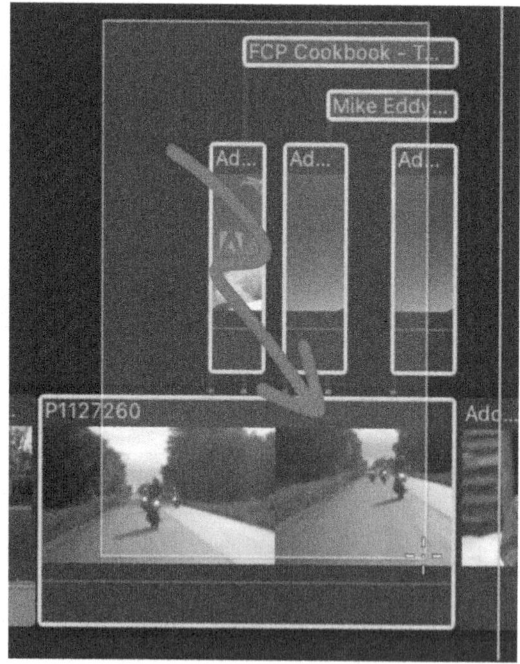

Figure 4.33: Click and drag across multiple clips to select them in the timeline

2. Right-click on any of the clips to see the **Clip** pop-up menu, where you should select **New Compound Clip**. Alternatively, use the keyboard shortcut *Option + G*.

3. In the pop-up window, give your compound clip a name to help with organization, and use the **In Event** drop-down menu to select the event you want it to land into. Then click **OK**.

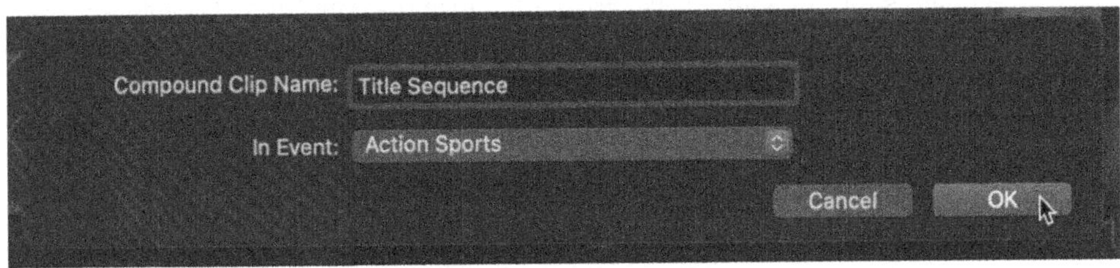

Figure 4.34: After naming your compound clip, click on the OK button

The compound clip will appear in the timeline as one clip. A compound clip is indicated by a unique icon in the upper-left corner that looks like several clips connected together.

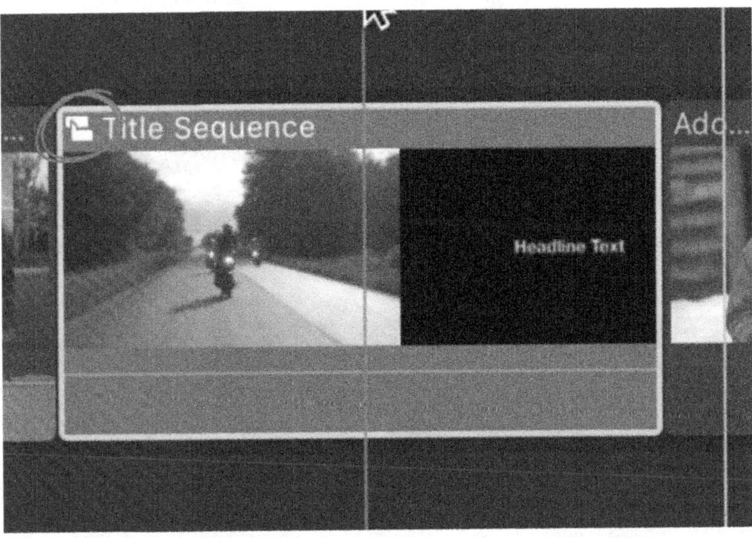

Figure 4.35: The icon representing a compound clip in the timeline

4. Your compound clips are also created in the Event Browser panel inside the event you specified. Scroll through your clips in your event displayed in the Event Browser panel. Or, select the compound clip in the timeline, right-click on it to bring up the **Clip** pop-up menu, and select **Reveal in Browser** at the bottom of the menu. Alternatively, use the keyboard shortcut *Shift + F*. Once found, notice that the clip in the Event Browser panel has the same icon in the upper-left corner.

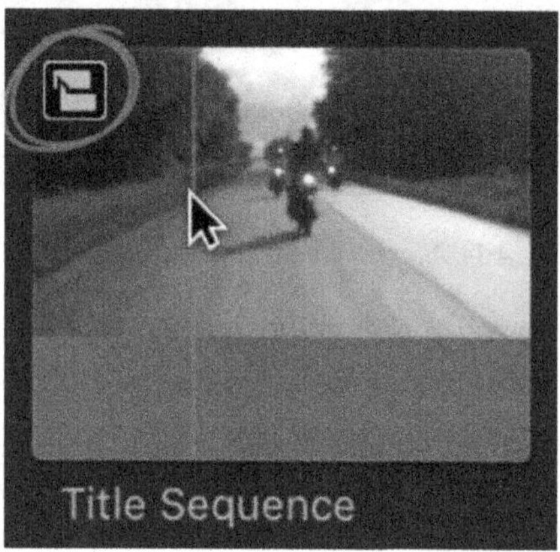

Figure 4.36: The icon representing a compound clip in the Event Browser

5. Let's say you want to make changes to the clips in a compound clip. Go back to the Timeline and double-click on your compound clip. It will open in a new Timeline and will fill the Timeline panel.

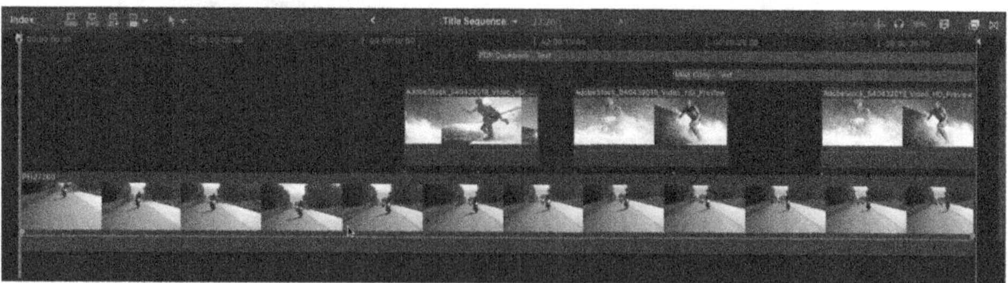

Figure 4.37: A compound clip opens in its own Timeline panel

6. At this point, you can edit as you normally would, and all changes will be updated in the compound clip in the larger timeline project.

7. You can go back to the larger timeline project by using the **Go back in Timeline history** icon (the arrow on the left side of the timeline project name shown in *Figure 4.38*).

Figure 4.38: Click on the Go back in Timeline history arrow icon

8. Likewise, to the right of the project name is the **Go forward in Timeline history** icon. With these, you can easily navigate through your compound clips and active timeline projects.

Color coding your clips

Color coding clips is like using different colored cutting boards in a kitchen – it helps keep everything organized and easy to identify at a glance. By assigning colors to different types of media or stages of your edit, you can visually separate interviews, B-roll, music, graphics, or anything else on your timeline. This simple yet powerful technique helps streamline your workflow, reduce errors, and make your timeline easier to navigate, especially in complex projects.

In this recipe, we'll explore how to assign and manage these roles, allowing you to categorize and visually distinguish different types of clips and elements within your timeline. Color me excited!

How to do it...

To color-code your clips, follow these steps:

1. We will start by changing the settings for the video and audio roles for the current library. Click on the **Modify** menu and select **Edit Roles…**. This brings up a dialog box listing current roles for video and audio media. Click on the **+ Video Role** button to add a video role.

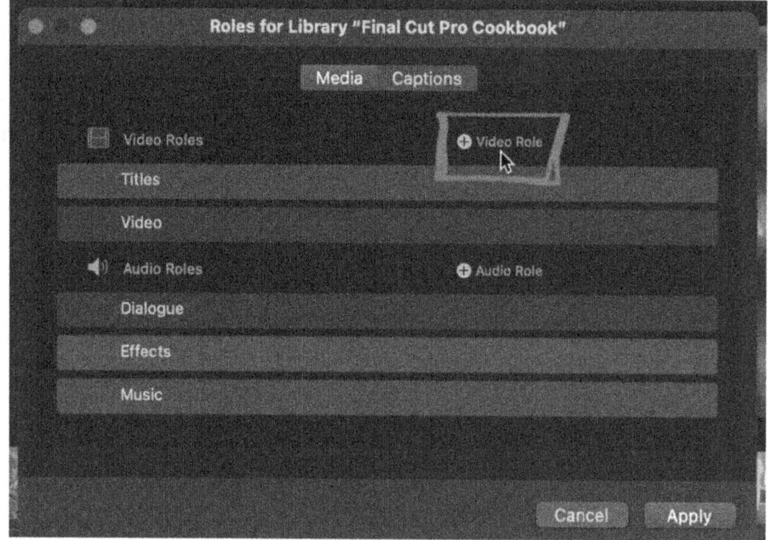

Figure 4.39: Click on the + Video Role button to add a video role in the library edit window

2. By clicking **+ Video Role**, a new line is added to the **Video Roles** area. The name of the video role is highlighted and ready to type over. For this example project, I want to distinguish the difference between winter and summer clips. So, I'm going to add a role called Winter.

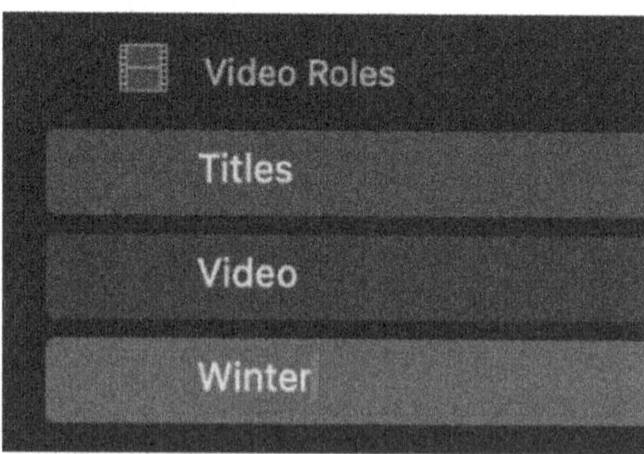

Figure 4.40: Type in a name for the new video role

3.   Next, click on the **Change role color** icon that looks like a color gradient circle.

Figure 4.41: Click on the Change role color icon

4.   This brings up a color palette of possible color choices. Let's make this sort of teal green.

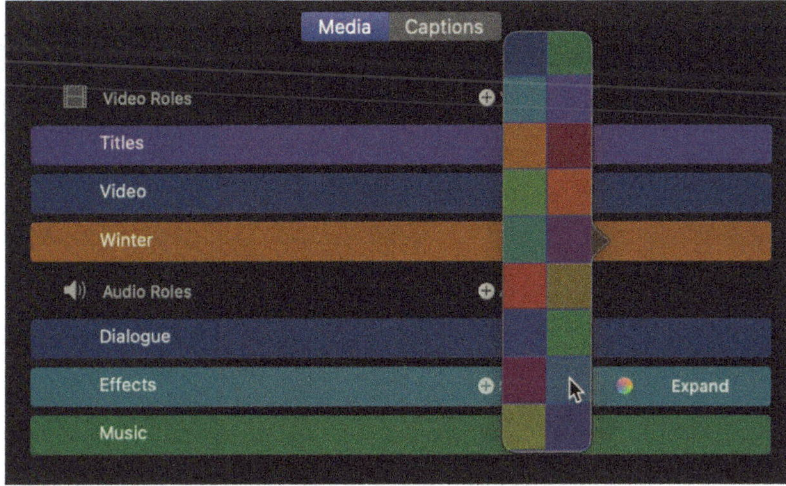

Figure 4.42: Choose from the color palette

5.   Let's add another video role with the **+ Video Role** button near the top right of the window. I will call this Summer. I'm going to leave it as the default orange, but you can explore the other colors available in the palette.

6.   Click on the **Apply** button at the bottom of the window. This applies the new role changes to this library. In my timeline, I've got multiple clips that alternate winter and summer action sports footage.

7.   Let's select some clips in the timeline and change their roles. You probably know that, on a Mac, you can select a file, hold the *Shift* key, and click at the end of a list to select the whole list. But did you know you can select discontinuous files? That is a big word to say they are not next to each other. So, click on a clip in your timeline, hold down the *Command* key, and click the specific clips you want – even if they are not next to each other in the timeline.

8. Right-click on any of the clips selected, and in the **Clip** popup menu, select **Assign Video Roles**, then the role you want – **Winter**, in my case.

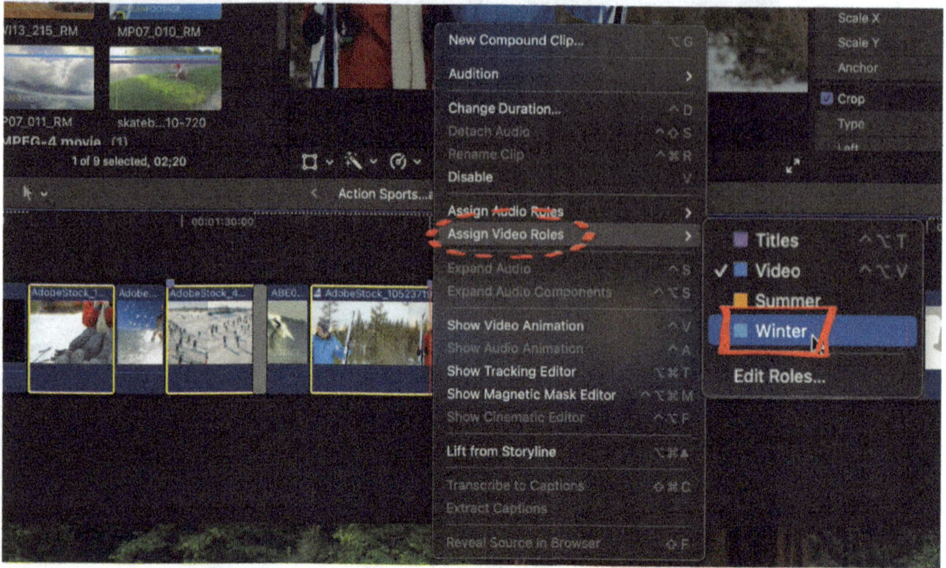

Figure 4.43: Select Assign Video Roles | Winter from the Clip pop-up menu

Those clips will now be color-coded with teal green.

9. Now, hold the *Command* key and click on some different clips. Right-click on any one selected clip, and from the **Clip** pop-up menu, select **Assign Video Roles**, then a different role. I will choose **Summer** this time. Observe that those clips have an orange color.

You can see both the **Winter** and **Summer** color coding here:

Figure 4.44: The color-coded clips in the timeline

So, you can organize clips with keywords, ratings, and Smart Collections in the Event Browser panel, and you can organize clips by color in the Timeline panel.

Using multicam editing

In live recording events, multiple cameras are fed into one video console, and the technician switches the video to one signal out. In **multicam editing**, multiple streams of the same action are recorded and saved ahead and time. Then, Final Cut Pro syncs the video streams together and allows an editor to switch the streams to one video out. Final Cut Pro supports mixed formats, mixed frame rates, and up to 64 camera angles.

The advantages of this approach include enhanced creative flexibility with the feeling of a live event, streamlined editing of complex shoots, and the ability to produce polished, multi-angle videos that captivate and engage your audience.

In this recipe, we'll delve into how to set up and use multicam editing, enabling you to efficiently manage and edit scenes shot from different angles or cameras.

Getting ready

In my example, I have four camera angles and an audio recording of two musicians. If you don't have access to professional recording equipment, it is okay to just experiment with several iPhones recording the same dialogue or action.

How to do it...

Capturing the action from multiple angles and then syncing it together can save a lot of time. So, we'd better get started:

1. Creating a multicam clip is a bit similar to creating a compound clip, in that you are going to select multiple clips at the same time. Import the multiple video files that you want to use in your multicam editing. In the Event Browser panel, select all the clips that you want to bundle together into a multicam clip.

2. Right-click on any of your selected clips and, from the event clip pop-up menu, select **New Multicam Clip….** A dialog box appears giving us the chance to edit the name of our multicam clip and to select what event it should go into.

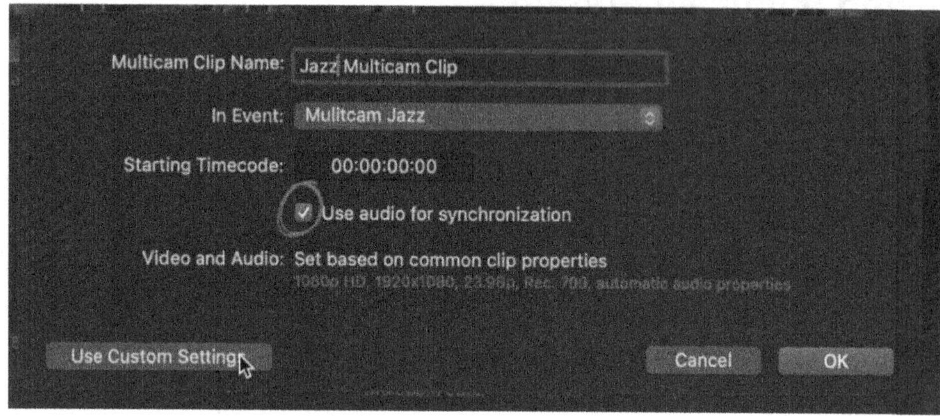

Figure 4.45: Enable the checkbox to use audio for synchronization in the multicam creation dialog box

3. Because Final Cut Pro uses audio waveforms to synchronize clips, it is important to record audio with all your cameras, even if they are not going to be the primary audio source. Make sure **Use audio for synchronization** is checked, and then click **OK**.

4. Final Cut Pro does a great job of analyzing and syncing video files with their waveforms, but sometimes there can be issues if the audio is unavailable or distorted. Let's take a slight detour and talk about other methods of synchronization. One of the easiest ways to do this is to go through the clips first and create a marker that you can use to visually sync the clips together. Pick a strong visual cue, like when someone's arm is at its highest point in a large gesture.

If this is the case, click on the **Use Custom Settings** button. We see an expanded dialog box. For **Angle Synchronization**, choose **First Marker on the Angle**. This will use a marker for synchronization.

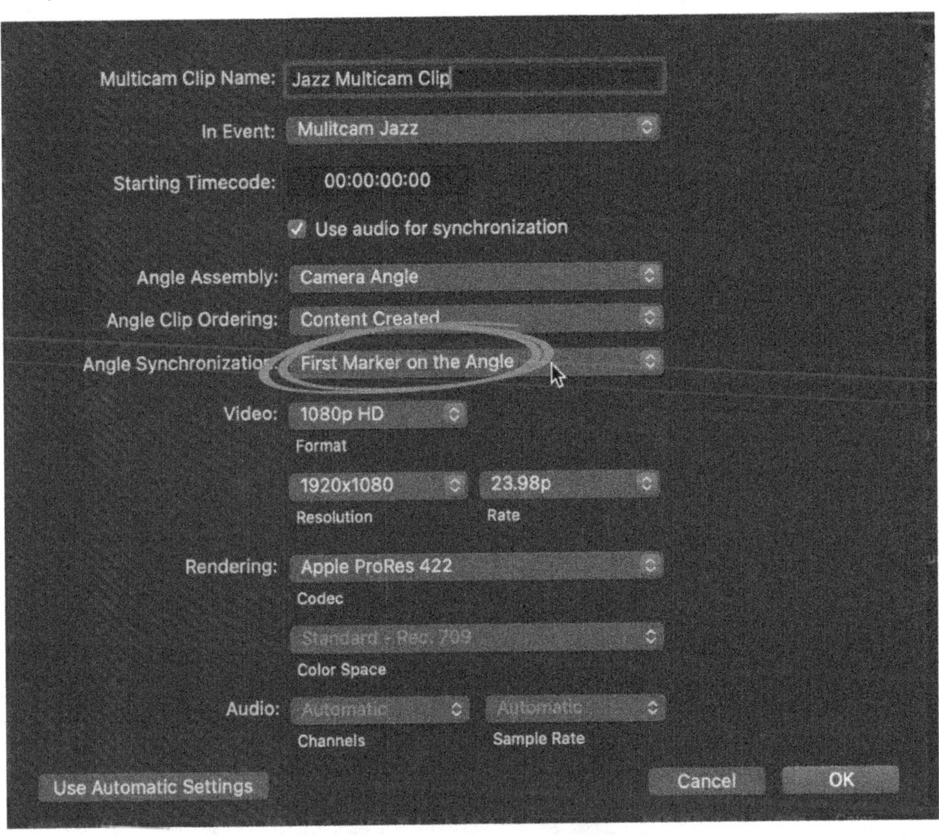

Figure 4.46: Select First Marker on the Angle for the Angle Synchronization parameter in the multicam custom dialog box

 If you're using just one marker, it does not have to be near the beginning of the footage. As long as your visual cue is the first marker on each clip, it will work.

For **Angle Assembly**, select **Camera Angle**, and for **Angle Clip Ordering**, select **Content Created**. Ultimately, how the angles are assembled and in what order is not as important as getting **Angle Synchronization** correct.

In my example, I know the audio recording is clean. So for this case, I don't need to use a marker for synchronization. If I had clicked on **First Marker on the Angle** for the **Angle Synchronization** setting, I could reverse out of it and go back to the original dialog box by clicking on the **Use Automatic Settings** button. And now, from the first dialog box, click **OK**.

You may see a message showing the progress of analyzing the footage and synchronizing the clips based on the audio waveforms. Once done, a new clip is created in the Event Browser panel, and you will notice that an icon in the upper-left corner with four squares represents a multicam clip bundled together.

Figure 4.47: The icon that represents a multicam clip in the Event Browser

5. Drag the multicam clip to a new Timeline panel and onto the primary storyline.

6. In the upper-right corner of the Viewer panel, click on the arrow next to **View** to open the **View** menu, then select **Angles** (or use the keyboard shortcut *Shift + Command + 7*).

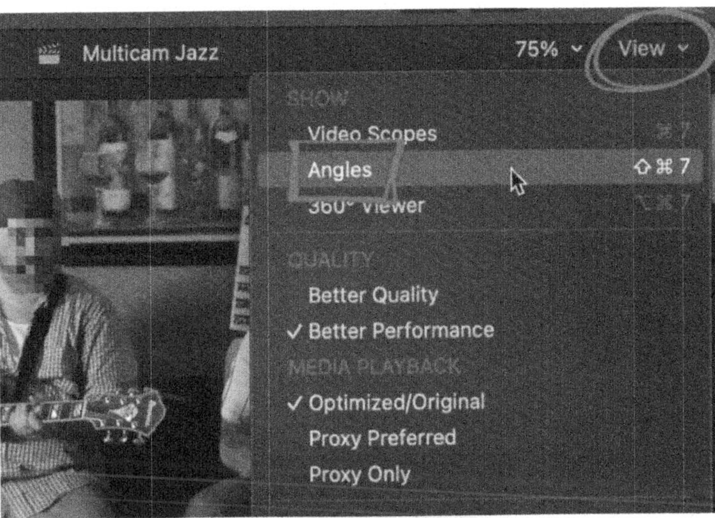

Figure 4.48: Select Angles from the View menu in the Viewer panel

7.   Another panel will open in the Viewer panel that has thumbnails of the clips from the multicam bundle now in the primary storyline. Click on the **Settings** menu in the upper-right corner of the Multicam Viewer panel. Depending on the number of clips you have, set the panel to display 2, 4, 9, or 16 angles. In my example, I have five clips – four clips are video and one is an audio file – so under **Display**, I will choose the **9 Angles** option to include all the clips.

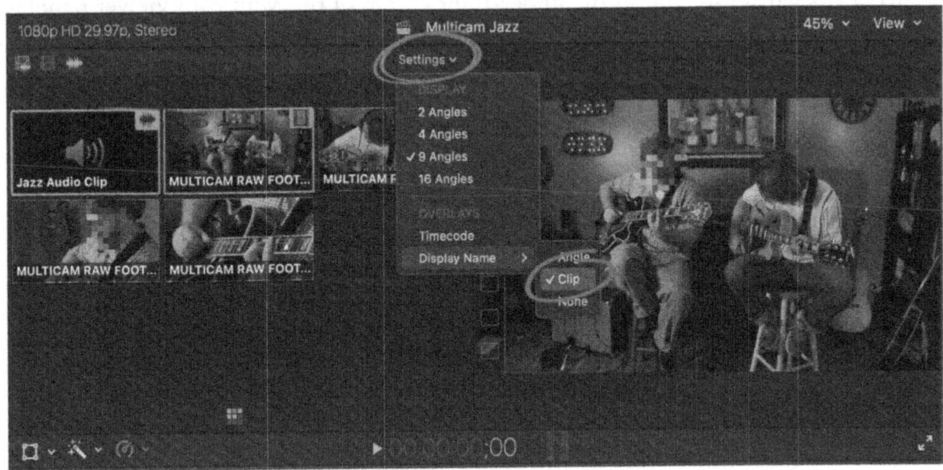

Figure 4.49: Select Display Name | Clip from the Settings menu in the Multicam Viewer panel

Still in the **Settings** dropdown, under **Overlay**, we can choose what text to display on the clips. We could choose to display the timecode, but I am not tracking this, so let's not include it. Instead, we will look at **Display Name** – I don't have any info in the **Angle** field for the clips, and I don't want to choose **None**, so I will choose **Clip**.

8. Now, skim through the primary storyline and notice that the clips in the Multicam Viewer panel play synchronously. They represent each camera recording the event. We want to switch back and forth between these clips.

9. Hover the mouse over the clips in the Multicam Viewer panel. Notice that the cursor changes to a pair of scissors. This indicates that when you click on that angle thumbnail, the multicam project stream cuts to that angle.

Figure 4.50: Note that the scissors cursor indicates cutting to that video angle

10. Let's get set to edit. In the upper-right corner of the Multicam Viewer panel are three icons – a filmstrip with an audio waveform, just a filmstrip, and just an audio waveform. These icons indicate what type of media will get changed when you cut between views.

Figure 4.51: The icons indicating which media will change at an angle cut

As is the case when creating most music videos, we have high-quality audio files that should always be used and not cut away from. So, that means we are going to lock the audio file and only switch the video signal. Because we synchronized our clips using their audio in an earlier step, we are confident that the video action of the clips will line up and be synchronized to the master audio file.

11. Place the playhead at the very beginning of the primary storyline in the Timeline panel. Click on the first button, which looks like a filmstrip with an audio waveform. The icon will turn yellow. This is the button to enable video and audio switching. Then, click on the master audio file so that it is enabled and also highlighted in yellow.

12. Next, click on the second icon, which looks like a filmstrip, to enable video-only switching. The icon will turn blue. Then, click on any of the other video clips. That camera angle becomes highlighted in blue, and the audio file remains highlighted in green. The camera angle you select becomes visible in the Timeline and Viewer panels. Essentially, we selected the master audio recording first, and then by choosing to only switch the video image, we locked the audio file in place.

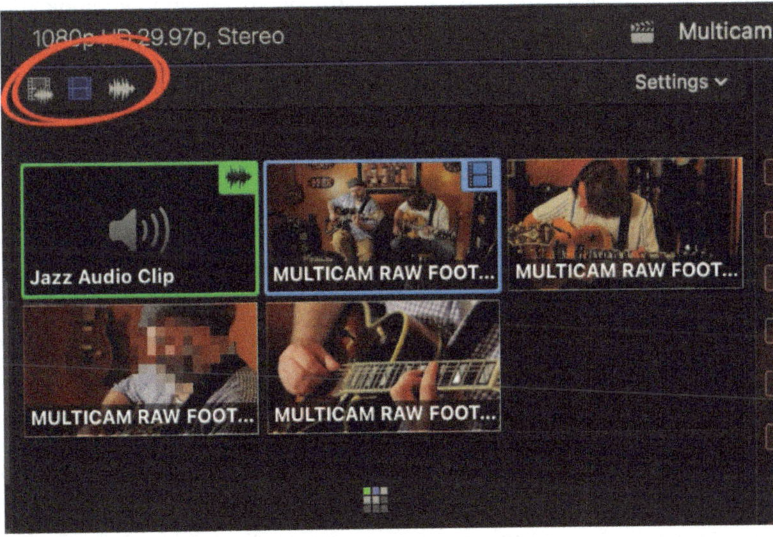

Figure 4.52: The blue filmstrip icon indicates that only video will be switched during cuts in the Multicam Viewer panel

13. In the primary storyline of my example, I see that they have recorded preparing to start the music. Even in the multicam clip with all the clips connected, we can click and drag the beginning of the primary storyline to the right and change the *in* point of the clip to when the music is starting.

14. Now comes the fun part. Place the playhead at the beginning of the primary storyline. Hover the mouse over the Multicam Viewer panel. Then, click on the **Play** icon – next to the time code counter, at the bottom edge of the Viewer panel – or use the *spacebar* shortcut to start playing the timeline.

15. As the footage plays, click on the various video clips to switch to that camera angle. The angles are switched in real time. The clips in the Multicam Viewer panel become highlighted in blue and are visible in the Viewer panel. In the timeline, the video image in the primary storyline changes too. If you like keyboard shortcuts, instead of clicking on the angles, you can simply press the number associated with that angle. In my example, I have 5 angles, and the audio track is locked in as angle 1. So, I would press *2, 3, 4,* or *5* to switch video angles. Note that the switch only works with single digits, so just *1* to *9*.

16. Now, press the *spacebar* again to pause the playback, and let's look at the primary storyline. Skim through the timeline and see how the Viewer panel and the Multicam Viewer panel change with the cuts you made between camera angles. Notice how the cuts are dotted-line edit points, indicating that no frames are missing when you've cut your view between the different angles.

17. Practice going through the project and switching between angles to the feel of the music. Watch the clips and try to anticipate when the camera is focusing on one of the performers.

18. Once you have completed a run-through of switching *live*, that is, clicking to select angles as the project is playing in real time, let's explore how to edit, or change, our angle cuts in the primary storyline. With the playback stopped, move the mouse to the timeline and over an edit point. The cursor may look familiar from the earlier recipe, *Getting to grips with ripple, roll, slip, and slide edits.* Click and drag on the edit point to change the adjoining clips as a rolling edit. That is, no frames will be dropped, and the length of the project will not change. This is a great way to make minor adjustments to your edits and produce a polished, multi-angle video.

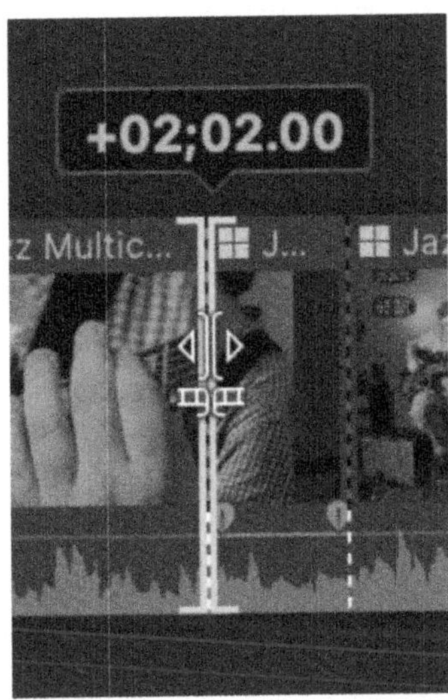

Figure 4.53: The cursor on edit points indicates a rolling edit within a multicam clip

19. If you want to completely change a segment to a different angle, turn on snapping and move the playhead to the beginning edit point of the clip you wish to change. Then, simply click on a different angle in the Multicam Viewer panel to change that sequence.

Multicam editing has the benefit of letting you cut between angles naturally to the flow of the action, but there is also the added benefit that you can go into the timeline and adjust your edit points to be just right.

5

Exploring Color Correction and Stylizing

Step into the vibrant palette of video enhancement, where color correction and stylizing are the spices that flavor your visual feast. We will explore how to breathe life into your footage and evoke emotion through color, from enhancing realism to unleashing creative flair.

Color correction and color grading are both essential parts of the post-production process but serve different purposes. Color correction involves adjusting footage to achieve accurate and natural-looking colors. It focuses on fixing issues such as exposure, white balance, contrast, and saturation to ensure the footage appears realistic and consistent across all shots. Color grading, on the other hand, is the creative process of enhancing or altering the color of your footage to create a specific mood, tone, or style. It goes beyond correction to establish a cinematic or artistic look, shaping the overall aesthetic of your video.

In this chapter, you will gain expertise in color correction and grading techniques within Final Cut Pro. You will tackle tasks such as white balancing and color matching. You will utilize various color tools such as Color Board, wheels, and curves, and create custom color looks. You will also learn about advanced methods, including using shape and color masks, adjusting exposure with the luma waveform monitor, applying secondary color corrections, and applying LUTs to RAW files, empowering you to enhance the visual appeal and narrative impact of your videos through precise and creative color manipulation.

In this chapter, you will complete the following recipes:

- Utilizing white balance
- Using the Match Color feature
- Using Color Board, Wheels, and Curves
- Using Shape Masks and Color Masks
- Fixing exposure with the luma waveform monitor
- Adding secondary color corrections
- Applying LUTs to raw files

Utilizing white balance

You wouldn't serve blue coffee or orange milk – white balance keeps your colors appetizing. By using the White Balance command, you can quickly adjust the temperature and tint to neutralize color casts, making the whites in your video appear true to life. The advantage of properly white-balancing clips is that it creates a consistent and professional look, ensuring that skin tones, landscapes, and objects appear natural and visually appealing across your entire project.

In this recipe, we will explore how to use the White Balance command to quickly repair clips in which the camera inadvertently set the wrong color tint.

Getting ready

For this recipe, we will use clips that were shot incorrectly. You may be able to find some on the web, or try using your camera to deliberately record some footage with the wrong white balance.

We will be using information, icons, and menus in the Inspector panel. Be sure this is open. The quick keyboard shortcut to open the Inspector panel is *Command + 4*. Note that the Inspector panel shows the details of whatever is selected. In addition, the Viewer panel shows the image of wherever the playhead is parked.

How to do it...

In my example, I have a clip that was shot indoors, where the milk looks a little orange, giving me the impression that the camera was still set for white balance outdoors. There are three methods that we can follow to color-correct this and find the right white balance:

1. Here's the first way. First, we need to see the clip to be corrected in both the Viewer panel and the Inspector panel – a shortcut to see both is to *Option + click* on the clip you are working on. Notice that this selects the clip and parks the playhead on the clip at the same time.

Figure 5.1: Select a clip in the Timeline panel

2. With the clip still selected, go to the **Modify** menu and select **Balance Color**, or use the keyboard shortcut *Option + Command + B*. That will balance the color. Boom!

It will make an indoor shot look less orange and more blue. Conversely, an outdoor shot balanced wrong will have a blue tint, and this command will make it look less blue and more natural. The goal is to make items in the shot that are white look more naturally white.

3. The second method to initiate this command is with the **Enhance** icon. The **Enhance** icon looks like a magic wand and is located in the lower-left corner of the Viewer panel. With the clip selected in the timeline, click on the **Enhance** icon to bring up a drop-down menu, and from there, select **Balance Color**.

Figure 5.2: Select Balance Color in the Enhance menu

4. So far, we have relied on Final Cut Pro to balance the color with an automatic setting. However, we can also set the white balance manually. This is the third method, which may give us a better result. Again, with the color-balanced clip selected, look at the Inspector panel. If it is not already selected and highlighted in blue, click on the **Show the Video Inspector** icon, which looks like a film strip, in the upper-left corner of the Inspector panel.

5. Then, near the top of the panel, in the **Effects** area, you will see the **Balance Color** effect. Next to **Method**, click on **Automatic**, and from the drop-down menu, select **White Balance** instead.

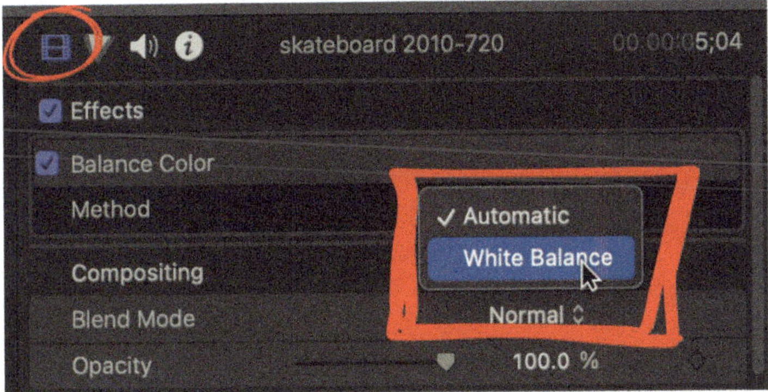

Figure 5.3: Select White Balance in the Balance Color method

6. By changing the balance color method to **White Balance**, the cursor changes to an eye-dropper. Use the eyedropper to click on an area in the image, in the Viewer panel, that should be white. The resulting color balance is much more true to life.

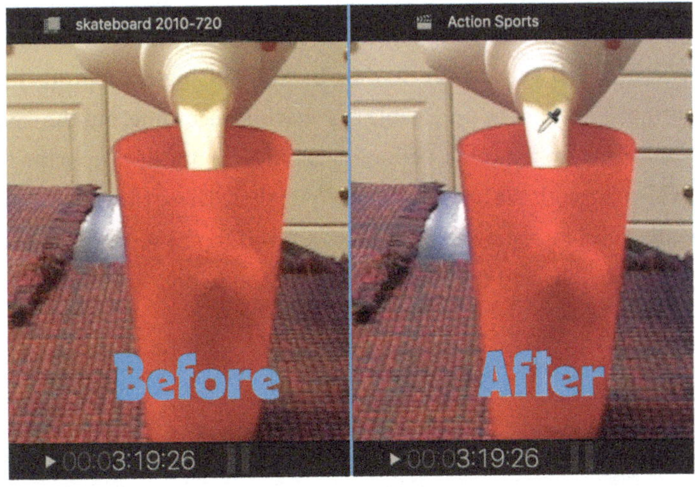

Figure 5.4: Use the eyedropper to select white in your image

How it works...

The color of light is measured on a scale called Kelvin (K). Light that is lower on the Kelvin scale is reddish, whereas light that is higher on the Kelvin scale is bluer. Daylight is measured at 5600K and is more blue than reddish indoor lights, which measure closer to 3000K.

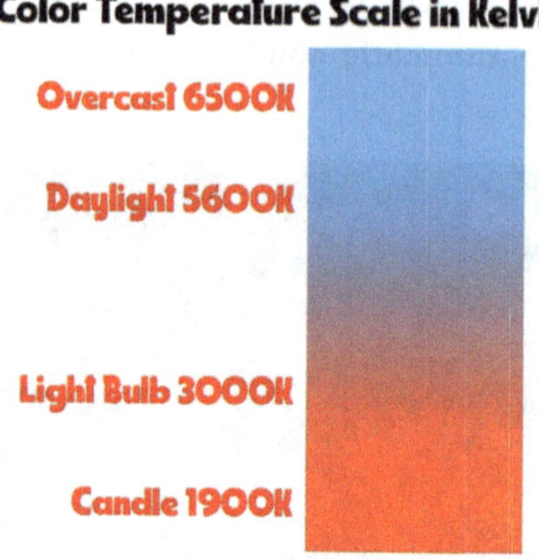

Figure 5.5: Color temperature scale in Kelvin

Our eyes and brain are amazingly created to see white objects as true white with rapid precision. But cameras have a narrower band of accuracy and need to have *white* identified to the censor. That's why using the white balance settings is important – inaccurate camera footage can be adjusted to the proper color.

There's more...

Although modern cameras have an auto white balance setting, most professionals do not leave it on while shooting. It may not be noticeable to you while recording, but the camera will constantly make fine adjustments to the color. Perhaps a cloud temporarily covers the sun or someone in a red sweater walks through the background of your shot. These things can affect the color. When you start to edit and place shots from different times in the recording next to each other, the difference will be obvious and cause extra work for you in post-production.

If you use a white card to manually set the camera's white balance, be sure to place it under the lights to be used. Or, sometimes I will set the camera to auto white balance and give the camera time to think for a moment and gauge the environment. Then I will use the K number that it settled on to set the color balance manually. When shooting with multiple cameras, make sure they are all using the same color balance number.

Also, note that in Final Cut Pro, when **Balance Color** has been set manually with the White Balance method, the effect can be copied and pasted to other clips. However, the effect cannot be copied when the **Balance Color** method has been set automatically. We will get more into copying and pasting attributes later in this chapter, in a recipe called *Using Color Board, Wheels, and Curves.*

Using the Match Color feature

The **Match Color** feature allows you to automatically match the color of one clip to another, ensuring consistency across your footage. This way, you can quickly achieve a uniform look, even if your clips were shot under different lighting conditions. This simplifies the color-grading process, saving time while maintaining visual continuity and enhancing the overall cohesiveness of your video.

In this recipe, you will select a reference clip and apply its color characteristics to a target clip.

Getting ready

For my example, I've got two clips in my timeline, and I want the plain lighting of one to match the sunset lighting of the other. Perhaps you can find two similar clips.

How to do it...

Matching the color of one clip to another used to be a very time-consuming manual process. Now it's only a few clicks away. So, let's hurry up and get to it:

1. *Option + click* on the clip that you want to change – this will both select it and park the playhead above it to see the changes in the Viewer panel.

2. Click on the **Enhance** icon, which looks like a magic wand and is located in the lower-left corner of the Viewer panel, and select **Match Color...** (or use the keyboard shortcut *Option + Command + M*).

Figure 5.6: Select Match Color… from the Enhance menu

3. The Viewer panel will change to a two-up display. In addition, the cursor changes to a camera icon when you skim over other clips. With the camera cursor, click once on the clip that you want to match. Note that in the Viewer panel, there are two images: on the left is the source clip with the desired color, and on the right is a preview of the result on the target clip. You can sample other clips at this point.

4. When you are satisfied with the change to your target clip, click on the **Apply Match** button in the Viewer panel. Now our clip has been changed to match that source color.

Figure 5.7: Select a matching clip and click on the Apply Match button

5. If at some point you want to change the **Match Color** effect, you can do this in the Inspector panel. With the changed clip selected, look in the Inspector panel at the **Match Color** effect in the **Effects** area. Next to **Source**, there is a **Choose...** button. Click on this to rematch your clip to a different source clip for a new color profile.

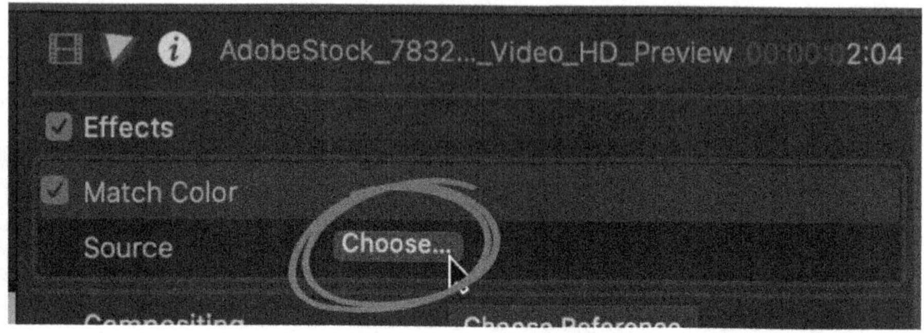

Figure 5.8: Click on the Choose... button to re-match the color of the clip

Using Color Board, Wheels, and Curves

Color Board, color wheels, and curves are powerful tools, giving you complete control over your footage's color:

*   **Color Board** allows you to adjust exposure, saturation, and color balance across shadows, midtones, and highlights
*   **Color Wheels** provide a more intuitive interface
*   **Curves** offer even more precision, letting you fine-tune specific color ranges or create custom tonal adjustments, enabling you to create a professional, polished look that aligns with your creative vision

In this recipe, we will explore using all three to correct and stylize the color of clips.

Getting ready

You will need several clips, including ones in which the color is off a bit – maybe they have a blue or red tint, or perhaps they are just bland.

How to do it...

As gourmet cooks know, there are several ways to fine-tune a dish. Let's explore several ways to fine-tune the color of your clips:

1. *Option + click* once on the clip that you want to change to both select it and park the playhead above it to see the changes in the Viewer panel. In the upper-left corner of the Inspector panel, click on the **Color Inspector** icon – it looks like a triangle, and when you click on it, you will see that it changes to a color gradient.

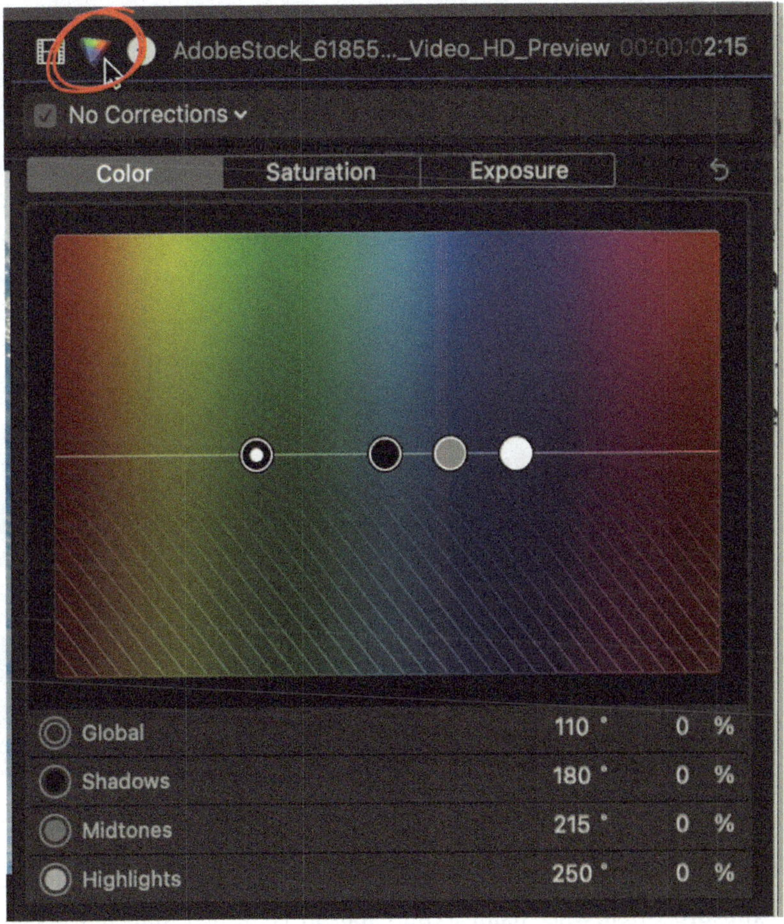

Figure 5.9: Click on the Color Inspector icon in the Inspector panel

2. We are going to add some color corrections. Near the top, click on the down arrow next to **No Corrections** and, from the **Add Color Corrections** drop-down menu, select **+Color Board**.

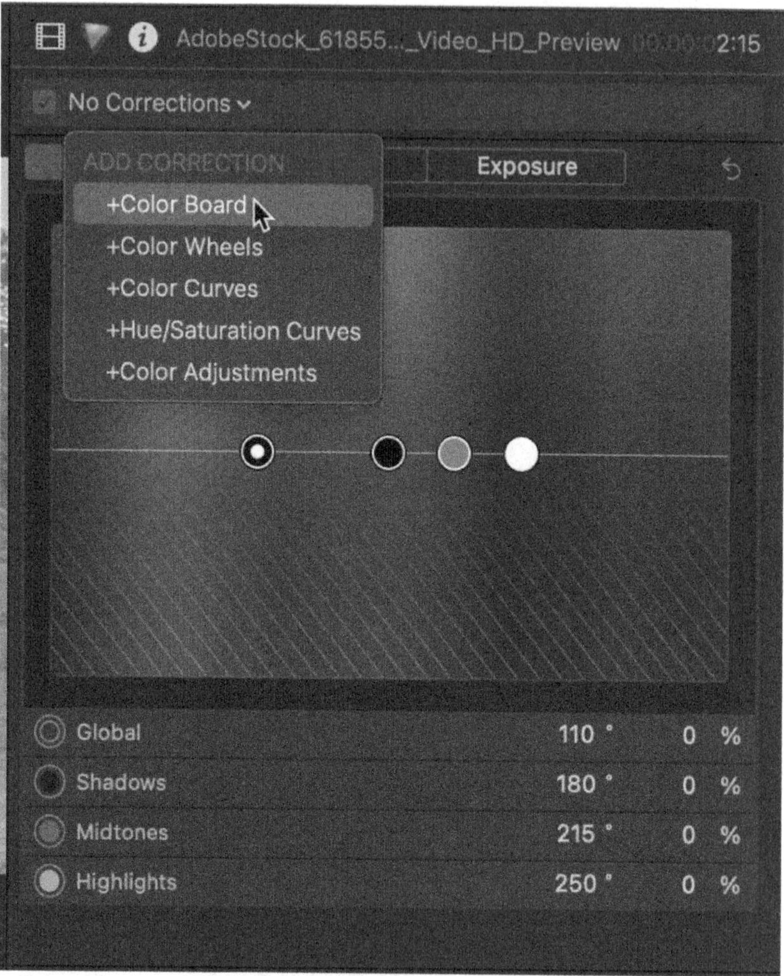

Figure 5.10: Select +Color Board from the Add Color Corrections menu

The Color Board area has three tabs along the top for adjusting **Color**, **Saturation**, and **Exposure**. Often, when fixing a clip, exposure is the first thing to work with:

3. Click on the **Exposure** tab. There are four round slider buttons in the center of the panel. These sliders correspond to the lines at the bottom with percentages.

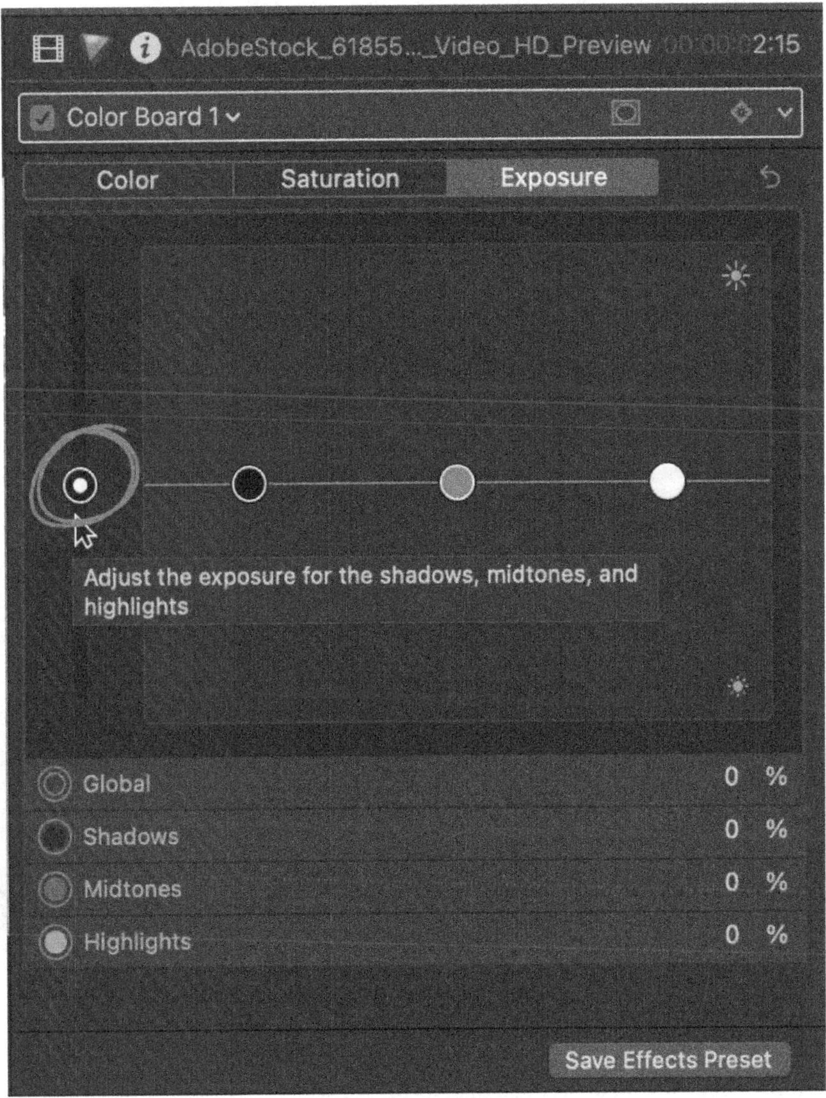

Figure 5.11: Use the global adjustment button for Exposure

4. The button to the far left adjusts the exposure globally for the entire image, while the three buttons in the panel – **Shadows, Midtones,** and **Highlights** – will adjust these settings separately. By bringing down a slider, it decreases that range. Dropping the shadows down a bit tends to increase the contrast. Go slow because a little bit goes a long way. Experiment with the sliders and watch the changes to your clip in the Viewer panel.

5. Next, click on the **Color** tab. There are also four buttons this time: **Global, Shadows, Midtones,** and **Highlights**. But in the Color Board, they do more than slide up and down. The circle button with the white center is the global adjustment button. In the Color Board, adjustments are made by dragging a button across the color spectrum and then up or down. Dragging a button above the center line adds that color, and dragging it below the center line subtracts that color.

    In my example, I am dragging the **Midtones** button above the center line in the blue spectrum, and a blue tint is added to my image in the Viewer panel:

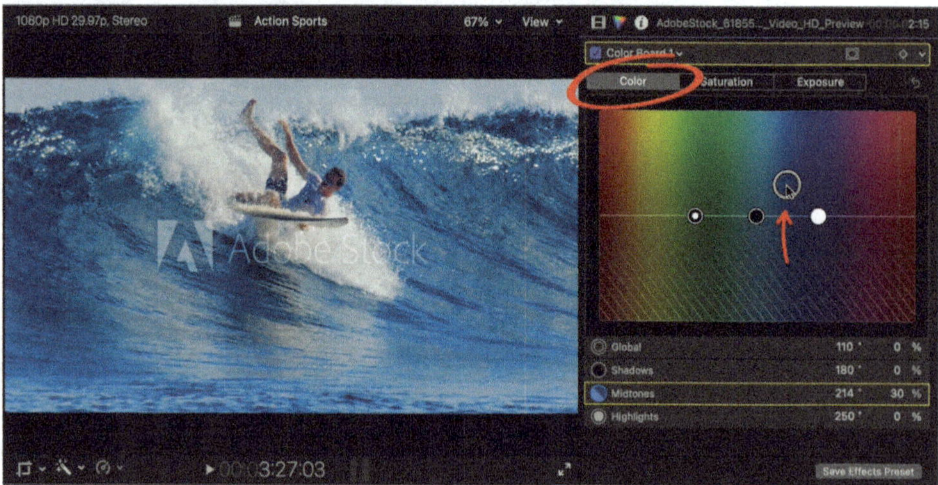

Figure 5.12: Make adjustments with the Color Board

Experiment with the other buttons to add or subtract a color. Clips can be corrected to look more natural or stylized in colorful ways.

6. Now, click on the **Saturation** tab. There are also four buttons that work in a similar way. Experiment with the color saturation of your clips. In all the tabs, drag the button slowly. Try sliding back and forth until you find just the right amount of correction or style.

7. Let's explore the other types of corrections. Near the top of the Inspector panel, click on the down arrow next to **Color Board 1**. Then, in the **Add Color Corrections** drop-down menu, under **ADD CORRECTION**, select **+Color Wheels**.

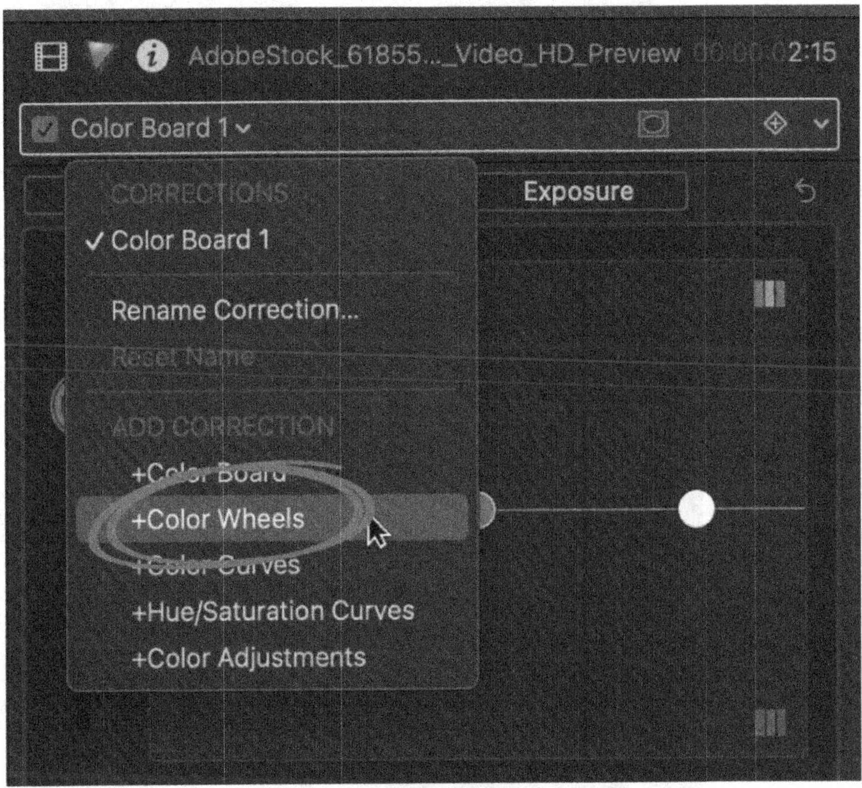

Figure 5.13: Add a color correction by selecting +Color Wheels

8. This interface may be a little more intuitive for some people. By grabbing the button in the center of a color wheel and dragging toward a particular color on the edge of the wheel, we increase that color and decrease the color that is opposite on the color wheel. In my example, I am dragging the **GLOBAL** center away from blue and toward orange. A little bit goes a long way, so the center buttons move slowly to the touch.

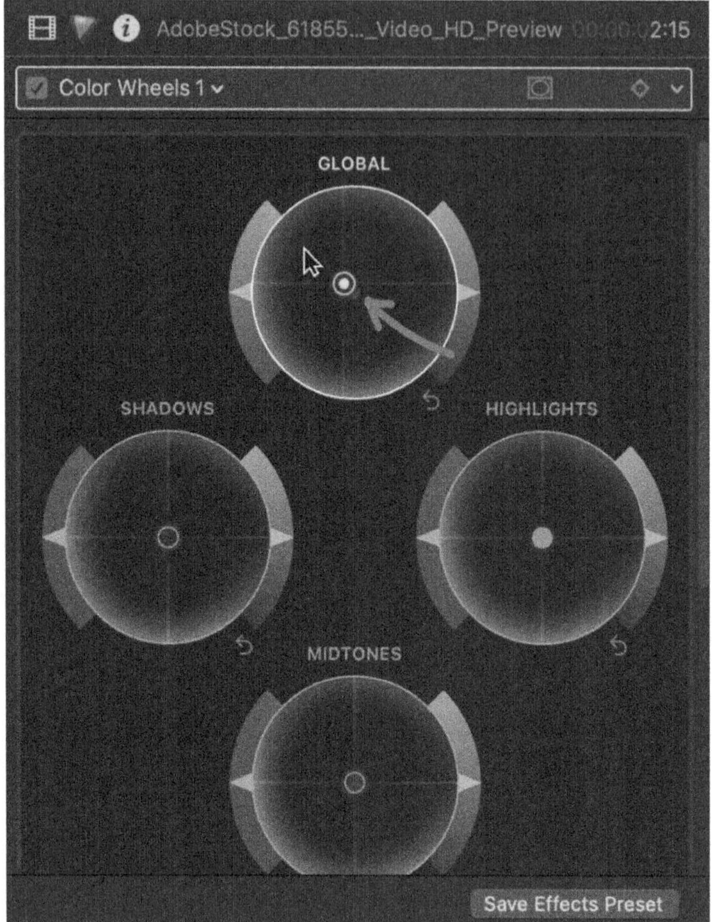

Figure 5.14: Drag the adjustment buttons in the Color Wheels panel

9. A spectrum Color Board and color complementary color wheels are two methods for adjusting color. Now, let's explore color curves. Near the top of the Inspector panel, click on the down arrow next to **Color Wheels 1** again to open the **Add Color Corrections** dropdown menu. However, this time, under the **ADD CORRECTION** section, select **+Color Curves** instead.

Color curves provide a more detailed method of adjusting color within a clip. The bottom left of each area controls the **Shadows** settings, the **Midtones** settings are controlled in the middle, and the **Highlights** settings are adjusted in the upper-right area. At the top of the curves interface is **LUMA**, which means lighting, or exposure.

In my example, I dragged the shadow control point below the center line to decrease the amount, making the image darker:

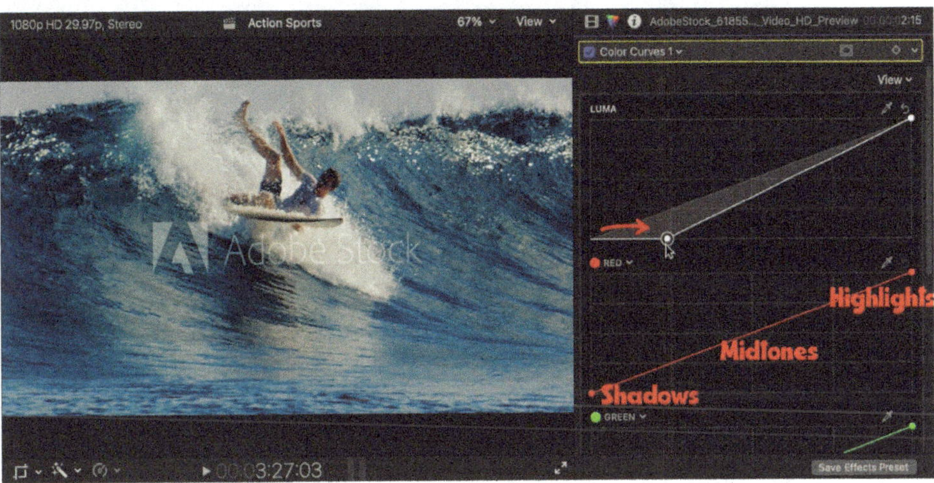

Figure 5.15: Drag corner adjustment buttons in the Color Curves panel

10. Click in the middle of the **RED** adjustment line to create a control point and drag down to decrease red in the midtones. Experiment to see that dragging above the original center line increases the color, and dragging below subtracts the color. Subtle changes can be made by adding multiple control points to your color adjustment line.

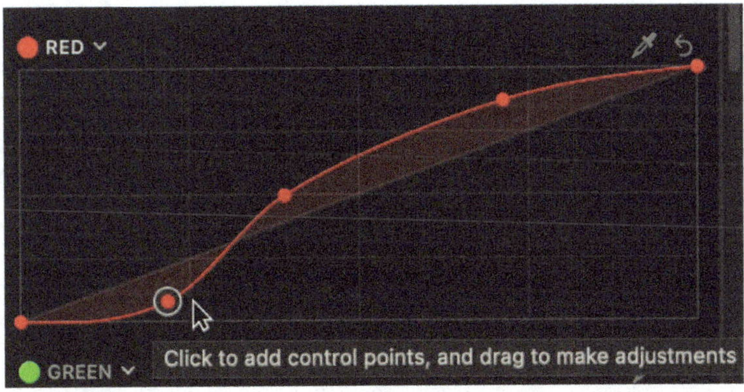

Figure 5.16: Click and drag control points for subtle adjustments

11. It is always good to know that adjustments are not permanent. In all the color correction methods – Color Boards, Color Wheels, and Color Curves – there is a way to revert the clip to its original version. In the upper-right corner, click on the **Reset** icon, which looks like a backward arrow. This will essentially take you *back in time* to reset your clip to the original settings.

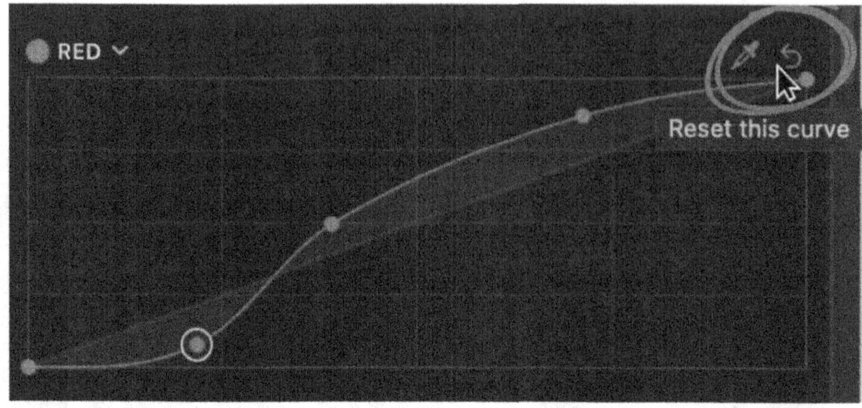

Figure 5.17: Click on the color adjustment Reset icon

12. Let's use color-correcting tools in combination with video scopes. With the Color Inspector panel still open, *Option + click* on a new clip in your timeline to select it and park the playhead over it at the same time. In the Viewer panel, click on the **View** menu and select **Video Scopes**.

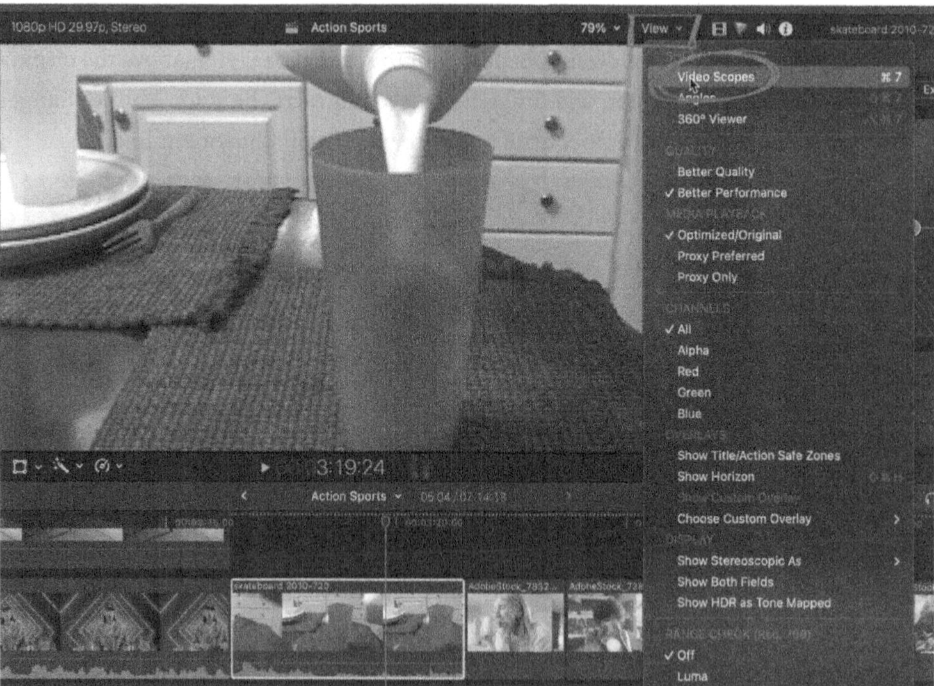

Figure 5.18: Select Video Scopes from the View menu

13. In the Video Scopes panel, click on the **Scope and Settings** icon that looks like a small scope and, from the menu, select **Waveform**, **RGB Parade**, and **IRE**.

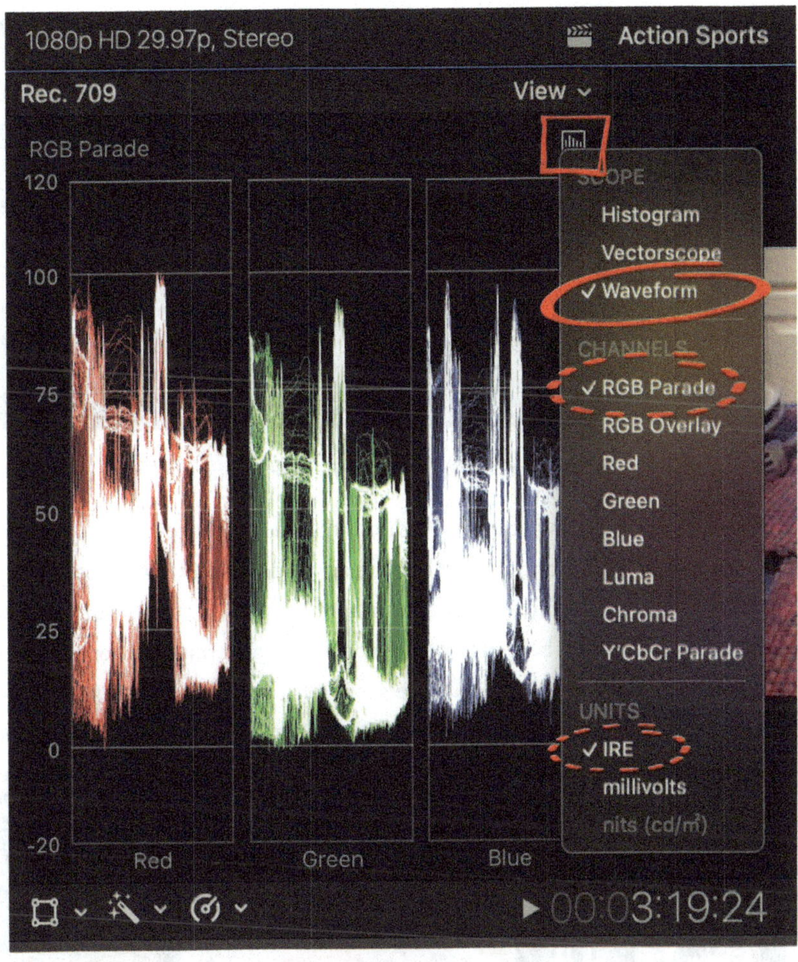

Figure 5.19: Select Waveform, RGB Parade, are IRE from the Scope and Settings menu

14. Our goal is to balance the red, green, and blue channels. In my example, the color balance is too warm. The red channel is more dominant.

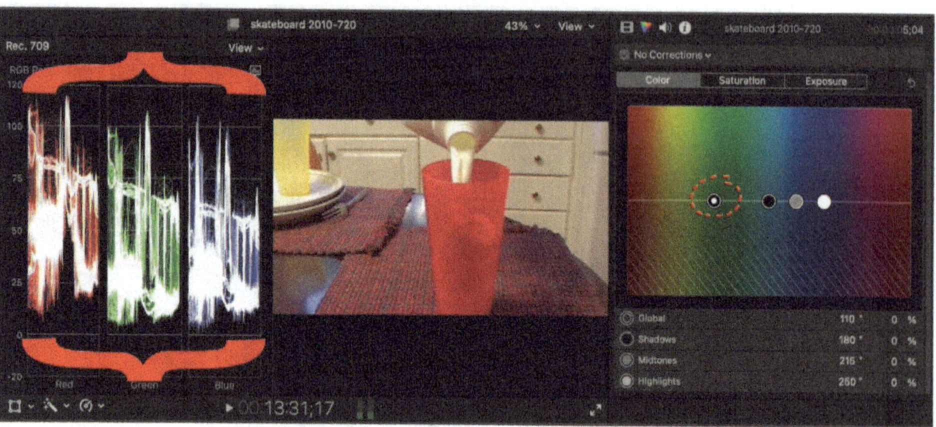

Figure 5.20: The dominant red waveform channel indicates improper color balance

15. To adjust this image, we can first work with the **Exposure** tab. Drag the **Highlights** button down until the channels in the scope are under 100 IRE. Also, let's drag the **Shadows** button down to add a little more contrast and depth. For the **Color** tab, select the **Global** button, drag it to the blue area of the spectrum, and raise it over the center line to add blue. Keep an eye on the RGB parade scope and adjust the color to where the red, green, and blue channel waves are of a more similar size and the color is balanced.

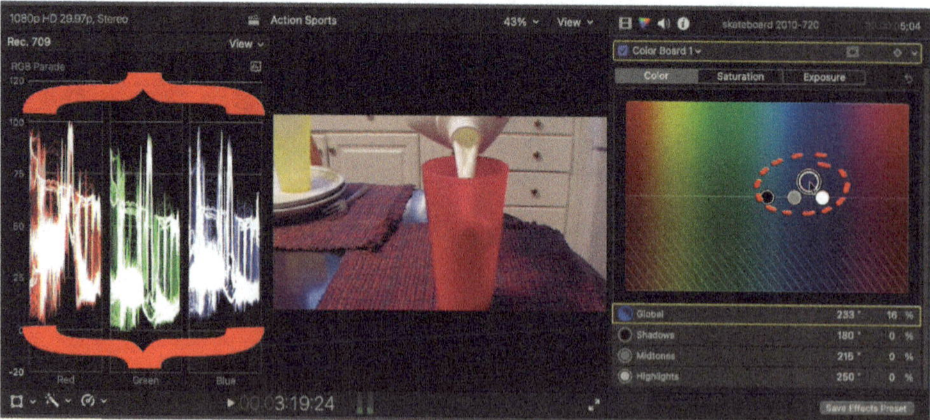

Figure 5.21: Drag the Global Color button above the center line in the blue area to adjust the RGB parade scope

There's more...

Often, you will have multiple clips in your timeline from the same camera angle that all need to be corrected. We only need to correct one and can then paste the color correction attribute into the other clips:

1. In my example, I have a series of clips from a dialogue scene. I have color-corrected the first clip using the tools in the **Exposure, Saturation**, and **Color** tabs. This will be my reference clip. With that clip still selected, use the keyboard shortcut of *Command + C* to copy it.

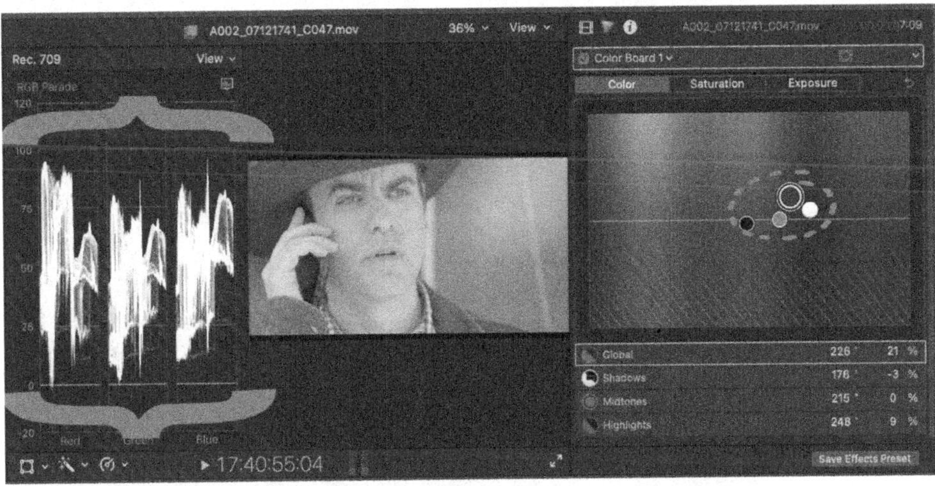

Figure 5.22: Copy the clip you have color-corrected

2. In the Timeline panel, hold down the *Command* key and carefully click on the other clips from the same camera angle to make a discontinuous selection of clips.

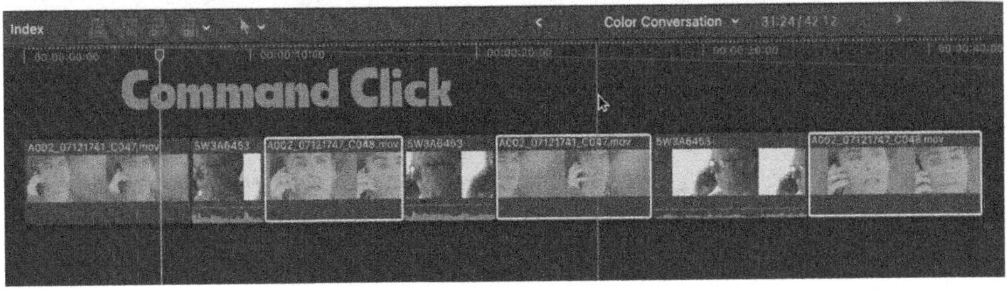

Figure 5.23: Hold down the Command key and click on similar clips

3. Under the **Edit** menu, select **Paste Attributes…**. Or, use the keyboard shortcut of *Shift + Command + V*. You are presented with a dialogue box. Use the checkboxes to select the attributes in the original clip that you want to paste into the clips you have selected. In my example, I am pasting the changes to **Color Board 1**. Click on the **Paste** button to add the attributes to the other clips that are from the same camera angle. Note that you should check each clip for consistency and make color adjustments as needed.

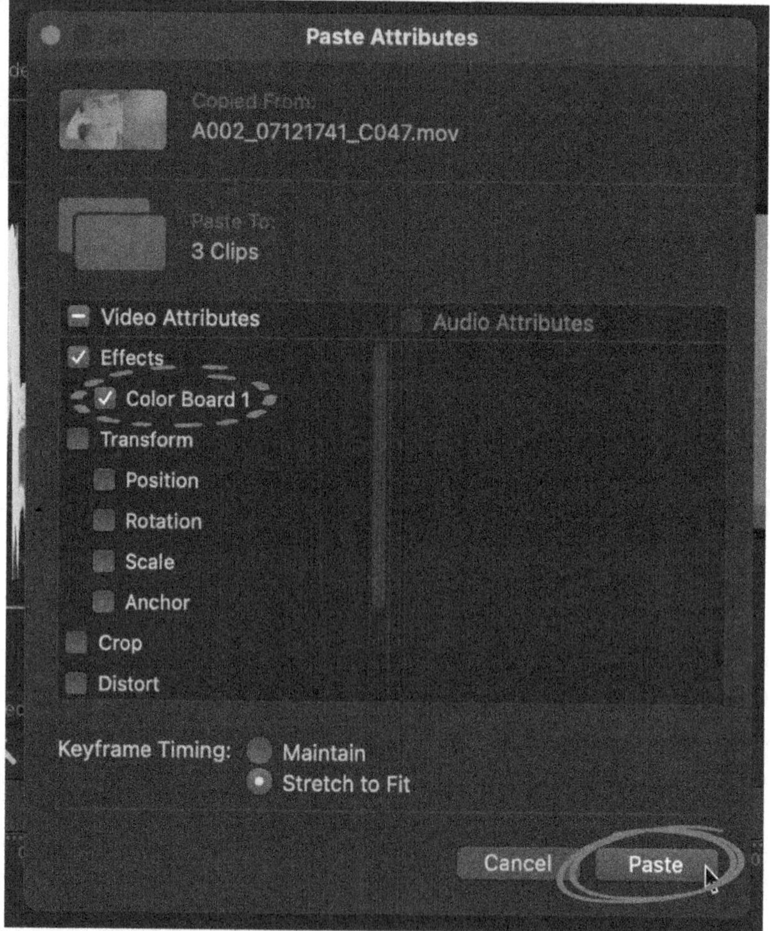

Figure 5.24: Select the Video Attributes or Audio Attributes checkboxes and click on the Paste button

4. Also, notice that, from the **Edit** menu, there is a **Remove Attributes…** option, or you can also use *Shift + Command + X*. You will be presented with the same dialogue box, in which you can select the attributes to remove.

5. But wait, there's more. When color-correcting clips, you may want to use a reference clip for comparison. Let's create a custom workspace with the Comparison Viewer panel. From the **Window** menu, select **Show in Workspace**, and in the sub-menu to the right, select **Comparison Viewer**. If they are not already selected, choose **Inspector** and **Timeline**. In my example, I added **Timeline Index**, but this is not necessary. If it is not already deselected, uncheck **Event Viewer**.

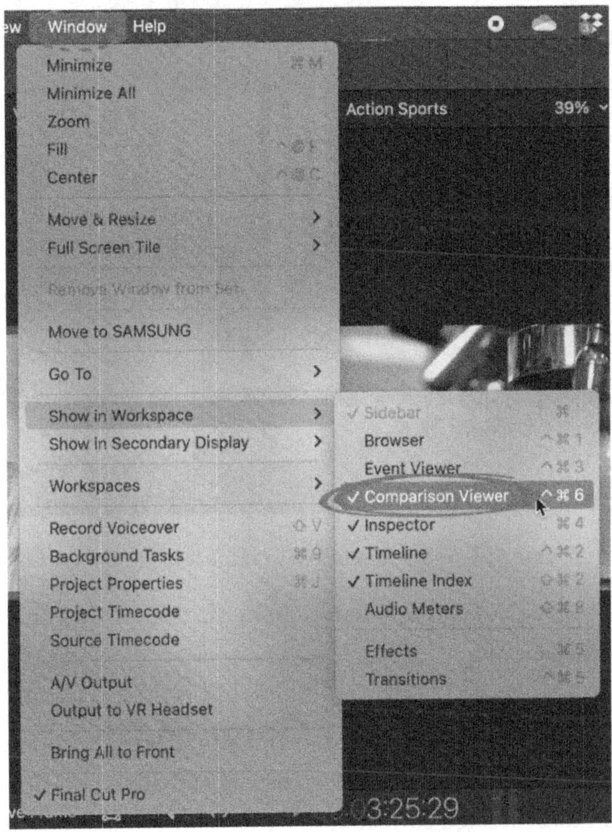

Figure 5.25: Select Comparison Viewer from the Window and Show in Workspace menu

6. Then, similar to our previous steps in this recipe, for the Comparison Viewer and the Viewer panel, click on the **View** menu and select **Video Scopes**. Turn on the RGB parade waveform. Along the top center of the Comparison Viewer are two tabs. We could choose the **Timeline** tab and use the Comparison Viewer to show the previous clip, but we want a reference image. Click on the **Saved** tab. *Option + click* on the primary clip you want to reference and click on the **Save Frame** button in the lower-right corner of the Comparison Viewer panel.

You can view a window of your saved frames by clicking on the **Frame Browser** button in the lower-left corner of the Comparison Viewer. *Option + click* on the clip you want to adjust and, in the Inspector panel, perform your color corrections. Use the original image and its RGB waveform for comparison. In my example, I am increasing the warm tones with the color wheels.

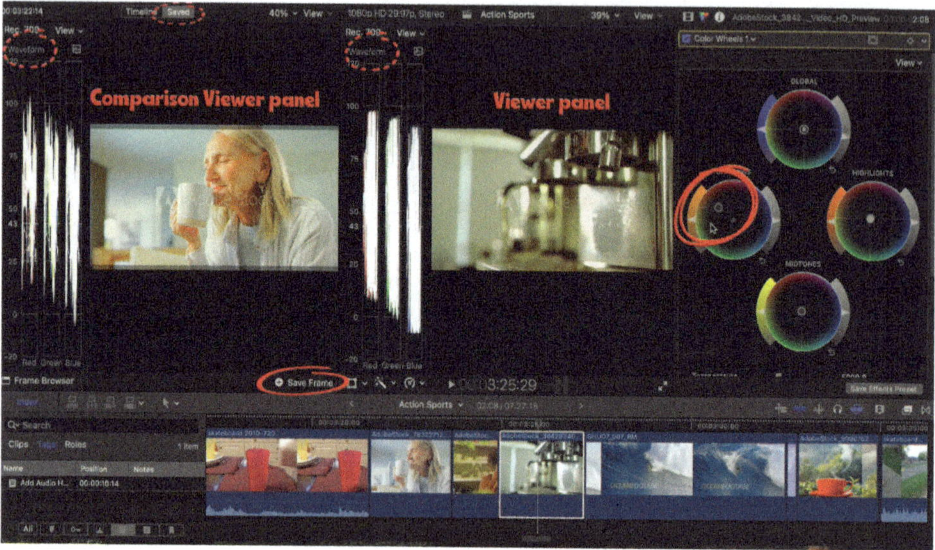

Figure 5.26: Notice the custom workspace in the Comparison Viewer panel

7. Be sure to save this custom interface from the **Window** menu. Select **Workspaces** and **Save Workspace as…**.

Using Shape Masks and Color Masks

Shape Masks and Color Masks allow you to isolate and adjust specific areas or colors within your footage for more targeted corrections. With Shape Masks, you can apply effects or color adjustments to defined geometric areas, while Color Masks let you focus on and modify specific hues within your shot.

The advantage of using these masks is that they offer precise control over localized edits, allowing you to refine your footage with greater detail, correct problem areas, and enhance specific elements without affecting the entire frame.

In this recipe, we will explore how to create a shape in which the inside and outside have different color styles. The same will be done by isolating a single color and adjusting it differently from the rest of the image.

How to do it...

Let's look at how to work with Shape Masks and Color Masks:

1. With a clip selected in your timeline and the playhead parked on top of it to see the results in the Viewer panel, select the triangular **Show Color Inspector** icon in the upper-left corner of the Inspector panel.

2. Near the top of the Inspector panel, click on the down arrow next to **No Corrections** and, from the **Add Color Corrections** drop-down menu, select **+Color Board**.

3. In the **Effects** area, the line for **Color Board 1** will be highlighted in yellow. Toward the right-hand side of the line is an icon that looks like an oval inside a square. This is the **Apply Shape or Color Mask** icon. Click it once and, in the drop-down menu, select **Add Shape Mask**.

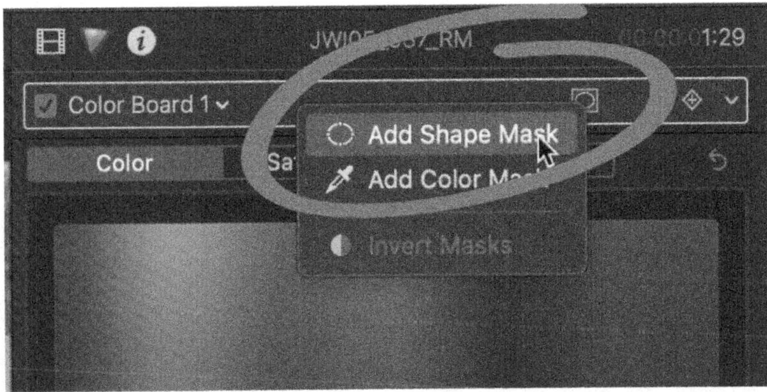

Figure 5.27: Click on the Apply Shape or Color Mask icon and select Add Shape Mask from the menu

The **Add Shape Mask** command creates a selected area in your clip. That's what a mask is – simply a selected area.

4. You will see a target area on your clip in the Viewer panel. Try moving the green buttons along the inner red edge to control the size of the mask. Then, try moving the outer red edge, which is the range of feathering from the inner mask edge to the outside.

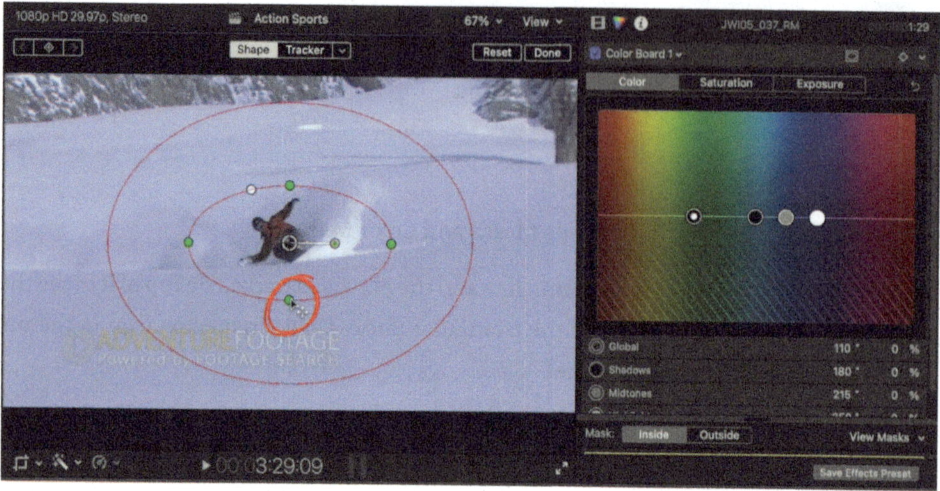

Figure 5.28: Adjust the size of the Shape Mask with the green control point button

5. Along the bottom edge of the mask's Inspector panel, there are two tabs: **Inside** and **Outside**. With the **Inside** tab selected, make a color adjustment and note that it is applied to what is inside that Shape Mask. For my example, to make this obviously different, I'm going to add the color blue on the inside of my Shape Mask. Now, click on the **Outside** tab and add a difference adjustment. I'm going to add the color red. Again, this is not a normal adjustment but is being done to show an obvious difference. Your examples might be more subtle.

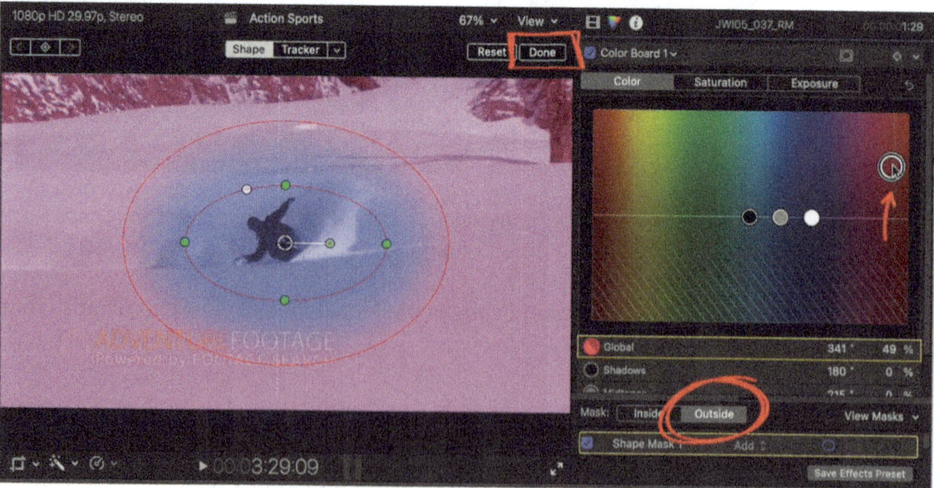

Figure 5.29: Click on the Outside tab to adjust the color outside of the Shape Mask

The Shape Mask is useful because you can adjust a targeted area in clips.

6. Adjustments using a Shape Mask can be done with the Color Board, Color Wheels, or Color Curves (check out the previous recipe in this chapter for more details on these topics). When you have completed your adjustment, click on the **Done** button in the upper-right corner of the Viewer panel.

7. To view the Shape Mask again and make adjustments, click on the **Enable Onscreen Controls** icon – it looks like an oval shape on the **Shape Mask 1** line located at the bottom of the Color Inspector panel.

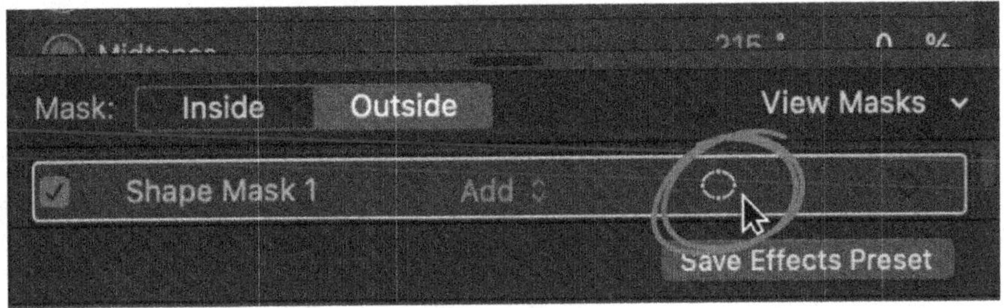

Figure 5.30: Click on the Enable Onscreen Controls icon to readjust a Shape Mask

A color adjustment mask can be created by producing a shape, but a mask can also be created from the *shape* of a particular color.

8. *Option + click* on a new clip in your timeline to select it and park the playhead over it at the same time. Let's start by adding a color adjustment with a Color Board. Near the top of the Inspector panel, click on the down arrow next to **No Corrections** and, from the **Add Color Corrections** drop-down menu, select **+Color Board**. On the **Color Board 1** line, click on the **Apply Shape or Color Mask** icon, which looks like an oval inside a rectangle. From the drop-down menu, this time select **Add Color Mask**.

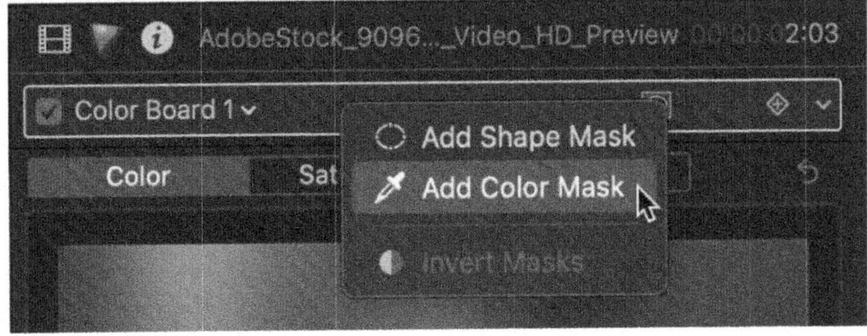

Figure 5.31: Select Add Color Mask from the Apply Shape menu

9. Hover the mouse over the Viewer panel and note that the cursor changes to an eyedropper. Click and drag the eyedropper on the color that you are using to mask. Drag the circle large enough so that you've selected as much of your color as you can without any of the other colors turning darker or becoming highlighted.

Figure 5.32: Select a color for the Color Mask

10. Like the Shape Mask, at the bottom of the Inspector panel are the **Inside** and **Outside** tabs. For my example, I'm going to increase the saturation inside the mask and decrease the saturation outside of the mask. This will give the image a peculiar look, with one color standing out and the rest of the scene black and white.

Figure 5.33: Desaturate the image outside of the Color Mask

11. To view the Color Mask again and make adjustments, click on the **Turn on Color Mask Onscreen Controls** icon – it looks like an eyedropper on the **Color Mask** line located at the bottom of the Color Inspector panel.

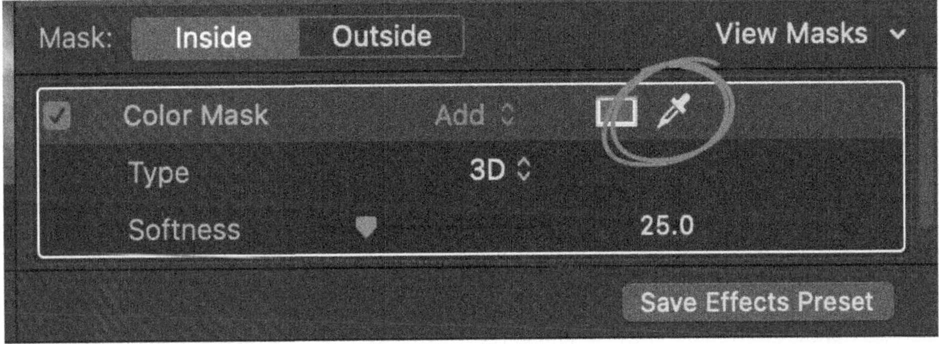

Figure 5.34: Click on the Turn on Color Mask Onscreen Controls icon to readjust a Color Mask

Fixing exposure with the luma waveform monitor

Similar to the way that over-modulated audio creates distortion, over-exposed images create visual distortion. This is especially true with broadcast television.

The luma waveform monitor provides a visual representation of your clip's light exposure levels, helping you accurately assess exposure across shadows and highlights. This allows for more accurate exposure control, helping you create visually appealing videos with consistent brightness, clear detail, and a professional finish.

 Remember – luma means light and chroma means color.

In this recipe, we will use the luma waveform monitor to analyze our clips and then use the exposure adjustment in the Color Board to bring the clips into balance.

Getting ready

You will need several clips, including ones in which the exposure is a little too bright. Most preview clips from stock media websites have been color-corrected and have had their exposure fixed already. You may have to broaden your search or shoot your own footage.

How to do it...

In my example, I have a clip that looks pretty good. But let's see if its exposure is broadcast-safe. Here is how to do it:

1. Select a clip to analyze in the timeline so that its information is visible in the Inspector panel. Then, park your playhead on top of it so that it is visible in the Viewer panel.

2. In the upper-right corner of the Viewer panel, click on the **View** menu, and in the drop-down menu, select **Video Scopes**.

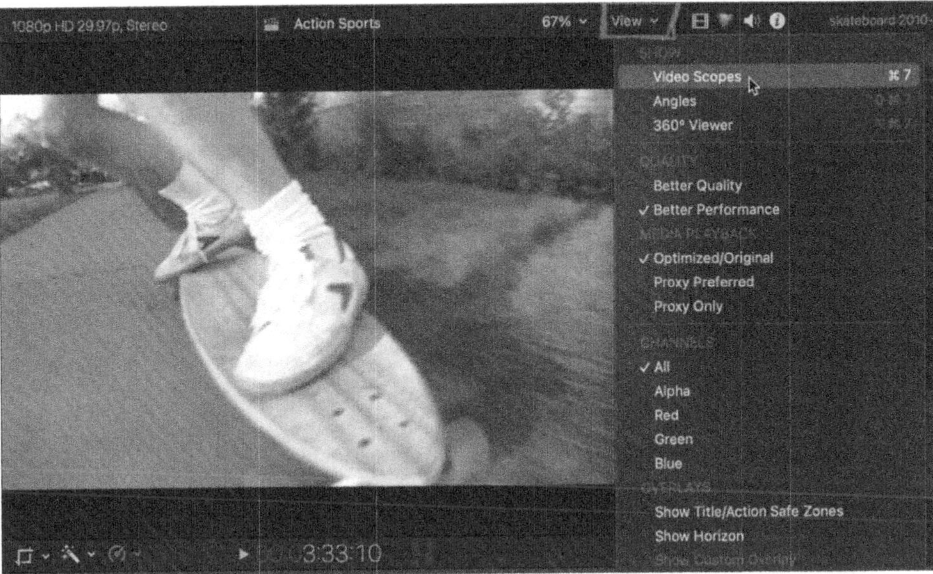

Figure 5.35: Select Video Scopes from the View menu

This command will open two areas in the Viewer panel – on the left will be an area of video scopes, and on the right will be the clip's image.

3. Near the upper-right corner of the Scopes panel, click on the **Scope and Settings** icon, which looks like a small chart. In Final Cut Pro, scopes are digital representations of devices that television engineers use to measure video signals. There are three **SCOPE** options available:

    - **Histogram** provides a statistical analysis of the image
    - **Vectorscope** shows the distribution of color in an image on a circular scale
    - **Waveform** shows the relative levels of light or color

    Depending on which scope you choose, the other settings in the drop-down menu will change. In our case, we will choose **Waveform**, which means we will see two more categories:

    - **CHANNELS**: Channels are like signals. They can be combined colors, individual colors, or the luma (light) values. We will choose **Luma** here.

- **UNITS:** These are the values used by the scope. Here, we want to use **IRE** because that is what broadcast television uses to measure exposure. (True nerds will know that the name is derived from the initials of the Institute of Radio Engineers.)

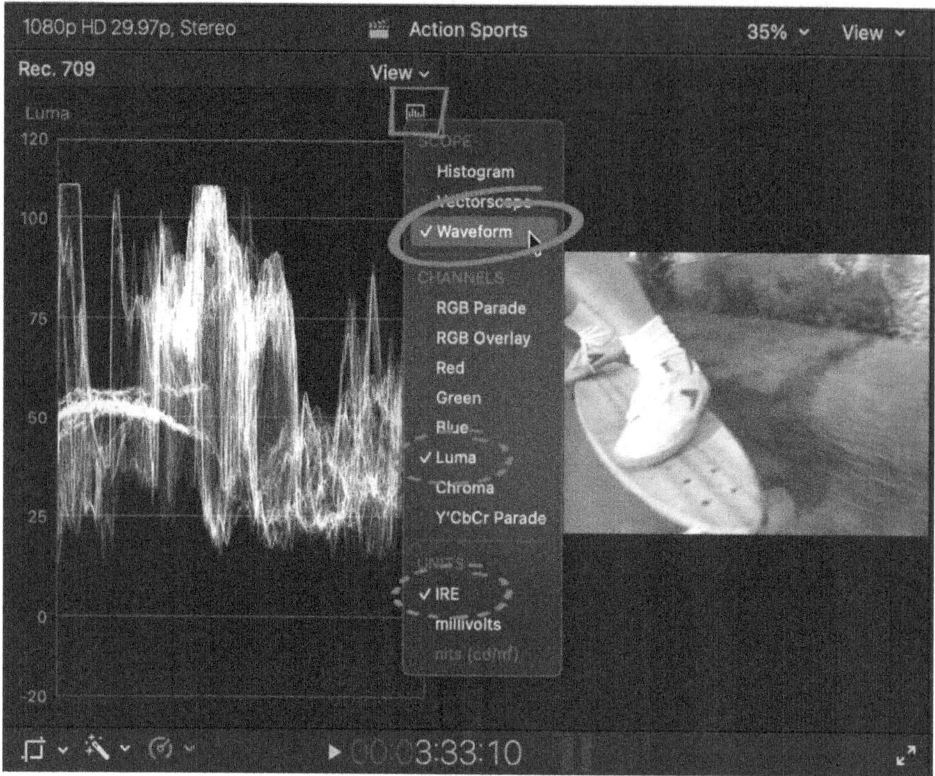

Figure 5.36: Select Waveform from the Scope and Settings menu

This will reveal a scope that has up-and-down waveform values. It shows the luma (light) channel and uses IRE as the unit of measurement. Skim your mouse through your clips in the timeline and notice how the waveform in the scope changes as it reads the amount of exposure, or luma, in each image.

As we said in the recipe introduction, over-modulation of video causes visual distortion. In my example, the footage is okay but overexposed a bit. Let's fix that.

4. With the clip you want to adjust selected in your timeline and the playhead parked on top of it to see the results in the Viewer panel, select the triangular **Show Color Inspector** icon in the upper-left corner of the Inspector panel.

5.   Near the top, click on the down arrow next to **No Corrections**, and from the **Add Color Corrections** drop-down menu, select **+Color Board**.

6.   Click on the **Exposure** tab along the top of the panel. Then, watching the scope, adjust the **Global** exposure slider down until the top of the luma waveform is at or under 100 IRE.

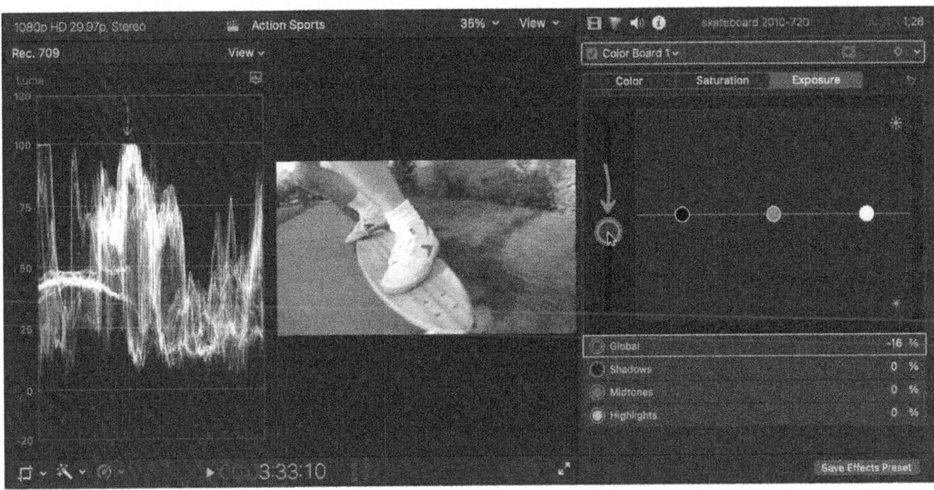

Figure 5.37: Adjust the Global exposure to under 100 IRE

Broadcast television has a limit of 100 IRE, which is why we should adjust the **Global** exposure slider to be at or under 100.

And with that, congratulations, your clip is broadcast-safe!

Adding secondary color corrections

In Final Cut Pro, adding secondary color corrections allows you to adjust specific colors or areas within a clip without affecting the rest of the image. This provides enhanced precision and creative control, enabling you to fine-tune specific elements for a more refined, professional look or to highlight key aspects of your footage without altering the overall composition.

You can do this by using tools such as Shape Masks, which can isolate particular hues, making targeted adjustments to saturation, brightness, or tint. Just like layering additional spices while cooking to add depth to a dish.

In this recipe, we will explore how to color-correct a clip and then introduce additional enhancements to feature particular colors and portions of the image.

How to do it...

"And you get a color, and you get a color!" Let's add some color correction:

1. Being able to make more than one type of color correction is a subtle difference that can add professionalism to your projects. In my example, I want to make special adjustments to a person's face as well as the overall image. So, with the clip you want to adjust selected in your timeline and the playhead parked on top of it to see the results in the Viewer panel, select the triangular **Show Color Inspector** icon in the upper-left corner of the Inspector panel.

2. Near the top, click on the down arrow next to **No Corrections**, and from the **Add Color Corrections** drop-down menu, select **+Color Board**.

3. Click on the **Exposure** tab. Then click, hold, and drag down the **Shadows** slider button to darken the shadows and add some contrast to this shot. This is starting to look good, but we can do more.

4. Adding a secondary correction is easy. Near the top of the Inspector panel, click on the downward arrow next to **Color Board 1**. From the **Add Color Corrections** drop-down menu, select **+Color Curves**.

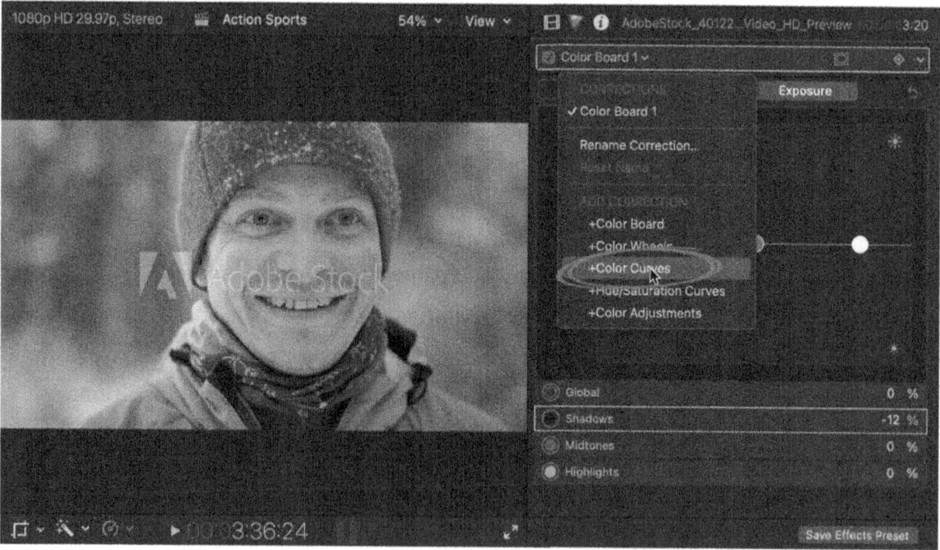

Figure 5.38: Add color curves as a secondary color correction

5. In my example, I want to highlight this person's red hat, but you may want to pick a color from your clip to accentuate. About three-quarters of the way up and to the right of the center line, click and drag a control point above the center line to add more color to the midtones/highlights portion of this shot.

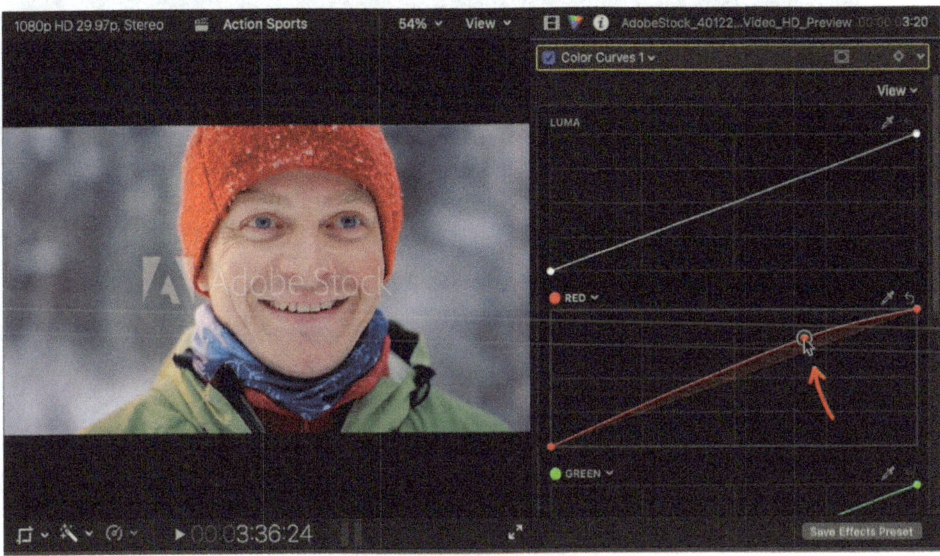

Figure 5.39: Increase the color with a control point above the center line

6. But I think this made the skin tones just a little bit red! In my example, I want to isolate the face with a Shape Mask. Near the top of the Inspector panel, click on the downward arrow next to **Color Curves 1**. From the **Add Color Corrections** drop-down menu, select **+Color Wheels**. We now have a row in the Inspector panel labeled **Color Wheels 1**.

7. In the **Color Wheels 1** row, click on the **Apply Shape or Color Mask** icon, which looks like an oval inside a rectangle. From the small drop-down menu, select **Add Shape Mask**. Near the bottom of the Inspector panel, check to see that the **Inside** tab is selected.

8. Now look at the Viewer panel, and notice the green control button for the size of the Shape Mask. In my example, I will drag the edges of the shape to be right inside the person's face, with the feather area relatively small.

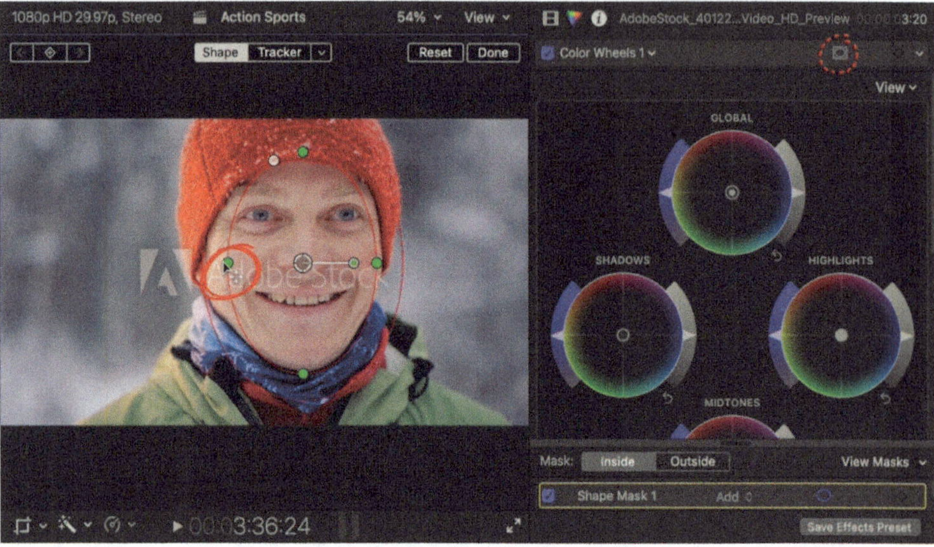

Figure 5.40: Add a Shape Mask to the Color Wheels adjustment

9. With the size of the Shape Mask set, go to the Inspector panel and select the **Midtones** wheel. Slide the center button right toward the blue spectrum visible around the inside of the circle. Remember, just a little change goes a long way. For my example, I have added blue inside the Shape Mask.

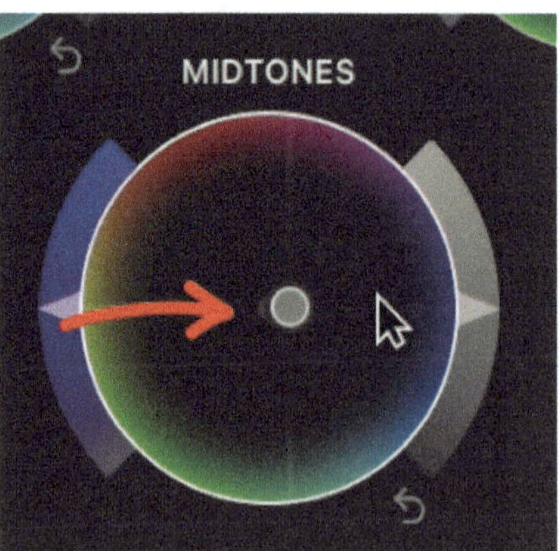

*Figure 5.41: Adjust the color by dragging the center button toward the color inside
the circle*

10. When you have completed your adjustment, click on the **Done** button in the upper-right corner of the Viewer panel.

11. Next, click on the **Show Video Inspector** icon, which looks like a film strip, near the top of the Inspector panel. Notice, in the **Effects** area, the different rows for the Color Board, Curves, and Wheels that were added. Experiment by checking them on and off to compare the results and see how these subtle changes can make a big difference. In my example, **Color Board 1** created contrast, **Color Curves 1** increased the red color, and **Color Wheels 1** had a Shape Mask to adjust the color of the face. Clicking rows on and off is a good way to see how they work together.

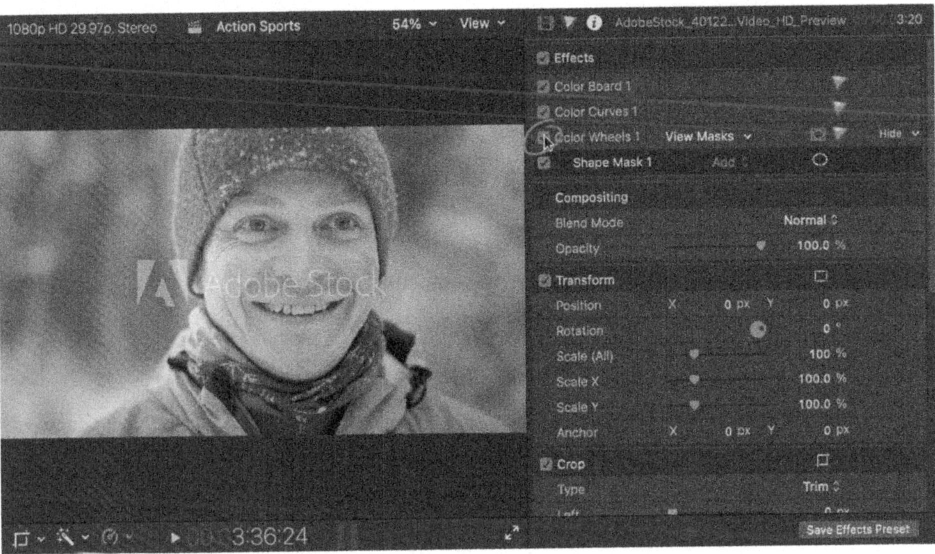

Figure 5.42: For comparison, use the checkbox to turn secondary color corrections on and off

There's more...

You can change the names of effects. This is helpful when you have several effects and want to remember what they specifically do. Double-click on the title of the effect, and it will become highlighted in blue, so you can type in a new name.

Figure 5.43: Change the names of effects

Applying LUTs to raw files

Applying a **Look-Up Table (LUT)** to raw footage mathematically converts the tons of data from the camera to a standard video color space. Camera LUTs can be used to replicate the camera's intended color profile.

Using built-in or third-party LUTs in Final Cut Pro to grade raw files helps you quickly translate the raw color data into a defined style, allowing you to achieve consistent, cinematic results while preserving the detail and flexibility of raw formats. They also speed up the grading process, offer a wide range of creative possibilities, and ensure precise, professional-quality color grading with minimal effort.

While applying a camera LUT is often one of the first steps in the grading process, additional color correction or style adjustments are usually made to refine the look further.

In this recipe, we will see how easy Final Cut Pro makes it to add a LUT to your footage.

Getting ready

You will need some footage that is in a raw or log format and that is *ungraded*. A few stock media websites will have some footage, but you may need to broaden your internet search.

Also, upon its initial installation, Final Cut Pro does not show the menu for adding camera LUTs to footage. Here's how to open it:

1. In the Event Browser panel, select your raw, *ungraded* clip.

2. Then, in the Inspector panel, click on the **Show the Info Inspector** icon – it's along the top edge, and looks like a circle with a lowercase i in the center.

3. Near the bottom of the Inspector panel, click on the **Metadata Views** button, which will probably be labeled as **Basic**. This will open a drop-down menu. From there, select **Extended**.

   Now you can see the camera LUT parameter we want to use to adjust our footage.

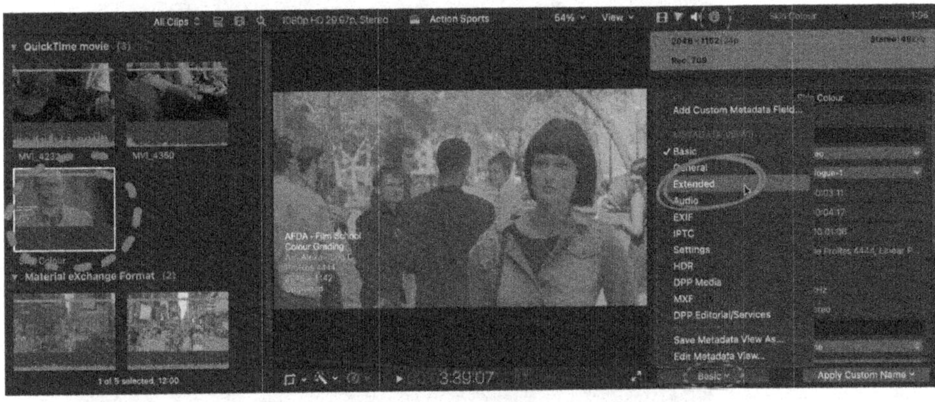

Figure 5.44: Select the Extended metadata view

How to do it...

The footage is in a raw format, so let's get cooking:

1. So, with the **Metadata Views** option in the Information Inspector panel set to **Extended**, we can see a metadata line for **Camera LUT**.

2. Click on the drop-down menu currently labeled as **None**. Notice that Apple has many built-in camera LUTs from various camera manufacturers. Select the camera LUT that corresponds with your selected footage. For my example, I am going to select **ARRI Log C**.

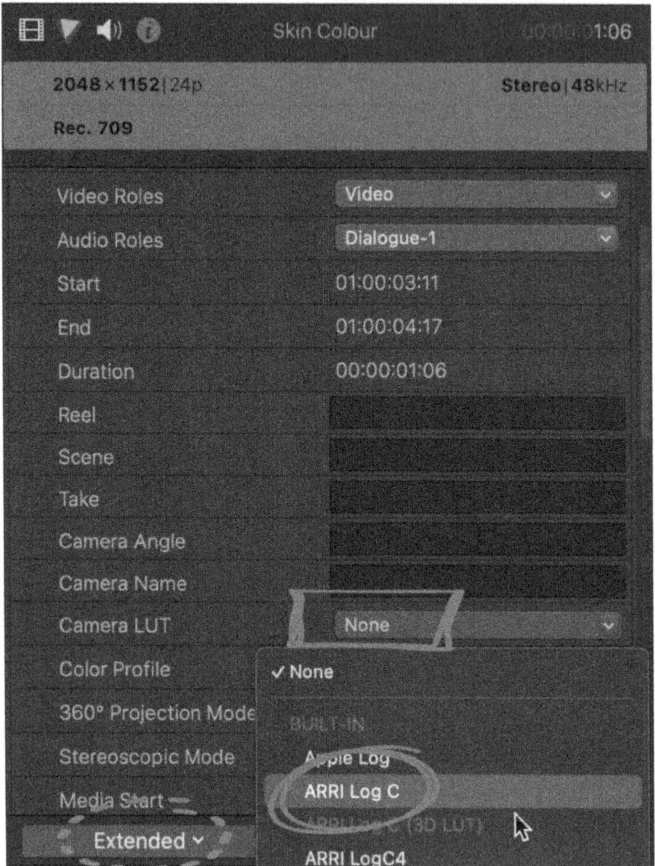

Figure 5.45: Select the camera LUT in the Extended Information Inspector panel

When we select a camera LUT, the clip colors are converted to our HD Rec. 709 color space. These LUTs are from the manufacturer and will get you 90 percent in the direction of your color correction, and you can use Curves and Color Boards to adjust your footage from here. It is good not to rely wholly on LUTs but to train your eyes to color-correct for the story you are trying to tell.

 If your camera's raw format is not listed in the built-in **Camera LUT** menu, check your camera manufacturer's support web page for the LUT file that works with Final Cut Pro. Look for a .cube file to download. Then apply it as a custom camera LUT.

3. Select another raw clip. Instead of applying a LUT to match the camera it came from, let's stylize it. In the Information Inspector panel, click on the **Camera LUT** drop-down menu. Near the bottom of the menu, select **Add Custom Camera LUT...**.

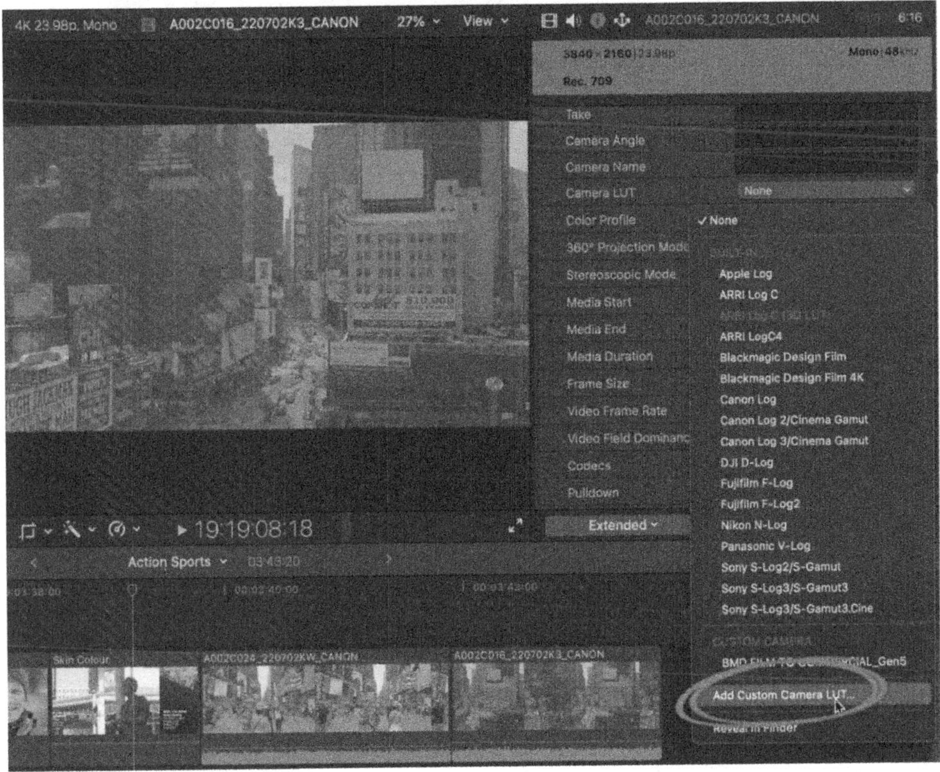

Figure 5.46: Select Add Custom Camera LUT... from the Camera LUT menu

4. There are many paid and free LUT files available for Final Cut Pro, but I'm going to add a LUT that I've downloaded for free. Note that .cube files are the files that will work as LUTs. Here's one called Matrix, which sounds cool. Let's apply it. Navigate to the LUT file you wish to apply, select it, and click **Open**.

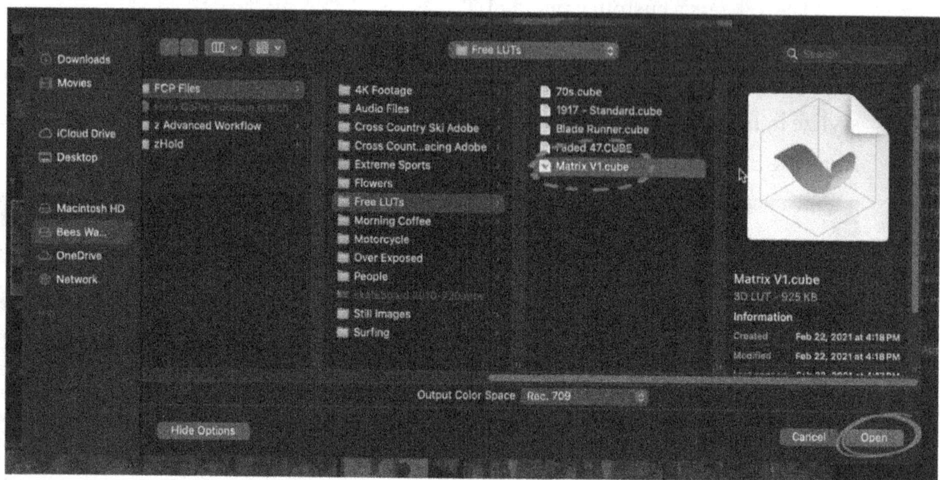

Figure 5.47: Select a LUT file to apply

5. Now, instead of using a color look-up table to convert the camera data to a normal HD color space, the data from the camera is converted to colors within a Matrix-style movie. In addition, the custom camera LUT – called **Matrix V1** – is added to your **Camera LUT** menu in the **Custom Camera** area.

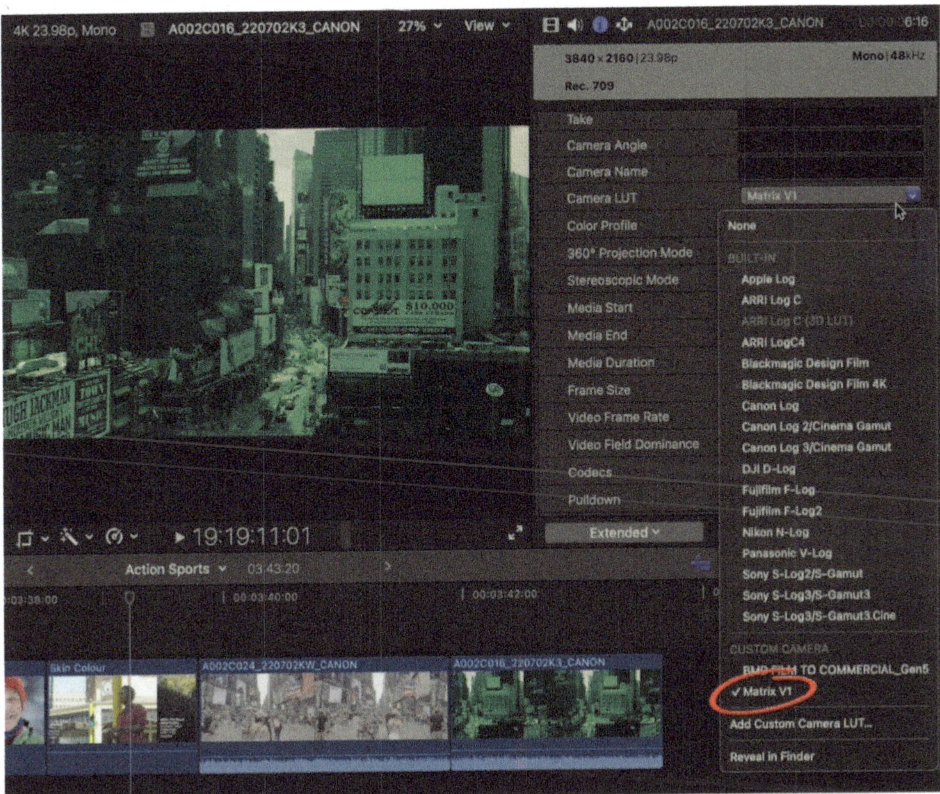

Figure 5.48: Note the custom LUT added to the Camera LUT menu

Note that at the bottom of the **Camera LUT** drop-down menu is a **Reveal in Finder** option. You'll be able to find the selected camera LUT file. That way, you can transfer LUTs to other computers and have all your LUTs ready to get cooking.

6

Applying Visual Effects

Enter the enchanting realm of visual effects, where Final Cut Pro becomes your magical kitchen of creativity. We'll explore how to sprinkle your projects with captivating effects, from subtle enhancements to amazing transformations.

In this chapter, you'll learn essential skills such as adding custom look-up tables (LUTs), individual clips, and creating and saving custom color presets. You will also explore advanced editing techniques, including utilizing blend modes for creative effects, applying effects to sections of clips through adjustment clips, and applying the amazing automatic Color Adjustments effect.

Remember, story drives production. So, effects are not added just because they are cool; they need to move your audience's attention to your message. Just like a signature dish, all the ingredients move the guest to a particular flavor profile.

In this chapter, you will complete the following recipes:

- Stacking visual effects
- Stacking adjustment clips
- Creating a custom Color Board preset effect
- Using the Color Adjustments effect
- Using the Custom LUT effect
- Using blend modes

Stacking visual effects

Think of visual effects like sandwich toppings – the more thoughtfully you stack, the tastier the result. The order makes a difference. Stacking visual effects allows you to layer multiple effects on a single clip, creating complex and dynamic visuals. The advantage of stacking effects is the creative flexibility it offers – by combining effects such as color adjustments, transitions, and filters, you can craft a distinctive look that enhances the mood or narrative of your video.

In this recipe, we will explore how the order of effects affects the look of your clips, giving you truly unique imagery.

How to do it...

Final Cut Pro applies effects to clips in a specific order. Let's find out how:

1. Add a clip to your project in the Timeline panel, then *Option-click* on it, so that both the clip is selected and the playhead is parked on top of it.

2. Open the Effects Browser panel with the **Effects Browser** icon, located at the upper right of the Timeline panel. It looks like two overlapping rectangles.

Figure 6.1: Click on the Effects Browser icon

3. Adding effects to a clip is quite easy. In my example, I will add two effects to a clip and test the order in which they are applied – a glass effect and a blur effect.

   There are quite a few effects, especially if you select **All** from **Effects Categories** in the left side panel, so I'm going to use the search field down at the bottom edge of the Effects Browser. Type in glass and we see an effect called **Glass Block**.

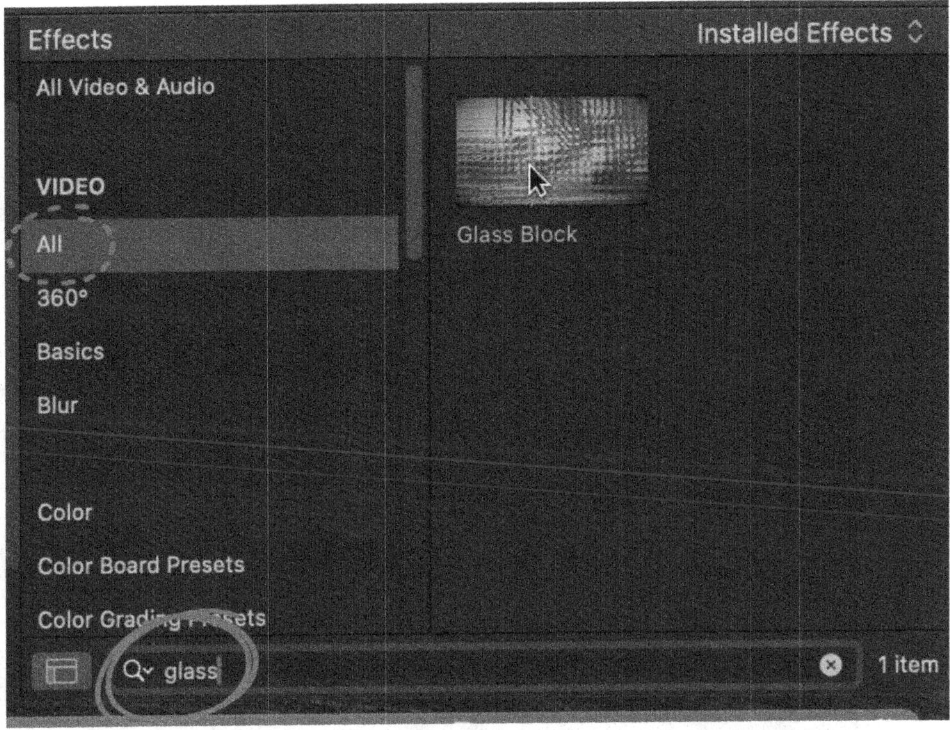

Figure 6.2: Search for an effect in the search field

When you use the mouse to skim over an effect in the Effects Browser panel, you will notice that a preview is shown in the Viewer panel to give you an idea of what that effect will look like.

Click on the **Glass Block** effect once and drag it on top of a clip in the Timeline panel. Boom, done!

4. To exit the search mode, click on the **X** button on the far right side of the search field.

5. Next, I want to add a blur effect. In the left panel, click on the **Effects** category labeled **Blur** and pick a blur that you like. I'm going to use a nice, smooth **Gaussian** blur. Drag the effect on top of the same clip.

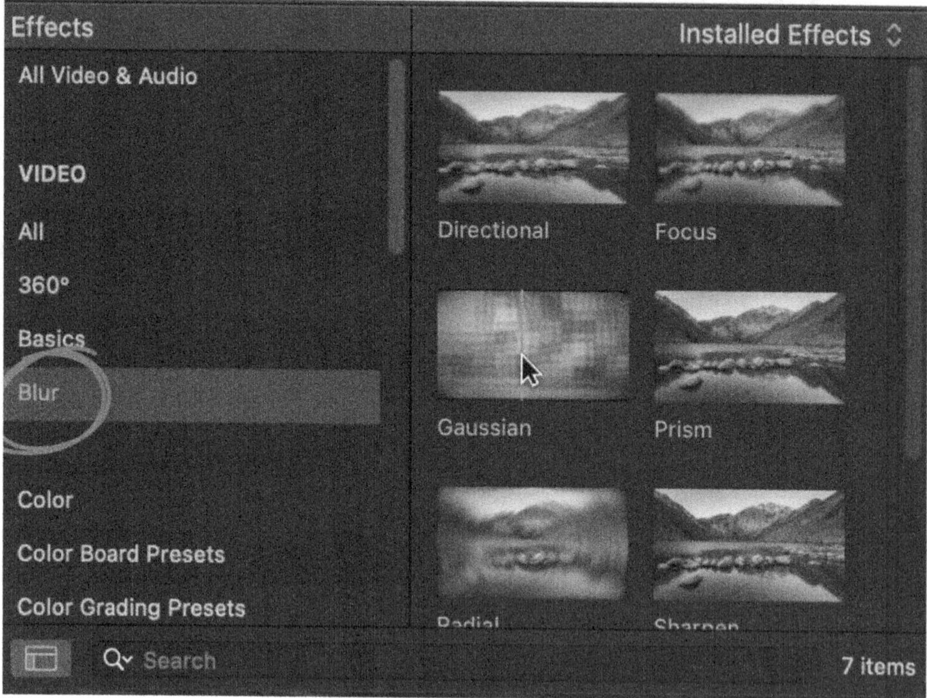

Figure 6.3: Select a Blur effect

Here's an alternative way to apply an effect – with a clip selected in the Timeline, simply double-click on an effect, and it will be applied to the selected clip. Multiple effects can be applied to the same clip.

6. In the Inspector panel near the top, under the **Effects** category, note that there are two sections of effects called **Glass Block** and **Gaussian**. Click on the title edge, that is, the top of the effect section with the name of the effect, and the effect section becomes selected with a yellow outline.

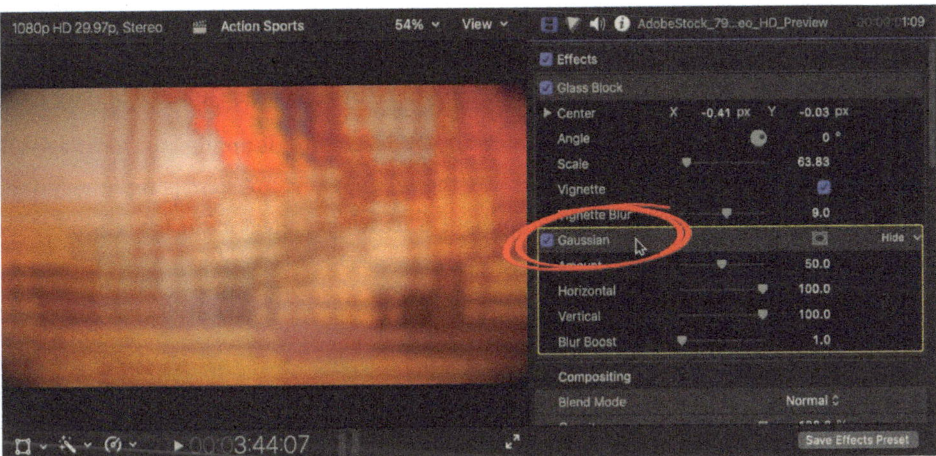

Figure 6.4: Select an effect in the Inspector panel

7. Effects are applied in order from the top down. Notice that previously, in *Figure 6.4*, **Glass Block** is applied first, and then the **Gaussian** blur is applied second, so that it blurs the edges of the glass block. However, let's swap the order. Click and hold on the title bar for the **Gaussian** effect and drag it above the **Glass Block** effect, as in *Figure 6.5*. It should snap into place like the Magnetic Timeline.

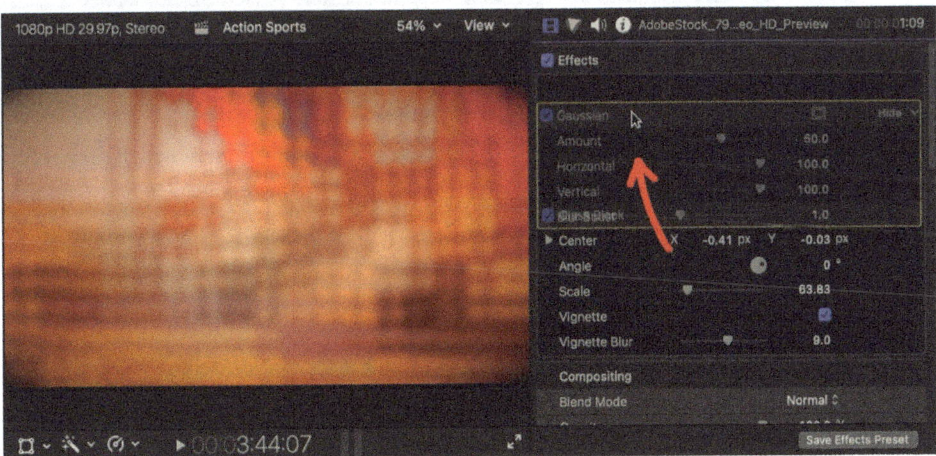

Figure 6.5: Move the order of effects

If you look at *Figure 6.6*, our clip in the Viewer panel looks different. So, the answer to the question of how effects are applied to a clip is that they are applied from the top down. The **Gaussian** blur is applied first, and then the **Glass Block** effect is applied second. The glass block edges are sharp because the **Gaussian** blur is applied to the image before the **Glass Block** effect. Explore reversing the order again and even using other effects to see that the first effect in the list is applied, and the next effect in the list is applied to the clip with the previous effect.

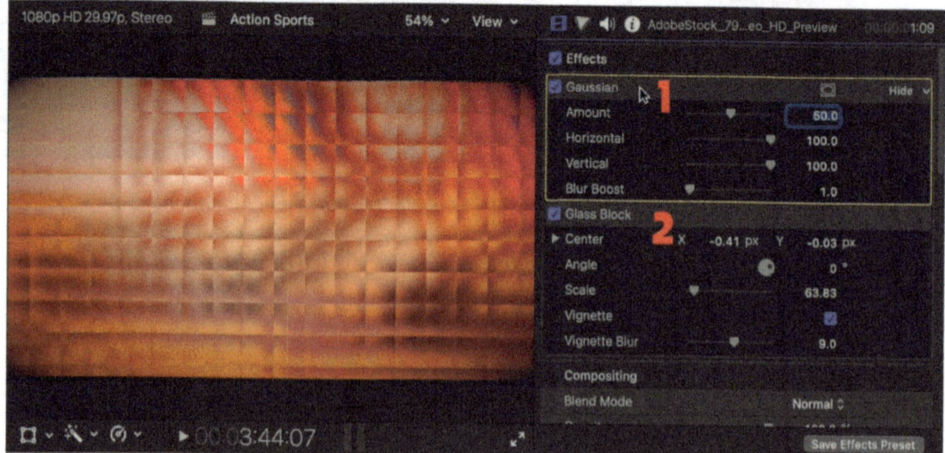

Figure 6.6: Effects are applied top-down

More than one effect can be applied to clips, and the order in which they are applied to the image makes a difference!

There's more...

You can also apply effects to clips in the Timeline from effects listed in the Inspector panel of another clip. Click on the title line of an effect in Inspector and drag it straight onto another clip in the Timeline.

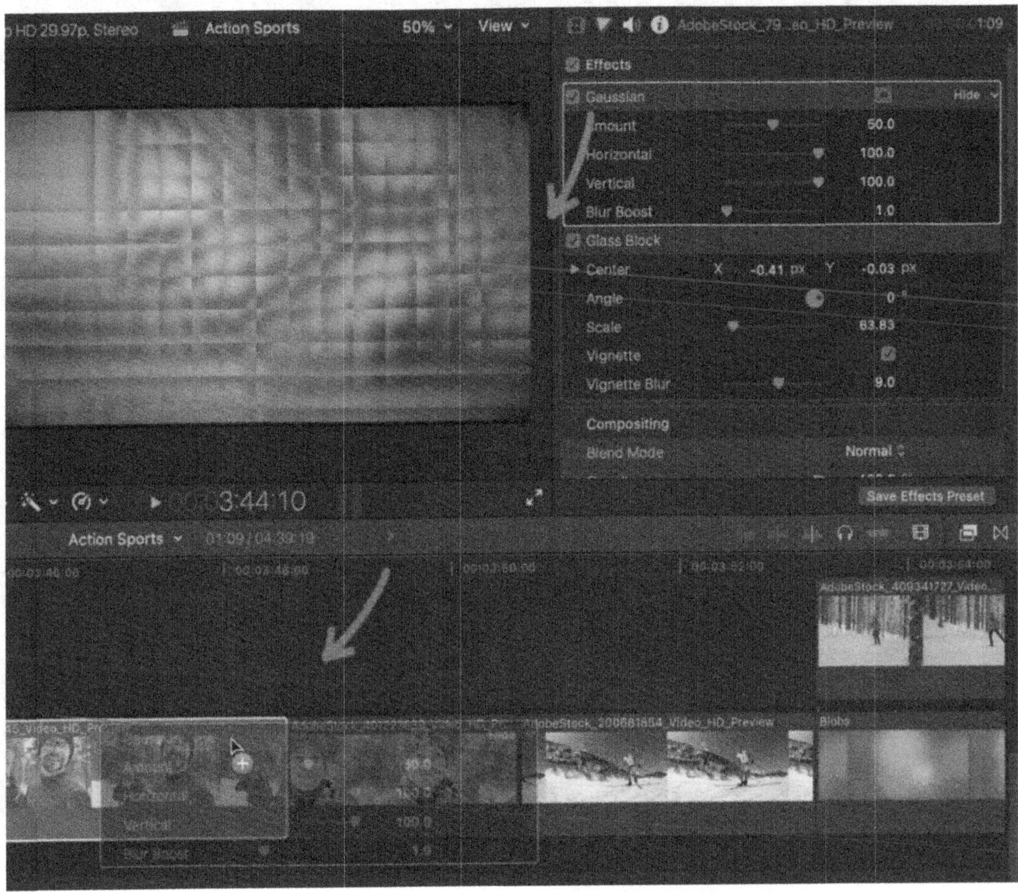

Figure 6.7: Drag the effect from the Inspector panel to another clip

In addition, effects can be copied from one clip to one or more clips. In my example, I have added a comic look effect and have scaled one clip in my Timeline project.

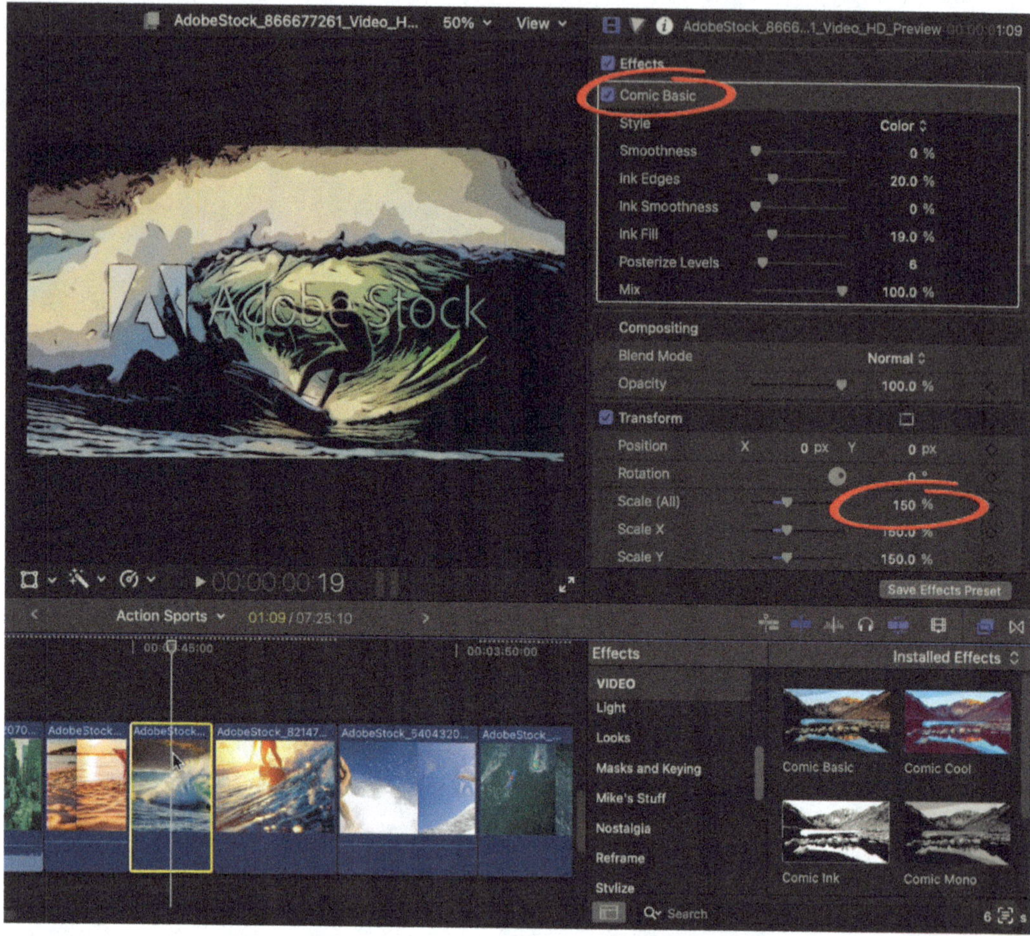

Figure 6.8: Note the Comic Basic effect and 150% scale applied to this clip

Let's copy these attributes to other clips. With the clip that has the effect selected, copy it with the keyboard shortcut of *Command + C*. Select one or more different clips in your project. To simply paste all of the effects from the first clip to the others, go to the **Edit** menu and select **Paste Effects** or use the keyboard shortcut *Option + Command + V*. Perhaps you only want to paste selected attributes. In that case, from the **Edit** menu, select **Paste Attributes...**, or use the keyboard shortcut of *Shift + Command + V*.

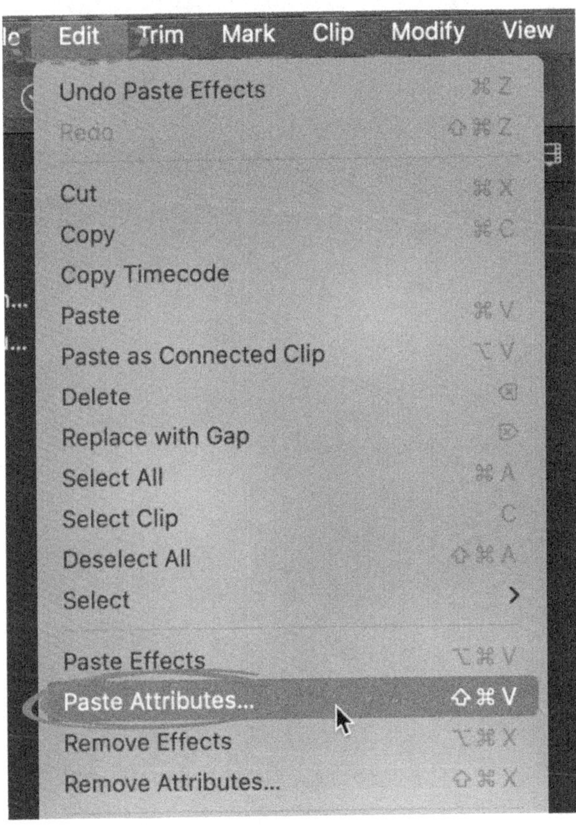

Figure 6.9: Select Paste Attributes... from the Edit menu

A dialog box is displayed. Select the video or audio attributes you want to transfer to the other clips and click on the **Paste** button.

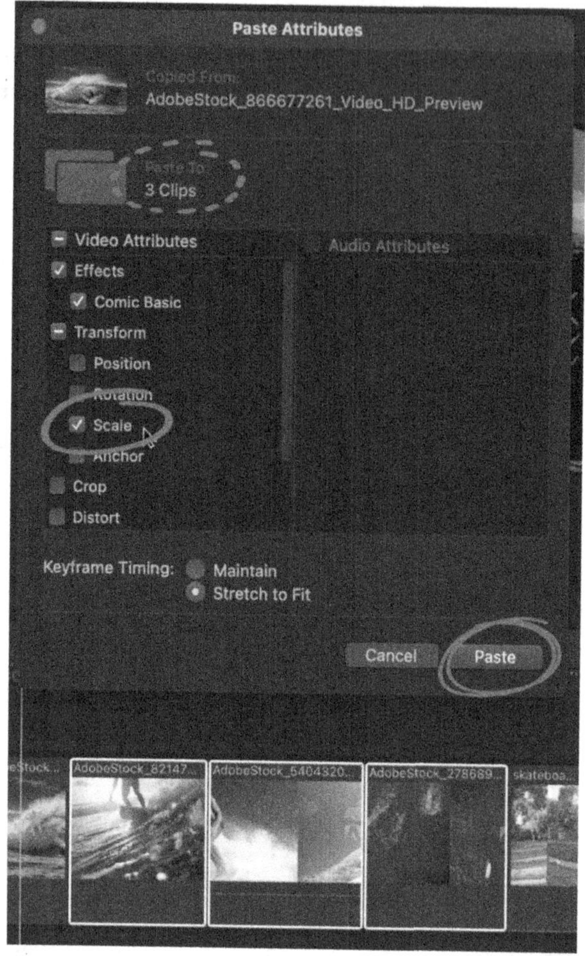

Figure 6.10: Select the video and audio attributes and click on the Paste button

Notice that from the **Edit** menu, you can also select **Remove Effects** and **Remove Attributes…**, which will, as you can probably surmise, remove all effects or display a dialog box to select certain effects to remove.

Stacking adjustment clips

Stacking adjustment clips in Final Cut Pro allows you to apply multiple effects, color corrections, or modifications across multiple clips at once, streamlining your workflow. This technique keeps your Timeline organized while making global changes easy to adjust or remove without affecting individual clips. By layering adjustment clips, you can experiment with different looks and effects non-destructively, enhancing flexibility and creativity in your edits.

In this recipe, we will explore how to quickly add adjustment clips and how their stacking order makes a difference.

How to do it...

Just like layering flavors in a perfect dish, stacking adjustment clips lets you blend multiple effects for a rich, polished final cut. Let's go:

1. An adjustment clip is an empty clip that receives effects and is connected on top of the primary storyline. The effects and other adjustments that it holds are then applied to the clips below it. You can add an adjustment clip by using the **Edit** menu and selecting **Add Adjustment Clip**, or use the keyboard shortcut *Option + A*. This connects a 10-second adjustment clip at the position of the playhead.

Figure 6.11: Note the adjustment clip above the primary storyline

2. Add an effect to the adjustment clip as you would any other clip. Select an effect from the Effects Browser panel and drag it onto your adjustment clip. In my example, I added the **Aged Paper** effect.

Figure 6.12: Select an effect and drag it onto an adjustment clip

3. Now, all the clips under the adjustment clip will display the same effect. There is a quick way to add an adjustment clip with an effect already applied. Click above a clip in your Timeline to park the playhead, and deselect any clips or adjustment clips. Select an effect in the Effects Browser panel, then press the keyboard shortcut of *Option + A*. This will add the adjustment clip at the position of the playhead and give it the name of the effect. In my example, I added an adjustment clip with the **Comic Mono** effect.

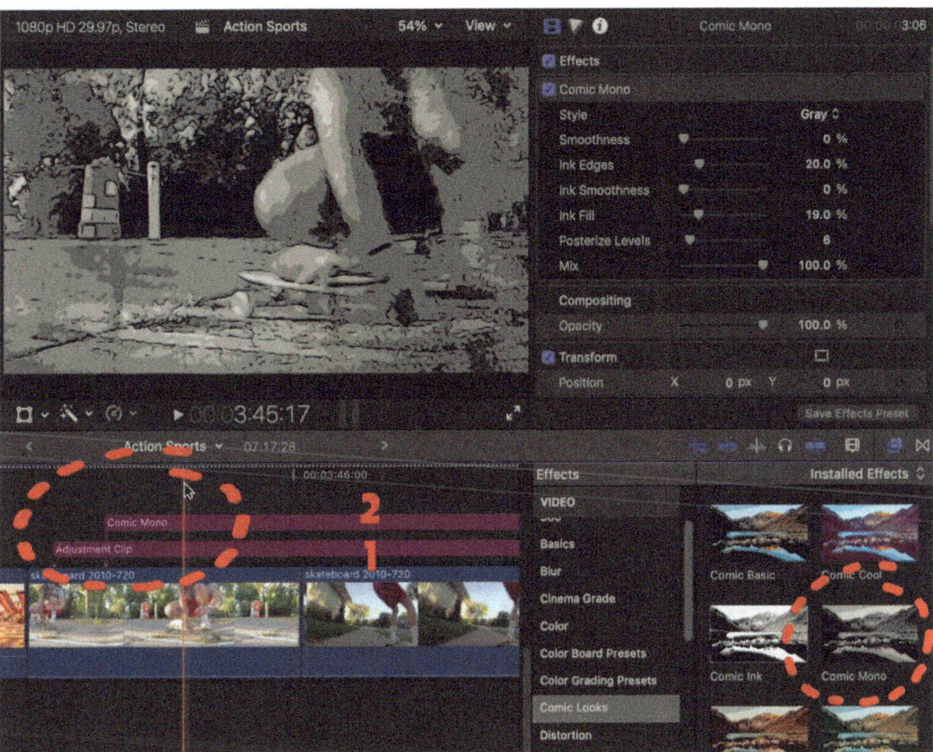

Figure 6.13: Select an effect and add it to the Timeline with the keyboard shortcut of Option + A

4. Experiment by stacking two adjustment clips on top of each other. In the previous recipe, we learned that when adding effects directly onto a clip, effects are applied from the top down, meaning the first effect in the **Inspector** window is applied, then the second. In contrast, when using adjustment clips in the Timeline, the effects are applied from the bottom up. The image flow starts with our actual clip, then, in my example, **Aged Paper**, and then a monochrome comic look. My resulting image is black and white.

5. Let's test this using a nifty keyboard shortcut to move adjustment clips to a different order. With your bottom adjustment clip selected, in my example, **Aged Paper**, press *Option +* ↑ (up arrow). This moves a clip up one layer and swaps places with the clip above it.

Figure 6.14: Use the keyboard shortcut of Option + ↑ (up arrow) to move an adjustment clip up one layer

6. Now we see that, after the base clip's image, the flow goes through the black and white comic mono effect, then the **Aged Paper** effect, which has the brown tint. The results have a brown tint. This confirms that our image flow is from the bottom up in the Timeline. Experiment with a few different effects and their order of being applied.

7. But wait, there is more. Adjustment clips can receive color correction, transformation, and other modifications that will be addressed in the other recipes in this chapter and the next. Almost anything applied to a clip can be applied to an adjustment clip and displayed in all the clips below it. But adjustment clips can also receive transitions. Change from the Effects Browser panel to the Transition Browser panel by clicking on the **Hide or Show Transitions Browser** icon that looks like a bow tie and is located in the upper-right corner of the Timeline panel. Select a transition of your choice and add it to your adjustment layer as you would a connected clip.

Figure 6.15: Click on the Hide or Show Transitions Browser button

8.   Experiment with various transitions, effects, and color corrections. Note that the effects are displayed with all the clips under a particular adjustment clip.

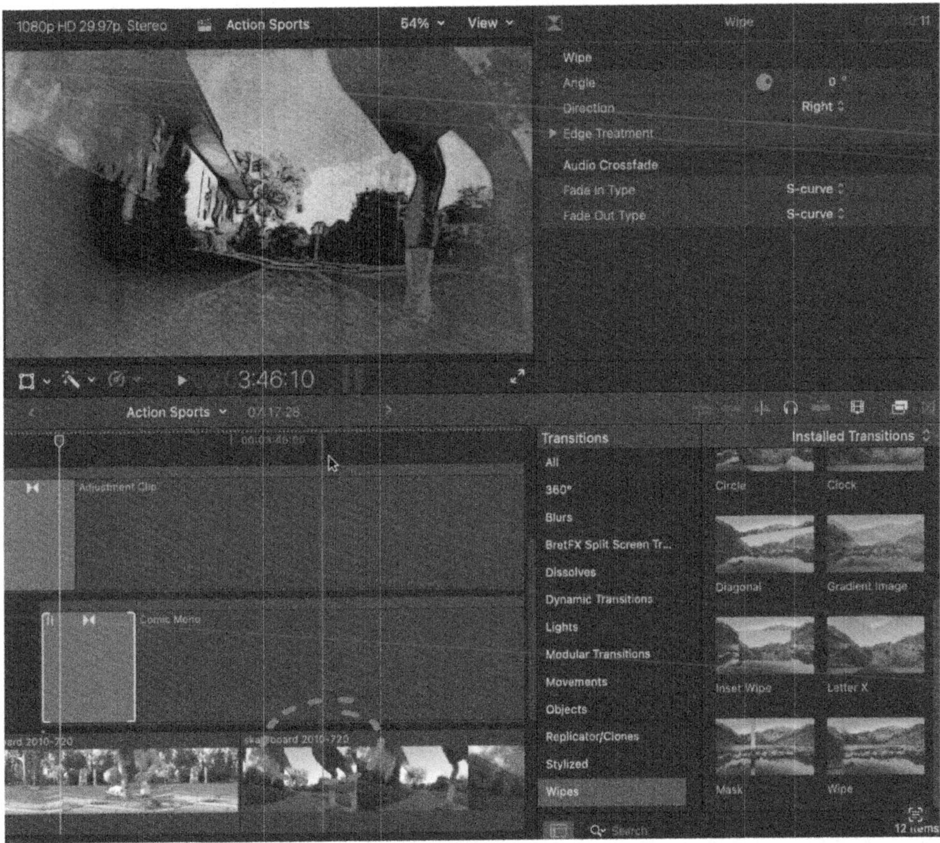

Figure 6.16: Note the effects displayed on all the clips under the adjustment clips

Creating a custom Color Board preset effect

Think of your custom color preset as your house dressing – once you've nailed your custom blend, it pulls the whole dish together. Creating a custom Color Board preset effect in Final Cut Pro involves applying specific color adjustments, such as LUTs, color wheels, or custom filters, to achieve a desired visual style or mood. By crafting a custom Color Board preset, you can give your footage a cohesive aesthetic, from warm and vintage tones to cool, modern styles, helping to reinforce the emotion or tone of your project. A custom Color Board preset brings consistency across your clips, elevating the professional quality of your video while enhancing storytelling through color.

In this recipe, we will explore using the Effects Browser panel to add color style to your clips and how to save the custom Color Board preset that you create.

How to do it...

Let's check out how to customize color effects:

1. Add a clip to your project in the Timeline panel, then *Option + click* on it so that both the clip is selected and the playhead is parked on top of it.

2. In the Effects Browser panel, select the **Color Board Presets** category. This is a collection of different stylized color looks with names that relate to how they will affect your clip. As you skim through the different effects, you can see a preview in the Viewer panel. Pick one that is a very distinctive effect to customize. In my example, I'm going to select a preset color look called **Night**. Drag an effect of your choice onto your clip to apply it.

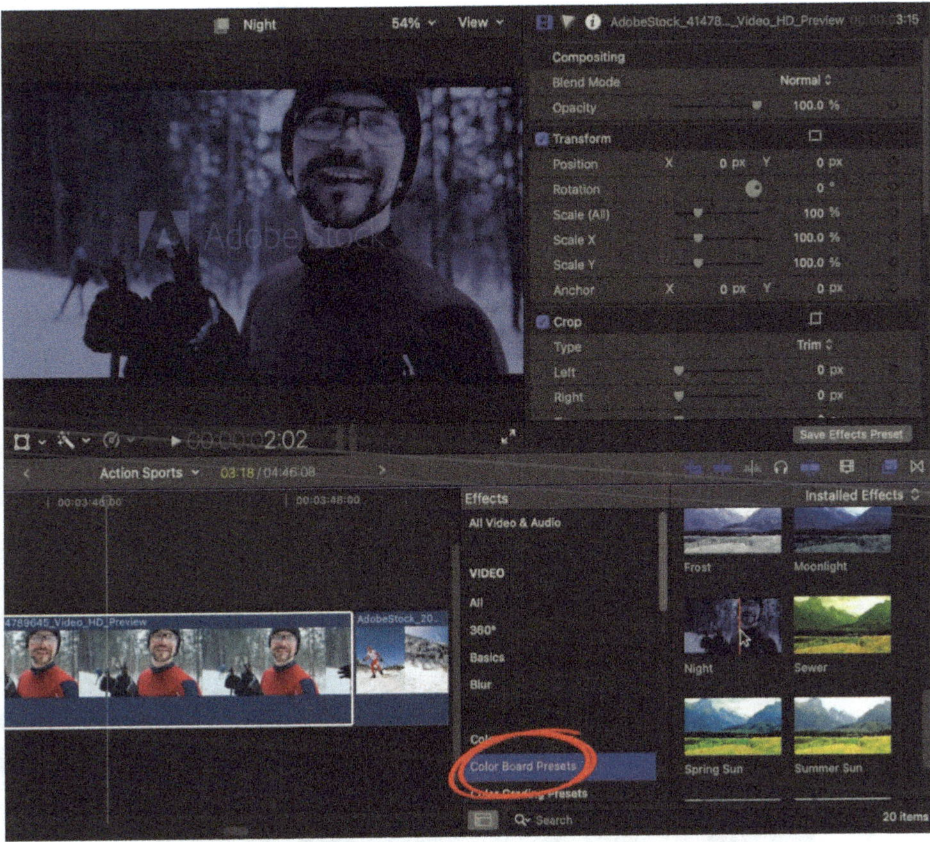

Figure 6.17: Browse the Color Board Presets options

3. In the Inspector panel, note that an effect called **Color Board 1** has been added. In the title row of **Color Board 1**, click on the **Color Inspector** icon, which looks like a color gradient triangle. This will switch to the **Color Inspector** view, and that is where we can customize the effect.

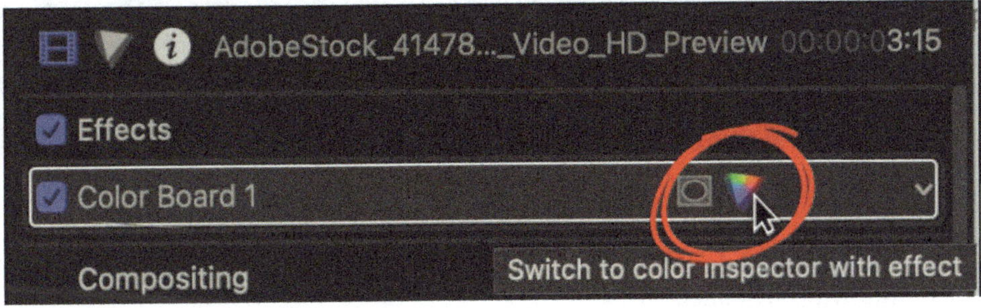

Figure 6.18: Click on the Color Inspector icon in an effect

4. If it is not already selected, click on the **Color** tab near the top of the Color Inspector panel. In my example, I can see that the shadows, mid-tones, and highlights are skewed toward the blue to make it look like night. Just to create a big difference, I'm going to change the color of the effect to be greener by sliding the **Global** button. You can choose any sort of change because this is mostly for an experiment in creating custom color looks. For more information on adjusting color, see *Chapter 5* and the recipe called *Using Color Board, Wheels, and Curves*.

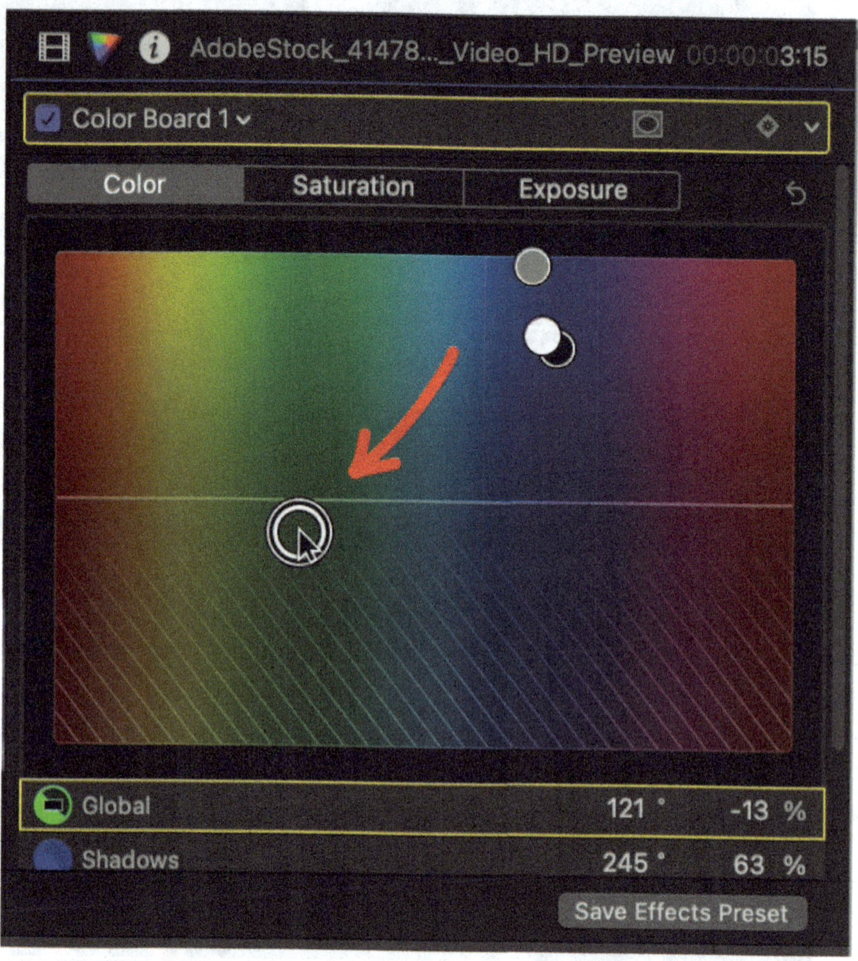

Figure 6.19: Change the Color preset

5. Once done, click on the **Save Effects Preset** button located in the lower-right corner of the Inspector panel.

6. A dialog box comes up with the chance to name this new custom color look. I'm going to call it My Night Look. Then, from the **Category** drop-down menu, select the **Effects** category in which you want the effect to be saved. In my example, I am going to put it with the others and select **Color Board Presets**. Click on the **Save** button in the bottom-right corner.

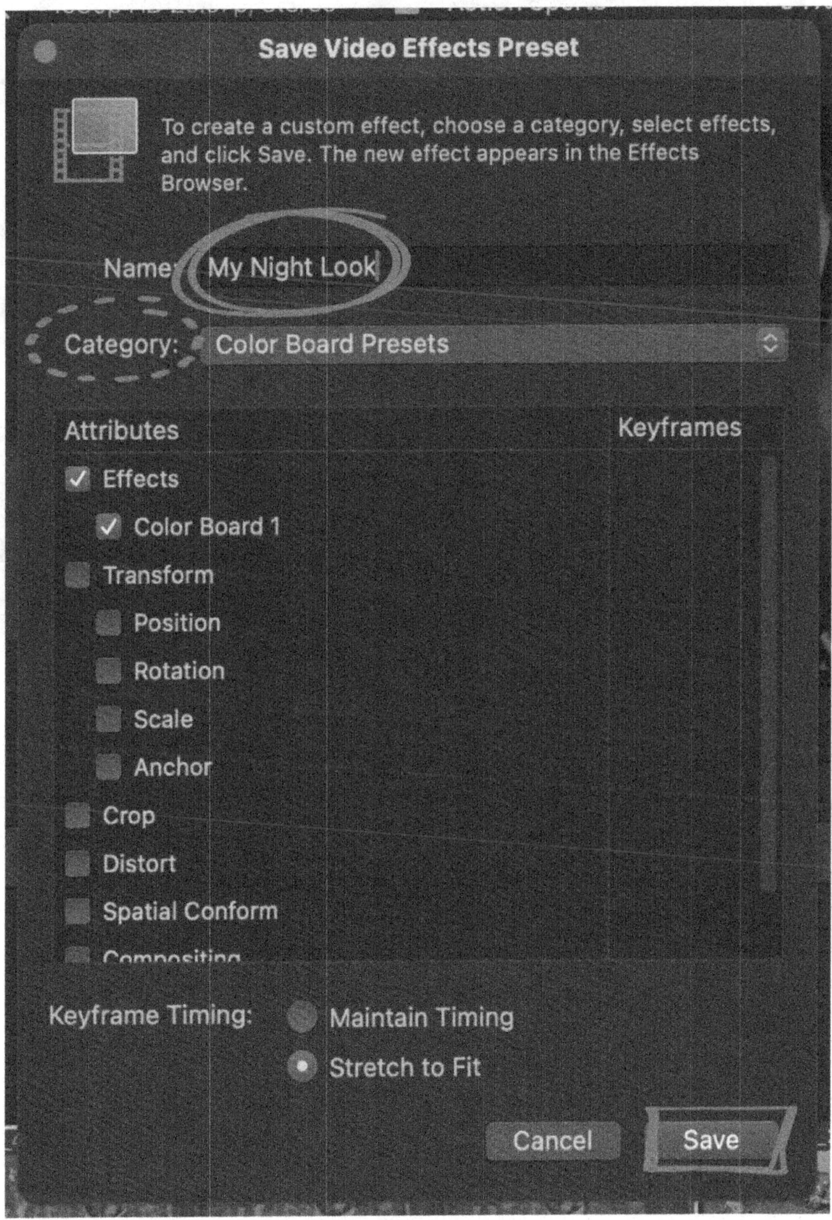

Figure 6.20: Save a custom Color look

Note that, in my example effect, **My Night Look** is saved as a preset within the **Color Board Presets** effects category.

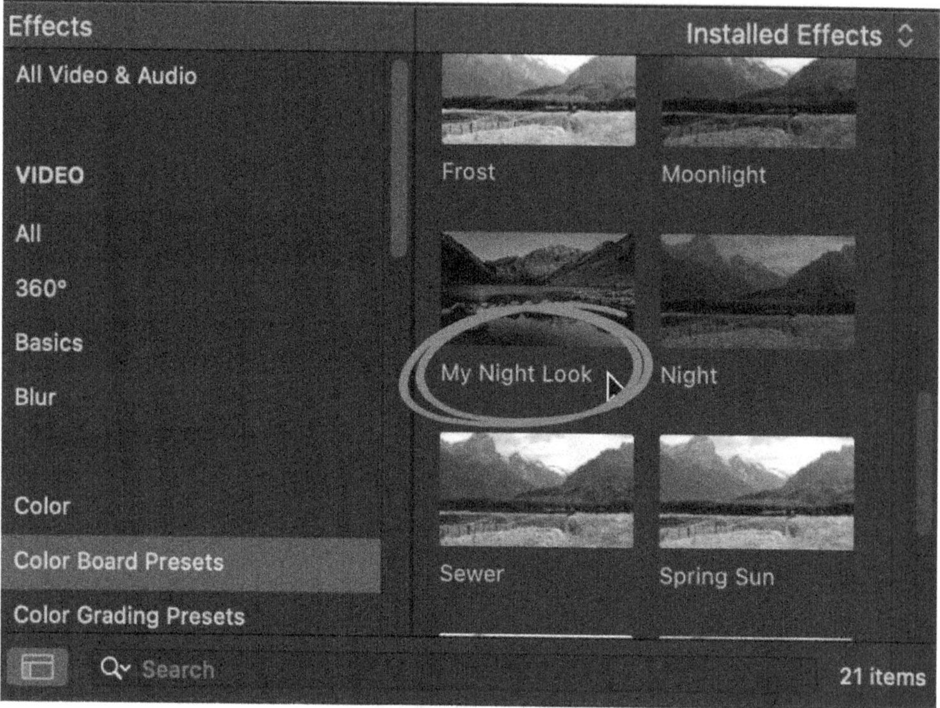

Figure 6.21: Saved custom colors appear in the Effects Browser panel

There's more...

Notice that you can *right-click* on the effect and select **Reveal in Finder**. It is in the Pro Apps folder of **Application Support**. This way, you'll be able to take that preset with you to other computers and always have your custom **Color Board** preset available.

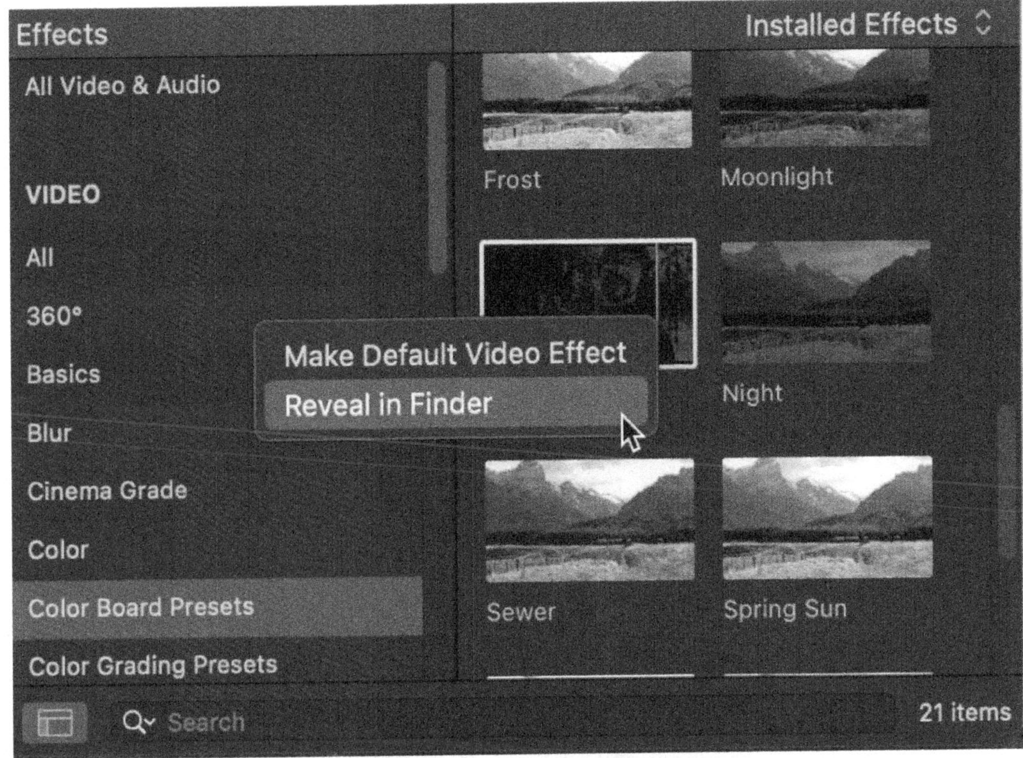

Figure 6.22: Locate your custom look in the Finder

Using the Color Adjustments effect

The **Color Adjustments** effect in Final Cut Pro provides a streamlined way to modify exposure, saturation, and color temperature all in one place, making color correction faster, more efficient, and more intuitive.

Within the **Color Adjustments** effect, **Enhance Light and Color** uses machine learning to analyze video clips and automatically enhance the tonal range of an image, removing any visible color cast. With a simple interface, you can quickly balance highlights, shadows, and midtones or adjust the overall warmth or coolness of your footage.

In this recipe, we will apply the **Color Adjustments** effect to clips using several different methods.

Getting ready

You will need some clips that require color adjustments in order to see the changes applied.

How to do it...

Is **Enhance Light and Color** the "one color adjustment to rule them all" (use Gandalf's voice)? Let's find out:

1. Add a clip to your project in the Timeline panel – this should be a clip in which the color is a little bit off and needs to be fixed. *Option + click* on it, so that both the clip is selected and the playhead is parked on top of it.

2. The **Color Adjustments** effect can be applied in several ways:

   - Here's the first method. Start by clicking on the **Enhancement** icon, which looks like a magic wand, located in the lower-left corner of the Viewer panel. In the drop-down menu, select **Enhance Light and Color**.

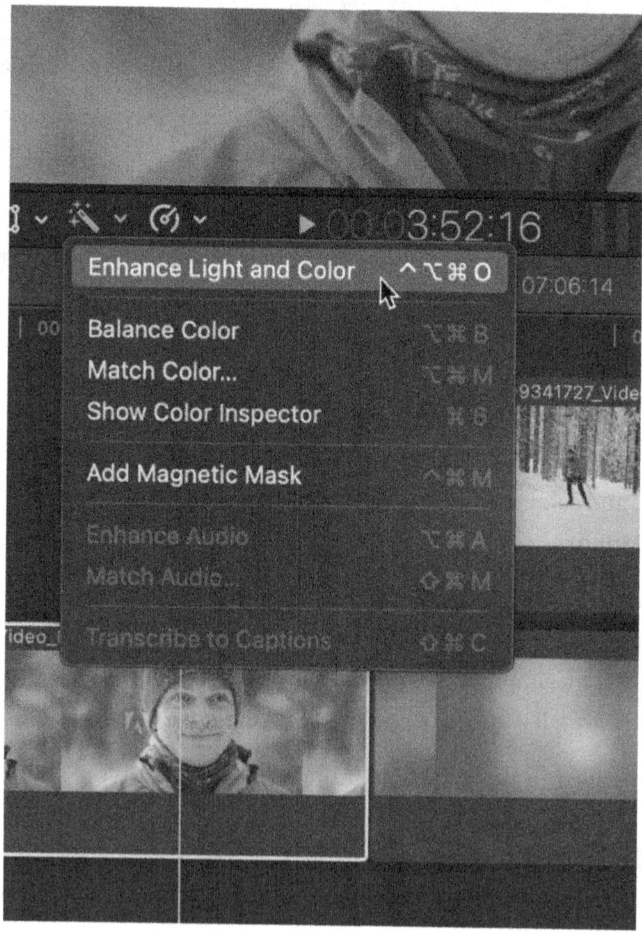

Figure 6.23: Select Enhance Light and Color from the Enhancement menu

In the Inspector panel, we can see a **Color Adjustments** effect with the **Enhanced Light and Color** interface. This is an effect that uses machine learning to analyze the image and make adjustments.

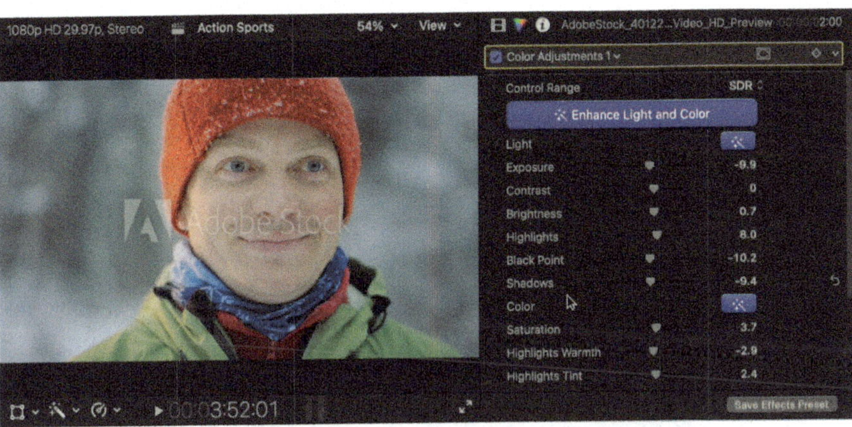

Figure 6.24: The Enhance Light and Color interface in the Color Adjustments effect

The **Control Range** option is used to select the correct brightness for both **standard dynamic range (SDR)** and high dynamic range clips. In my example, **SDR** was automatically selected for **Control Range**.

Also, notice that in the middle of the interface, there are two magic wand icons that indicate automatic adjustments separately for **Light** and **Color**. You can manually adjust any of the enhancement sliders. Note that when you make a change, the automatic **Color** or **Light** magic wand icons turn gray.

- The second method of adding this effect is from the Effects Browser panel. In the Effects Browser panel, click on the category of **Color** and select the **Color Adjustments** effect. Apply this to a clip by double-clicking on the effect or dragging it onto a clip in the Timeline.

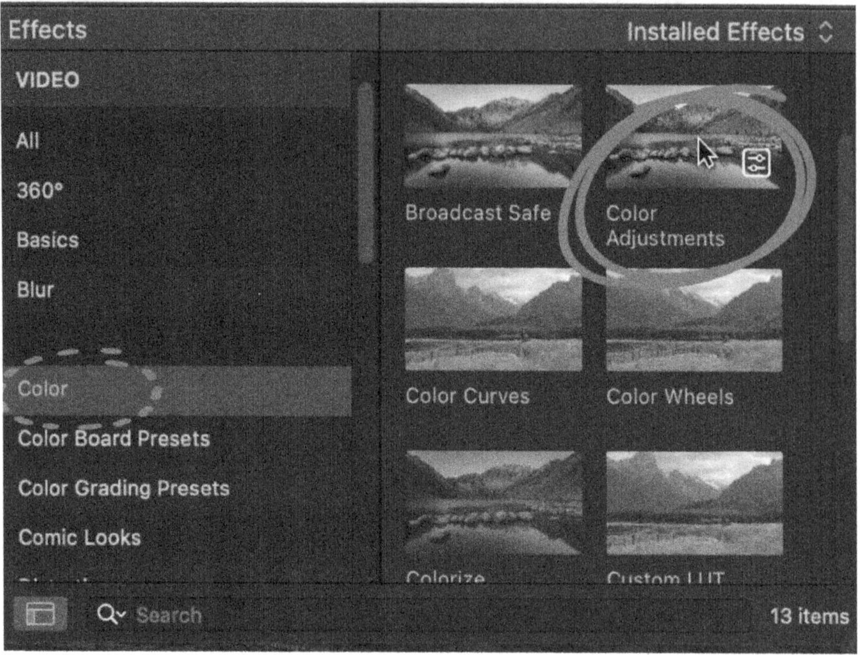

Figure 6.25: Select the Color Adjustments effect from the Color category

This will apply the same **Color Adjustments** effect and display the same **Enhanced Light and Color** interface in the Inspector panel.

- The third way to apply this effect is in the **Color Inspector** area of the Inspector panel. In the upper-left corner of the Inspector panel, click on the **Color Inspector** icon. It looks like a triangle and, when you click on it, you will see that it changes to a color gradient. Click on **No Corrections** to bring up the **Add Color Corrections** drop-down menu, then select **+Color Adjustments**.

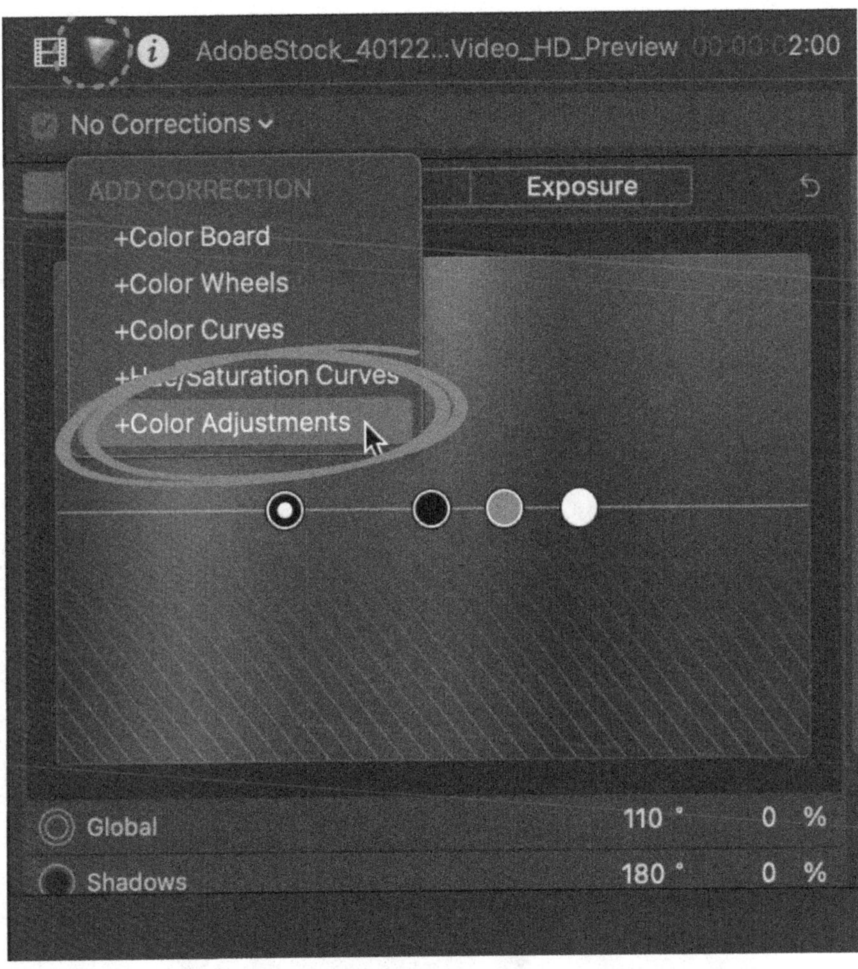

Figure 6.26: Select +Color Adjustments from the Add Color Corrections menu

3. Regardless of how the effect is added to a clip, the **Enhance Light and Color** interface is
    the same. If you were to make manual adjustments to the effect, the blue **Enhance Light
    and Color** turns gray to reflect that it is no longer set by the software. Also, note that you
    can save this custom **Color Adjustments** effect by clicking on the **Save Effects Preset**
    button in the lower-right corner of the Color Inspector panel. This will bring up a dialog
    box to name your effect and save it into a category in the Effects Browser panel.

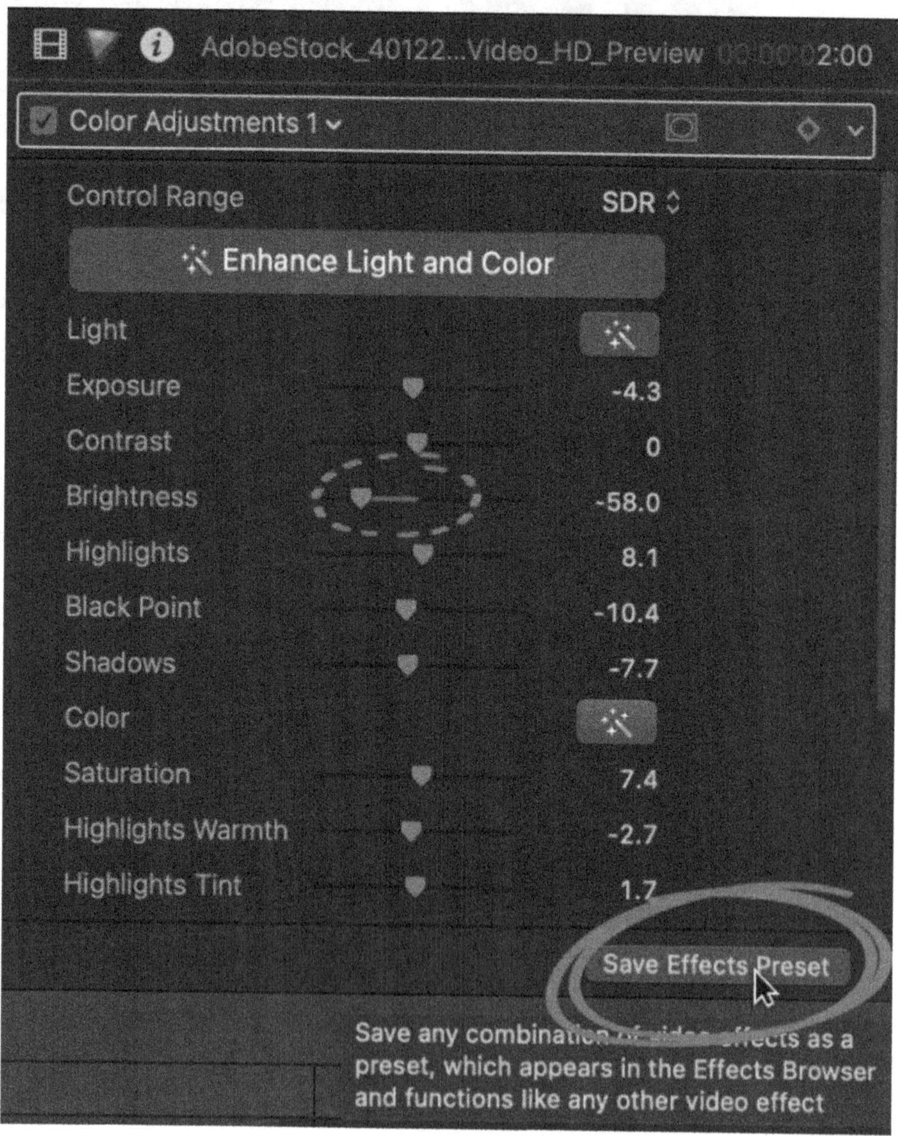

Figure 6.27: Save Effects Preset from the Color Adjustments effect

There's more...

The **Color Adjustments** effect uses machine learning to analyze the frame of video from the position of the playhead in order to automatically enhance the tonal range of the clip. To reset the analysis, click on the **Enhance Light and Color** button to turn it off – the button will turn gray. Then, move the playhead to a new position in the clip. Click on the **Enhance Light and Color** button again to turn it on – the button will turn blue again. This will reanalyze the image and change the color adjustment settings.

Using the Custom LUT effect

Custom LUTs are your made-from-scratch frosting – adding that perfect, polished finish to your visual cake. In Final Cut Pro, the **Custom LUT** effect allows you to apply a specific LUT to a single clip, transforming its color and tone based on a preset or custom color profile. By using a Custom LUT, you can quickly achieve a stylized or professional-grade look, whether you're aiming for a cinematic feel, matching footage from different cameras, or applying a specific visual mood.

In this recipe, we will use the Custom LUT effect to apply a LUT to a clip in a Timeline project without affecting the footage the clip is part of.

Getting ready

To follow along with this recipe, you will need some footage that is in a raw or log format and that is *ungraded*. A few stock media websites will have some footage, but you may need to broaden your internet search.

See *Chapter 5* and the recipe called *Applying LUTs to raw files* for more information about working with footage in the Event Browser panel.

How to do it...

Adding a LUT to a specific clip is straightforward. Let's get to it:

1. Add a clip to your project in the Timeline panel. *Option + click* on it, so that both the clip is selected and the playhead is parked on top of it.

2. In the Effects Browser panel, select the **Color** category and scroll down to find the effect called **Custom LUT**. Double-click on that effect or drag it to your clip to apply it.

3. In the Inspector panel, under the **Effects** category, there's a title row called **Custom LUT**. Click on the **LUT** drop-down menu. By default, **None** will be selected, but select **Choose Custom LUT...** instead.

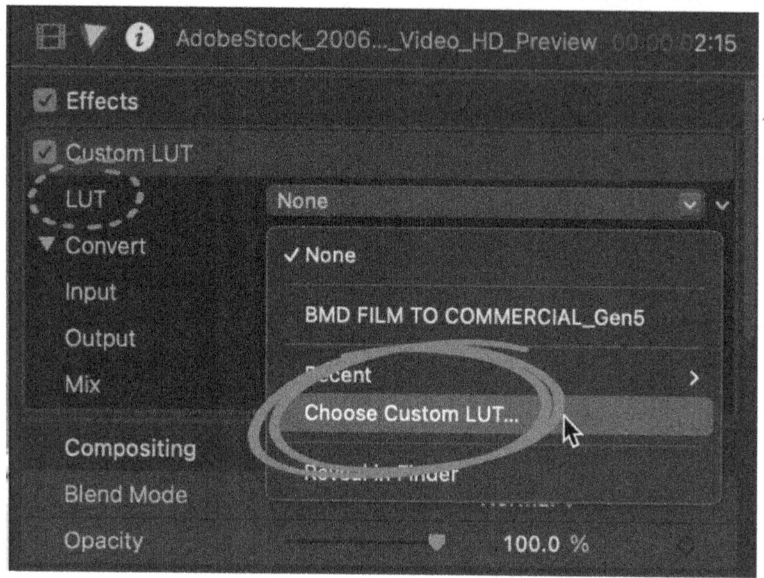

Figure 6.28: Select Choose Custom LUT... from the LUT menu

4. I'm going to add a LUT that I've downloaded for free. There are many paid and free LUT files available for Final Cut Pro on the interwebs. Check out Color Grading Central, Motion Array, or Envato, to name just a few. Notice that these files will be .cube files. Often, LUTs are used to set proper color settings based on a camera's specifications. In my example, I want to stylize my clip. I have a LUT file called Matrix that sounds cool. In the dialog window, navigate to the LUT file you wish to apply, select it, and click on the **Open** button. That LUT is applied to just that clip and not all the footage in the Event Browser.

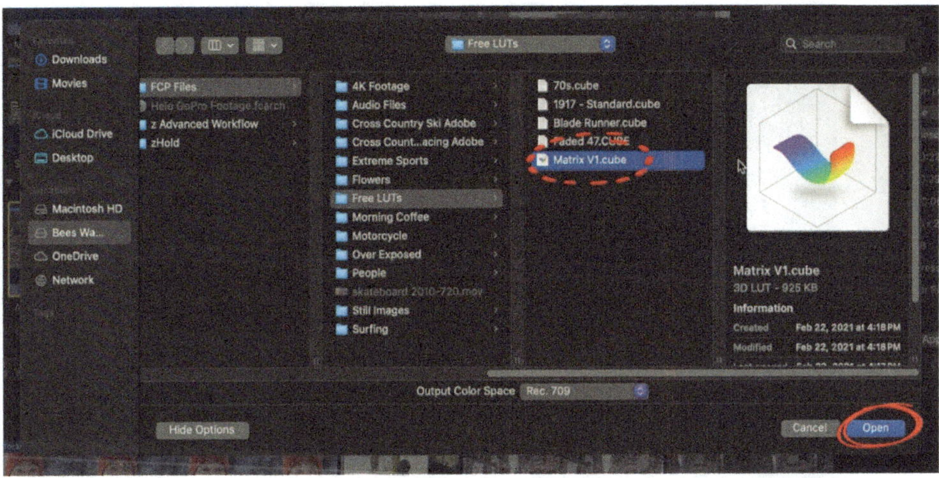

Figure 6.29: Select a LUT file to apply

5. Now, instead of using a color LUT to convert the camera data to a normal HD color space, the data from the camera is converted to colors within a **Matrix**-style movie.

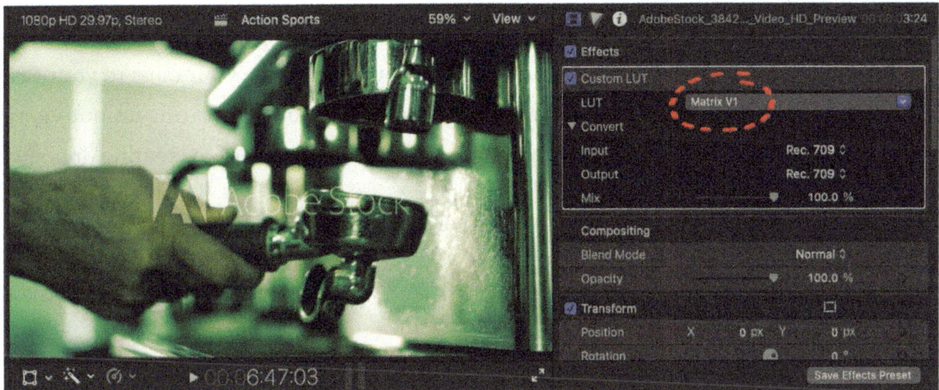

Figure 6.30: The result of applying a Custom LUT effect

6. The LUT is added to your **LUT** parameter drop-down menu in the **Custom LUT** effect. In addition, at the bottom of the **LUT** drop-down menu is the ability to select **Reveal in Finder**. You'll be able to find the selected camera LUT in the **Application Support** | Pro Apps folder. That way, you can transfer LUTs to other computers and have all your LUTs ready to get cooking.

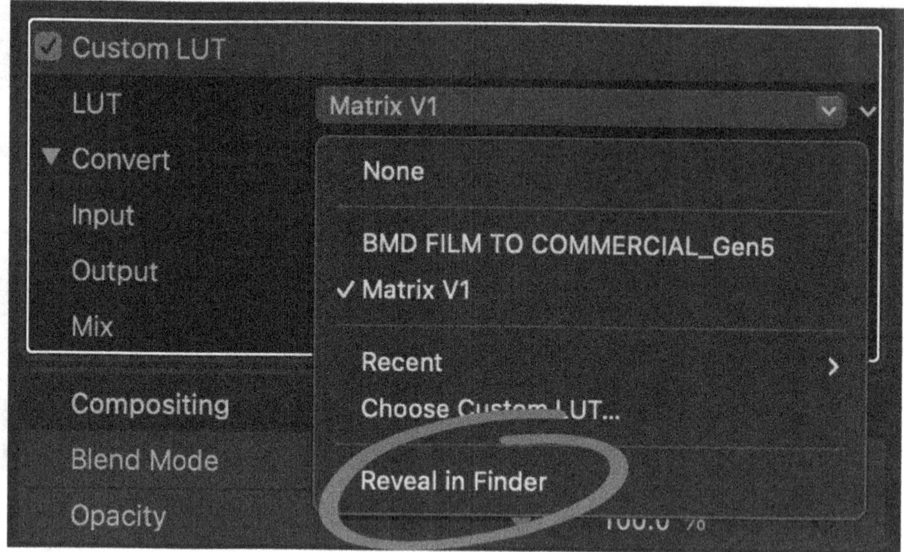

Figure 6.31: Find the Custom LUT in the Finder

Using blend modes

It's all in how you mix them. Blend modes allow you to combine your clips to your taste by adjusting how the pixels from one layer interact with those below it, creating unique visual effects. You can achieve a variety of looks, from enhancing contrast and color to creating dreamy overlays or stylized textures.

The advantage of blend modes is their ability to add depth and complexity to your compositions, providing creative control to achieve professional, eye-catching effects without the need for additional plugins or tools.

In this recipe, we will experiment with blend modes such as **Overlay** and **Darken** to discover the interaction of one image with another.

Getting ready

You will need a high-contrast clip of someone moving that was shot with a tripod.

How to do it...

Blend modes are the fusion cuisine of video editing. Let's mix it up:

1. A straightforward way to experiment with blend modes is to blend an image clip with a background graphic. Let's start by adding a generator to your Timeline. We explored some generators in *Chapter 4* in the recipe called *Using gap clips and placeholder clips*. In the upper-right corner of the Final Cut Pro interface, click on the **Show Titles and Generators** icon (it looks like a square with a T in it on top of another square). From **Generators**, select the **Backgrounds** category. These are nice because they loop and can be placed in a series. Select one and add it to your Timeline. In my example, I've added the orange **Blobs** generator to the primary storyline.

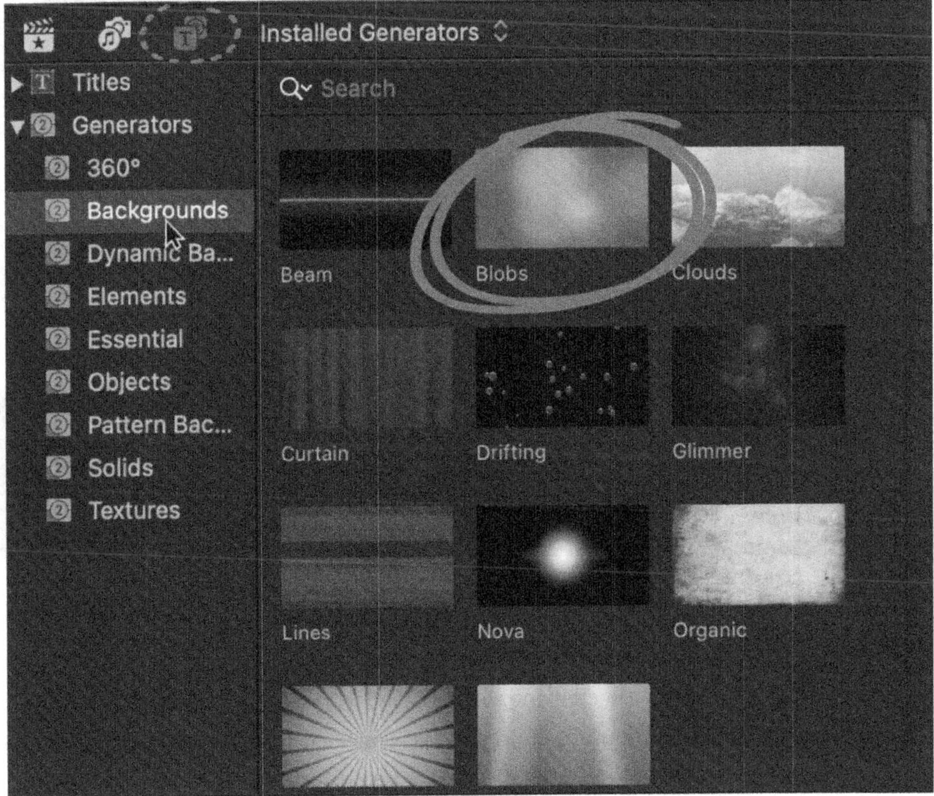

Figure 6.32: Select a background generator

2. Next to the **Show Titles and Generators** icon, click on the **Show Libraries** icon (it looks like a star on a movie slate). From your current library and event, select a clip from your Event Browser panel and connect it on top of the generator we just added to the project. In my example, I have a clip of a skier. Edit the size of the generator and the new clip to be the same size, as shown in *Figure 6.33*.

Figure 6.33: Connect a clip on top of a generator

3. Now, we want to blend the clip and the generator together. *Option + click* on the clip on top so that it is both selected and the playhead is parked on top of it. That's the clip that's going to get the blend mode change. This is because blend modes are applied to the top clip and blended down, not up.

4. In the upper portion of the Inspector panel is a section called **Compositing**. The drop-down menu for **Blend Mode** starts with **Normal**. Click on the **Normal** line to see a long menu. We can experiment with all the various blend modes, but oftentimes, the first thing to try is **Overlay**. Select **Overlay** from the menu.

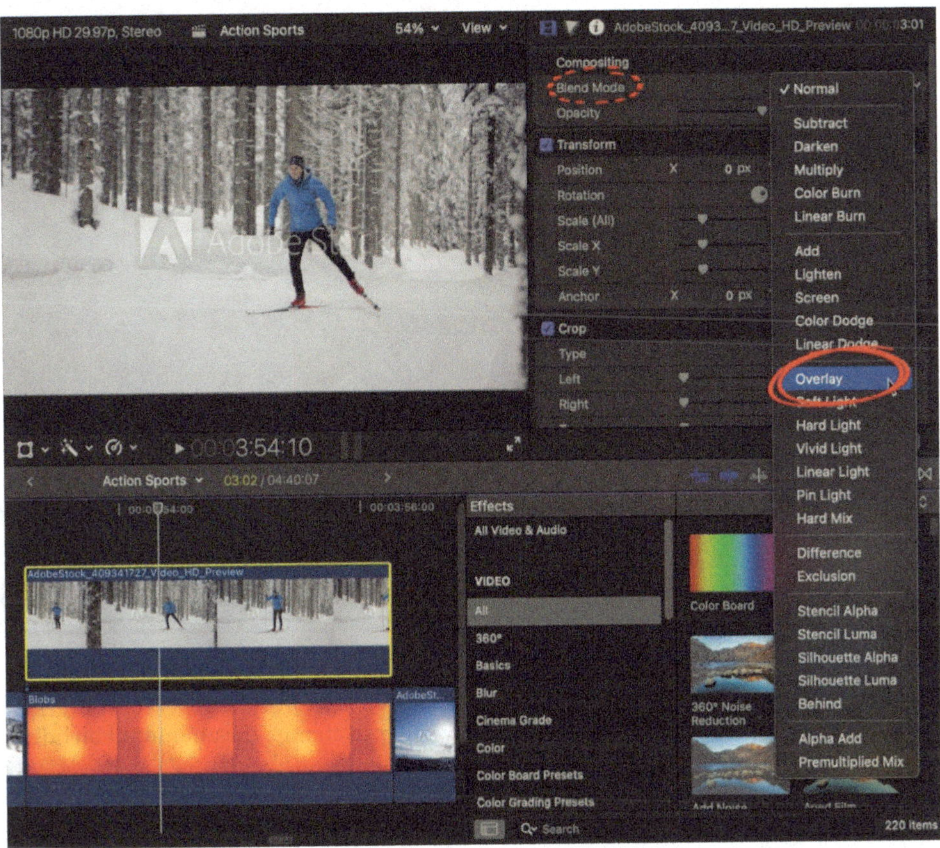

Figure 6.34: Select Overlay from the Blend Mode menu

Overlay is often the best blend mode to try first because it strikes a balance between enhancing contrast and preserving detail in your footage. It combines elements of **Multiply** (darkening) and **Screen** (brightening). **Overlay** makes darker areas richer and lighter areas more vibrant without overwhelming the original image. This makes **Overlay** a good starting point for adding texture and blending layers in a way that feels natural yet impactful.

The results can be amazing. The pixels of the two images are compared and interwoven according to the blend manner specified. Sometimes, the results are unsubstantial because of the way the pixels interact, but the result is always unique and creative.

Figure 6.35: The results of the Overlay blend mode

5. In the Inspector panel, use the **Opacity** slider to change the amount of blending the top image has on the image below.

    You can experiment with the various blend modes to find one that works for the story that you're trying to tell. Perhaps experiment with text for dramatic results.

Creating a freeze-frame effect

Let's use a blend mode to make a fun freeze-frame effect:

1. Add the high-contrast clip mentioned in the *Getting ready* section to your Timeline.

2. In the clip, find just a few places in which we want to see a freeze frame and add a marker in those spots with the keyboard shortcut *M*. See *Chapter 4* and the recipe called *Using markers and the Timeline index*.

3. We are going to connect some freeze frame clips to the Timeline at the markers, so make sure that **Snapping** is turned on. See *Chapter 1* and the recipe called *Taking advantage of the Magnetic Timeline and Position tool* for more information about turning **Snapping** on or off.

4. We're going to do a number of keyboard shortcuts, so get your fingers loosened up. Snap the skimmer to the first marker. *Option + click* on the clip so that it is both selected and the playhead is parked on top of it.

5. Press the keyboard shortcut *Shift + F*. This is a unique shortcut that selects the specific frame of the clip in the source footage in the Event Browser panel. Then, press *Option + F*. This is also unique. It creates a four-second freeze frame clip of that frame and automatically connects it to the Timeline at the position of the playhead.

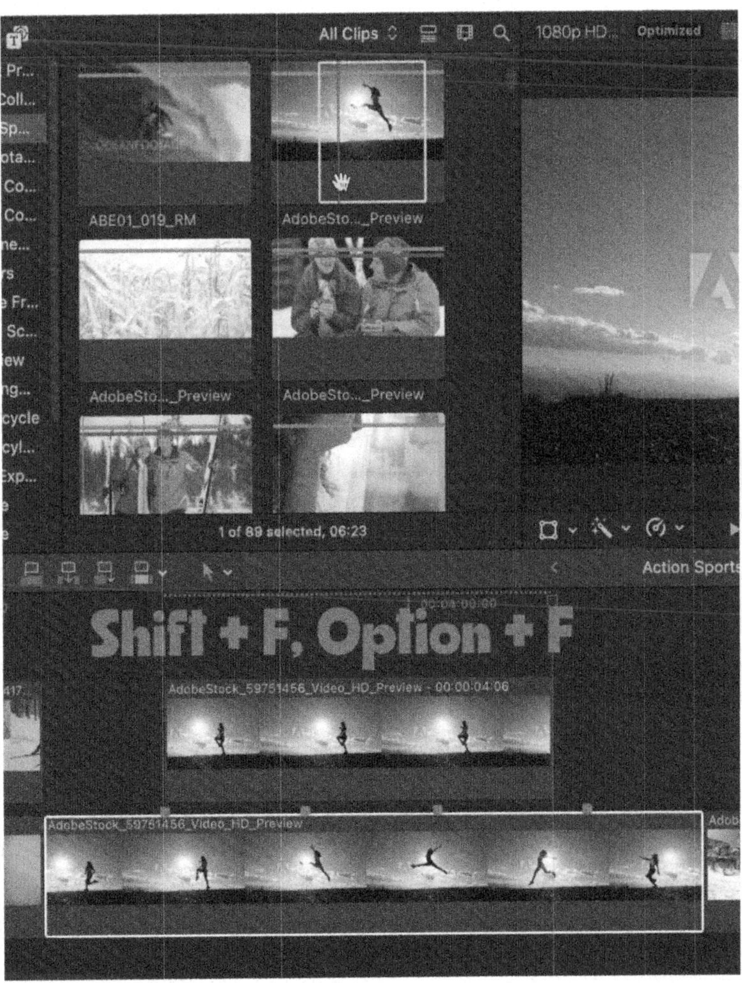

Figure 6.36: Use keyboard shortcuts to select frames and connect them to the Timeline

6. Go back to the Timeline and slide the skimmer to the second marker. Hold down the *Option* key while clicking on the bottom clip so that it is selected and the playhead is parked at the second marker. Repeat the keyboard shortcuts *Shift + F*, then *Option + F* to add a second freeze frame starting at the second marker. You don't have to worry about the length of the clips; we can adjust those later.

7. Do this for each marker that you have. The connected clips might start stacking up, making it hard to see them all. Let's use an applicable keyboard shortcut. Press *Option + Shift + Z*; this will expand or reduce the height of the clips to fit the height of the Timeline panel. And just to remind you, the partner keyboard shortcut of *Shift + Z* will expand or reduce the length of the clips to fit the length of the Timeline panel. Try them out.

8. Adjust the end point of each clip to snap to the end of the original clip in the Timeline. We want to adjust the blend modes of the new connected freeze frames. Hold down the *Command* key and click on each of your connected clips so that they all remain selected.

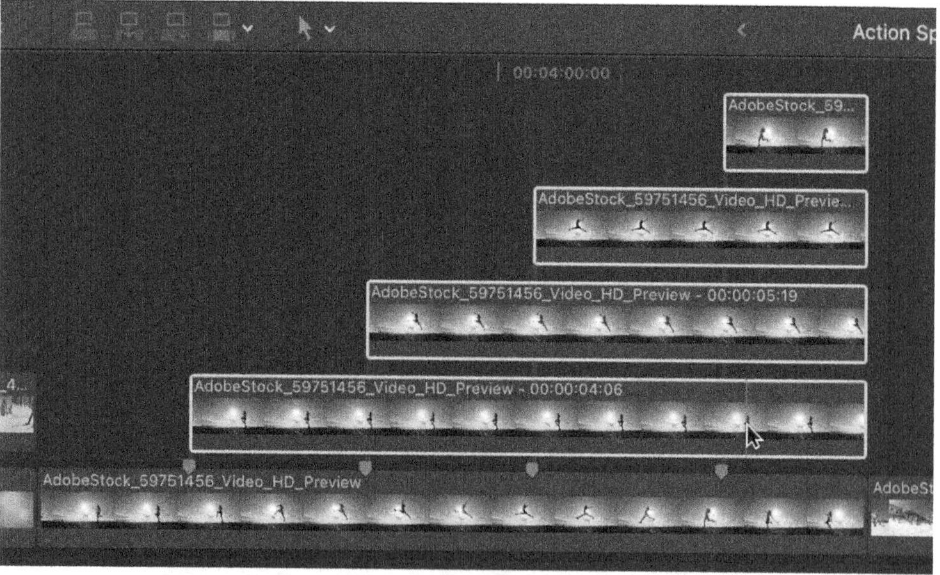

Figure 6.37: Select the connected freeze frame clips

9. In my example, I have four connected clips selected, and at the top of the Inspector panel, it says **Inspecting Four Items**. Use this to verify that all your freeze frame clips are selected. Then, in the Video Information Inspector panel, under **Compositing**, click on the **Blend Mode** drop-down menu and select **Darken**. The blend mode will be applied to all the selected clips.

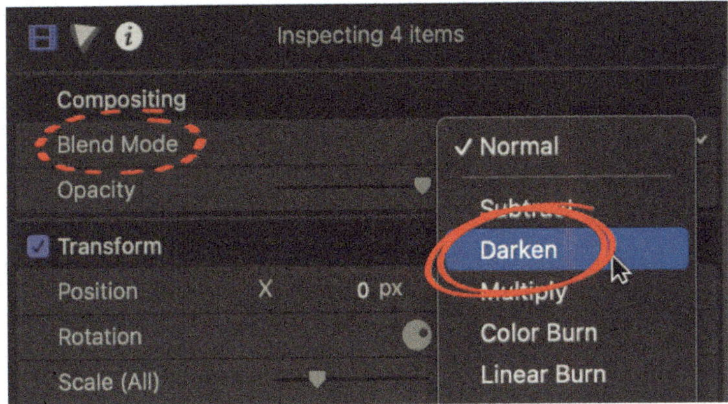

Figure 6.38: Select Darken from the Blend Mode menu

The **Darken** blend mode will show the dark pixels from the images. Because the dark ground did not change, the blend will not be noticed, but the dark pixels of the woman jumping will be added. When we play this clip, it appears that the frozen poses from the image are left behind as the person moves across the screen.

Figure 6.39: The result of freeze frames blended together

10. Note that if your subject is light on a dark background, you'd select the **Lighten** blend mode. In addition, you can also reverse the freeze frame effect and start the freeze frames together at the beginning of the base video clip. This will look like your subject is catching up to the images!

How it works...

There are many blend modes available. They fall into several categories to make it easier to find the right one:

- **Normal**: This is basically a *dissolve*-style blend and does not affect the color of the clips. Use the **Opacity** slider to adjust the visibility of the top clip.

- **Darken**: These modes, such as **Multiply** and **Darken**, are based on darker grayscale values. The category is called **Darken**, and there is a specific **Darken** blend mode. They reduce the brightness of the blend by keeping only the darkest parts of overlapping layers, like adding a deep, rich flavor to your dish.

- **Lighten**: Modes such as **Screen** and **Lighten** are based on lighter grayscale values. The category is called **Lighten**, and there is a specific **Lighten** blend mode. They brighten the image by preserving the lightest parts, much like balancing a recipe with a touch of sweetness or zest.

- **Midtone**: **Overlay** and **Soft Light** are based on mid-tone gray values. They blend layers by enhancing contrast, adding sharpness and depth, similar to balancing textures and spices in a meal for maximum impact.

- **Color**: These modes, including **Difference** and **Exclusion**, are based on color values and compare layers to create striking, often inverted effects – ideal for creative or experimental visual twists, like unexpected flavors in fusion cooking.

- **Alpha** and **Luma**: Modes such as **Stencil** and **Silhouette** are based on transparency. An **Alpha** channel is transparent. While full-screen video does not contain any transparency, text clips do. With text, whatever part of a text clip doesn't contain text is transparent. **Luma**, or light, works by blending images of black-and-white shapes with video clips, much like adding just the right missing ingredient to a dish.

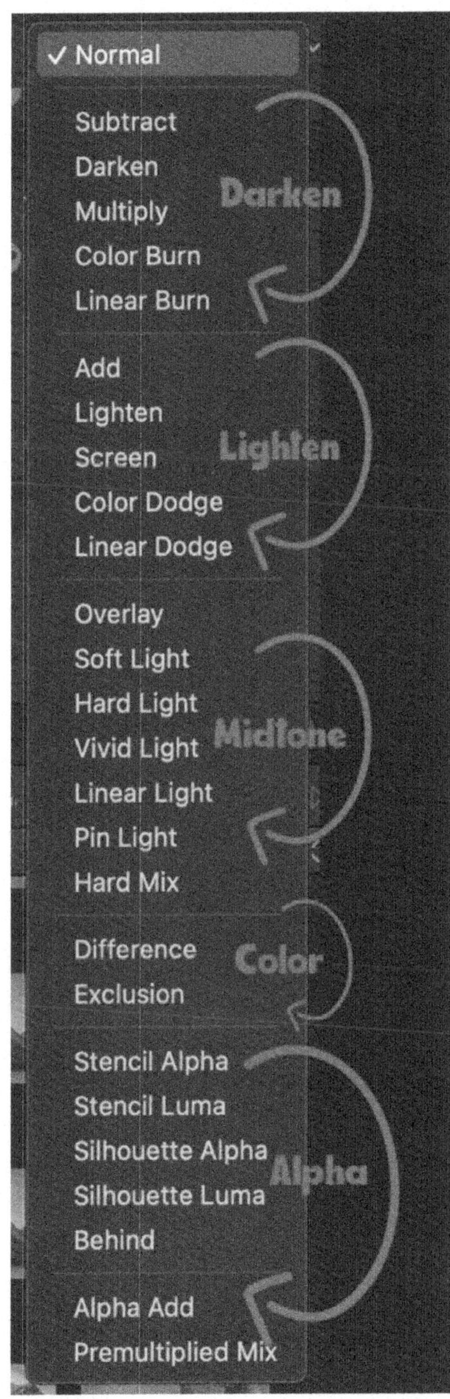

Figure 6.40: Blend mode categories

7

Transforming Visual Elements

Some dishes aren't complete until you've trimmed, plated, and garnished them just right – and the same is true for your video edits. In this chapter, you'll learn how to shape, position, and refine your visual ingredients with the precision of a seasoned chef preparing a final presentation.

We'll explore masks for isolating parts of an image, green screen keying for placing subjects in new environments, and keyframing for custom motion. You'll gain confidence in manipulating clips in space and time – whether it's reframing for composition, stabilizing for clarity, or retiming for emphasis. In addition, we will study the techniques behind cropping, distorting, and the iconic Ken Burns effect for immersive visual storytelling. These are the tools that give editors not just technical control, but expressive freedom.

Just like a well-balanced plate, these refinements are about more than aesthetics – they shape how your audience experiences the story. And in your role as editor-chef, mastering these tools gives you the creative edge to make each frame count.

In this chapter, you will complete the following recipes:

- Unmasking the mystery of masks
- Using the Green Screen Keyer effect
- Using the Magnetic Mask effect
- Keyframing clip position and effects
- Retiming clips
- Stabilizing clips
- Reframing clip resolution
- Cropping, distorting, and who is Ken Burns anyway?

Unmasking the mystery of masks

Behold, the mystery revealed: Masks are simply selected areas of a clip and function sort of like a picture-in-a-picture feature on a TV. Masks in Final Cut Pro allow you to isolate specific areas of a clip for targeted adjustments, such as applying effects, color corrections, or blurs to only part of the image.

By using shape masks or custom-drawn masks, you can create precise edits, hide unwanted elements, or direct focus to key parts of a scene. They enhance creative control, offering a non-destructive way to refine your visuals, improve composition, and elevate storytelling through selective visual treatments.

In this recipe, we will simplify the concept of a mask so that you can readily apply it to advanced effects.

How to do it...

Masks are simple yet impactful. Let's go:

1. Start by placing two clips in your project timeline, one connected on top of the other. *Option + click* on the top connected clip so that it is both selected and the playhead is parked on top of it.

2. Click on the down arrow next to the **Transform** icon in the lower-left corner of the Viewer. From the drop-down menu, select **Transform**.

Figure 7.1: Click on the Transform icon to see the Transform drop-down menu in the Viewer

3. The clip image in the Viewer will have blue buttons along the edge of its bounding box. Click, hold, and drag one corner in toward the center to make the clip smaller. As the connected clip is made smaller, we can see the clip behind it.

Figure 7.2: Drag the corner of the bounding box to make the clip smaller

Think of this as a picture in a picture, but the edges of the small connected clip are cut straight and are rather uninteresting.

4. This may be fine in some cases, but not here. So, click on the **Reset** button in the upper-right corner of the Viewer, then click on the **Transform** icon again to turn off the selection.

5. Now, in the Effects Browser, scroll down to the **Masks and Keying** category, and from there, choose the **Shape Mask** effect.

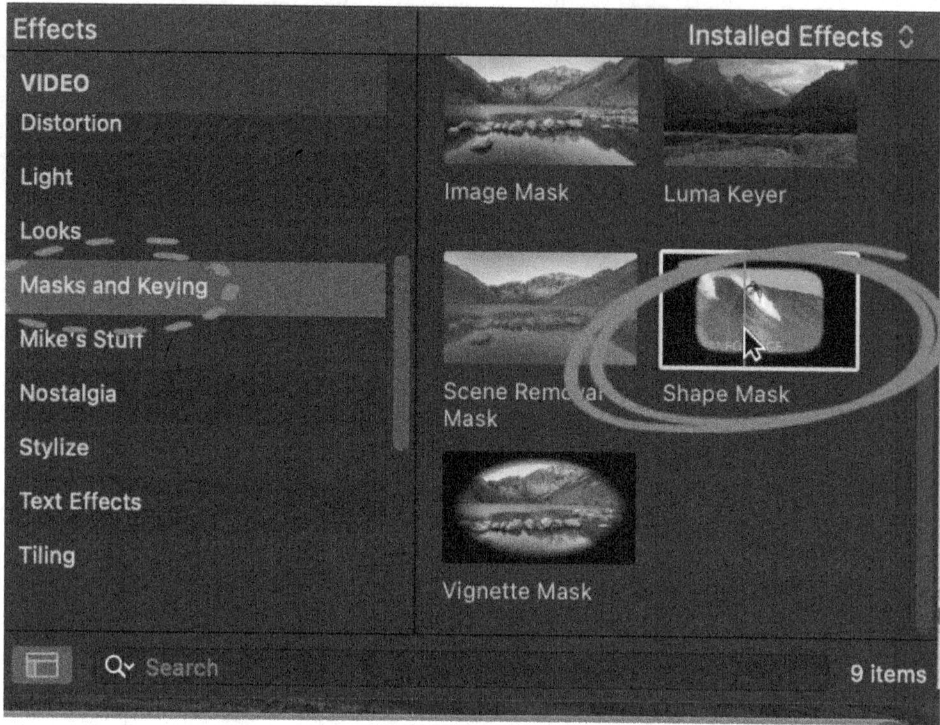

Figure 7.3: Select the Shape Mask effect from the Masks and Keying Effects category

6. Apply this to the connected clip. This time, we have the same picture-in-picture concept, but the shape can be changed, and the edges can be much more interesting, with a graduated, feathered edge. Plus, there are quite a few parameters to experiment with in the Inspector. Explore the various sliders and controls, particularly the slider control for **Feather** – this will blend the edge of the mask and make it more gradual.

Figure 7.4: Note the parameters of the Shape Mask effect in the Inspector

7. In the Inspector, specifically note the **Invert Mask** checkbox. Clicking on the checkmark reverses the parameters of the inside or the outside of our mask shape. Now it's more like a doughnut (another food analogy!) where there is a hole in the top clip showing the clip underneath in the middle.

Figure 7.5: Select the Invert Mask checkbox

As you can see, a mask is not that mysterious after all. Have fun exploring all the mask effects in Final Cut Pro.

Using the Green Screen Keyer effect

The **Green Screen Keyer** effect in Final Cut Pro allows you to easily remove green or blue backgrounds, enabling seamless compositing of your subject onto a new backdrop or environment. By applying this effect, you can quickly isolate your subject and fine-tune the transparency settings for a clean, professional result.

The advantage of using the Keyer effect is its efficiency in achieving high-quality chroma keying, offering a powerful way to integrate multiple elements into a single scene and expand your creative possibilities without complex workflows.

In this recipe, we will apply the Green Screen Keyer effect to a clip and explore the settings that will make it look picture-perfect.

Getting ready

You will need some footage shot against a green screen. Many stock media websites have preview clips available to download.

How to do it...

Fresh greens are *key* to an editor's healthy diet. See what I did there?

1. As we saw in recipes in the previous chapter, blend modes work on the top clip downwards. This is also the case with keying effects. We apply the effect to the top clip to reveal the clip underneath. In order to create a new background, let's start by adding a generator clip to your timeline. In my example, I've added clouds. In the upper-right corner of the Final Cut Pro interface, click on the **Show Titles and Generators** icon, which looks like a square with a T in it on top of another square. From **Generators**, select the **Backgrounds** category. Select one and add it to your timeline.

2. Place the clip that has been shot in a green screen environment on top of the generator clip in your timeline. You can adjust the edit points of these so that they are the same length. *Option + click* on the green screen clip so that it is both selected and the playhead is parked on top of it.

Figure 7.6: Select the connected green screen clip

3. In the Effects Browser, scroll down to the **Masks and Keying** category and select the **Green Screen Keyer** effect.

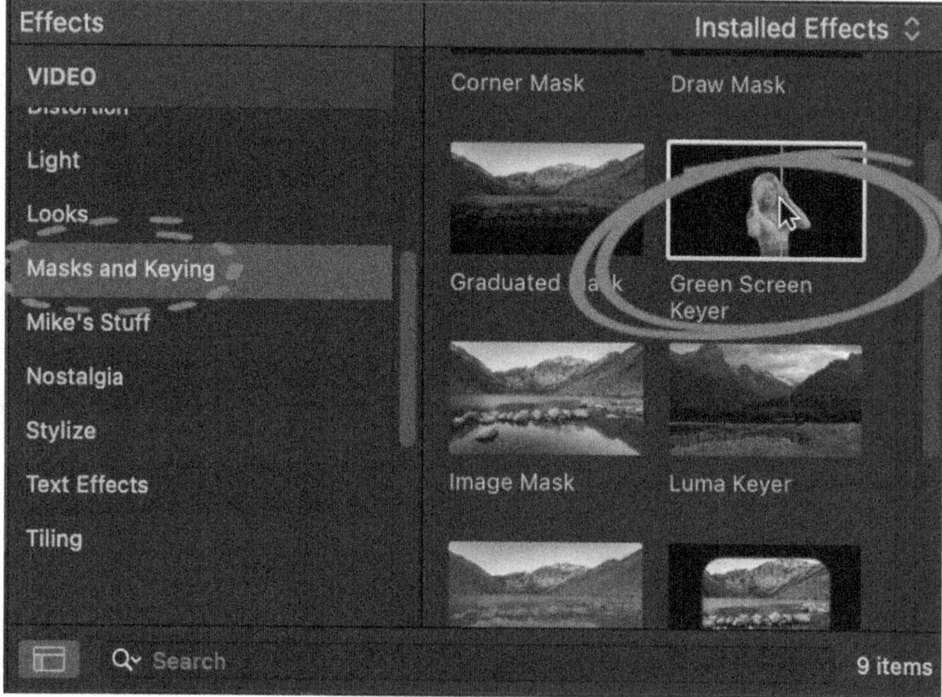

Figure 7.7: Select the Green Screen Keyer effect from the Masks and Keying category

4. Apply the **Green Screen Keyer** effect to your footage shot in a green screen environment. This effect is optimized to select the color green. The word *Key* means to affect. So, this *effect* will *affect* anything that is green and make it transparent. Hopefully, your talent did not wear anything green. The Green Screen Keyer effect does most of the work, so well-shot green screen footage looks great right from the start.

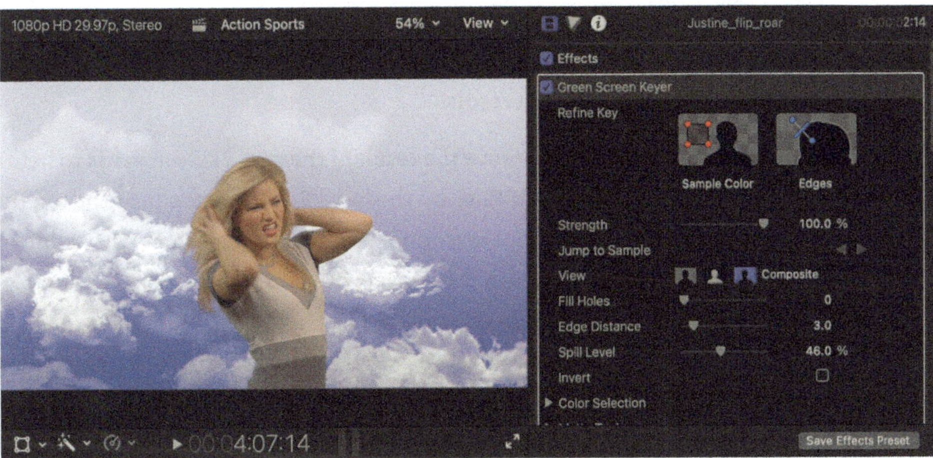

Figure 7.8: The Green Screen Keyer effect does most of the work

5. But there are several things you can do to improve it. In the Inspector, go to the **Green Screen Keyer** effect parameters, and click on the large **Sample Color** button near the top that looks like a red square next to a head. The cursor will change to a small red square. You will use this to tell the effect which shade of green is the best sample. Select a small area to sample the background.

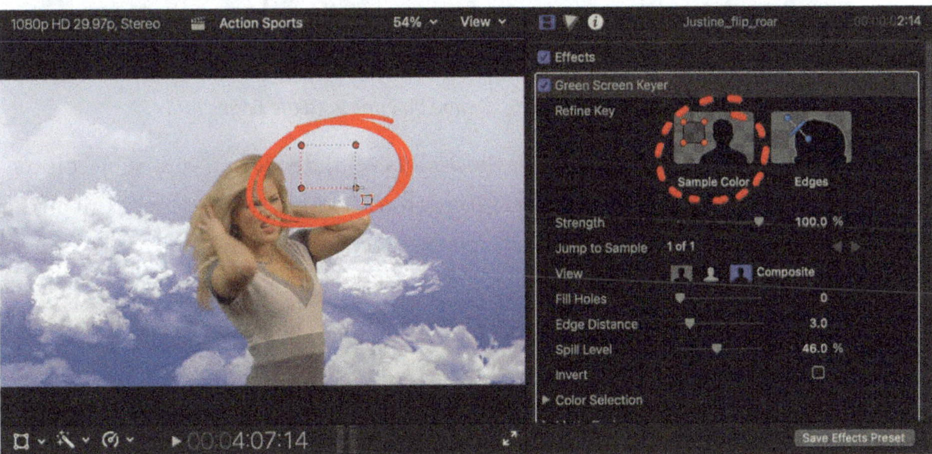

Figure 7.9: Select a sample square with the Sample Color tool

Often, the green background is not a perfect shade of green because of uneven lighting or wrinkles, and so on. You will want to choose the green on the original background that is next to your subject for the best result.

6. Another thing you can do to improve the result of the green screen key is to help the tool detect the edges of your subject. Click on the large **Edges** button near the top that looks like a blue line across a head. The cursor will change to a crosshair with a line next to it. Draw a line across a difficult area in the Viewer with one end of the line in the area to keep and the other in the area to remove.

Figure 7.10: Define an edge with the Edges tool

7. Another thing to keep in mind is the **Spill Level** slider. When your subject is too close to the green screen, the green light reflects onto them and causes a green tint on their edges. To fix this, **Spill Level** increases or decreases a magenta tone – magenta is opposite green on the color wheel and counteracts any green tint that spills onto your subject. Be careful, though, a little bit goes a long way. In my example, I have turned **Spill Level** up too much to show the magenta tint.

Figure 7.11: Test Spill Level by turning up the percentage to show a magenta tint

There are lots of advanced settings that can be used to help fix green screen footage, but this tutorial is not meant to get into all of them. I will mention that sometimes it's helpful to include a **Draw Mask** effect along with a green screen. You may see this referred to as a *garbage mask*, which can be used to hide equipment or shadows in the green background.

8. To create a *garbage mask*, temporarily turn off the Green Screen Keyer effect by clicking on the blue checkbox next to the **Green Screen Keyer** title.

9. Then, in the Effects Browser panel and from the **Masks and Keying** effects category, select the **Draw Mask** effect and apply it to the green screen clip.

10. Move your mouse over the Viewer and see that the cursor changes to a pen tool with a plus sign. Click the mouse to create control points around your subject. Make the control points close enough to mask out any unwanted background, but not so close that you clip off the movement of your subject, such as their arms. Note that when you circle around and hover the mouse over the first control point, the cursor changes to a pen tool with a circle.

Figure 7.12: Draw a mask around your subject

11. Click on the first control point to close the shape, and the mask is complete. Anything outside of the drawing becomes transparent.

Figure 7.13: The image outside of the Draw Mask effect is transparent

Use the Draw Mask effect in combination with the Green Screen Keyer effect for professional results.

There's more...

Editing green screen footage gets easier if the media is lit correctly:

- Make sure that the green background is smooth with minimal wrinkles.

- Make sure the lighting is smooth as well. Avoid hot spots and shadows by using soft, diffused lights.

- Move your subject far enough away from the green screen to avoid the green tint from reflecting on them.

- You may need to back up your camera and zoom in.

Also, if you do not have the opportunity to shoot against a green screen, the **Scene Removal Mask** effect might do the trick. There are several things that will help ensure some success:

- Shoot your subject in a bright, evenly lit place, preferably indoors, and a visually simple static background using a stationary camera

- Shoot with space and contrast between the foreground subject and background with no similar colors, textures, or strong shadows

- Shoot a few extra frames at the beginning or end of the shot, showing the background without the foreground subject present, so that the effect can analyze the difference between the static background and the moving subject

Using the Magnetic Mask effect

The **Magnetic Mask** effect in Final Cut Pro offers a fast and intuitive way to isolate specific areas of your video by automatically detecting edges within the image of your clip. This tool makes masking precise, even on complex subjects, significantly reducing the time spent on manual adjustments. The result is cleaner selections that enhance tasks such as color grading, compositing, or applying localized effects, giving your edits a polished, professional look with minimal effort.

In this recipe, we will apply the Magnetic Mask Keyer effect to a clip and explore how to make your clips stunning.

Getting ready

You will need some footage with the subject differentiated from the background by a fair amount of contrast. Many stock media websites have preview clips available to download for free.

The Magnetic Mask effect uses edge detection on a person or object to mask out the background. So, to prepare for this, place a plain clip or generated background on the primary storyline. Connect the clip you want to mask on top of the background clip. A clip in which the subject is in contrast to the background will work best.

How to do it...

Just like an induction cooktop targets the perfect pot, the Magnetic Mask effect locks onto your subject with precision – no extra stirring required. Let's go:

1. *Option + click* on the clip to be masked so that the clip is selected and the playhead is parked on top of it. Pick a point at which the subject is clearly visible and stands out from the background.

2. In the Effects Browser, click on the **Masks and Keying** category and select **Magnetic Mask**.

3. There are several ways to apply this effect. We can double-click on the effect to apply it to the selected clip. Or, as we have with other effects, drag the effect directly onto the clip in the timeline. But in this case, we can drag the effect directly onto the subject in the Viewer. Immediately, the Magnetic Mask effect detects edges in the image and reveals the mask in red.

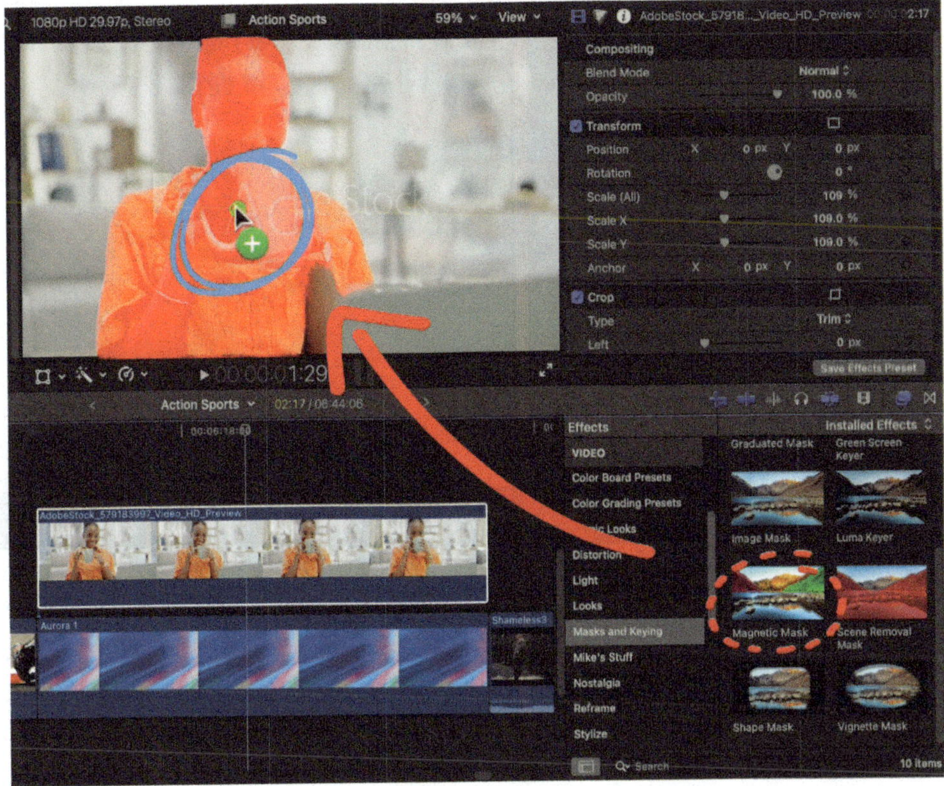

Figure 7.14: Drag the Magnetic Mask effect directly onto the subject in the Viewer

4. Notice that the cursor changes to an arrow on top of a green control point dot, with a green plus sign next to it. Release the mouse and note the onscreen control tools along the top edge of the Viewer.

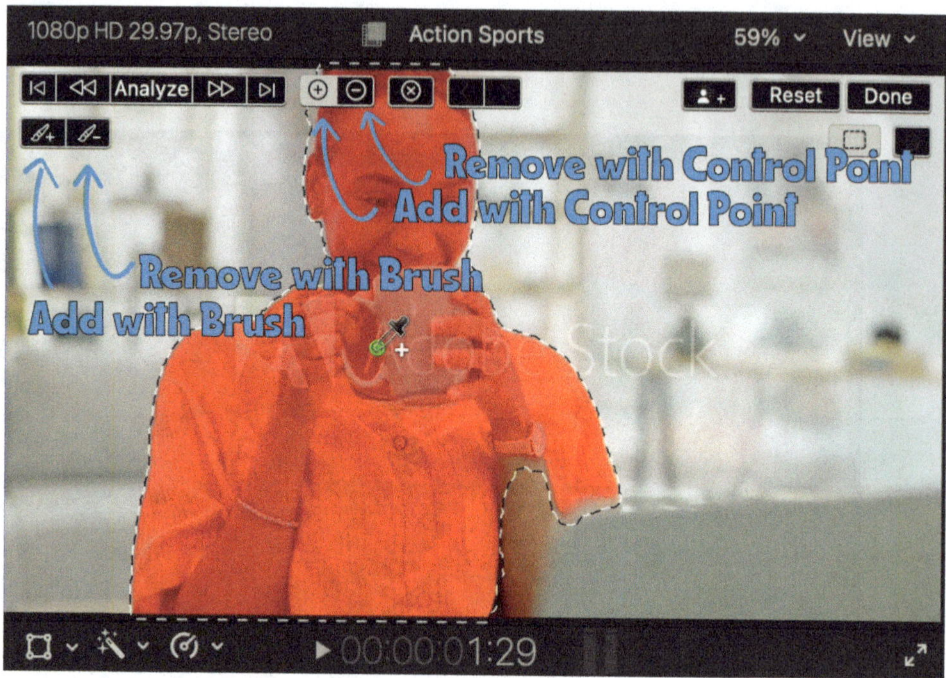

Figure 7.15: Use the onscreen controls to add or remove mask edge detection

5. To add to the mask, place the cursor over a portion of the image to add. When the **Add Mask Control Point** tool is active, the cursor looks like an eyedropper with a plus sign. Click to add a mask control point. Notice that another green dot has been placed at that point.

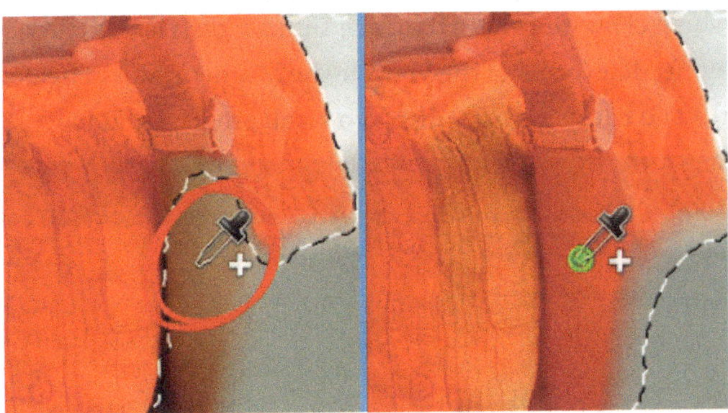

Figure 7.16: Click with the plus eyedropper to add a control point

6.   In my example, I need to click on this person's arm to add that edge to the mask as a control point. When using the **Add Mask Control Point** tool, there is a keyboard shortcut you can use. Hold down the *Option* key, and the cursor switches to the **Remove Mask Control Point** tool.

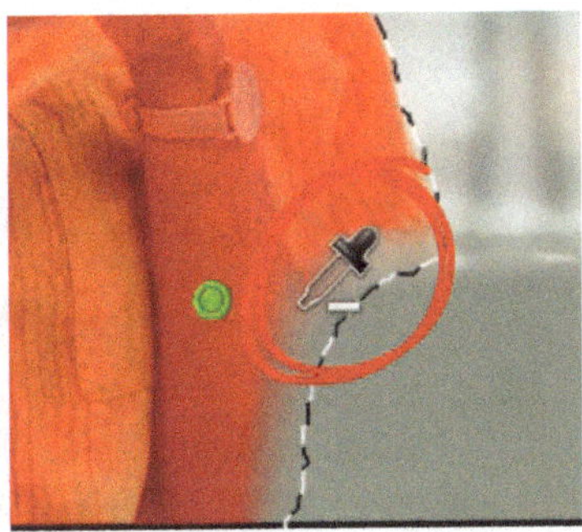

Figure 7.17: Hold down the Option key to switch to the Remove Mask Control Point tool

7. When you feel like the image has been sufficiently selected, click on the **Analyze** button in the upper-left corner of the Viewer. The Magnetic Mask effect will analyze the image forwards and backwards and display a small progress window.

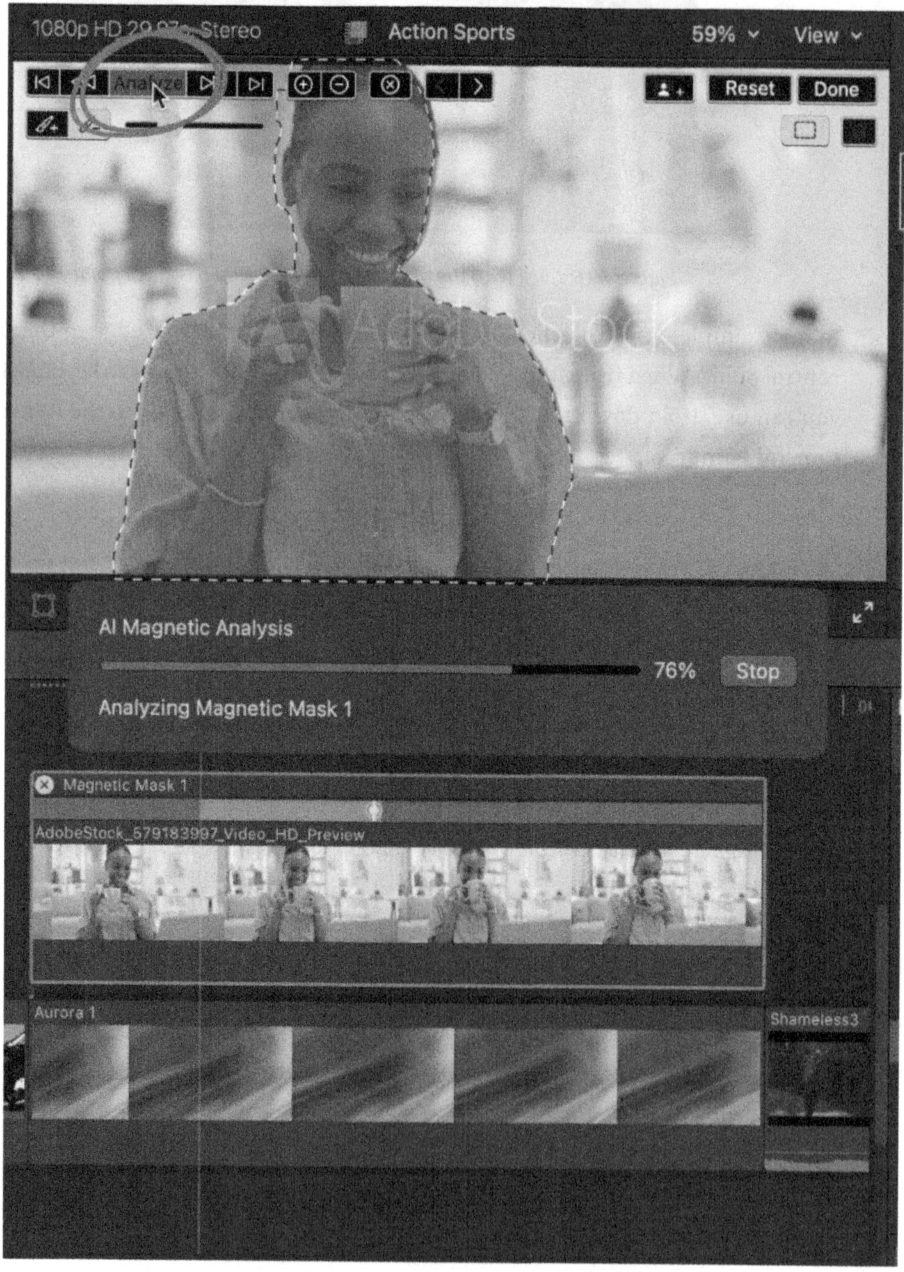

Figure 7.18: The Magnetic Mask effect will analyze the clip image

8. Skim through the clip and look for any gaps or any inadvertent additions. Add or remove the mask at those points.

9. You can add an additional mask by clicking on the **Add New Mask** icon that looks like a silhouette of a person with a plus sign located in the upper-right corner of the Viewer. Note that in the **Magnetic Mask** section of the Inspector, another Magnetic Mask effect has been added with a different color. Click on the **Mask Blend Mode** drop-down menu to select whether you choose to **Add, Subtract,** or **Intersect** the new mask with the first mask. There is also a slider to control the edge **Feather** parameter. This is a gradual blend on the edge of the mask area.

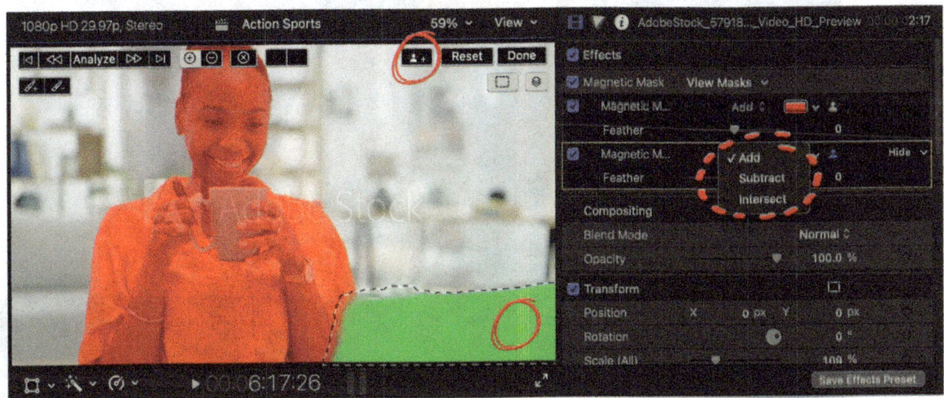

Figure 7.19: Add an additional mask and choose to add, subtract, or intersect it with the first mask

10. When you are happy with the analysis of the mask, click on the **Done** button in the upper-right corner of the Viewer.

Figure 7.20: The Magnetic Mask effect easily removes the background from the subject

 **Pro tip**: If you know you will be masking the subject when you shoot the video, you can improve the mask accuracy by lighting your subject well and creating contrast with the background.

Keyframing clip position and effects

Keyframing in Final Cut Pro allows you to animate changes by setting specific values at different points over time. This provides precision and flexibility, enabling detailed control over how elements evolve in a scene, adding professional-level motion and fluid transitions to your projects.

Think of a paper flip-book animation – books that have slightly different drawings on the edge of each page, which look like an animation when flipped through quickly. Now, imagine if you only needed to draw the first and last frames, and a magical book would fill in all the progressive drawings in between. The frames you drew would be keyframes.

By creating keyframes with inspector parameters, you can let Final Cut Pro smoothly move a clip across the screen, adjust its size, or gradually increase the intensity of an effect, giving your edits dynamic movement.

In this recipe, we will create animations from keyframes of a clip's position in space and the visibility of an effect.

How to do it...

Animation is just parameters changing over time. We are going to think big but start small:

1. Add a clip in the primary storyline in the timeline. Click on it so that it is selected and highlighted in yellow. Slide the playhead and snap it to the beginning of the clip. We can tell it's the beginning of the clip because of the bracket shape in the lower-left corner of the image in the Viewer.

2. It will also be helpful at this point to zoom out in the Viewer to see the space outside of the video screen. Click on the **Viewer Zoom** button located in the upper-right corner of the Viewer. It will have a percentage number. From the drop-down menu, select a percentage that is smaller than the current view.

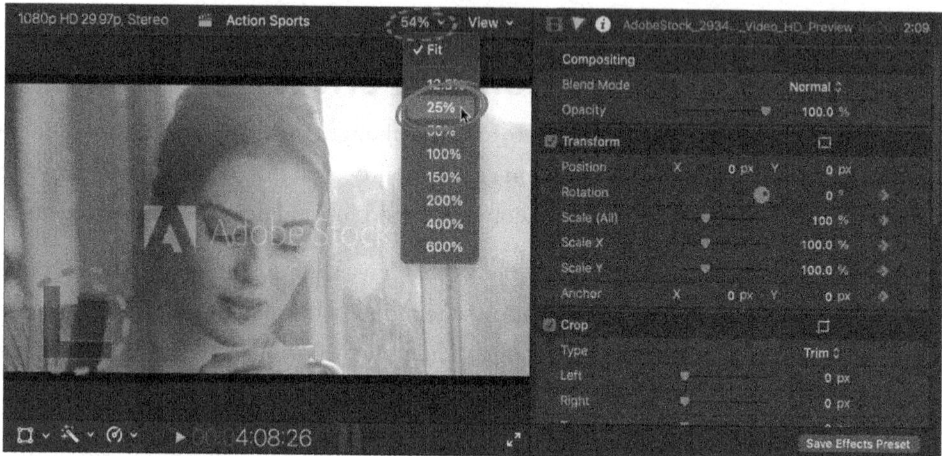

Figure 7.21: Zoom out in the Viewer

3. Click on the **Transform** icon, located in the lower-left corner of the Viewer, which looks like a small square with dots in the corners. The button will be highlighted in blue. In addition, the image of your clip will have a blue bounding box with control points in the corners and on the sides.

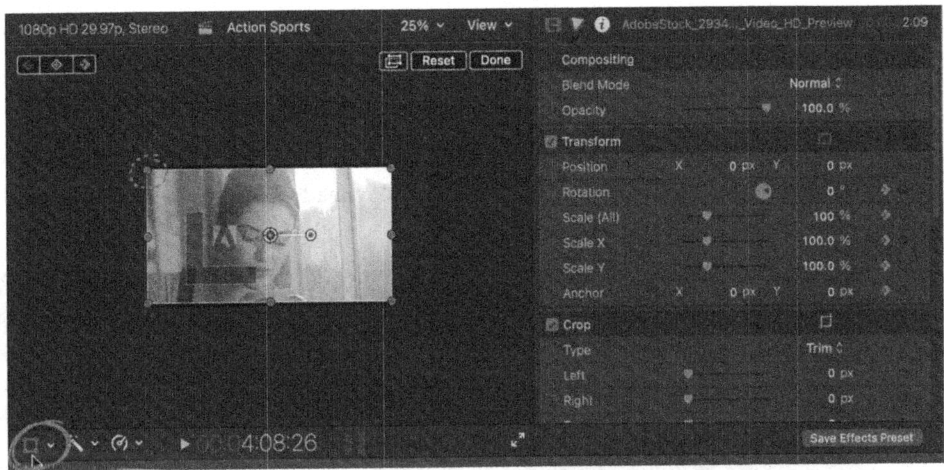

Figure 7.22: Click on the Transform icon and note the control points around the image

4.   Click near the center of the image and drag the clip off-screen. This will be the start of
     our animation. Let's create a keyframe at this starting position. In the Inspector, in the
     Transform area, for the **Position** parameter, click on the **Keyframe** icon (which looks like
     a little diamond with a plus sign inside).

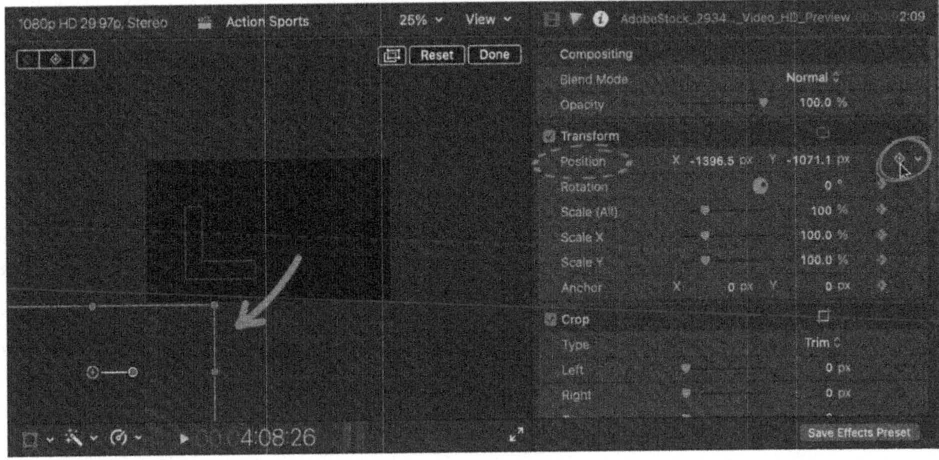

Figure 7.23: Add a keyframe for Position at the start of the clip

5. Next, in the timeline, slide the playhead to the end of the clip. Note that if there is another clip after this one in the timeline, the playhead will snap to the beginning of the next clip. Now, press the *left arrow* key once to go back just one frame. We can tell this is the end frame of our clip, even though the clip is not visible in the video frame, because of the bracket in the lower-right corner. With the playhead still moved ahead in time, click and drag your clip to a new position off-screen.

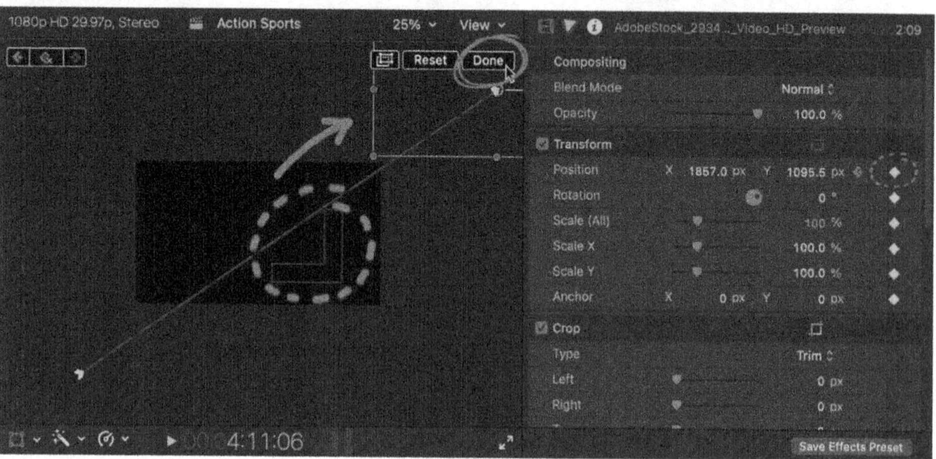

Figure 7.24: Drag the clip image to a new position at the last frame

6. Click on the **Done** button in the upper-right corner of the Viewer. Skim through your clip or move the playhead back to the beginning and use the keyboard shortcut of pressing the *spacebar* to play through your clip.

7. Because we were sort of in keyframe creation mode, Final Cut Pro automatically added the last keyframe for us on our last parameter change. To smoothly create keyframes, make changes in this order: Set the starting frame with the playhead, set the starting parameters in the Inspector, then, importantly, first change the playhead position, then change parameters for that position. This way, Final Cut Pro will help set the final keyframe for you.

8. Let's animate an effect. Place a clip into your timeline. Click once on the clip to select it and slide the playhead to the first frame. We can tell it's the first frame because of the bracket in the lower-left corner in the Inspector.

9. From the Effects Browser, select an effect and apply it to your clip. In my example, I am going to use the **Comic Basic** effect.

10. I would like to animate this effect to gradually increase as it plays from the first frame to the last frame. In the Inspector, under **Effects**, are the controls for the **Comic Basic** effect. Drag the **Mix** percentage to 0%. On the far right of the **Mix** parameter, click on the **Add Keyframe** icon, which looks like a diamond with a plus sign in it. This places a keyframe of zero effect at the beginning of our clip.

Figure 7.25: Add a keyframe for the Mix parameter at 0%

11. Now, slide the playhead to the last frame of the clip. With snapping turned on, the playhead will automatically go to the first frame of the next clip click. Press the *left arrow* key to go back exactly one frame to the end of our clip. We can tell it's the last frame because of the bracket in the lower-right corner of the Viewer.

12. In the Inspector, in the **Comic Basic** effect parameters, move the **Mix** slider to **100%**. Final Cut Pro should automatically add a keyframe at this position.

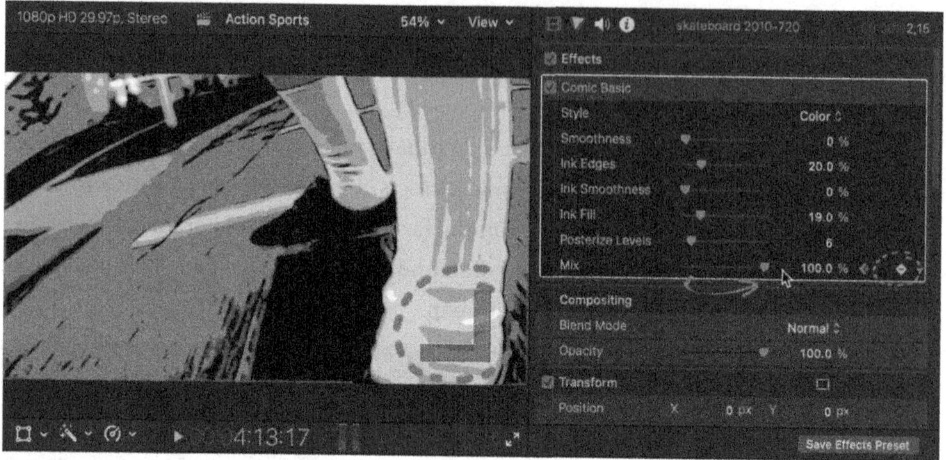

Figure 7.26: Slide the effect mix to 100% on the last frame of the clip

13. Skim through your clip and notice how the effect gradually increases with time. Note that the percentage increases on the **Mix** slider. **Position** and **Mix** are just two of numerous parameters that can be keyframed to change over time.

    We started small, and now you can think big. Start exploring all the various parameters that can be keyframed to animate your clips to support your story.

There's more...

Just to be clear, the starting and ending keyframes do not have to be on the first and last frame of a clip. You can set keyframes anywhere, and you can have multiple keyframes as set points along the way. You can also set the keyframe of your ending first and work backwards. As long as you set the parameter, add a keyframe, change the time, and then set a new parameter, it will work great.

Retiming clips

With retiming, you're the chef of time itself, stretching or squeezing moments to taste. Retiming clips in Final Cut Pro allows you to adjust the speed of your footage, enabling you to create dramatic slow-motion sequences or fast-paced time lapses. By utilizing tools such as the retime editor, you can easily manipulate clip speed, add speed ramps, and create unique visual effects that enhance storytelling and engagement.

The advantage of retiming clips is the capacity to evoke emotions and emphasize key moments, providing editors with a powerful technique to control pacing and rhythm in their projects while maintaining visual coherence.

In this recipe, we will explore how to adjust the speed of a clip and how to build in multiple speed changes.

How to do it...

We'll make a clip play fast, slow, fast! Let's get moving:

1. Add a clip that has some action to your project in the timeline. *Option + click* on it so that the clip is selected and the playhead is parked on top of it.

2. Click on the **Retiming** icon, located in the lower-left corner of the Viewer panel. It looks like a speedometer. A drop-down menu will be displayed. At the bottom, select **Show Retime Editor** or use the keyboard shortcut of *Command + R*.

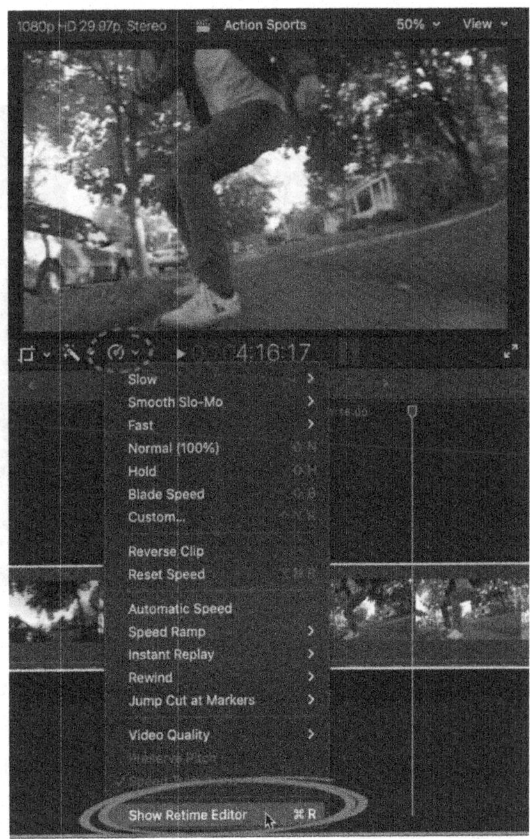

Figure 7.27: Select Show Retime Editor from the Retiming menu

The retime editor is a colored bar on top of the clip. Its normal state is green and 100%. On the right-hand side of the retime editor bar is a small line, and as we hover the mouse over it, the cursor changes to an arrow with a speedometer.

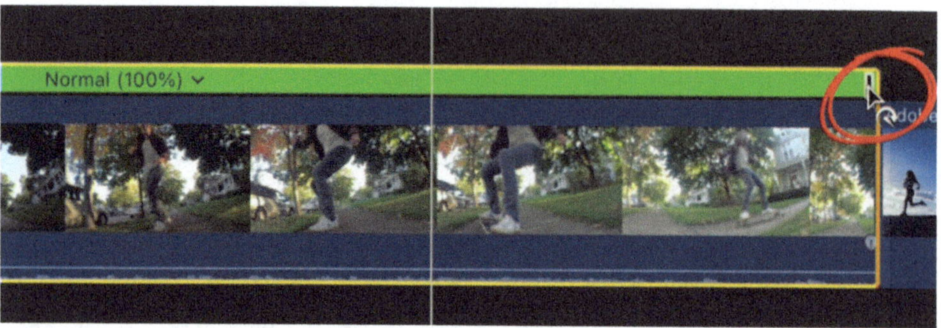

Figure 7.28: Note the cursor for the retime editor slider

3. Click, hold, and slide that line to the left to shorten a clip and make it play faster. As you do so, note that the retime editor bar is blue. Now drag the line to the right, and it lengthens the clip to play it slower. Note that the retime editor bar is now orange.

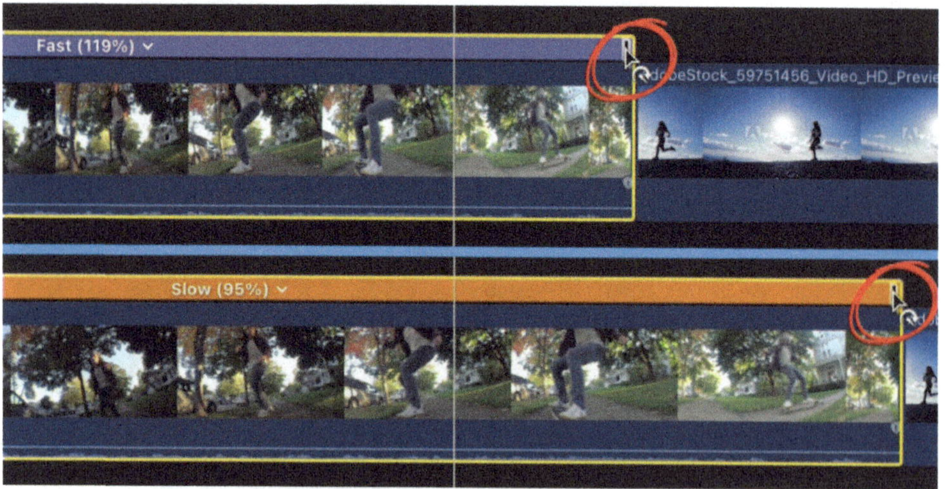

Figure 7.29: Move the retime editor slider left for faster and right for slower

4. Drag the slider back to the original 100% mark. A cool effect is to have a clip play fast, then slow motion, and then fast again. A great way to do this is with different speed sections in the retime editor, rather than cutting the clip into three different clips.

5. At the start of the action in which you want slow motion, park the playhead, and from the **Retiming** menu, select **Blade Speed**.

Figure 7.30: Select Blade Speed from the Retiming menu

6. This cuts a section in the retime editor bar. Slide the playhead forward a little bit to the place where you want to stop the slow motion. Just a little bit will do because the portion that we slow down will extend out to the right. Let's make another cut in the retime editor bar with the keyboard shortcut *Shift + B*.

Figure 7.31: View speed sections in the retime editor bar

7. Now, let's use the retiming sliders to make our fast-slow-fast multiple speed sections in the retime editor bar. Take the first section slider and move it to the left so the clip is faster. Take the middle section slider to the right to make it slower. And take the last section and slide it to the left to make it faster.

Figure 7.32: Use the Retime sliders to adjust clips to play fast, slow, fast

8. Play your clip from the beginning and change the retime editor sliders as you prefer.

9. Notice the gray areas between the speed change sections. Those are transitions. In my example, I'm transitioning from 187% to 57%. You can shorten the amount of time that the speed ramp will change by shortening that transition. Click on the edge of the gray and, with the cursor that looks like an editing tool, slide left or right.

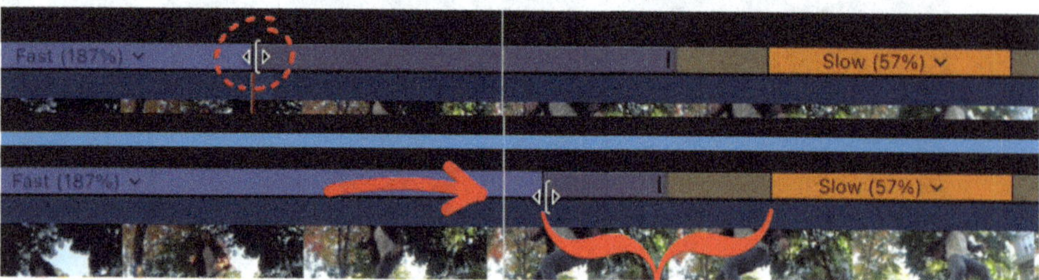

Figure 7.33: Use the editing tool to adjust the length of speed transitions

10. You can also change the edit points at which the speed changes happen. Double-click on one of the retime editor sliders, and a pop-up dialog box will appear. For **Source Frame**, simply click on the **Edit** button.

Figure 7.34: Edit Source Frame of the Retiming section

11. Now, the **Source Frame** editing slider looks like a film frame with an arrow at the bottom. You can drag that right or left to change the source point at which the speed change happens.

Figure 7.35: Move the Source Frame slider right or left

12. Double-click on the **Source Frame** editing slider again to lock your changes in place.

13. There are many other items in the **Retiming** menu with which you can experiment, including setting the **Video Quality** of your slow-motion clips to **Best (Machine Learning)**. This method creates new frames using a bidirectional optical flow algorithm to reduce artifacts, said the nerd, pushing up his glasses. As expected, analysis and rendering will take longer than the other methods. Note that this option requires a Mac with Apple Silicon. Otherwise, the best method is **Optical Flow**. It also uses an algorithm to create new in-between frames.

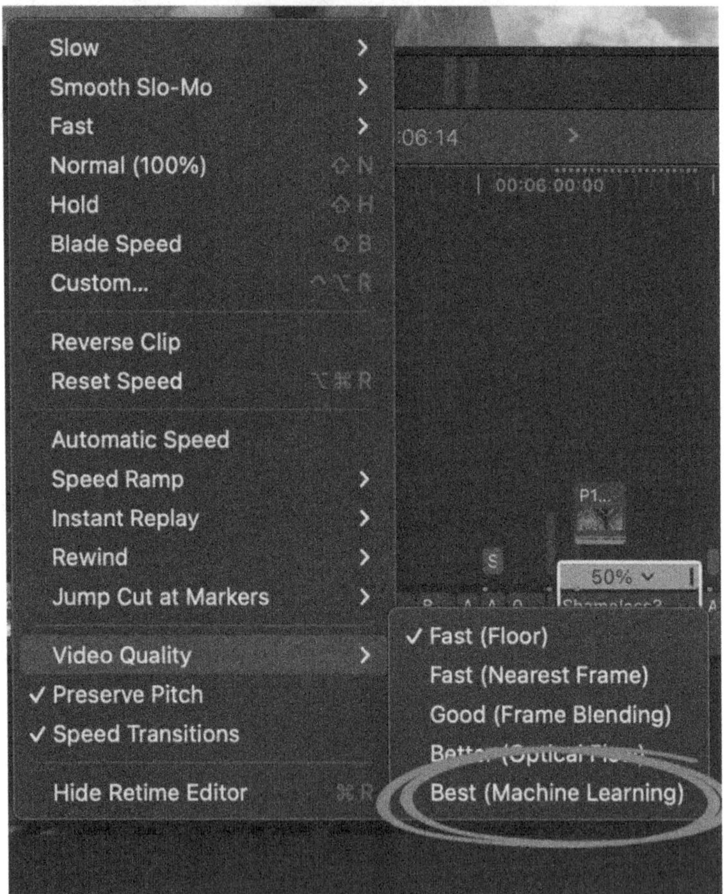

Figure 7.36: Select Best from Video Quality in the Retiming menu

Retiming clips has great storytelling value. Perhaps you might speed up sections of a training video or slow down sports action. Or, maybe your hero needs to walk in slow motion while something huge explodes behind them. Most definitely, we need a huge kitchen explosion.

Stabilizing clips

Story drives production, so you don't want flawed production to divert your audience's attention from your story. Stabilizing clips in Final Cut Pro is a powerful feature that helps smooth out shaky footage, resulting in a more professional and polished final product. By analyzing the motion of a clip and applying stabilization effects, you can eliminate unwanted camera jitters and vibrations, making your shots appear steadier and cinematic, maintaining audience engagement.

In this recipe, we will see how easy it is to allow Final Cut Pro to analyze a clip and apply the appropriate stabilization method.

Getting ready

You will need some footage that was shot handheld and needs some smoothing. Don't use footage that contains erratic panning.

How to do it...

Keep it smooth, real smooth. Here's how:

1. Add a clip to your project in the timeline that has been shot handheld. *Option + click* on the clip you want to work with so that it is both selected and the playhead is parked on top of it.

2. In the Inspector, scroll down a little bit until you see the **Stabilization** section. Click on the **Stabilization** checkbox. At this point, Final Cut Pro analyzes the clip and determines the best method for stabilization. You don't have to.

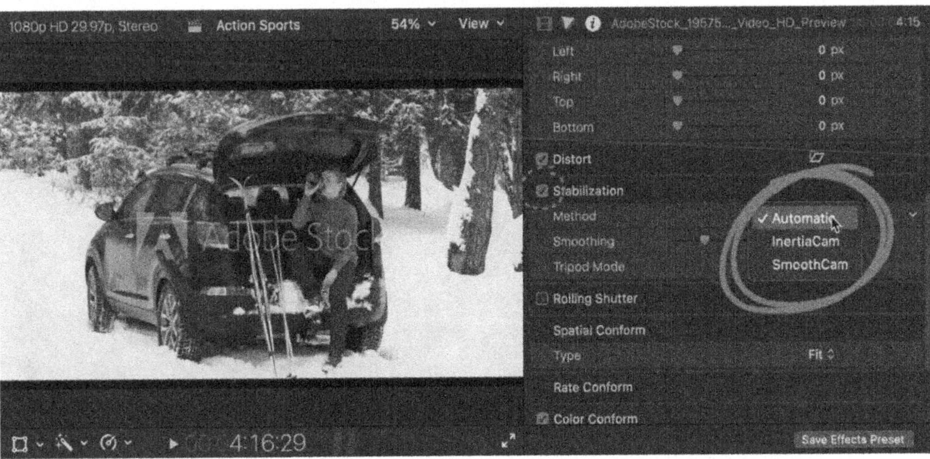

Figure 7.37: Click on the Method drop-down menu in Stabilization

3. One of the **Stabilization** parameters is called **Method**. Open the drop-down menu, and you will see three options:

- **Automatic** (the default option) allows Final Cut Pro to choose the most appropriate stabilization method (either **InertiaCam** or **SmoothCam**).

- **InertiaCam** is good for smoothing pans and zooms:

  - Use the **Smoothing** slider to adjust the amount of the effect.

  - When **InertiaCam** is chosen by FCP, if the footage is not overly shaky, a **Tripod Mode** checkbox is available to create the look of a static camera mounted on a tripod.

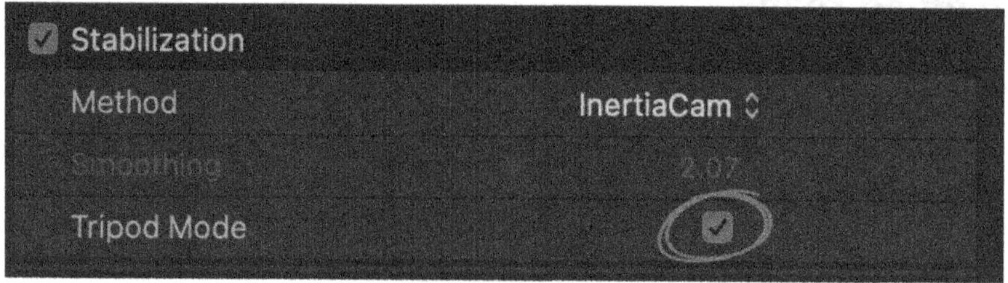

Figure 7.38: The InertiaCam parameters of Stabilization

- **SmoothCam** applies stabilization for pans and zooms as well as rotation, and scale:

  - Adjust the pan and tilt of your image by dragging the **Translation Smooth** slider.

  - Adjust the rotation around the center point of the image by dragging the **Rotation Smooth** slider.

  - Adjust the scale movement by dragging the **Scale Smooth** slider.

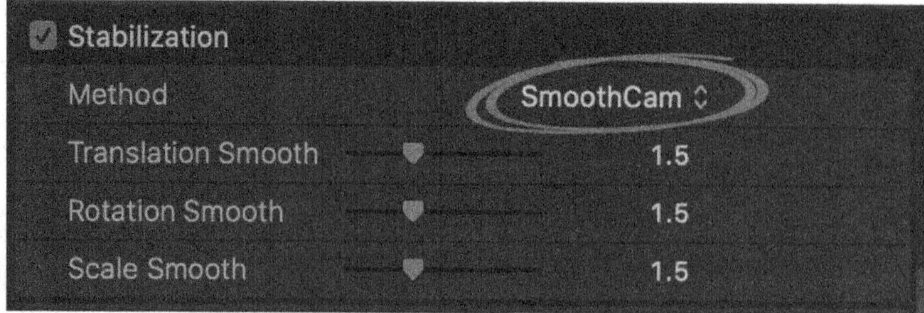

Figure 7.39: The SmoothCam parameters of Stabilization

4. Notice that the process of stabilization zooms in on the clip in order to have margins where it stabilizes the image. If the shot is too shaky, the stabilization effect will have to zoom in so much that the resolution of the image may be compromised. Check to see if the image quality is reduced. In addition, if your footage is too shaky, the black edges outside the clips may be visible as the stabilization analysis tries to steady the shot.

Figure 7.40: Stabilization zooms in on a clip

There's more...

As you know, story drives production, but sometimes your story needs the opposite of stabilization. Even if you recorded your footage using a steady tripod, you may want a bit of the energy that comes from a handheld camera. If so, in the Effects Browser, go to the **Stylize** category and select the **Handheld** effect. Apply it to your clip by simply dragging it from the Effects Browser on top of your clip. Then, alter the **Shakiness** parameter – be careful though, as a little bit goes a long way.

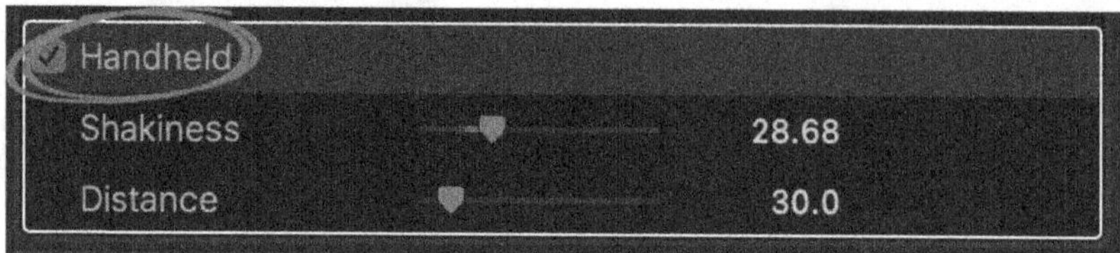

Figure 7.41: The Handheld effect gives energy

Reframing clip resolution

Reframing 4K clips in Final Cut Pro allows you to adjust the framing and composition of your shots without sacrificing image quality, thanks to the high resolution that 4K footage provides. The advantage of reframing 4K clips is that it enables you to creatively explore different perspectives and compositions by zooming in, panning, or repositioning elements within the clip images. You can create dynamic visuals or focus on specific details, offering greater flexibility during the editing process while ensuring that your final output maintains crispness and clarity.

In this recipe, we will show how to quickly set a 4K clip to its original size and reposition it within the video frame.

Getting ready

You will need some footage that is larger than your project size. Let's create some projects that are smaller than the footage you have:

1. From the **File** menu, select **New** and **Project**, or use the keyboard shortcut of *Command + N*.

2. In the dialogue box, click on the **Use Custom Settings** button in the lower-left corner.

3. From the **Video** section, click on **Format**. Choose **1080p HD** if you have larger footage to work with, such as 4K, or choose **720p HD** if you have footage that is 1080 in size.

4. Once done, click **OK**.

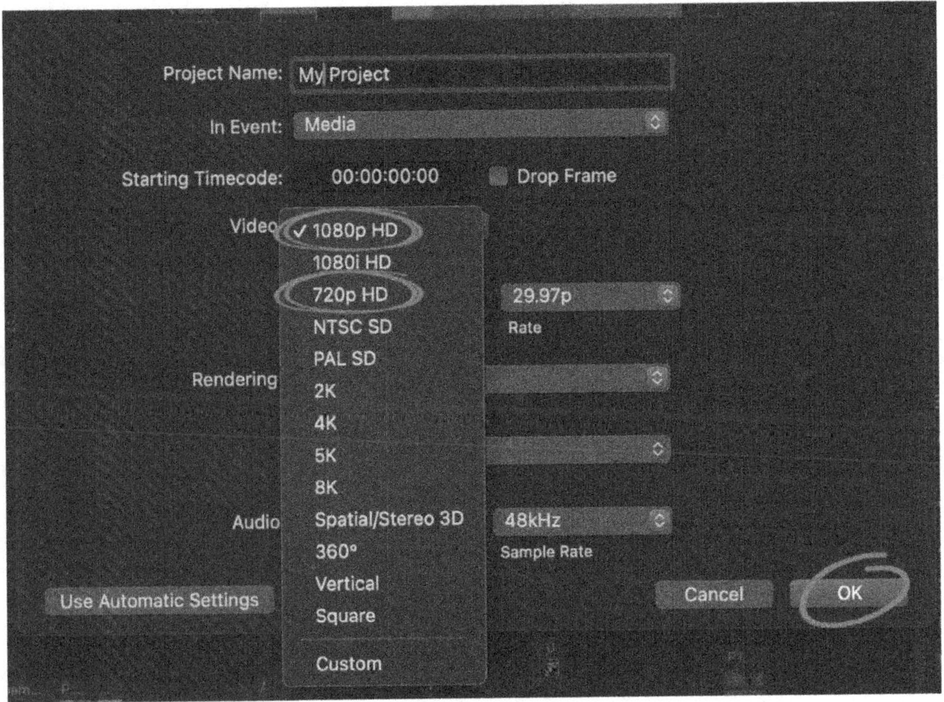

Figure 7.42: Create a new project that is smaller than your footage

How to do it...

Just like scaling up a fabulous recipe, you can't afford to lose any quality. Here's how:

1. Add a large-resolution clip to your project in the timeline. In my example, I have a clip that was shot in 4K, and my project size is 1080p HD. *Option + click* on the clip so that it is selected and the playhead is parked on top of it.

2. In the Inspector panel, scroll down to the **Spatial Conform** section. **Spatial Conform** can be best understood by how it functions with standard definition footage. As you may know, SD clips are relatively square, with a 4:3 aspect ratio. Most current projects are relatively rectangular, with a 16:9 aspect ratio.

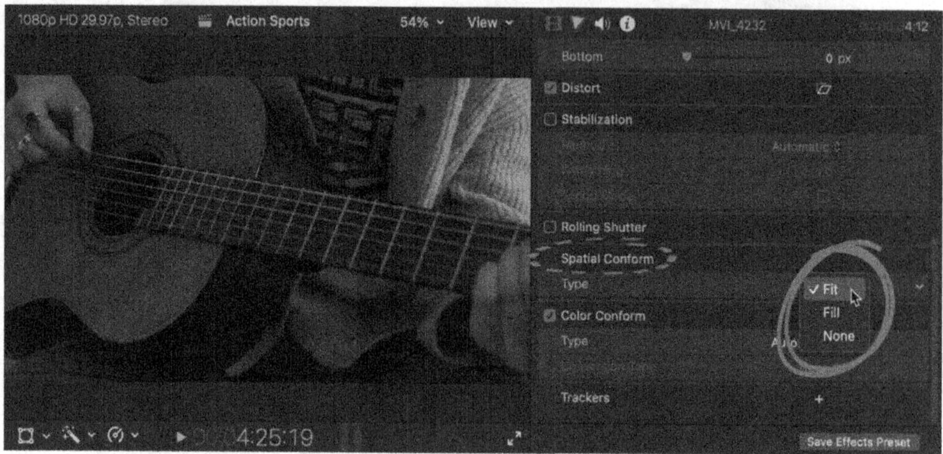

Figure 7.43: Select Fit from the Type drop-down menu for Spatial Conform

3. For the **Type** parameter, open the drop-down menu, and you will see three options:

- **Fit**: This will scale your footage so that it all fits within the boundaries. Square clips, such as SD footage, will fit at the top and not lose any of the image, but there will be black bars on the sides of a rectangular frame. The content fits in a way that none of the image is lost.

- **Fill**: This will scale up your footage to fill the rectangular aspect ratio and cut off some of the image at the top and bottom, but there will be no black bars on the sides. The frame will be filled.

- **None**: This leaves the clip's frame size unchanged. If the clip's frame size is larger than the project's frame size, the clip appears cropped. If the clip's frame size is smaller than the project's frame size, black bars surround the clip.

For my 4K example, **Fit** shows the whole clip in the frame, but I want to zoom in without losing quality. I'm going to select **None**. This makes the clip its natural large size.

4. Because the size of the clip is now larger than the frame of the Viewer, let's change the view percentage. In the upper-right corner of the Viewer, click on the **View Zoom** menu. Select a small percentage, such as **25%**.

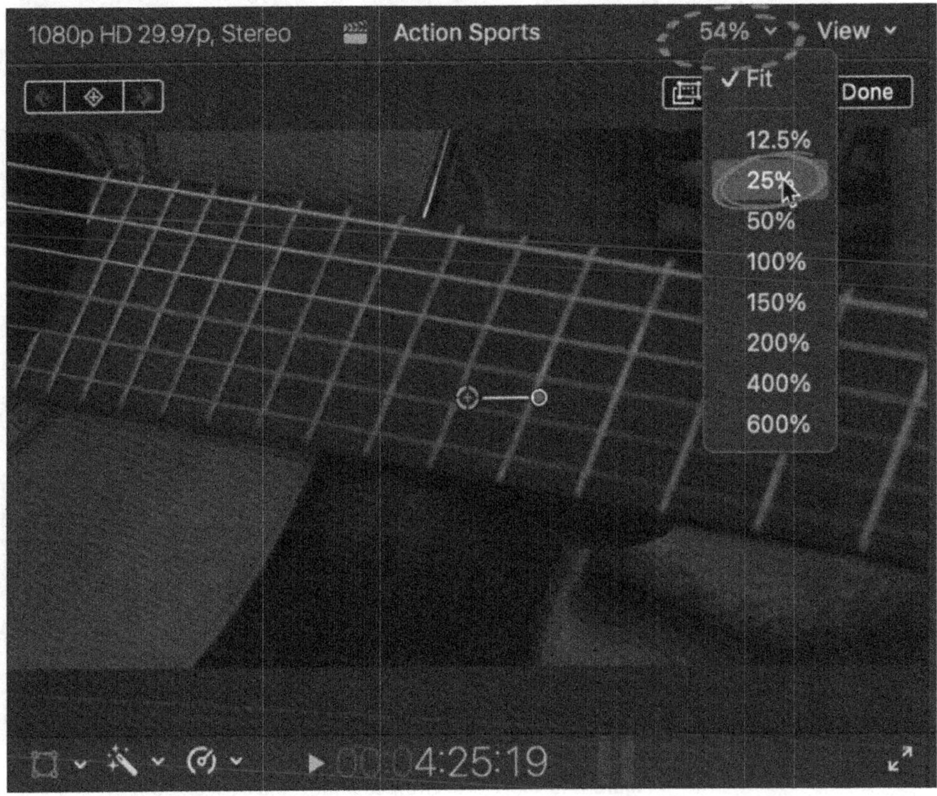

Figure 7.44: Select a smaller percentage from the View Zoom menu

5. In the Viewer, click on the **Transform** button – it's in the lower-left corner and looks like a square with dots in the corners. You will see the bounding box around the clip image with blue control dots. In my example, the image of the clip is much larger than the frame size of my project, and I want to focus on the hand playing the guitar. Move the larger image within the Viewer.

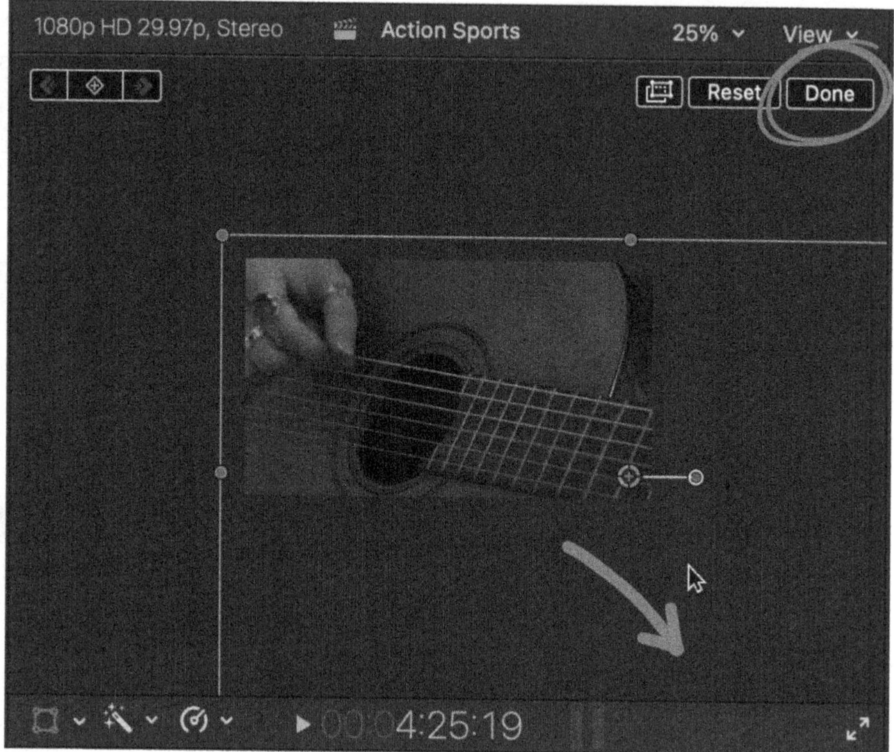

Figure 7.45: Move the reframed image and click on Done

6. We can reframe this without losing any resolution. Click on the **Done** button in the upper-right corner of the Viewer.

Cropping, distorting, and who is Ken Burns anyway?

Cropping, distorting, and using the **Ken Burns** effect in Final Cut Pro provides editors with versatile tools to enhance the visual storytelling of their footage. Cropping allows you to focus on specific areas of a clip, while distortion can create unique visual styles, and the Ken Burns effect adds dynamic motion by panning and zooming across still images or clips. The advantage of these techniques is that they can transform static content into engaging narratives, drawing viewers' attention to important details and creating a more immersive experience.

In this recipe, we will explore the different tools within the **Transform** menu and how they function.

Getting ready

For this recipe, you will need at least one still image, preferably in a horizontal format.

How to do it...

You can insert your own cropping, chopping, and trimming cooking pun here. Let's get started:

1. Add a clip to your project in the timeline, then *Option + click* it so that the clip is selected and the playhead is parked on top of it. In the Viewer, click on the down arrow next to the **Transform** icon that's in the lower-left corner and looks like a square with dots in the corners.

2. You may remember that we used the **Transform** menu in the *Unmasking the mystery of masks* recipe earlier in this chapter. From the **Transform** menu, select **Transform**. In the Viewer, the outer edge of the clip will be highlighted in white, and there will be blue control points in the corners and along the sides. Click and drag one corner, and notice how the corners keep the aspect ratio of the image intact as you enlarge or shrink the image.

Figure 7.46: The Transform corners keep the aspect ratio of the image

3. The side control points condense or elongate the image. Try squeezing the image from the side or bottom.

Figure 7.47: The Transform sides condense or elongate the image

4. The control point on the arm coming out of the center of the image will spin the image. Try this out.

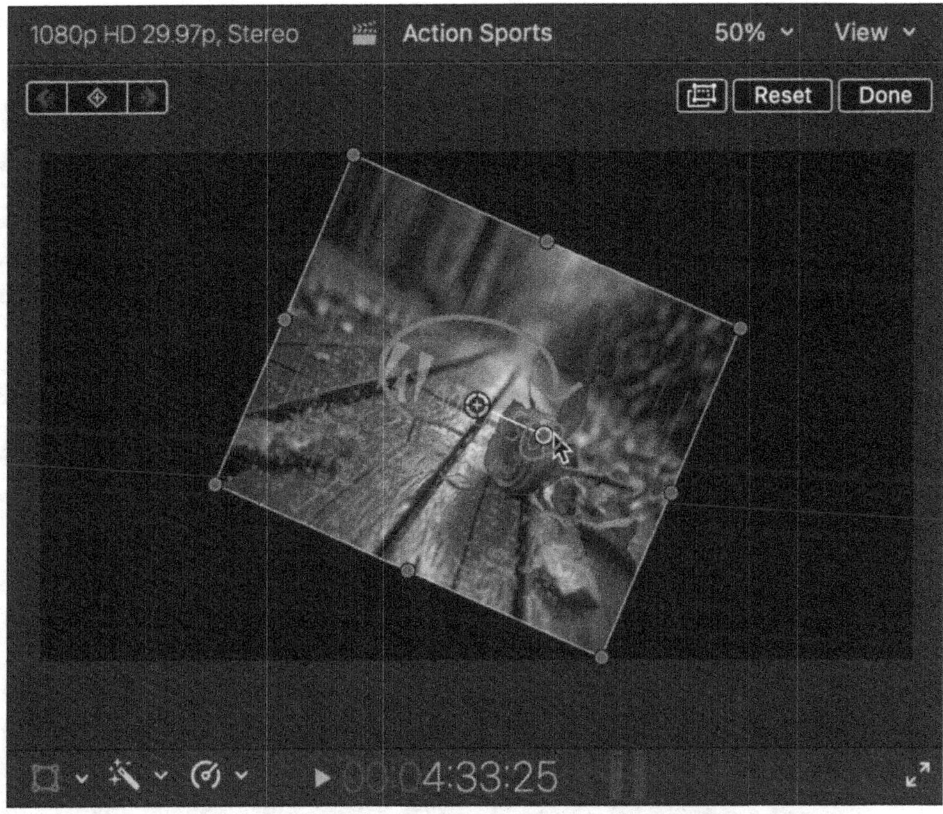

Figure 7.48: The Transform center spins the image

5. Click on the **Reset** button in the upper-right corner of the Viewer.

6. From the **Transform** menu, select **Distort**.

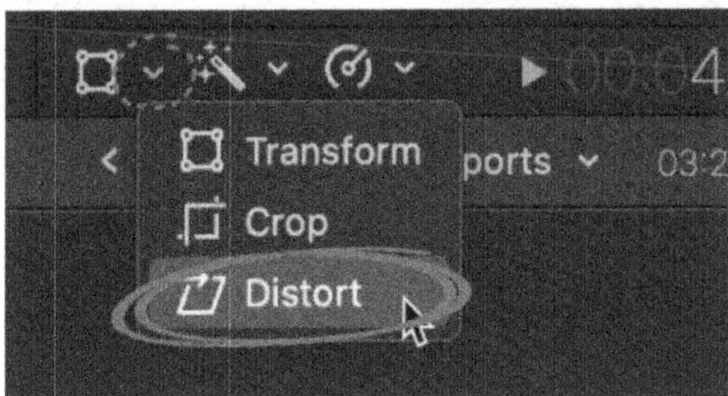

Figure 7.49: Select Distort from the Transform menu

7. The **Distort** command, as you can imagine, moves the control points of the bounding box independently. Explore how the corners can move.

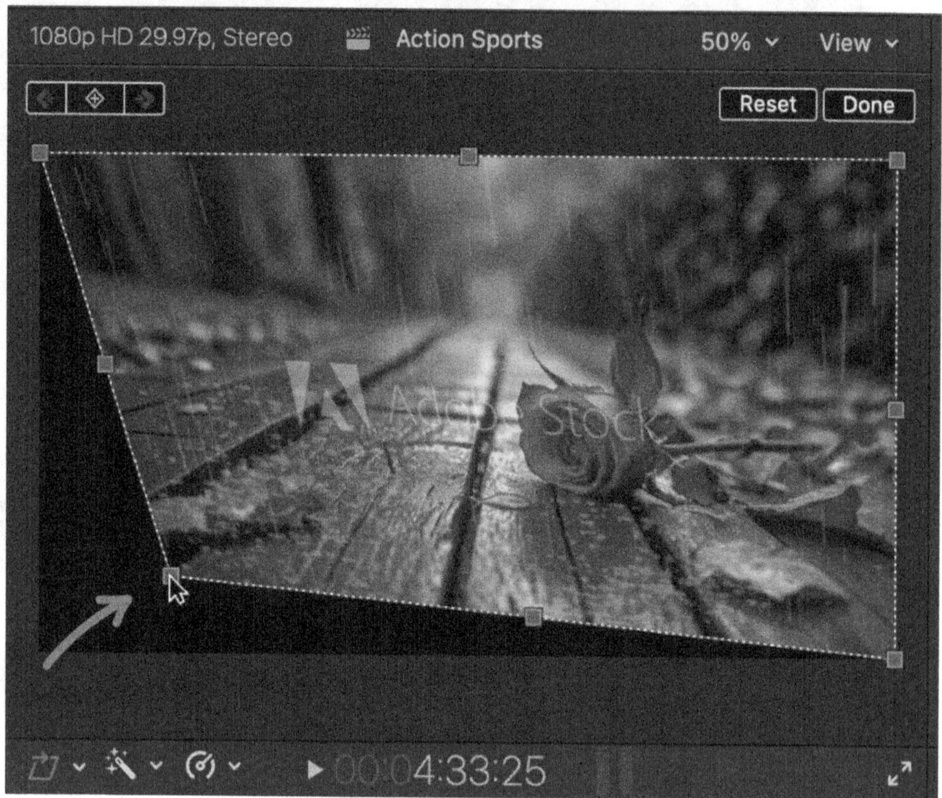

Figure 7.50: Move the Distort control points independently

8. Now click the **Reset** button again.

9. Click on the **Transform** menu again and select **Crop**. The **Crop** section has three options: **Trim**, **Crop**, and **Ken Burns**.

10. Select the **Trim** tab. In contrast to the other tools, **Trim** will not change the aspect ratio of the clip but rather cut the video. That is to say, the image is not zoomed or changed, just trimmed off. This works well for split screens.

Figure 7.51: The Trim tool cuts the image

11. Click **Reset** before continuing.

12. Now, click on the **Crop** tab. **Crop** keeps the aspect ratio and zooms into the image. Here, click and drag a corner to zoom into a portion of the image.

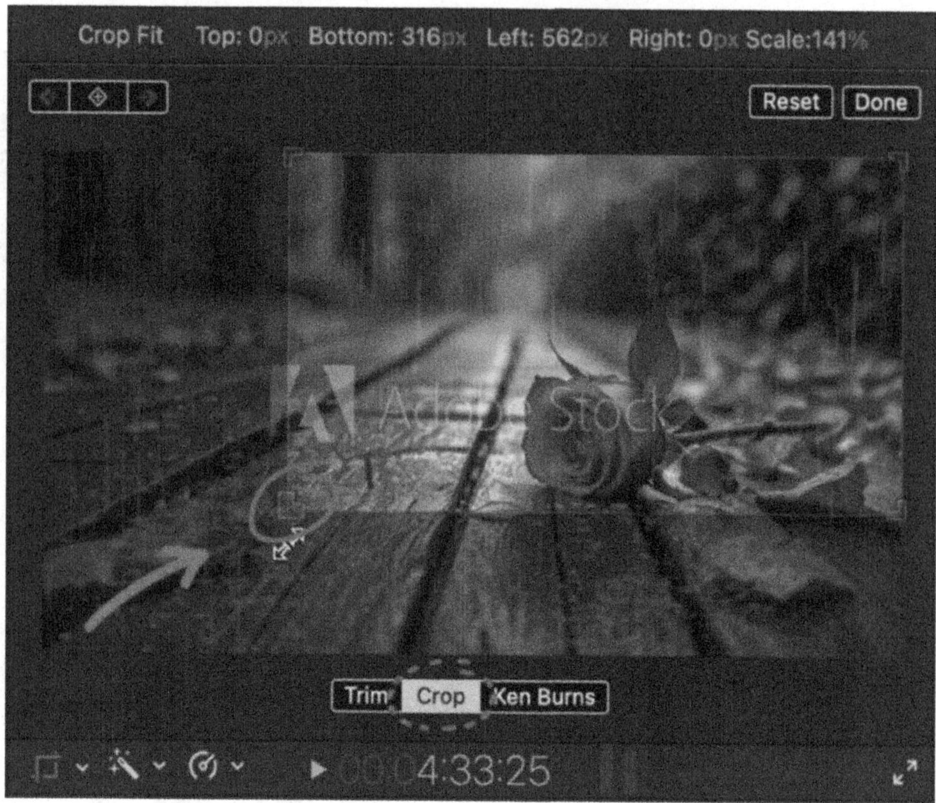

Figure 7.52: The Crop tool keeps the aspect ratio of the image

Notice that when you click on **Done**, the new corners of the image spring to the frame size of the project. The image zooms into the portion that has been cropped, but the aspect ratio of the clip is consistent.

13. The last tab is called **Ken Burns,** named after the famous documentary filmmaker. In 1990, he made a series called The Civil War. Burns had no moving pictures of the American Civil War to use in the film; however, luckily, that period of history was extensively documented through photography. So, with only photos to work with, Ken Burns created the technique of slowly panning and zooming over the photos to add motion and interest to his storytelling. It became so popular that Apple added it as a crop effect.

When you click the **Ken Burns** tab, notice that the green bounding box is the starting point of the clip and the red bounding box is the end point of the clip. There is no need to change **Spatial Conform** in the Inspector. The effect automatically conforms the starting frame of the clip to fill the screen. See the *Reframing clip resolution* recipe earlier in this chapter. This effect creates a pan and zoom from the starting frame to the end frame.

In my example, I'm going to make the end frame much smaller. Notice a white arrow in the middle of the screen, indicating the direction from the center cross of the green start to the center cross of the red end.

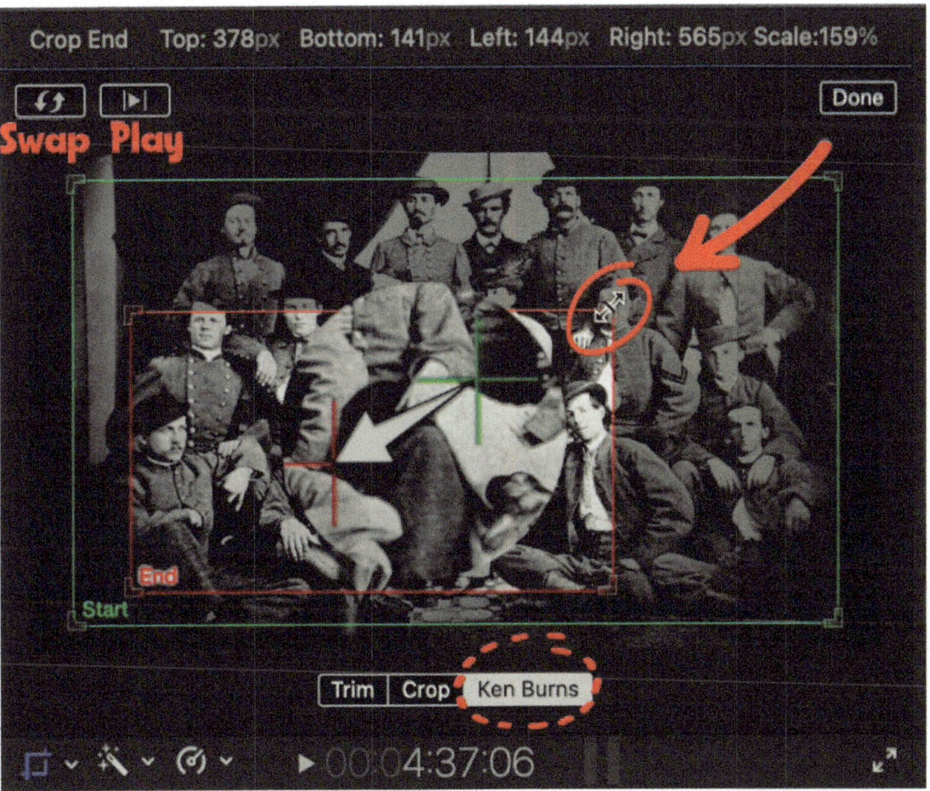

Figure 7.53: The Ken Burns effect creates a slow pan and zoom

14. Now click on the **Play** icon in the upper-left corner, and it will preview your effect. In my example, the distance the full screen moved was too great from the start to the end for the length of time the clip was playing. The zoom was too fast. The **Ken Burns** effect is meant to be a gentle pan and zoom. Resize the end frame to be closer in size to the start frame for a smooth animation.

15. Depending on your story, sometimes you may want the image to start large and zoom in to emphasize a character. Or, the story may call for the starting image to be smaller and zoomed out for perspective. Click on the **Swap** icon in the upper-left corner, which looks like two arrows turning around. This will swap the position of the start and the end frames. So, instead of zooming in, the effect can zoom out.

16. When you have positioned your start and end as you like, click on the **Done** button in the upper-right corner of the Viewer and enjoy your creation. Well done – you have preserved history.

8

Correcting and Enhancing Audio

The symphony of sound in the kitchen of video editing, where audio serves as the distinctive ingredient to a savory experience. There is a saying, *"Audio is half of what you see."* In other words, don't underestimate the importance of audio in the viewer's experience of your story.

We'll explore how to balance music and dialogue, as well as enhance audio with effects and equalize the soundscape of our clips. Get ready to immerse yourself in the art of audio editing and discover how it truly completes the sensory experience of your videos.

In this chapter, you will cover tasks such as setting audio roles, utilizing the **Range** tool to control audio levels, adjusting levels efficiently with keyboard shortcuts, and keyframing audio spikes for precise control over sound dynamics. Additionally, you'll learn techniques including using the **Audio Enhancement** functions, syncing audio from external recorders, recording scratch audio, applying audio effects, and fixing mono recordings, ensuring your projects sound polished and professional.

So, in this chapter, we will cover the following recipes:

- Setting audio roles
- Using the Range Selection tool to duck audio
- Adjusting levels with keyboard shortcuts
- Keyframing audio spikes
- Using the Audio Enhancement functions

- Syncing audio from an external recorder

- Recording scratch audio

- Using audio effects

- Fixing a mono recording

Technical requirements

This chapter will discuss how to adjust the volume level of your clips. Video projects should be exported with the average audio volume level at **-12** dB. To monitor your volume level easily, click on the small audio meter in the lower center of the Viewer panel.

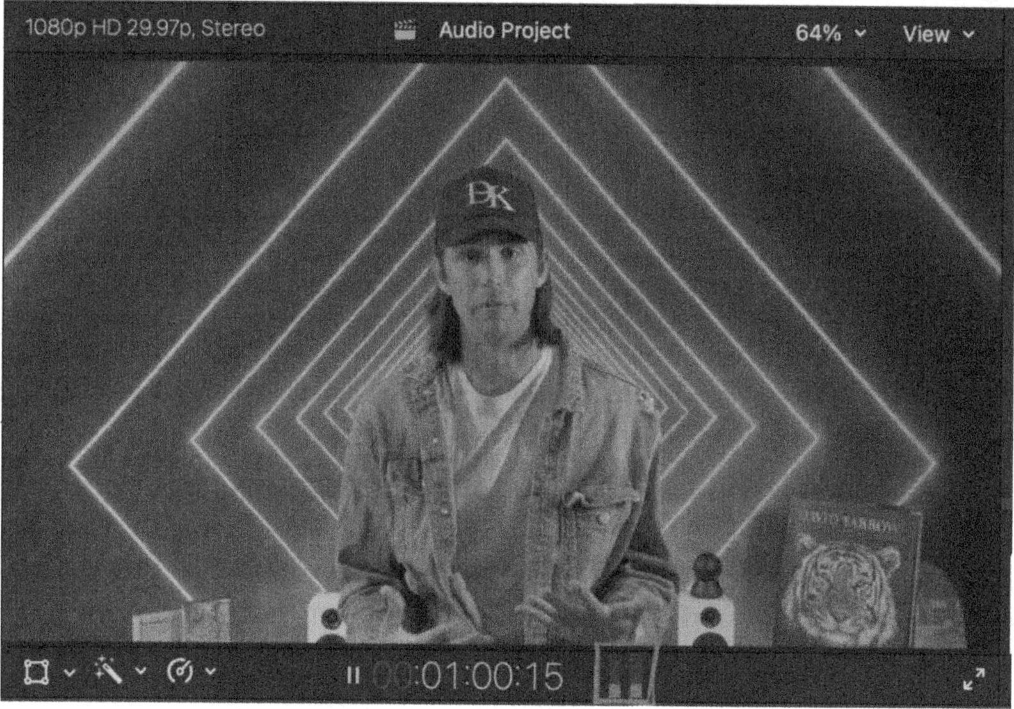

Figure 8.1: Click on the small audio meter in the Viewer panel

This will display a larger audio meter on the right side of the Timeline panel. You can drag the edge of the panel to adjust the size of the Audio Meter panel.

Figure 8.2: Adjust the size of the audio meter in the Timeline panel

Professional broadcast levels should average at **-12** dB and, on some occasions, peak at **-6** dB. Levels should never reach **0** dB, which indicates distortion and is displayed in red. It is a good practice to go by the audio meter readings you see and not the volume you hear. You may even take off your headphones and set your audio level by sight in the audio meter. Then, put on your headphones and adjust your system settings to a comfortable listening level. Remember this profound truth: green is good, red is bad.

When video images are stacked on each other, the topmost clip covers – and in a sense, cancels – the images underneath. In contrast, when audio files are stacked together, the volume is added together. So, when layering clips that include audio with music and so on, it is important to monitor the overall audio level with a close eye on the audio meters.

It should also be noted that when working with audio, clips can be listened to individually:

1. *Option + click* on the clip you want to work with so that it is both selected and the playhead is parked on top of it.

2. Click on the **Solo** icon, which looks like a pair of headphones located in the upper-right corner of the Timeline panel, or use the keyboard shortcut of *Option + S*. This will disable the audio of all clips except the one selected.

3. Now you can use the nifty shortcut of *Shift + ?* to play for 2 seconds on either side of the skimmer. You can also use the **Audio Skim** icon, which looks like a skimmer line with audio waveforms on either side. Click on this to hear your audio scrubbed as you skim through your clips. I don't have this one on all the time, but it is useful for finding just the right audio sequence.

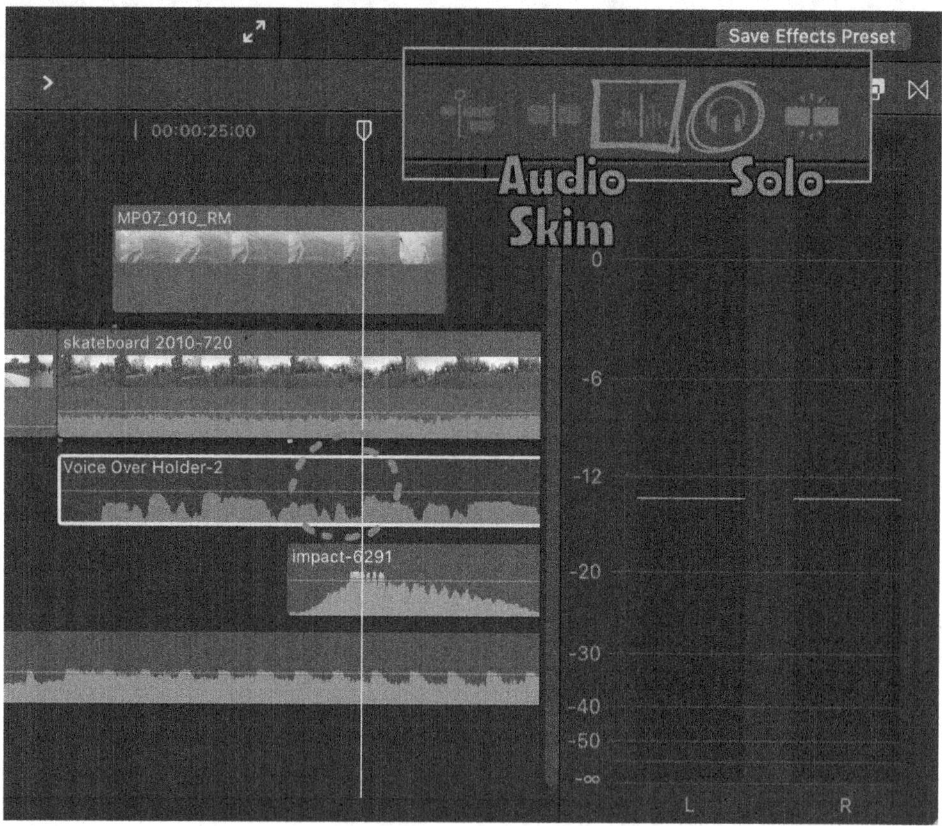

Figure 8.3: Note the Solo and Audio Skim icons

There is one more item to mention in preparation for this chapter on audio enhancement. It is helpful to extend the Inspector panel to see the many parameters available for adjustment. Click on the **Show Audio Inspector** icon in the upper-left corner of the Inspector panel, which looks like a speaker with sound waves coming out of it. Then, double-click on the top title bar of the Inspector panel. The panel will extend lower to show all of the adjustment parameters.

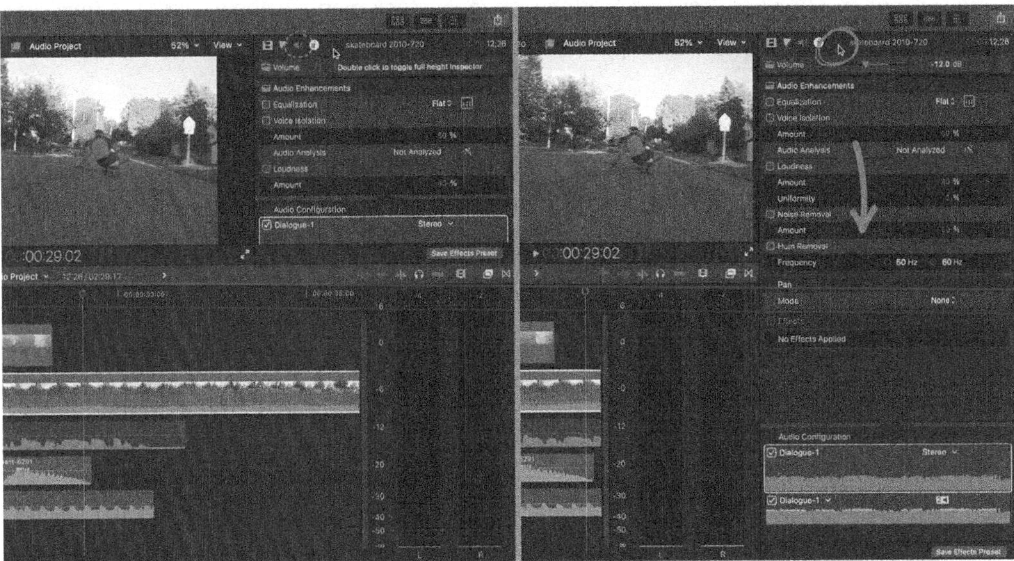

Figure 8.4: Double-click the title bar to extend the Inspector panel lower

Setting audio roles

Set your audio roles like setting the table – everything in its place for a flawless feast. Setting audio roles in Final Cut Pro allows you to categorize and label different audio elements, such as dialogue, music, and effects. By assigning roles, you can visually manage your audio tracks more efficiently, enabling faster editing and mixing workflows. The advantage is that it streamlines the process for better organization and control, making collaborative projects and complex edits easier to handle.

In this recipe, we will explore how to properly label and organize different types of audio media.

Getting ready

Make sure the **Audio Inspector** options are expanded, as mentioned in the *Technical requirements* section.

It would be helpful to import music and sound effects files, as well as video files that have an audio component. Preview media is available on most stock media websites. See the *Importing media into Final Cut Pro* recipe in *Chapter 2*.

How to do it...

Not to be confused with freshly baked rolls, let's see how to set audio roles:

1. There are several ways to view and change the audio role of a clip: the Inspector panel, a right-click pop-up menu, the Final Cut Pro menu, and keyboard shortcuts. Let's start with the Audio Inspector panel. *Option + click* on the clip you want to work with so that it is both selected and the playhead is parked on top of it. Look to the lower portion of the Audio Inspector panel. Click on the down arrow in the lower Stereo Signal Waveforms panel. A pop-up menu will appear. Select **Music -1** from the list.

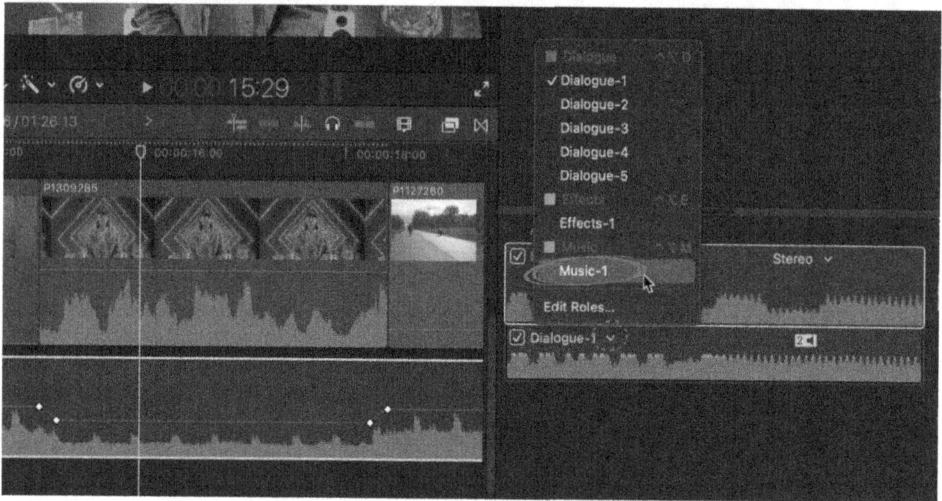

Figure 8.5: Select Music-1 from the waveform pop-up menu

2. *Option + click* on a different clip so that it is both selected and the playhead is parked on top of it. In my example, I am going to use a sound effect. Right-click on the clip and, from the **Clip** pop-up menu, select **Assign Audio Roles** and **Effects-1**.

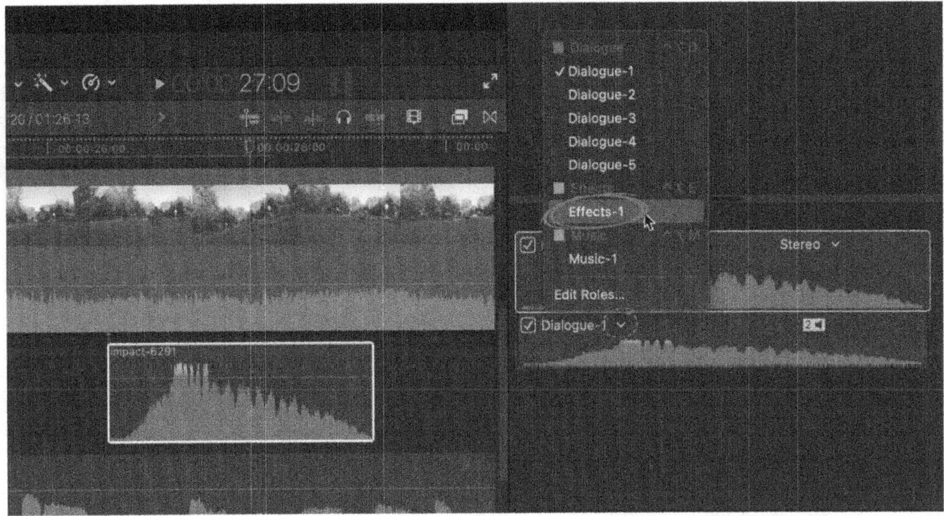

Figure 8.6: Select Effects-1 from the right-click pop-up menu in the Timeline panel

3. The Final Cut Pro menu has this command as well. With another clip selected, from the **Modify** menu, select **Assign Audio Roles** and **Effects-1**.

4. As you have probably noticed by now, you can use keyboard shortcuts. With a clip selected, press *Control + Option + D* to assign the **Dialog** role, press *Control + Option + E* to assign the **Effects** role, and press *Control + Option + M* to assign the **Music** role.

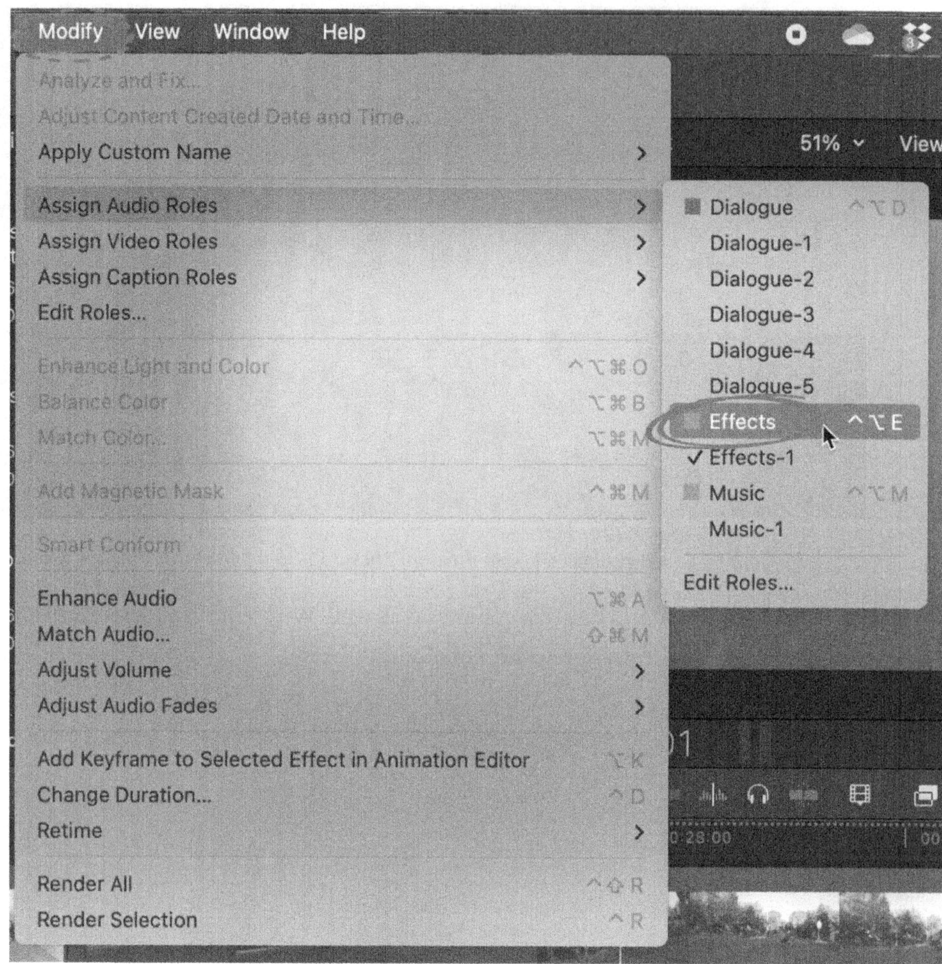

Figure 8.7: From the Modify menu, select Assign Audio Roles and Effects-1

Now, with those roles assigned properly, we can explore the ways that Final Cut Pro can visually help keep our media arranged. See how similar media are grouped together and given different colors. In my example, the timeline is not very complicated, but you will be able to see how large projects with multiple layers can be quickly organized to let you focus on a particular audio type when editing.

5. Start by opening the timeline index by clicking on the **Timeline Index** button, which is a rectangle that says the word **Index** and is located at the top of the left corner of the Timeline panel.

6. Then, near the top of the timeline index, click on the tab for **Roles**, and at the bottom of the panel, click on the **Show Audio Lanes** button.

7. Finally, click the **Focus** icon for effects, which is on the right side of the **Effects** line in the center of the panel and looks like a round dot. Notice how the **Dialog** and **Music** lanes are reduced to simple lines to allow the editor to focus on **Effects** in the Timeline panel.

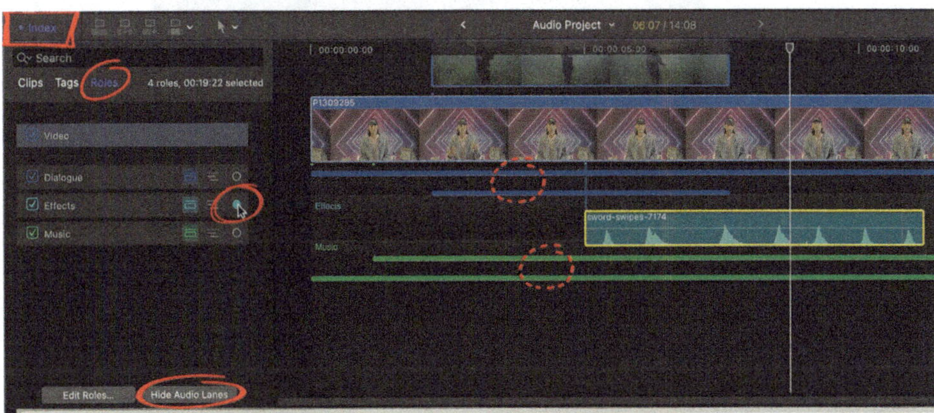

Figure 8.8: Click on the Focus effects icon in the timeline index

8. Spend some time exploring how to focus on, or collapse, different audio roles.

There's more...

It is possible to have audio roles assigned when importing your media. Near the bottom of the right-hand **Settings** panel, under the **Assign Audio Role** section, there is a drop-down menu – your choices are **Automatically, Dialogue, Effects**, and **Music**. If you know you have a specific media type, you can assign it accordingly. Or, if you have a mix of media types, you can leave the setting on **Automatically**.

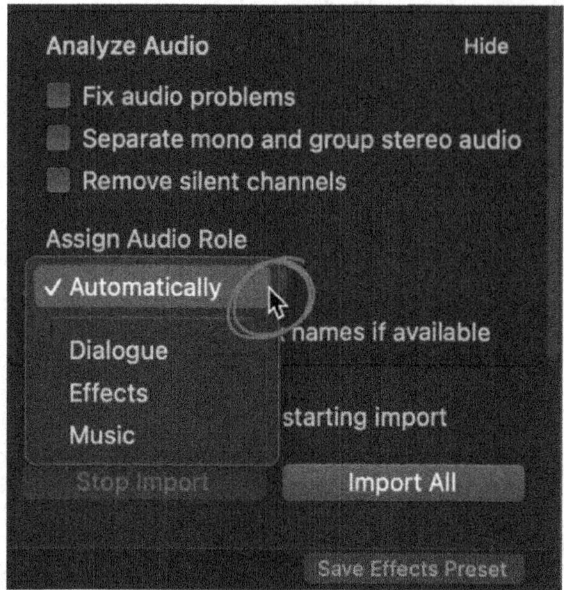

Figure 8.9: Select Automatically or a specific audio role when importing media

If the media is all dialogue, for example, it works well. If there is mixed media and import is set to **Automatically**, it does not always work properly. So, it is always a good idea to review your footage and reassign it as needed. This can be done in the Event Browser panel as well as the Timeline panel.

Using the Range Selection tool to duck audio

As we said in the *Technical requirements* section of this chapter, when audio files are stacked together, the volume is added together. So, when layering clips that include dialogue with music and so on, it is important to monitor the overall audio level. Audio levels should average at **-12** dB and, on some occasions, peak at **-6** dB. The difference between professional productions and amateur productions is the attention to detail like this. When you have a music bed (i.e., instrumental music) playing under dialogue, it is important to duck, or lower, the volume of the music so that the dialogue is understandable.

Using the **Range Selection** tool allows you to quickly select a specific portion of the audio and adjust its levels, perfect for ducking music or sound effects beneath dialogue. This technique helps create smooth transitions between audio elements, enhancing the clarity of spoken words without manually keyframing every adjustment. It also speeds up the workflow and offers precise control, ensuring balanced audio throughout your project.

In this recipe, we will show how the **Range Selection** tool can make quick work of ducking your music.

How to do it...

Ducking audio is way easier than preparing a roast duck feast. Check it out:

1. Prepare a project in the Timeline panel in which the primary storyline clips alternate between dialogue and non-dialogue with a music file playing underneath.

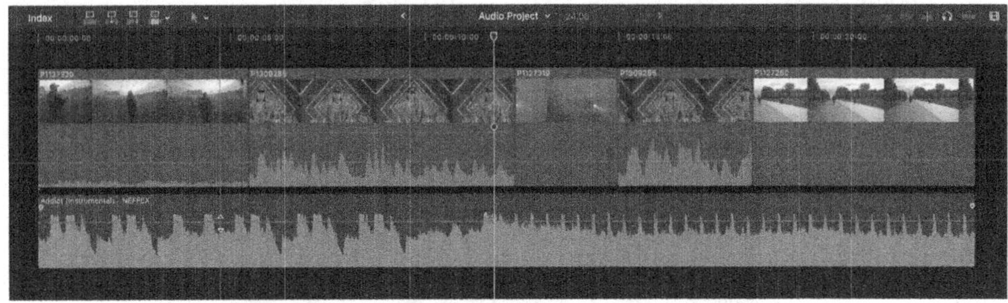

Figure 8.10: Prepare alternating dialogue clips over a music bed

2. Here, we are going to adjust the volume of the music without the **Range Selection** tool. Notice that when you move the cursor over the **Adjust Volume** line in the middle of the audio waveform, the cursor changes to up and down arrows. Click and drag the **Adjust Volume** line up and down to see how the volume of the whole clip is affected. We want to adjust only a portion of the music under the dialogue.

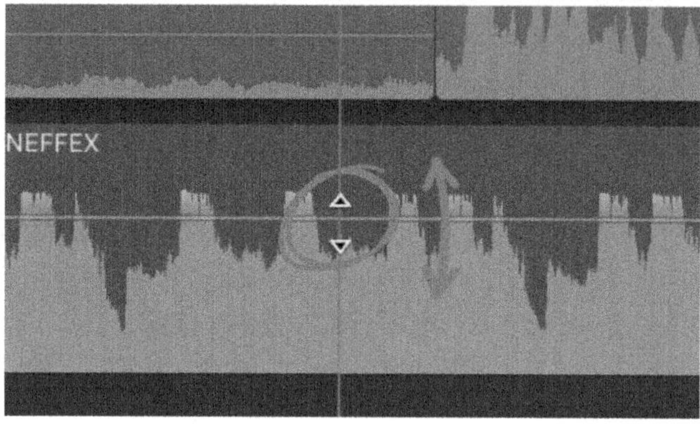

Figure 8.11: Drag the Adjust Volume line up or down

3. We want to duck, or lower, the volume under the dialogue but leave the music up during the non-speaking scenery. Let's start by adjusting the volume manually. While holding down the *Option* key, keep the mouse over the **Adjust Volume** line in the music clip. Notice that the cursor changes to an arrow with a plus sign in a diamond shape. Click once just before the start of the dialogue clip above the music. This will create a keyframe control point.

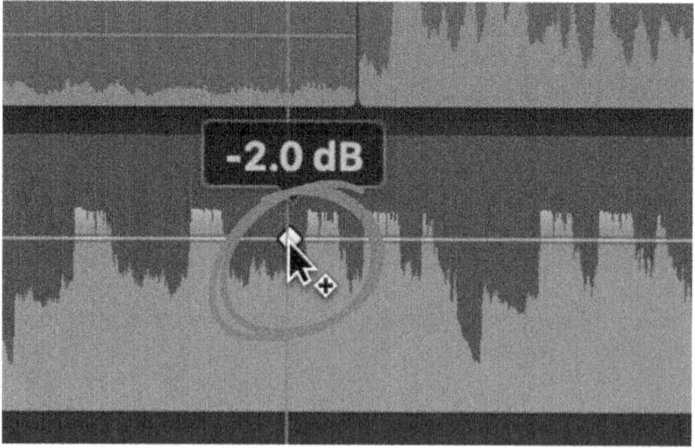

Figure 8.12: Click the Adjust Volume line while holding the Option key to create a keyframe

4. Add three more keyframe control points along the music clip's **Adjust Volume** line under either side of the dialogue clip above it. They are called *keyframes* because they are key, or primary, to our volume adjustment. We set these, and the computer will calculate the in-between slope of change.

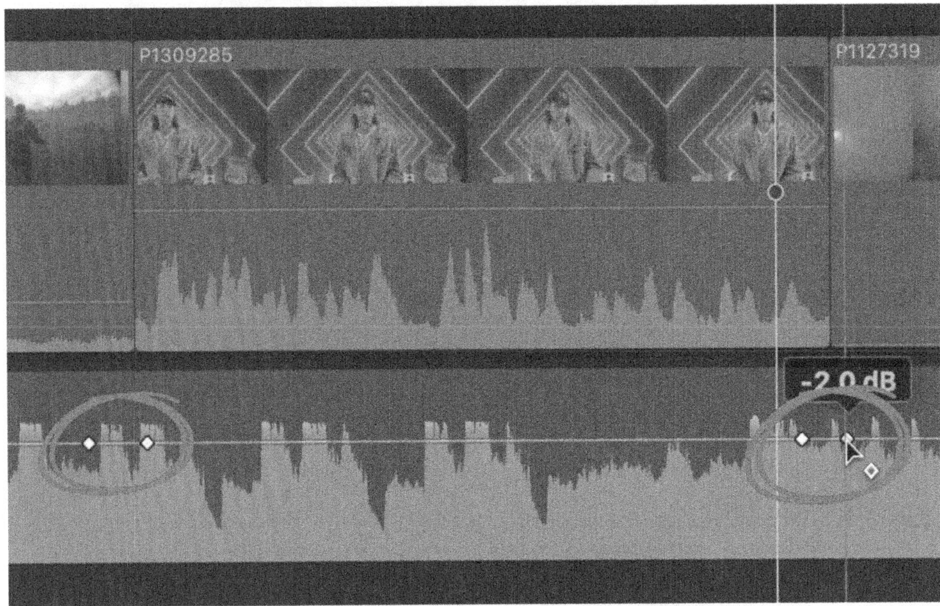

Figure 8.13: Create keyframes by Option + clicking on the Adjust Volume line

5. Move your mouse over the **Adjust Volume** line between the center keyframe points. Notice that the cursor changes to four arrows. Drag the **Adjust Volume** line down and see that the volume gradually adjusts a fade between the other keyframe control points.

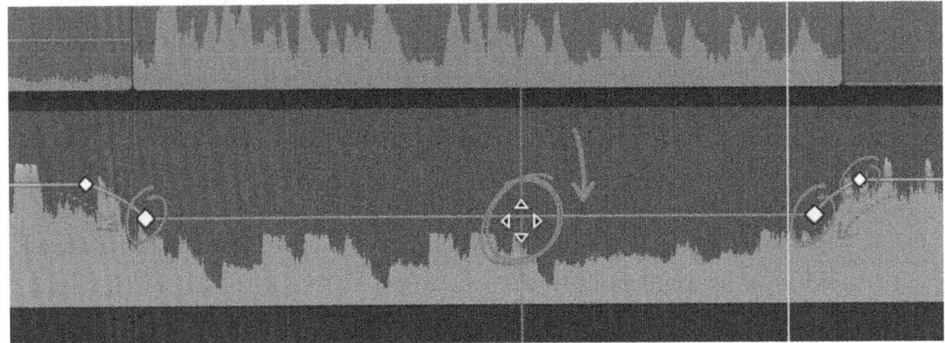

Figure 8.14: Drag down the Volume Adjust line between Keyframes

Congratulations, you have ducked your audio! But there is a faster way to do this.

6.   Move to a different part of your project that has not had the audio adjusted. Near the upper-left corner of the Timeline panel, click on the **Tools** icon and select **Range Selection**. Or, faster yet, skip the tool menu and simply press the keyboard shortcut *R*.

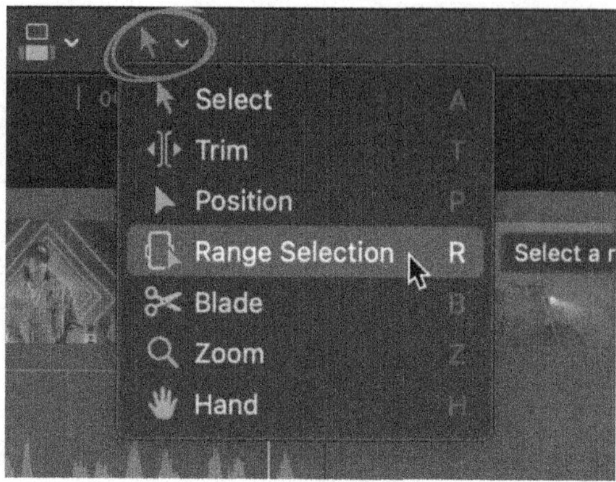

Figure 8.15: Select the Range Selection tool

7.   Now, in the music file, click and drag to select a portion of audio that's right underneath the dialogue clip.

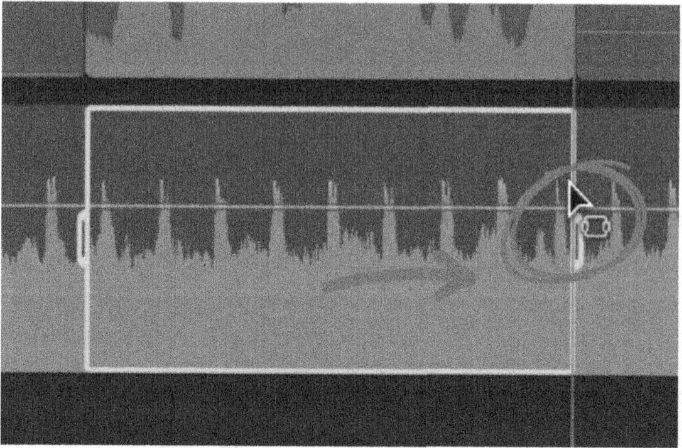

Figure 8.16: Select a range in the music file

8.   Now, simply drag the **Adjust Volume** line down, and Final Cut Pro automatically creates keyframes for that audio fade.

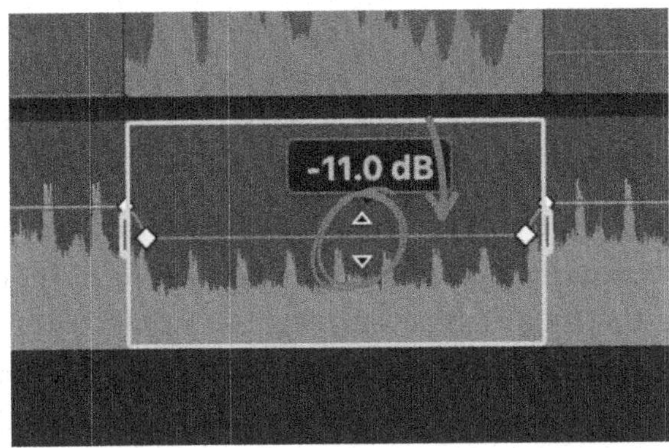

Figure 8.17: Keyframes are automatically created when dragging down the Adjust Volume line

9.   Press the *A* key to go back to the regular **Selection** tool. That's fast. Nice work.

Adjusting levels with keyboard shortcuts

By using keyboard shortcuts, you can raise or lower audio levels in small increments, making it easy to achieve the perfect balance between dialogue, music, and effects without needing to open additional menus or tools. This helps speed up the editing process, giving you more time to focus on creative decisions and ensuring consistent sound levels across your timeline.

In this recipe, we will explore several methods for adjusting audio volume and how you can use them to edit faster.

Getting ready

In this recipe, we need an audio clip with keyframe volume adjustments. To save time, my example will be the music clip edited in the previous recipe. You can do the same.

How to do it...

Great chefs know some shortcuts to speed up their work, and it is no different for editors. Here is how to speed up your audio editing skills:

1. First, let's check where to find the volume adjustments that have associated keyboard shortcuts. Click on the **Modify** menu, then **Adjust Volume**, and notice the keyboard short-cuts for the **Up (+1 dB)** and **Down (-1 dB)** commands. Adjusting the volume up by one decibel at a time uses the shortcut *Control + =*, while adjusting the volume down one decibel at a time is *Control + -*. You can think of it as the plus and minus keys with *Control* as the modifier key.

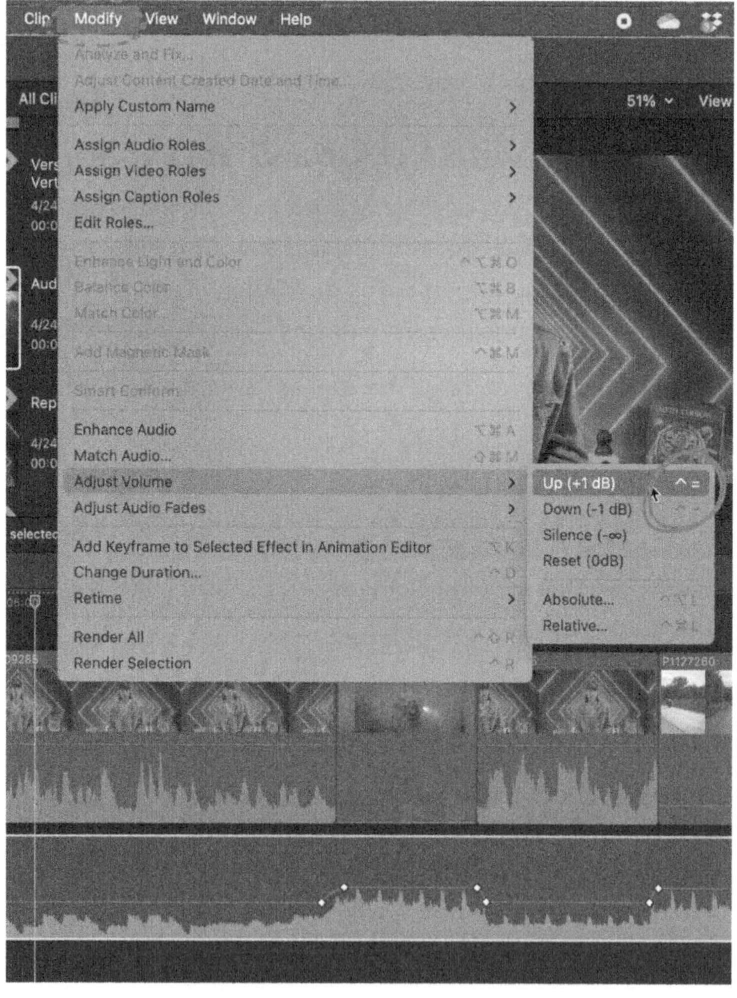

Figure 8.18: Notice the audio keyboard shortcut in the Modify menu

2. In my example, I am using the music clip from the previous recipe, mentioned in the *Getting ready* section, in which we made keyframe control points to duck the music under dialogue clips. Let's say I want to increase the overall volume of the music clip. It would be a pain to select each Keyframe and raise it up. Instead, click on the music clip to select it and press the keyboard shortcut of *Control + =* several times. As you adjust the volume level with the keyboard shortcut, note that the level of the waveform in the Timeline panel moves up and down while keeping the relative position of the keyframes intact.

3. In fact, we can adjust the volume on the fly. Move your skimmer to the beginning of the music clip and press the *spacebar* to play the sequence. Keep an eye on your audio meter and adjust the volume up or down by quickly pressing our new keyboard shortcuts until your mix is averaging **-12** dB. Nice.

4. Pause your playback, and let's explore how to adjust the volume across an entire clip by using a relative volume adjustment. Select a clip that has some volume adjustments with keyframe control points, such as the music clip from the previous recipe. Press the keyboard shortcut *Control + Command + L*. Notice that at the bottom of the Viewer panel, there is a symbol that looks like a variated waveform representing a relative volume change. There is also a plus sign and a space. Type 3 and press the *Return* key.

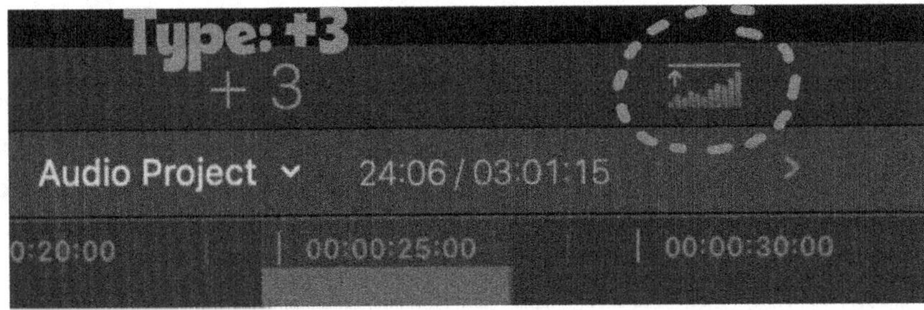

Figure 8.19: Increase the relative volume of a clip

It brings our relative audio volume up by three decibels from the current level. Note that this is from the current level, or what had been the most recent change. This will work well when you are adjusting volume and want to keep the keyframe control points or adjust the overall volume from your last adjustment. The default adjustment is a plus sign to increase the volume. To increase the volume, you only need to type in the number of the decibel increase. If you are decreasing the volume, you would also need to type the - (minus) sign along with the number of the decibel change. Also, if you type in an amount but want to cancel it, simply press the *Esc* (escape) key.

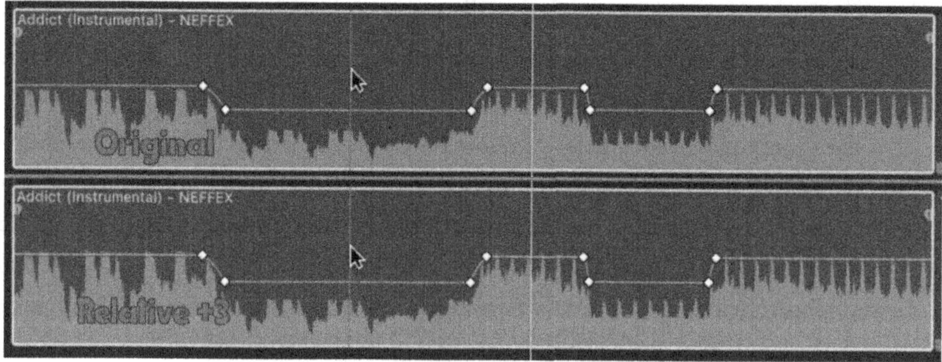

Figure 8.20: Note the result of a relative volume increase

5. Now, let's explore an absolute volume adjustment. Select a clip that has some volume adjustments with keyframe control points, such as the music clip from the previous recipe. Press the keyboard shortcut *Control + Option + L*. Notice that at the bottom of the Viewer panel, there is a symbol that looks like a straight waveform representing an absolute volume change. Again, there is a plus sign and a space. Type 3 and press the *Return* key.

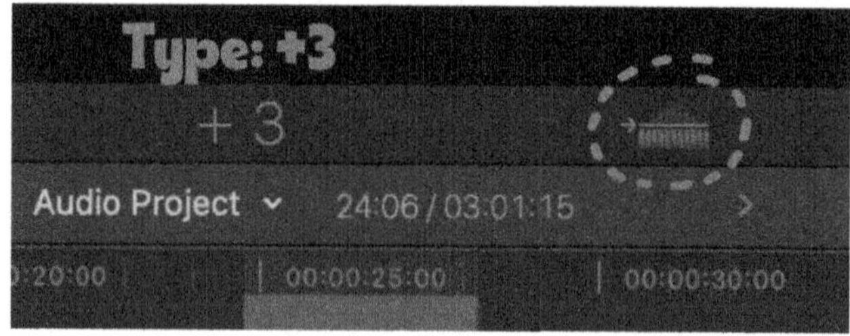

Figure 8.21: Increase the absolute volume of a clip

Whoa, this may not be what you expected. This command brings our absolute audio volume up by three decibels from the original level. Note that this is from the original level, and not what had been the most recent change. It is clear from *Figure 8.22* that this does not work well when you are adjusting volume and want to keep the keyframe control points or adjust the overall volume from your last adjustment. Keyframes are canceled. But it does work well if you know the original volume level or have not changed it yet, and want a quick way to change the overall volume level, or if you quickly want to set multiple clips to silent. Select the desired clips and set the absolute volume to **–100**.

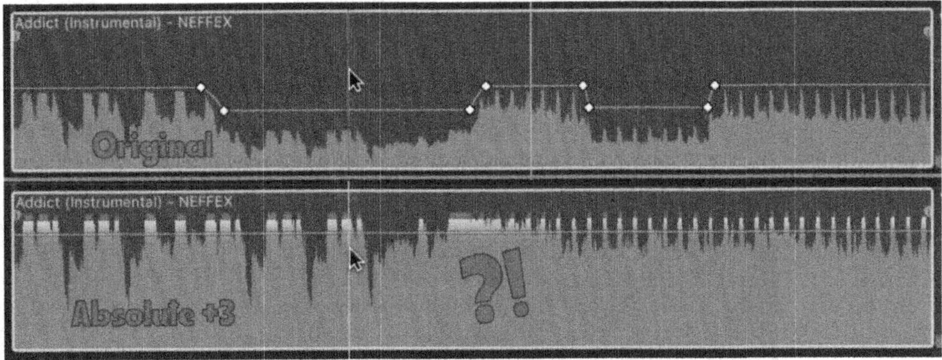

Figure 8.22: Note the result of an absolute volume increase

6. In my example, I did not want to lose my audio keyframes. Good thing there is an **Undo** command! Press *Command + Z* to undo this change.

> The absolute adjustment uses the same input method as the relative adjustment. You can refer back to *step 4*.

7. There is one more audio keyboard shortcut to mention, and that is **Match Audio**. This feature does not match levels but, rather, equalization – or some may say sound tone. This works well in a situation where you might have the same person talking but at different times in different rooms, but you want the tone to match.

Start by setting the volume levels of the two clips to be about the same. There are several ways to access the **Match Audio** feature:

- From the **Modify** menu, select **Match Audio...**

- Press the keyboard shortcut *Shift + Command + M*

- Click on the **Enhancement** icon, which looks like a magic wand located in the lower-left corner of the Viewer panel, then select **Match Audio...**

- You can also use the Audio Inspector panel. *Option + click* on the clip you want to work with so that it is both selected and the playhead is parked on top of it. This is the clip that has the subpar audio. Then, at the top of the Inspector panel, if it is not already selected, click on the **Show Audio Inspector** icon, which looks like a speaker with sound waves coming out of it. Next, in the **Equalization** parameter, there is a drop-down menu with the default setting of **Flat**.

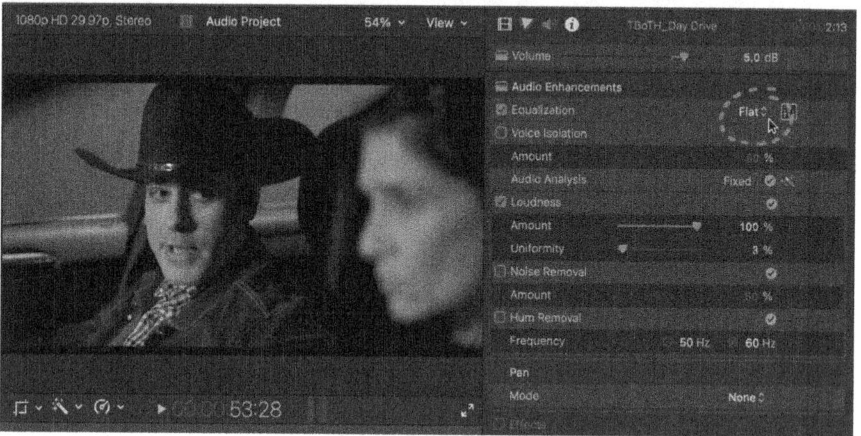

Figure 8.23: Note that the default of the Equalization menu is set to Flat

Click on this drop-down menu and, at the bottom of the list, select **Match**.

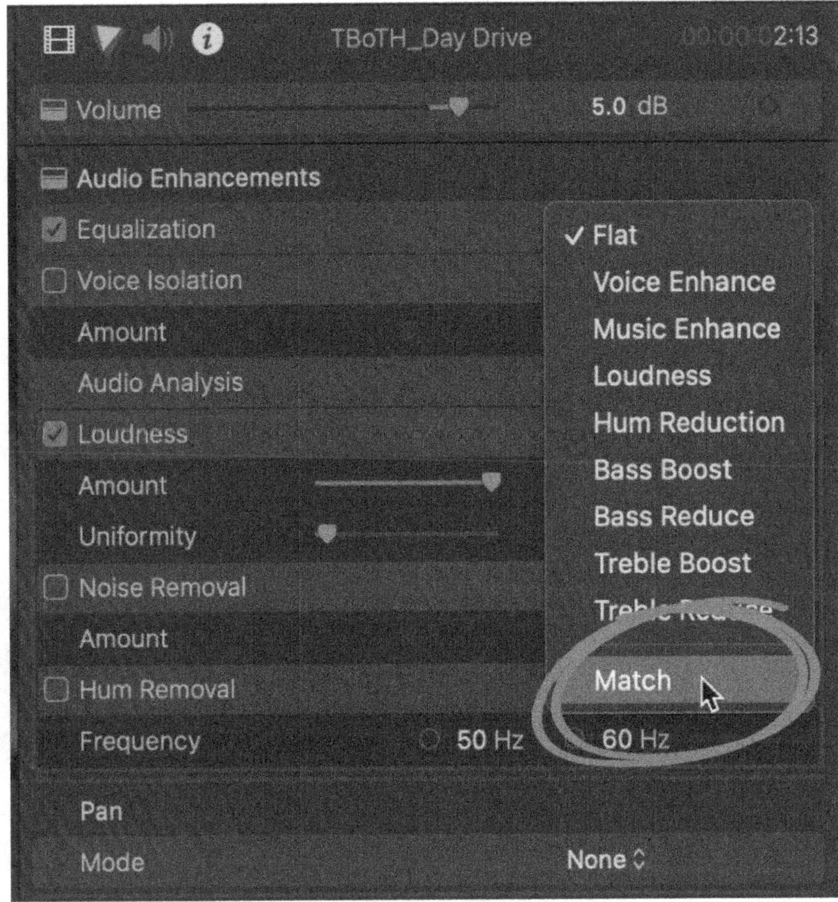

Figure 8.24: Select Match from the Equalization menu

However, you initiate the **Match Audio** feature, at this point, the Viewer panel changes to a two-up display similar to the **Match Color** command discussed in *Chapter 5* and the recipe called *Using the Match Color feature*. The clip we want to change is on the right, and the clip you are selecting for the match is on the left.

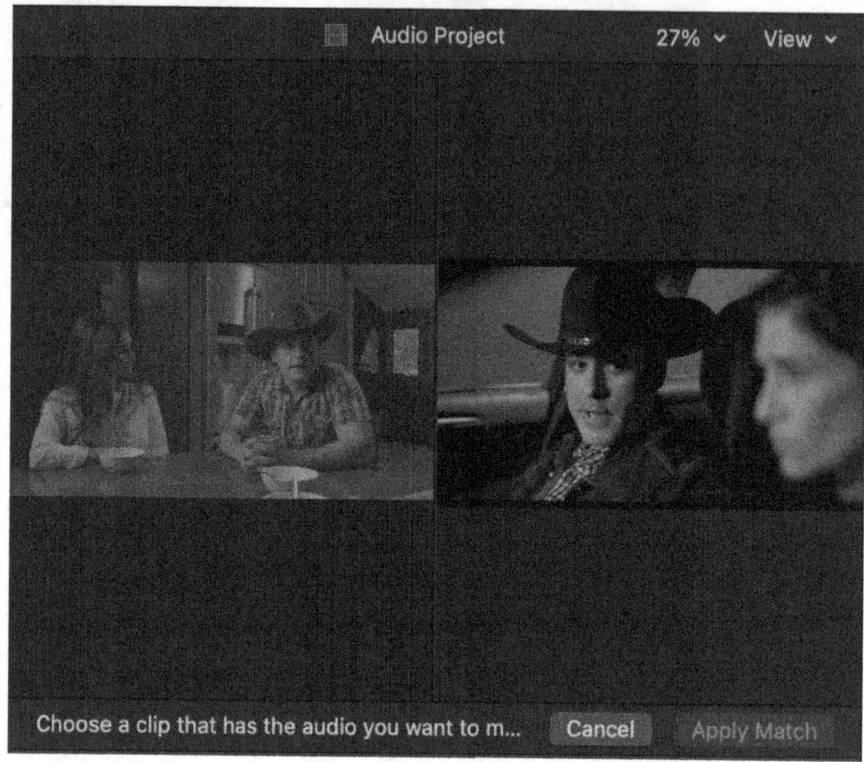

Figure 8.25: When matching, the Viewer panel shows a two-up display

8. Click on the clip in the Timeline panel with the audio you want to use. Notice that the cursor changes to a small rectangle with audio faders to indicate the selection process is active.

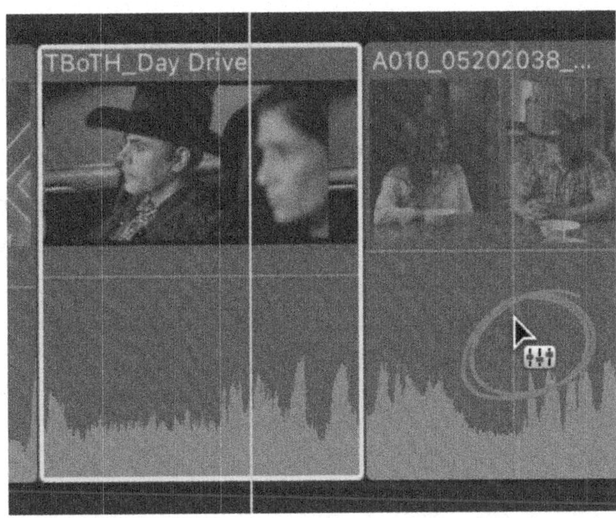

Figure 8.26: Note that the cursor changes to audio fades when selecting a matching clip

9. Now, clip on the **Apply Match** button located at the bottom right of the Viewer panel. This completes the audio equalization matching process.

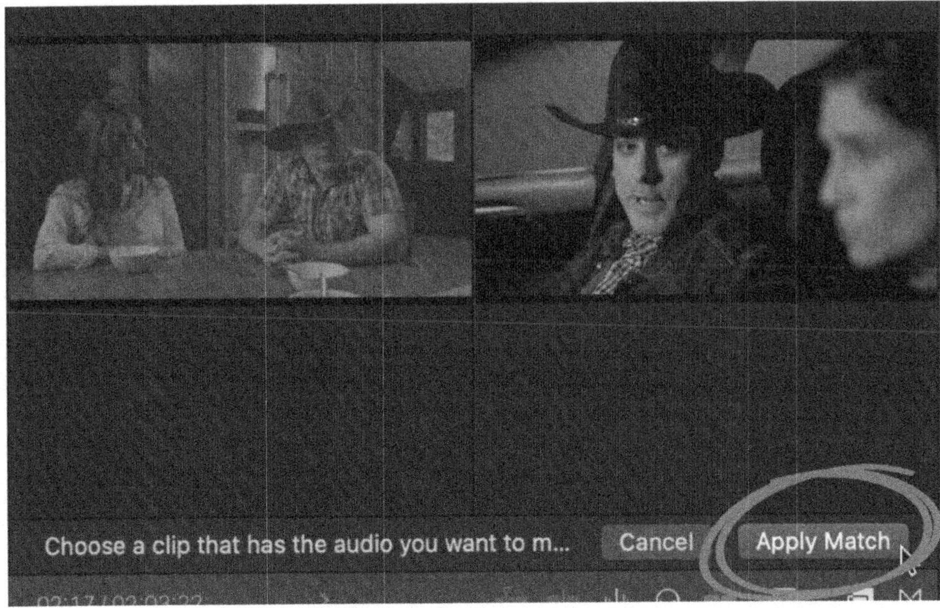

Figure 8.27: Click on the Apply Match button to complete the equalization match

10. If, at any point, you want to undo the match, simply select **Flat** from the **Equalization** menu, and the equalization of the clip will return to its original state.

Keyframing audio spikes

You can manually adjust volume levels with keyframes at specific points in your timeline to smooth out sudden loud noises or emphasize key moments. By setting keyframes, you can create gradual transitions in volume, avoiding jarring spikes or pops in the audio. The advantage of this approach is that it offers precise control over dynamic sound adjustments, resulting in a polished, professional audio mix that enhances the viewer's experience.

In this recipe, we will demonstrate the technique of leveling out jolting audio pops.

Getting ready

To follow along, use audio that contains clicks or pops. Alternatively, try recording yourself/ someone coughing or bumping the microphone, and use that audio.

How to do it...

A sudden spike of the wrong spice, or audio pop, can jolt your audience away from your story. Let's see how to mellow it out:

1. Add a clip to your project in the Timeline panel and adjust the volume of the audio so that it is averaging **-12** dB. Now listen to the audio, watching the audio meter, until you hear the audio jolt. If an audio file goes above zero into the red, the audio meter will leave a red rectangle light on above the meter with a positive number indicating the amount over zero that was reached. Remember our profound truth: green is good, red is bad. Spikes into the red will be distorted.

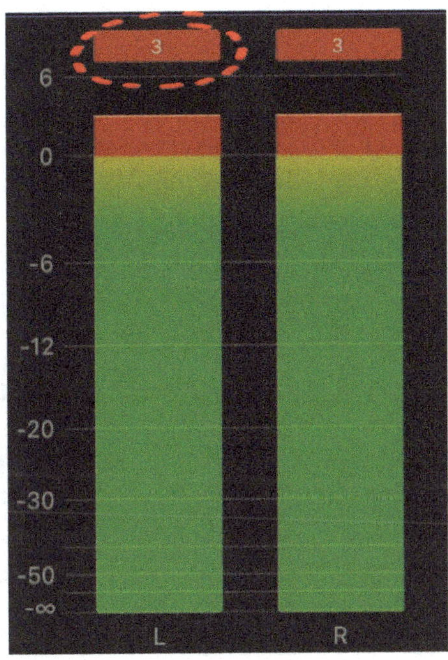

Figure 8.28: Note that an audio spike is visible in the audio meter

2.   This needs to be fixed. Click on the Timeline panel so that it is selected. Move the skimmer line over the offending blip and use the keyboard shortcut *Command + +* (plus) to zoom into the audio waveform to find the red spike. Holding down the *Option* key, carefully click on the **Adjust Volume** line to create three keyframe control points. Position the center keyframe near the center of the spike.

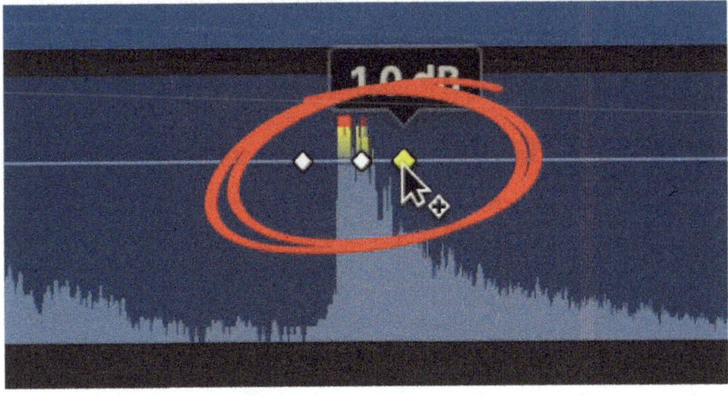

Figure 8.29: Option + click on the Adjust Volume line to add three keyframes

3. Drag the center keyframe down so that it is no longer red. You may be inclined to drag the offending sound down to zero, but a blank sound can be just as jarring as a bump. It is usually the case that you cannot completely eliminate audio mistakes. You just want to minimize bumps and pops to the point that they are not distracting. Go through your project carefully to find any other places that need adjustment.

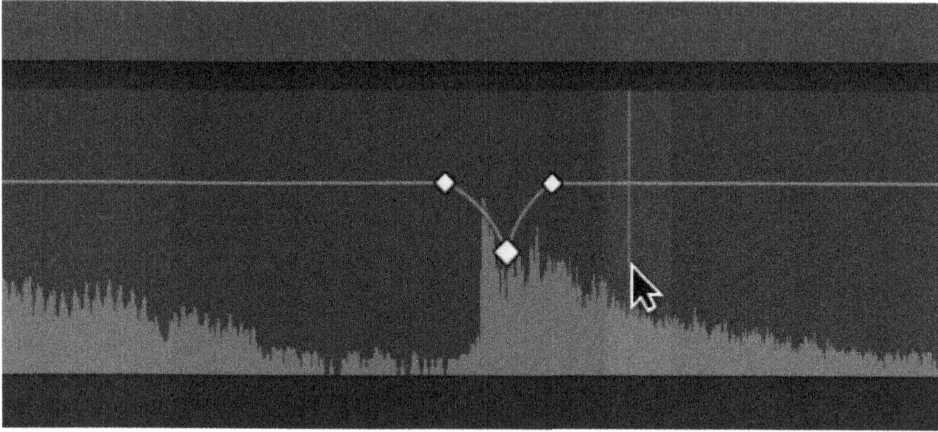

Figure 8.30: Drag the center keyframe down to minimize an audio spike

Using the Audio Enhancement functions

Using built-in audio tools is like reaching for your trusty kitchen gadgets – fast, reliable, and essential for a polished final dish. The **Audio Enhancement** functions in Final Cut Pro analyze and improve the quality of your audio by reducing background noise, hums, or boosting low levels. With just a few clicks, you can clean up dialogue or ambient sounds, ensuring clearer audio without manually adjusting every setting. This simplifies the audio editing process, saving time while delivering a professional sound mix with minimal effort.

In this recipe, we will explore the **Audio Enhancement** section of the Audio Inspector panel. There are three areas we will look at: **Equalization**, **Voice Isolation**, and **Audio Analysis** (the latter includes **Loudness**, **Noise Removal**, and **Hum Removal**). We will also look at the **Pan** setting.

How to do it...

There is a lot to cover, let's get to it:

1. Start by selecting an audio clip in your timeline so you can monitor the result of our enhancements.

2. At the top of the Inspector panel, if it is not already highlighted in blue, click on the **Show Audio Inspector** icon, which looks like a speaker with sound waves coming out of it. Also, double-click on the top title bar of the Inspector panel. The panel will extend lower to show all of the adjustment parameters.

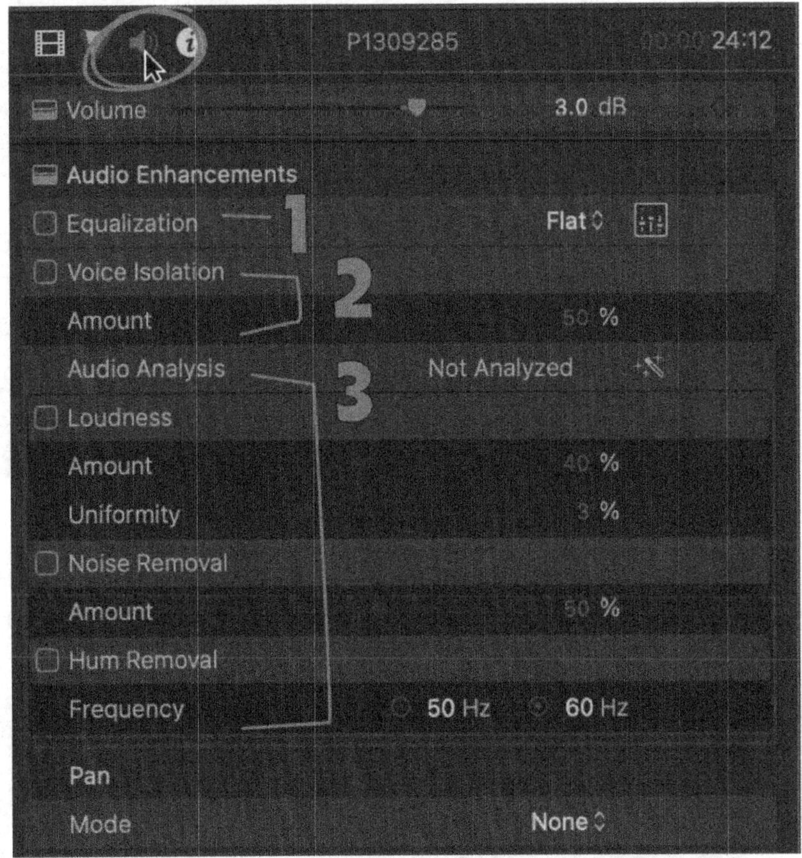

Figure 8.31: Note the three areas of Audio Enhancements in the Audio Inspector panel

Looking at the top of the panel, you can adjust the volume of your clip in the first parameter line in this panel, but it's the **Audio Enhancements** section that we're most interested in at this point.

3. First, let's start with the parameters for **Equalization**. **Equalization (EQ)** is one of the most commonly used audio processes. It shapes the sound of audio by changing the volume level of specific frequency bands. There is a checkbox to turn it on or off, and the drop-down menu, which is currently set to the default of **Flat**. Click on the drop-down menu to see some **Equalization** presets. For example, **Voice Enhance** will increase the volume of mid-range frequencies, which matches the pitch of people's voices. **Music Enhance** will boost low and high frequencies and reduce the mid-tones to enrich the tonal range of music.

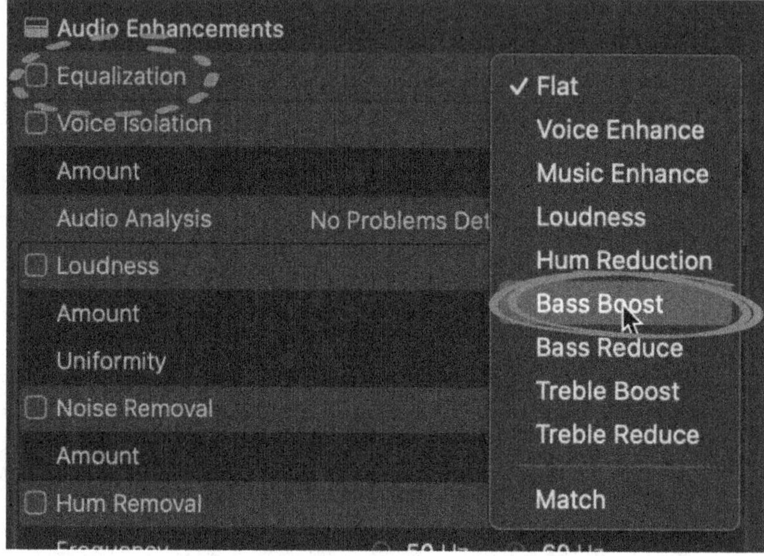

Figure 8.32: Note the presets in the Equalization drop-down menu

In the **Equalization** parameter, you can also click on the **Advanced Equalizer UI** icon, which looks like a small set of fader sliders and is located to the right of the drop-down menu:

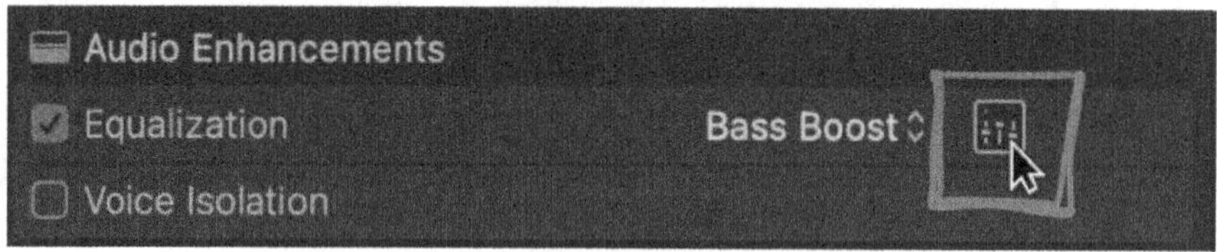

Figure 8.33: Click on the Advanced Equalizer UI icon

It brings up a unique **Graphic Equalizer** interface. The main use of this interface is to use the slider buttons to increase or decrease the volume of sound at 10 frequency ranges covering 32Hz to 16kHz, which is the primary range that humans can hear. There is also a duplicate drop-down menu of the **Equalization** presets located in the upper-left corner.

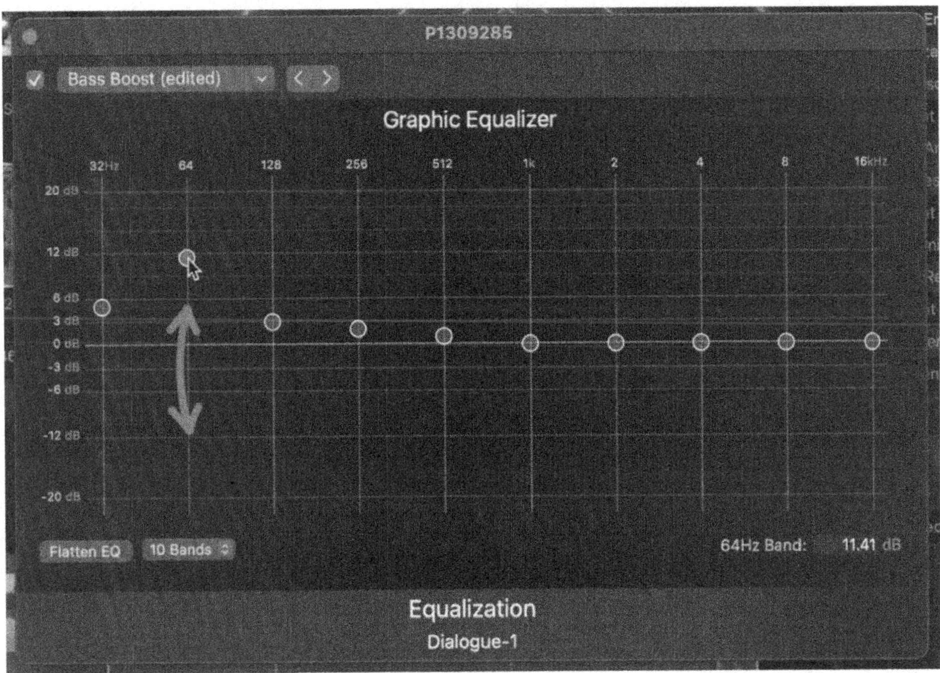

Figure 8.34: Slide the volume buttons of specific frequencies in the Graphic Equalizer interface window

Notice that low bass tones are on the left and high-pitched tones arc on the right. In my example, you can see that the **Bass Boost** preset only increases the volume of low tones on the left. Take some time to go through the presets and see how the **Graphic Equalizer** interface displays the raising and lowering of frequency ranges for that setting. There is also a **Flatten EQ** button to quickly set the equalization back to normal.

4. Second in the **Audio Enhancements** section is **Voice Isolation**. This function prioritizes human voices over other parts of the audio signal. It does an amazing job of analyzing the clip and understanding the human voice to isolate it from the background, which might be useful when working with footage of an interview. There is a checkbox to turn it on. Experiment with the **Amount** slider because you do not want to increase it to the point that the voice sounds like a robot.

Figure 8.35: Use the checkbox to turn on the Voice Isolation enhancement parameter

Equalization and **Voice Isolation** are turned on manually with a checkbox in the **Audio Enhancements** section of the Audio Inspector panel.

5. The third area of **Audio Enhancements** is **Audio Analysis**. These enhancements are designed to correct common audio problems either automatically or with minor manual adjustments.

As with many of the commands in Final Cut Pro, there are several ways to start the analysis of a clip. You could click on the **Enhancement** icon, which looks like a magic wand and is located in the lower-left corner of the Viewer panel, and from the drop-down menu, select **Enhance Audio**. Or, from the **Modify** menu, select **Enhance Audio**. Of course, there is the keyboard shortcut of *Option + Command + A*, but as we are already working in the Audio Inspector panel, let's click on the small **Analyze Audio** icon, which looks like a small magic wand in the **Audio Analysis** title line.

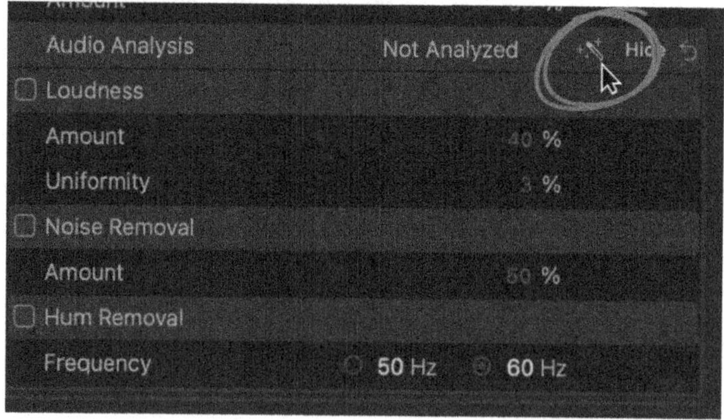

Figure 8.36: Click on the Analyze Audio icon in the Audio Inspector panel

6. The analysis process will start, and some progress wheels may spin. When it is finished, a green checkmark will appear, and the status in the **Audio Analysis** title line will change from **Not Analyzed** to **No Problems Detected**. If issues with the clip are detected, the status will be listed as **Fixed**, and a checkbox will be filled in next to the enhancement in which the fix was completed.

7. After that, let's look at some of the **Audio Analysis** options:

   - **Loudness** improves the main audio signal and makes it more uniform.

   - **Noise Removal** is similar to **Voice Isolation** but different in that it works to understand and remove background noise. Be careful not to increase this one too much, or it will make your clip sound robotic.

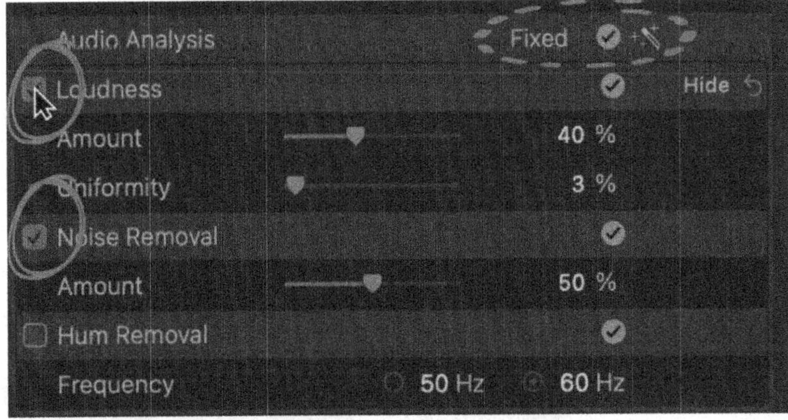

Figure 8.37: Use checkboxes to turn on functions

   - **Hum Removal** is specific to two particular frequencies, **50 Hz** and **60 Hz**, caused by electrical interference. Use the checkbox to enable this enhancement and the bullet button to choose the frequency. A **60 Hz** cycle is the common frequency of electricity in North, Central, and much of South America, along with a few other countries. The rest of the world uses a **50 Hz** electrical cycle.

Sometimes during recording, audio cables will pick up a hum when they are closely placed in parallel to electrical cables. When setting up a recording session, try to keep electrical cables and audio cables away from each other. If they need to cross, place them perpendicular to one another.

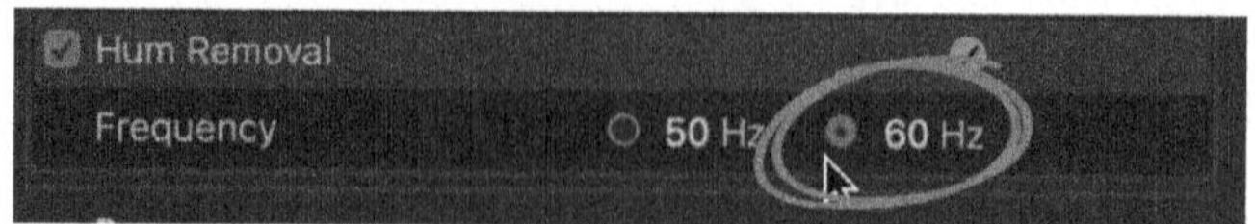

Figure 8.38: Select a specific frequency to remove hum caused by electrical interference

To turn off an enhancement, deselect its checkbox. A yellow warning triangle may appear in the Inspector panel, indicating potential problems. Then, you can choose to turn the enhancement on or off.

8. Note that **Audio Analysis** with the **Enhance Audio** command can be performed on whole media files in the Event Browser panel as well. In addition, we can also analyze audio at the point of importing by clicking on the checkbox for **Fix audio problems** in the **Analyze Audio** section of the Import Settings panel.

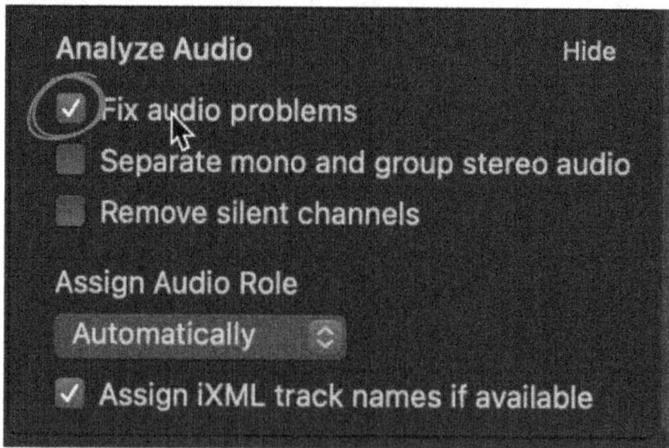

Figure 8.39: Check Fix audio problems to analyze your audio when importing

9. Although not part of the **Audio Enhancements** section, **Pan** is an audio technique that can really add high production value to your story and is worth mentioning in this recipe. Panning is when a sound changes in volume across stereo or surround sound speakers.

    Click on the drop-down menu for the **Mode** parameter, which should be labeled as **None**. Unless you are editing for a surround sound system, select **Stereo Left/Right**.

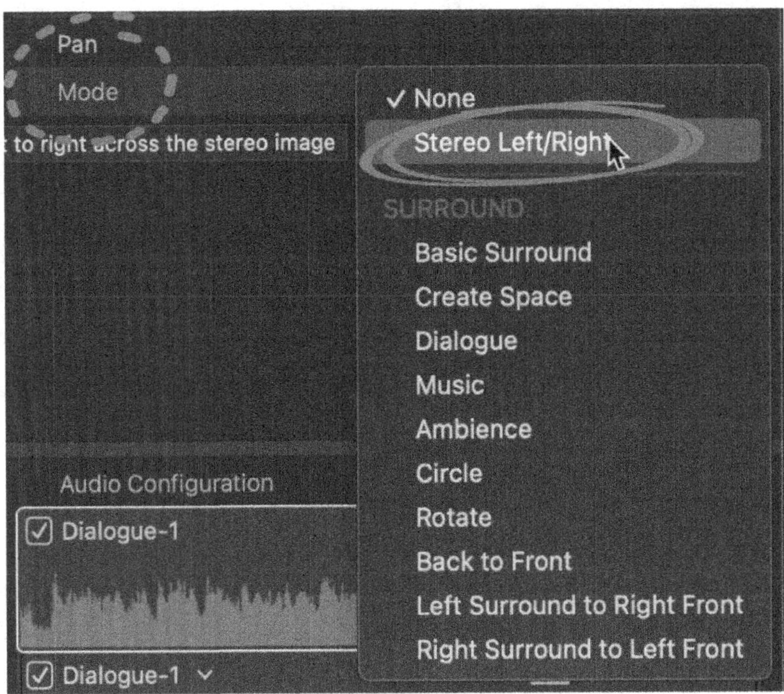

Figure 8.40: Select Stereo Left/Right from the Mode drop-down menu

10. As an example, let's say you have a sound effects clip of footsteps and you want the left-to-right movement of the actor to have matching audio movement. Place the playhead at the point in the clip when the actor starts walking from the left. Then, under **Pan**, slide the **Amount** slider to the left to about **-80**. Click on the **Add Keyframe** icon on the far right. This sets a control point of **Left Stereo** at 80%.

 See *Chapter 7* and the recipe called *Keyframing clip position and effects* for more information on setting keyframes.

Next, move the playhead to the end of the clip, or when the actor stops walking on the right side of the screen. Slide the **Amount** slider to the right to about **80**. Final Cut Pro understands the process and automatically creates another keyframe at this point. Now, the volume of the sound will pan from left to right across the keyframe control points.

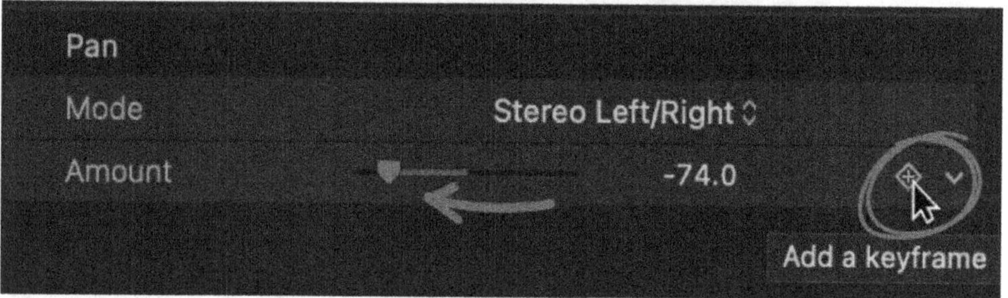

Figure 8.41: Use the Amount slider to create keyframes to pan sound volume from left to right

 Do not pan your sounds the full 100 percent because that actually becomes a little unsettling to your audience and would distract from your story.

There's more...

Let's say you have tried the **Loudness** enhancement and some other functions, but your clip is just not loud enough. Here is a trick you can try. Right-click on the low-volume clip and, from the **Clip** pop-up menu, select **Detach Audio** (or use the keyboard shortcut *Control + Shift + S*).

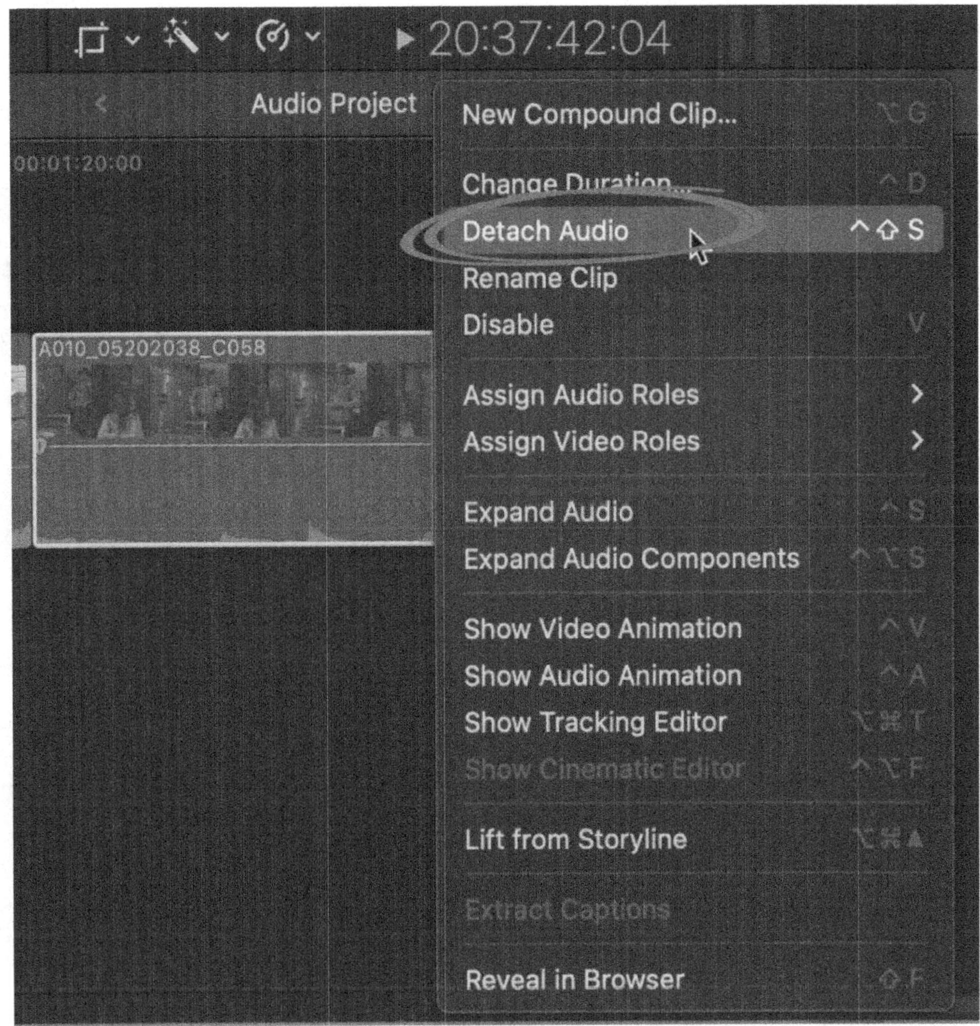

Figure 8.42: Select Detach Audio from the Clip pop-up menu

This will separate the audio component from the video component. The audio is still connected and will move with the video clip, but they are now separate clips.

Next, while holding down the *Option* key, click on the audio clip and drag it straight down. Notice that the cursor changes to an arrow with a green plus sign. The *Option* key is sort of a universal shortcut for duplication. The audio volume is increased because you have two audio clips playing together. Make sure they snap together and play at the same time.

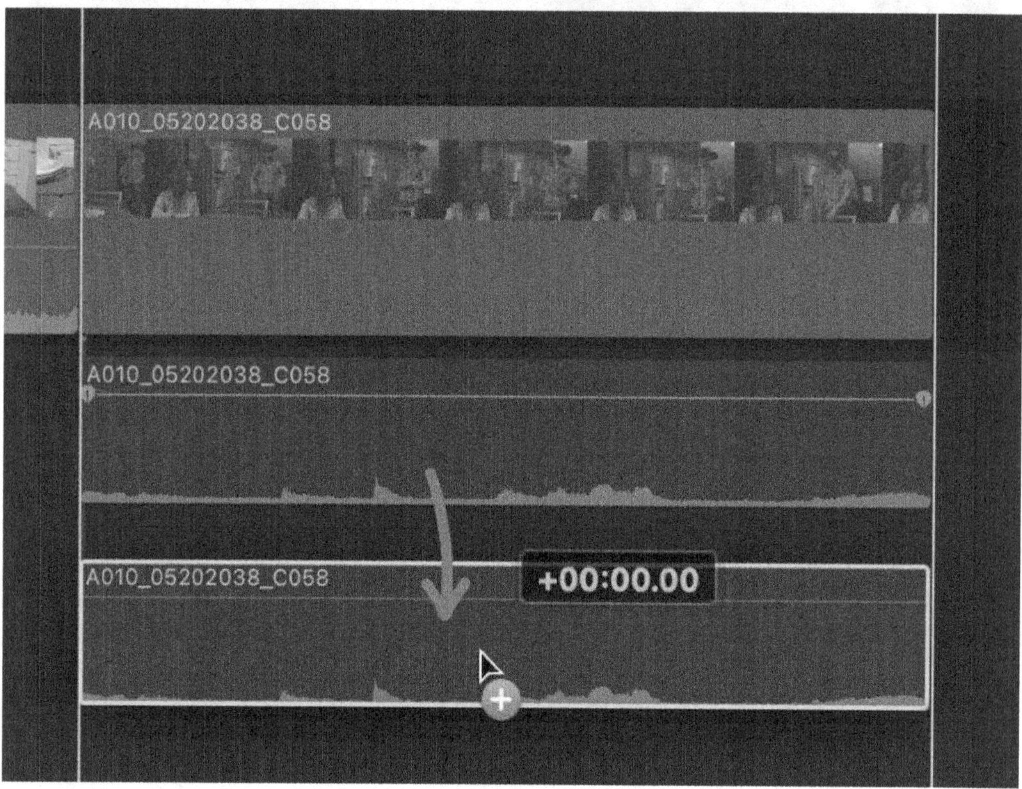

Figure 8.43: Option + drag the audio clip to create a duplicate clip

If only the *Option* key could duplicate a French silk chocolate pie!

Syncing audio from an external recorder

External recorders with professional microphones provide superior sound quality compared to on-camera microphones or low-quality stereo connectors on DSLRs. This results in clearer dialogue, richer soundscapes, and an overall polished production. Syncing audio from an external recorder in Final Cut Pro allows you to combine high-quality audio clips with your video footage for a more professional result, and by using the Final Cut Pro automatic synchronization feature, you can quickly align external audio precisely with your visuals.

In this recipe, we will see how easy it is to synchronize an audio file with a video file.

Getting ready

When recording on a separate external audio recorder, there are some things that will help the clip synchronization process in the editing room:

- Make sure that the camera is also recording audio while recording video. Final Cut Pro can analyze the waveforms of the video and audio files and create a match.

- Create a succinct snapping sound from a slate or even someone making one loud clap with their hands – anything to distinguish the waveforms from the two or more devices to match more easily.

How to do it...

Affogato blends two ingredients (espresso over vanilla gelato). The **Synchronize Clips...** command also blends two ingredients. Let's see:

1. Import the video media and the associated externally-recorded sound file.

2. In the Event Browser panel, select both files. Then, right-click on either file and select **Synchronize Clips...** (or use the keyboard shortcut *Option + Command + G*).

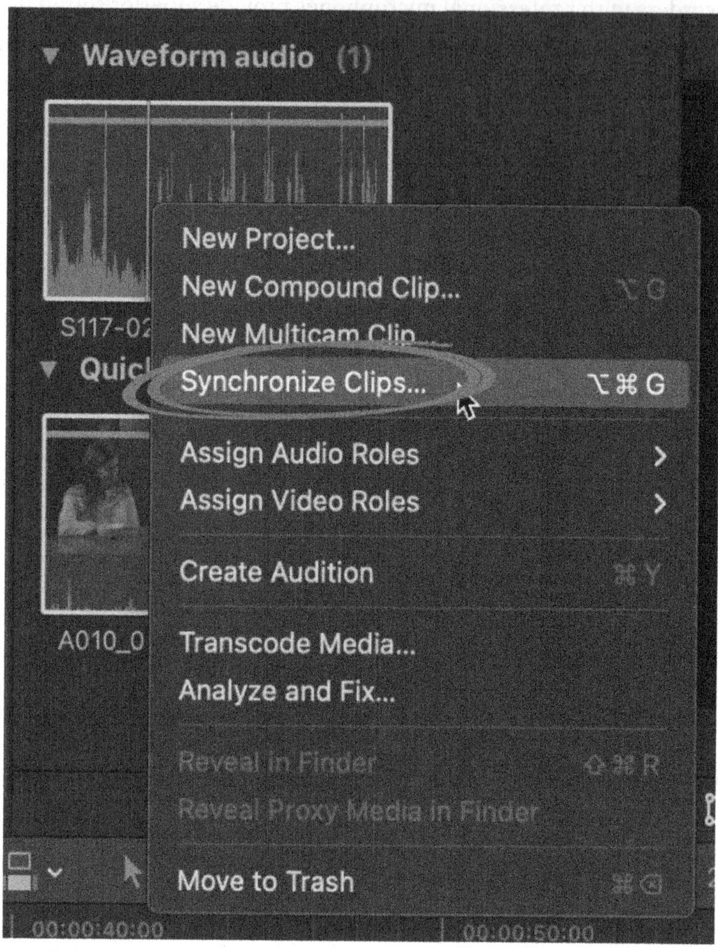

Figure 8.44: Select both clips and select Synchronize Clips... from the Clip pop-up menu

3. We are presented with a dialog box. At the top of the window, you will see **Synchronized Clip Name**. The default is to use the name of the video clip with - `Synchronized Clip` added to the end, but you can change it further if you wish.

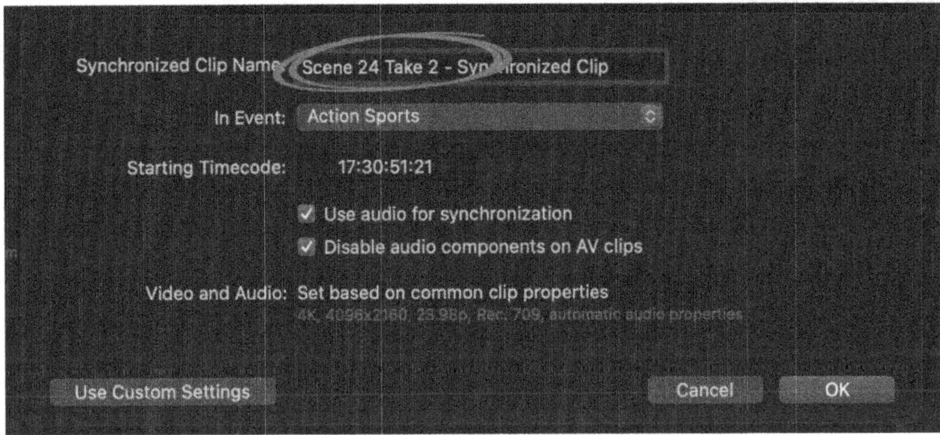

Figure 8.45: Change the name of the clip and click on Use Custom Settings if you need to improve synchronization

4. Verify that the **In Event** parameter is using the event you're currently working in, and be sure there is a checkmark in front of **Use audio for synchronization**.

5. Click on the **OK** button in the lower-right corner. Final Cut Pro will create a new clip with the video and audio combined. The clip will have an icon in the upper-left corner that looks like two ovals looped together.

Figure 8.46: Note that a synchronized clip is identified by an icon of two looping ovals

6. Add this clip to your timeline and work with it as you would any other clip. You don't have to deal with separate audio files.

There's more...

Season your sound to perfection – because great audio is the secret ingredient of every unforgettable dish. Here are some pro tips to help you out:

- If you are not using high-quality XLR audio equipment, you may want to investigate a portable audio recorder with XLR inputs from Zoom, Tascam, or other manufacturers.

- When recording audio (dialogue in particular), ask everyone on set to be silent for a minute so that you can record the room tone – that is, the audio of the background sound at that location. This can be a lifesaver if there is an audio glitch, cough, or extra speaking recorded in a studio, and you need to mask it with ambient sound.

- Also, sometimes the analysis of the two waveforms does not work. In that case, the best option is to manually create a marker in each clip at a place you can hear fits together. Then, right-click on the clips again to return to this dialog box. In the bottom-left corner, click on the **Use Custom Settings** button. From the **Synchronization** parameter, click on the drop-down menu, which will be set to the default of **Automatic**. From the menu, select **First Marker on the Clip**. Then, click on the **OK** button in the lower-right corner.

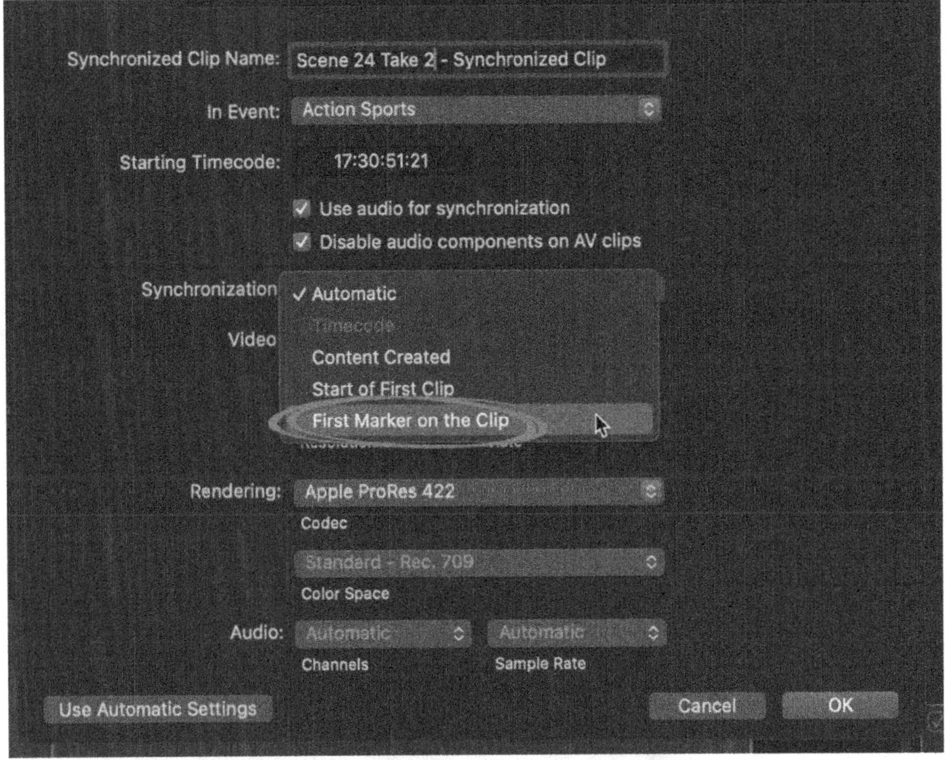

Figure 8.47: Selecting the First Marker on the Clip is a good way to manually synchronize clips

Recording scratch audio

Not to be confused with baking a cake from scratch, *scratch* audio is slang for a recording that will soon be scratched, or replaced, with a better recording. It is a placeholder that you can conveniently record while in the editing workflow. The advantage is that scratch audio serves as a reference point for timing, dialogue, and synchronization, making the final editing process smoother.

In this recipe, we will explore the **Record Voiceover** interface and how clips are inserted into the project timeline.

Getting ready

You will need a working microphone. Most Macs will have a built-in microphone. If not, you will need a USB-connected mic.

How to do it...

We've hardly scratched the surface of all the cool stuff Final Cut Pro can do, so let's get started:

1. In the Timeline panel, place the playhead at the point where you want your recording to start. Then, from the **Window** menu, select **Record Voiceover** or press the keyboard shortcut *Shift + V*.

2. You are presented with a **Record Voiceover** floating window. From here, you can give your clip a name. Then, if the window is not already expanded, click on the disclosure triangle next to the **Advanced** section to bring up more parameters.

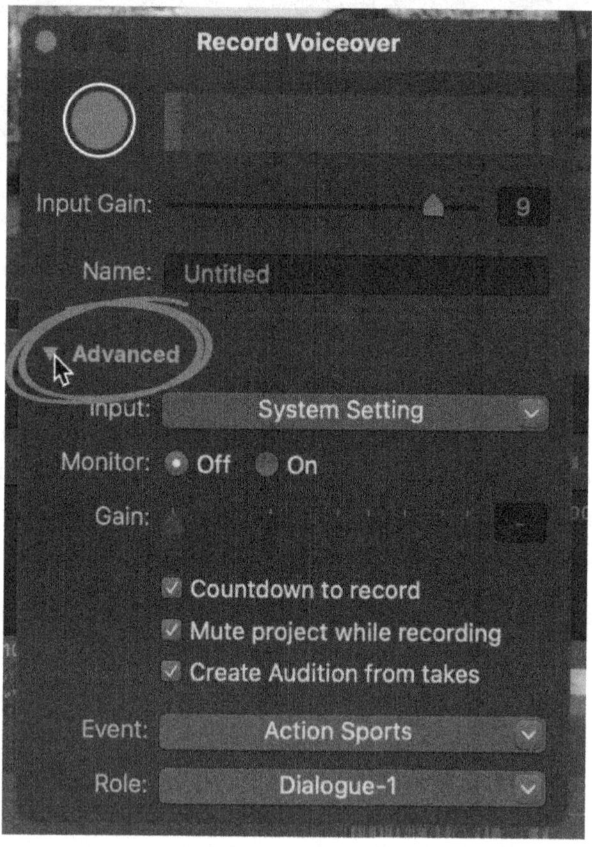

Figure 8.48: Open the Advanced section of the Record Voiceover window

3. Near the middle of the window, click on the drop-down menu for **Input**, which, by default, might say **System Setting**, and there will be your list of potential audio inputs. If you've got a USB microphone connected, it will show up in this list. For my example, I'm going to stay with the system setting of the built-in microphone.

4. With your input set, turn your attention to the top of the window and the **Input Gain** slider. Gain is more than just volume; it is increased amplitude. Volume is how loud the output of the channel is. Gain is how loud the input of the channel is.

5. Experiment by talking out loud the way you will record and move the **Input Gain** slider. Watch the green bar fluctuate. Vary how close you are to the mic. You want the recording to be strong and close to the right side, but not reach the end to cause any red distortion. Remember: green is good, red is bad.

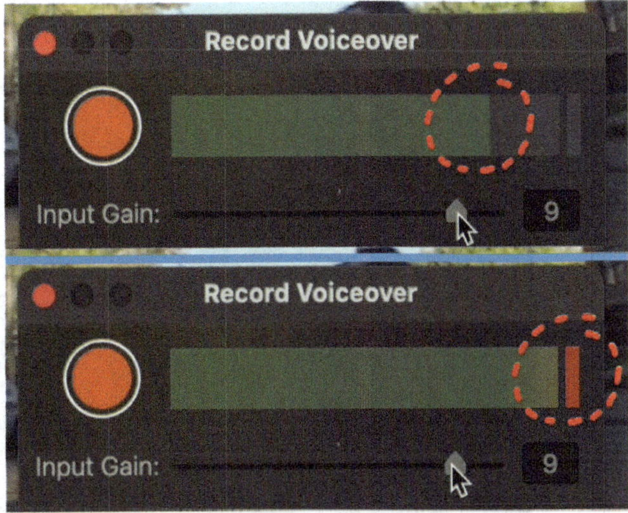

Figure 8.49: Note that recording levels should be strong but not red

6. Once you have the input selected and the recording level dialed in, we are almost ready to record. Before we do that, let's review a few things in the **Advanced** section, even though we may not change them:

    *   For the **Monitor** setting, I am going to click on the **Off** button. I don't want to hear myself in the system speakers and have the potential for feedback.

    *   If I had a sound system connected, I might have monitoring on, and then I would use the **Input Gain** slider to adjust the volume.

    *   Let's keep **Countdown to record** checked. This gives a three-second countdown before recording. We will see how that works.

- Let's keep **Mute project while recording** checked too. This is because we don't really need to hear the music clip or anything else while recording. In some cases, you might, but not this time.

- **Create audition from takes** is a nice feature. As you might try different recordings, Final Cut Pro will put those takes into an **Audition** bundle to keep the project timeline less cluttered. See *Chapter 4* and the recipe called *Creating an audition* to learn more about video clip **Audition** bundles.

- The default **Event** should be the event you are already working from, but check this too.

- The default audio role is probably **Dialogue-1**, unless you are making Star Wars *pew-pew* blaster sounds, in which case, set the role to **Effects-1**.

7. You are ready! Click on the big orange **Record** button in the top-left corner of the window.

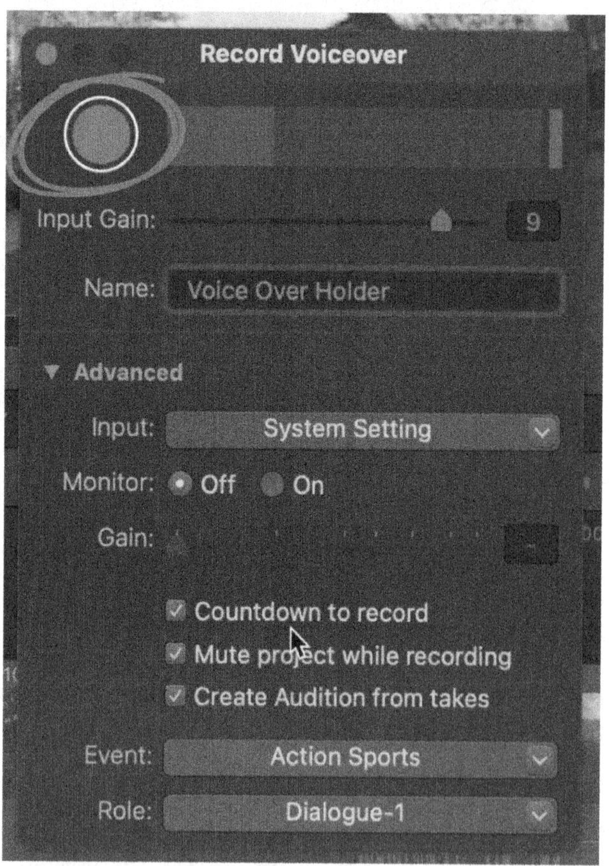

Figure 8.50: Click on the Record button when ready

Final Cut will back up three seconds and start playing the project with countdown numbers in the Viewer panel.

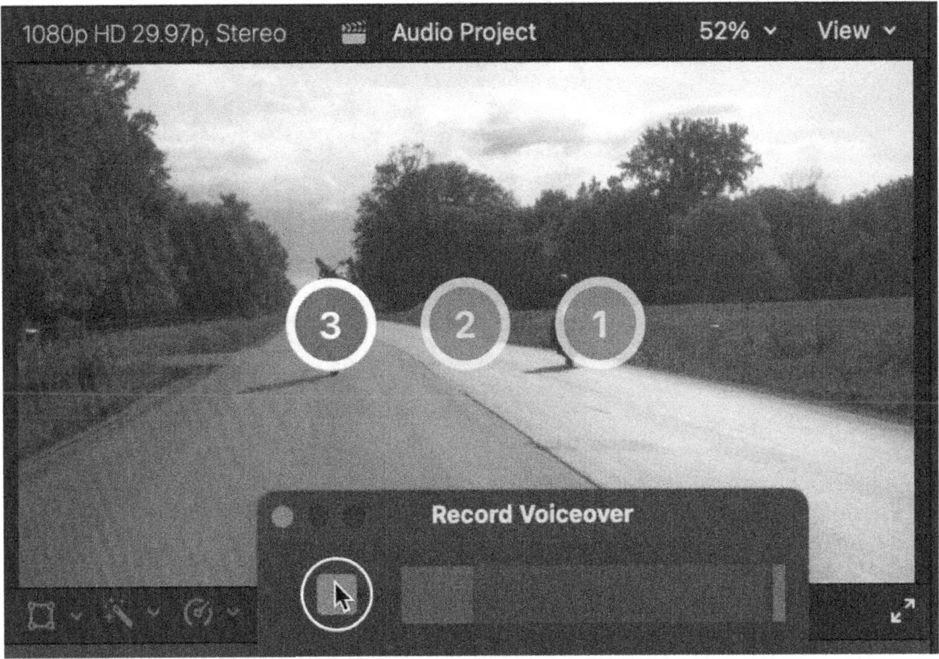

Figure 8.51: The three-second countdown is your cue to start speaking

8. When it hits zero, start talking or making sound effects, and then, when you are done, click on the same button, which is now an orange square. The clip is added to the project timeline at that location with the name you have assigned it!

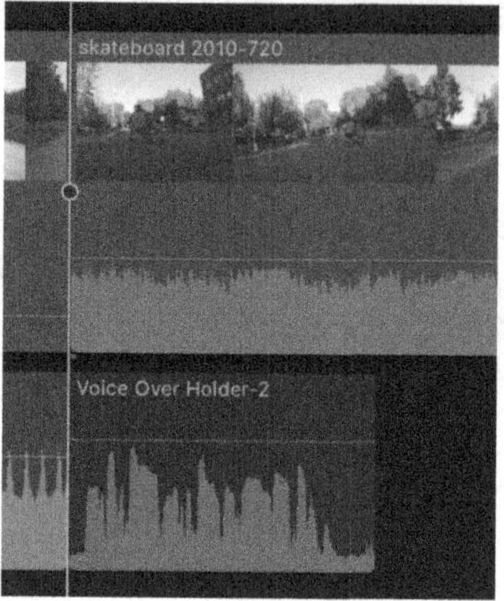

Figure 8.52: Note that the recorded clip is added to the timeline

See also

Similar to how Scratch Audio creates a placeholder, Final Cut Pro has a video generator that is a placeholder. It is described in *Chapter 4* in a recipe called *Using gap clips and placeholder clips*.

Using audio effects

Using audio effects in Final Cut Pro allows you to enhance and polish sound by adding reverb, EQ, and more to your audio clips. These effects help fine-tune or add creative flair to dialogue, music, or ambient sound, creating a more immersive and engaging experience for your audience.

In this recipe, we will see how easy it is to add effects to audio clips and explore just two of the many possibilities.

Adding audio effects to clips is straightforward and similar to adding video effects. For more information on that, see *Chapter 6* and the recipe called *Stacking visual effects*.

How to do it...

Resistance is futile (read with an alien voice). Let's get started:

1. *Option + click* on the clip that you want to work with in your timeline so it is selected and the playhead is parked on top of it. We will need to see lots of information in the Audio Inspector panel, so double-click on the title bar to extend it down all the way.

2. Click on the **Show Effects Browser** icon, which looks like two overlapping rectangles located in the upper-right corner of the Timeline panel. In the Effects Browser panel, scroll down past the **VIDEO** effects to the **AUDIO** effects section.

3. Click on the **All** category. There are quite a few installed audio effects. Some can be fun, such as making someone sound like an alien or a cartoon animal. Take some time to explore the selection. It is all about the story you are telling.

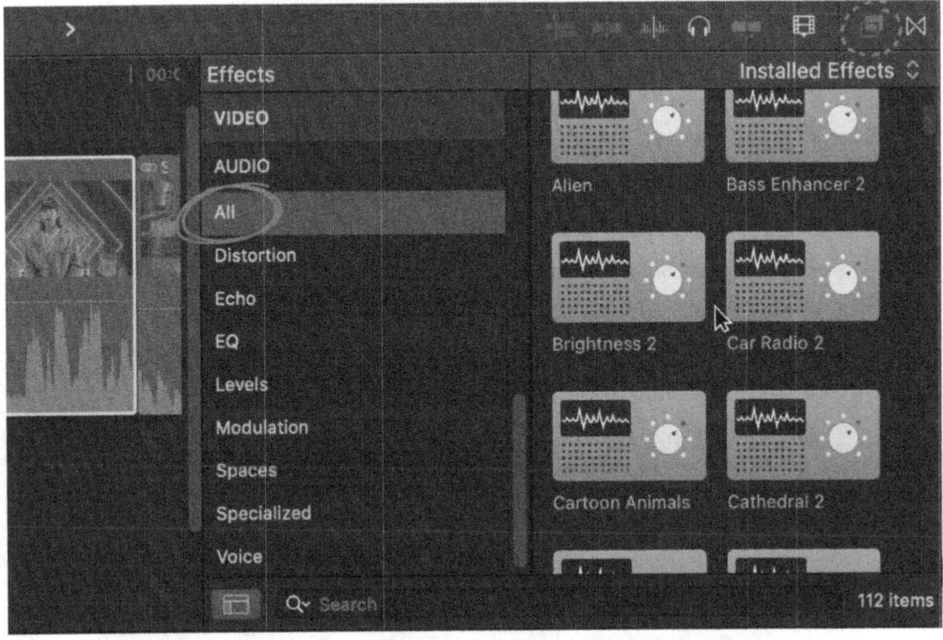

Figure 8.53: Open the Effects Browser panel and select All audio effects

Some effects are useful in storytelling. Perhaps you want your characters to speak from a car radio or on a telephone. In these situations, it is actually hard to record bad audio. It is easier to use your camera or audio gear to record good audio and then give it an effect that will make the clips sound like a low-resolution playback device. There are also quite a few effects that help with fixing audio – for example, adding less bass or less treble frequencies.

4. It is easy to preview an effect. With your clip selected, place the skimmer on top of the effect in the Effects Browser panel and press the *spacebar* to play the preview.

Figure 8.54: Place the skimmer over the effect icon and press the spacebar to preview the effect on your clip

5. Here's an interesting audio effect: **Quantec Room Simulator**. *Option + click* on a clip in your timeline. Then, in the Effects Browser panel, in the **AUDIO** section, click on the **Spaces** category. Select **Quantec Room Simulator** and drag that onto your selected clip in the timeline.

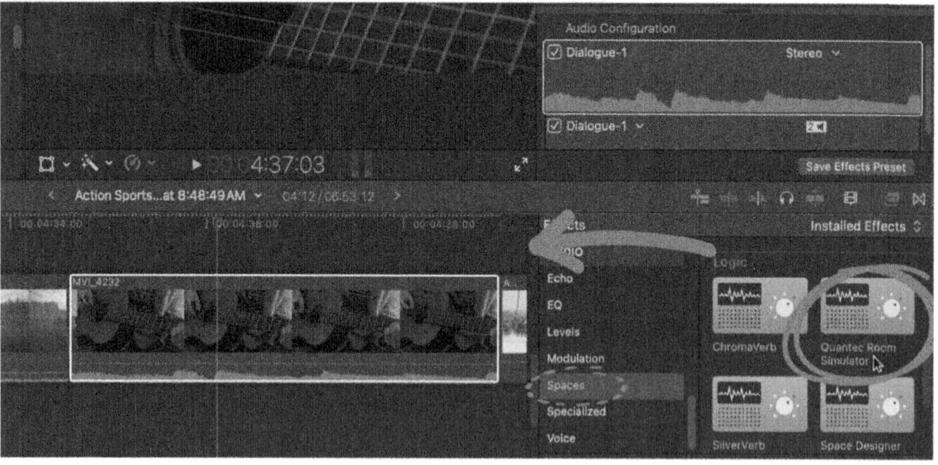

Figure 8.55: Add the Quantec Room Simulator effect to a clip in your timeline

6. In the Audio Inspector panel, within the **Quantec Room Simulator** effect area, click on the **Advanced Effect Editor UI** icon, which looks like a little mixing board.

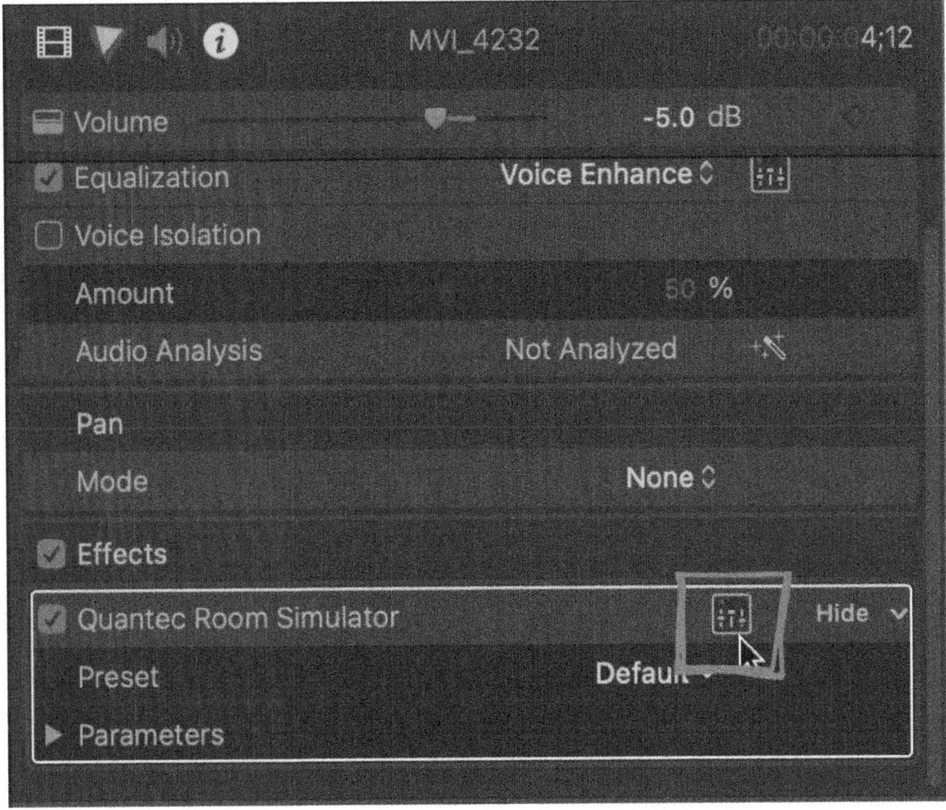

Figure 8.56: Click on the Advanced Effect Editor UI icon

7. This brings up a graphical interface window. If you really want to geek out, click on the **Quantec** logo, and this brings up a message window with information about the original inventor of the QRS reverb effect and how Apple has simulated the original code into its software.

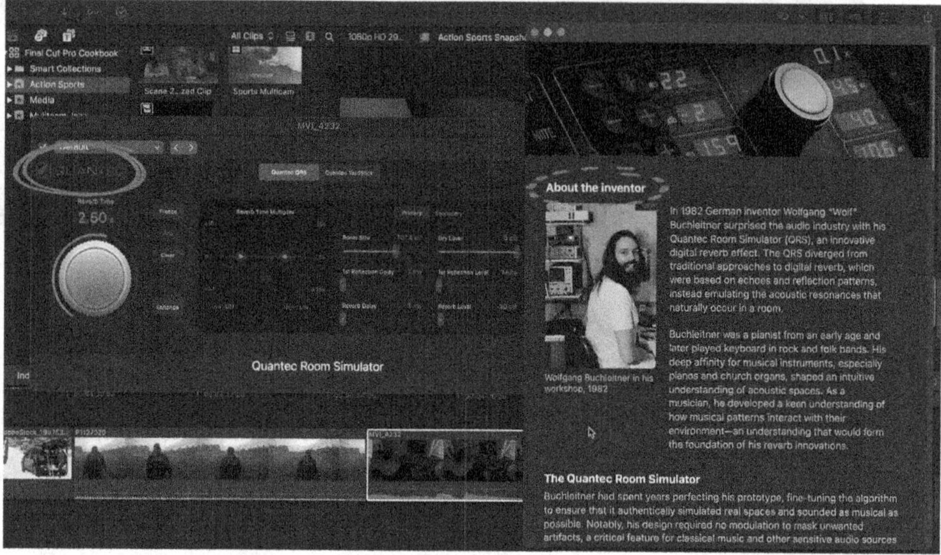

Figure 8.57: Click on the Quantec logo for information about the effect's origin

8. From the drop-down menu in the upper-left corner of the advanced interface window, select a room size. In my example, I am selecting **02 Medium Rooms** and **Grotto**.

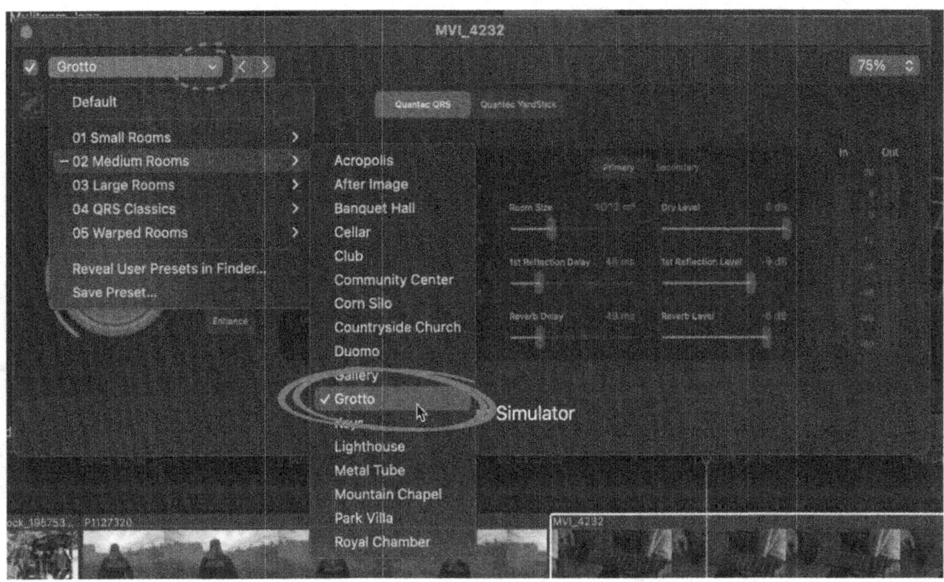

Figure 8.58: Select Grotto from 02 Medium Rooms in the room size menu

9. You can also use the arrow icons to advance through the room size menu options.

Figure 8.59: Use the arrow icons to cycle through the room size choices

10. Have fun experimenting with the room choices and changing the adjustments to parameters, such as **Room Size.** This is a very realistic and advanced room reverb simulator with a long history in the audio editing industry.

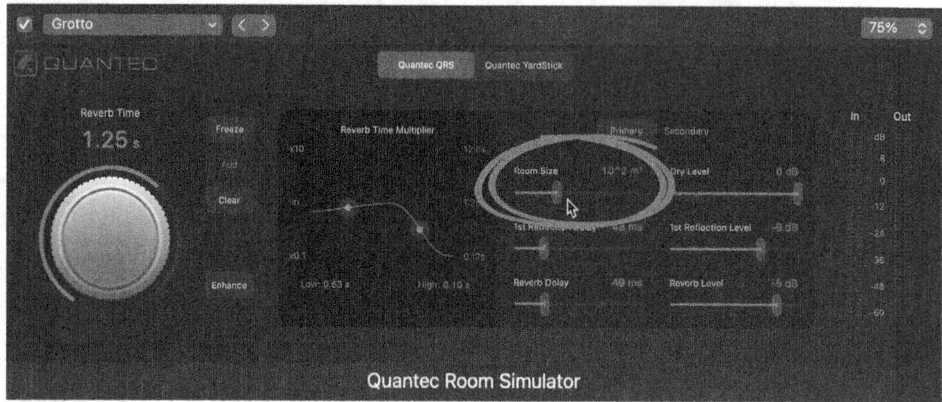

Figure 8.60: Experiment with the parameters in the advanced interface window

11. Notice that you can save custom presets and reveal them in the Finder. That way, you can take them with you to install them on a different computer. This way, you will have your presets with you wherever you go, like always keeping your favorite hot sauce in your pocket.

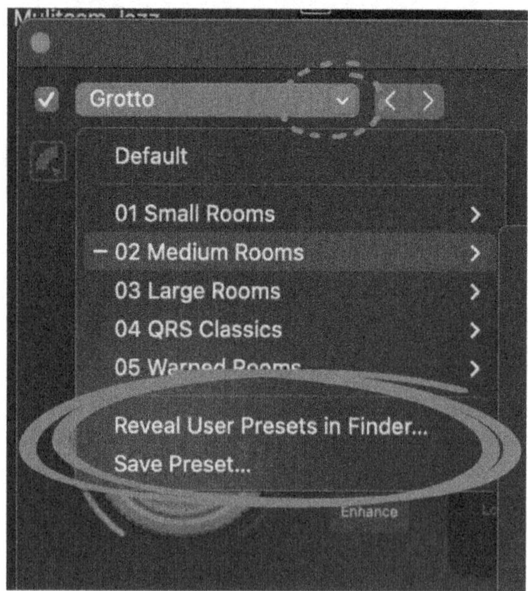

Figure 8.61: Save custom presets and install them into other Final Cut Pro systems

Fixing a mono recording

Although Cola de Mono, a traditional Chilean holiday beverage, sounds delicious, that is not the mono we are talking about. Professional XLR microphones are, by nature, mono audio devices. When connecting a mic to a video camera that has two audio input ports, the camera needs to have its preferences set to extend the one-mic recording across both stereo channels.

A mono audio recording is the result of not properly setting the camera preferences, and the audio signal is only recorded on one channel of a stereo clip. Fortunately, we can still fix it in Final Cut Pro. It's easy when you know where to look.

In this recipe, we will dig into a clip's **Audio Configuration** waveform to fix a mono recording.

Getting ready

To follow along, you may need to track down a mono recording or experiment with your camera to intentionally create one.

How to do it...

I'm still thinking about that Chilean holiday drink, so we'd better get started:

1. *Option + click* on the clip you want to work with so that it is both selected and the playhead is parked on top of it. We will need to see lots of information in the Audio Inspector panel, so double-click on the title bar to extend it down all the way.

2. We are also paying particularly close attention to the large audio meter. Click on the small audio meter in the lower center of the Viewer panel to display the large audio meter. Play the clip and notice that the audio signal, the green bar, is only playing on one channel.

Figure 8.62: Observe that the mono signal is on only one side of the audio meter

3. In the lower portion of the Audio Inspector panel is the **Audio Configuration** section and a display of the audio waveform for the clip. In the upper-right part of the waveform image is a drop-down menu that has the default of **Stereo**. Click on this menu and select **Dual Mono**. Bam! The one mono signal is duplicated onto the other channel. This is our fix. Both sides of the stereo signal are filled with the same audio.

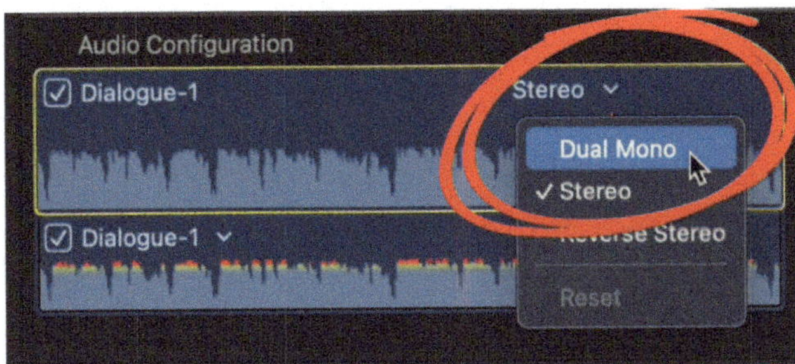

Figure 8.63: Select Dual Mono from the Audio Configuration waveform drop-down menu

4.   Play the clip again and notice the green bar visible on both the right and left channels. Note that the clip is not true stereo with the subtle variations that two channels can have. This is a straight duplication, but it is much better than having the sound on only one speaker during playback.

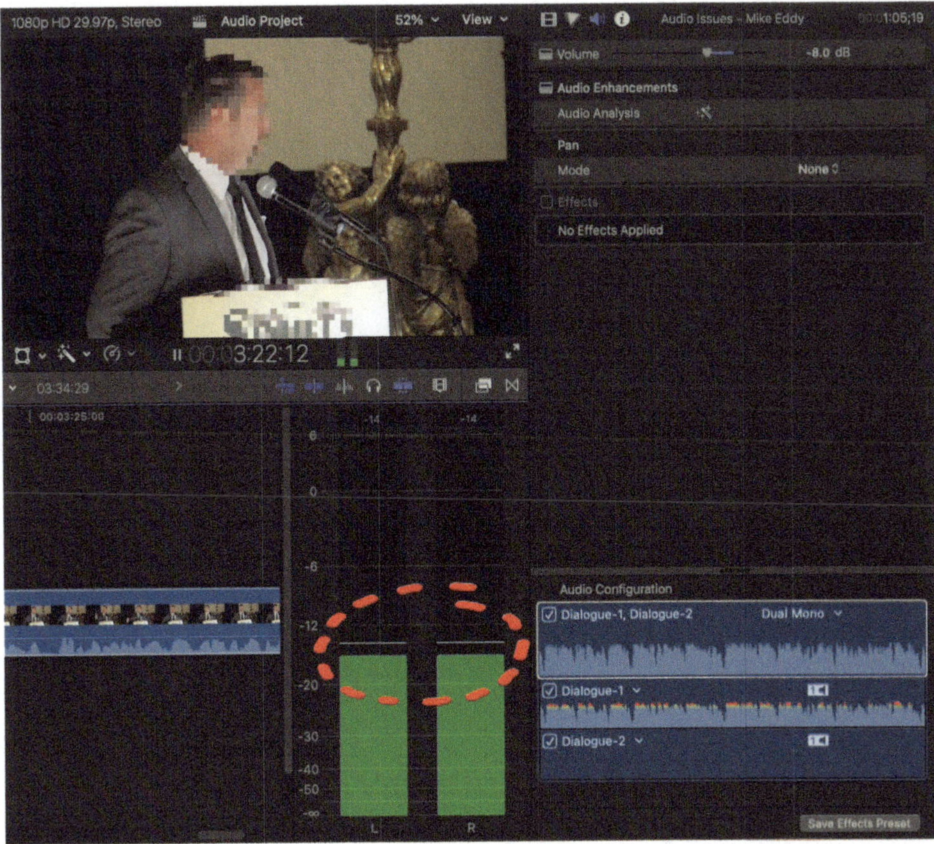

Figure 8.64: Observe that the mono signal is duplicated on both sides of the audio meter

9

Building Titles

Step into the spotlight of title design, where Final Cut Pro becomes your stage, and creativity shines as brightly as the marquee. In this chapter, we'll illuminate the art of crafting captivating titles that command attention and set the stage for your story. We'll explore how to customize fonts, animate text, and add flair to your titles with finesse. Whether you're branding your content or adding context to your narrative, get ready to see your name in lights and make a lasting impression with Final Cut Pro.

In this chapter, you will learn vital troubleshooting techniques, such as fixing blank text fields and understanding safe zones, to ensure that their titles and graphics display correctly across various platforms. Additionally, you'll explore creative options for title creation, including replacing titles, utilizing generators and themes, and even mastering advanced techniques such as creating and tracking titles to objects and creating a dramatic text reveal.

In this chapter, you will complete the following recipes:

- Customizing titles
- Replacing titles
- Using safe zones
- Using themes in titles and generators
- Creating a title object tracker
- Revealing text animation

Customizing titles

Adding text in Final Cut Pro allows you to overlay titles, captions, and other text-based elements to enhance storytelling or provide essential information. With various text fields, you can easily customize the font, color, alignment, and animation to match the visual style and tone of your project. By mastering text fields, you gain control over creative formatting, making it simple to create impactful, professional-looking titles that engage and inform your audience. In addition, knowing how to deal with empty text fields will alleviate a lot of headaches.

In this recipe, we will review some ways to customize text and then show you the simple way to use text fields that are empty.

How to do it...

Titles in Final Cut Pro are much easier than trying to write with icing on a cake, believe me. Let's get to it:

1. In the sidebar panel, click on the **Show Titles and Generators Sidebar** icon. Then, click on the **Titles** category. From here, scroll through the sample titles and imagine the possibilities.

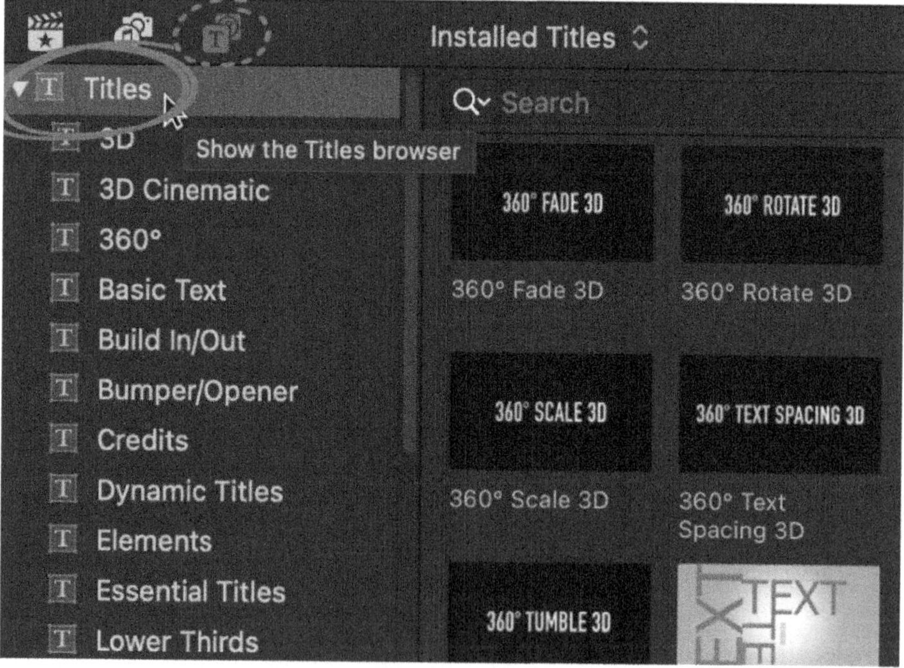

Figure 9.1: Click on Titles in the Titles and Generators sidebar

2. As you skim through the sample titles, you can see a preview in the Viewer panel. For my example, I'm going to select a title that has a few text fields built into the animation. I selected one called **Ferris Wheel**, and I've dragged this down and connected it on top of a clip that is in the primary storyline. Do the same and then skim the mouse in the Timeline panel above the clips, and we will see the animated text on top of the video clip.

Figure 9.2: Review the animated text by skimming above the clips

3. Now, with the **Ferris Wheel** title selected, click on the **Title Inspector** icon – it looks like a square with a capital T inside of it at the top left of the Inspector panel. Notice that there are sections for each of the four text lines available in this animation. Select the text in each field and add your own. For my example, I'm going to use Step Into Adventure and put each of the three words into separate text fields. **Text Line 1** will contain Step, **Text Line 2** will contain Into, and **Text Line 3** will contain Adventure. You can use this or create your own phrase.

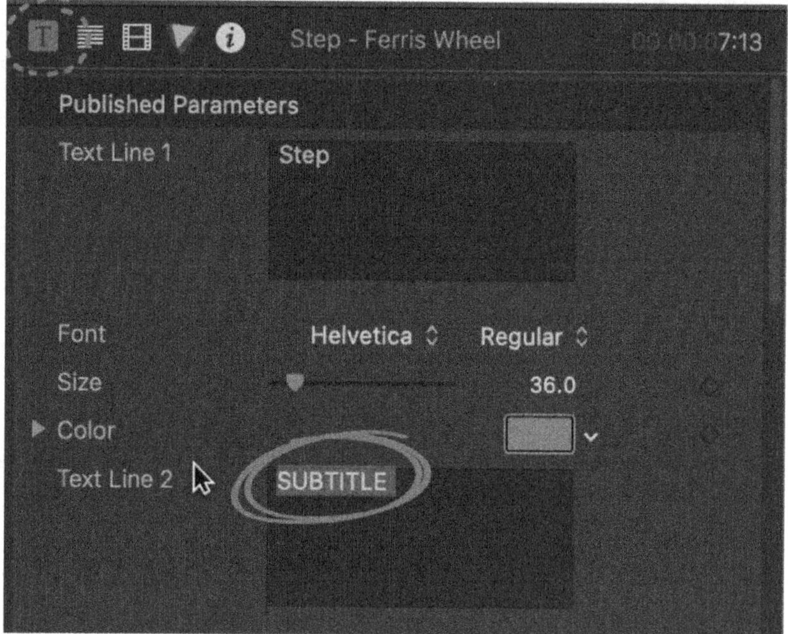

Figure 9.3: Edit text fields in the Title Inspector panel

4. You will see that each **Text Line** section has changeable drop-down menus for parameters such as the following:

   - **Font:** This lets you change the font type and style (**Regular, Bold, Italic**, etc.).
   - **Size:** This can be adjusted using the slider.

- **Color**: Click on the down arrow to the right of the sample color rectangle; it brings up a Spectrum panel. Wherever you click, it will set that color for your text.

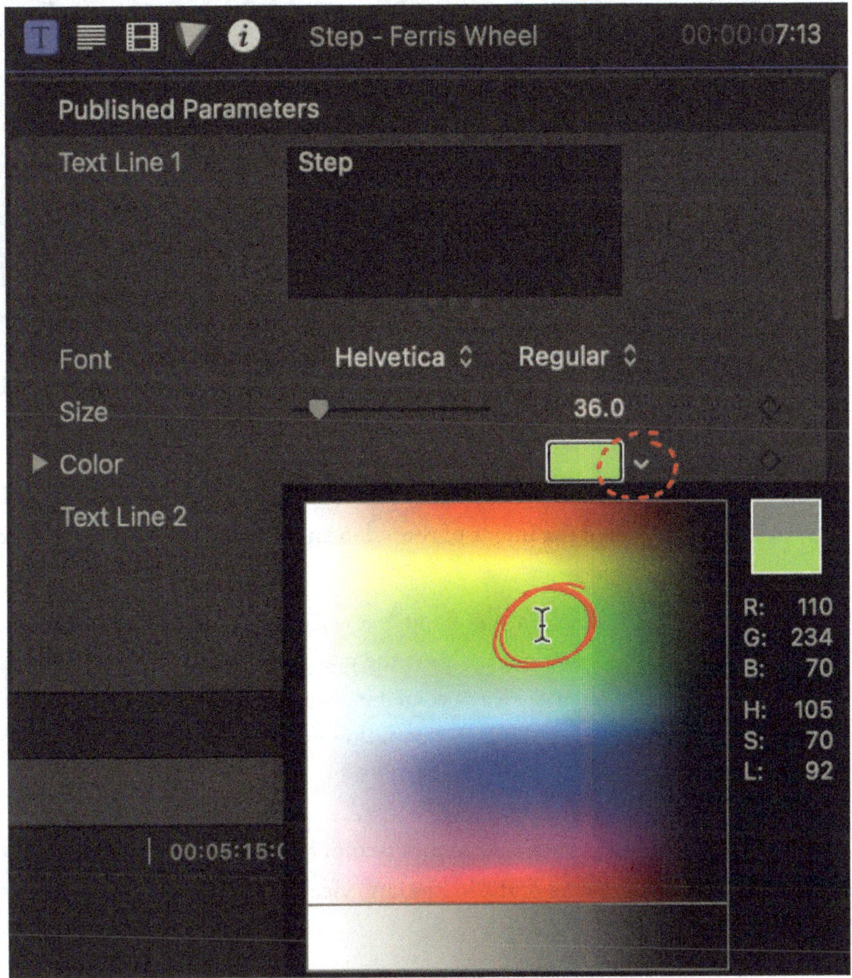

Figure 9.4: Click to choose a color in the Spectrum panel

5. Additionally, if you click on the sample color rectangle itself, it brings up the macOS **Colors** window. This small window, which can be moved around the screen, has several different types of color palettes across the top. The primary one is the color wheel located on the far left. Click and drag the targeting circle around the color wheel to select a color. Now, click on the eyedropper down near the bottom-left corner of the window.

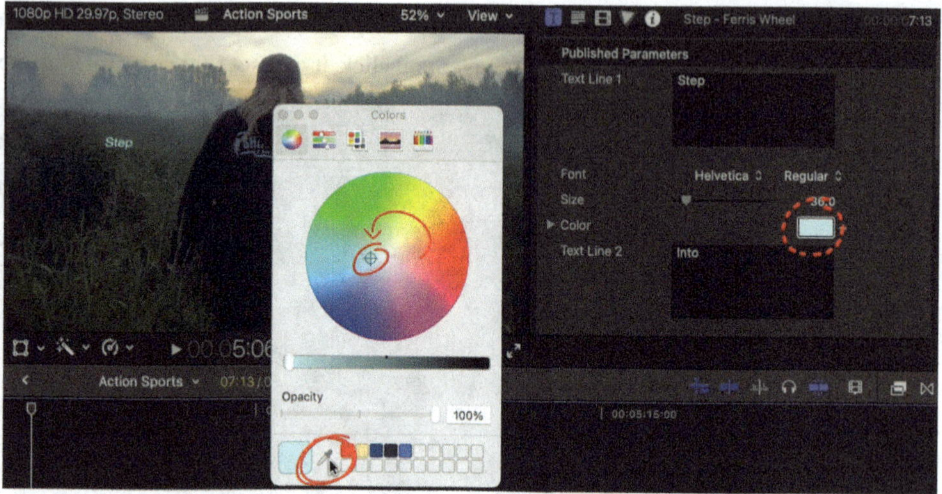

Figure 9.5: Select the eyedropper in the macOS Colors window

6. The cursor will change to a magnified circle with a one-pixel square in the center. Move the cursor around the image of the video and notice how it displays the colors.

Bonus tip: A method that will create design unity is something called **correspondence**. This is the practice of repeating an element already in the design, such as a color. Instead of choosing simple white or black for a text color, a subtle design technique is to use the eyedropper and find a color within your image.

For my example, I am going to pick a color from the sunset. You can choose a light color for text in a dark area of the image, and vice versa.

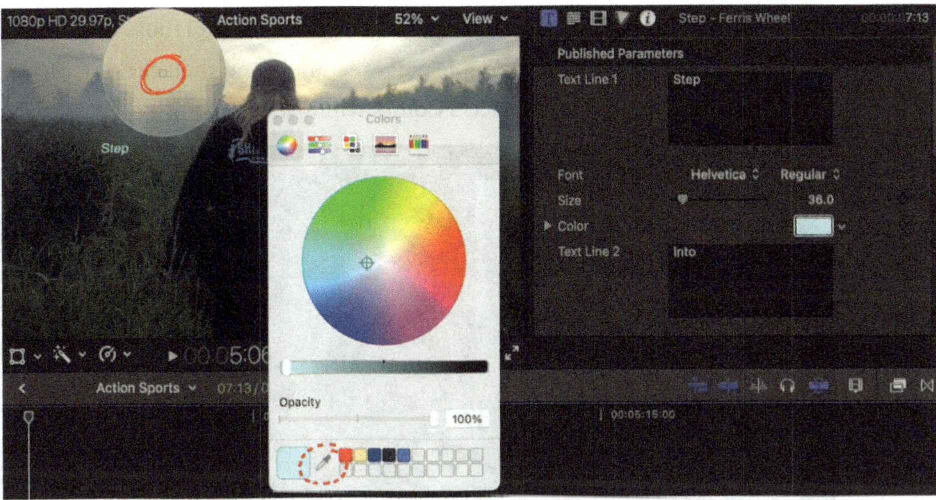

Figure 9.6: Use the magnification circle to choose a color in your image

7. You can save that color for future use by dragging it to the little color-saver squares to the right of the eyedropper. This is useful if you are using the color in your brand and want to save it for use in other applications where the macOS **Colors** window is also accessible.

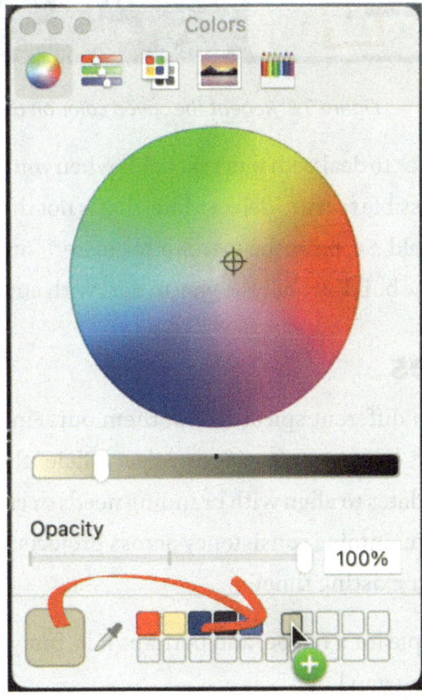

Figure 9.7: Save the current color for use in other applications

8. Now that we have saved our color, let's go ahead and make all of those text fields the same color by clicking on the default sample color rectangle and then clicking on the colored square that we've saved in the macOS **Colors** window.

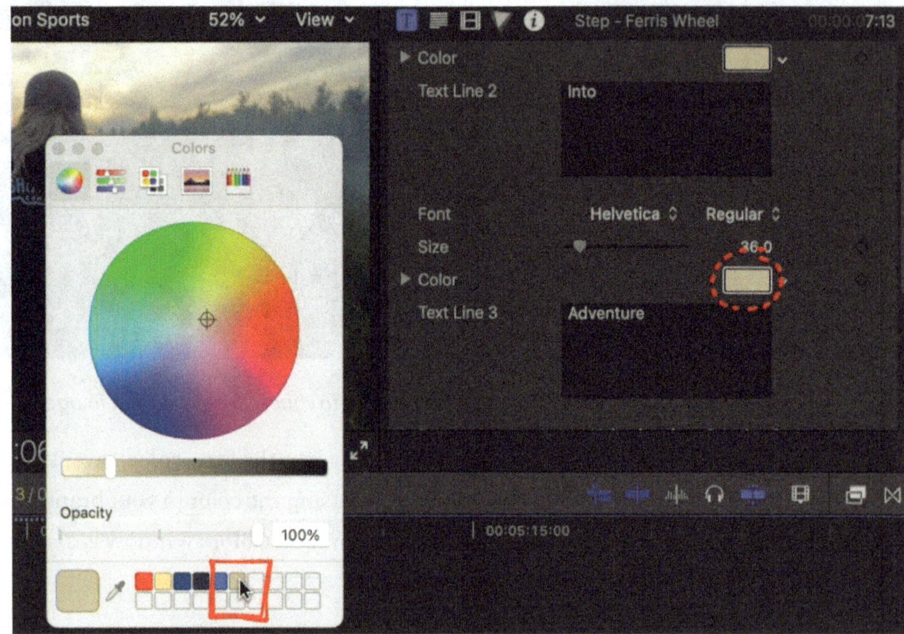

Figure 9.8: Repeat the saved color on other text fields

9. Now, here's the trick to deal with four text fields when you only have three words for your text. It's virtually impossible to try to delete a line; that is not the solution. Instead, just put a space in the extra text field. So, press the *spacebar* to create " " in the text field, which will be invisible. Sorry for all the build-up, but the way to deal with empty text fields is just to add a space.

Replacing titles

If only you could swap in different spices to test them out. Final Cut Pro offers the flexibility to update and refine the text elements of a video project efficiently. By swapping out titles, you can quickly make stylistic updates to align with branding needs or creative direction. This method not only saves time but also maintains consistency across projects, ensuring that edits don't disrupt the design or flow of your existing timeline.

This might seem too simple for a recipe, and perhaps it is, but you may not know this is possible without someone showing you how.

In this recipe, we will see how easy it is to replace a title but keep the existing content.

How to do it...

It seems too easy to be true. Let's go:

1. In the Sidebar panel, click on the **Show Titles and Generators Sidebar** icon. Then, click on the **Titles** category. From the Title and Generator Browser panel, watch the animated previews and select a title that has several text fields. Add it to your project and type in some text.

2. For my example, I'm going to select the **Ferris Wheel** title used in the previous *Customizing titles* recipe.

3. Select another title – this time, from the **Text** category – that also has several text fields. In my example, I'm going to use a title called **Rack Focus**.

4. To replace a title with another title, simply click, hold, and drag the new title from the Title and Generator Browser panel directly on top of the old title in the Timeline panel. The cursor changes to an arrow with a green plus sign.

Figure 9.9: Drag the new title directly onto the original title

5. You can tell you have the new title directly on the old title when the old title becomes highlighted in white. Let go of the mouse click, and a pop-up menu will be displayed. Select **Replace** from the pop-up menu.

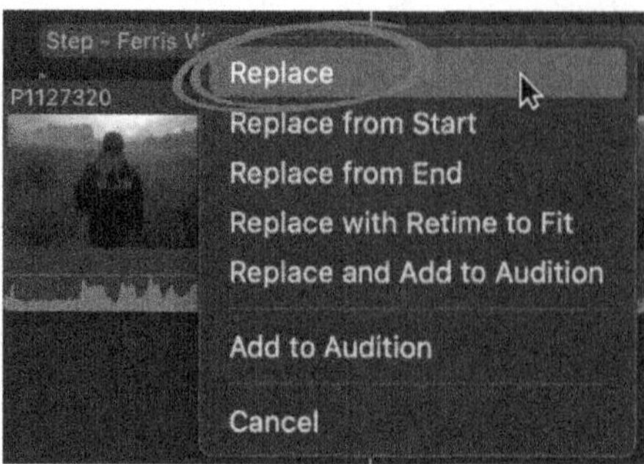

Figure 9.10: Select Replace from the pop-up menu

6. The old title will be replaced with the new title, and, conveniently, the text you had typed into the original text fields will persist into the new title. Skim through your project to confirm that the text was transferred to the new title.

For more information about replacing clips or titles from the start or end, or how to retime to fit, see *Chapter 3* and the recipe called *Replacing clips*. In addition, see *Chapter 4* and the recipe called *Creating an audition* for the other items in this pop-up menu.

Explore other titles to see how easy it is to transfer text between titles.

Using safe zones

Safe zones in Final Cut Pro help ensure that text and critical visual elements remain visible across various playback screens and devices by placing guidelines on the Viewer panel that mark the *title-* and *action-safe* areas within the frame. By keeping essential information within these boundaries, you avoid your audience potentially missing your story from the unintended overscan cropping that might occur on older TVs or displays. Using safe zones ensures that your project maintains its intended composition, delivering a more professional and visually cohesive final product.

In this recipe, we will see how to display the safe zone markers and where your titles need to land.

How to do it...

Keeping the outside edge of your serving plate clean looks professional. The same is true for your titles:

1. Add a clip of a person to your project timeline. Let's identify who this person is with the use of a title (as we have seen in the previous two recipes).

2. In the **Titles** sidebar, click on the category for **Lower Thirds**. Lower thirds have this name because these titles are located in the lower third of the video screen. They're basically used for the names and job titles of the people in your documentary, newscast, or promotional video.

3. Take a little time to explore all the available animated **Lower Thirds** titles. I have a favorite called **Snap Left**, and I'm going to drag it to the Timeline panel and connect it on top of my surfing clip. Park the playhead on top of the lower third and the clip so they are both visible in the Viewer panel.

4. In the upper-right corner of the Viewer panel, click on the **View** drop-down menu. About halfway down the menu is the **Overlays** section. Select **Show Title/Action Safe Zones**.

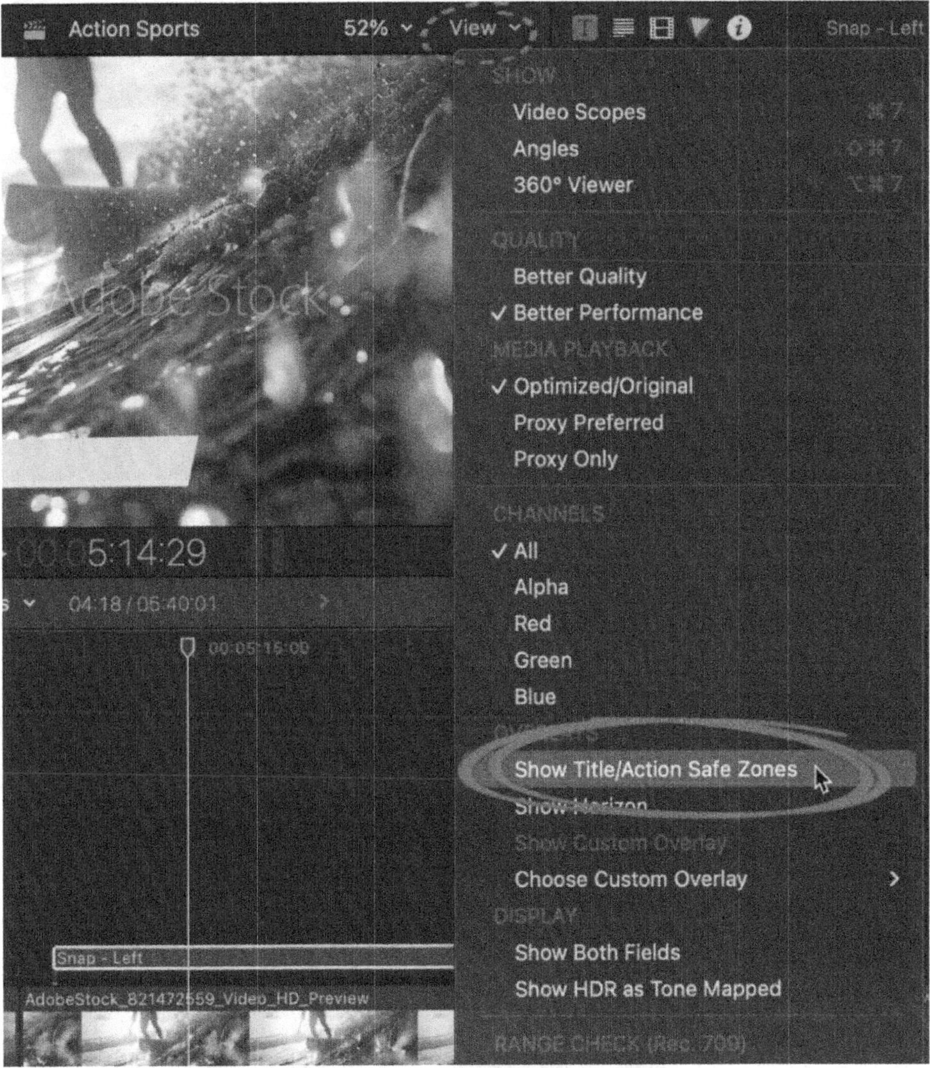

Figure 9.11: Select Show Title/Action Safe Zones from the View drop-down menu

This places an overlay around the edge of the Viewer panel screen with two rectangles in faint yellow lines.

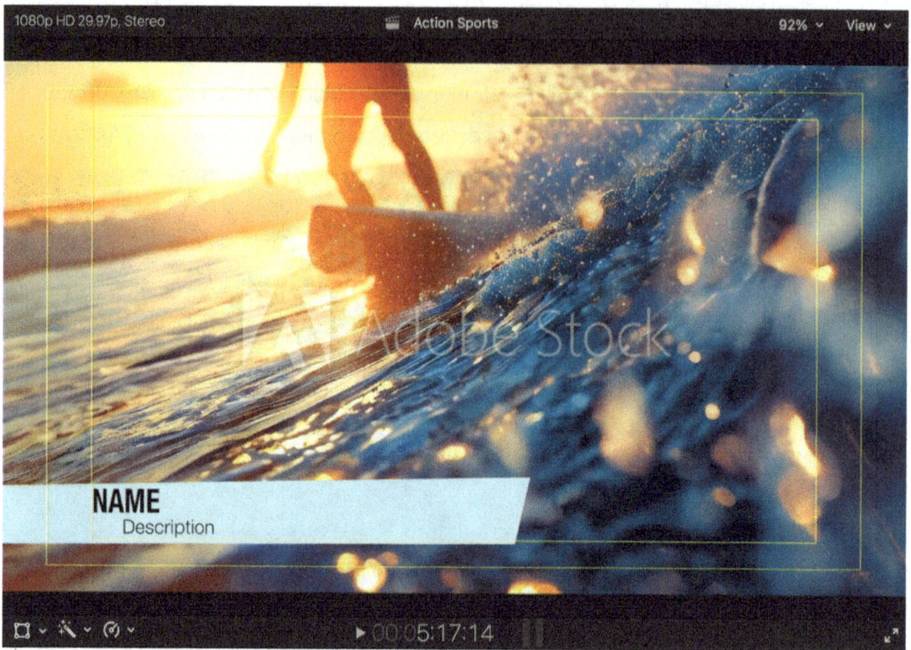

Figure 9.12: The title-/action-safe zones are displayed in the Viewer panel

The outer line indicates the outside edge of the action-safe zone. Professional productions will keep their primary action within the action-safe area so viewers don't miss a thing.

The inner line indicates the outside edge of the title-safe zone. This zone is further from the edge of the screen. Just in case a TV is showing your image improperly, you don't want the names of your important characters to be unread.

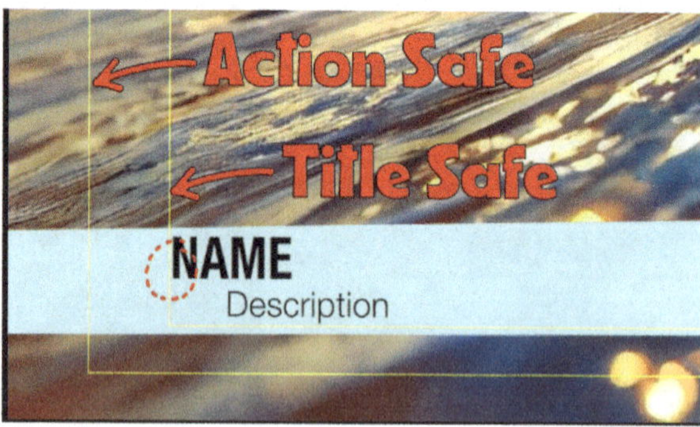

Figure 9.13: Note the outer action-safe line and the inner title-safe line

Notice that the text in all of the built-in lower thirds stays within the title-safe zone. When creating Lower Third titles, keep them in the title-safe zone. Using the **Title/Action Safe Zones** overlays is another example of small attention to detail that you can do to make your productions more professional.

In addition, it will speed your workflow if you build the habit of adjusting the Final Cut Pro interface to conform to your current editing process, like quickly turning on the **Title/Action Safe Zones** overlay to check your titles.

Using themes in titles and generators

Just as a fine restaurant would use matching colors with a table setting, an editor would use themes to coordinate the look of their project. Using generator and title themes in Final Cut Pro brings cohesive design and branding into your video projects with minimal effort. These preset themes provide a variety of styles and effects that can be applied consistently, from lower thirds to titles, ensuring a polished and unified look throughout the project.

Leveraging these tools enhances both productivity and visual appeal, enabling editors to focus on storytelling while keeping their graphics visually consistent and professional.

In this recipe, we will explore the themes available across the **Titles** and **Generators** categories of animated graphics.

How to do it...

Keep it all looking coordinated. Let's do this:

1. In the **Titles** and **Generators** sidebar, click on the main **Titles** category. Within the Titles Browser panel, scroll down to the bottom, and you'll notice that different titles are grouped together with a theme name. It might be **Scrapbook** or **Skylight**. There are many that can enrich the flavor of your storytelling. Take some time to explore the themes.

2. For my example of a surfing TV show, I'm going to pick a theme called **Kinetic**. Notice that this theme has a left lower third, an upper third title, some end pages, and a reveal animation. It also has **Bug**, which is slang for the animated channel title that pops up in the lower-right corner on a lot of cable and broadcast TV shows. Take time to skim through the title thumbnails to see what the animations do.

3. Drag the **Left** title down to the Timeline panel and connect it on top of a clip. I think this lower third title will work well with my example show on surfing. I can use it to display the name of who will be surfing next.

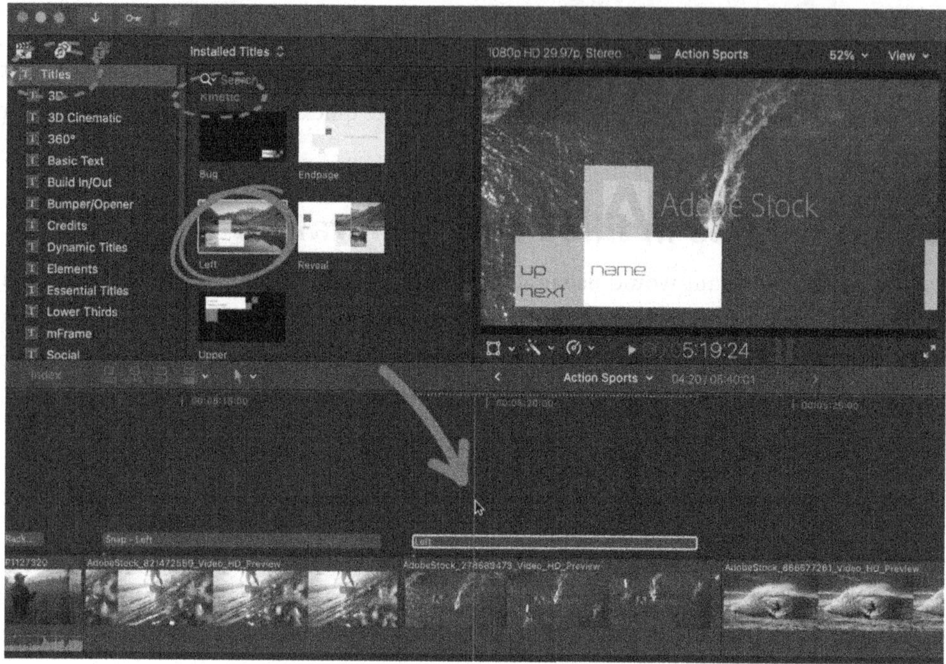

Figure 9.14: Connect a themed lower third title on top of your video clip

4. Now, in the **Titles** and **Generators** sidebar, click on the **Generators** category. Then, in the Browser panel, scroll to the bottom and notice that there are a few themes that are the same within **Titles** and **Generators – Kinetic** is one of them. Take a look at the other themes with background generators. Under **Kinetic**, click once on the generator called **Build** to select the entire clip. Add or insert it into your timeline project like you would any other clip.

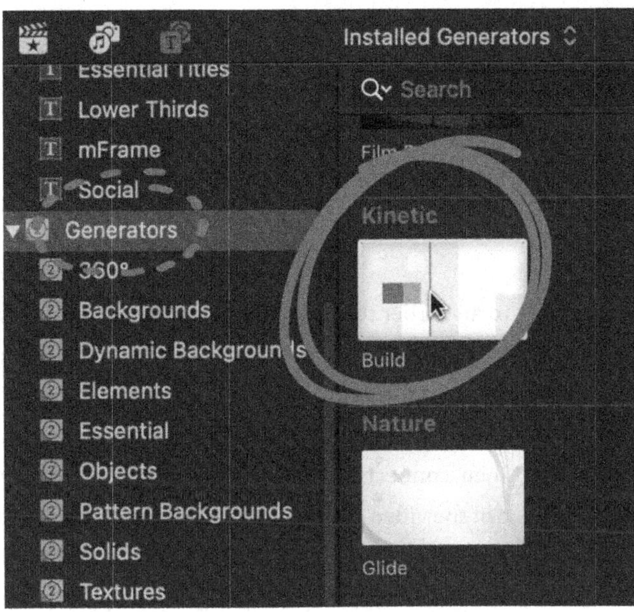

Figure 9.15: Add a themed generator clip to your project

5. Here is something cool. The ending frame of many of the generator backgrounds matches the beginning frame. Add or insert another copy of your generator background right after the first one. You should have two background graphics in a row.

6. Now, place the skimmer at the edit point between the two duplicate background generators and use the *Shift + ?* (question mark) shortcut. This shortcut plays two seconds before and two seconds after the current position of the skimmer. Notice that the two backgrounds work seamlessly together. Nice.

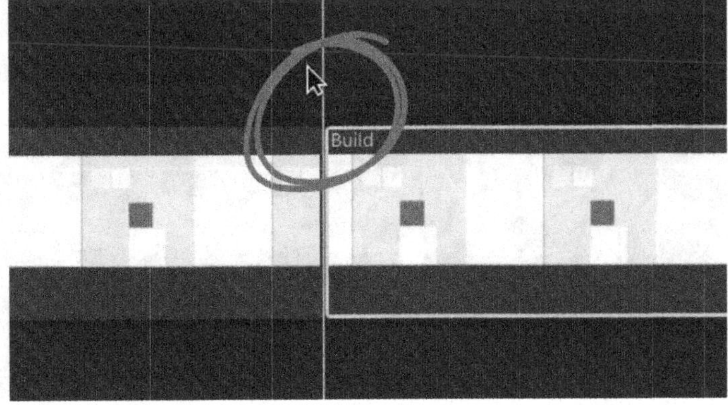

Figure 9.16: Many generators have matching endings and beginnings

There's more...

In my example, the generator is exactly 10 seconds, but sometimes you need more than 10 seconds of an animated background, so piecing these together can create a longer animation. Maybe you need a full-screen background graphic to run under some headline titles that introduce an instructional video, or perhaps run underneath the edge of some still photos or Keynote or PowerPoint slides.

1. I'm referring back to an earlier recipe in this chapter called *Using safe zones*. Keynote and PowerPoint slides tend to have information that goes right to the edge of the screen. You don't want any important information to get cut off and missed by your audience. So, when slides need to be added to a video, you would first export them as JPEGs and import them into Final Cut Pro. Then, connect each slide on top of a background generator, which, most likely, will be on top of the video of the person speaking. With the slide image selected, go to the Inspector panel. In the **Transform** section, use the **Scale** parameter. You could use the slider control, but it is easier to click directly on the percent field and type 90 for the exact amount of scaling. This sizes the image right at the edge of the action-safe zone. Nice.

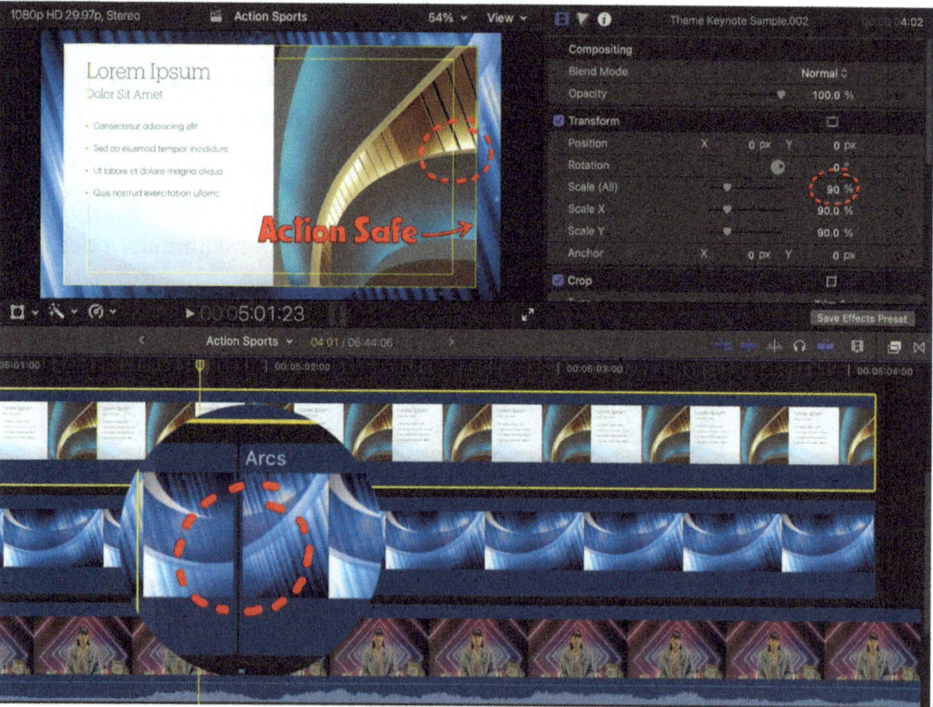

Figure 9.17: Use linked themed generators with slide graphics

Creating a title object tracker

Creating a title object tracker in Final Cut Pro allows your text to follow moving subjects, adding a dynamic and professional touch to titles. By setting tracking points, you can ensure that the title stays aligned with the action on screen, enhancing clarity and visual interest. This feature is particularly useful for highlighting key elements in documentaries or instructional videos, giving viewers a seamless and engaging viewing experience.

In this recipe, we will investigate the steps to track an object and attach text to follow that object.

Getting ready

Object tracking works best in images with contrast. The easiest clip to work with might be of someone in dark clothes moving against a light background.

How to do it...

Like a sous chef following the head chef's every move, let's get some text to follow an object:

1. Add a clip of someone in contrast to your timeline project. *Option + click* on the clip you want to work with so that it is both selected and the playhead is parked on top of it. In my example, I'm using a video of a runner, and I'm going to create some text that will follow him on screen.

2. In the Video Inspector panel, scroll down to the bottom of the **Trackers** parameter and click on the plus sign icon to add a tracker.

Figure 9.18: Click on the plus sign icon to add a tracker to your clip

3. This will add **Object Track** under the **Trackers** category. For the **Analysis Method** param-
    eter, click on the drop-down menu that has the default of **Automatic** and select **Machine
    Learning**. This is the best method to analyze a clip and create an object tracker.

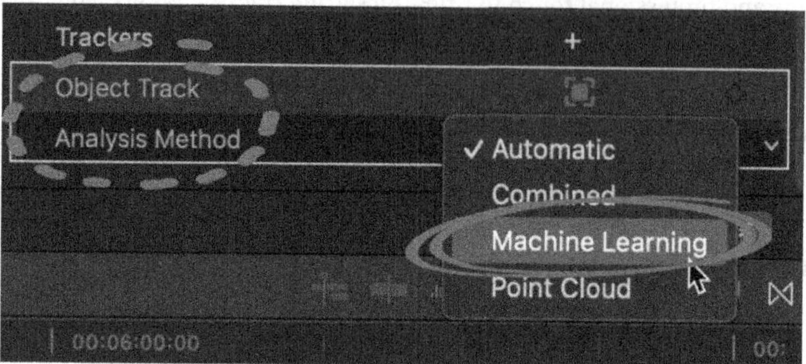

Figure 9.19: Select Machine Learning from the Analysis Method drop-down menu

4. An object tracker grid is displayed on the clip in the Viewer panel. Move the grid over the
    area in your image to analyze. Shape the grid with the on-screen control points. Use the
    orange dots on the sides to size the object tracker and use the white dot in the upper-left
    corner to smooth the corner into a circle. In my example, I am creating a little bit of an
    oval around this person's head

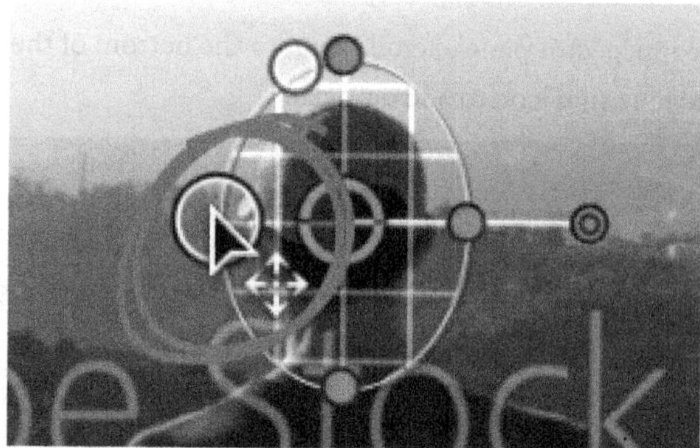

Figure 9.20: Use control points to adjust the size of the object tracker

5. In the left corner of the Viewer panel, click on the rectangle **Analyze** button. This will an-
    alyze the clip to the end and then to the beginning in order to find and track the contrast
    of the selected object – in my example, the person's head.

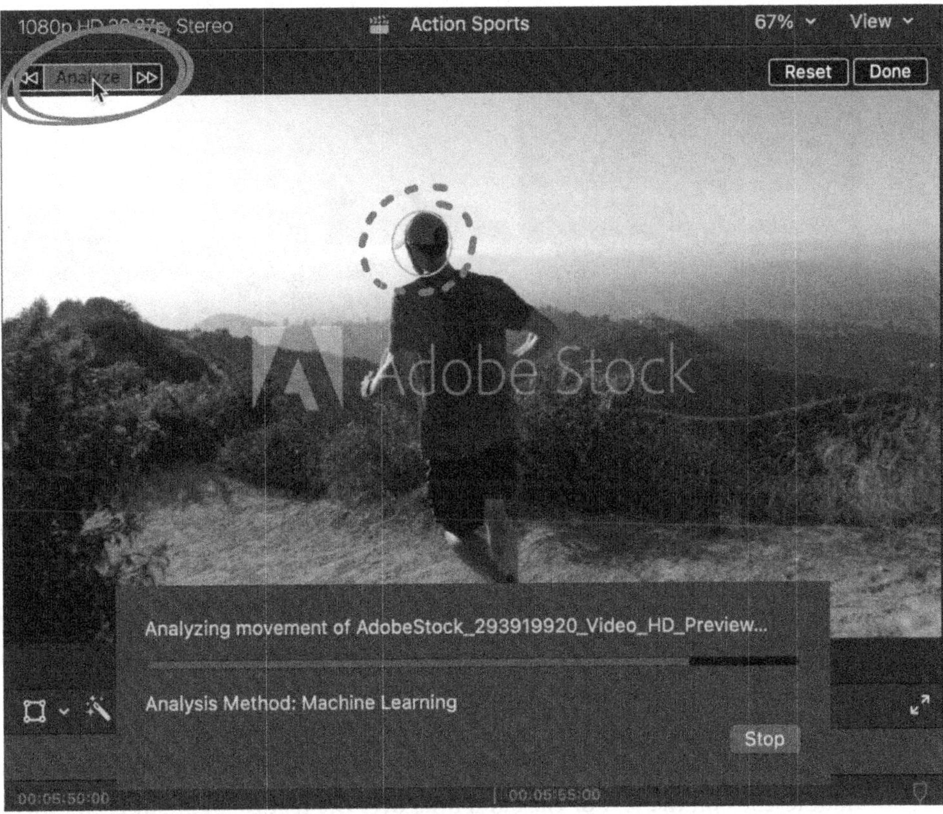

Figure 9.21: Click on the Analyze button in the upper-left corner of the Viewer panel

6. Once the object tracker has been created in the base clip, we want to connect some text on top of it. In the Titles sidebar panel, click on the **Basic Text** category. Let's keep it simple. Scroll down to the title called **Text** (yes, very exciting) and drag that on top of our analyzed clip. If you need to edit the length of the text to match the length of your clip, do so by simply dragging the edges of the text clip.

Figure 9.22: Connect a basic Text title on top of our analyzed clip

7. Click on the **Text** field so it's selected. You can edit the text directly in the Viewer panel; double-click on the text or click and drag over the text to highlight it and then type in the text of your choice. I'm going to use Step into Adventure. To escape, or to end our editing of the text directly in the Viewer panel, press the escape key, *Esc*, on your keyboard.

8. With the text clip still selected, click on the **Transform** icon in the lower-left corner of the Viewer panel (it looks like a square with control points on the corners). Then, in the top center of the Viewer panel is a new button that says **Tracker**. We are going to link the **Title** clip to the **Tracker** grid created in the earlier clip.

*Figure 9.23: Click on the Transform icon in the lower-left corner of the Viewer panel
to display the Tracker button*

9. Next to the **Tracker** tab is a down arrow icon. Click on this to open a drop-down dialog
    box. Check the following options:

    - Verify that **Tracker Source** is your clip with the object tracker grid. In my example,
      it is the Adobe Stock image of the runner.

    - The **Tracker** parameter drop-down menu should be changed from the default
      None to the name of the object tracker we created in the base clip. We used the
      default name, so select **Object Track**. When we select **Object Track**, Final Cut will
      close this dialog box and link the text to the object tracker grid.

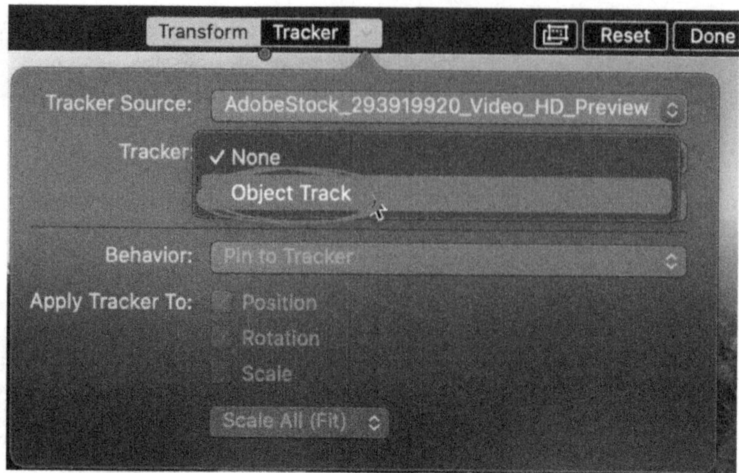

Figure 9.24: Select Object Track from the Tracker drop-down menu

10. Click on the **Tracker** down arrow again to bring up the same dialog box:

- Verify that **Behavior** is set to **Offset from Tracker**. This is because we don't want the text to be directly on top of the tracked object. We want the title to follow our runner off to the side.

- Note the **Apply Tracker To** parameter. Only add checkboxes to the things that need to be applied. In my example, with just tracking the head of our subject, the text should follow **Position**, but I don't need **Rotation** or **Scale**.

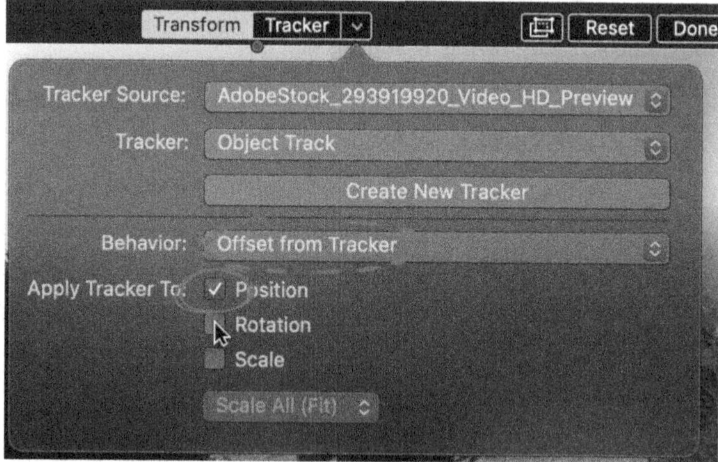

Figure 9.25: Verify that Behavior is Offset from Tracker and check Position

With those options set, close the dialog box by clicking elsewhere in the Viewer panel.

11. Drag your text directly into the Viewer panel and position it next to your object.

12. The default color of this text is white. That will not look good in my example with a light sky. Along the top of the Inspector panel, click on the **Text Inspector** icon, which looks like multiple small lines of text. This is where you can change the font and size of your text.

13. Scroll down to the section called **Face**, meaning the front part of our font. If this section is not already open, hover over to the right side to reveal a button called **Show**. Click on the **Show** button to open the color details for the **Face** font.

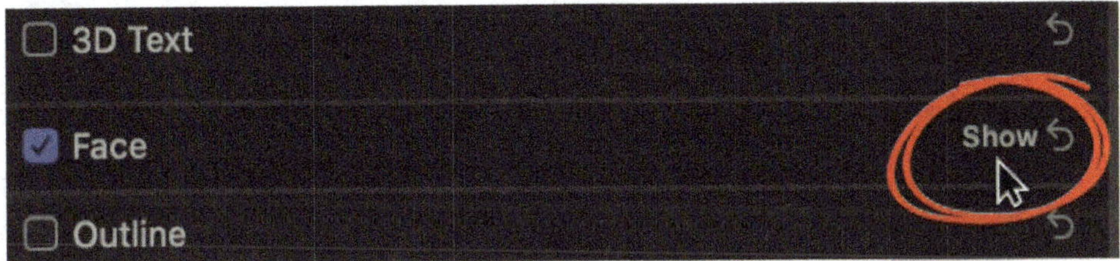

Figure 9.26: Click on the Show button for the Face parameter

14. Click on the sample color rectangle, which brings up the macOS **Colors** window. Now, click on the eyedropper down near the bottom-left corner of the window, and the cursor will change to a magnified circle with a one-pixel square in the center. Move the cursor around the image of the video and notice how it displays the colors. Instead of choosing simple white or black for text, a subtle design technique is to use the eyedropper and select and repeat a color within your image. For my example, I am going to pick a color out of the trees, such as a nice dark green. Find your color and click.

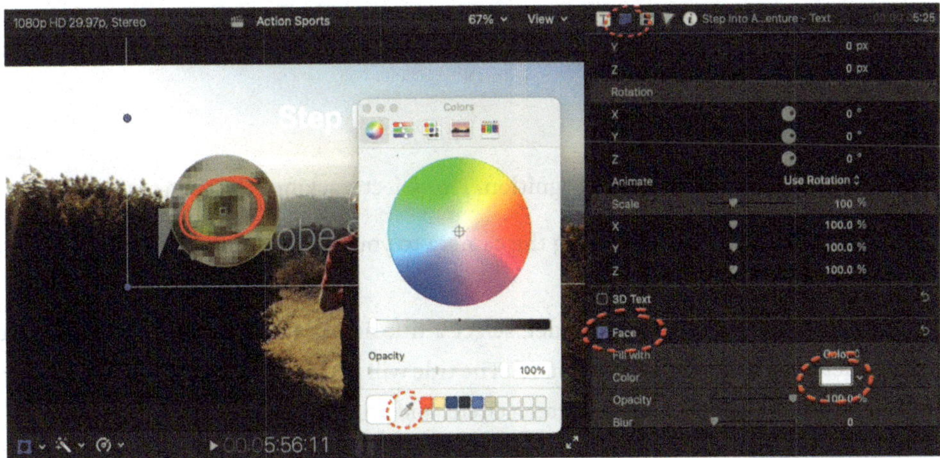

Figure 9.27: Select a dark color with the magnified circle from the image background

15. Close the macOS **Colors** window and click on the video image in the Viewer panel. Click on the **Done** button in the upper-right corner.

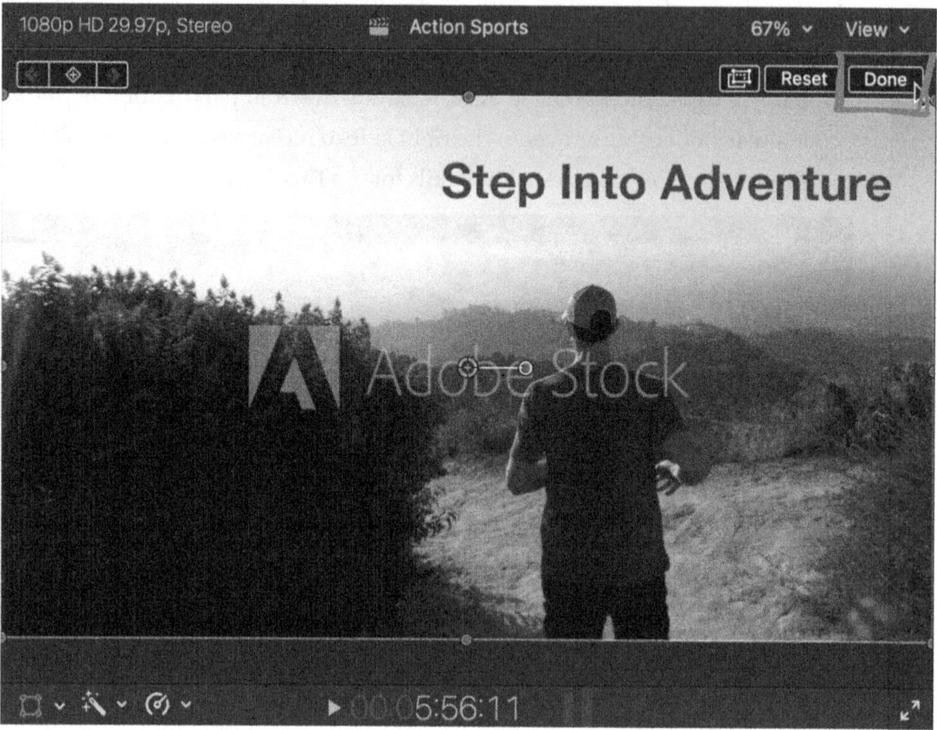

Figure 9.28: Select the video clip and click on the Done button

16. Play through your project. The linked text will follow along with your object, like someone running on a trail. Very nice.

There's more...

Final Cut Pro has built-in facial recognition. The object tracking effect can take advantage of this:

1. Add a clip of a person facing the camera to your timeline project. Place the playhead at the beginning of the clip.

2. From the Titles Browser panel, select a title and drag it directly onto the image of the person's face in the Viewer panel. The title will detect a face. The cursor will change to an arrow with a plus sign in a green circle, and an oval tracker grid will be created.

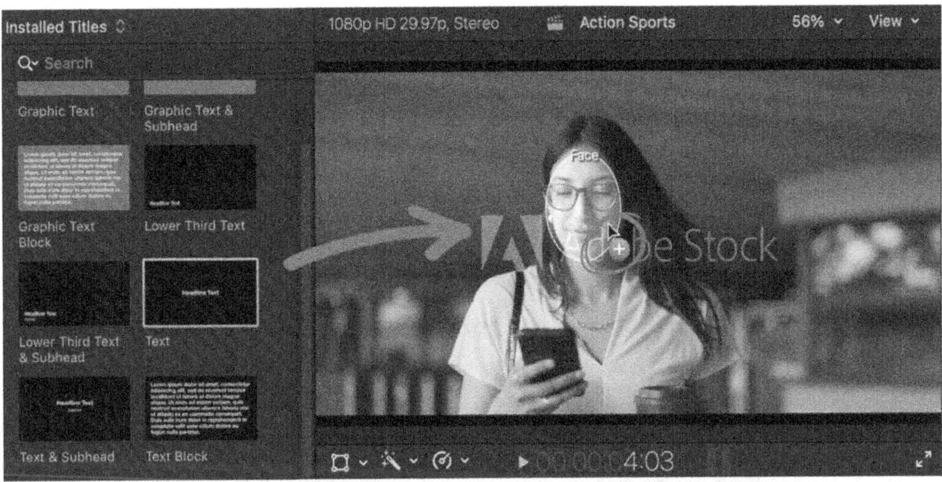

Figure 9.29: Drag a title directly onto a face to create a tracker

3. When you release the mouse, the **Tracker** control buttons will be displayed at the top of the Viewer panel. Click on the **Analyze** button in the upper-left corner of the Viewer panel.

Figure 9.30: Click on the Analyze button to start the facial recognition process

Final Cut will analyze the face in the clip forward and backward.

4. When it is finished. Click on the down arrow icon next to the **Tracker** tab.

5. Verify that **Tracker Source** is your person clip and that **Face Track** is the default name of your **Tracker**.

6. Check that the **Behavior** is **Offset from Tracker**.

7. Then, you can check the appropriate items for **Apply Tracker To**. Normally, I would probably just use **Position**, but for my example, I am also going to check **Rotation** to see how it looks.

8. Click on the **Done** button in the upper-right corner.

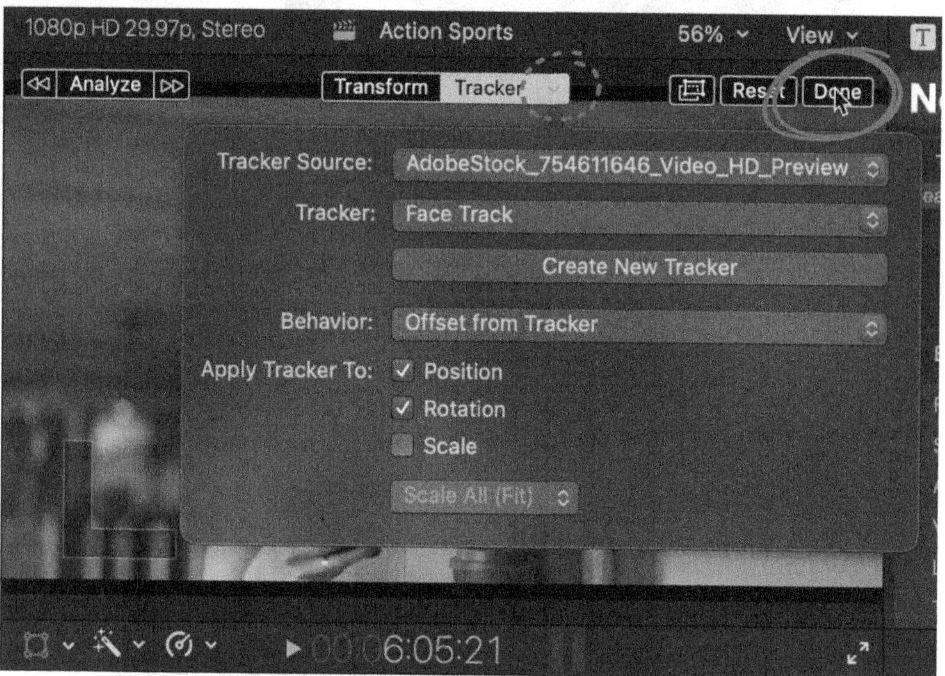

Figure 9.31: Verify the tracker parameters and click on the Done button

9. The result is amazing and so fast. You can adjust the length of your title and the text, font, color, and so on after this. Next to the person's face, I left the default text of **Headline Text**. Get it? Headline?

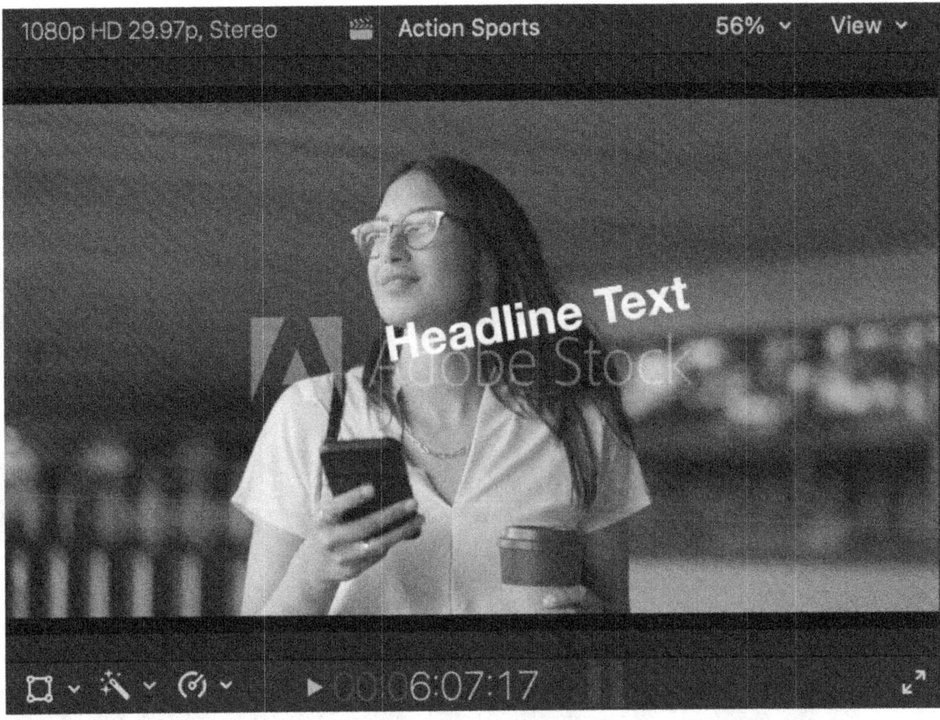

Figure 9.32: Note the amazingly fast result of a title detecting a face and making a tracker

Revealing text animation

The **Magnetic Mask** tool in Final Cut Pro lets you precisely shape and animate a mask that clings naturally to the edges of your footage, creating a seamless way to reveal text creatively. By crafting your mask to follow specific contours or movements, you can add dynamic flair, such as text appearing through a doorway or tracing along an object. This technique elevates your storytelling, making your text integration feel visually engaging.

In this recipe, we will create a cool animation with an object-revealing text.

Getting ready

You will want a clip of an object with some contrast moving through the frame.

How to do it...

Get your chef hats on, we are going to make a text sandwich:

1. Add your clip to the primary storyline in the Timeline panel. We want to duplicate it. While holding down the *Option* key, click on the clip and drag up. Notice how the cursor changes to an arrow with a plus sign in a green circle, and a copy of the clip is created.

Figure 9.33: Duplicate a clip by dragging up while holding down the Option key

2. The top clip is going to get a mask. In the Effects Browser panel, scroll down to the **Masks and Keying** section. Select **Magnetic Mask** and drag it onto the duplicated clip. You will see the cursor change to the arrow with a plus sign in a green circle again.

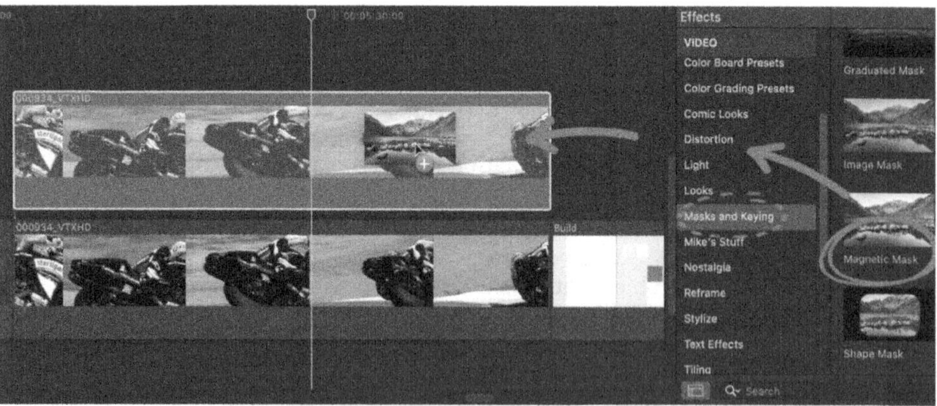

Figure 9.34: Apply the Magnetic Mask effect to the duplicated clip

3. When the effect has been applied, the Viewer panel will change, and the cursor will change to an eyedropper with a plus sign. Click on the object in the image that you want to apply the mask to.

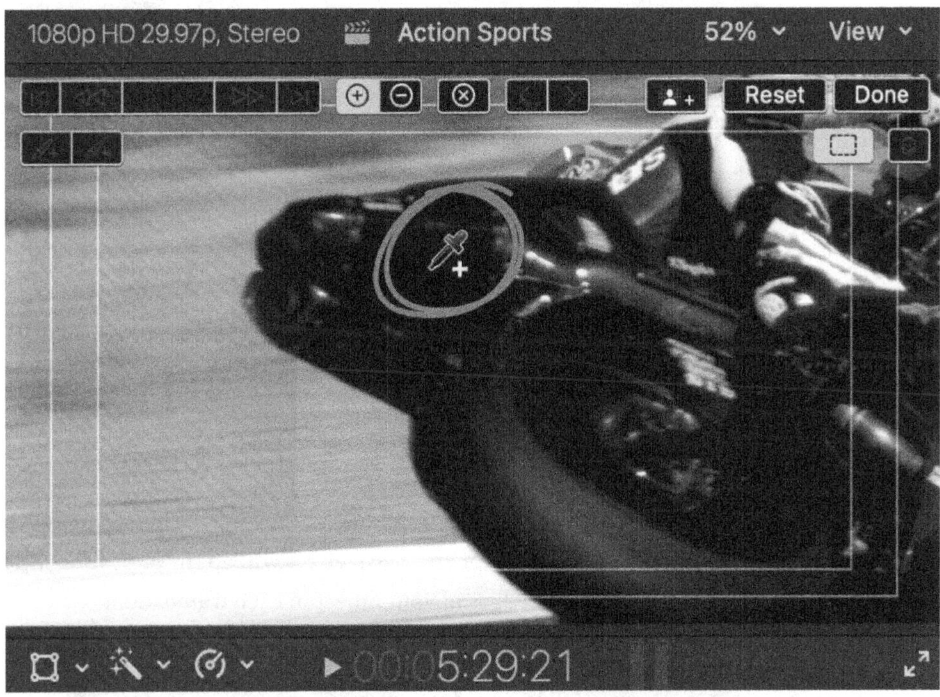

Figure 9.35: Use the eyedropper to select the object in the image you want to mask

4. The Magnetic Mask effect will find the edges of the object and use a red color to indicate what has been selected. Wherever you click, a green control point will be added. Keep clicking on the object until the entire object is masked in red. If a portion of the image is added but not part of the object, hold down the *Option* key, and the cursor will change to an eyedropper with a minus sign. Click on the areas to subtract from the mask.

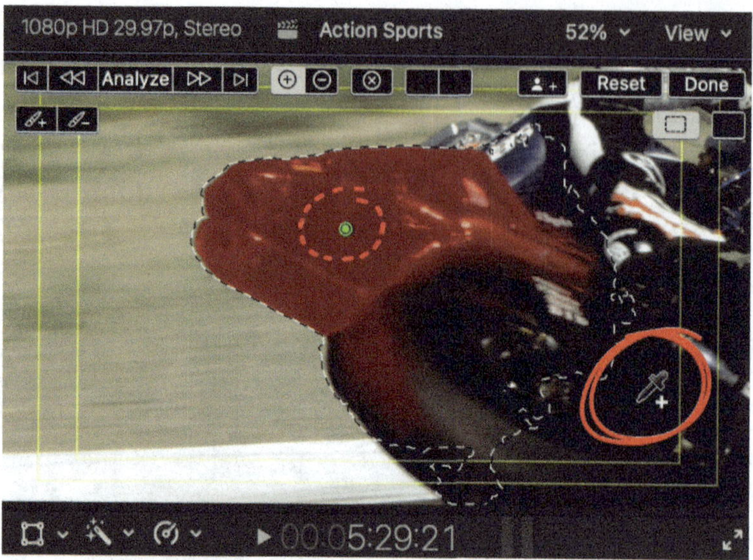

Figure 9.36: Click with the eyedropper to add mask control points to your object

5. When you are happy with the mask selection, click on the **Analyze** button in the upper-left corner of the Viewer panel. The Magnetic Mask effect will go through your clip forward and backward and analyze the edges of your object in each frame. Cool!

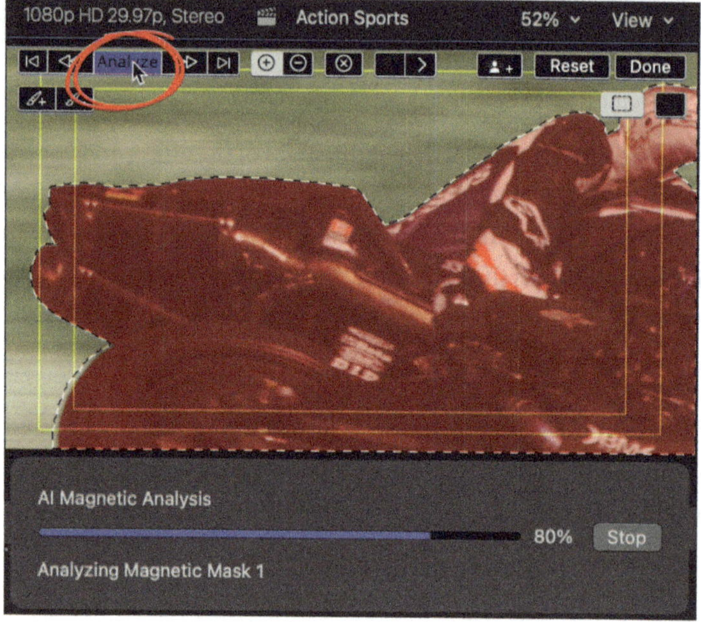

Figure 9.37: Click on the Analyze button

6. Let's add some text. Start with a basic title without a lot of animation. See the previous recipe in this chapter called *Creating a title object tracker*, in which we used a basic title. Connect the title on top of your two clips. Type in something clever. You can use `Mike Is Cool`. With the text clip selected in the timeline, you can drag it in the Viewer panel to position it so that your object will reveal the text about halfway through the timing of the clip.

Figure 9.38: Position your text to be revealed by your object

7. Let's use a nifty keyboard shortcut to move our text down one layer. With the **Title** clip selected, press *Option + ↓* (down arrow). This moves a clip down one layer and swaps places with the clip below it. You are pretty smart, so you have probably already guessed that *Option + ↑* (up arrow) will move a clip up one layer. Way to go! Give these a try.

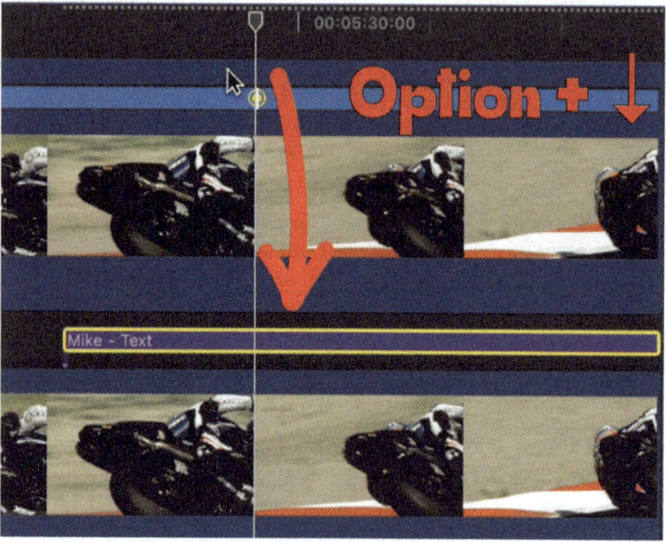

Figure 9.39: Press Option + ↓ to move the Title clip down one layer

8. In the Timeline panel, click on the top clip on which we applied the Magnetic Mask effect. Click on the **Done** button in the upper-right corner of the screen.

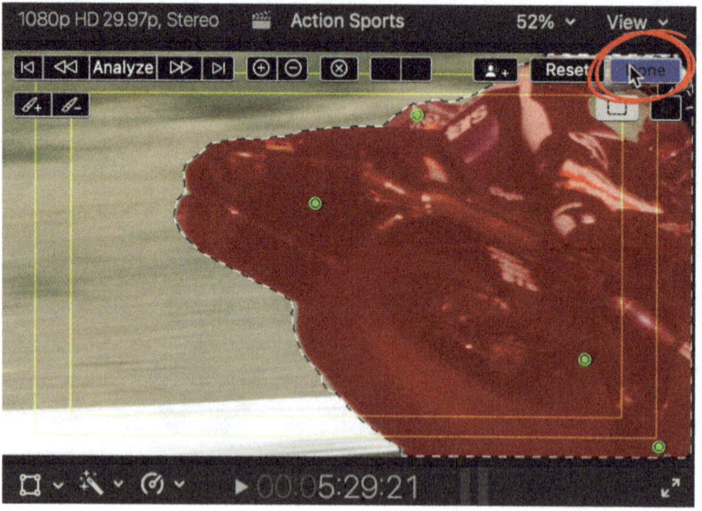

Figure 9.40: With the mask clip selected, click on the Done button

Voila! You have made a text sandwich. The object in the top clip is masked off, but because there is a duplicate underneath, the background matches. The **Title** clip is on top of the background but under the object with the mask until the object passes and reveals the text!

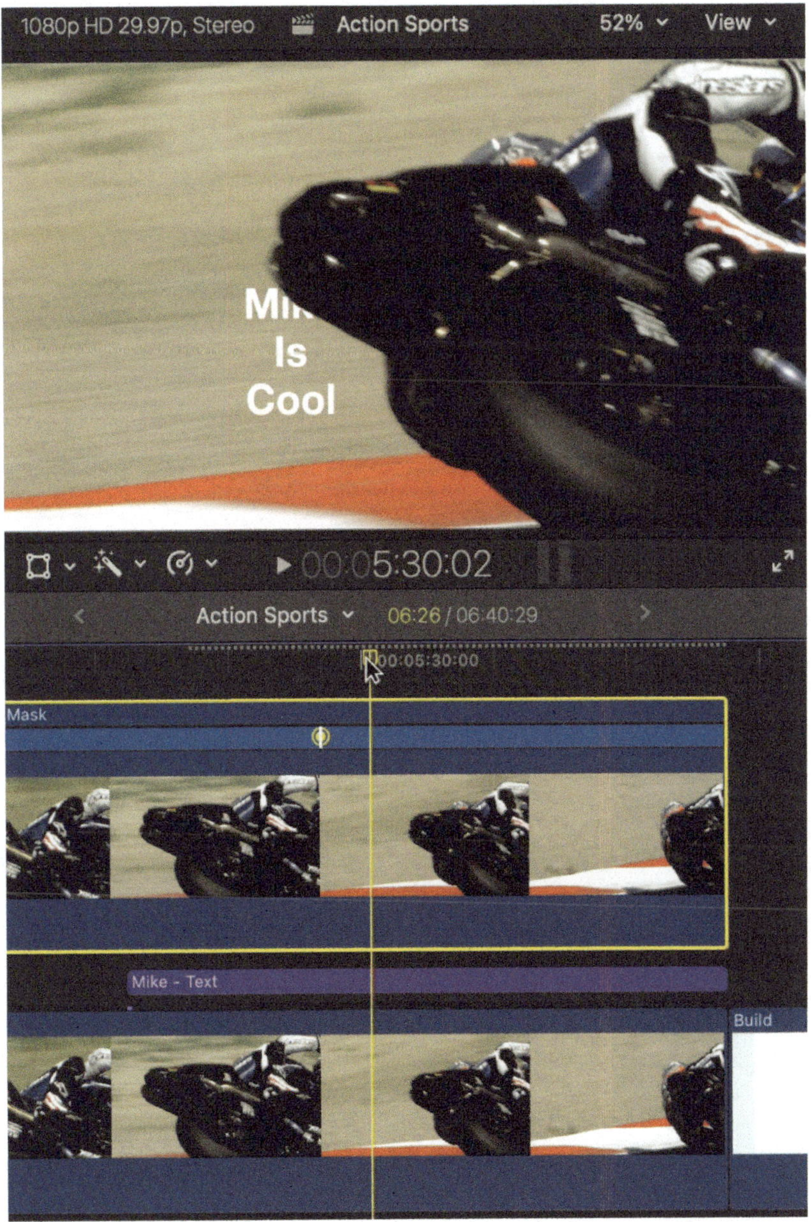

Figure 9.41: Observe the result of the Magnetic Mask effect revealing text between duplicated clips

There's more...

When selections have been made with the Magnetic Mask effect, you can also apply color adjustments or other effects to those selections. See the *Chapter 7* recipe called *Using the Magnetic Mask effect* for more information.

10

Accelerating Real-World Projects

Stride confidently into the kitchen of Final Cut Pro practicality, where seasoned advice becomes the special ingredient to your editing success. In this chapter, we serve up a feast of real-world tips and tricks, handpicked to inspire your editing palate and elevate your projects. We'll explore strategies for project management, workflow optimization, and problem-solving in the editing studio.

In this chapter, you will discover techniques for managing project versions effectively, ensuring organized and streamlined editing workflows. You'll also learn how to create repeatable video introductions and how to enhance project versatility. You will study a valuable way to gather accurate client feedback and implement closed captions, empowering you to deliver profession-al-quality videos tailored to client specifications with precision and ease.

In this chapter, you will complete the following recipes:

- Creating assets for a workgroup
- Controlling project versions
- Planning for project versatility
- Creating a repeatable project intro and outro
- Creating closed captions
- Gathering accurate client feedback

Creating assets for a workgroup

When working in a collaborative environment, importing media into a shared folder rather than directly into the library keeps your assets accessible and organized. When importing media from an SD card, Final Cut Pro saves files in one of two places: inside the library or outside the library. If it's inside the library, it's hard for other people to access. So, we want to save some files outside of the library. This method ensures that team members can easily access and update files without duplicating media, saving storage space, and maintaining consistency. By centralizing assets in a shared location, you streamline the workflow, reduce potential conflicts, and make collaboration more efficient.

In this recipe, we will demonstrate how to import footage in a way that your workgroup can access it right from the start.

Getting ready

To follow along, you will need to have an SD card with footage recorded from a video camera.

How to do it...

Just as a great sous chef preps ingredients for their team of chefs, you can prepare footage for your whole workgroup to access, as follows:

1. Let's say our work group has a connected server. Make a new folder to receive the footage. In my example, I am going to call my folder `Helicopter GoPro Footage`.

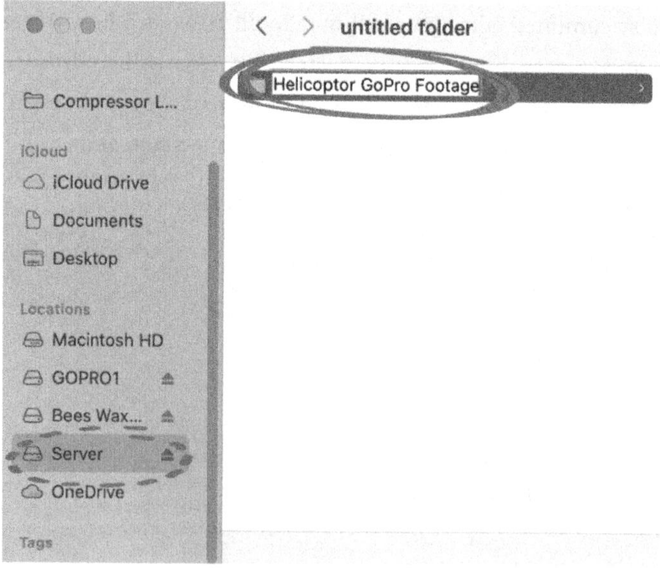

Figure 10.1: Create a folder to receive the imported footage

2. Now, in Final Cut Pro, from the **File** menu, select **New | Library...**. In my example, I am going to call this `Extract Helo Footage Only`. It can be saved anywhere. I'm just going to save it into my **Movies** folder on the hard drive. I am naming it this way because we are not going to edit anything, just import the footage.

Just a quick note to express, as we did in *Chapter 2*, in the recipe titled *Importing media into Final Cut Pro*, that SD cards are *not* computer disks. The media needs to be extracted and converted with a software program such as Final Cut Pro or iMovie.

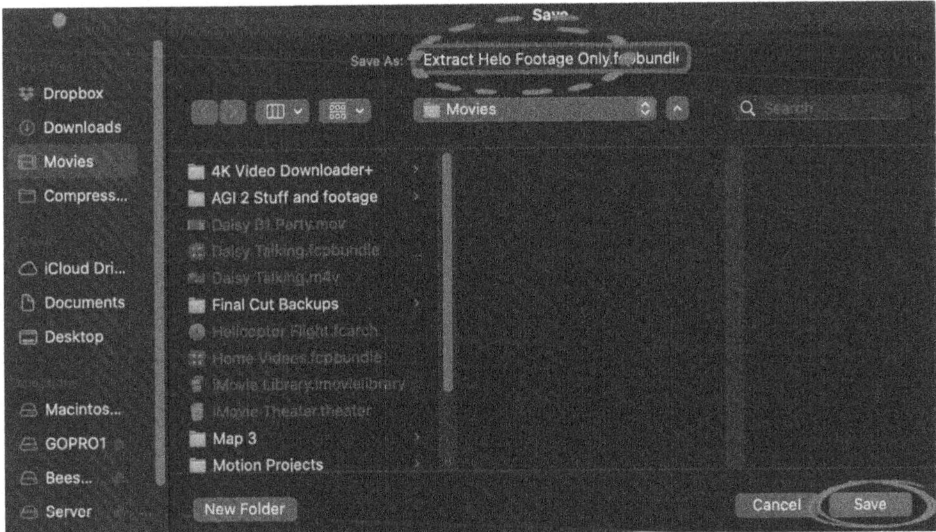

Figure 10.2: Create a library to just extract the footage

3. It is important to make sure that the library is selected. Then, go to the Inspector panel and, next to **Storage Locations**, click on **Modify Settings**.

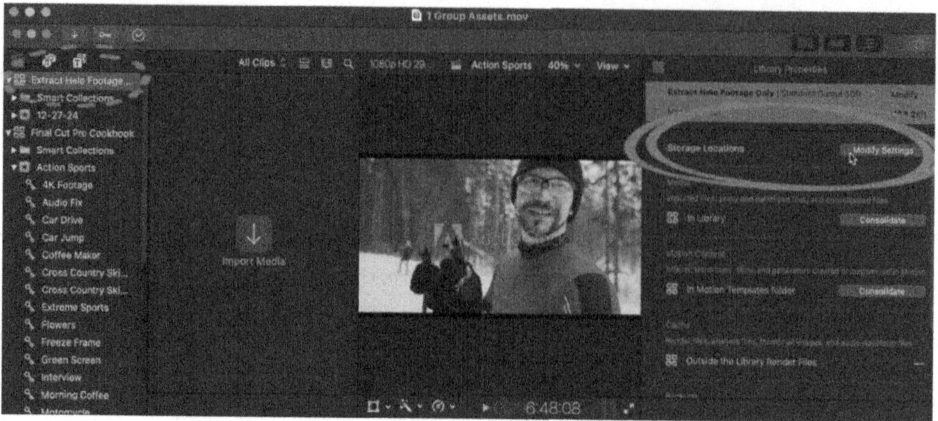

Figure 10.3: Modify the storage settings of the library

4. You are presented with a dialog box. The default storage location is to save media into the library, so we have to change the setting. Click on the drop-down menu for **Media** and select **Choose…**.

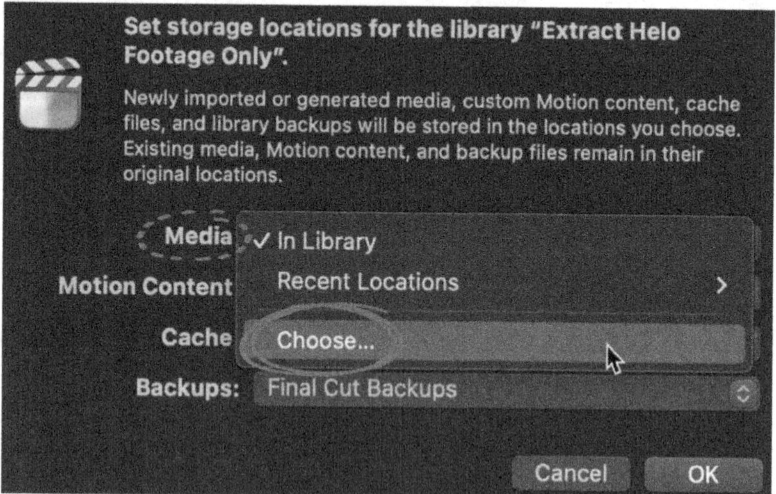

Figure 10.4: Choose the folder to receive the media

5. You are presented with a new window. Navigate to the folder that you have already designated. In my example, it is called `Helicopter GoPro Footage`, located on a shared server. Then, click on the **Choose** button in the lower-right corner.

6. Notice that the dialog box indicates that newly imported or generated media will be stored in the folder you just created. The other settings for **Motion Content, Cache**, and **Backups** can remain the default. Click on the **OK** button.

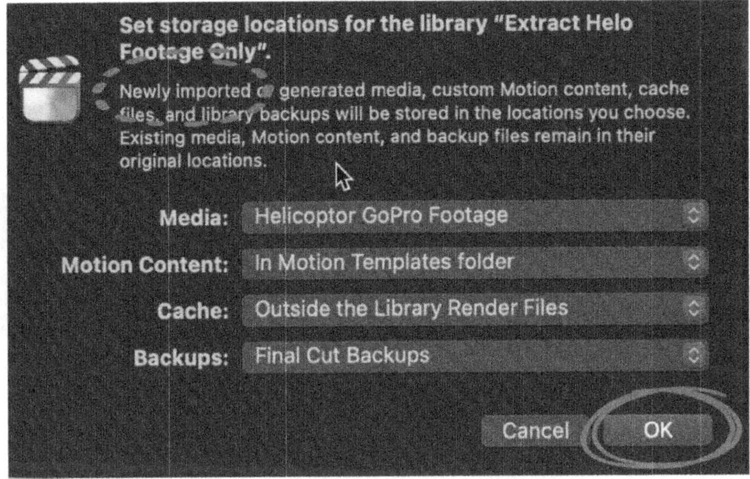

Figure 10.5: Verify the storage location settings

7. With the extracting library still selected, use the keyboard shortcut of *Command + I* to open the **Media Import** window. Select your SD card from the **Camera** section in the upper-left corner. Verify that in the **Files** section, the selection dot indicates files will *be copied to* the folder you designated and not to the library. Be sure to make your selections for **Analyze Video**, **Transcode**, **Analyze Audio**, and so on. Refer to *Chapter 2*, which has several recipes regarding importing and transcoding media. Then, click on the **Import All** button.

Figure 10.6: Select your SD card and verify that the import will go into your designated folder

8. Check to see that the footage is inside the extracting event.

9. Go to the Finder and verify that **Final Cut Original Media** is in the designated folder on the server.

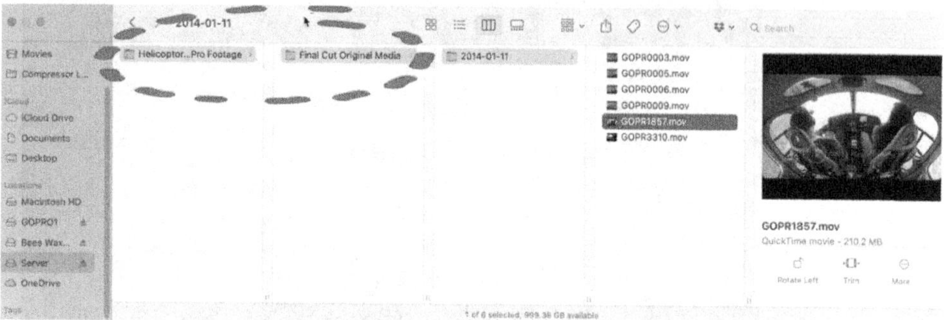

Figure 10.7: Verify that the media is in your designated folder

Nice work! Now your group can access the files for their own libraries.

 A note of clarification: You can store Final Cut Pro libraries on shared storage systems that use the NFS or SMB protocol.

Controlling project versions

Managing project versions in Final Cut Pro ensures you always have a backup of your work while giving you the flexibility to explore creative options without fear. By creating duplicate project versions, you can experiment with edits, effects, or alternate timelines without compromising the original. Duplicated projects do not take up extra space on your hard drive. This approach streamlines collaboration, supports iterative revisions, and saves valuable time by letting you revert or compare changes effortlessly.

In this recipe, we will describe the three flavors of project duplication and discuss their differences:

*   **Duplicate Project**

*   **Duplicate Project As...**

*   **Snapshot Project**

In addition, there are three methods to select a duplication flavor:

*   From the **Edit** menu

*   By right-clicking on a project to open a pop-up menu

*   By using keyboard shortcuts

Getting ready

To follow along, you will need to create a project in a library. See *Chapter 1*, the recipe titled *Taking advantage of the Magnetic Timeline and the Position tool*, for information about projects.

How to do it...

Great chefs are always tweaking their recipes, but never delete the original. Here is how to keep track of your editing changes and versions:

1. Double-click on a project in the Event Browser panel to not only select it but also open it in the Timeline panel. Now, in the **Edit** menu, about halfway down, you'll see a group of three duplication commands. Select the first one, **Duplicate Project**.

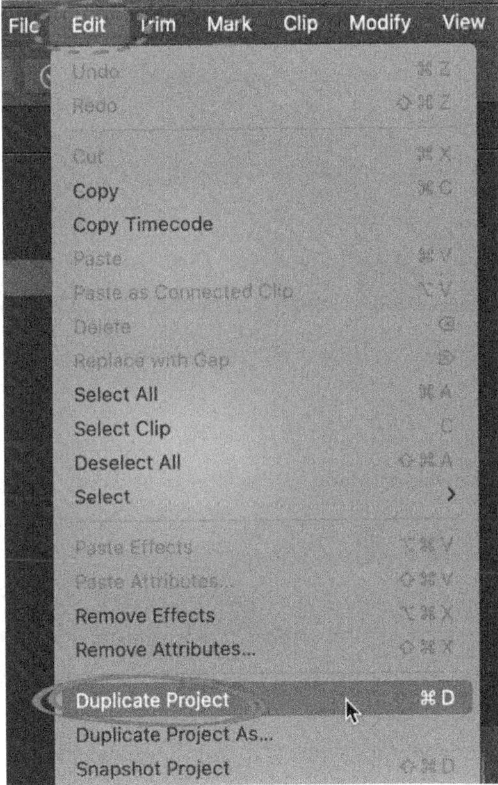

Figure 10.8: Select Duplicate Project from the Edit menu

This simply duplicates the project and adds an incremental number to the name. Notice that if you were to duplicate that project again, it would keep adding numbers to the duplicates. Click once on your original project to select it.

2. Right-click on your project, and from the pop-up menu, select **Duplicate Project As...**. This brings up a dialog box in which you can change the settings of your project, along with the name. We'll get more into some of these details in the recipe titled *Planning for project versatility* later in this chapter. For now, let's give this project a different name and adjust some settings to create a different version of the project. Click on the **OK** button.

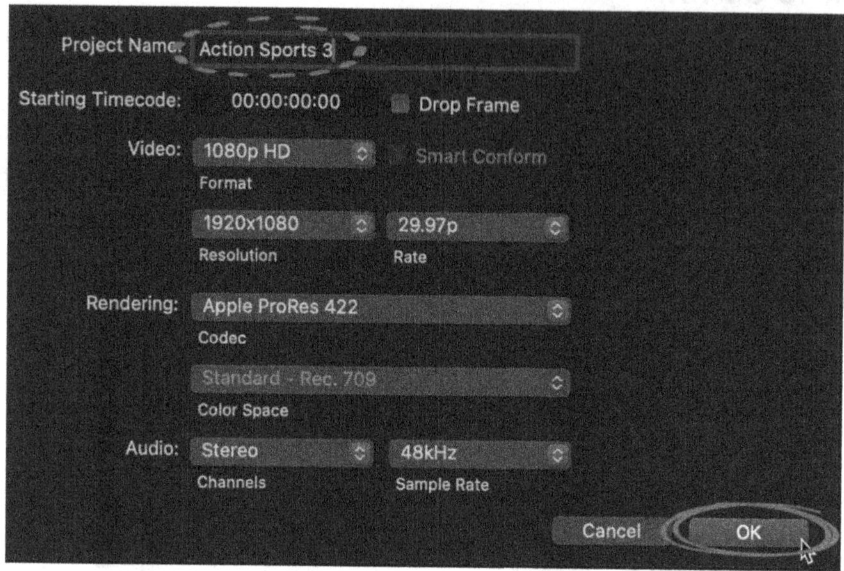

Figure 10.9: Duplicate Project As… allows you to change settings

The **Duplicate Project** and **Duplicate Project As...** commands have something in common in that they treat **compound clips** as their original form. Compound clips are almost like little projects unto themselves. In other words, if you were to make a change to a compound clip that is shared by the duplicated projects, that change would be visible in these duplicates. So, your versions will always include any updates or changes you make to compound clips that are incorporated into those timelines. Contrast that with the Snapshot Project command. This duplication creates a totally separate and independent project along with any shared compound clip. It's a snapshot in time that does not get updated with any changes to original projects or compound clips that are incorporated into the timeline.

3. Let's take a closer look at the snapshot. Click once on your original project and perform the *Shift + Command + D* keyboard shortcut to activate the `Snapshot Project` command. It takes the name of the project and at the end adds the word *Snapshot* along with the date and time that it was created.

A snapshot can become a saved version at a particular juncture: perhaps when you are about to try a new variation to your story, or when a client or supervisor signs off on a level of progress. A snapshot is a version frozen in time. To come back to our cooking analogy, you've placed it in the deep freezer.

Also to be noted is that when projects are duplicated in these three ways, the original project remains open in the Timeline panel. The duplicate is saved and set aside. The intent is that you will keep editing the current version in the Timeline panel. To open one of the duplicates, you must double-click on it in the Event Browser.

We will discuss long-term project archiving and backups in *Chapter 11*, in the recipe titled *Saving a project archive*.

Planning for project versatility

Planning for project versatility is about thinking ahead and making yourself more valuable to your clients and colleagues. Consider ways to adapt the media created from this project. Think of the variety of delivery platforms that might be utilized. Perhaps you plan to edit a promotional video from 2 minutes to 30 seconds, or even 6 seconds. Perhaps you find ways to repurpose all the interviews you did into extended versions. There are so many different opportunities on social media to let consumers experience and drill deeper into your content. Final Cut Pro uses a process called **Smart Conform** to analyze action within clips. This is valuable when repurposing your footage for social media, maximizing your project's reach and usability.

In this recipe, we will explore how Smart Conform analyzes action in clips and adjusts a clip's position when converting it from a horizontal to a vertical orientation.

Getting ready

To follow along, you will need several clips with action or movement of the subject.

How to do it...

With a few adjustments, great chefs can adapt quality ingredients to multiple purposes, and nothing goes to waste. You can do the same with your projects:

1. Create a new project that is horizontal in orientation. I have a project here that I've called Versatile Action, and it has the **Video** setting set to **1080p HD**. That is a normal video project setting. Click on the **OK** button.

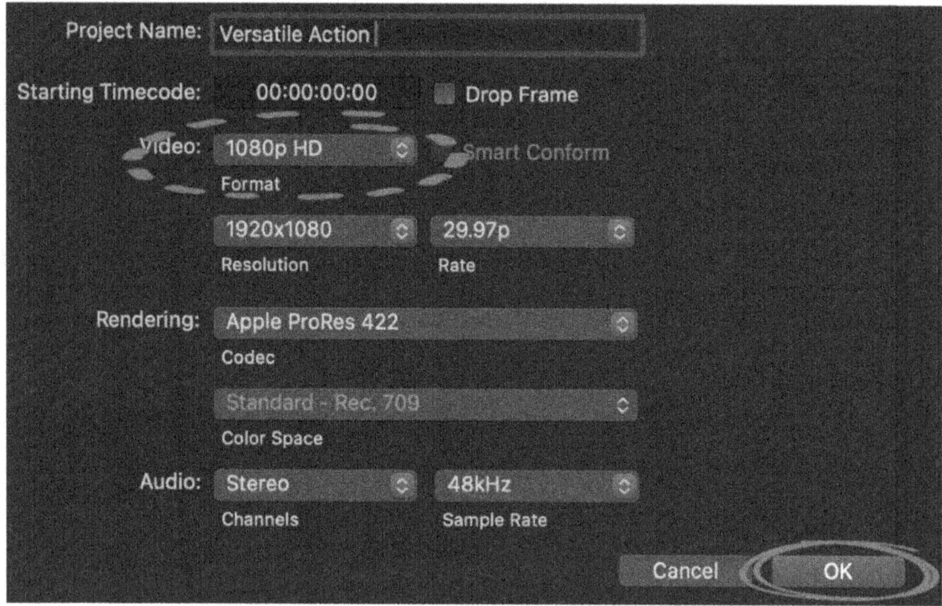

Figure 10.10: Start with a horizontal project

2. Add several clips in which the subject is moving. In my example, I've got several clips with action movement.

Figure 10.11: Add clips with action to your project timeline

3. Let's say we want to repurpose this project to social media in a vertical format. We are going to revisit some steps from the previous recipe in this chapter, *Controlling project versions*. Right-click on that project in the Event Browser panel and from the pop-up menu select **Duplicate Project As...**. In the dialog box that is presented, add the word Vertical to the name. Under the **Video** option, click on the pop-up menu and change this to **Vertical**. Now, here is the special command. To the right of the **Video** parameter, click on the checkbox for **Smart Conform**. Click on the **OK** button.

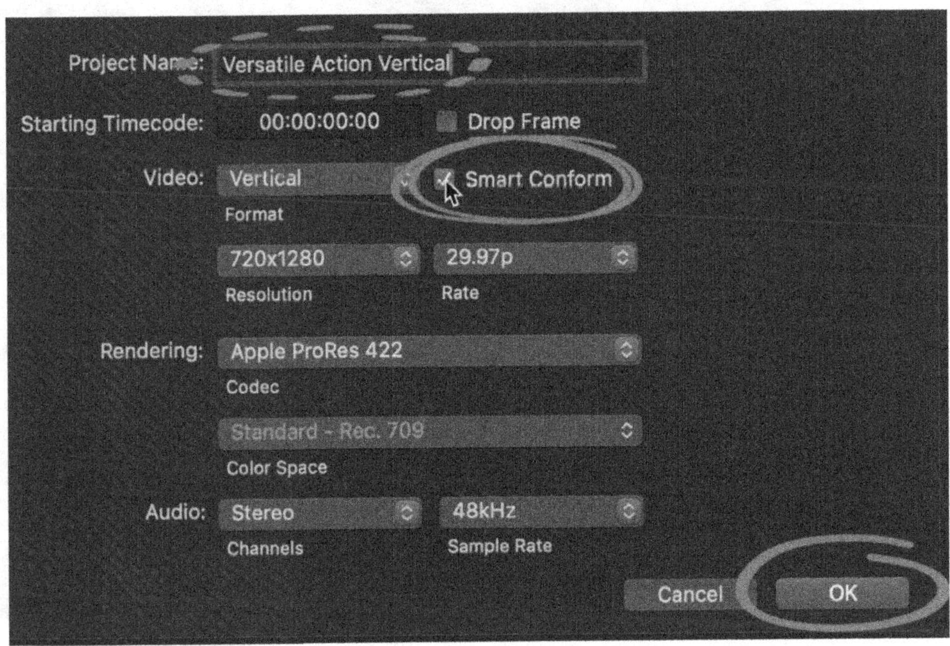

Figure 10.12: Click on the Smart Conform checkbox when converting videos to a vertical orientation

4. Final Cut Pro will analyze the subject movement in your clips. A duplicate project has been created in the Event Browser, but the original project is still displayed in the Timeline panel. In the Event Browser panel, double-click on the new project to open it in the Timeline panel. We'll see how it adjusted the frames.

5. Click on the **Transform** icon, which is located in the lower-left corner of the Viewer panel and looks like a square with dots in the corners, to see the bounding box around your clips. To get a better view, click on the **Viewer Zoom** drop-down menu located in the

upper-right corner of the Viewer panel. Let's zoom out by selecting a smaller percentage number. Let's also click on the **Show Full Video Image** icon to show the video image behind the vertical video bounding box. It is located in the upper right and looks like a rectangle on top of another.

Figure 10.13: View the video behind the bounding box by clicking on the Show Full Video Image icon

6. Review your clips to check that each clip is analyzed and the vertical component is positioned to include as much of the subject's action as it can. In my example, the vertical clips are positioned on the runners and the motorcycle, and are in a different place from each other in relation to their original videos.

Figure 10.14: FCP positions vertical orientation on subject movement

7. That was easy. But let's say you want the vertical component to follow more of the action. In my example, the motorcycle action moves outside of the vertical viewing space. This can be readily adjusted with **keyframes**. We also talked about keyframes in *Chapter 7*, in the recipe titled *Keyframing clip position and effects*. In the Timeline panel, position the playhead at the first frame of the clip. In the Inspector panel, in the **Transform** section, create a keyframe for the **Anchor** parameter by clicking on the **Add Keyframe** icon, which looks like a diamond with a plus sign in it.

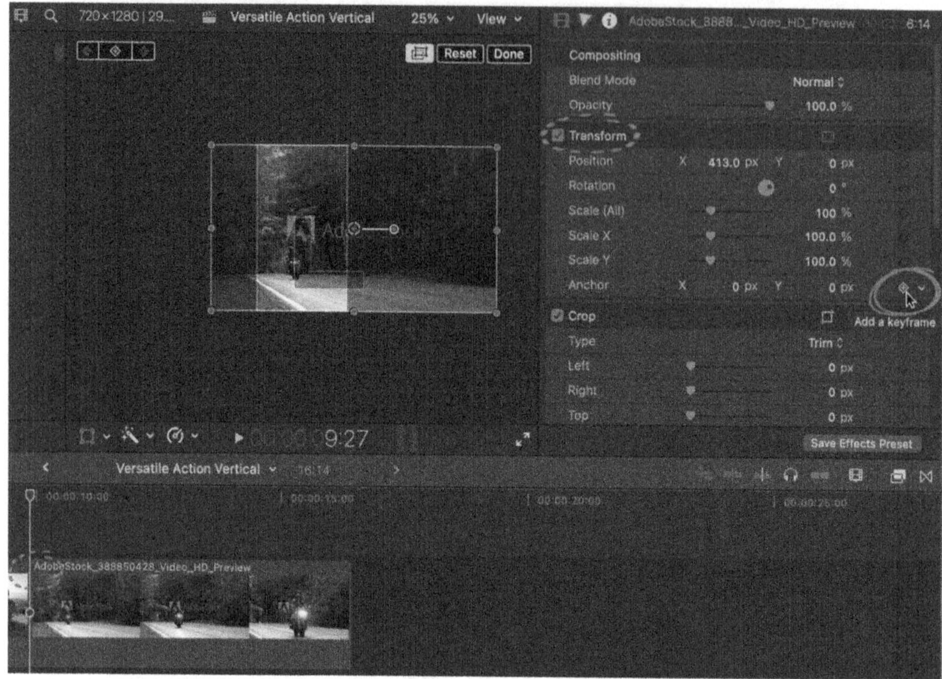

Figure 10.15: Add a keyframe to Anchor at the first frame of the clip

8. In the Timeline panel, move the playhead to the last frame of the clip. Click, hold, and drag up on the number, probably 0, that is the parameter for the **X** pixel position. Keep dragging up until the vertical component has moved over the subject in the last frame of the clip.

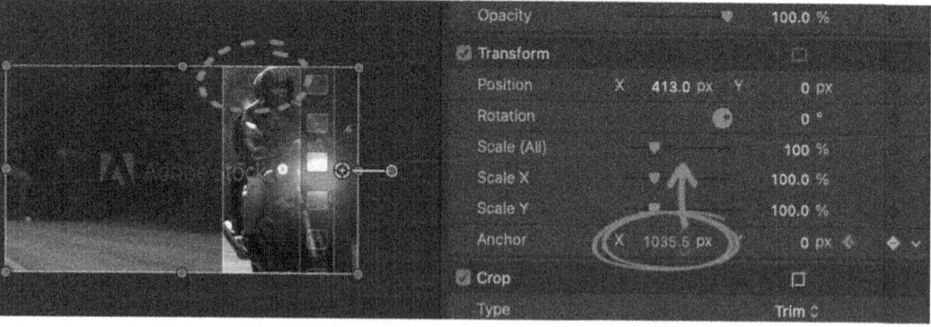

Figure 10.16: Drag up on the X pixel position number field

9. Release the mouse, and Final Cut Pro will make a keyframe at this anchor position. Slide the playhead to the beginning of the clip and skim through the action.

Nice!

Creating a repeatable project intro and outro

Capturing someone speaking on camera is the bread and butter (or, you might say, *roti and dal*, *miso and rice*, or *frijoles and arroz*) of business videos. At any rate, a quick way to create multiple videos with the same intro and outro can be a huge time-saver. Keyframing the music bed in your project intro and outro allows you to create smooth, precise audio transitions that align perfectly with your visuals. This technique not only enhances the viewer's experience but also makes your intro and outro reusable, ensuring consistent quality across multiple projects.

In this recipe, we will create a sample business project and explore techniques for quick reusability.

Getting ready

To follow along, you will need several clips of someone talking and some instrumental music that lends itself to a business video music bed.

How to do it...

Get those butter knives out, here we go:

1. Let's start by creating a new project. Click once on the event in which you want to locate your project, and then use the *Command + N* keyboard shortcut. Use the settings you prefer.

2. In my example, I've called my project `Repeatable Project` (yes, I know, very original. I'm sure you will come up with something much more creative!). In the Timeline panel, add a graphic or a full-screen background generator as the first clip on the primary storyline. We used generators back in *Chapter 9*, in the recipe titled *Using themes in titles and generators*.

3. Next, add an interview or somebody talking in a promotional video demonstration. Place the same background graphic after your person is talking. We're going to make bookends around the talking video.

4. Add a transition between the video and the background graphics. I like to use a transition called **Cube**. It provides an interesting movement from one clip to another.

5. Now, let's add some music to the primary storyline. You can get music from **Audio Library** in the YouTube Studio area of your YouTube channel. Alternatively, there is a lot of free music available on the internet or from a subscription service. I've got a song that's got some good ups and downs to it. I'm going to cut the song in the middle because I want to use the ending that the composer planned for the song. You don't want to just fade the song down at the end of your video. That's not very professional.

Figure 10.17: Bookend a graphic and music around a speaking clip

6. Having the audio meters visible is important so we can adjust the volume of the music properly. If your audio meter is not already open, click on the small audio meter just to the right of the timecode number at the bottom of the Viewer panel. The volume of professional videos should average at -12 decibels and peak at -6 decibels. We covered more about Final Cut Pro audio in the *Technical requirements* section at the start of *Chapter 8*.

7. I have found that, although at the same level, music seems louder than dialogue. So, I'm going to keep my music level just below -12 decibels. As I start to edit my intro music, I can tell the volume of this clip is going to increase, so I'm going to keyframe some volume changes. *Option + click* on the **Adjust Volume** line and place several control points. The cursor will change to an arrow with a plus sign.

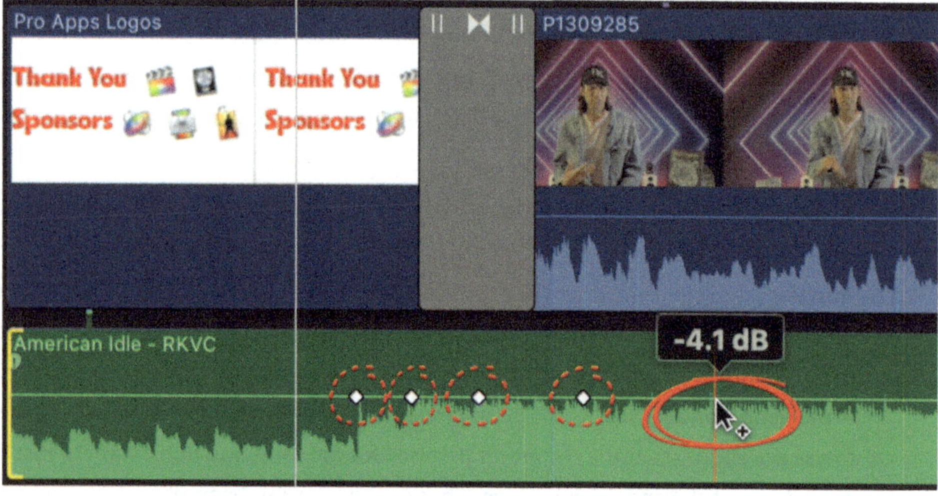

Figure 10.18: Option + click on the Adjust Volume line to add keyframes

8. The first keyframe is like an anchor holding the volume just below -12 decibels, then you want to start bringing it down when the speaker starts. But I don't fade it out completely; I like to have a little bit of music while they're introducing themselves and then have it fade out after that. Make sure the music is not too loud and that the speaker is understood. You will need to play this several times in order to watch the audio meter and get the volume just right.

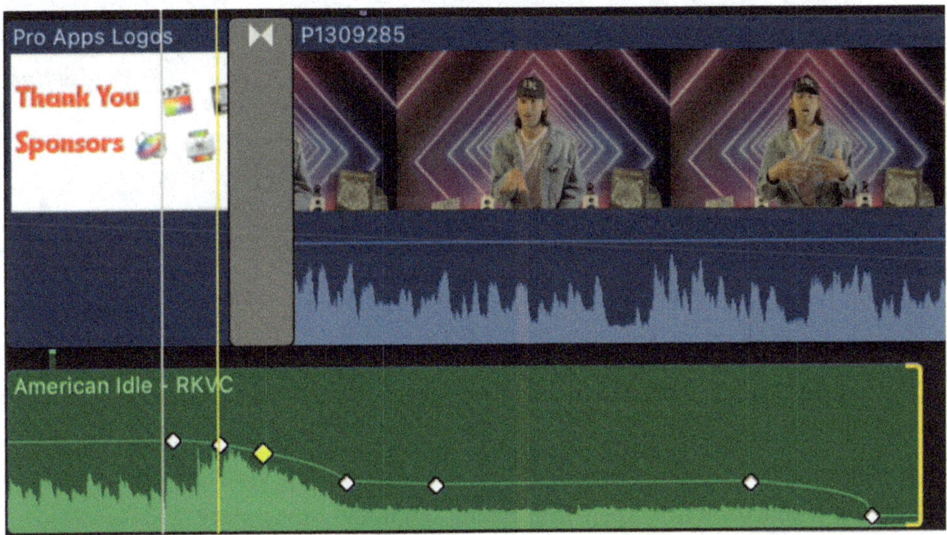

Figure 10.19: Let some music play during the speaker's introduction

9. We're going to do the same sort of keyframes on the audio level as the project ends. Add a cross-dissolve to the very end. This cross-dissolve will match the natural fade out of the music. As your speaker starts concluding their talk, bring in a little bit of music, ducked underneath. Then, gradually bring the music up so that when the final graphic is on screen, the music is at the normal level of -12 decibels. Be sure to play this several times to check the volume level. You don't want the audience to miss the speaker's closing sentence.

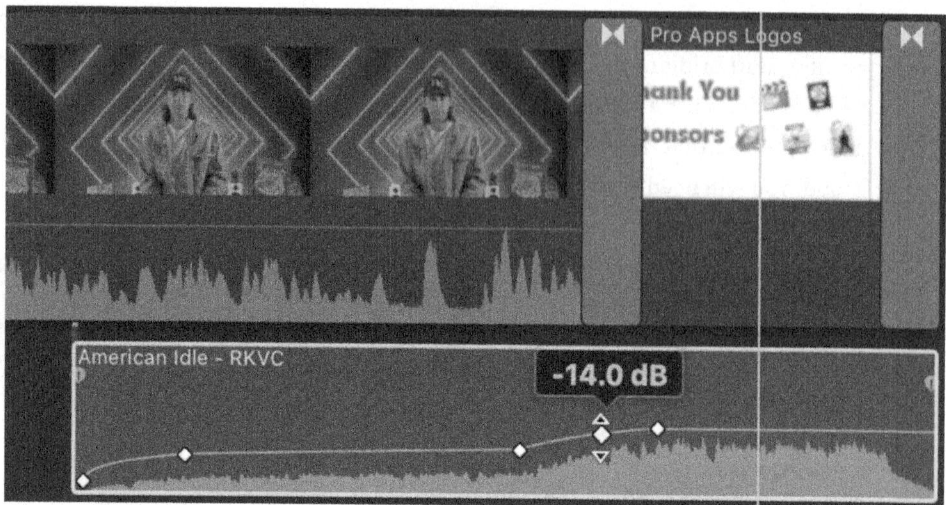

Figure 10.20: Let some music play during the speaker's conclusion

Now, here is one of the key tips to creating this graphic and music bookend for a repeatable project. Notice that the default is for the ending music clip to be connected to the primary storyline at its beginning. Also, notice that this is connected to the clip of the person speaking. If we were to add a different clip of someone speaking, that music would still try to link itself to the person speaking, but in the wrong place.

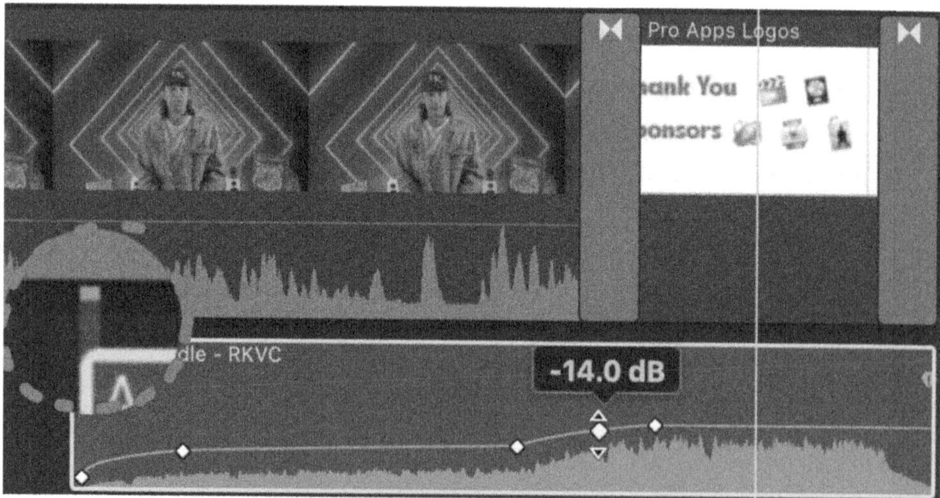

Figure 10.21: The default is for a clip to be connected to the previous clip at its start

10. We want the music to link itself to the end graphic and stay connected. So, here's the trick. Click once on the background graphic in the primary storyline to select it. Now, hold down the *Option + Command* keys and click on the music file just below the graphic. Voilà, the music file is now linked to the graphic clip and not the person speaking. By the way, we mentioned this earlier, in *Chapter 3*, in the *There's more…* section of the *Creating secondary storyline transitions* recipe.

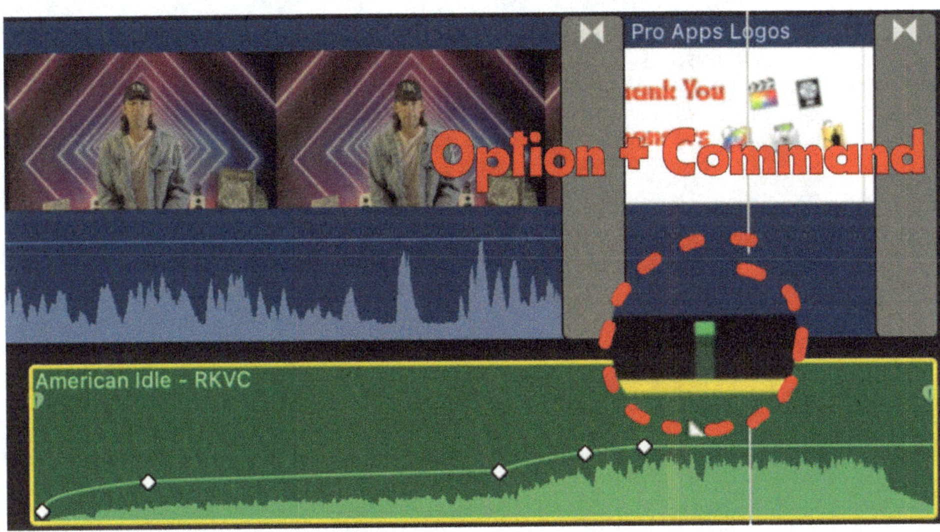

Figure 10.22: Hold down Option + Command and click on the music file to create a new connection

11. Let's also add a lower third Title to identify our person. Click on the **Show Titles and Generators** icon at the top of the Sidebar panel. It looks like a square with an uppercase "T" on top of a video countdown frame. Under **Titles**, click on the category of **Lower Thirds**. I like the lower third called **Snap Left**. It's fun and has lots of energy to it. We also used this title in *Chapter 9*, in the recipe titled *Using safe zones*. Oftentimes in interview videos like this, the person will say "Welcome" and start to introduce themselves. You should make a lower-third title visible while they are saying their name. The title should be visible for around 4 seconds. You need enough time for someone to read it for the first time.

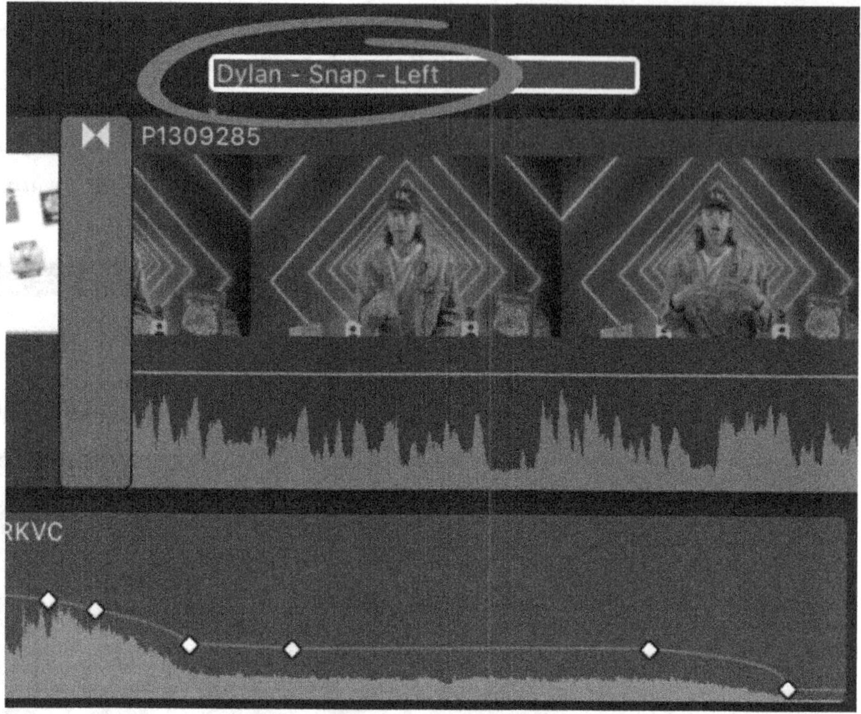

Figure 10.23: Add a lower-third title

12. So now, with that background graphics and music bookended around the person speaking, let's test out our repeatable intro and outro. In the Event Browser panel, select another clip of a person speaking. Make sure you have set in and out points that include a buffer to account for the transition from and to the full-screen graphic.

13. Click, hold, and drag the new clip from the Event Browser onto the original clip on the Timeline panel. The cursor will change to an arrow on top of a film strip with a white plus sign in a green circle.

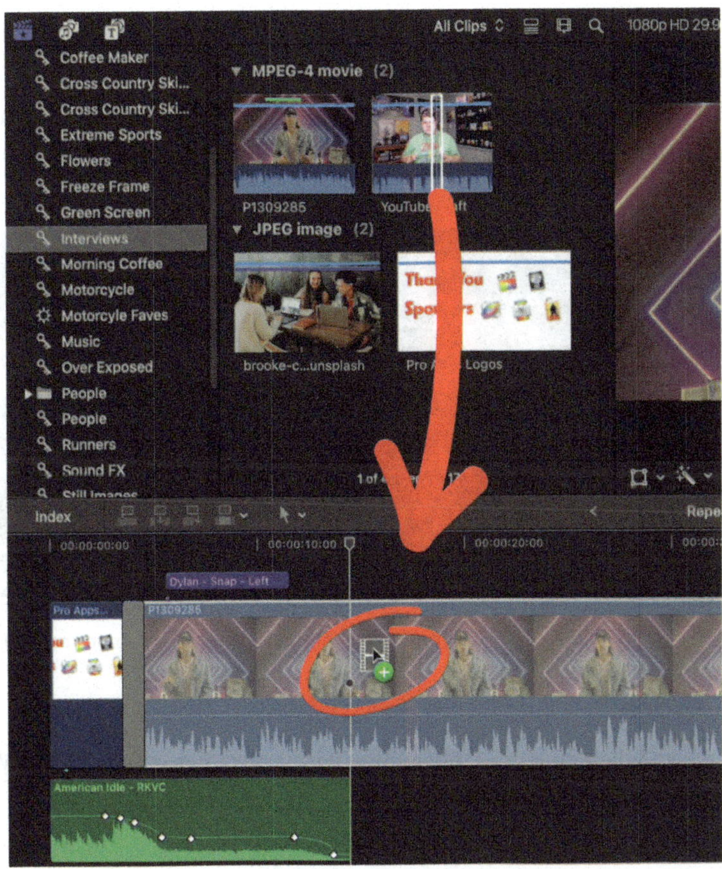

Figure 10.24: Drag a new clip on top of the original clip in the Timeline panel

14. When you let go, a pop-up menu appears. Click on **Replace**. This will replace the clip in the Timeline panel and scale the project to the size of the new clip.

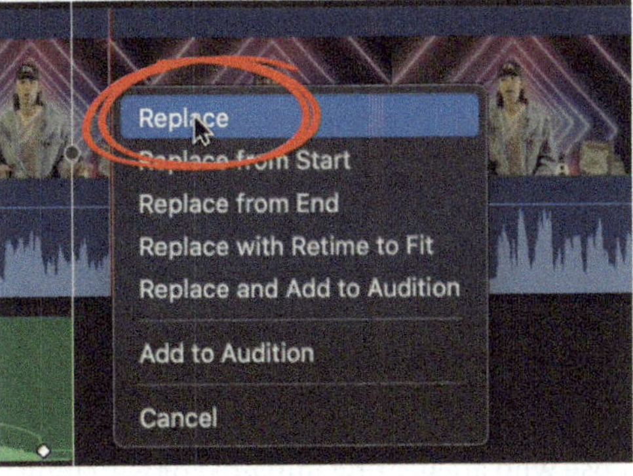

Figure 10.25: Select Replace from the pop-up menu

Boom, we replaced the first speaker with a different speaker, but the graphics and music stayed bookended; all we have to do is change the name in the lower-third intro title. You may, however, need to adjust the length of the music depending on how long different speakers introduce themselves or summarize their closing statements. Play these through to check.

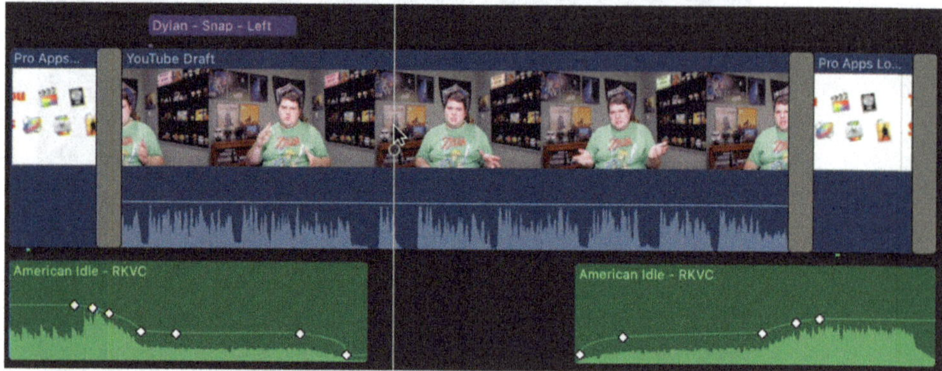

Figure 10.26: The repeatable intro and outro stay in place as bookends

There's more...

Here's a little tip when changing the volume with keyframes on the **Adjust Volume** line. Hold down the *Command* key while dragging a keyframe control point up and down, and the cursor will move in smaller increments, giving you more control.

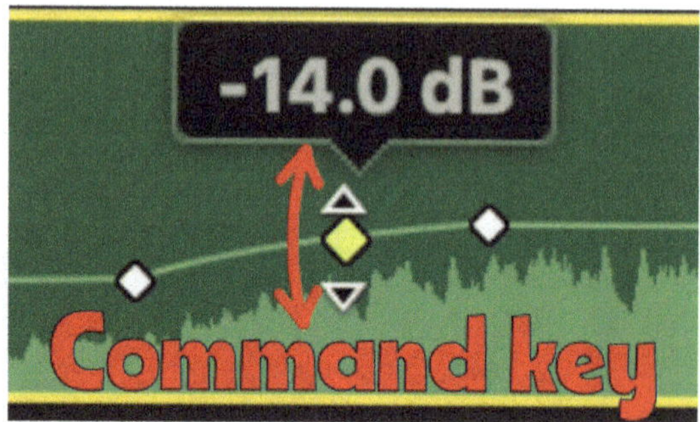

Figure 10.27: Hold down the Command key for more precision

Creating closed captions

Creating **closed captions** in Final Cut Pro ensures your video content is accessible to a wider audience, including those who are hearing impaired or watching without sound. With tools for transcribing, editing, and exporting captions, Final Cut Pro makes it easy to craft accurate, professional captions that enhance viewer comprehension. Additionally, the option to burn captions directly onto the video ensures compatibility across all platforms, even those that don't support separate caption files.

In this recipe, we will explore how to transcribe a clip into captions, how to edit the text of the captions, and how to edit the way caption clips align with the audio.

Getting ready

To follow along, you will need a clip of someone talking, which can be the same clip from the previous recipe. Transcribing clips works on an M1 Mac and Sequoia or newer.

How to do it...

Captions allow everyone to enjoy your video. Let's see how to add them:

1. Let's start by having Final Cut Pro transcribe a clip into captions. As with most commands in Final Cut Pro, there are four ways to transcribe a clip:

   - From the **Edit** menu, and near the bottom, select **Captions | Transcribe to Captions**

   - From the **Enhancement** icon menu, which is the magic wand in the lower-left corner of the **Viewer** window. Select **Transcribe to Captions**

   - Right-click on the clip that you are working with, and from the pop-up menu, select **Transcribe to Captions**

   - Use the *Shift + Command + C* keyboard shortcut

2. From the Timeline panel, click once on the clip you wish to transcribe. Choose one of the methods listed previously. Final Cut Pro analyzes the clip and creates caption clips in the caption lane along the top edge of the Timeline panel.

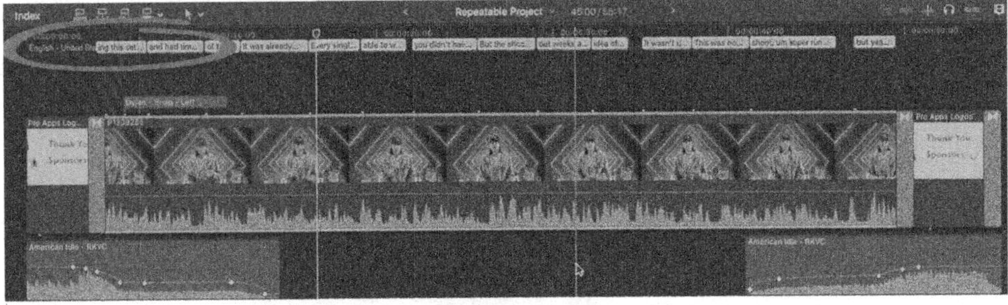

Figure 10.28: Caption clips are created in the caption lane

3. Note that the text data is local to your computer and not in the cloud. You can edit the text in a caption clip by double-clicking on it. This displays a **Caption Edit** window. If you feel like the line of text is too long, you can use the *Return* key to make two lines.

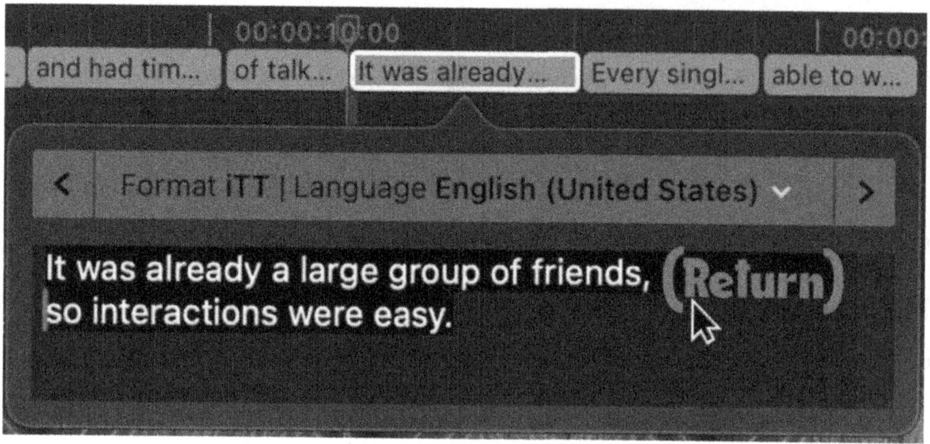

Figure 10.29: Use the Return key to make two lines of text in the Caption Edit window

4. Click anywhere off of the **Caption Edit** window to exit editing mode and save the changes. You can convert a clip with two lines of text into two separate caption clips. Right-click on the clip, and from the pop-up menu, select **Split Captions**. Likewise, you can combine two clips. Select both clips. Right-click on one, and from the pop-up menu, select **Join Captions**.

    You edit the position, or alignment, of caption clips like you would video clips. You can slide clips and edit the length of edges.

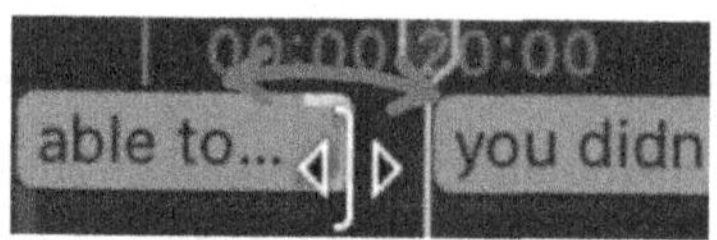

Figure 10.30: Adjust the length of a caption

5. If two captions are next to each other, use the *T* keyboard shortcut to switch to the **Trim** tool. Use it to roll the edit point to line up the captions exactly where you want them. Press the keyboard shortcut of *A* to switch back to the **Select** tool.

Figure 10.31: Adjust two adjoining captions with the Trim tool

6. A quick way to review your caption clips is to use the **Timeline Index** panel. Click on the **Index** button, located in the upper-left corner of the Timeline panel. Click on the **Captions** categories.

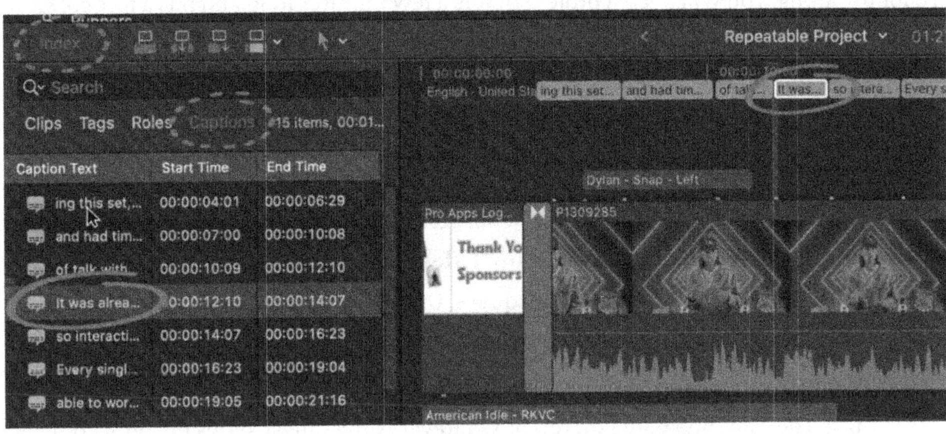

Figure 10.32: Use the Timeline Index to review caption clips

7. Use the up and down arrow keys to easily switch between captions. If you see something that needs to be edited, you can double-click on the caption listed in the **Timeline Index** panel. The **Caption Editing** window will open in the Timeline panel.

8. When exporting your project, you can have **closed captions**, which the consumer can turn on or off, or you can have **burned-in captions**, which are always displayed. But that, my fellow chefs, is a topic for another chapter: *Chapter 11*, in fact, in a recipe titled *Sharing closed and burned-in captions*.

Gathering accurate client feedback

So, you are ready to send a version of your project to the client. Great! Gathering accurate feedback is essential for creating a project that meets expectations while minimizing revisions. But this isn't necessarily easy. If the client has exact changes to edit points, such as cutting out something someone is saying or changing the timing of some action, it's difficult to do if the time they're indicating is vague. You might spend too much time hunting for that exact thing they're talking about. Back in the day, we used a timecode generator machine during the recording process that could burn a timecode onto the lower portion of the video. The term *window burn* has stuck. Adding a Final Cut Pro timecode generator to create a window burn ensures that clients can reference specific moments in the footage with precision. This approach not only streamlines communication but also saves time by reducing misunderstandings and back-and-forth adjustments.

In this recipe, we will see how quick and easy it is to add this step to your workflow.

Getting ready

To follow along, you will need a project that is a few minutes long and has a few connected clips.

How to do it...

Just like the delicious, burned sugar crust on the classic French dessert *crème brûlée*, we are going to burn the project timecode onto our video:

1. Start by opening the **Titles** and **Generators** sidebar. In the upper-right corner of the Final Cut Pro interface, click on the **Show Titles and Generators** icon, which looks like a square with a *T* in it on top of another square. Under **Generators**, select the **Elements** category. Find the element called **Timecode**.

2. We want this to be visible on the top layer of our project. Drag the **Timecode** element into the Timeline panel on top of whatever is the tallest series of connected clips in the project you have prepared.

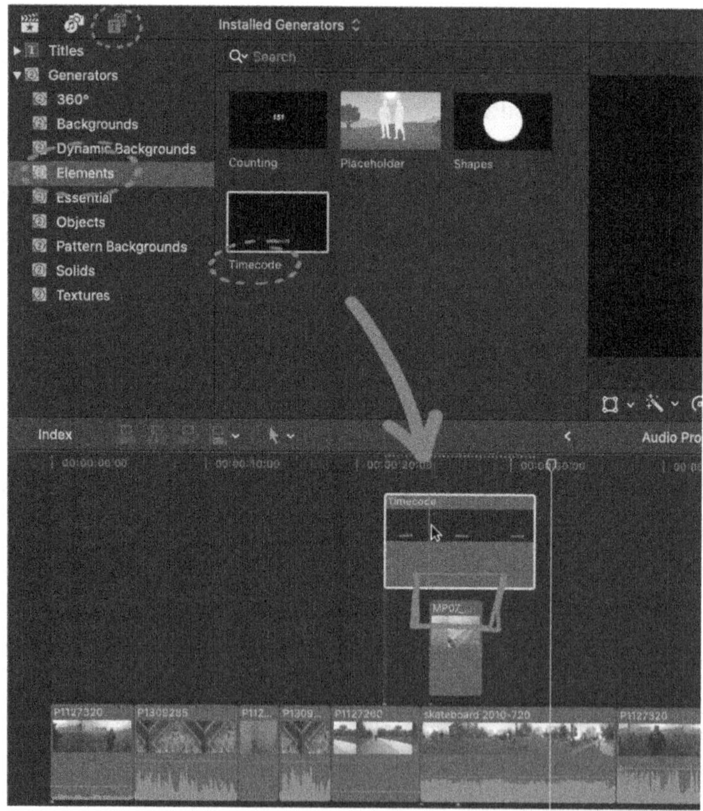

Figure 10.33: Drag the Timecode element on top of a connected clip

3. Click anywhere in the Timeline panel to make sure it is selected, and press the *Shift + Z* keyboard shortcut to fit the project to the size of the Timeline panel. Then, while you can see the whole project, drag the edges of the **Timecode** element to the beginning and end of the project.

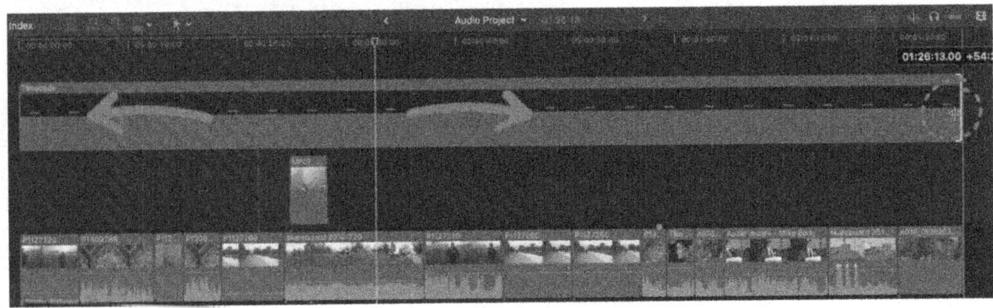

Figure 10.34: Extend the size of the Timecode element to the length of the project

4. With the **Timecode** element selected, look at the Inspector panel. The first parameter at the top is **Format**; we want **HMSF**, which is the industry standard. This stands for **hours, minutes, seconds,** and **frames**. That way, you can get accurate feedback down to the frame number.

5. Keep the **Font** option the same, as this is the industry standard as well.

6. You want **Timecode Base** to be set to **Project**. This will be the ongoing time of the whole project and not the source clips, which is the other option.

7. In the text field for **Label**, it currently says **Project** because we selected **Project** for **Time-code Base**. But instead of just **Project**, I like to type in Rough Draft. Be sure to add a space between your text and the timecode. Believe me when I say that you can't assume that the AV department of a university system will know that having a timecode running through a video means it is a rough draft and that they should play the other version you sent them for the meeting. I advise that you add Rough Draft, or Review Only, or Don't even think of playing this version at the board meeting, or something like that.

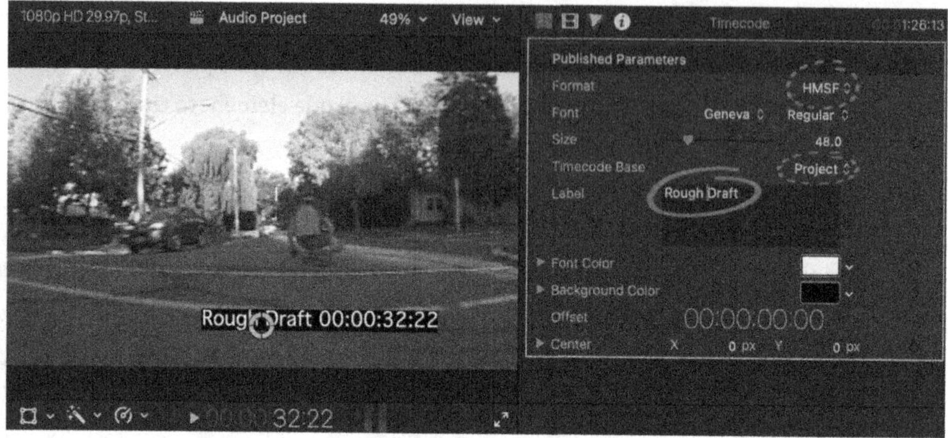

Figure 10.35: Label the draft in the Timecode element

8. Nice cooking; well burned. Remember, when you are editing your project and the **Timecode** element seems to block your view of the clips, it is easy to hide it. Simply right-click on it (or any clip), and from the clip pop-up menu, select **Disable**, or use the *V* keyboard shortcut to enable or disable a clip's visibility.

9. But you will want the **Timecode** element to be visible when you send it to your client. Conveniently, we'll talk about exporting options in the next chapter, *Chapter 11*, and suggestions on sharing your project with a client in the *Technical requirements* section of that chapter.

 **Bonus tip:** When the client gives you a list of changes based on the timecode numbers in the window burn version you sent, start making your changes at the end instead of the beginning. It is a little counterintuitive, but if you start making changes at the beginning, it'll throw off the timecode correlation for the rest of the project. So, start at the end and work backward. That way, the timecode numbers in your project will remain consistent with the notes, as some of the changes may affect the timing of your project. By the way, before making changes such as this to your project, it is a good idea to make a snapshot backup to keep track of versions. See the recipe titled *Controlling project versions* earlier in this chapter for information on how to snapshot a project.

11

Sharing Your Projects

Your story is complete, and now it is time to delve into the art of sharing in Final Cut Pro. We'll explore how to spread the flavor of your projects far and wide, from engaging with collaborators to delivering your masterpiece to the world. Get ready to pass the plate as we unveil techniques for social media sharing, customizing share settings, and bundling sharing destinations.

In this chapter, you will learn how to tailor your exports to specific needs and formats. You'll explore advanced sharing techniques such as sharing separate roles, sharing closed captions, and creating share bundles for streamlined processing.

In this chapter, you will complete the following recipes:

- Sharing for Apple devices
- Sharing for other devices
- Customizing share settings
- Sharing roles
- Sharing closed and burned-in captions
- Exporting an XML project
- Saving a project archive

Technical requirements

To follow along, you will need some imported media and projects. We will assume your project is *broadcast*-ready – that is, the audio is set to -12 dB (see *Chapter 8* and its *Technical requirements* section) – and the video's brightness is below 100 IRE (see *Chapter 5* and the recipe called *Fixing the exposure with the luma waveform monitor* for more information).

In addition, here are a few thoughts about sharing files with clients and colleagues. Sharing large files over the web can be challenging. There is no easy answer. It's not like a spreadsheet where you can just attach your file in an email. Sure, you can use an internet service such as iCloud, Dropbox, and so on. But when you have a cornucopia of gigabytes, don't discount the old-fashioned Sneak-ernet. That is, use your sneakers to walk the files on a hard drive to their destination. If, however, you need someone remote to review your video, I suggest sending a link. Check out *Chapter 10* and the recipe called *Gathering accurate client feedback*. In that recipe, we put a timecode window burn on a video. That way, the client can give you feedback for changes that are frame-accurate. But, of course, you don't want them to have the file itself and accidentally use it as they would a final version. Instead, you want them to review it and give feedback. A good method is to put the video on your YouTube account and set the viewing to *Unlisted*, not *Public*. That way, only people with a link can see it. Make sure the name and description indicate that it is a draft. Because it is viewed in a web browser, the size of 1080p would be good, but even 720p would be fine and would take less time to upload.

Sharing for Apple devices

Exporting projects for Apple devices ensures your video is optimized for iPhones, iPads, and Apple TVs, delivering the highest quality playback tailored to their screens and capabilities. By using the specific Apple device settings in Final Cut Pro, resolution and encoding are preset to match the requirements of your target devices. This streamlined process saves time, eliminates guesswork, and guarantees a seamless viewing experience for Apple users.

This includes sharing projects for Vision Pro devices, which allows you to create immersive content tailored to Apple's cutting-edge spatial computing technology. By exporting in high resolution and optimizing for 3D and spatial audio, your videos will take full advantage of the Vision Pro's capabilities, offering a truly engaging experience.

In this recipe, we will explore the *share* destinations for Apple devices that are preloaded into the *destination* preferences. This includes the sizes of 720p, 1080p, and 4K, as well as the HEVC and Vision Pro formats.

How to do it...

Polish that Macintosh apple because here we go:

1. In the Event Browser panel, double-click on a project to open it in the Timeline panel. Let's see the list of preloaded *Share* destinations. In the upper-right corner of the Final Cut Pro interface, click on the **Share** icon, which looks like a square with an arrow pointing up. This brings up the menu of destinations. I find it interesting that the *Import* icon is a down-pointing arrow and is the first icon at the top left of the Final Cut Pro interface. Correspondingly, the **Share** icon is the last icon on the right. I will also mention that you can use the destinations from the **File** menu and select **Share**.

Figure 11.1: Click on the Share icon to see the list of destinations

2. Let's explore the destinations. The first item in the list, **Export File (default)...**, is listed first because it is a default format. But it is not specifically for Apple devices and fits better with the next recipe, *Sharing for other devices*. So, I am going to save it for later.

3. Select the second item in the list, **Apple Devices 720p....** You are presented with a window detailing the information about the file to be exported. Note that the **Info** tab is highlighted along the top center of the window. There is a thumbnail image of the video taken from the position of the playhead in the Timeline panel. There is also the name of the project, **Description, Creator**, and **Tags**. Tags are the keywords that you added to your project. See *Chapter 2* and the recipe called *Using keywords* for more information. Along the bottom of the window is information about the video specs, including the expected file size. As this destination has the smallest dimension of the Apple devices, **720p**, it creates output files with the lowest data rates and smallest file sizes. Click on the **Settings** tab at the top center of the window.

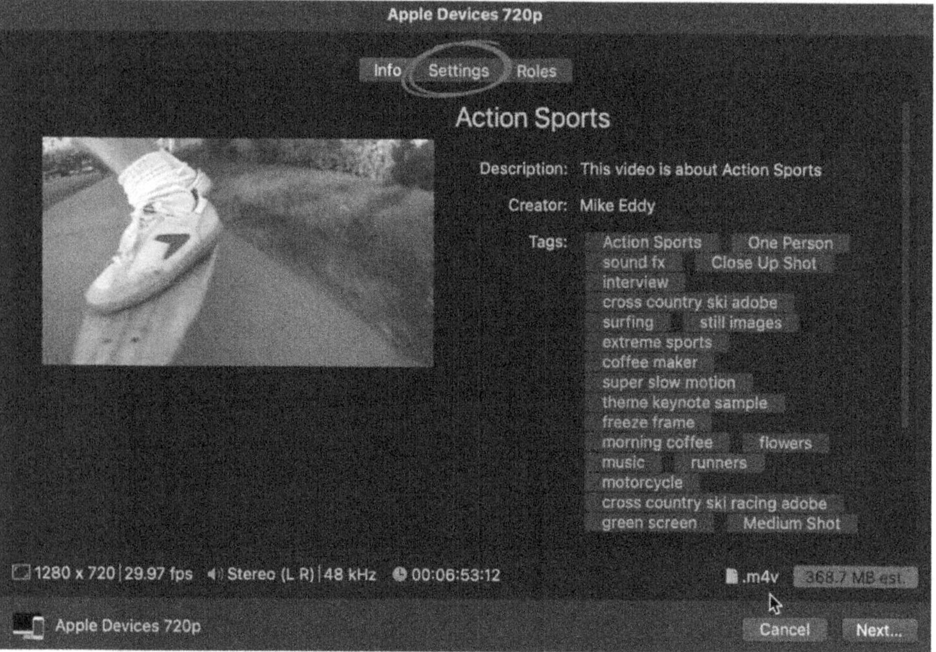

Figure 11.2: Note the information about the export file and click on the Settings tab

4. In the **Settings** window, the **Format, Video Codec**, and **Resolution** settings can all be changed from drop-down menus. But these Apple destinations are meant to be quick, pre-loaded, settings geared to Apple devices. Changing settings is exactly what we will cover in the next recipe. So, at this point, don't change any of the settings. Here is the special thing about videos exported for Apple devices: notice that the extension for the video file will be **.m4v**. When you buy or rent TV shows or movies in the iTunes Store, you can find that those videos are stored in the M4V format. M4V videos are opened in iTunes by default. If this is your intention, perfect. Click on the drop-down menu for the **Action** parameter.

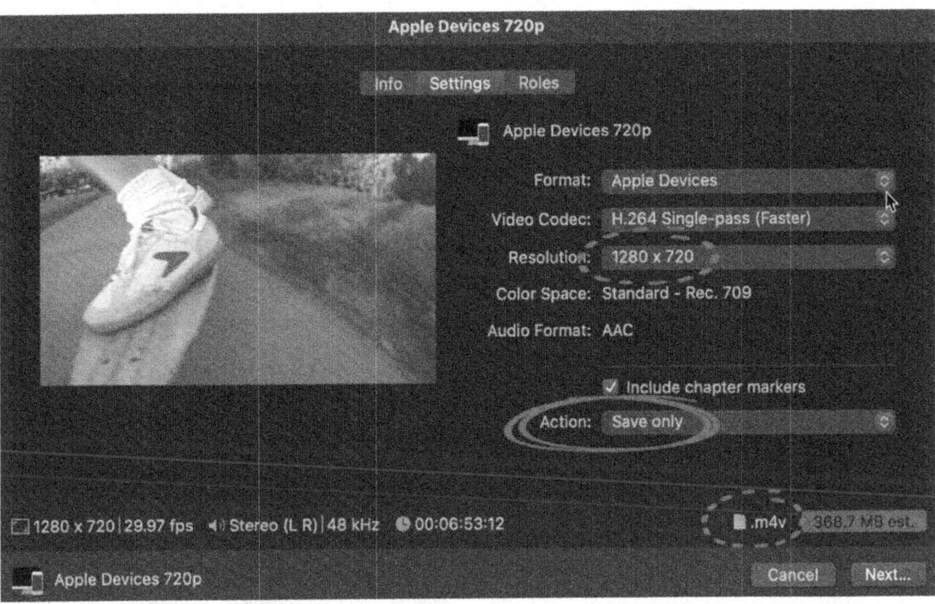

Figure 11.3: Apple device settings for .m4v export and the Action parameter

5. The **Action** menu will be displayed. This is a menu of things that will happen when the compression and export have been completed. The **Action** menu is unique to various destination types. For Apple devices, instead of only saving the file, you can specify an application to open the video, such as the **TV.app** application, or you can specify that the file be added to your **Photos** library or added to the TV app folder. Let's add it to **TV.app**; select **Home Videos** from the menu.

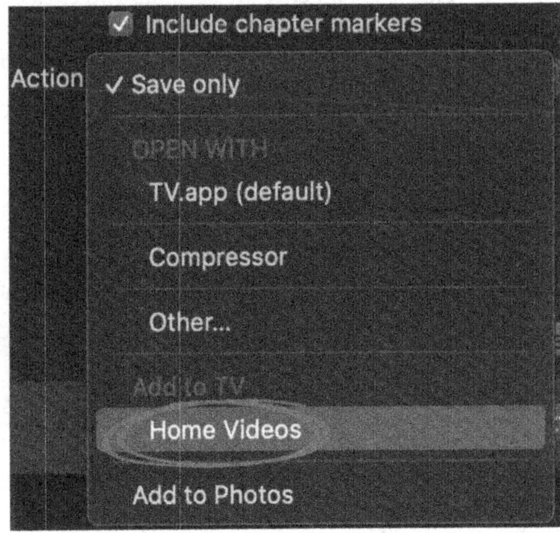

Figure 11.4: Select Home Videos from the Action menu

6. This will make the video easily accessible from the TV application. Click the **Next...** button. The video is processed, and the file is saved in the **User Home | Movies | TV | Media | Home Videos** folder.

7. Click on the **Share** icon again to bring up the **Destinations** menu. Select **Apple Devices 1080p....** This destination is very much like the **720p** destination. Click on the **Settings** tab. You can verify that this destination creates output files with dimensions up to 1920 x 1080. Keep the **Action** parameter set to **Save only**. Click on the **Next...** button.

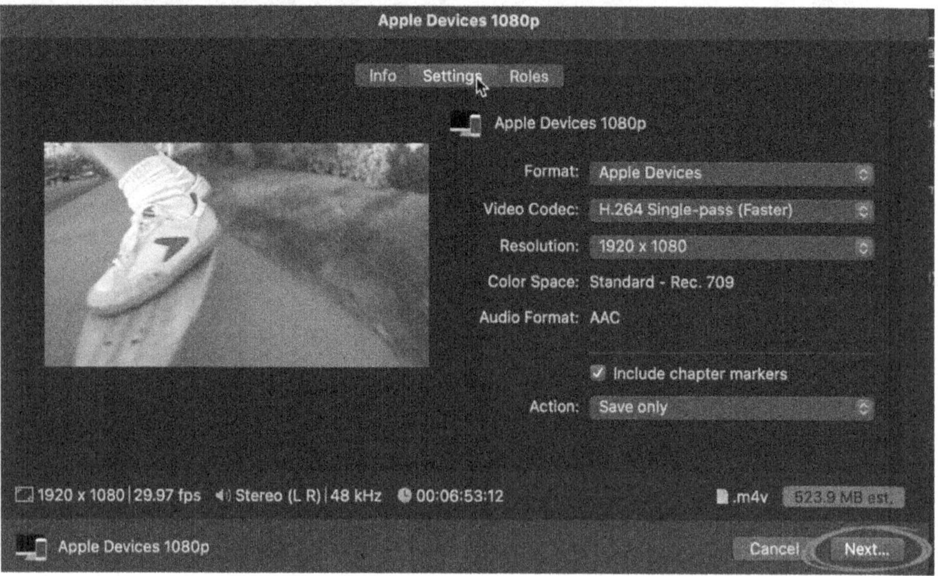

Figure 11.5: Verify the settings and click on Next...

8. This will start saving the video file. If this is the first time you have shared a video, Apple has an annoying habit of displaying an abbreviated dialog box. Click on the down arrow icon to expand the dialog box.

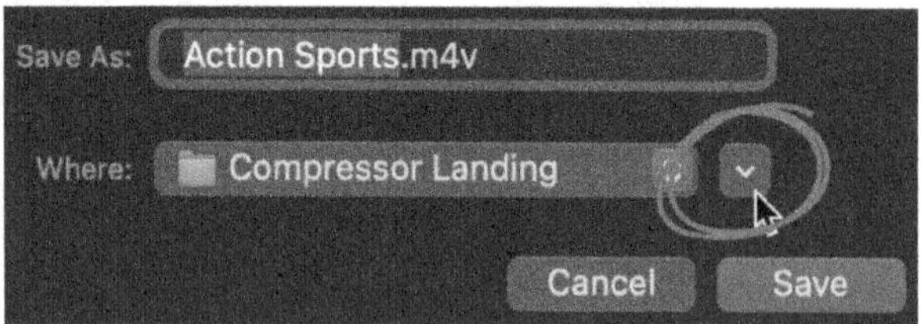

Figure 11.6: Expand the dialog box by clicking on the down arrow icon

9. With the dialog box expanded, it probably looks more familiar. Navigate to the folder where you want to save your video. Click on the **Save** button.

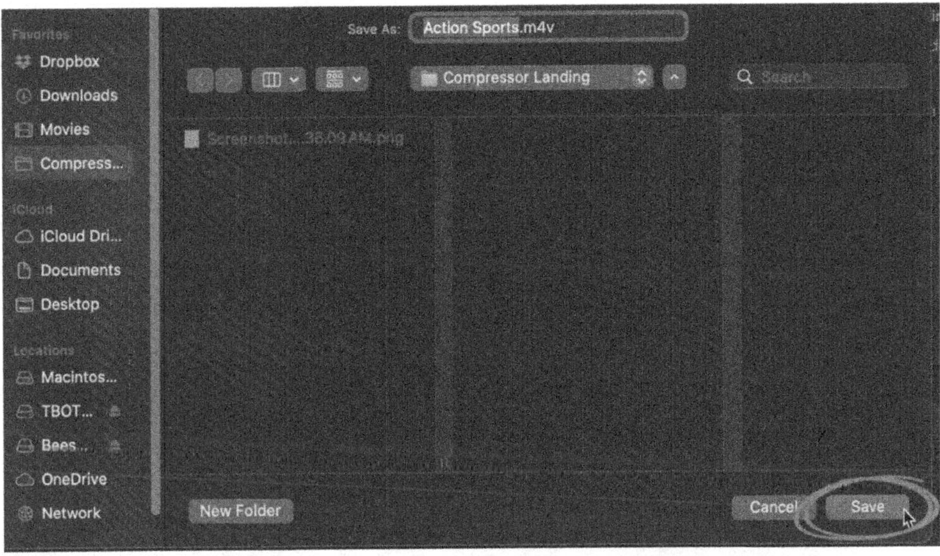

Figure 11.7: Navigate to your destination and click on Save

10. With the **Save** dialog box dismissed, click on the **Background Tasks** icon, which looks like a closing circle and is located in the upper-left corner of the Final Cut Pro interface. This will reveal a pop-up window listing many tasks that could be processed in the background. Check the percentage progress of your **Sharing** project. Close the window by clicking on the red button in the upper-left corner of the window.

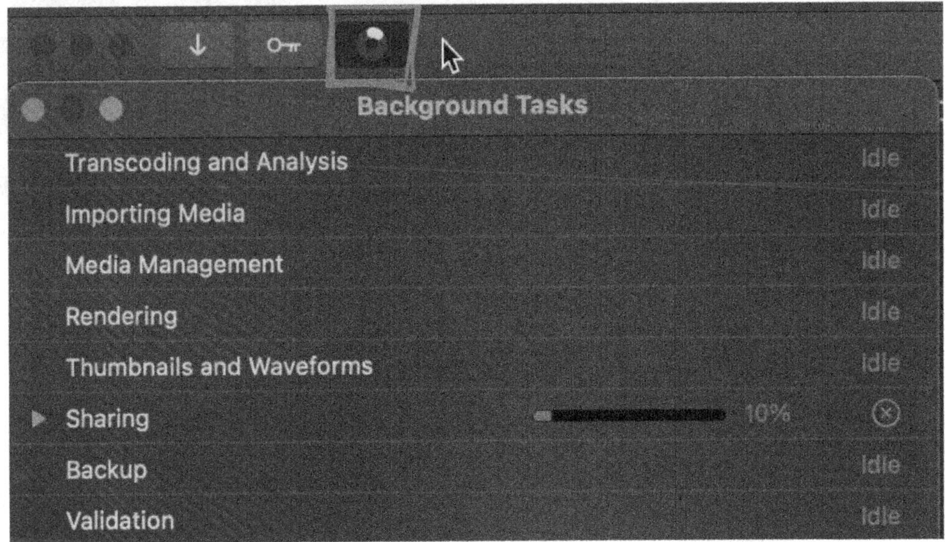

Figure 11.8: Display Background Tasks by clicking on the Background Tasks icon

11. Notice that you can keep working in Final Cut Pro while tasks are happening in the background. Click on the **Share** icon again to bring up the **Destinations** menu again. Select **Apple Devices 4K....** Like the other two Apple device destinations, this destination exports files for playback on recent models of iPhone, iPad, and Apple TV. The **Apple Devices 4K** option creates output files with dimensions up to 4K. Of the three **Apple Devices** options, this option creates files with the highest data rates and largest file sizes. Note that you are limited to the size of your project settings. Unless you have created a project with 4K size settings, you will not be able to export a video that is 4K in size. Final Cut Pro will not upscale your video.

12. In my example, the Action Sports project I created was 1080p in size. So, in the **Apple Devices 4K** settings, the **Resolution** parameter limits me to **1920 x 1080**. You can click on the **Cancel** button or proceed with saving a video.

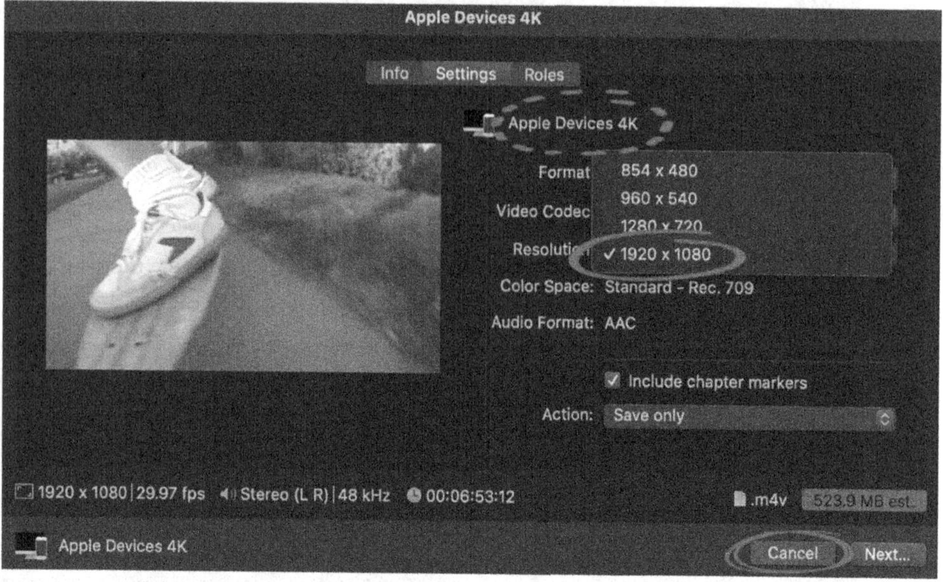

Figure 11.9: Even in the 4K destination, you are limited by your project size settings

13. The destination of **Social Platforms** is a preloaded destination but not necessarily targeting Apple devices, so I am going to save it for the next recipe.

14. But we are going to work with the next destination even though, technically, it is not Apple-specific either. Click on the **Share** icon again to bring up the **Destinations** menu. Select **HEVC - High Efficiency Video Coding....**

15. HEVC, also known as H.265, exports smaller file sizes and better data compression at the same video quality as H.264. It was invented as the ideal format for cell networks. But, for most of us, we are not supplying media directly to cell networks. Instead, we are uploading files to YouTube or other social media sites. These sites automatically convert the files we send them into a variety of different codecs. So, unless you are creating files that play directly from a cellular network, HEVC is not useful. It is interesting that the HEVC **Format** option is set to **Computer** and the file extension is **.mp4**. *MP4* is the short name for *MPEG-4 Part 14*, said the video nerd, as they pushed their taped glasses up their nose.

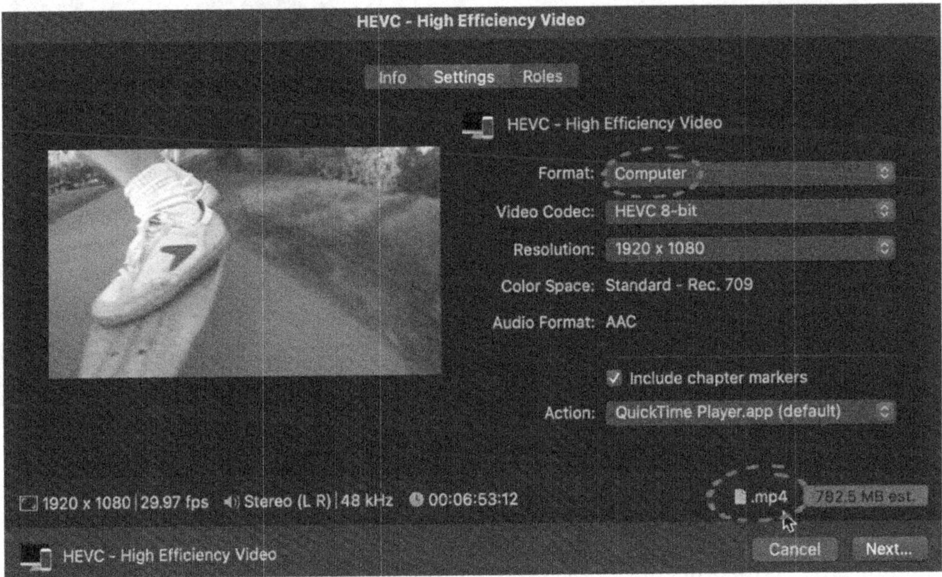

Figure 11.10: The HEVC destination creates a computer .mp4 file

16. Click on the **Share** icon again to bring up the **Destinations** menu. Select **Apple Vision Pro (MV–HEVC)....** The MV-HEVC format is similar to HEVC, except that it stores the two views (one for each eye) in separate layers. Cool. But again, in my example of the `Action Sports` project, **Resolution per eye** is limited by my project size. In addition, in the lower-left corner, there is an indication of an error. That is because my source file is not stereoscopic. Creating videos for the Apple Vision Pro device is just a bit beyond the scope of this particular cookbook. For now, click on the **Cancel** button.

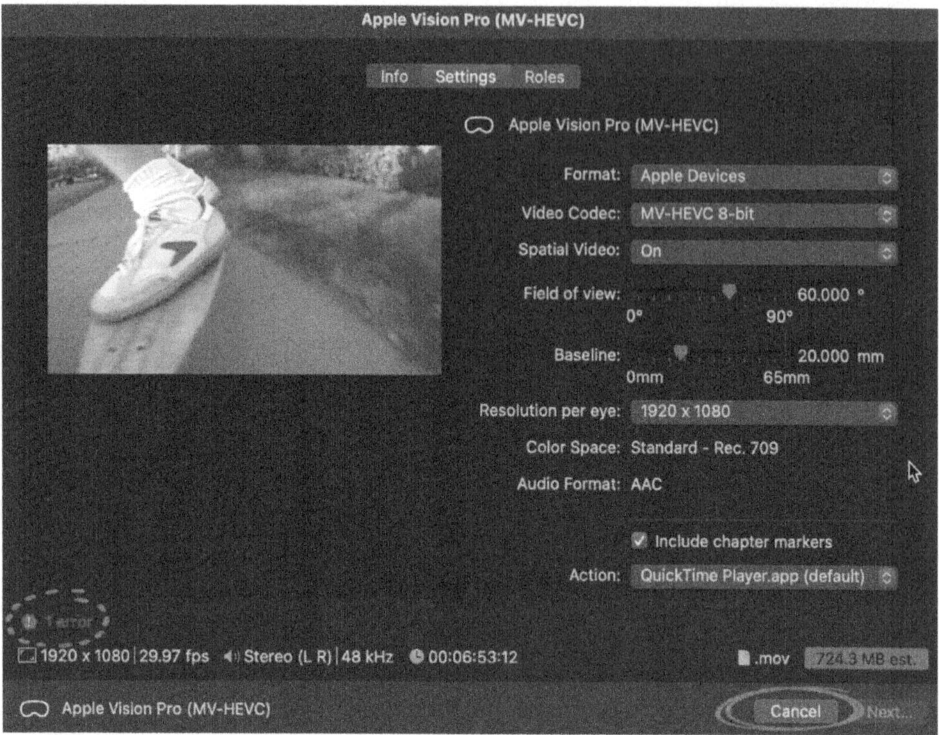

Figure 11.11: Apple Vision Pro devices are a possible destination

Sharing for other devices

Sharing projects for other devices lets you optimize your content for diverse platforms, ensuring compatibility and easy access. Whether exporting for email, preparing for social media, or setting up live streams, you can tailor your exports to meet specific technical requirements. This flexibility ensures your audience experiences the flavor of your content in the best possible quality, no matter the platform or device.

In this recipe, we will explore the other destinations available through the *Share* presets. We will look at the **Export File (default)** settings, the **Social Media** settings, and the settings for email, images, image sequences, and HTTP live streaming.

How to do it...

Like great chefs plating their dish before they serve it up, attention to detail is the key. Let's go:

1. We are revisiting the first item in the preset list. In the Event Browser panel, double-click on a project to open it in the Timeline panel. In the upper-right corner of the Final Cut Pro interface, click on the **Share** icon, which looks like a square with an arrow pointing up. This brings up the menu of Share destinations. Select **Export File (default)…**, which is listed first because it is a default format. You can also apply the **Export File (default)** destination with the keyboard shortcut of *Command* + *E*. Click on the **Settings** tab at the upper center of the window.

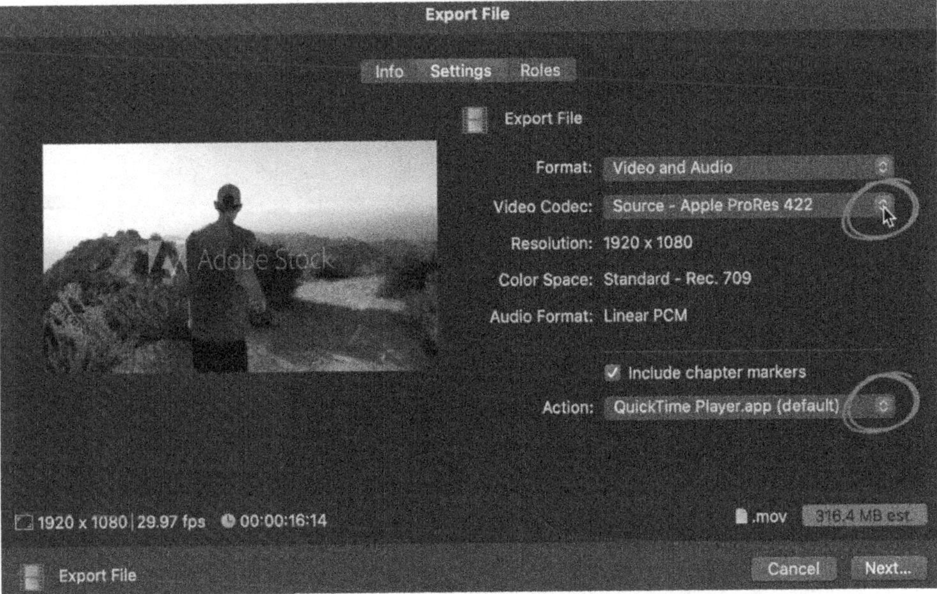

Figure 11.12: Keep the default settings for the default destination

2. Notice that the **Video Codec** parameter is set to **Source - Apple ProRes 422**. ProRes 422 is the native format that Final Cut Pro uses when importing footage. Check out *Chapter 2* and the recipe called *Understanding optimized versus proxy media*. So, this source setting is, for all practical purposes, uncompressed. Every frame is an iFrame, there is no interpolation between images. There are other formats you can set in the **Video Codec** drop-down menu, but I suggest you keep the default as the source. We will dig into how to create custom format destinations in the next recipe.

3. Click on the parameter menu for **Action** to display a drop-down menu. The default action to be performed when the export is complete is to open the file with the QuickTime Player application. This is good to leave as the default, as it will give you one more chance to watch your video before you send it out. Click on **QuickTime Player.app (default)** to keep it selected.

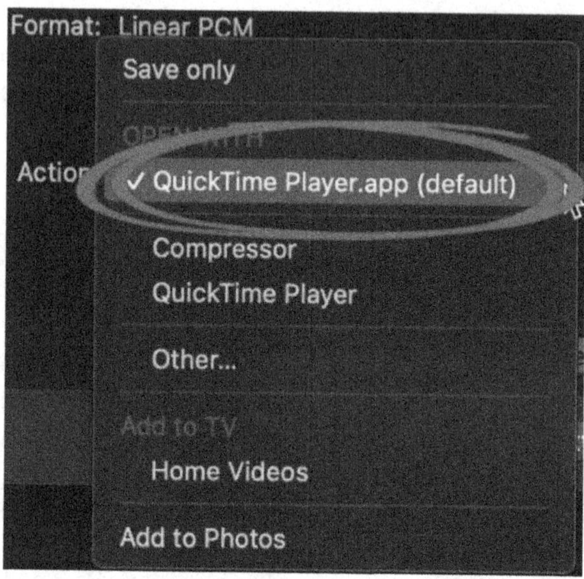

Figure 11.13: Open the file with QuickTime Player to review one more time

4. Be aware that because this format is the same as the source and uncompressed, the file size will be larger than other *Share* destinations. Click on the **Next...** button and save the video file to the location of your choice.

5. Click on the **Share** icon again to bring up the menu of *Share* destinations. Select the other destination that we saved for this recipe, **Social Platforms....** This destination is tailored to prepare your projects and clips to upload them to video-sharing websites. Click on the **Settings** tab at the upper center of the window.

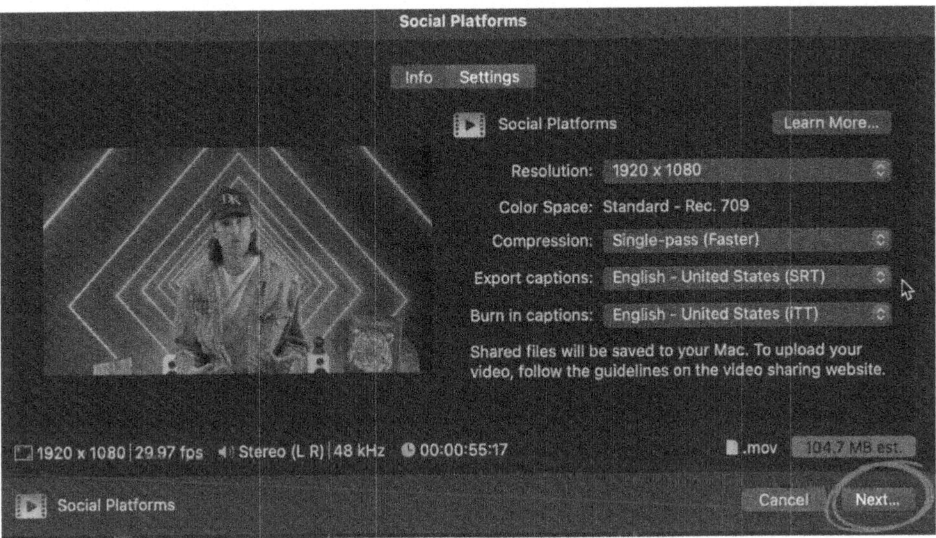

Figure 11.14: Captions are included in the Social Platforms settings

6. Let's look at the settings for the **Social Platforms** destination. The parameter selection for **Resolution** depends on the resolution size of the project when you created it. Most editors want their videos to be viewed as large as they can, but Final Cut Pro can't upscale your project. Note that many, but not all, social media websites work well with 4K projects. Social media website servers reformat your video for the variety of devices that will view it. You are just delivering a clean version for them to process.

7. For the parameter of **Compression**, choose **Single-pass (Faster)**. It compresses quicker, and there is not a huge difference in quality between **Single-pass** and **Multi-pass**.

8. Now, you can turn closed captions on or off. The settings for captions are a unique component of the **Social Platforms** destination. Closed captions are displayed with a video from text in a separate file that you upload with the video file to the social media website. Closed captions are the setting for **Export captions**. Choose the parameter of **SRT** because this type of file usually keeps the formatting you set up in Final Cut Pro.

9. You can also choose **Burn in captions**, which, as the name suggests, are always on the video. Users cannot turn these off. The best parameter to select for this is **iTT**. Many consumers watch videos with their devices on silent, so burned-in captions can be very advantageous. See *Chapter 10* and the recipe called *Creating closed captions* for more info on how to transcribe videos and create captions. In addition, we will explore captions in a bit more detail in another recipe in this chapter called *Sharing closed and burned-in captions*.

10. Click on the **Next...** button and save the video file to the location of your choice.

11. There are more destinations to explore, and they can be reached from the Final Cut Pro **Settings** window. Click on the **Share** icon again to bring up the **Destinations** menu. This time, select **Add Destination...** from the menu.

Figure 11.15: Open the Final Cut Pro Settings window by selecting Add Destination…
from the Share menu

12. The Final Cut Pro **Settings** window is opened, and the **Destinations** tab is selected. Note that you can open the **Settings** window with the keyboard shortcut of *Command + ,* (comma). There are several new preset destinations in the Destinations Browser panel. To add a destination to the **Destinations** menu, drag a destination icon into the **Destinations** menu sidebar. Notice that the cursor changes to an arrow with a plus sign in a green circle, and a blue line indicates where the destination will land in the menu.

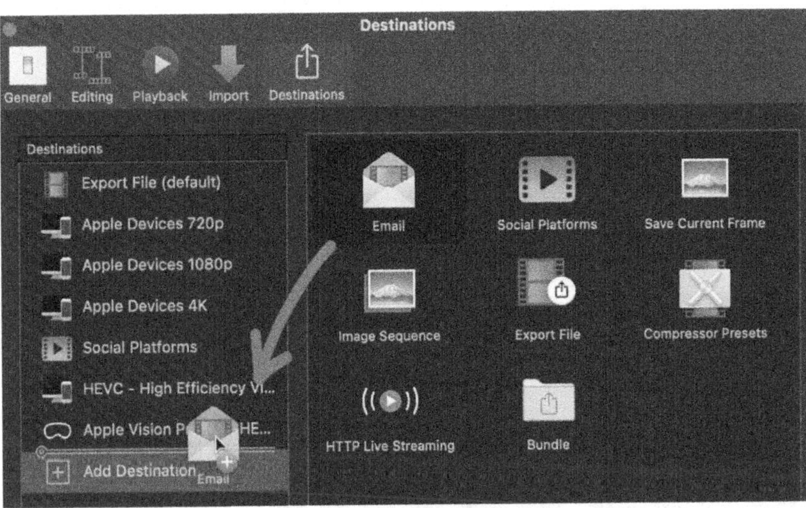

Figure 11.16: Drag a destination icon to the Share menu sidebar

13. Release the mouse, and the destination is added to the **Destinations** menu. In the Destination Browser panel, you are presented with the settings for the selected destination. The settings for the **Email** destination are fairly straightforward. It will try to compress your video as small as it can. When you use this destination, Mail (Apple's email application) will open, and the video will be included as an attachment. But videos can only be compressed so much, and most email programs have a limit of 10 MB, so this destination is not always practical. See the *Technical requirements* section at the beginning of this chapter for thoughts on sharing files.

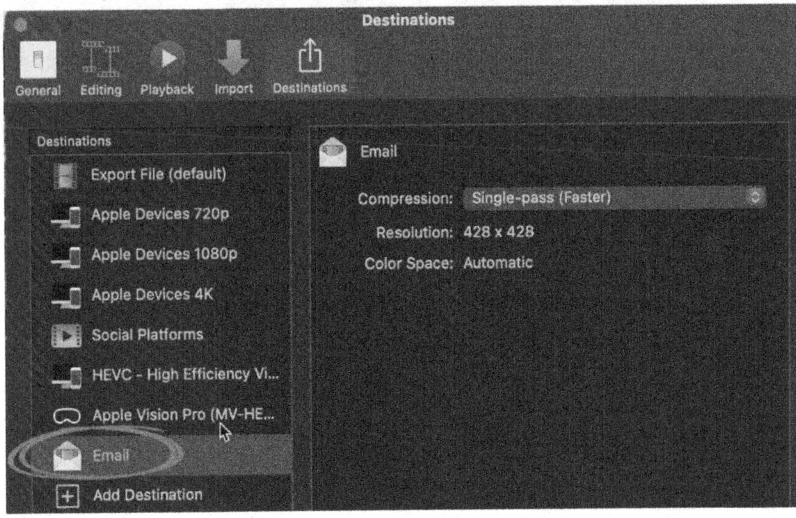

Figure 11.17: The settings for the Email destination are displayed in the Destinations panel

14. Click on **Add Destination** in the **Destinations** menu sidebar. Select the destination of **Save Current Frame** and drag it to the **Destinations** menu sidebar.

15. You are presented with the settings for the selected destination in the Destination Browser panel. Click on the drop-down menu for the **Export** parameter. There are several formats to choose from, depending on your final usage. Normally, you would leave the checkbox for **Scale image to preserve aspect ratio** selected, unless you have an unusual project that uses a non-square pixel format, such as 1440 x 1080.

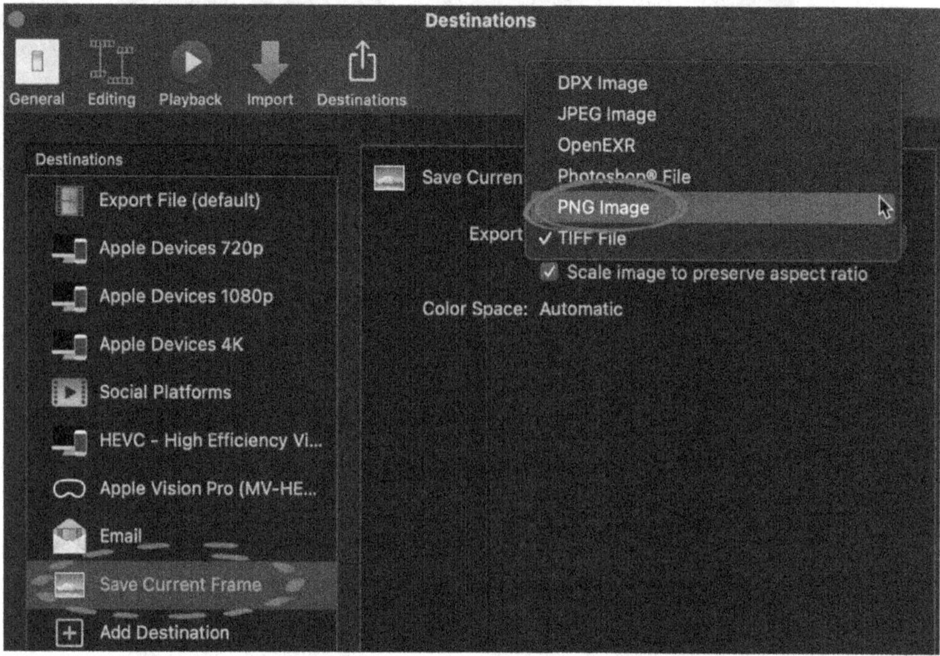

Figure 11.18: Choose the file format to export the current frame from your Timeline

16. Click on **Add Destination** in the **Destinations** menu sidebar. Select the destination of **Export Image Sequence** and drag it to the **Destinations** menu sidebar.

17. You are presented with the settings for the selected destination in the Destination Browser panel. An image sequence is a set of sequentially numbered still-image files that are compatible with many professional finishing, compositing, and grading apps. When saving this export, you are able to name the folder in which the images will be located. Click on

the drop-down menu for the **Export** parameter. Notice that, just like the **Save Current Frame** destination, there are many formats to choose from. Normally, you would leave the checkbox for **Scale image to preserve aspect ratio** selected, unless you have an unusual project that uses a non-square pixel format.

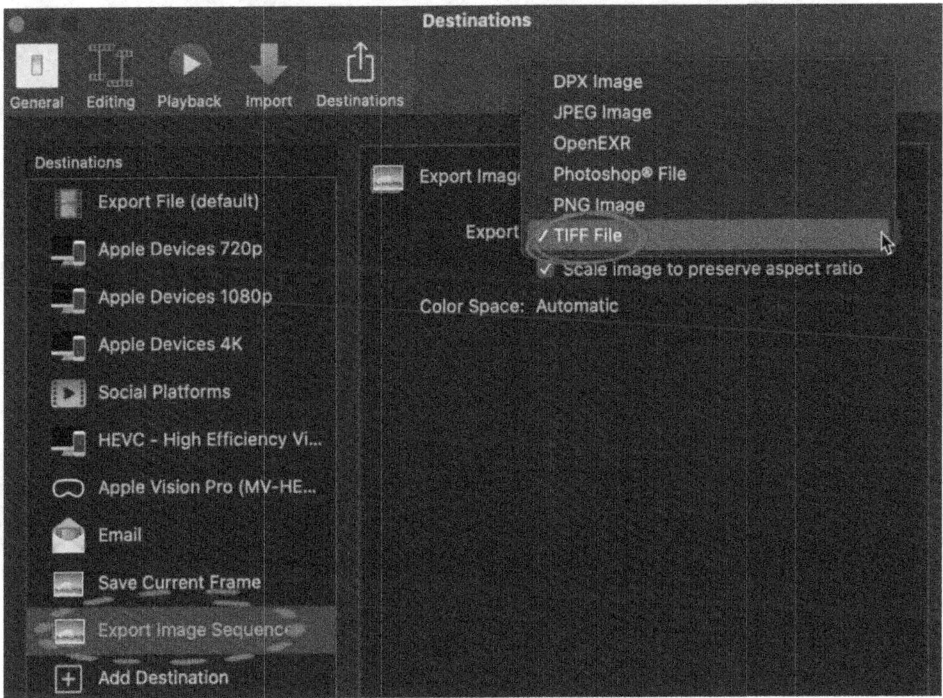

Figure 11.19: Choose the file format to export into an image sequence

18. Click on **Add Destination** in the **Destinations** menu sidebar. Select the destination of **Export for HTTP Live Streaming** and drag it to the **Destinations** menu sidebar.

19. You are presented with the settings for the selected destination in the Destination Browser panel. Select one or more network types on which the movie will be streamed. For the parameter of **Versions to export**, select the checkboxes for **Cellular** and **Broadband**. When this destination is processed, your video is transcoded, and the exported segments are saved in folders. An `index.html` file and a `readme.html` file containing information on how to post your project to your website are included in the export. You may need to work with your server administrator.

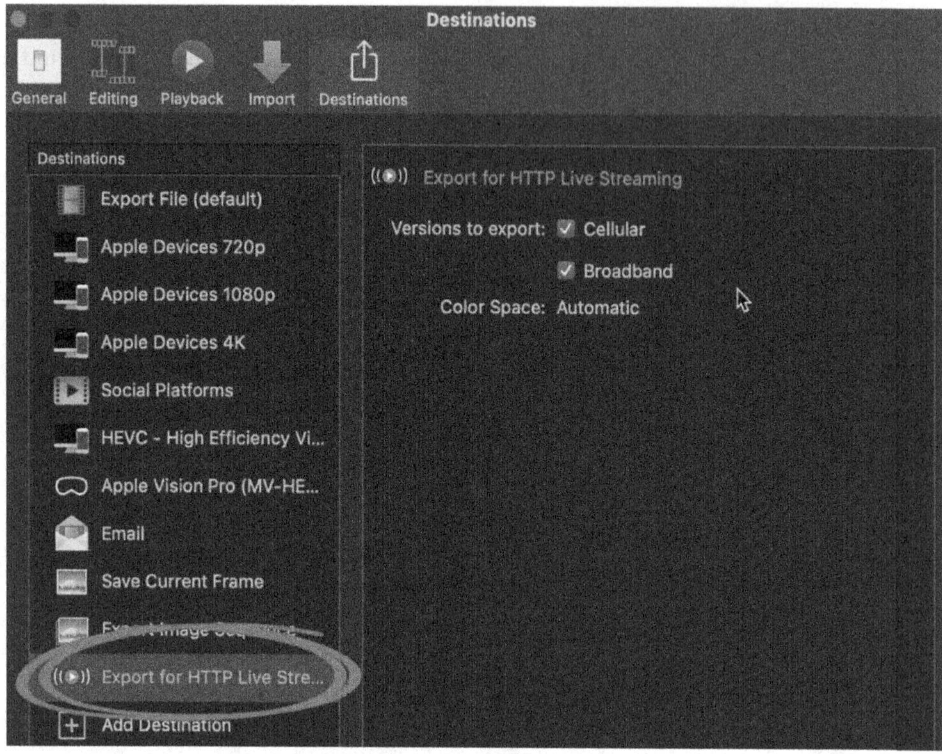

Figure 11.20: Choose the streaming versions to export

20. Click on **Add Destination** in the **Destinations** menu sidebar. Select the destination of **Bundle** and drag it to the **Destinations** menu sidebar.

21. The **Bundle** destination is a folder that can hold several destinations. Drag destinations from within the **Destinations** menu sidebar into the **Bundle** folder. In my example, I added **Social Platforms** and **Apple Devices 1080p** together. This way, I can process both destinations with one menu selection. Click on each item in the **Bundle** folder and note that you can access the settings in the Destination Browser panel.

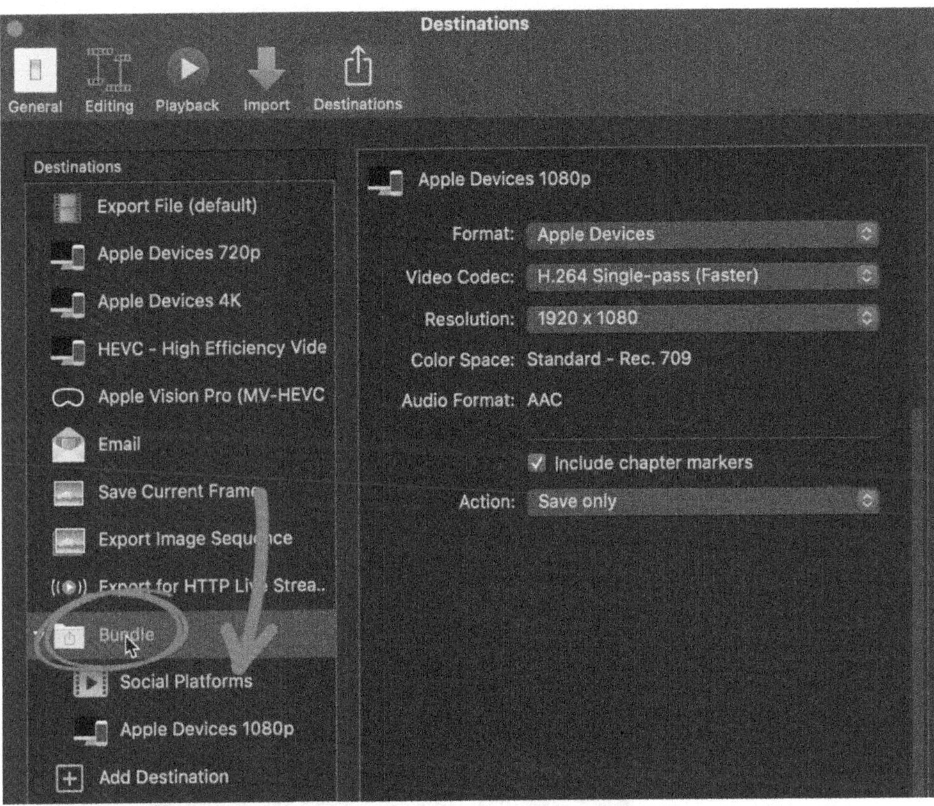

Figure 11.21: Drag destinations together into a Bundle folder

22. Speaking of menu selections, we have been building our list of destinations in the **Destinations** menu. Let's get to using them. Again, this is the **Destinations** tab in the Final Cut Pro Settings window. Close the window by clicking on the red dot in the upper-left corner of the window.

23. Click on the **Share** icon again to bring up the **Destinations** menu. Select an item that we just added from the menu.

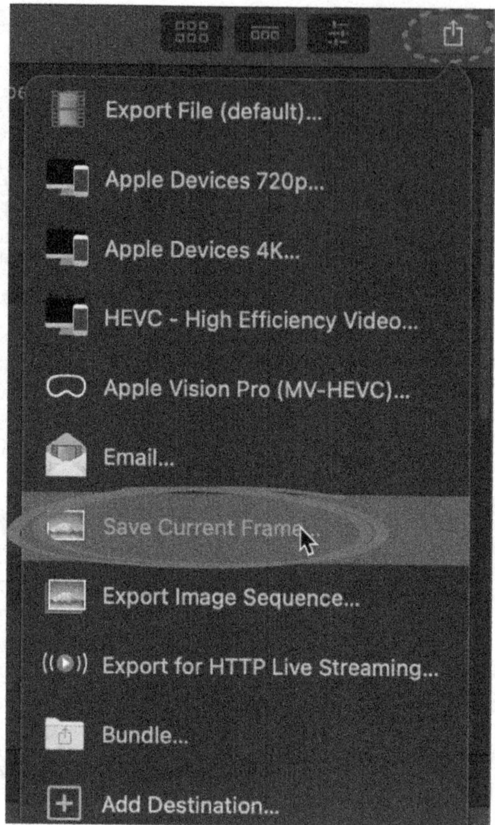

Figure 11.22: Select a destination from your Destinations menu

24. From the **Destination Export** window, check the **Settings** tab. Verify that the settings are the way you expected. Click on the **Next...** button and save your export to the folder of your choice. Nice job.

There's more...

You may run into this situation, like I did, in which an actor needed a blemish removed and the tools in Final Cut Pro just won't accomplish it. Follow these steps:

1. Use the **Range** tool, keyboard shortcut *R*, to select the range of frames that need fixing, and use **Export Image Sequence** to save them as images. The images will have sequential file names.

2. Go through each file and use the healing tool in your favorite image editing application. By the way, the healing tool in the Mac Photos app does a nice job. Yes, I know, this will be very tedious, but it needs to be done.

3.   Import the folder with the fixed images back into Final Cut Pro. Make sure to check **Keywords – From folders.** Make sure your Event is sorted by the name of the clips. See *Chapter 1* and a recipe called *Changing the Event Browser's appearance* for more information on working with the Event Browser panel. Select the keyword collection created from the folder name. Click on one of the images and then select them all with the keyboard shortcut *Command + A*.

4.   Now, the default time for still images is 4 seconds, but you don't have to mess with settings. Go ahead and add all the images to a new project that can be a landing spot with the shortcut *E*, for append, and select all the images with the shortcut *Command + A*.

5.   Then, use the shortcut *Control + D* to initiate a change in the duration. Type in 1, for one frame, and press *Return*.

6.   The images are now one frame in size, just like the way they were exported, and they snap together with no gaps. With the clips still selected, use the shortcut *Option + G* to make a compound clip. Give it a name.

7.   Select the compound clip and copy it, *Command + C*, go to the original project, and paste it in place, *Command + V*.

Congrats! You just saved the day.

Customizing share settings

Customizing share settings in Final Cut Pro allows you to streamline your workflow by creating tailored share destinations. By setting up specific export presets for platforms or clients, you save time and ensure consistent output. Explore and test different export settings of your own footage to see the visual and file size differences to decide which setting is best for you and your process.

In this recipe, we will work through the process of creating a custom destination and explore various settings.

How to do it...

Custom export settings, like a deli sandwich made-to-order:

1.   We are headed back to the Final Cut Pro Settings window. In the upper-right corner of the Final Cut Pro interface, click on the **Share** icon, which looks like a square with an arrow pointing up. Select Add Destination... from the menu.

2.   You will be presented with the Final Cut Pro **Settings** window with the **Destinations** tab selected. Select the **Export File** destination from the Destination Browser panel and drag it to the **Destinations** sidebar. You can place it anywhere in the list.

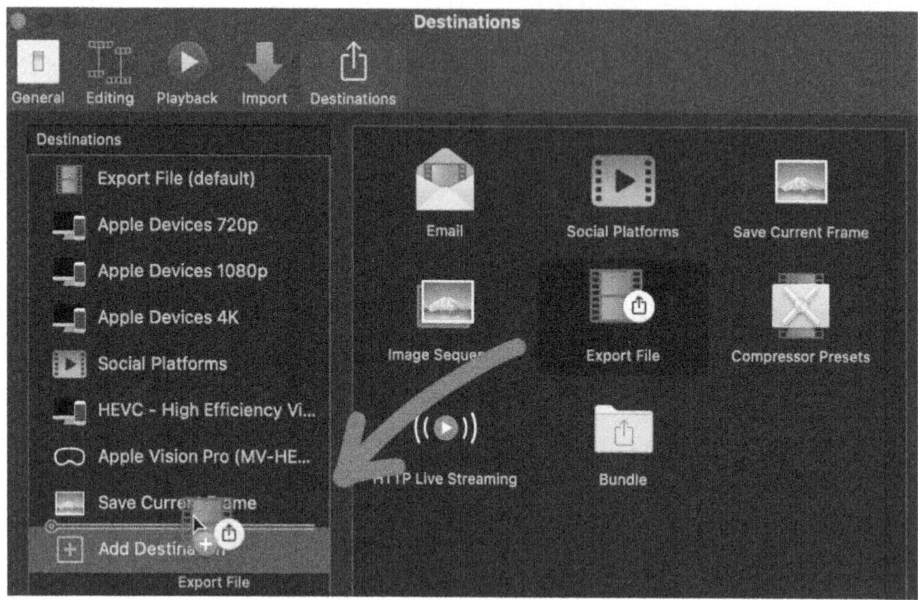

Figure 11.23: Drag the Export File icon to the Destinations sidebar

3. In the **Settings** panel for the **Export File** destination, click on the drop-down menu for the **Video Codec** parameter. Note the list of possible formats. For now, choose **H.264**. I like having an H.264 destination to quickly access from the *Share* menu.

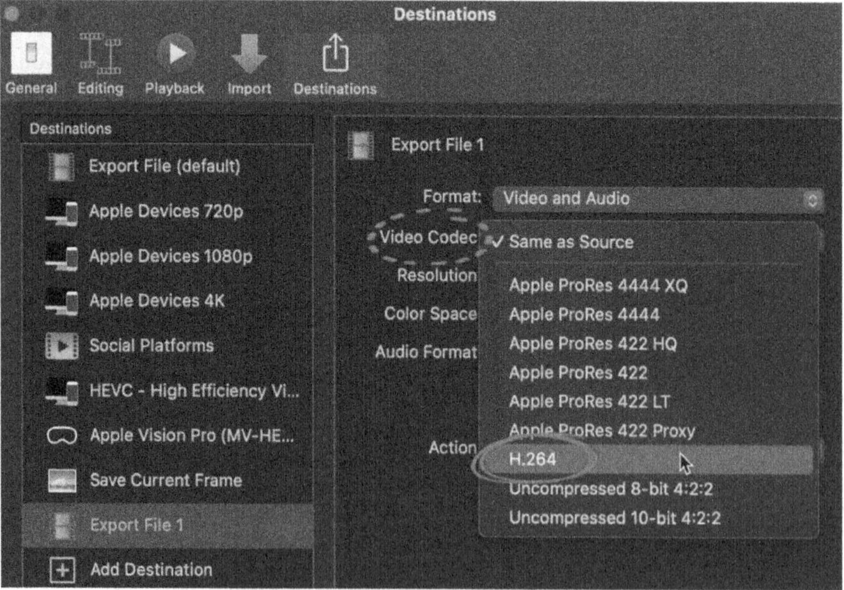

Figure 11.24: Choose H.264 from the Video Codec parameter menu

4. Let's rename this destination. Click once on the **Export File 1** destination in the sidebar. The text will become highlighted. Go ahead and type in a new name. For my example, I am going to name it `Custom Export`. Yes, I know, very creative. But I can always change it again later.

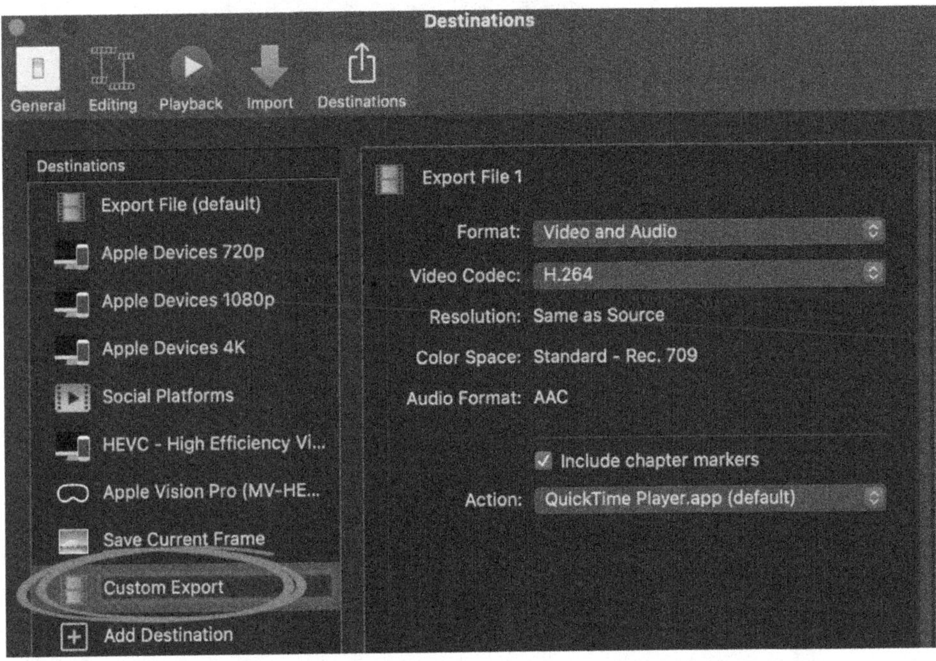

Figure 11.25: Type in a new name for your custom export destination

5. We have been adding destinations to the **Destinations** menu, and we need to close the **Settings** window before we can use our new destinations. Close the **Settings** window by clicking on the red dot in the upper-left corner of the window. Now, click on the **Share** icon in the upper-right corner of the Final Cut Pro interface and, from the **Destinations** menu, select **Custom Export....**

Figure 11.26: Select Custom Export… from the Destinations menu

6.   You are presented with a window that displays the share information. Let's click on the **Settings** tab at the upper center of the window. Click on the drop-down menu for the **Video Codec** parameter. Notice that there are many more video formats available, albeit a bit unusual.

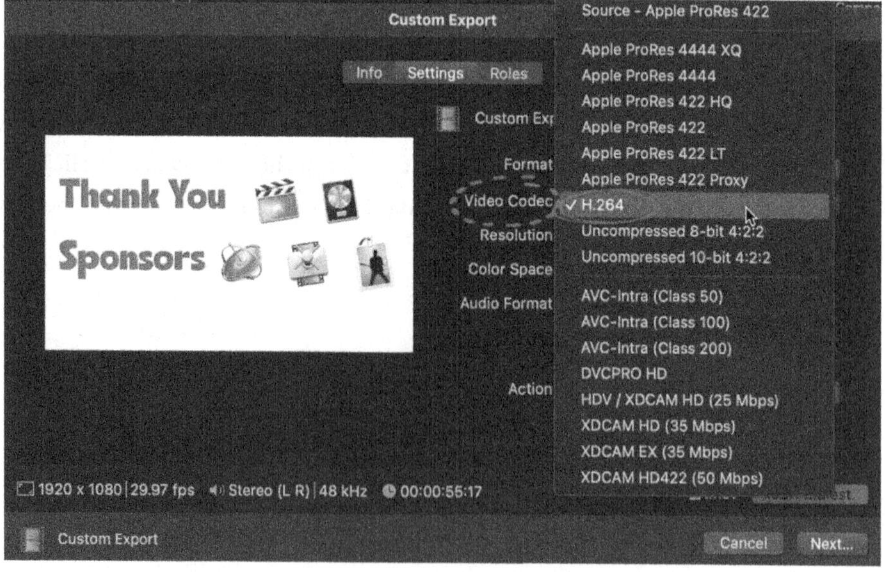

Figure 11.27: Many options for the Video Codec parameter

7. From the **Format** parameter menu, there are three categories: **MASTERING**, **PUBLISHING**, and **BROADCAST**. The **MASTERING** category is understandable. It displays the options to export both video and audio, or to export video only, or audio only. From the menu, select **Audio Only**.

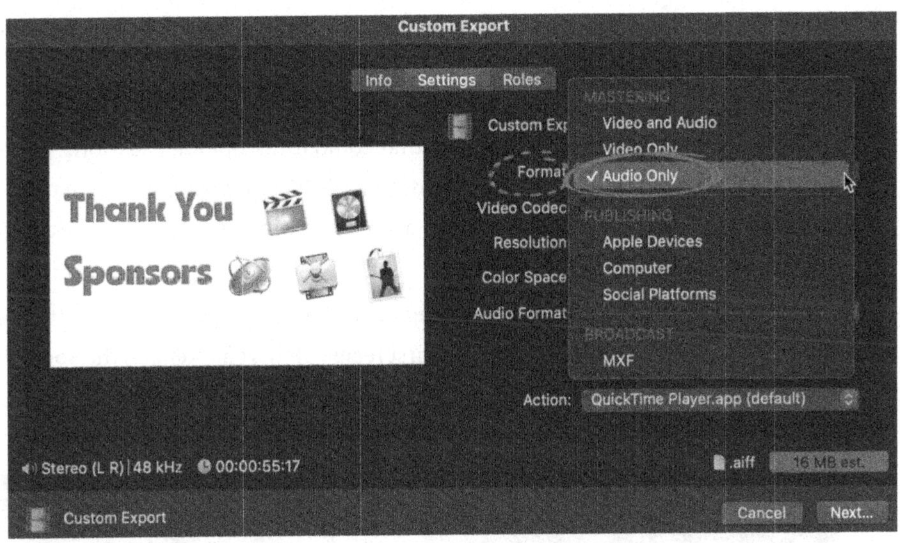

Figure 11.28: Select Audio Only from the Format parameter menu

8. Previously, when the format was for video and audio, the audio format defaulted to **Automatic**. Now, the **Audio Format** parameter menu has several formats to choose from.

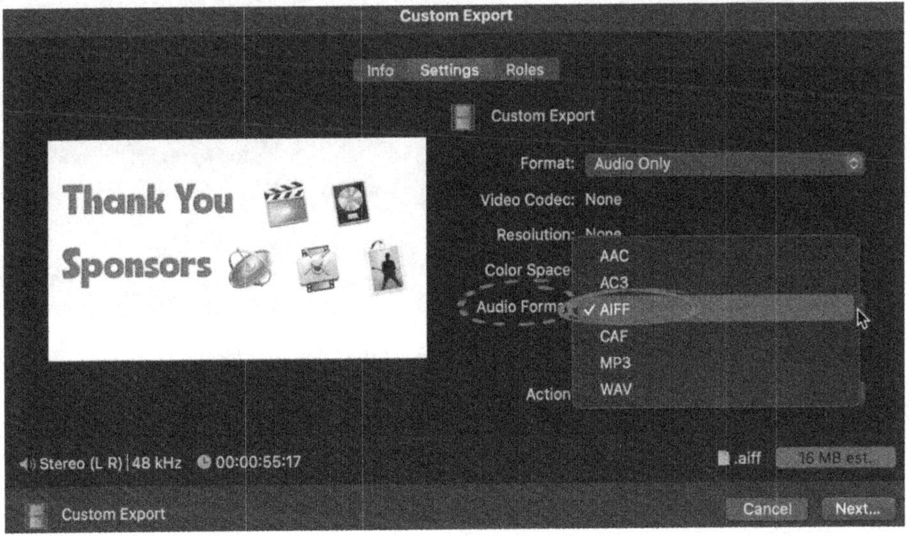

Figure 11.29: Several audio formats are available when exporting audio only

9. For online streaming and social media, **AAC** is ideal due to its high-quality compression and small file size, typically used in MP4 or MOV files. For DVDs, Blu-ray, and broadcast TV, **AC3** (Dolby Digital) is the industry standard, supporting multi-channel audio for surround sound. If you're working on professional audio editing or music production, **AIFF** and **WAV** are the best choices, as they are uncompressed and maintain full audio fidelity, usually exported at 24-bit or 32-bit with a sample rate of 48 kHz or higher. For long recordings, such as interviews or live events, **CAF** (**Core Audio Format**) is useful because it eliminates file size limitations that could interrupt long sessions. If your project requires general playback on common devices, **MP3** is a great option due to its universal compatibility and small file size, with a standard bitrate of 192 kbps or a high-quality setting of 320 kbps.

10. Click on the **Format** parameter menu again and note the **PUBLISHING** category. We explored the **Apple Devices** format in the first recipe of this chapter and the **Social Platforms** format in the second recipe. Select the **Computer** format. We touched on the **Computer** format briefly in the first recipe when we were specifying the HEVC video codec.

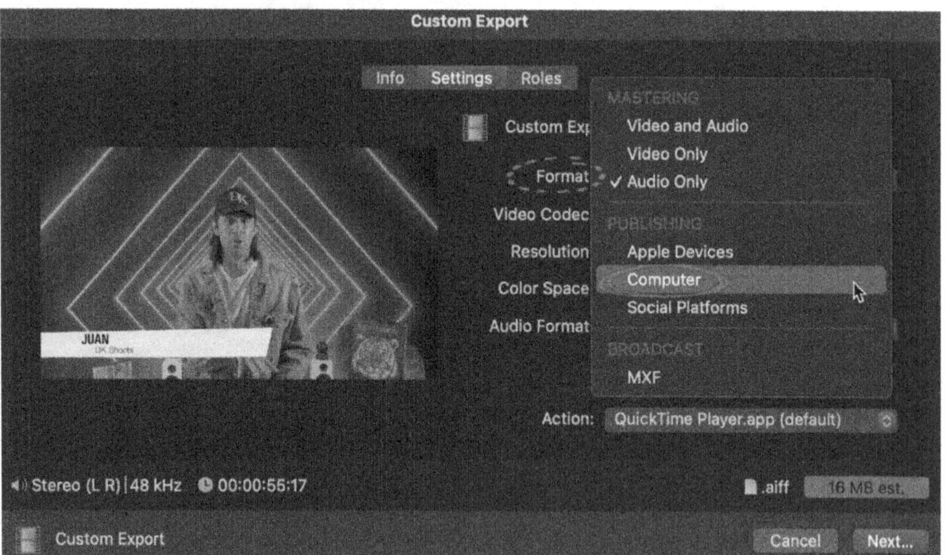

Figure 11.30: Select the Computer format

11. Now, when we have specified **Computer** as the format, several variations of the HEVC codec are available in the **Video Codec** parameter menu. Also note that the extension for this format is **.mp4**.

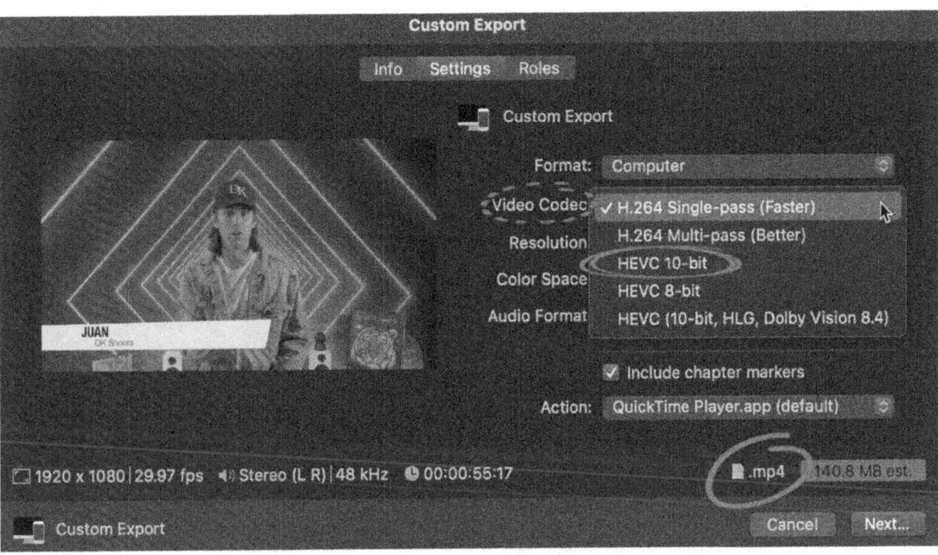

Figure 11.31: The HEVC codec is available in the Computer format

12. Click on the **Format** parameter menu again and note the **BROADCAST** category. From this category, select **MXF. MXF (Material eXchange Format)** is an industry-standard file format for video and audio suitable for broadcast or theatrical release. Like QuickTime files, MXF files contain metadata including frame rate, frame size, creation date, and custom data added by a camera operator. When you export MXF files, you can use audio roles to configure eight audio channels – six 5.1 surround channels and two stereo channels.

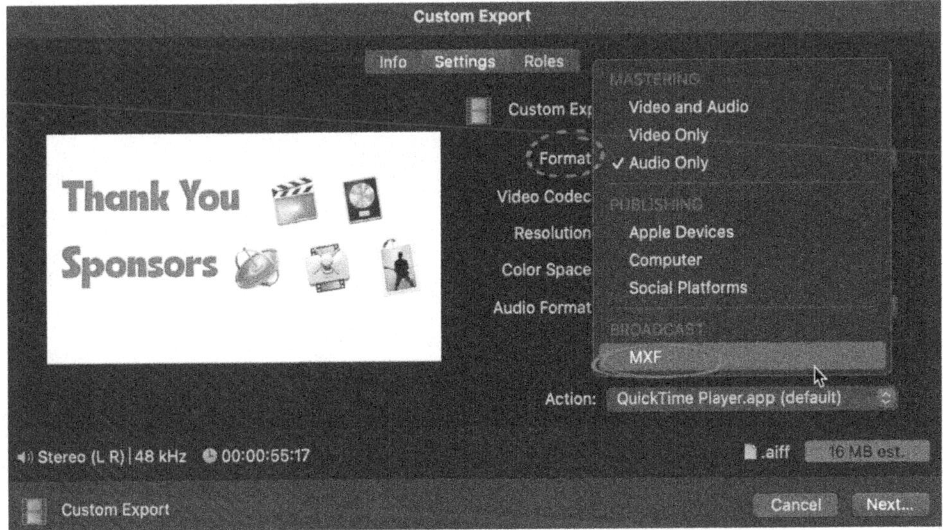

Figure 11.32: Select MXF from the BROADCAST category of Format

13. Click on the **Video Codec** parameter menu and note that the MXF format defaults to the highest resolution ProRes codec.

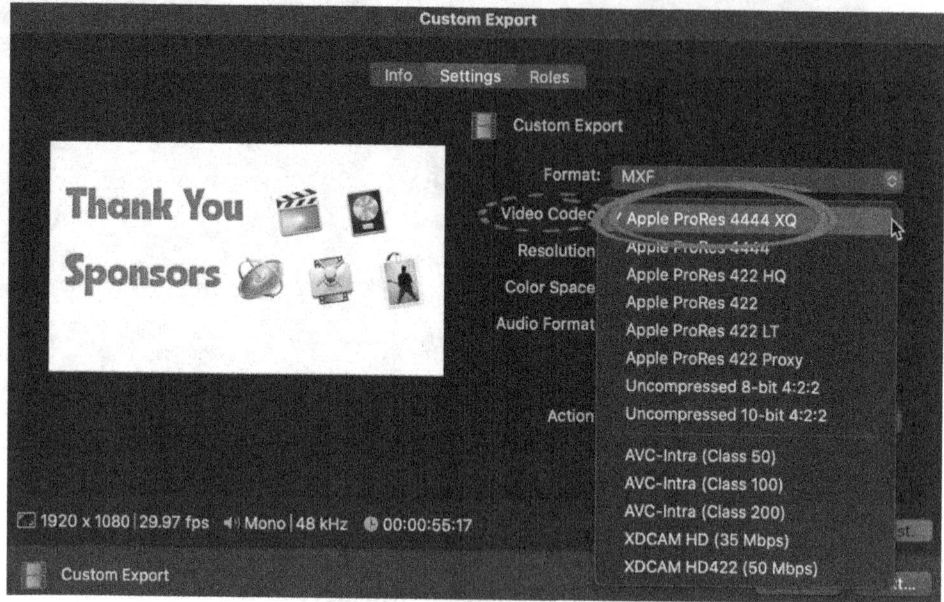

Figure 11.33: The MXF format defaults to the highest resolution ProRes codec

14. Click on the **Roles** tab at the upper center of the window. Note that the parameter of **Roles as** has been set to **Multitrack MXF File**.

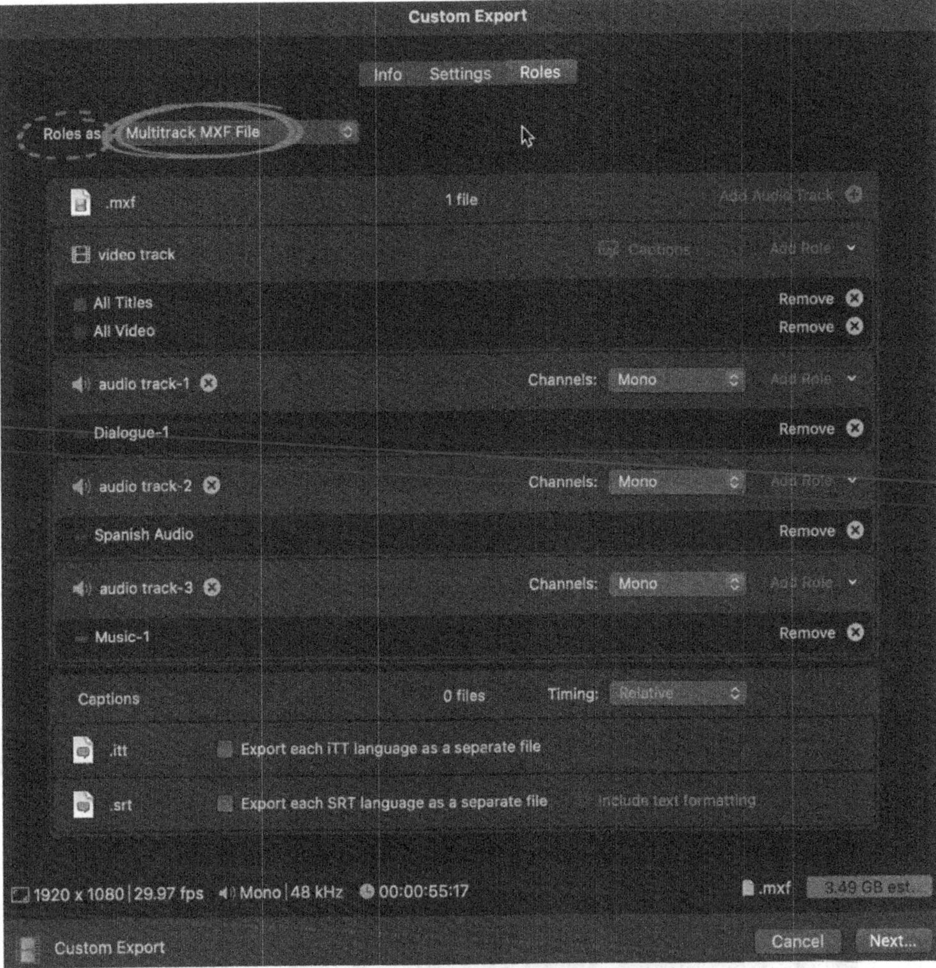

Figure 11.34: The Roles as parameter is set to Multitrack MXF File

15. Click on the **Settings** tab in the upper center of the window. The MXF format can be saved as a custom destination in Final Cut Pro. However, a complete explanation of how to create projects for MXF exporting is beyond the scope of this cookbook.

16. One last thing to mention is that you can export destinations that you have created from your Mac to another, from the Final Cut Pro **Settings** window and the **Destinations** tab. Drag a destination from the **Destinations** list in the sidebar to a location in the Finder. The destination file is appended with the filename extension of .fcpxdest.

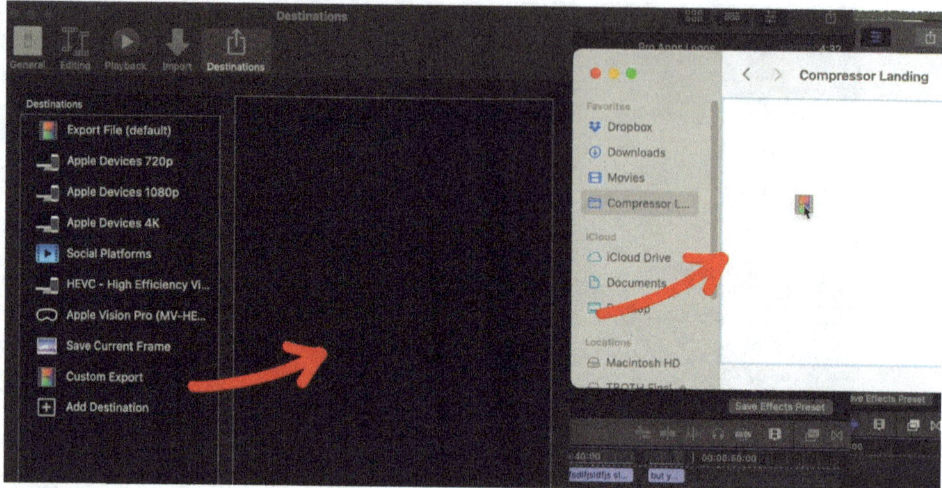

Figure 11.35: Drag a destination from the sidebar to the Finder

17. To import a destination, simply drag a destination file from the Finder to the **Destinations** list in the sidebar of the **Destinations** window.

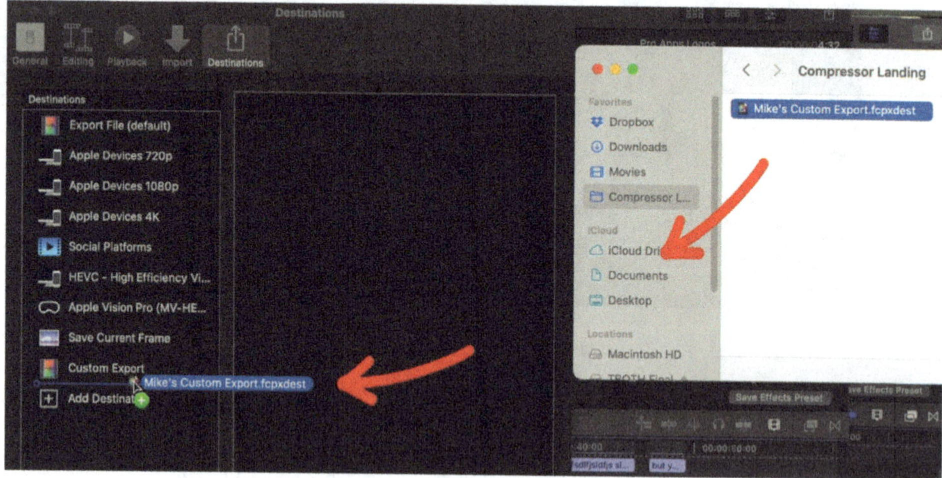

Figure 11.36: Drag a destination from the Finder to the sidebar

18. The destination you added appears in the **Destinations** list and is available when you click the **Share** icon in the toolbar. Now, you can have all your favorite destinations with you anywhere you go.

There's more...

In Final Cut Pro, you can customize the metadata (also called attributes) included with exported files:

1. Select a project in the Event Browser panel. Now, in the Inspector panel, click on the **Share Inspector** icon, which looks like three arrows pointing up. Explore the fields that can be edited.

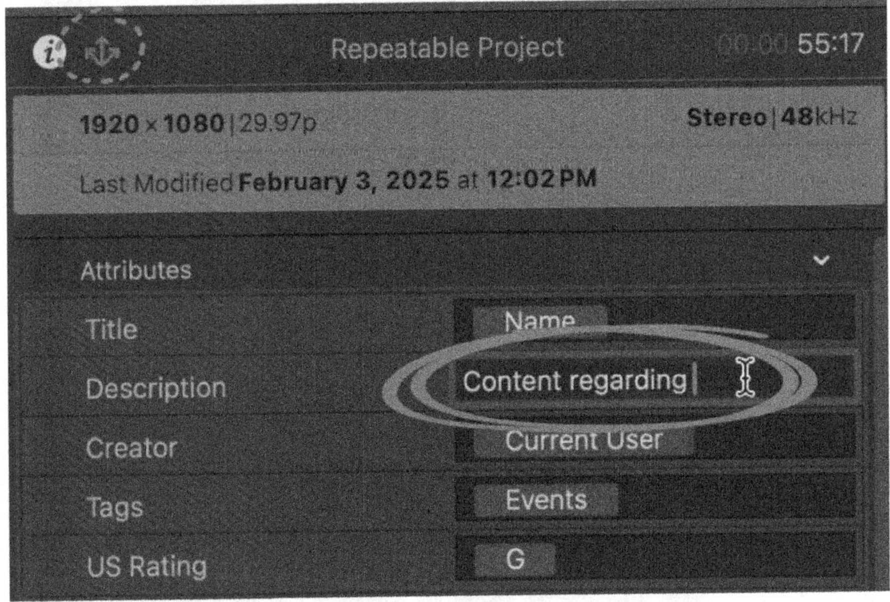

Figure 11.37: Edit export attributes in the Share Inspector panel

2. Click on the down arrow icon to the right of the **Attributes** parameter to display a drop-down menu. At the bottom of the menu, select **Edit Share Fields...**.

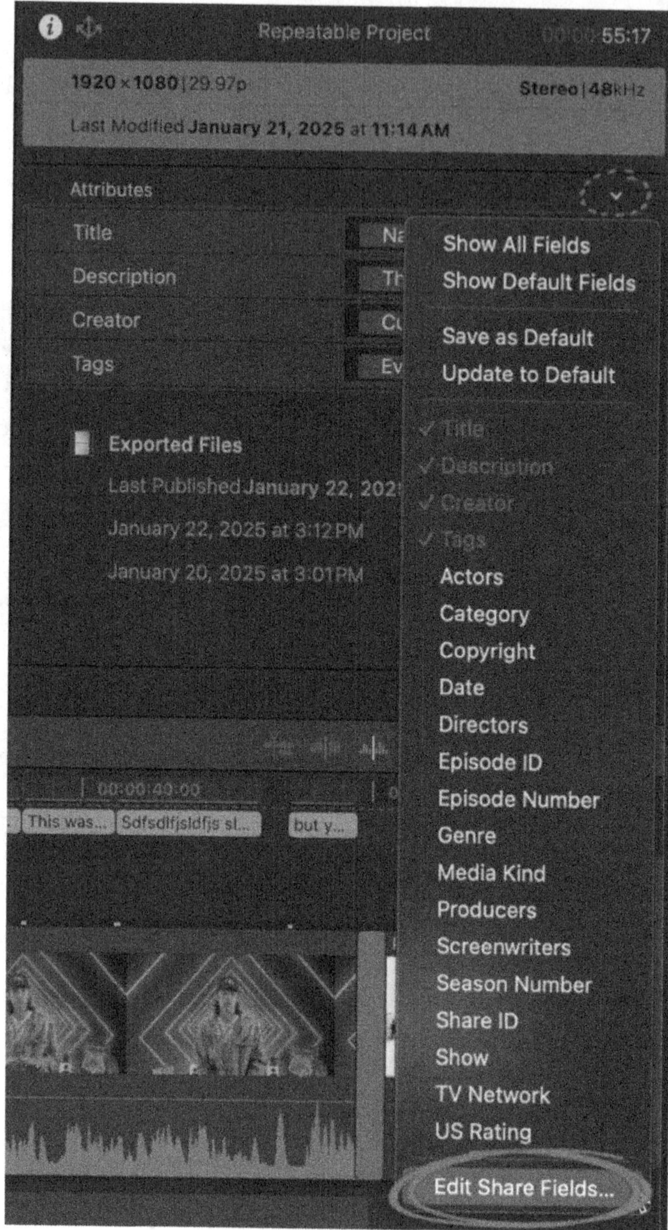

Figure 11.38: Select Edit Share Fields… from the Attributes menu

3. In the **Edit Share Fields** dialog box, select an attribute field from the list on the left. The attributes assigned to the selected field appear in the **Format** field on the right. Explore how these attributes can be edited. Click on the **OK** button when you are finished.

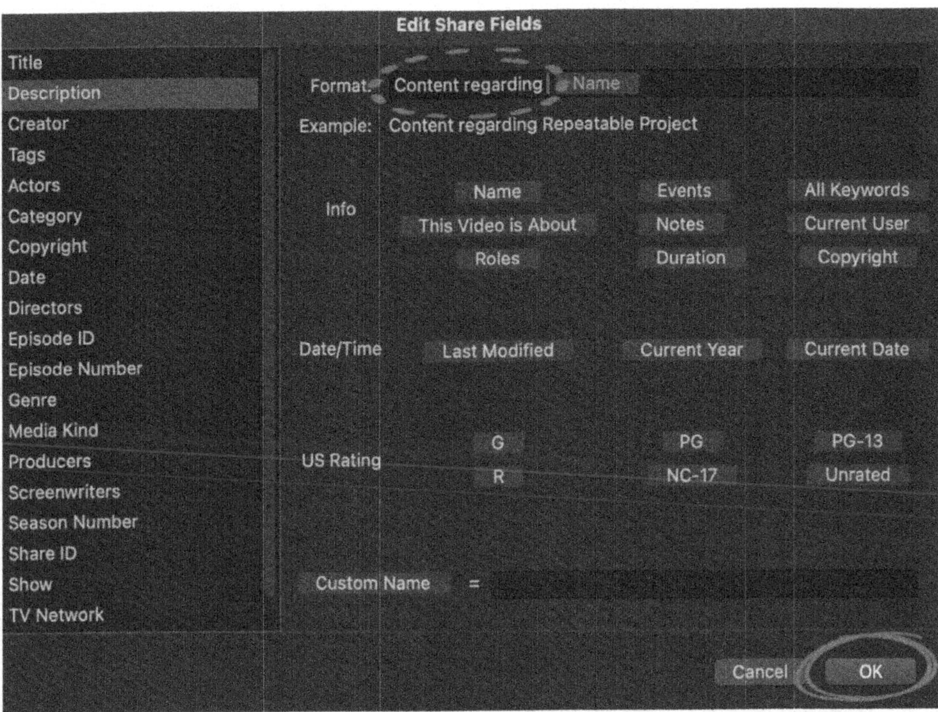

Figure 11.39: Explore the variety of share fields that can be edited

Sharing roles

Sharing roles in Final Cut Pro gives you the flexibility to select and export specific audio, video, or caption roles tailored to your project's needs. This feature is especially useful for delivering multiple language versions or isolating audio stems for post-production. By customizing and managing roles at export, you can create professional, organized outputs that meet the exact specifications of your audience or clients.

In this recipe, we will explore how to select certain audio tracks and titles for exporting.

Getting ready

To follow along with this recipe, we are going to set up a project to have an alternate language. I am starting with a project created in *Chapter 10* and a recipe called *Creating a repeatable project intro and outro*, but you can use any project that has some dialogue and titles. You may need to have your audio translated. There are several online resources for translating audio and text files, such as Maestra, Google Translate, and TurboScribe. For a title, I just duplicated the Lower Third title I had and changed the name.

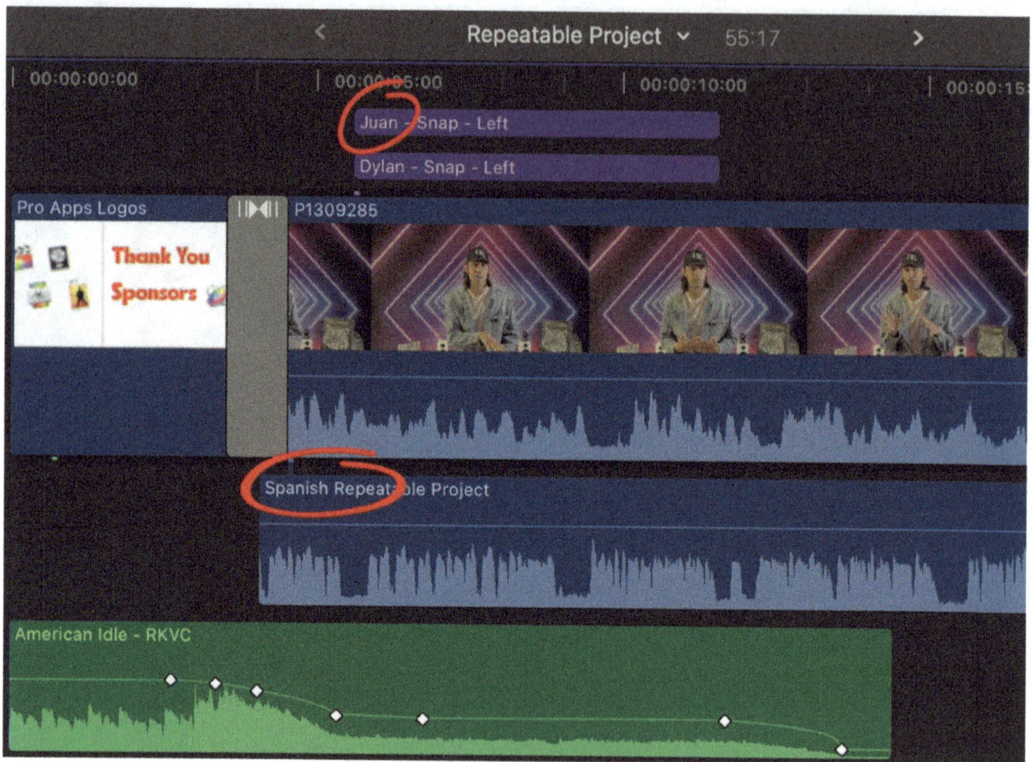

Figure 11.40: Explore the variety

With an audio file and a title added to your project, let's add some roles. From the **Modify** menu, select **Edit Roles...**, and you are presented with the list of roles in the library you are working on. In the **Video Roles** section, hover over the **Titles** bar and click on **+ Subrole**. In my example, I am adding an alternative Spanish version of my project, so I am calling this title subrole `Spanish Titles`. Also, in the **Audio** section, hover over the **Dialogue** bar and click on **+ Subrole**. I am going to name my new audio role `Spanish Audio`. Click on the **Apply** button in the lower-right corner of the window.

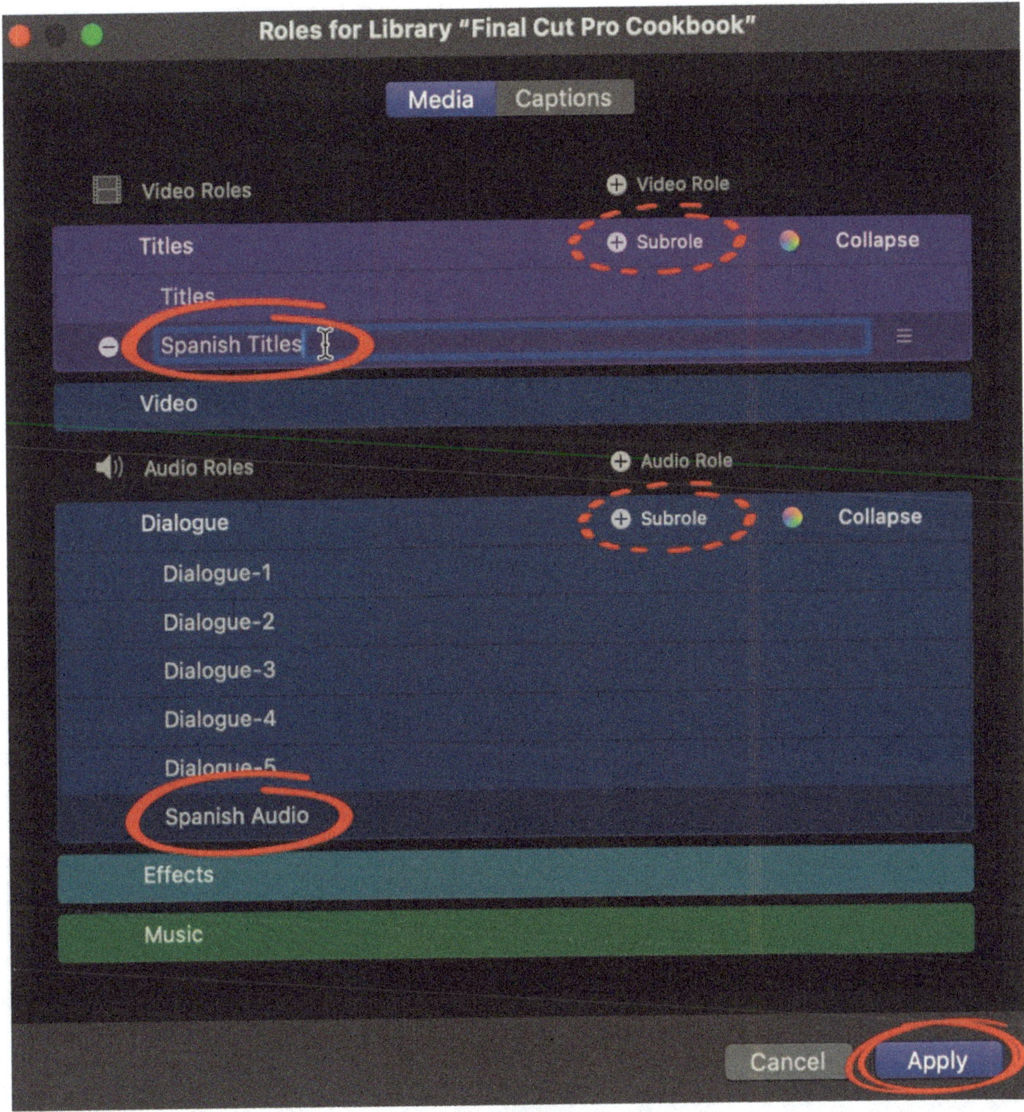

Figure 11.41: Add alternative title and audio roles to your library

Now that we have created roles for our alternative media, we need to assign the roles to the clips. Right-click on the Spanish title you have added to the project in your Timeline panel. From the clip drop-down menu, select **Assign Video Roles**, and from there, select **Spanish Titles**.

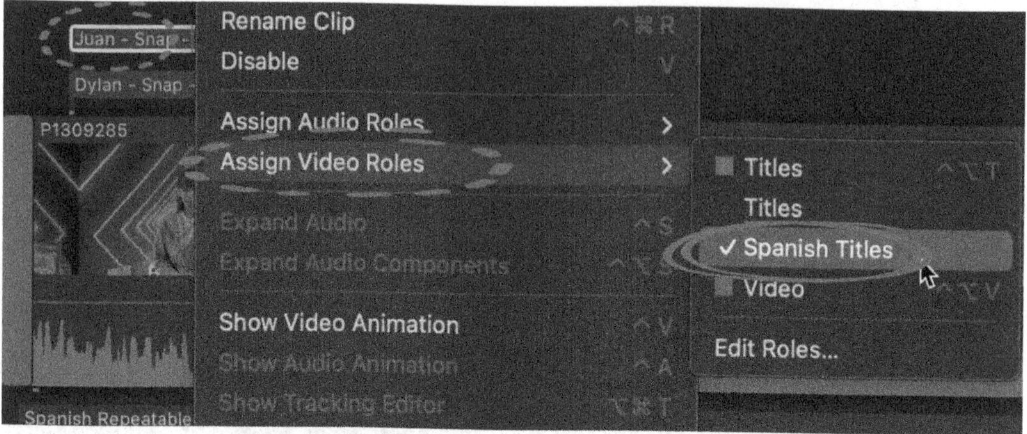

Figure 11.42: Assign the Spanish Titles role to your alternative title clip

Likewise, right-click on the Spanish audio clip you have added to the project on your Timeline panel. From the clip drop-down menu, select **Assign Audio Roles**, and from there, select **Spanish Audio**, or select the role names that you created for your library.

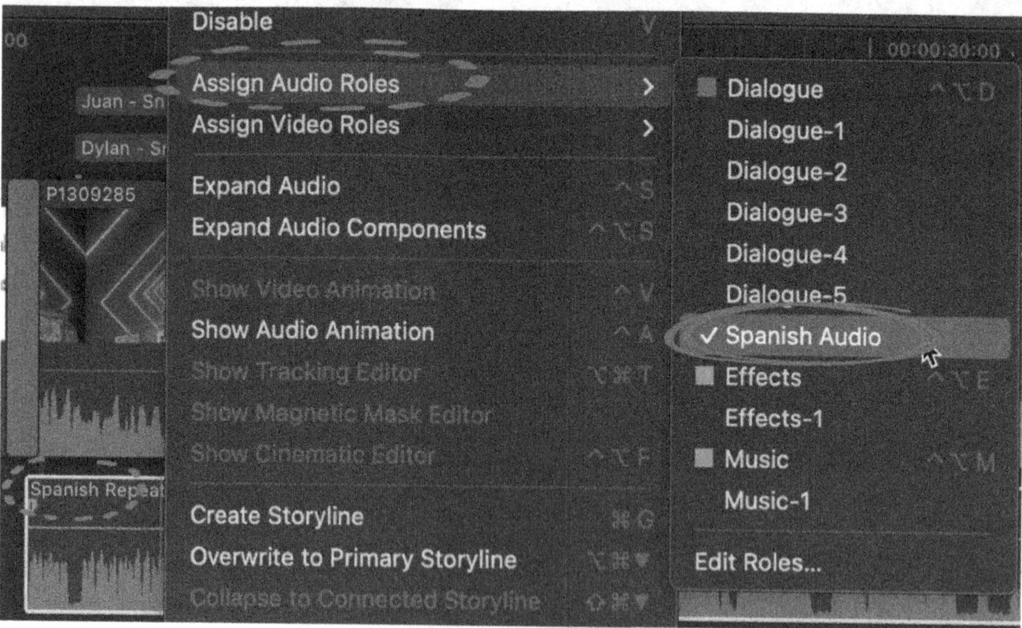

Figure 11.43: Assign the Spanish Audio role to your alternative audio clip

Good, we are ready to go.

How to do it...

Pass the hot sauce, we're getting an alternative language infusion:

1. With your project selected in the Timeline panel, click on the **Share** icon in the upper-right corner of the Final Cut Pro interface, which looks like a square with an arrow pointing up. From the **Destinations** menu, select the first item, **Export File (default)....** You can also apply the **Export File (default)** destination with the keyboard shortcut *Command + E*. Within the **Export File** information window, click on the **Roles** tab in the upper center.

2. In the **Roles** pane, click the **Roles as** drop-down menu and select **Multitrack QuickTime Movie**. This exports the roles you specify as a single QuickTime video file.

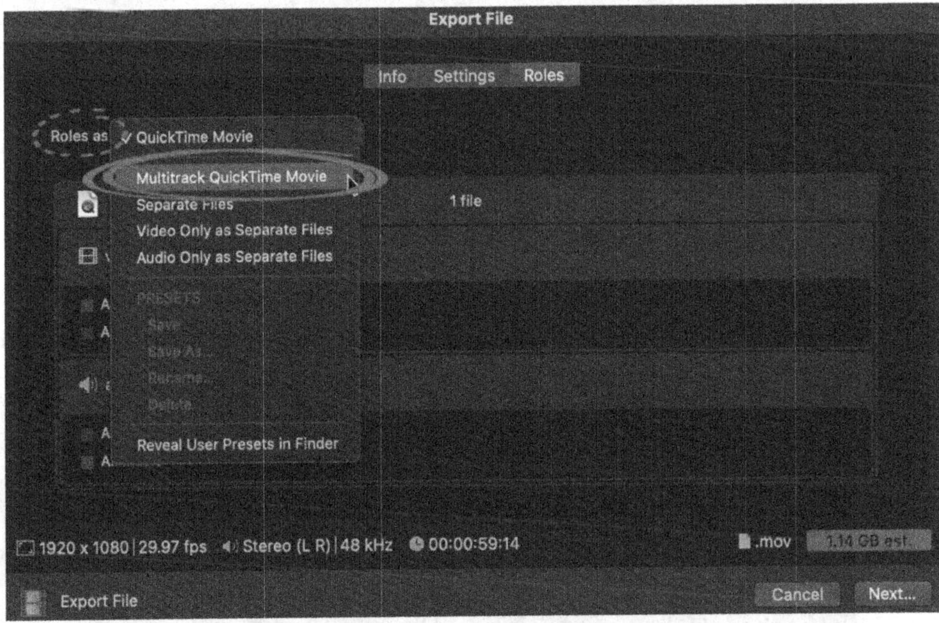

Figure 11.44: Select Multitrack QuickTime Movie from the Roles as drop-down menu

3. In the **video track** area on the right side of the window, click on the **Add Role** button. From the **Video Roles** drop-down menu, select **Spanish Titles,** or the title you created earlier.

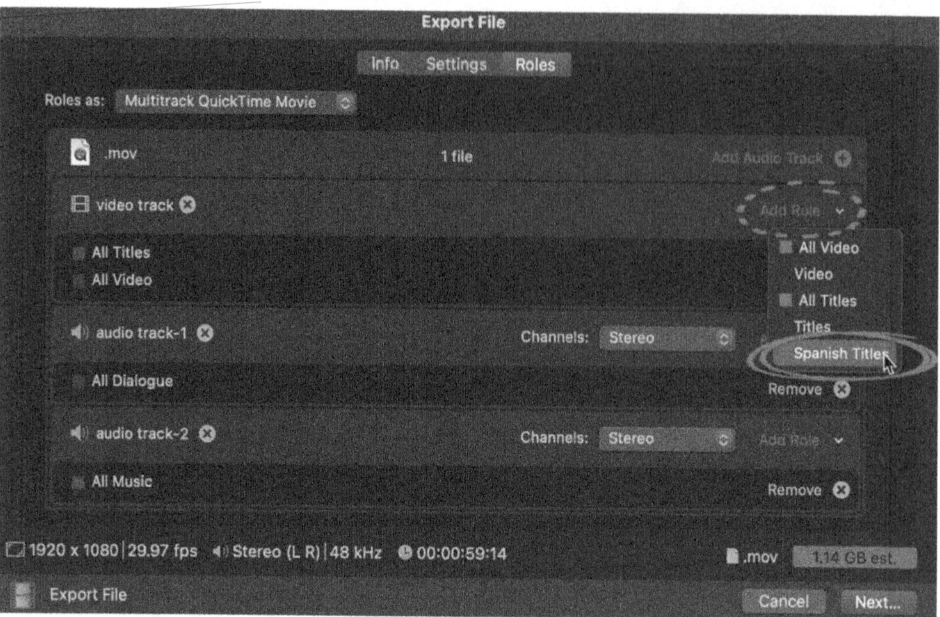

Figure 11.45: Add the Spanish Titles role to export

4. Now, in the **audio track-1** area, which contains **All Dialogue**, on the right side of the window, click on the **Add Role** button. From the **Audio Roles** drop-down menu, select **Spanish Audio**.

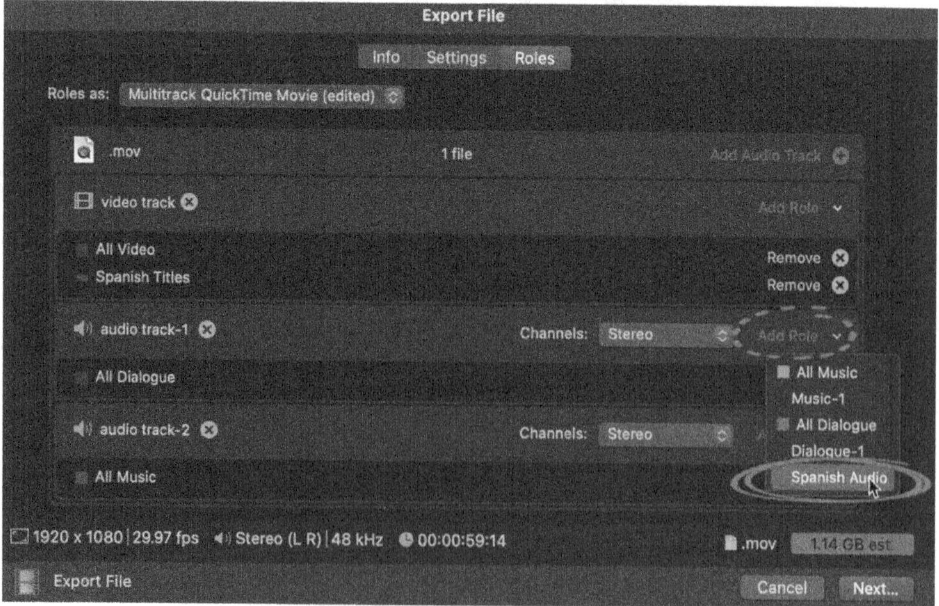

Figure 11.46: Add the Spanish Audio role to export

5. In addition, you can save the role settings that you have made. Click the **Roles as** drop-down menu, and from the **Presets** area, choose **Save As...**.

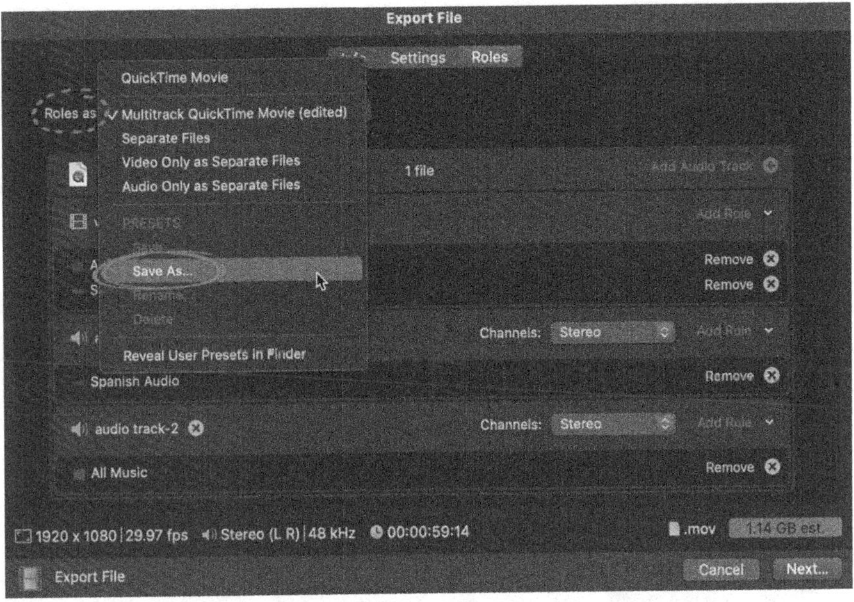

Figure 11.47: Select Save As… from the Roles as drop-down menu

6. You can give this set of roles a proper name. In my example, I am going to label it Spanish Multitrack QuickTime Movie. Click on the **Save** button.

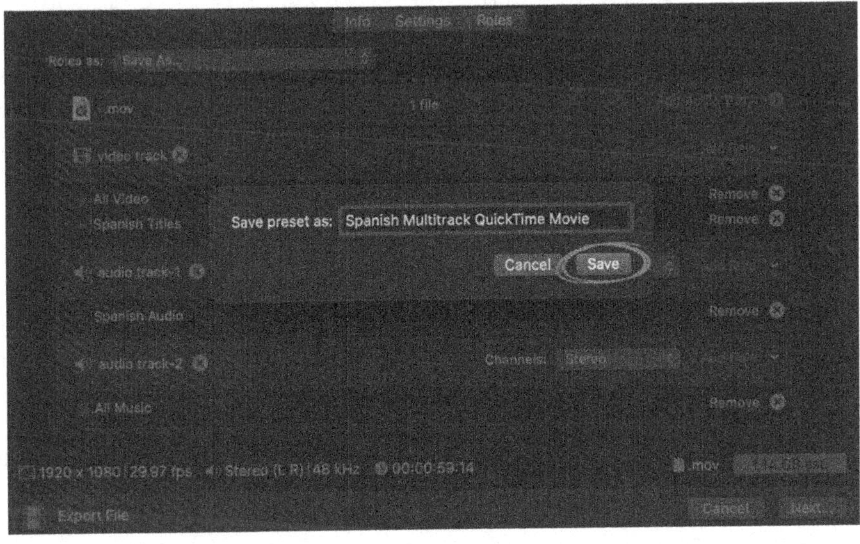

Figure 11.48: Name your preset and click on the Save button

7. Furthermore, you can select **Reveal User Presets in Finder** from the **Roles as:** drop-down menu, and you will be able to take that `.rolespreset` file with you wherever you go.

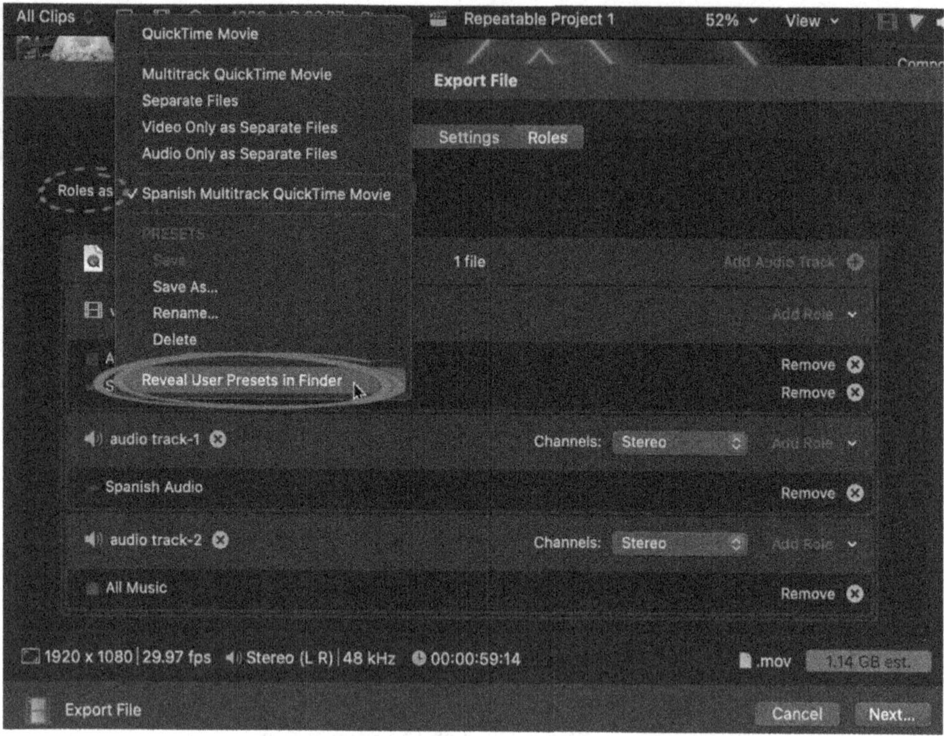

Figure 11.49: Select Reveal User Presets in Finder from the Roles as: drop-down menu

Being able to share specific roles in a project is incredibly efficient. You no longer have to make separate projects for different languages and worry about version control. You can build one project and customize your exports. Muy bien.

Sharing closed and burned-in captions

Sharing closed and burned-in captions allows you to tailor your video for accessibility and specific viewing platforms. With Final Cut Pro, you can export captions as a separate file for flexible use or burn them directly into the video for guaranteed visibility across all devices. This ensures your content is inclusive, platform-compliant, and professional, meeting the needs of diverse audiences.

In this recipe, we will export a project to include captions that are burned into the video or that are included as a file so that customers can turn captions on or off.

Getting ready

In this recipe, we will need to prep a project to have captions. For my example, I am going to use the project we created in *Chapter 10* and the recipe called *Creating closed captions*. In that project, we transcribed our dialogue into captions. But in this export recipe, we need two different types of caption formats.

From the Event Browser panel, double-click on the project we created in *Chapter 10*, or another project that has captions, to open it in the Timeline panel. Click on one of the caption clips in the captions lane. Select all the captions in that lane with the keyboard shortcut *Command + A*. Right-click on one of the selected caption clips and, from the clip pop-up menu, select **Duplicate Captions to a New Format**. And, because Final Cut Pro sets **iTT** (short for **iTunes Time Text**) as the default caption format, select **SRT** from the submenu.

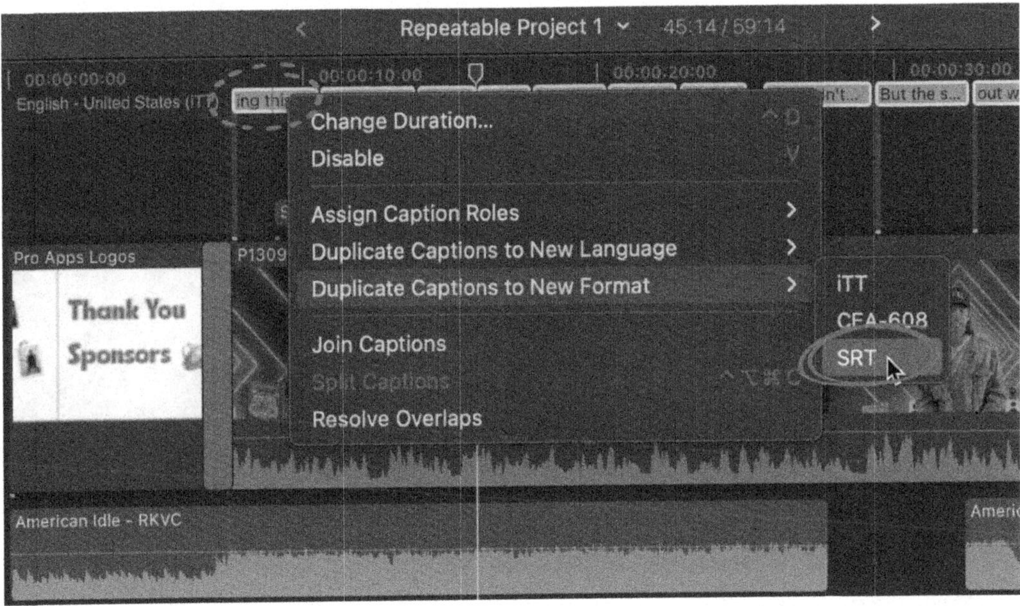

Figure 11.50: Select SRT from Duplicate Captions to New Format in the clip pop-up menu

Now we have the two formats we need to export.

How to do it...

Earlier, we said that captions are like a perfectly sealed container. Everyone can savor the full flavor of your video. Well, now is the time to pop the top and share:

1. Let's start by exporting our project for social media with burned-in captions because so many people watch videos on their phones with the sound turned off. With your project selected in the Timeline panel, click on the **Share** icon in the upper-right corner of the Final Cut Pro interface, which looks like a square with an arrow pointing up. From the **Destinations** menu, select **Social Platforms....** In the export window, click on the **Settings** tab in the upper center. From the **Burn in captions:** parameter, click on the drop-down menu and select your language version that is in the **iTT** format. This is the best format for burned-in captions. Click on the **Next...** button in the lower-right corner. From there, you can select where on your Mac to save your video file.

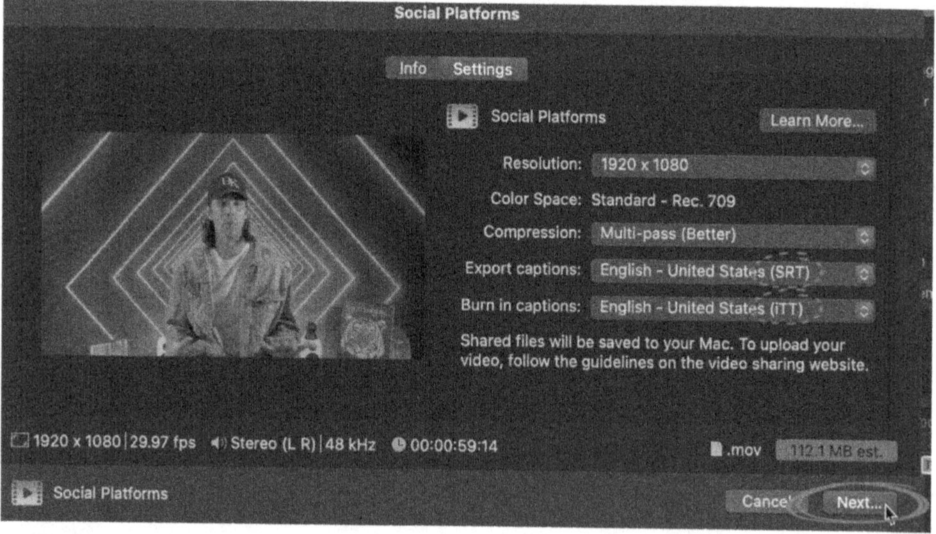

Figure 11.51: Select SRT for Export captions: and iTT for Burn in captions:

2. If, instead, you prefer to have closed captions that consumers can turn on or off, it is a good idea to export your own caption file and not rely on the social media platform to accurately transcribe your video. I suggest setting the **Export captions:** parameter to your language version and the **SRT** format. As the parameter suggests, Final Cut Pro will create a separate `.srt` file that has the text of your captions with time codes. You will need to

upload this file to the social media site along with your video. But the closed captions will match the dialogue in your video much better. Click on the **Next...** button in the lower-right corner. From there, you can select where on your Mac to save both your video file and your closed caption text file.

3. What if you are exporting your video in another format and want captions? Again, make sure your project is selected in the Timeline panel and click on the **Share** icon in the upper-right corner of the Final Cut Pro interface, which looks like a square with an arrow pointing up. From the **Destinations** menu, select **Export File (default)....** Click on the **Roles** tab in the upper center of the window. Within the **Roles** tab of the **Export File** window, in the **video track** area on the right side, click on the **Open Caption Settings** button, which looks like a purple text bubble next to the word **Captions**.

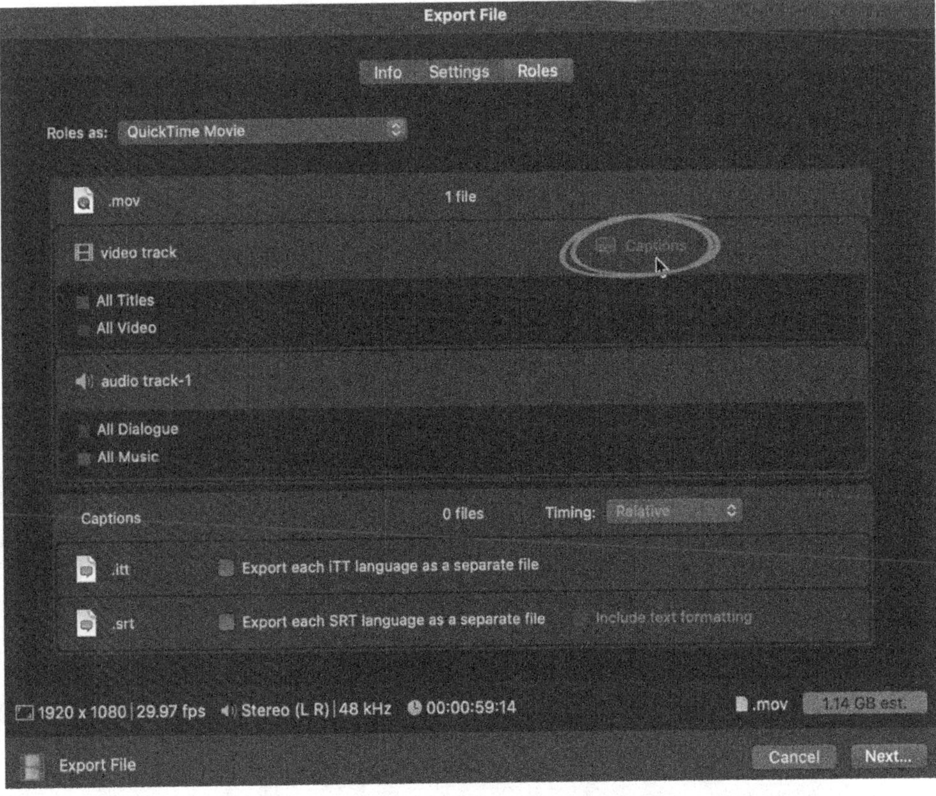

Figure 11.52: Click on the Open Caption Settings button in the Roles window

4. This will bring up a small dialog box. From the **Burn in captions:** parameter, click on the drop-down menu and select the **iTT** format for your language version. Click on the **OK** button.

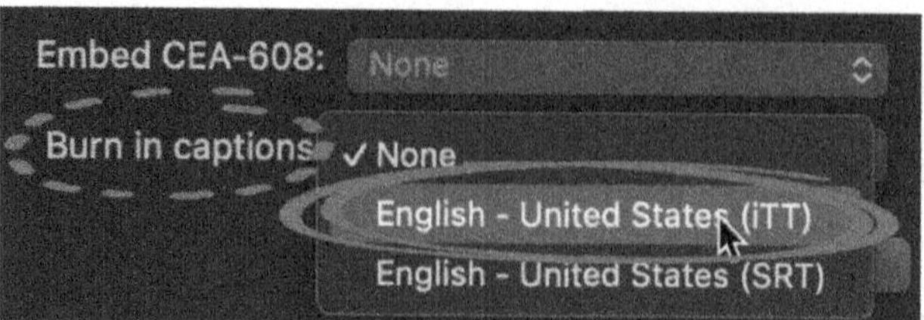

Figure 11.53: Select the iTT format for Burn in captions

5. As we said earlier, if you prefer to have closed captions that consumers can turn on or off, it is a good idea to export your own caption file and not rely on the social media platform to accurately transcribe your video. In that case, I suggest selecting the checkbox next to the **.srt** parameter labeled **Export each SRT language as a separate file** in the **Captions** section near the bottom of the window. Also, click on the drop-down menu for the **Timing:** parameter and select **Absolute.** This will use each caption's actual start time, regardless of the project's start time. In addition, don't check **Include text formatting.** This has to do with text color, which makes no difference in a separate file. As indicated near the bottom-right corner of the window, Final Cut Pro will create two files: the video file and a separate . srt file that has the text of your captions with time codes.

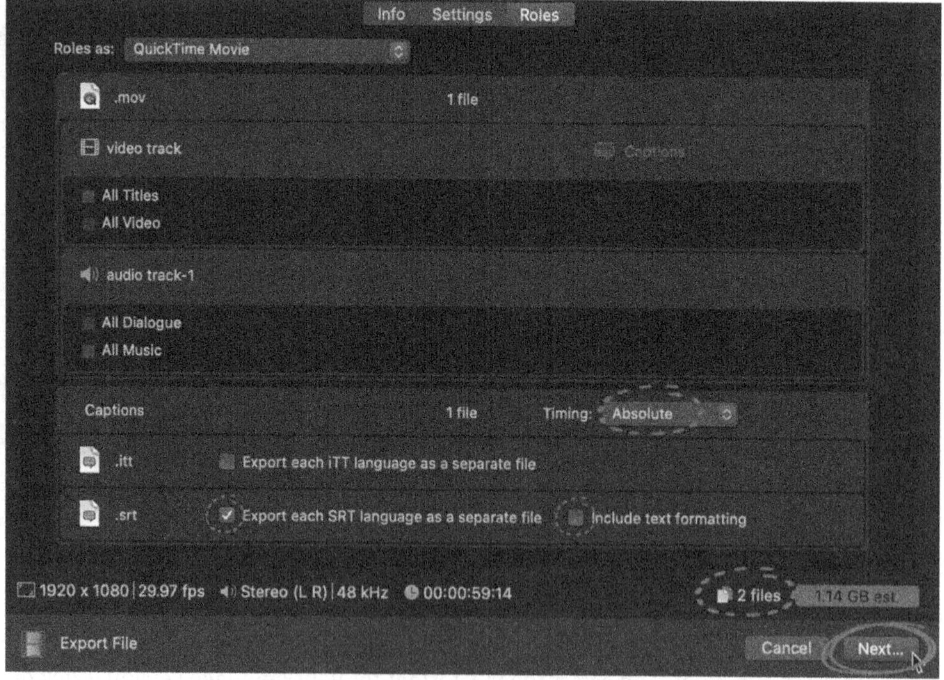

Figure 11.54: Export SRT captions as separate files with Absolute timing

6. Click on the **Next...** button in the lower-right corner. From there, you can select where on your Mac to save both your video file and your closed caption text file.

There's more...

It is possible to just export your captions without the video file. From the **File** menu, select **Export Captions...**. You are presented with a dialog box in which you can name the file and select where on the hard drive it will be saved. From the **Role** list, select the checkbox next to **SRT**, and for the **Start Time** parameter, select **Absolute**. When finished, click on the **Export** button.

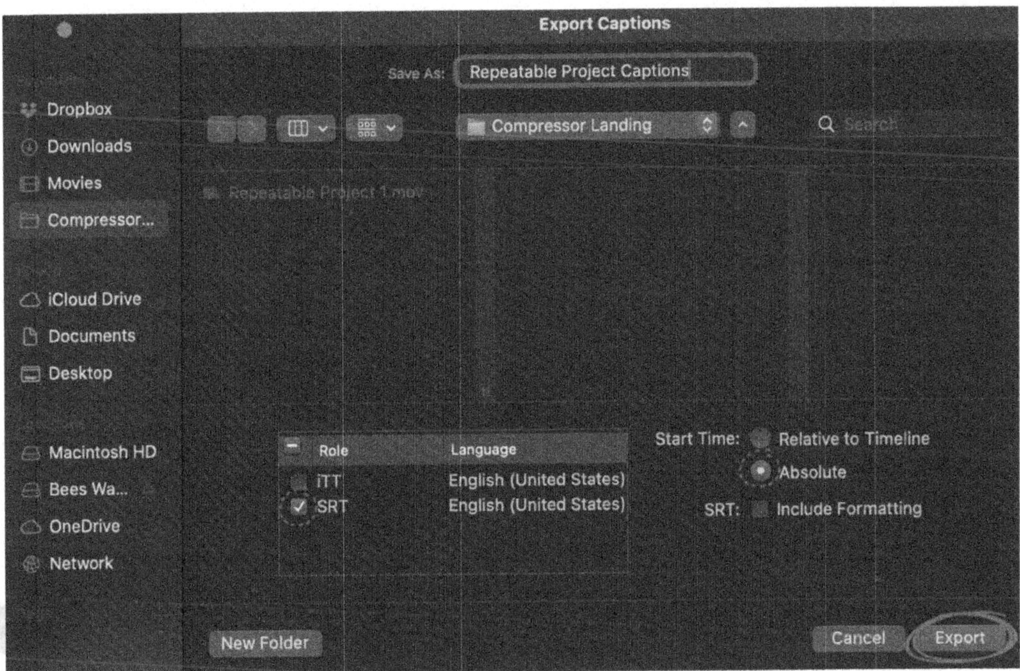

Figure 11.55: Export captions separately from the File menu

Exporting an XML project

Exporting an **XML** (short for **eXtensible Markup Language**) file of a project provides a streamlined way to collaborate with other editors by sharing only the essential project data. By sending just the XML file, you can avoid transferring large media files, assuming the recipient already has access to the same source footage and Final Cut Pro library. This approach saves time, reduces file size, and ensures a smooth workflow when working on shared projects.

In this recipe, we will review how easy it is to export an XML file of a project.

Getting ready

The reason this works is because the XML file of your project is so small. An XML file has no footage. It is just a text file, not unlike HTML web files, that contains instructions on what to do with footage.

When you send someone an XML file from your project, they can import it into their library, and it functions with all your edits because they already have the large library and footage files. You will need to get those files to your colleague somehow. As described in the *Technical requirements* of this chapter, you may need to use a Sneakernet and physically give them a copy of the library and footage on a hard drive. That way, you know the library is structured properly. This leads to the topic of structure and how your library *contains* the footage. As we learned in *Chapter 2* and the recipe called *Importing media into Final Cut Pro*, when you import footage into a library, you can choose to have it copied inside the library or left on the hard drive and linked to the library. As a project grows, you may end up with files scattered across various hard drives, including the internal Movies folder. Think of collaborating with another chef. Before you go, the ingredients that are scattered around the kitchen have to be consolidated into a nice, neat tote bag.

Media can be consolidated into the library itself or a folder linked to the library. Neither is right nor wrong, just your preference. Into the library makes just one file, a large file, but only one thing to manage. The folder method makes the library smaller, but you need to keep the folder and the footage inside it accessible to the library.

Here is how to consolidate a library:

1. Click on your library in the Sidebar panel on the far left of the Final Cut Pro interface. Look to the Inspector panel on the far right of the Final Cut Pro interface. Across from the **Storage Locations** heading, click on the **Modify Settings** button.

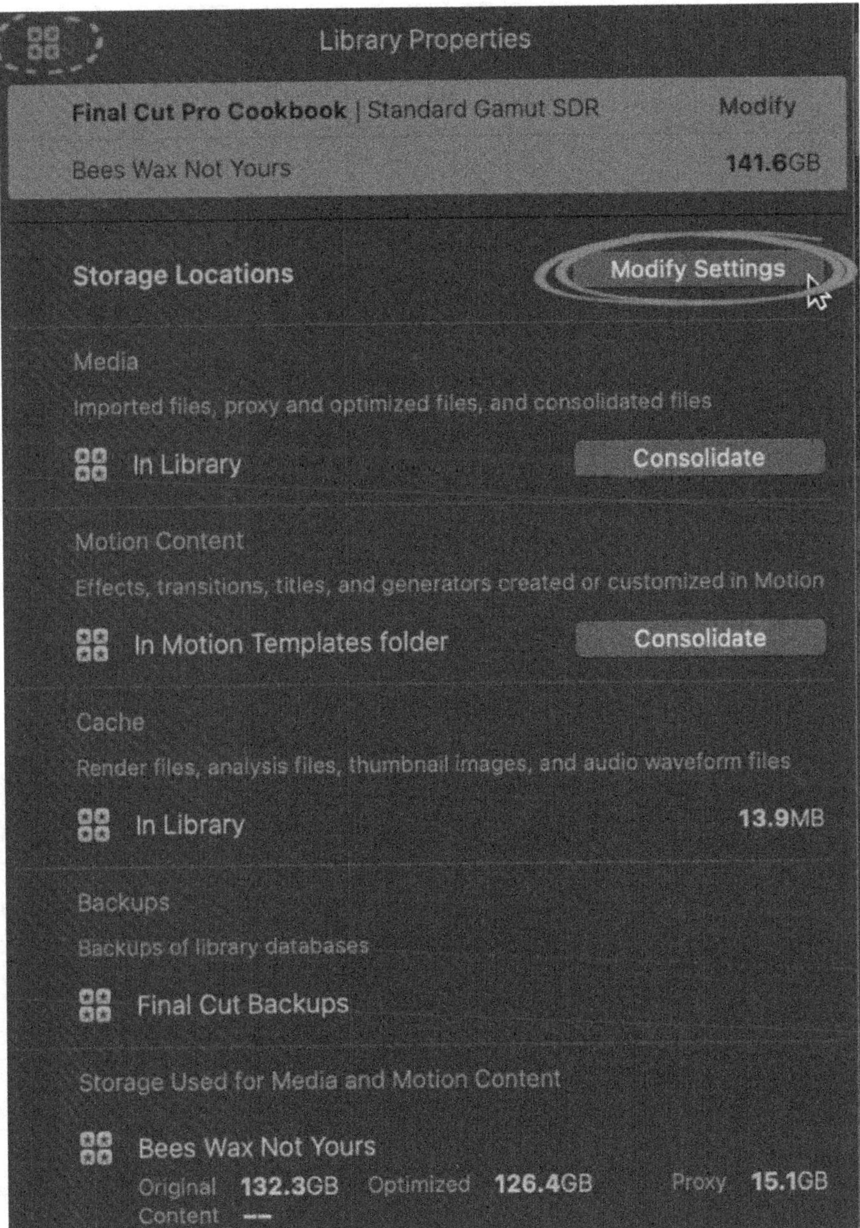

Figure 11.56: Click on the Modify Settings button

2. The default location settings for **Motion Content, Cache,** and **Backups** are fine and do not need adjusting. We are interested in the location of **Media**. Click on this menu. The default setting for this menu is **In Library**.

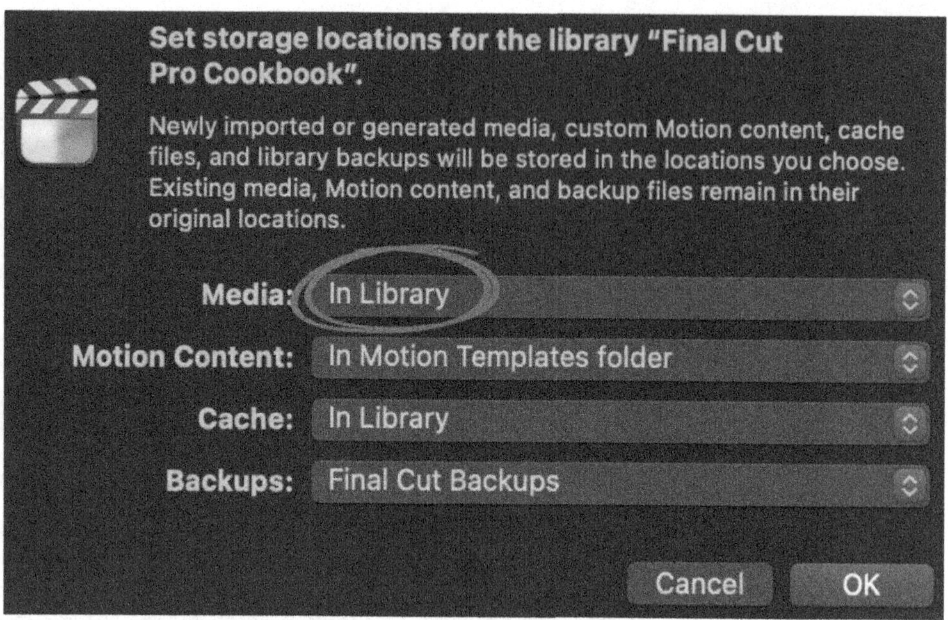

Figure 11.57: Click on the Media drop-down menu to change the location

3. To set the media location to a folder, select **Choose...** from the drop-down menu.

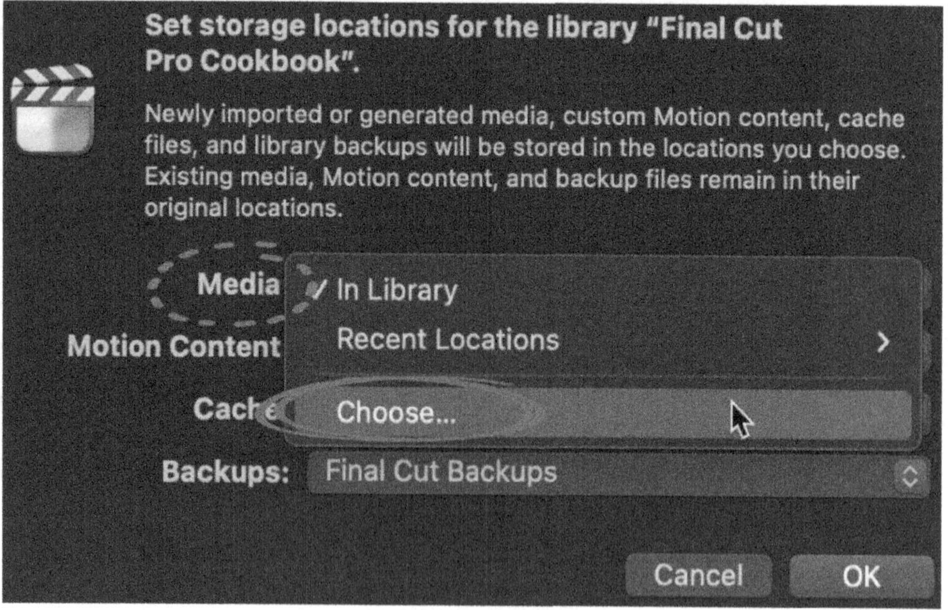

Figure 11.58: Select Choose... from the Media drop-down menu

4. You will be able to select a folder or create a new one. Then, click on the **Choose...** button. Remember, this step was just to change the setting of where the media would go moving forward. Now, we need to do the consolidate command. In the Inspector panel, in the **Media** section, click on the **Consolidate** button.

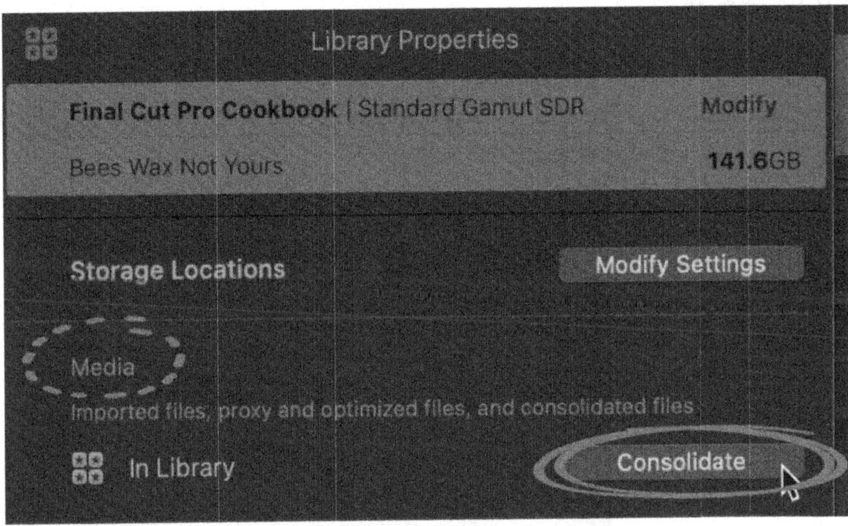

Figure 11.59: Click on the Consolidate button in the Media section

5. Verify that **Media Destination** is set correctly: a folder or the library. In my example, I want to consolidate all the media into one library file. Also, check the media types to include in the consolidation. Then, click on the **OK** button.

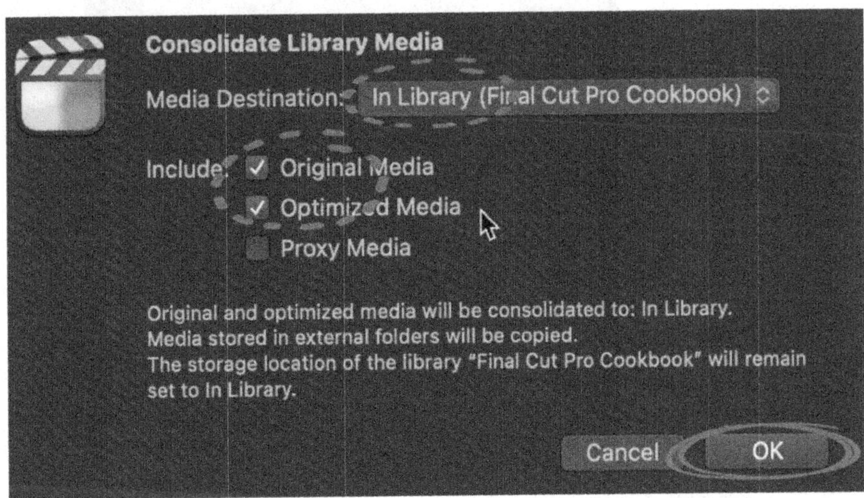

Figure 11.60: Click on the OK button to consolidate your media

It will be easier to get your library and media to your colleague now that your files are consolidated into one place. To follow this recipe, you will not necessarily need a colleague with the same Final Cut Pro Library and footage, but you will need a library with media, an event, and a project.

How to do it...

You don't have to send your fellow chef all the ingredients, just the recipe card. Here's how:

1. Select the project you want to send to your colleague in the Event Browser panel. From the **File** menu, select **Export XML...**.

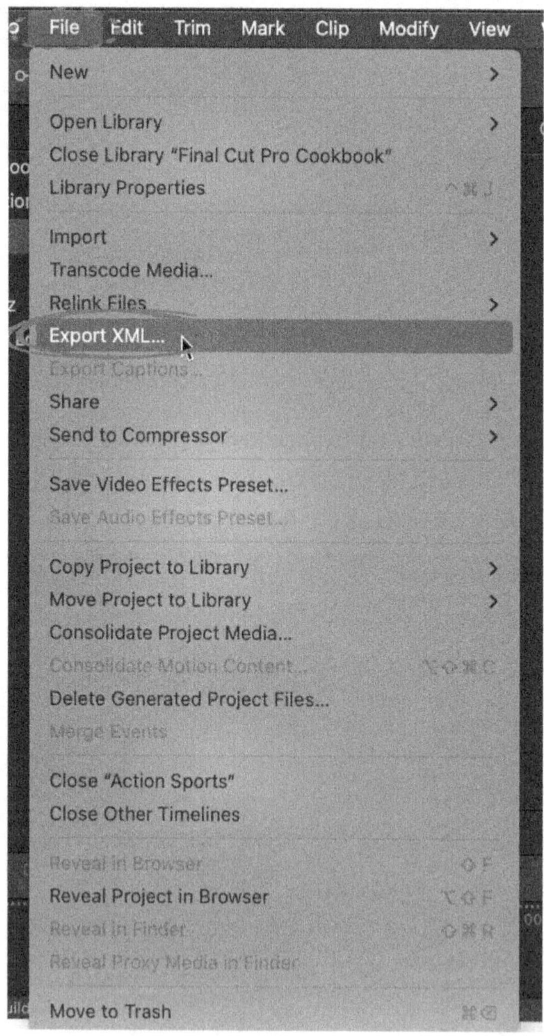

Figure 11.61: Select Export XML... from the File menu

2. In the dialog window, give the file a name or leave it as the name of the project, and navigate to the location you want to save the file. From the **Metadata View** drop-down menu, select **Extended**. This will provide all the data needed to share a project with a colleague.

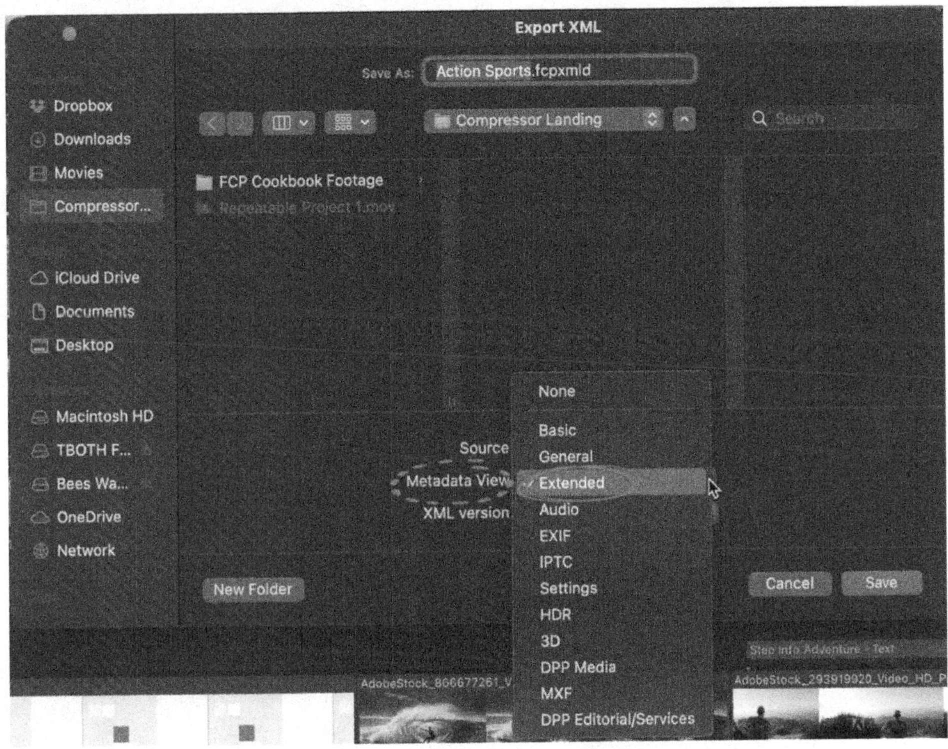

Figure 11.62: Select Extended from the Metadata View drop-down menu

3. From the **XML version** drop-down menu, select whatever is the current version and click on the **Save** button.

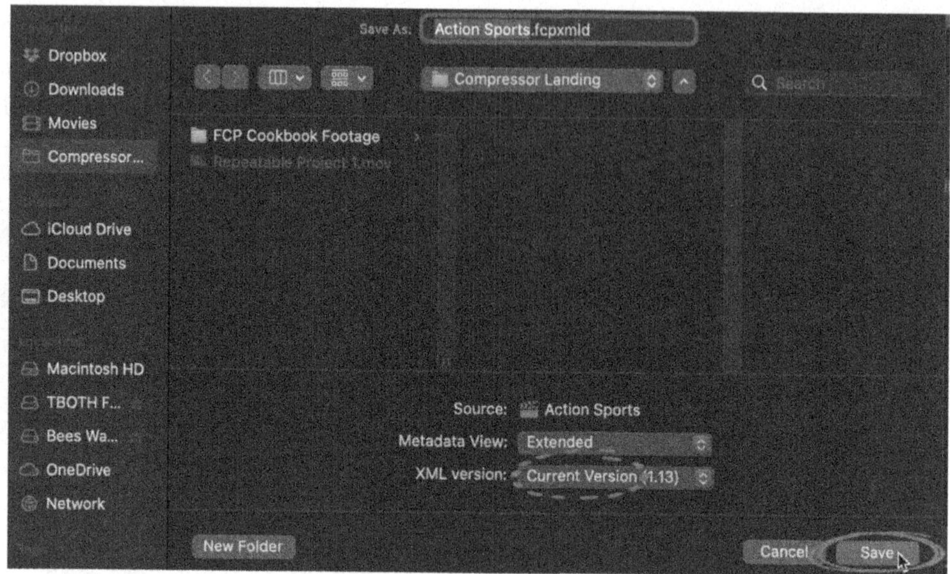

Figure 11.63: Click on the Save button

4. You have saved a small file that can probably be emailed, and now your colleague can view your latest editing master dish. How can I import an XML project or file, you might ask? Simple, from the **File** menu, select **Import** and **XML…**.

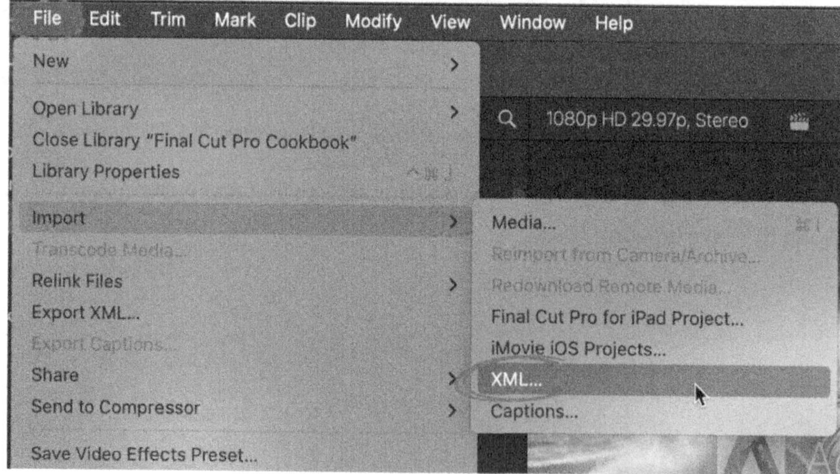

Figure 11.64: From the File menu, select Import and XML…

5. Navigate to the file and click on the **Import** button. Great, once you and a colleague have the same Final Cut Pro library and media files, you can exchange project versions as much as you want.

Saving a project archive

As we bid adieu to our editing endeavors and masterpiece, let's wrap up with finesse. Like a great chef, we will ensure every detail of our finished project is impeccably seasoned before starting on the next editing creation. From archiving media to organizing project files, we will explore the essential project management tasks in Final Cut Pro to ensure efficient workflow management.

In this recipe, we will review the steps to creating card archives, consolidating media, sharing projects, and exporting XML versions. The most convenient ingredients are the library and the media, along with an exported final version. You can jump right back into editing. But these take up the most disk space. Smaller in size are the card archives and XML files, but then there is a bit more effort to recreate your project.

How to do it...

That's a wrap! Your grand chef d'oeuvre deserves a grand archive:

1. Let's start with exporting the final version of your project. In the Event Browser panel, double-click on a project to open it in the Timeline panel. In the upper-right corner of the Final Cut Pro interface, click on the **Share** icon, which looks like a square with an arrow pointing up. This brings up the menu of *Share* destinations. Select **Export File (default)...,** which is listed first because it is a default format. You can also apply the **Export File (default)** destination with the keyboard shortcut *Command + E*. Click on the **Settings** tab in the upper center of the window.

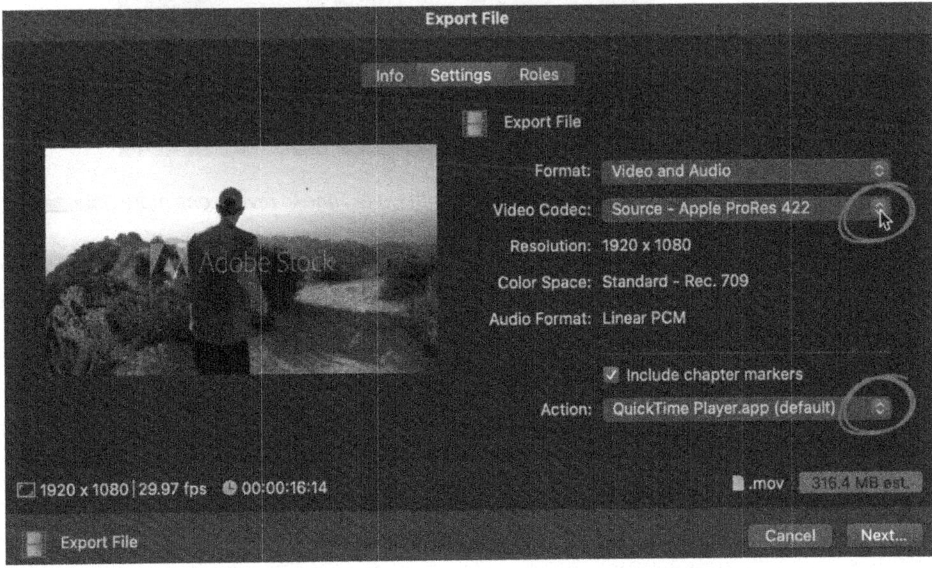

Figure 11.65: Keep the default settings for the default destination

2. Notice that the **Video Codec** parameter is set to **Source - Apple ProRes 422**. ProRes 422 is the native format that Final Cut Pro uses when importing footage. Check out *Chapter 2* and the recipe called *Understanding optimized versus proxy media*. So, this source setting is, for all practical purposes, uncompressed. Every frame is an iFrame, there is no interpolation between images. There are other formats you can set in the **Video Codec** drop-down menu, but as I suggested earlier, you should keep the default as the source.

3. Click on the parameter menu for **Action** to display a drop-down menu. The default action to be performed when the export is complete is to open the file with the QuickTime Player application. This is good to leave as the default, as it will give you one more chance to watch your video before you send it out. Click on **QuickTime Player.app (default)** to keep it selected.

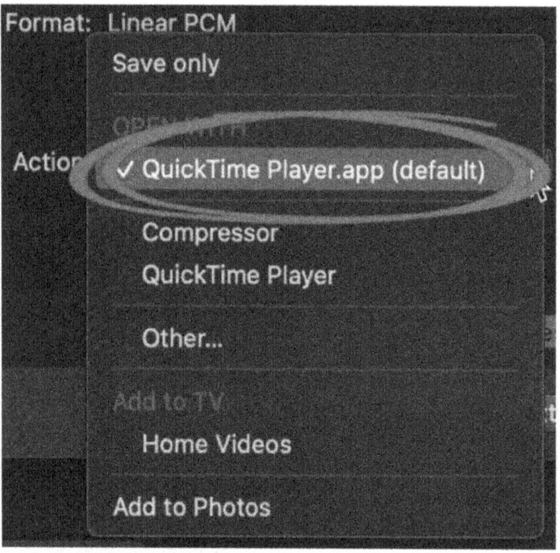

Figure 11.66: Open the file with QuickTime to review one more time

4. Be aware that because this format is the same as the source and uncompressed, the file size will be larger than other *Share* destinations. Click on the **Next...** button and save the video file to the location of your choice.

5. Next, let's consolidate the library in order to keep all the media in one place. For the purposes of archiving, it is easier to have the media in one folder linked to the library. Click on your library in the Sidebar panel on the far left of the Final Cut Pro interface. Look to the Inspector panel on the far right of the Final Cut Pro interface. Across from the **Storage Locations** heading, click on the **Modify Settings** button.

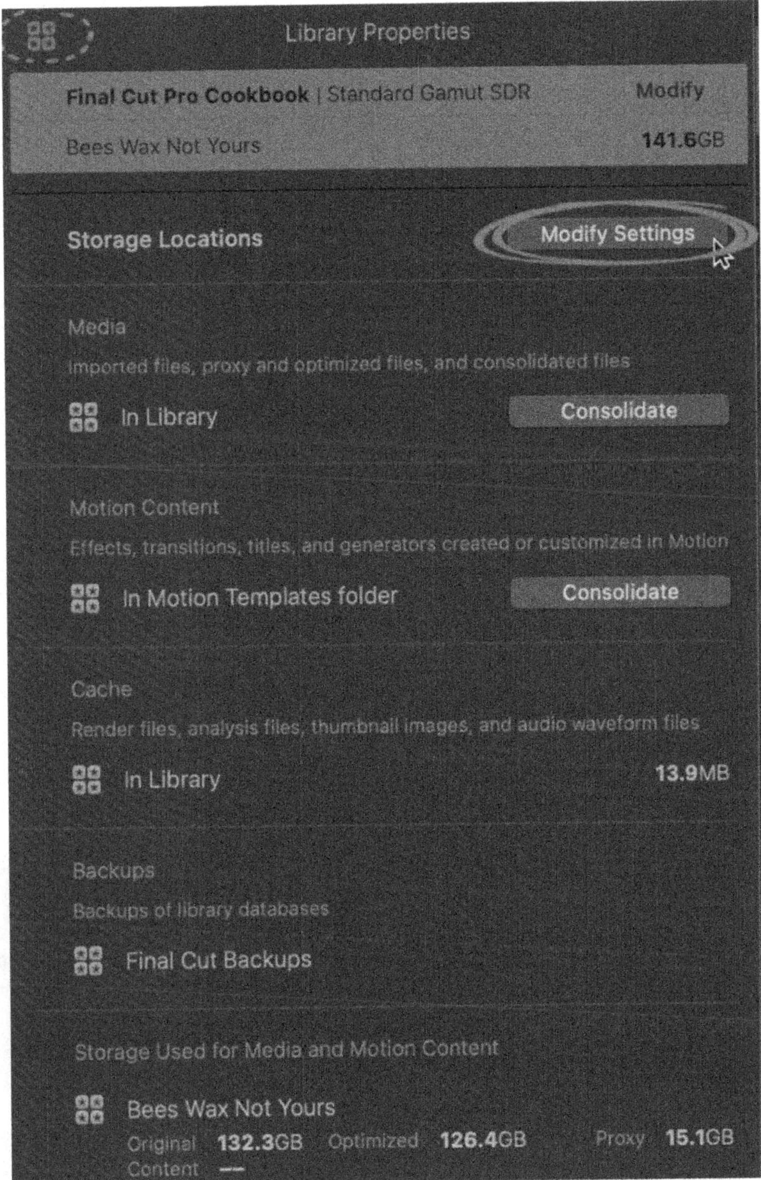

Figure 11.67: Click on the Modify Settings button

6.   The default location settings for **Motion Content, Cache,** and **Backups** are fine and do not need adjusting. We are interested in the location of **Media**, so click on the drop-down menu.

7. To set the media location to a folder, select **Choose...** from the drop-down menu.

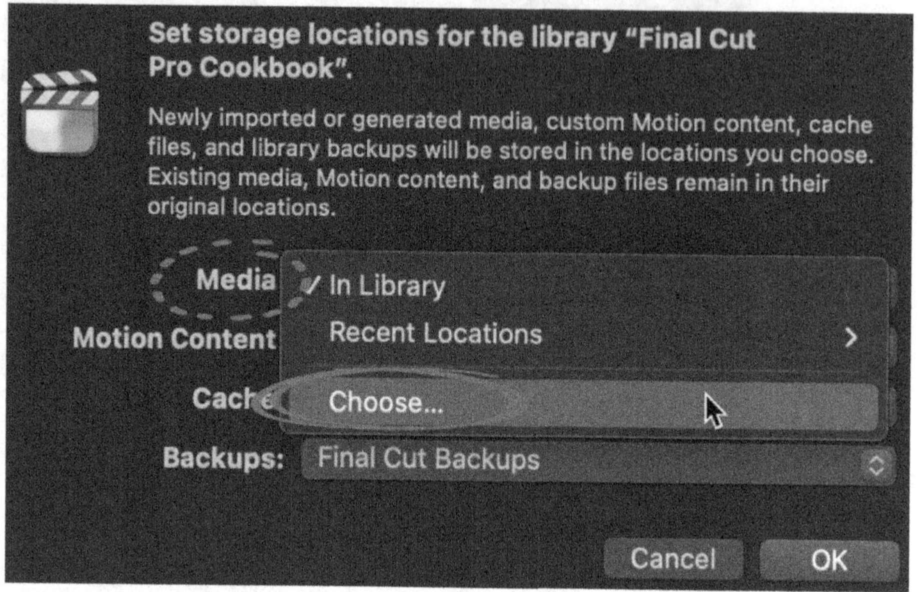

Figure 11.68: Select Choose… from the Media drop-down menu

8. You are presented with a window in which you will be able to select a folder or create a new one. Then, click on the **Choose...** button. Verify that the **Media** location is the folder you selected and click on the **OK** button.

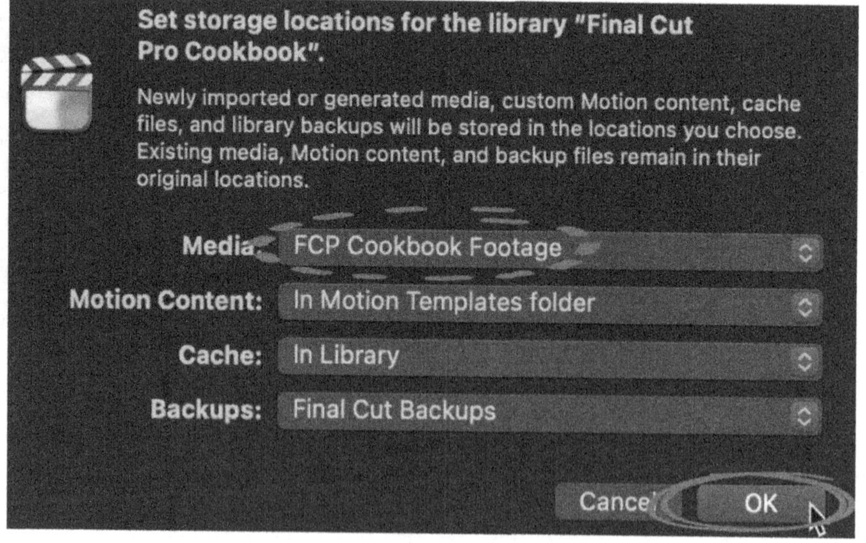

Figure 11.69: Verify that the Media: location is the folder you selected

9. Remember, this step was just to change the setting of where media would go moving forward. Now, we need to do the consolidate command. In the Inspector panel, in the **Media** section, click on the **Consolidate** button.

10. Verify that **Media Destination** is set correctly to the folder you selected. As an archive, I suggest that you do not include **Optimized Media** because those will be large files. You can optimize the media later if you need to change anything in your project. Then, click on the **OK** button.

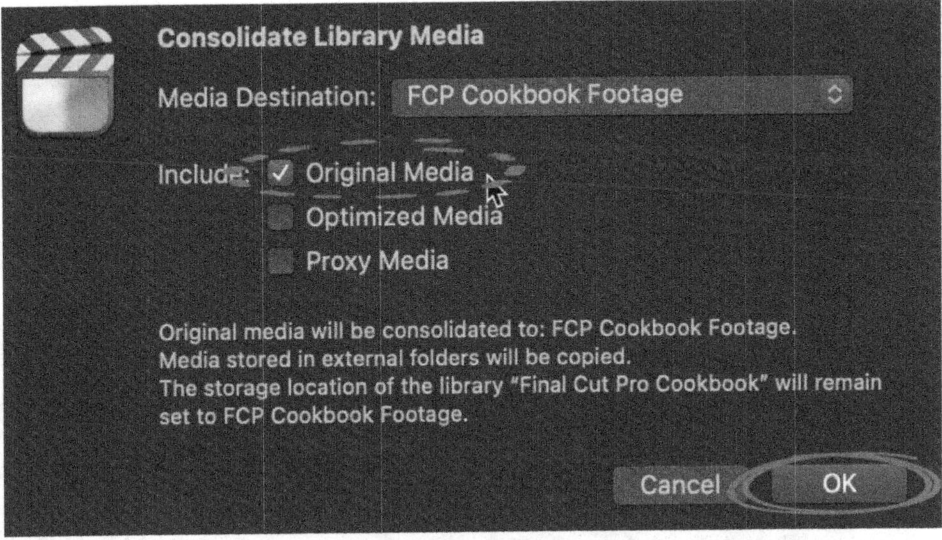

Figure 11.70: Click on the OK button to consolidate your media

11. You have now saved the uncompressed final version of your project, the library, and the media. These can be in medium-term storage. You may need to make changes, and you don't want these files to be too hard to get to.

12. Now is the time to gather the components for long-term storage. Let's work on the card archive first. I hope that you saved archives of your camera footage as a first step before importing the footage into the library. Review *Chapter 2* and the recipe called *Creating a camera archive* for more info.

13. If you have not already done so, here are the steps. With Final Cut Pro already launched, insert an SD card from a camera. The **Media Import** window should open up automatically. If it doesn't, click on the **Import Media** icon, which is an icon of an arrow pointing down located in the upper-left corner of the Final Cut Pro interface, and from the drop-down menu, select **Media...**. Alternatively, from the **File** menu, select **Import** and **Media**, or use *Command + I* as the keyboard shortcut. The SD card should show up in the list of cameras located in the upper-left corner of the **Media Import** window.

Figure 11.71: Select the SD card in the Import window

14. The first step is to make a card archive. This creates a disk image of the SD card, the entire SD card, and all the footage that's on it. With the SD card selected, click on the **Create Archive...** button located in the lower-left corner of the interface. This will make a disk image of that SD card.

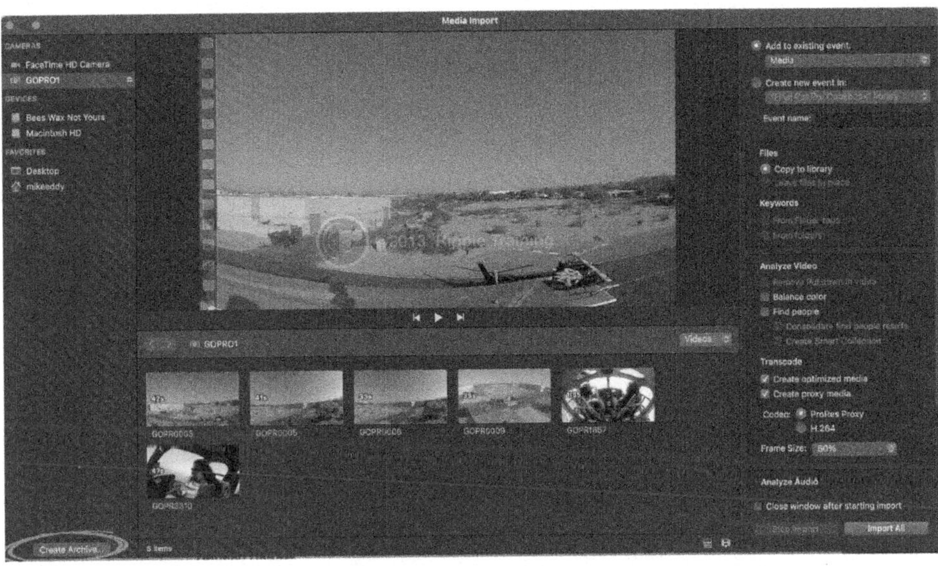

Figure 11.72: Click on the Create Archive button

15. You can give this disk image a different name that might give more information and help organize the footage. It is as simple as that. Place the card archives in your long-term storage location.

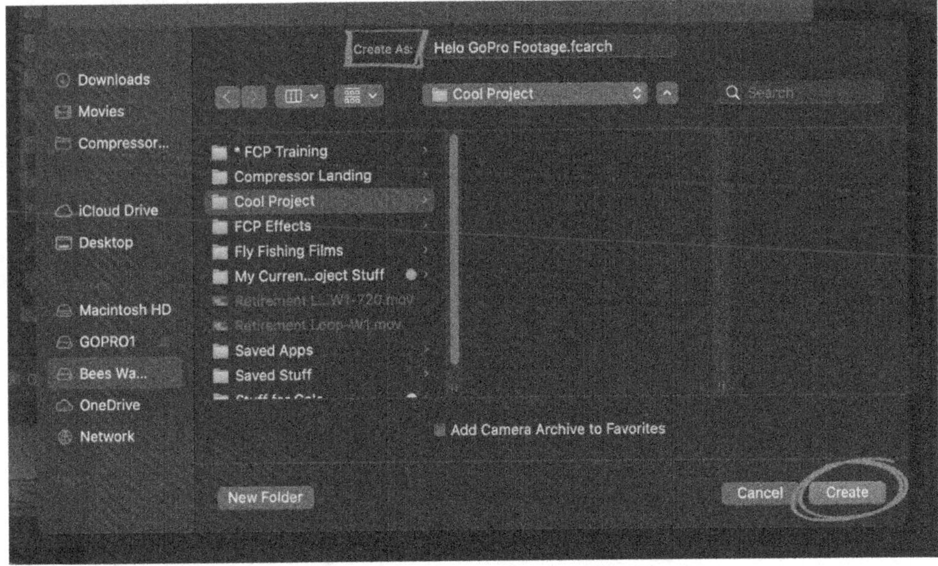

Figure 11.73: Give the card archive a new name

16. Now, let's make a backup of the library. We are going to export an XML file that, not unlike HTML web files, does not contain footage, but rather, instructions on what to do with footage. You can check out the *Getting ready* section of the previous recipe called *Exporting an XML project*, for more information.

17. Select the library we are archiving in the Sidebar Browser panel. From the **File** menu, select **Export XML...**.

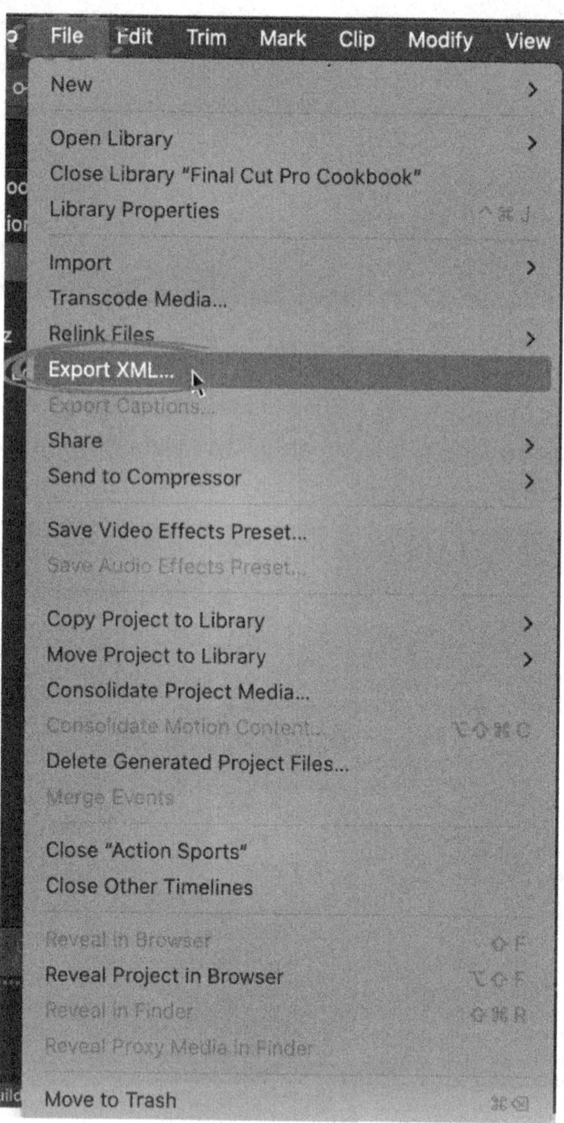

Figure 11.74: Select Export XML... from the File menu

18. In the dialog window, give the file a name or leave it as the name of the library and navigate to the long-term storage location. From the **Metadata View** drop-down menu, select **Extended.** This is a safe choice as it contains a broad range of metadata. This includes the possible transfer to another editing application. There is more information about the **Metadata View** menu options later in the *How it works...* section.

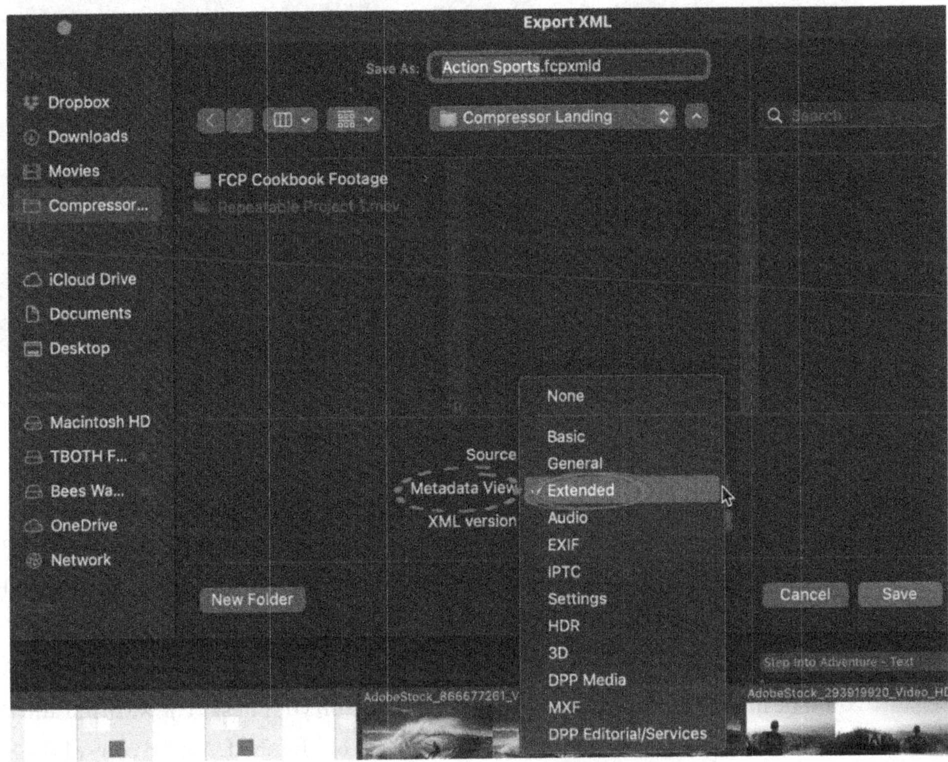

Figure 11.75: Select Extended from the Metadata View drop-down menu

19. From the **XML version** drop-down menu, select whatever is the current version and click on the **Save** button.

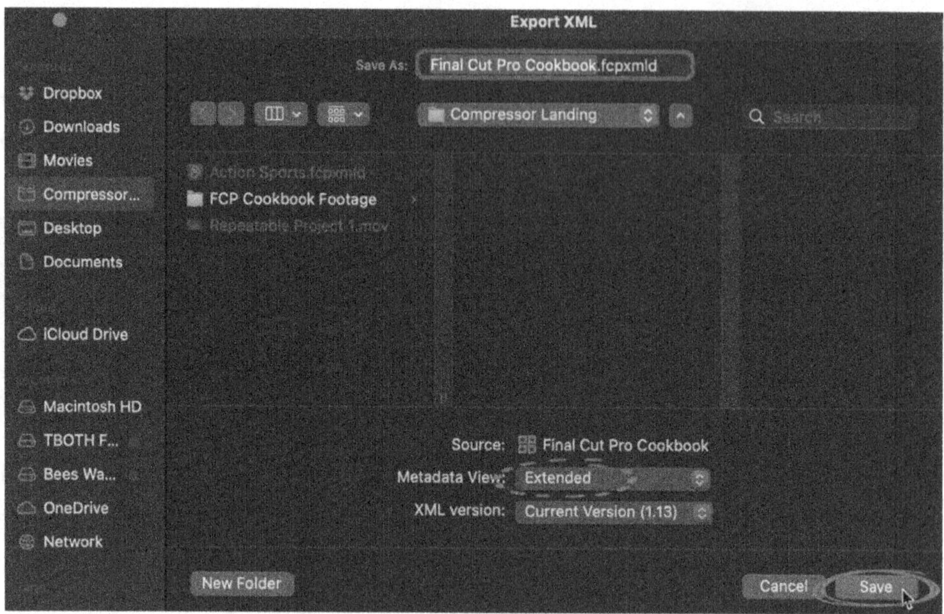

Figure 11.76: Click on the OK button

20. The XML file will be small and, paired with the card archives of your footage, you will be able to recreate your project. In addition, if you have the library but not the media, you can import the media from the card archives and resume your editing. A good backup practice is to remember 3-2-1. Three copies, in at least two locations, and at least one on a different type of media. Your library, the media files, and the export of your final version could be in medium-term storage on a hard drive on your desk. The XML file and the card archives are in long-term storage on a hard drive on the shelf. A third copy of the XML file and card archives can be on a server, which is both a different location and a different type of media. But this is not 100% foolproof; even unused hard drives sitting on a shelf can fail.

How it works...

Here's an explanation of the **Metadata View** options available in Final Cut Pro's XML export, along with their usage:

- **Basic**: Includes essential project and clip information, such as clip names, time code, and duration. Best for simple project transfers where only fundamental metadata is needed, keeping the XML file lightweight.

- **General**: Expands on **Basic** by including broader clip details such as frame rate, resolution, and creation date. Suitable for general project sharing, ensuring important clip attributes are maintained without excessive data.

- **Extended**: Adds even more metadata fields, such as reel names, scene numbers, and camera angle details. Useful for editors working on complex, multi-camera projects where detailed metadata is needed for organization.

- **Audio**: Focuses on audio-related metadata, including audio channels, bit depth, sample rate, and audio format. Best when working with audio post-production teams, ensuring all necessary sound information is included.

- **EXIF** (short for **Exchangeable Image File Format**): Contains camera-specific metadata such as lens type, aperture, shutter speed, and ISO settings. Essential for photographers and cinematographers who need to maintain precise camera settings for grading or archival purposes.

- **IPTC** (short for **International Press Telecommunications Council**): Includes copyright, author, description, keywords, and other metadata useful for media asset management. Commonly used in journalism and stock footage workflows to track ownership and content descriptions.

- **Settings**: Captures key project settings such as codec, resolution, frame rate, and aspect ratio. Helpful when sharing projects between different editors or software to ensure consistency in technical specifications.

- **HDR** (short for **High Dynamic Range**): Includes metadata related to HDR color space, brightness levels, and gamma settings. Necessary for HDR workflows to maintain proper color accuracy and dynamic range information.

- **3D**: Stores stereoscopic 3D metadata, including left/right eye information and convergence settings. Used in 3D film production to ensure correct alignment and depth settings during post-production.

- **DPP Media** (short for **Digital Production Partnership Media**): Supports DPP-compliant metadata fields for media assets, including technical and descriptive details. Required for broadcasters and media companies that follow DPP standards for content delivery.

- **MXF** (short for **Material Exchange Format**): Provides metadata for MXF-wrapped files, such as format type, track layout, and encoding parameters. Useful for broadcast and archival workflows that rely on the MXF format for media exchange.

- **DPP Editorial/Services**: Includes metadata specific to editorial and service-based workflows, such as content ratings, compliance notes, and delivery instructions. Primarily used in professional broadcast environments where detailed content tracking is required.

Bonus tip: Some of you might be used to writing dates by *day/month/year* or *month/day/year*. But to keep track of projects chronologically in the alphabetical organization of the Mac filesystem, you need to use *year-month-day* – for example, *2023-04-14* for April 14th in 2023. It won't matter how many seconds you can shave off your editing time with keyboard shortcuts if you can't find your client's files. As any chef knows, knife skills won't matter if you keep losing your jar of kosher salt. Thanks.

packtpub.com

Subscribe to our online digital library for full access to over 7,000 books and videos, as well as industry leading tools to help you plan your personal development and advance your career. For more information, please visit our website.

Why subscribe?

- Spend less time learning and more time coding with practical eBooks and Videos from over 4,000 industry professionals
- Improve your learning with Skill Plans built especially for you
- Get a free eBook or video every month
- Fully searchable for easy access to vital information
- Copy and paste, print, and bookmark content

At www.packt.com, you can also read a collection of free technical articles, sign up for a range of free newsletters, and receive exclusive discounts and offers on Packt books and eBooks.

Other Books You May Enjoy

If you enjoyed this book, you may be interested in these other books by Packt:

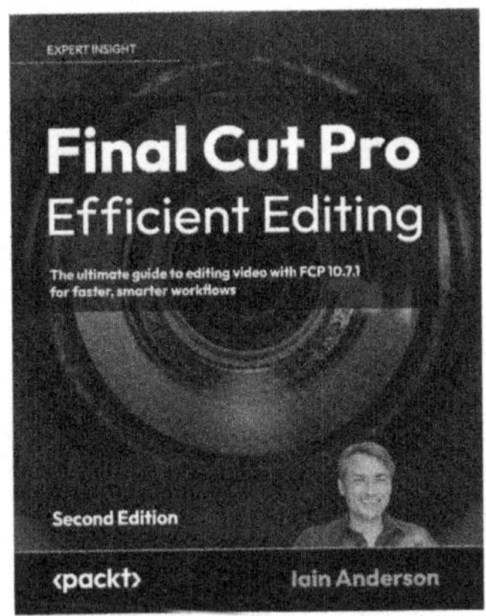

Final Cut Pro Efficient Editing, Second Edition

Iain Anderson

ISBN: 978-1-83763-167-4

- Organize and manage media from multiple sources
- Edit and manipulate video with an intuitive interface and powerful tools
- Streamline your workflow with customizable workspaces and keyboard shortcuts
- Sync and edit multicam interviews with ease and learn advanced trimming techniques
- Use advanced audio and color grading tools to achieve a professional-quality finish
- Work with other editors using the built-in collaboration tools
- Create stunning visual effects and complex motion graphics titles
- Export video projects in a variety of formats for delivery to multiple platforms and user devices

Packt is searching for authors like you

If you're interested in becoming an author for Packt, please visit authors.packtpub.com and apply today. We have worked with thousands of developers and tech professionals, just like you, to help them share their insight with the global tech community. You can make a general application, apply for a specific hot topic that we are recruiting an author for, or submit your own idea.

Share your thoughts

Now you've finished *Final Cut Pro Cookbook*, we'd love to hear your thoughts! Scan the QR code below to go straight to the Amazon review page for this book and share your feedback or leave a review on the site that you purchased it from.

https://packt.link/r/183588847X

Your review is important to us and the tech community and will help us make sure we're delivering excellent quality content.

Index

Symbols

4K clips
resolution, reframing 286-290

A

accurate client feedback
gathering 413-416

adjustment clips
stacking 220-224

Apple devices
sharing 418-425

assembly edit 66-68

assets
creating, for workgroup 390-394

audio
ducking, with Range Selection tool 309-313

audio effects
using 344-350

Audio Enhancement functions
using 324-334

audio roles
assigning 308
setting 303- 307

audio spikes
keyframing 322-324

audition
creating 143-149

B

big close-up (BCU) 135

Blade tool
using 114-116

blend modes
using 240-248

burned-in captions
sharing 456-461

C

camera archive
creating 32-35

clip position and effects
keyframing 271-276

clips
appending 78-83
connecting 78
duration, changing 116-119
inserting 78
overwriting 78-83
replacing 94-97
retiming 276-282
selecting, with keyboard shortcuts 85-88

skimming 84

stabilizing 283-286

closed captions

creating 410-413

sharing 456-461

Color Adjustments effect

using 231-237

Color Board 176

color coding clips 153-157

color correction 167

color grading 167

color of clips

color correction attribute 187-189

fine-tuning 177-186

color wheels 176

Compositing 243

compound clips

creating 150-153

continuous timeline scrolling

exploring 24-26

Core Audio Format (CAF) 442

correspondence 360

curves 176

custom Color Board preset effect

creating 226-230

Custom LUT effect

using 237-239

D

dailies 66

Digital Production Partnership Media (DPP Media) 479

Draw Mask effect 261

E

Equalization (EQ) 326

Event Browser

appearance, changing 10-15

filtering order, customizing 15-21

Event Browser List view

using 58-66

Exchangeable Image File Format (EXIF) 479

exposure

fixing, with luma waveform monitor 196-199

eXtensible Markup Language (XML) file

exporting, of project 461-468

external recorder

audio, syncing from 335-338

F

Final Cut Pro

media, importing into 36-46

Final Cut Pro interface 1

Event Browser panel 4

Inspector panel 4

sidebar panel 3

Sidebar panel 3

Timeline panel 4

viewer panel 4

Viewer panel 4

working with 2-5

workspaces 2-10

G

gap clips

using 127-135

generators

themes, using 367-370

Green Screen Keyer effect
using 256-264

group of pictures (GOP) 52

H

High Dynamic Range (HDR) 479

High-Efficiency Image File (HEIF) 132

I

International Press Telecommunications Council (IPTC) 479

iTunes Time Text (iTT) 457

J

J- and L-cuts
creating 135-138

K

Ken Burns effect
cropping 290-297
distorting 290-297
using 290-297

keyboard shortcuts
levels, adjusting with 313-322

keyframes 311, 401

keywords
using 53-58

L

Look-Up Table (LUT) 211
applying, to raw files 204-209

luma waveform monitor
exposure, fixing with 196-199

M

Magnetic Mask effect
using 264-271

Magnetic Mask tool 381-388

Magnetic Timeline 21
exploring 22, 23

markers
using 139-143

masks
mystery, unmasking 252-255

Match Color feature
using 173-176

Material eXchange Format (MXF) 443, 480

media
importing, into Final Cut Pro 36-46
importing, with drag and drop 46-50
relinking 72-75

metadata 53

mono recording
fixing 351-353

multicam editing
using 157-165

O

optimized media
versus proxy media 50-53

P

placeholder clips
using 127-135

Position tool 21
exploring 23, 24

Precision Editor view
  working with 26-30

project archive
  saving 469-480

projects, for other devices
  sharing 426-437

project versatility
  planning for 397-402

project versions
  controlling 394-397

proxy media
  versus optimized media 50-53

R

Range Selection tool
  using, to duck audio 309-313

repeatable project intro and outro
  creating 403-410

ripple edit 124

roles
  sharing 449-456

rolling edit 125

S

safe zones
  using 364-367

scratch audio
  recording 339-344

secondary color corrections
  adding 199-203

secondary storyline transitions
  creating 106-113

Shape Masks and Color Masks 190
  working with 191-195

share settings
  customizing 437-448

slide edit 126

slip edit 126

Smart Collections
  creating 68-72

Smart Conform 397

standard dynamic range (SDR) 233

T

text animation
  revealing 381-388

themes
  using, in titles and generators 367-370

timeline appearance
  adjusting 89-93

timeline index
  using 139-143

title object tracker
  creating 371-380

titles
  customizing 356-362
  replacing 362-364
  themes, using 367-370

transitions
  adding 97-105
  dissolve transition 106
  fade to black 106
  ripple dissolve 106

Trim tool
  using, techniques 122-127

V

visual effects
stacking 212-220

W

white balance
utilizing 168-172

Download a Free PDF Copy of This Book

Thanks for purchasing this book!

Do you like to read on the go but are unable to carry your print books everywhere?

Is your eBook purchase not compatible with the device of your choice?

Don't worry, now with every Packt book you get a DRM-free PDF version of that book at no cost.

Read anywhere, any place, on any device. Search, copy, and paste code from your favorite technical books directly into your application.

The perks don't stop there, you can get exclusive access to discounts, newsletters, and great free content in your inbox daily.

Follow these simple steps to get the benefits:

1. Scan the QR code or visit the link below:

https://packt.link/free-ebook/9781835888469

2. Submit your proof of purchase.
3. That's it! We'll send your free PDF and other benefits to your email directly.

Made in the USA
Monee, IL
07 July 2026